MILLER'S

COMPANION TO
ANTIQUES &
COLLECTABLES

MILLER'S

COMPANION TO
ANTIQUES &
COLLECTABLES

Miller's Companion to Antiques & Collectables

First published in Great Britain in 2006 by Miller's,
a division of Mitchell Beazley, imprints of
Octopus Publishing Group Ltd,
2–4 Heron Quays, London, E14 4JP

Miller's is a registered trademark of Octopus Publishing Group Ltd
Copyright © 2006 Octopus Publishing Group Ltd

The publishers will be grateful for any information that will assist
them in keeping future editions up to date. While every care has
been taken in the preparation of this book, neither the author nor
the publisher can accept any liability for any consequence arising
from the use thereof, or the information contained therein.

ISBN-13 978-1-84533-190-0
ISBN-10 1-84533-190-7

A CIP record for this book is available from the British Library

Set in Berkeley Book and Frutiger

Produced by Toppan Printing Co., (HK) Ltd
Printed and bound in China

Senior Executive Editor Anna Sanderson
Executive Art Editor Rhonda Summerbell
Project Editor Catherine Emslie
Editor Theresa Bebbington
Copy Editor Clare Peel
Design Vanessa Marr
Proofreader Naomi Waters
Production Jane Rogers
Picture Research Jenny Faithfull

Front cover, clockwise from top left: blue-and-white plate by
Ridgway, in the "British Flowers" pattern, c.1825; silver tankard from
the 1690s, decorated in the 19thC; chair with baluster-style back;
glass vase designed by Per Lütken for Holmegaard, c.1959; silver *lion
passant* hallmark.
Back cover, left to right: diecast Mercury No.26 Lancia D24 racing car,
c.1960, Chiltern/Chad Valley (smaller) and Merrythought bears.
Page 3 (title page): NIDERVILLER figure of an apple vendor, c.1775.
Page 5 (contents page): WILLIAM DE MORGAN, rare, covered vase
decorated by Joe Juster, c.1888.

CONTENTS

HOW TO USE

Miller's Companion to Antiques & Collectables is the ideal "companion" to the budding collector and antiques enthusiast, and could not be simpler to use. Whenever you need to remind yourself of the difference between soft- and hard-paste porcelain, or to check when Tiffany & Co. was founded for instance, just turn to the relevant entry – organized alphabetically – where you will find invaluable information, including collecting tips. In addition to the main alphabetical section of the book, at the back there is a section giving advice on buying and selling antiques, as well as an appendix containing further information on styles, marks, and forms found in the principle collecting areas.

FINDING YOUR WAY AROUND
Clear running heads enable you to refer quickly to the entry you are seeking.

ILLUSTRATIONS
Colour photographs illustrate selected entries, with concise caption information.

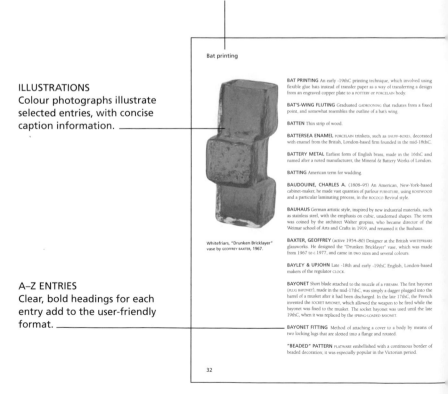

Bat printing

Whitefriars, "Drunken Bricklayer" vase by GEOFFREY BAXTER, 1967.

BAT PRINTING An early -19thC printing technique, which involved using flexible glue bats instead of transfer paper as a way of transferring a design from an engraved copper plate to a POTTERY or PORCELAIN body.

BAT'S-WING FLUTING Graduated GADROONING that radiates from a fixed point, and somewhat resembles the outline of a bat's wing.

BATTEN Thin strip of wood.

BATTERSEA ENAMEL PORCELAIN trinkets, such as SNUFF-BOXES, decorated with enamel from the British, London-based firm founded in the mid-18thC.

BATTERY METAL Earliest form of English brass, made in the 16thC and named after a noted manufacturer, the Mineral & Battery Works of London.

BATTING American term for wadding.

BAUDOUINE, CHARLES A. (1808–95) An American, New-York-based cabinet-maker, he made vast quanties of parlour FURNITURE, using ROSEWOOD and a particular laminating process, in the ROCOCO Revival style.

BAUHAUS German artistic style, inspired by new industrial materials, such as stainless steel, with the emphasis on cubic, unadorned shapes. The term was coined by the architect Walter gropius, who became director of the Weimar school of Arts and Crafts in 1919, and renamed it the Bauhaus.

BAXTER, GEOFFREY (active 1954–80) Designer at the British WHITEFRIARS glassworks. He designed the "Drunken Bricklayer" vase, which was made from 1967 to c.1977, and came in two sizes and several colours.

BAYLEY & UPJOHN Late -18th and early -19thC English, London-based makers of the regulator CLOCK.

BAYONET Short blade attached to the muzzle of a FIREARM. The first bayonet (PLUG BAYONET), made in the mid-17thC, was simply a dagger plugged into the barrel of a musket after it had been discharged. In the late 17thC, the French invented the SOCKET BAYONET, which allowed the weapon to be fired while the bayonet was fixed to the musket. The socket bayonet was used until the late 19thC, when it was replaced by the SPRING-LOADED BAYONET.

A–Z ENTRIES
Clear, bold headings for each entry add to the user-friendly format.

BAYONET FITTING Method of attaching a cover to a body by means of two locking lugs that are slotted into a flange and rotated.

"BEADED" PATTERN FLATWARE embellished with a continuous border of beaded decoration; it was especially popular in the Victorian period.

WITHDRAWN

CERAMIC MARKS

One of the most useful marks on later ceramics is the Design Registration Mark. Registration began in 1839 following the Copyright of Design Act but the insignia shown on the right was used from 1842. The table on the right shows which piece of information each area of the insignia represented and which letters were used to denote the years and months of registration (which were not used in sequence). The positioning in the insignia changed after 1867 and from 1884 consecutive numbers were used to represent the year instead, nearly always prefixed by "Rd" or "Rd No." A guide to the year from the number is given in the table below:

REGISTRATION MARKS 1842–83

1842–67	1868–83
a – class	a – class
b – year	b – day
c – month	c – bundle
d – day	d – month
e – bundle	e – month

1842–67

A =1845		N = 1864	
B = 1858		O = 1862	
C = 1844		P = 1851	
D = 1852		Q = 1866	
E = 1855		R = 1861	
F = 1847		S = 1849	
G = 1863		T = 1867	
H = 1843		U = 1848	
I = 1846		V = 1850	
J = 1854		W = 1865	
K = 1857		X = 1842	
L = 1856		Y = 1853	
M = 1859		Z = 1860	

1868–83

A =1871		L = 1882	
C = 1870		P = 1877	
D = 1878		S = 1875	
E = 1881		U = 1874	
F = 1873		V = 1876	
H = 1869		W = 1878	
I = 1872		(1–6 March)	
J = 1880		X = 1868	
K = 1883		Y = 1879	

Month letters for both periods are as follows:

A = December
B = October
C or O = January
D = September
E = May
G = February
H = April
I = July
K = November
(and December1860)
M = June
R = August
(and 1–19 September 1857)
W = March

TABLE OF REGISTRATION NUMBERS 1884–2003

1 = 1884	658988 = 1917	860854 = 1950	978426 = 1977
19754 = 1885	662872 = 1918	863970 = 1951	982815 = 1978
40480 = 1886	666128 = 1919	866280 = 1952	987910 = 1979
64520 = 1887	673750 = 1920	869300 = 1953	993012 = 1980
90483 = 1888	680147 = 1921	872531 = 1954	998302 = 1981
116648 = 1889	687144 = 1922	876067 = 1955	1004456 = 1982
141273 = 1890	694999 = 1923	879282 = 1956	1010583 = 1983
163767 = 1891	702671 = 1924	882949 = 1957	1017131 = 1984
185713 = 1892	710165 = 1925	887079 = 1958	1024174 = 1985
205240 = 1893	718057 = 1926	891665 = 1959	1031358 = 1986
224720 = 1894	726330 = 1927	895000 = 1960	1039055 = 1987
246975 = 1895	734370 = 1928	899914 = 1961	1047799 = 1988
268392 = 1896	742725 = 1929	904638 = 1962	1056078 = 1989
291241 = 1897	751160 = 1930	909364 = 1963	2003720 = 1990
311658 = 1898	760583 = 1931	914535 = 1964	2012047 = 1991
331707 = 1899	769670 = 1932	919607 = 1965	2019933 = 1992
351202 = 1900	779292 = 1933	924510 = 1966	2028115 = 1993
368154 = 1901	789019 = 1934	929335 = 1967	2036116 = 1994
385180 = 1902	799097 = 1935	934515 = 1968	2044227 = 1995
403200 = 1903	808794 = 1936	939875 = 1969	2053121 = 1996
424400 = 1904	817293 = 1937	944932 = 1970	2062149 = 1997
447800 = 1905	825231 = 1938	950046 = 1971	2071520 = 1998
471860 = 1906	832610 = 1939	955342 = 1972	2080158 = 1999
493900 = 1907	837520 = 1940	960708 = 1973	2089210 = 2000
518640 = 1908	838590 = 1941	965185 = 1974	2098500 = 2001
535170 = 1909	839230 = 1942	969249 = 1975	3000500 = 2002
552000 = 1910	839980 = 1943	973838 = 1976	3009770 = 2003
574817 = 1911	841040 = 1944		
594195 = 1912	842670 = 1945	After a European Directive was implemented in the UK in December 2001, the numbering started again at 3000000.	
612431 = 1913	845550 = 1946		
630190 = 1914	849730 = 1947		
644395 = 1915	853260 = 1948		
653521 = 1916	856999 = 1949		

MOTIFS & DEVICES

There are many motifs used in ceramic marks. Such marks might be used to help distinguish a company from others, and they can be very useful in dating a piece as variations often occur throughout a company's manufacturing period. Here are some examples.

Scroll marks

Coalport Porcelain This "ampersand" mark appeared painted in gilt c.1861–75.

Sèvres Crossed "L"s, for Louis XV and XVI, were used from 1749, with date letters inside them from 1753.

Anchors

Geminiano Cozzi This factory ran from 1765 to 1812. An anchor mark in red, or more rarely gold, was used.

Squares

Worcester This mark varies in style. It was hand-painted in underglaze blue c.1755–75 and on reproductions.

Triangles

Hubaudière Hubaudière took over this faience factory in 1782 (d.1794). Also used in the 19thC.

Globes

Minton The standard printed Globe mark, without "S" or the crown, was used c.1863–72, and this version from c.1873, with "England" added from 1891.

Crowns

Royal Worcester This mark was used from 1891, when "Royal Worcester England" was added.

Derby Porcelain This mark dates from 1861–1935. The intials "S" and "H" stand for "Stevenson & Hancock".

Animals

Ulysee Cantagalli Cantagalli made maiolica reproductions 1878–1901. The cockerel mark appears in various forms, and can be very abstract.

Belleek Pottery This standard mark was used 1863–91, and one with the addition of "Co. Fermanagh" and "Ireland" is still used.

Swords

Meissen First used in 1724, the crossed swords mark went through various changes. The first mark shown here (left) generally appeared between 1763 and 1774. This version from 1774 until 1814 the star below the handles denoted the Marcolini period. From 1818 until 1924 the swords were long with slightly curved blades.

Crescents

Hanau This painted mark was used on tin-glazed wares by this German company (est. 1661) 17th–18thC.

Beauty spot

BEADING A decorative border of compact beads, either cast and applied, or embossed. Also a term used for moulding – either a small, plain, half- or quarter-round, wooden moulding, or moulding in the form of a string of beads.

BEADWORK Decoration on material using GLASS beads of different colours.

BEAKER A drinking vessel without a handle, stem, or foot. The basic cylindrical form has changed little since the 15thC. Most 16th and early 17thC beakers are plain, with bands of ARABESQUES, stylized flowers, or foliage; later 17thC examples feature embossed-and-chased flowers and leaves, often with engraved initials or armorials. From the 17thC, particularly in Continental Europe, beakers were sometimes produced in groups, known as "nesting" sets, where the individual vessels fitted into one another for storage. In the 18thC, it was common for beakers to be made in pairs. Complete sets are most valuable; a pair will be worth more than twice the value of a single vessel. Vessels in novelty forms were a popular concept in the Victorian and Edwardian periods, examples include little beakers resembling sewing thimbles and used to measure "thimblefuls" of liquor.

BEAR-RARY Rare toy made in 1911 by Louis S. Schiffer, based in New York, USA. One half is a BISQUE-head DOLL, the other side is a TEDDY BEAR.

BEARER See LOPER.

BEAR JUG English STONEWARE JUGS made in the 18thC in the shape of a bear. They were first made in Derby and Staffordshire, but were widely copied.

BEATLES MEMORABILIA Items owned by or marketed for the music group The Beatles, pioneers of the pop music that epitomized the sounds of the 1960s. They have a unique place in the history of pop music; no previous group had enjoyed such enormous and lasting success. Almost any object associated with the group is of interest to collectors. The wide range of Beatles merchandise made during the 1960s and 70s reflects the group's phenomenal popularity. Among the diverse Beatles objects that come up for sale are furnishings, jewellery, clothing, games, books, wigs, and even confectionary. Drawings by John Lennon, who also wrote and illustrated two books, are among the most desirable Beatles memorabilia, and can fetch high prices. Look out for handwritten lyrics to famous songs; autographed and handwritten letters; autographed photographs (these are often faked, so beware); artwork for record sleeves; and animation cels from Yellow Submarine. See also CELEBRITY DOLLS and ROCK AND POP EPHEMERA.

1960s record player decorated with a BEATLES design.

BEAUTY SPOT Applied beauty marks typical on late-17thC dolls. Pretending to have a "mole" to offset a beautiful complexion began as a way to cover up smallpox scars. Beauty spots became fashionable at the French Court in the

---

APPENDIX
Artworks and text provide further invaluable information that will help with identifying and dating, and which may whet the appetite for more detailed reference works such as *Miller's Antiques Encyclopedia*.

CROSS REFERENCES
Words that have their own entries are highlighted in upper case, and *"See also"* notes direct you to other relevant entries.

Laminated birch cantilevered
and upholstered armchair by
ALVAR AALTO, 1930s.

AALTO, ALVAR (1898–1976) Finnish ART DECO architect and furniture designer, noted for his bentwood chairs, made from the 1930s onward.

ABADEH From Iran, brightly coloured Persian CARPETS, often incorporating a Tree of Life, lozenge patterns, and stick-like animal and human figures.

ABRASH (Arbrush) In Oriental CARPETS, colour variations caused by using wool dyed with different batches of vegetable-based dye.

ABSTBESSINGEN German FAIENCE produced in this town in the 18thC.

ACACIA Whitish-yellow wood with brown veins. Used for INLAY and BANDING.

ACANTHUS Classical stylized leaf design based on the scalloped leaves of the acanthus plant. Used in carved decoration and metal MOUNTS on furniture.

ACID ENGRAVING A glass-decoration technique introduced commercially in the 19thC. The glass is covered with a resist – an acid-proof coating such as wax or resin – and the design cut through using a pointed stylus. The object is then dipped into hydrofluoric acid, and a matt design is created by the acid dissolving the surface of the exposed glass. Also known as acid-etching.

ACID GILDING A 19thC technique for decorating POTTERY, whereby the surface is etched with hydrofluoric acid and the low-relief pattern gilded.

ACID POLISHING Process to create a shiny finish by dipping the GLASS into a mixture of hydrofluoric and sulphuric acids.

ACORN CLOCK Early 19thC MANTEL CLOCK in an acorn shape from New England, USA.

ACORN KNOP Wineglass stem moulded in the shape of an upturned acorn.

ACTION MAN The first British DOLL designed for boys. It has a variety of military, sporting, and dare-devil outfits, and the value almost doubles if the doll has its original box. "Action Soldier" was first made in 1966. Earlier dolls have static hands and painted hair, and are better quality than later models. In the 1970s, real-looking hair and gripping hands were introduced, followed by frowning, moving eyes. "The Footballer" is one of the most popular types, then "Red Devil" and "Superman". Action Man is marked on the back "Made in England by Palitoy under licence from Hasbro", with the date 1964.

ACT OF PARLIAMENT CLOCK An 18thC wall-hung CLOCK with a large dial, no glass, and a trunk below to house the weights. So-called because privately owned timepieces were taxed by an Act of Parliament passed in 1797, so most people relied on public clocks, often hung in taverns.

ADAM, ROBERT (1728–92) Scottish architect who, with his brother James, influenced furniture design in the late 18thC and was a pioneer of the NEO-CLASSICAL STYLE. Their Classically inspired forms for dining-room furnishings, typified by motifs such as PALMETTES and FESTOONS, influenced other designers and created a look known as "Adam style". They worked in MAHOGANY and SATINWOOD, decorated with rich INLAY. Their designs were published in 1775.

ADAM SISTERS American, New York-based makers of RAG DOLLS.

ADAMS Family of English potters who owned factories including Greengales, Hanley, in Staffordshire in the 18th and 19thC. Famous for PARIAN busts of famous (or infamous) people in the 19thC.

ADAMS & CO. Glassmaker founded in Pittsburgh, America, in 1851. The company made clear pressed and cut FLINT GLASS until the late 19thC.

ADDERLEYS LTD British, Staffordshire-based pottery, established in 1906. The firm produced affordable teaware, including TRIOS, and porcelain figures.

ADMIRAL JUG Originally made to commemorate Lord Howe's victory over the French in 1794, a TOBY JUG depicting an admiral.

AEROGRAPH DECORATION Late-19thC invention for applying patterns onto POTTERY using a mechanical airbrush.

AESTHETIC MOVEMENT A development of the design-reform movement, popular in Europe and the USA from *c*.1875 to the late 1880s, in which "Art for Arts sake" was the chief impulse. Following the invasion of Japanese territorial waters by the US Navy in 1853, all things Oriental came into fashion. The Aesthetic style was influenced by Japanese decoration, with elegant forms and stark, unadorned designs. Simple forms and uncluttered surfaces were a reaction to the highly elaborate products of mainstream Victorian taste, while ornament was often placed asymmetrically. Typical motifs included sunflowers, fan shapes, peacock feathers, and bamboo. In the late 19thC, following the introduction of Japanese art to the West, firms, such as the GORHAM MANUFACTURING CO., TIFFANY & CO., and DOMINICK & HAFF, employed Japanese metalworkers to create Oriental-style silver vessels.

Satinwood, painted, two-tier, occasional table in the AESTHETIC style, 19thC.

AIR-TWIST **stem wine glass, 18thC.**

AFFENKAPELLE German for MONKEY ORCHESTRA. Refers to PORCELAIN figures first made in the mid-18thC at MEISSEN and copied by other manufacturers.

AFFLECK, THOMAS (d.1795) Scottish-born cabinet-maker who moved to Philadelphia, USA, where he worked to the designs of Thomas CHIPPENDALE.

AFSHAR Persian nomadic tribe of the Shiraz-Kerman area. They make bright red, blue, and ivory woollen RUGS with stylized flowers and diamond patterns.

AGATA Mottled decoration in GLASS resembling the mineral agate. The effect is achieved by sprinkling alcohol onto the molten surface, and was first used by the NEW ENGLAND GLASS CO. in America in the late 19thC. It was much copied.

AGATE GLASS First developed by the Romans, an opaque GLASS made to resemble agate, jasper, and CHALCEDONY by combining two or more colours of glass. It was refined by 15thC Venetian and 19thC Bohemian glassmakers.

AGATEWARE Made in Staffordshire, England, during the 18thC, POTTERY resembling the veined or marbled effect of agate. Layers of different-coloured clays were rolled together and sliced to build up mingled layers resembling agate, then moulded into wares. Lead and salt glaze were used. Desirable items include teaware, jugs, COFFEE- and CHOCOLATE-POTS, and shell-shaped wares.

AGRA Town in India and site of the Taj Mahal. Produced large CARPETS, usually with floral patterns in green, blue, and brown.

AIR-BEADED GLASS containing bubbles of air, like strings of beads.

AIR-TWIST STEM A helical decoration found in the stem of a DRINKING GLASS popular from the 1740s to the 1760s. The twist is formed by making air bubbles in the GATHER of molten glass, then stretching and rolling it to draw them out into fine threads. One or two bubbles may extend slightly further than the others, because they are not all the same size. In early examples, the bowl and stem were made as one piece, with the twist at the top of the stem extending into the bowl. The most common type of air twist was the multiple spiral, made from up to 12 filaments. Stems with single spirals are known as single-series air twists, while those with two different patterns of spiral, such as a "corkscrew" and a "cable", are double-series air twists. Air-twist glasses often have bowls that feature diamond-point or wheel engraving of ARMORIALS, patriotic and political mottoes and slogans, commemorative themes, vine-leaf patterns, and hops and barley. KNOPS add to the value. *See also* MIXED-TWIST STEM and OPAQUE-TWIST STEM.

ALABASTER Artificial material made of lime or gypsum and coloured white, yellow, or red to resemble marble.

ALABASTER WARE PORCELAIN and GLASS, made to resemble ALABASTER.

ALBANY SLIP Using clays from Albany, New York, reddish-brown glaze used inside 19thC American STONEWARE vessels to make them watertight.

ALBARELLO (-i) Derived from Islamic POTTERY, a tin-glazed DRUG JAR with a narrow waist and without a spout. It was used for storing dry drugs.

ALBUM QUILT (Also known as an autograph or friendship quilt.) A mid-19thC American patchwork QUILT, with each section designed and made by a separate person.

ALCOCK, SAMUEL & CO. Based at Cobridge and Burslem in Staffordshire, England, c.1828–59, a maker of PARIAN, EARTHENWARE, and PORCELAIN.

ALCORA WARE MAIOLICA made in Alcora, Spain, in the mid-18thC, and decorated with blue and white, purple, and yellow figures, and grotesques.

ALDER Pinkish-brown wood with a knotty grain, used in country furniture.

ALE GLASS Used for consuming ale, a DRINKING GLASS with a tall stem and tall, narrow bowl. During the 18thC the bowls were small, because the beer contained a higher level of alcohol than today. Ale glasses can be identified by the engraved decoration of hops and barley on the bowls and were widely produced in England from the early 18thC to the early 19thC. They are more affordable than glasses with decorative stems.

ALEXANDER DOLL CO. Based in the USA, Beatrice Behrman set up the Alexander Doll Co. in 1923, trading as MADAME ALEXANDER. However, she became famous for her hard plastic and vinyl DOLLS only after 1945. The dolls all had names, although different types were from the same moulds. Identified by the name of the first doll produced from each mould, the most common include "Margaret", "Maggie", and "Cissie". The most popular type are the "Little Women Dolls". These hard plastic dolls may have the same type of face as either a "Margaret" or a "Maggie"; they were also made in cloth. The dolls were marked on the heads or bodies with "Alex", "Alexander", or "Mme Alexander". Some have name-tags on their clothes. Elaborate dresses increase the value.

ALEXANDER DOLL: Jo from *Little Women*, in its original box, c.1958.

ALEXANDRITE GLASS Made in the late-19th and early 20thC by THOMAS WEBB & SON, decorative GLASS with shades from amber and blue to deep pink.

ALLEN PEPPERBOX An American, early-19thC pistol with six revolving barrels made by leading gunsmith, Ethan Allen of Massachusetts.

ALLER VALE *See* DEVON POTTERIES.

ALLGEYER German manufacturer of flat-cast toy soldiers, 1790–1896.

ALT, BECK & GOTTSCHALCK From 1854 this Nauendorf-based German firm made all-BISQUE DOLLS and bisque heads, including 1920s' heads for the "BYE-LO" babies. Their dolls have square faces, small features, and flat, painted eyebrows. Foreshortened thighs create FLAPPER LEGS.

ALUMINIA ART NOUVEAU range of FAIENCE wares produced by the ROYAL COPENHAGEN porcelain factory at the end of the 19thC. They were decorated with airbrushed colours and stencils showing Japanese influence.

ALUMINIUM (Aluminum) Metal used pure or in alloys from the mid-19thC for medallions, plaques, and figure groups; mass-produced after 1914.

AMBERINA GLASS Heat-sensitive, coloured GLASS, with graduating shades ranging from light amber at the base to dark ruby at the top of the vessel. The process was invented by the glassmaker Joseph Locke at the NEW ENGLAND GLASS CO., USA, and patented in 1883. "Amberina" was later made by other firms.

AMBOYNA Imported from the West Indies in the 18thC, amboyna (*Pterospermun indicum*) is a richly coloured, yellowish-brown, burred wood with a tight grain. It was used as a veneer on expensive FURNITURE, and is found on pieces made in the Regency and Continental Empire periods.

AMBROTYPE A photograph made by exposing a glass plate treated with light-sensitive wet collodion. The negative was made positive by backing with black paper or paint.

AMBULANTE A small, portable piece of French FURNITURE.

AMEN GLASS Some of the most notable mid-18thC English DRINKING GLASSES are those that feature verses from Jacobite hymns ending in "Amen" (hence the name) in DIAMOND-POINT ENGRAVING. These glasses were made in support of the Old Pretender (James Edward Stuart) and the Young Pretender (Charles Edward Stuart) to the thrones of England and Scotland. Only two dozen authentic examples exist, and these were widely copied in the 19thC. Copies are larger than the originals. *See also* JACOBITE GLASS.

AMERICAN ART POTTERY The fashion for painted CERAMICS in the years following the Centennial Exposition in Philadelphia in 1876 gave rise to the American Art Pottery Movement, which flourished *c.*1875–1920. Two prominent Cincinnati women were responsible for its development. Mary Louise MCLOUGHLIN created Cincinnati FAIENCE, based on the slip-painted wares of LIMOGES and on Japanese wares, and founded the Cincinnati Pottery Club. Maria Longworth Nichols established the ROOKWOOD POTTERY in 1880.

AMERICAN ART POTTERY Rockwood floor vase, with grapevine and fruit design by Charles Stuart Todd, *c.*1915.

Other prominent American Art potteries include GRUEBY of Boston, the DEDHAM POTTERY, Massachusetts, and the NEWCOMB POTTERY, founded in 1895 at Sophie Newcomb Memorial College for Women in New Orleans by Mary G. Sheerer. Other leading American art potters include Louis Comfort TIFFANY, TECO, FULPER, and George OHR.

AMERICAN ARTS AND CRAFTS Formerly known as MISSION STYLE, a genre that developed in the eastern and mid-western states in the USA between 1890 and the 1920s. Influenced by contemporary designers in Europe – as well as North American colonial history and Native American culture – designers in the USA such as Gustav STICKLEY created FURNITURE and decorative arts using simple, plain forms.

AMERICAN CERAMICS The development of the American CERAMICS industry was hampered by imported foreign wares and a shortage of skilled manpower. The first American PORCELAIN is hard to distinguish from the imported wares it copied and is rarely marked. Wares made by BONNIN & MORRIS in Philadelphia between 1770 and 1772 copied BOW; TUCKER PORCELAINS made in Philadelphia between 1826 and 1838 were based on French 18thC designs; D. & H. Henderson's Jersey City STONEWARE is mistaken for that made by RIDGWAY; brown-glazed wares from BENNINGTON, Vermont, are similar to DERBY wares; while BELLEEK made in Trenton, New Jersey, rivalled Irish Belleek and ROYAL WORCESTER. The mid-19thC English fashion for PARIAN figures crossed the Atlantic, and Parian was produced in Bennington, the Greenpoint section of Brooklyn, New York, and in Trenton. Despite the gradual burgeoning of potteries in the 19thC, American ceramics shown at the Centennial Exposition in Philadelphia in 1876 received little notice. However, interest in American ceramics has grown. Among the most popular are items of 18thC slip-decorated REDWARE, produced from c.1750 onward in New England, and SALT-GLAZED STONEWARE, developed by immigrant French and German potters from c.1750. English imported pottery such as SPATTERWARE is also popular. Innovative forms and decorations that are hallmarks of American art pottery from the late 19thC are collected too. *See also* ANGLO-AMERICAN CERAMICS.

AMERICAN CHIPPENDALE (Also known as American Rococo.) Mid-18thC FURNITURE that was inspired by the designs of Thomas CHIPPENDALE, but without the GOTHIC details and with a greater use of ROCOCO motifs.

AMERICAN FLINT GLASS produced in quantity in Boston, Massachusetts, USA, in the mid-19thC. Not true FLINT GLASS.

AMERICAN LOWESTOFT Chinese pottery imported into the USA in the 18thC and mistaken for LOWESTOFT wares.

AMERICAN TERRA COTTA & CERAMIC CO. *See* TECO POTTERY.

ANEROID BAROMETER with exposed
mechanism, mounted on an
electrotype group of greyhounds
and a hare, Victorian.

AMORINI Cupids or cherubs used in decoration.

AMPHORA Originally an ancient Greek two-handled jar, often decorated with black or red figurework and with a bulbous body and strap handles from the shoulder to neck. Later, more common, Roman examples consist of coarse wine jars with pointed bases to push into the earth floor of cellars.

AMSTEL WARE Late 18thC POTTERY from factories along the Amstel river, Amsterdam. Similar to wares by MEISSEN.

ANABORI Form of NETSUKE with deeply recessed interior carving.

ANATOLIA Region of Turkey noted for its woollen PRAYER RUGS.

ANCHOR ESCAPEMENT Invented c.1670 and named after its anchor-shaped mechanism, which engages with the escape wheel on a CLOCK.

ANDERSEN, DAVID Founder (in 1876) of a Norwegian, Oslo-based firm, noted for ART NOUVEAU and ART DECO FURNITURE and METAL.

ANDIRONS Two iron supports designed to hold logs over an open fire. They were made from the 17thC in wrought iron, and ornamented with brass finials from the 18thC. *See also* FIREDOGS and FIRECATS.

ANEROID BAROMETER An instrument that measures air pressure using a vacuum chamber with an elastic lid linked to the indicator needle.

ANGLE BAROMETER An instrument with the upper part of the tube bent nearly at right angles, so that the mercury moves further than in a vertical column. Gives more accurate measurements than a standard barometer.

ANGLO-AMERICAN CERAMICS Hand-painted and transfer-printed CERAMICS made in England in the 19thC for export to the USA. Not long after TRANSFER-PRINTING was invented, potteries in the northwest English port of Liverpool made jugs, MUGS, bowls, and PLATES decorated with sailing ships and patriotic subjects to appeal to visiting seamen. In central England, Staffordshire potters also produced pitchers with transfer-printed naval battles and portraits of heroes. After the War of 1812, hundreds of American views were transfer-printed in underglaze blue on various domestic items.

ANGLO-JAPANESE STYLE Style in vogue during the 1870s and '80s that showed a Japanese influence on Victorian designs. Examples are Japanese motifs, bamboo legs, fretwork, and lacquering. *See also* AESTHETIC MOVEMENT.

ANGOULÊME FAIENCE Late-18thC French TIN-GLAZED POTTERY figures.

AN HUA So-called "secret" designs in shallow-moulded relief below the glaze in MING PORCELAIN. They are visible when held to the light.

ANILINE DYE A chemical dye introduced into the manufacture of CARPETS c.1870. It lacks the warm tone of vegetable dye.

ANIMALIER A sculptor of animal forms.

ANNEALING Slow cooling of hot GLASS that reduces internal stresses that may cause cracking once the glass is cold. Also, a process for restoring the malleability of SILVER or other metals made brittle by hammering. The metal is heated until red hot, then immersed in cold water.

ANNULATED Ringed; often used to describe the stem of a GLASS.

ANODIZED Metalwork given a final protective coating by electrolysis.

ANSBACH German factory specializing in large, colourful FAIENCE ornaments from the 1730s, and PORCELAIN tableware from the late 18th and 19thC.

ANTHEMION Originating in Classical Greek architecture, a stylized floral motif based on a honeysuckle flower. It is often found on OAK FURNITURE.

ANTIMACASSAR Textile covering designed in the 19thC to protect the head-rest on upholstered FURNITURE from being stained by Macassar hair oil.

ANTIQUE As a guide, an item that is 100 years old or more.

ANTIQUITIES Generally accepted to mean objects made before AD 600 in Europe, and of ancient Egyptian, Greek or Roman origin. Also used to cover the pre-Columbian era in the Americas and the products of civilizations now extinct. Those from Egypt are often valuable, but there are exceptions such as simple REDWARE vases, small Egyptian limestone carvings, Roman TERRA-COTTA oil lamps, and small examples of Cypriot POTTERY. Ancient Greek pottery is often decorated with scenes from Classical mythology. Later attic VASES, where the image colours have been reversed (background black and figures red), are known as RED-FIGURE VASES. Glass from the 2ndC is often no more expensive than that of the 18thC; subtle colours and iridescence is typical of much Roman glass. Export laws exist in most countries where antiquities originate, so always make sure that the piece is being sold legally. Beware: antiquities are fragile, and condition affects value, but some damage is to be expected – be suspicious of anything that seems too perfect. Avoid objects with heavy restoration – particularly if it is on the face of a piece of sculpture or a painting. Avoid badly corroded bronzes – their detail may have been irreparably damaged.

SÈVRES coffee cup and saucer decorated in gold and platinum with ANTHEMION borders, c.1826

AOGAI Japanese method for inlaying MOTHER-OF-PEARL into lacquered wood.

AO KUTANI Japanese STONEWARE with patterns in green, yellow, and purple glaze. It was made at Kutani in Kaga province in the 17thC.

APOSTLE SPOON Produced in vast numbers, so-called because the cast finial on the SPOON portrays one of the twelve apostles, each identified by the emblem carried in his right hand. Apostle spoons were made in England from the mid-15thC, but the fashion for them had waned by the mid-17thC. Such spoons were originally made in sets of 12 or 13 (including Christ), but complete sets are rare. They were often given as christening presents to boys, with the child receiving the spoon bearing the apostle after whom he was named. Sometimes dedications or initials and dates are found engraved on the backs of the faceted stems. Apostle spoons tend to command high prices. Beware of fakes made by shaping the bowls of tablespoons into the fig shape typical of the bowls of apostle spoons and attaching a reproduction apostle finial. You can spot a fake by the stiffness of the figure.

APOTHECARIES' DRUG JAR *See* DRUG JAR.

APPLE A light, reddish-brown FRUITWOOD with an irregular grain, which is sometimes quite knotty.

APPLIED DECORATION Ornamental motifs made separately from the main body and attached to it to provide decoration. On SILVER, it may also strengthen the work. One technique found on silver is CELTIC STRAPWORK; another is CUT-CARD WORK. Cast ornament may also be applied to silver, as may beaded or reeded wires, soldered around the body or applied to the rim, foot, and edges for decoration and strength.

APPLIQUÉ In textiles, a decorative technique of applying one piece of fabric to a surface of another piece of fabric to make a design.

APREY French factory, founded mid-18thC, producing FAIENCE decorated with birds and flowers.

APRON Concealing skirt of wood beneath the seat-rail of chairs and sofas or between the drawers and legs of case furniture and dressers-on-stands.

AQUATINT Made in the 18thC, engravings that were taken from etched copper plates and printed using resinous gums to imitate the subtle gradations of true watercolour or Indian ink drawings.

ARABESQUE Intricate design of branches, leaves, geometrical patterns, and scrollwork combined into a flowing frieze. The more stylized and fantastical forms are known as "Mooresque". Also the floral motif of Islamic origin found on CARPETS and characterized by complex patterns of linking tendrils.

ARBOR (1) Any spindle within a clockwork mechanism, especially with the mainspring attached. It may have a squared end for winding up the spring.

ARBOR (2) The axle on which a wheel is mounted in a CLOCK movement.

ARBRUSH Alternative name for ABRASH.

ARCH Often found after the 17thC above the dial in LONG-CASE CLOCKS.

ARCHITECT'S TABLE A TABLE with a hinged top, which can be raised to provide an angled working area for making architectural drawings. Most are made of MAHOGANY, but there are examples made of WALNUT.

ARDEBIL Town in northern Iran noted for densely woven CARPETS, often of reds and blue with central medallions.

ARDUS French factory, founded in the 18thC and specializing in FAIENCE wares decorated with fruit, flowers, and portraits.

ARGAND LAMP A LAMP that produced a bright flame, it was invented by Aimé Argand in Switzerland in 1784. Costly when first produced, they retain their value today if complete with their original parts. The glass lamp covers or shades were ideal for protecting the candle or wick from the elements without reducing the amount of light emitted.

ARGENTINE SILVER White metal alloy of nickel, copper, and zinc, used instead of less-durable copper for SILVER PLATE from the 19thC.

ARGONAUT A drinking vessel made from the shell of a nautilus, mounted in SILVER to resemble a sailing ship.

ARGYLL (Or argyle.) Supposedly conceived in the mid-18thC by one of the Dukes of Argyll who disliked cold gravy, the Argyll is a small vessel designed to keep gravy hot. By using an internal device, such as a cylinder into which a hot iron was placed, a double wall to create a sleeve for hot water, or a burner, the Argyll was more efficient at keeping gravy warm than the SAUCEBOAT. Argylls were made in a variety of shapes and sizes, with the vase shape being common 1785–95, but most resemble covered COFFEE-POTS with handles and spouts. The spout rests at the bottom of the bowl, ensuring that the liquid of the gravy pours out ahead of the fatty layer on top. The handle was insulated to prevent hands from burning. Argylls were produced until the Victorian period in silver and SHEFFIELD PLATE. They are collectable.

An ARGAND LAMP with a single arm, patinated bronze, and bright bronze decoration.

An 18thC ARITA **Imari moulded plate.**

ARGY-ROUSSEAU, GABRIEL (b.1885) French ART NOUVEAU glassmaker, specializing in PÂTE-DE-VERRE.

ARITA A centre of Japanese PORCELAIN production named after the region in northern Kyushu, where many kilns were centred. At the beginning of the 17thC the majority of Japanese porcelain was produced in or near near Arita. By the middle of the 17thC white wares with underglaze blue were being exported to Europe, and from later in the century KAKIEMON and IMARI wares were made. *See also* POTTERY AND PORCELAIN, JAPANESE

ARK A term generally used to describe a gabled CHEST.

ARMADA CHEST German iron-bound CHEST for storing valuables from the 16thC. It usually has metal bandings and an elaborate lock.

ARMADA JUG From *c.*1860 CLARET JUGS or WINE EWERS in SILVER or cut GLASS with silver mounts. They had slim necks, scrolling handles, and pedestal feet.

ARMCHAIR First developed in the 18thC, an upholstered CHAIR with arms. Although seats were stuffed rather than sprung, many had loose feather-filled cushions that made them comfortable. Armchair design was led by the French, and many English armchairs produced in the 18th and 19thC are based on French prototypes of the Louis XV and Louis XVI periods. Deciding whether a 19thC armchair is English or French can be difficult. Chairs made by leading manufacturers in the 19thC were occasionally marked with their names. If you can find the maker's stamp (often under the seat rail or inside the back leg), it can increase the value of the chair. GILLOW (of Lancaster) was a leading maker of the period; also look for labels by Howard & Sons (London), Krieger (Paris; stamped on the arm), Lexcellent (Paris), Maple (London), and Thomas Schoolbred (London). However, a label from a British firm may represent a retailer or repairer, not necessarily the manufacturer. French chairs often had wooden casters, so that they did not scratch wooden floors. In England, where carpets were favoured, casters in the 18thC were often made from brass with leather-bound wheels; later, wheels were made just of brass. Some examples were stamped by their makers (Cope & Collinson are well known). In the 19thC, less-expensive chairs were made with ceramic casters and these are of less interest to collectors. Pairs are sought after and usually cost more than twice the price of a single chair. Note: never remove the old casters from a chair, as this will reduce its value. *See also* ARMCHAIR, BUTTON-BACK; ARMCHAIR, WINGED; BÉRGÈRE; and EASY CHAIR.

ARMCHAIR, BUTTON-BACK An ARMCHAIR with buttons adorning the upholstery. Before buying a Victorian button-back, turn the CHAIR upside down and look for a manufacturer's mark or label; these add to its value. Howard & Sons' labels are desirable – they made the "Rolls-Royce" of chairs.

ARMCHAIR, CLUB An open ARMCHAIR with upholstered arms and back rail, made in MAHOGANY, OAK, or ROSEWOOD, and used in gentlemen's clubs.

ARMCHAIR, WINGED First made in the early 18thC, a popular armchair with side panels to keep out draught. Before *c*.1830 the upholstery on CHAIRS was made from thin layers of horsehair, and padding supported by webbing covered with fabric. Upholstery using coiled metal springs covered with padding and webbing was made from *c*.1830. Antique upholstered furniture can sometimes be less expensive than modern counterparts. The wooden frame is the most important part of antique chairs, so never buy a chair with a damaged frame. Generously shaped wings can add to a chair's value. It is rare to find a chair with its original covering. Do not worry about the condition of upholstery, because this can be restored. However, take the cost of re-upholstering into account before you buy a chair in poor condition – re-upholstering can be expensive and can more than double the cost of the chair. Provided that you choose a good-quality fabric in a style appropriate to the chair, the re-upholstering should not affect the value. If a chair is recently re-covered, ask if there are photographs of the frame. Marks left by the original upholstery nails on the side of the chair are a good indication that it is an original and not a more recent reproduction. Do not put springs in an 18thC chair that originally had a stuffed seat. See also ARMCHAIR; ARMCHAIR, BUTTON-BACK; BÉRGÈRE; and EASY CHAIR.

ARMILLARY SPHERE Globe that demonstrates the movements of the planets and constellations in relation to each other.

ARMITAGE SHEFFIELD American silver-plated wares made in Philadelphia *c*.1800 by the Armitage brothers, originally from Sheffield, England.

ARMOIRE Used for storing clothes, a type of French tall CUPBOARD or WARDROBE with one or two doors. Long, outset brass hinges and cockerel-head escutcheons are typical of the stylish metalware found on French furniture made during the reign of Louis XVI. ROCOCO carving will make a French armoire more desirable than simple decoration. Dutch armoires made in the 18thC are always plain. If you find one with MARQUETRY inlay, it is a modern reproduction, or it might have been "improved" in the 19thC.

ARMORIAL An engraved design showing a crest or coat of arms on CERAMIC, SILVER, or SILVER-PLATE pieces. The form of the shield and the design of the CARTOUCHE can provide evidence for determining the date of an item.

ARMOUR A protective, usually metal, outfit or covering worn by soldiers. Most pieces available today date from the 16thC onward. Swashbuckling armour from the English Civil War (1642–9) is sought after by collectors; "lobster-tailed" cavalry helmets, pikeman's pots (simple helmets), breastplates,

A fine Victorian WINGED ARMCHAIR in early 18thC style.

backplates, and gauntlets are especially desirable. Complete suits of original armour rarely come up for sale, so even good 19thC reproductions are valuable. Much fine-quality armour of this period was made in Germany, France, and Spain. Most antique armour has been repaired at some stage. Full sets of armour are rare and extremely valuable – the majority are incomplete and are MARRIAGES between pieces from different periods. Assuming that you realise that the set is a composite and this fact is allowed for in the price, marriages are acceptable. Look out for: armourer's marks (these add to value); small dents in the breastplate (made from a pistol ball fired to test the armour's strength) – a good sign of age; and funerary helmets (worn at funerals). Treat rust with equal quantities of turpentine and paraffin, and a little methylated spirit. Polish armour with newspaper and protect with wax.

ARNOLD, JOHN One of two highly regarded London clockmakers of the same name. One was active 1760–95; the other, his son John Roger, 1800–30.

ARROW BACK American term for a WINDSOR CHAIR.

ART DECO One of the most significant decorative arts movements to emerge in the early 20thC, from c.1918–40, Art Deco swept through Europe, Britain, and the USA. Named after the 1925 Paris Exposition Internationale des Arts Décoratifs et Industriels Modernes, the style embraces two different approaches to the applied arts. On the one hand, French designers made luxurious objects of the highest quality in exotic woods. On the other hand, modernists such as the BAUHAUS in Germany developed clean, simple shapes suitable for mass production using "new" materials such as tubular steel and chrome. The style is characterized by bold geometric forms and angular architectural outlines, in reaction against the curvaceousness of ART NOUVEAU. Prototypes from the leading furniture designers, Marcel BREUER and Ludwig MIES VAN DER ROHE, and "Jazz Age" designers in the USA, Frank Lloyd WRIGHT, Donald DESKEY, and Paul T. FRANKL, are collectable, as are any pieces that exemplify the spirit of the age. The work of Art Deco studio potters commands high prices, but the colourful geometric designs of Clarice CLIFF and CARLTON WARE are increasingly popular. Look for pre-1935 pieces and rare shapes and patterns. LALIQUE is the dominant glass designer of the Art Deco period; his glassworks produced more than 10 million pieces – most of these are marked, to a high standard, and very collectable. Other noted makers are Genet & Michon, André Hunebelle, and Verlys. Look for powder compacts, cigarette cases, and brooches, especially those signed by Jean Després.

ART GLASS Term for decorative rather than functional GLASS made from the mid-19thC onward, with an emphasis on design and quality. Émile GALLÉ and DAUM FRÈRES are known for their art glass, and firms in the USA made colourful AMBERINA and BURNESE GLASS.

ARTIST BEAR Collective term for TEDDY BEARS made by bear lovers inspired to create their own designs, including the sleepy examples of Sue Quinn in Renfrewshire, Scotland (Dormouse Designs), and the Lilliputian Wareham Bears of Mary Hildesley in Dorset, England. "Little Mutt", who has one leg shorter than the other and wears an orthopaedic boot, is popular. In the USA these bears range from the realistic "Den's Den" animals of Vietnam veteran Denis Shaw to the more traditional Kaleb Designs by Barbara Wiltrout.

ART NOUVEAU A significant 19th and early 20thC movement in Europe, Britain, and the USA. In 1896 the antiques dealer Samuel BING opened a gallery in Paris that acted as a forum for the avant-garde work of designers opposed to the mechanization of the mid- to late 19thC. "Art Nouveau" derives its name from Bing's shop, La Maison de l'Art Nouveau, which retailed glass and furniture designed by such innovatory figures as René LALIQUE, Emile GALLÉ, and Louis C. TIFFANY. The style first appeared in Belgium c.1892 before spreading to France at the end of the 19thC. Inspired by nature, the style is dominated by sinuous fluid forms such as the shape of flowers, asymmetrical lines, insect motifs, ethereal maidens, and opalescent colours, and, in Britain, simple, straight-lined designs with a vertical emphasis.

ART POTTERY A term for hand-crafted POTTERY made in the late 19th and 20thC, usually by small firms such as POOLE POTTERY, MARTIN BROTHERS, ROOKWOOD, and FULPER. DOULTON and MINTON also produced handmade wares.

ARTS AND CRAFTS MOVEMENT In reaction to the industrialization of the 19thC, designers such as William MORRIS, Ernest GIMSON, and C.F.A. VOYSEY placed greater emphasis on hand craftsmanship and FURNITURE of simple design that was unspoiled by staining or similar preparations. Likewise, wares in GLASS were made to reflect the intrinsic beauty of that material, with simple forms. In the late 19thC this led to a revival in traditional methods of construction popular throughout Europe. The Arts Workers' Guild was founded in 1884; four years later the Arts and Crafts Exhibition Society held its first show. Hammered surfaces, CABOCHONS, ENAMELLING, and organic- and Celtic-style ornament are all characteristic of the style on metal wares. *See also* Charles Robert ASHBEE and Archibald KNOX.

ASH A close-grained, whitish-grey wood, ash (*Fraxinus excelsior*) was used in solid form for cheap COUNTRY FURNITURE, particularly the hooped backs of WINDSOR CHAIRS, and for drawer linings, and was at its height from 1750 to 1850. It was also used as a burred veneer. It is vulnerable to woodworm.

ASHBEE, CHARLES ROBERT (1863–1942) Craftsman who in 1888 in London founded the Guild of Handicraft, a working, medieval-style guild, where masters taught apprentices. It moved to Chipping Campden in 1902. Ashbee is noted for ARTS AND CRAFTS JEWELLERY and metalwork.

An ARTS AND CRAFTS Liberty pewter vase from the Tudric range by Archibald Knox, early 20thC.

ASPARAGUS TONGS Similar to SUGAR TONGS, but with small ridges along the inner face for holding asparagus spears; used from *c.*1750 to *c.*1830.

ASSAY MARK In the United Kingdom, a mark stamped on SILVER and gold by one of the assay offices (e.g. London, Birmingham, Chester, Exeter, Sheffield, Newcastle, York, Glasgow, Edinburgh, or Dublin) to signify that the metal is of the standard required by law. The symbol, which is often based on the city's coat of arms, is usually accompanied by a year mark.

ASSOCIATED When one part of an object is of the same period and style as the rest of the piece but not originally made for it – e.g. a teapot and associated stand. Also, when referring to weapons, any part that is not original.

ASTRAGAL Convex moulding used as glazing bars on a CABINET or BOOKCASE.

ASTROLABE A SCIENTIFIC INSTRUMENT for plotting altitude and charting the relative moments of planets and constellations. It consists of a telescope sight, a movable, brass measuring ring, and a PLANISPHERE.

ASTRONOMICAL CLOCK A fine, 18thC instrument that shows the phases of the moon and other astronomical phenomena.

ASUKA The period of Japanese history AD 552–645.

A.T. DOLLS The firm of A. Thuillier, known as A.T., operating in Paris, France, from 1875 to 1890, and known for its BÉBÉS. DOLLS were sold dressed and undressed with KID, COMPOSITION, and PAPIER-MÂCHÉ jointed bodies. A.T. sometimes used bodies and heads made by other dollmakers such as STEINER and GAULTIER. "Paperweight" eyes with pink shading behind are features of A.T. dolls. Some bébés have open mouths with two rows of teeth. These dolls command high prices because of their rarity and beauty.

ATLANTA A male figure used as a support or as a motif during the 17thC.

ATMOS CLOCK An instrument that uses slight changes in barometric pressure to rewind the main spring, hence it never needs manual winding.

ATTERBURY & CO. (Also known as the White House Works.) American, Pittsburgh-based glassworks, 1859–93. Made pressed and cut-glass TABLEWARE.

ATTWELL, MABEL LUCY (1879–1964) British illustrator of children's books, postcards, and NURSERY WARE, as well as MONEY BOXES and biscuit tins.

AUBUSSON French town in which TAPESTRIES and tapestry-weave CARPETS with a flower-filled pattern have been made since the 17thC; formal

A Shelley nurseryware teapot decorated by MABEL LUCIE ATTWELL, *c.*1926

workshops were founded *c.*1743. The most sought-after Aubussons are flat-woven on a loom. The design was built up one colour at a time. When a new colour was added, a vertical split was left between the wefts, and this was stitched up by hand. Aubussons were made with wide, plain borders and were intended to fit right up to the walls and to be cut to fit around fireplaces. Slightly worn small rugs or fragments may be available for more modest sums.

AUGER FLAME American term for flame-type finials found on CABINETS.

AUMBRY Medieval CUPBOARD, sometimes raised on a stand, and used for storing weapons or food. Also called a hutch.

AURENE GLASS An iridescent-coloured glassware developed by English-born Frederick Carder at STEUBEN GLASSWORKS in New York, USA. Produced from 1904 to 1934, "Aurene" GLASS is found in two main varieties: gold and blue (the latter ranging from pale and silvery to dark blue).

AURICULAR Derived from the Latin for "ear"; relates to any shell-like motif.

AUTOMATON A mechanical TOY with moving parts, usually powered by a clockwork mechanism, and popular during the 18th and 19thC. Those made between 1870 and 1914 in the factories of BING, MÄRKLIN, Lehmann, and CARETTE in Germany, Martin and Rossignol in France, BASSETT-LOWKE in the UK, and Ives in the USA are particularly collectable.

AUTOMATON CLOCK One of the most varied, valuable types of novelty CLOCK, a timepiece that contains a moving mechanical figure or device, which perform on the strike. Most surviving samples are from the 19thC, although they have been produced from the 16thC, especially in Germany.

AUTOPERIPATETIKOS CRYING DOLL Greek for "self-walking"; a type of walking, talking DOLL developed by STEINER. A cardboard conical skirt under the doll's dress hides bellows and a stop-start mechanism, which causes the wheels in the wooden base to rotate and the doll to "walk".

AVENTURIN Powdered gold found on some JAPANNED items.

AVENTURINE Italian for "chance"; decoration with flecked metallic particles of brown or blue quartz with gold inclusions. Also, anything that resembles the mineral, such as aventurine GLASS (blue with minute threads of gold) and LACQUER work of gold strands on a red or black background.

AXMINSTER Knotted-PILE CARPETS made at Axminster, England, in the late 18th and early 19thC and imitating Oriental and French styles. Not to be confused with the same factory's more recent cut-pile carpets.

BACCARAT **glass paperweight, dated 1848, with animal silhouettes within floral canes.**

BACCARAT Established in Meurthe, France, in 1764, and still flourishing today, an important maker of crystal GLASS. The firm imported labour from many factories in Europe in the late 18thC, and made superb crystal table glass. It is known for its fine-stemmed TABLEWARE of incredible thinness, and for stressing form over decoration. VASES and TAZZAS in OPALINE glass are characteristic of Baccarat's products. Baccarat is also famous for its 19thC PAPERWEIGHTS. One typical design includes a butterfly hovering over a clematis flower with a cluster of leaves. The rods in their paperweights may include tiny silhouettes of a dog, a horse, or a deer, all designs typical of the factory. Other common silhouettes include arrowheads and shamrocks. Baccarat weights featuring a snake or lizard are particularly rare today. Overlay weights usually have five facets. Baccarat paperweights often include signed and dated canes. The firm's trademark, registered in 1860, is still in use as a label, or acid-etched on the piece. *See also* DRINKING GLASS, FRENCH.

BACCHUS, GEORGE & SONS A major 19thC English GLASS manufacturer, established in Birmingham in 1840 and noted for its ornamental GLASS BOWLS. The firm exhibited wares at the Great Exhibition of 1851, including champagne glasses with curling colour-twist stems, inspired by 15th and 16thC Venetian glass. They also produced PAPERWEIGHTS from 1848 to *c.*1850. The firm's best MILLEFIORI designs have concentric patterns of canes set around a central white floret. Colours are typically rose-pink, turquoise, and blue, and are more muted than those used by leading French makers. Star canes around the edge of the weight are typical.

BACHELDER, EZRA American clockmaker, active 1793–1840.

BACHELOR'S CHEST Designed for a gentleman's dressing room, a small CHEST OF DRAWERS with a hinged, fold-over top to provide a working surface.

BACKBOARD The wood (often unpolished) used to infill the back of items of FURNITURE made to stand or hang against a wall.

BACKPLATE (1) Brass plate that protects a drawer front from being damaged by the BAIL or by the hand as the bail is grasped.

BACKPLATE (2) Also called back stop, or back piece; the metal plate extending from the POMMEL to the guard of a SWORD.

BACKPLATE (3) The rearmost of two plates supporting a CLOCK mechanism. It is usually engraved with the maker's name.

BACKSTOOL A 16thC rudimentary CHAIR – essentially a stool with a back.

BACKSWORD SWORD with only one edge for cutting.

BADEKIND Literally "bathing child", a 19thC china DOLL used as a bath toy.

BADGE A metal or fabric emblem identifying a soldier's position in the military. Officers' headdress badges are larger than most others, and are sought after; examples can be found dating to the mid-19thC. Before that date, there were no standard cap badges in England, although a King's Crown badge appeared on SWORDS, belts, buckles, and shoulder plates. British regimental badges are identifiable by a crown in the design. Some badges struck abroad were crudely made, and even cast in lead. American metal badges are less numerous than British ones, but there is a wide range of fabric unit and other insignia. Badges will show evidence of their age. Fakes usually weigh less, and feel waxy.

BADLAM, STEPHEN (1751–1815) An American cabinet-maker based in Dorchester, Massachuesetts. He made quality NEO-CLASSICAL-STYLE furniture.

BAEHR & PROESCHILD German makers of BISQUE-head dolls, from the late 19thC to 1930.

BAFF Persian name for the knot used in the manufacture of CARPETS.

BAGNEUX SHADE Originally made in Bagneux, France, a GLASS dome used in the 19thC to protect ornaments from dust.

BAGUETTE In JEWELLERY, a small stone cut into a rectangular shape.

BAIL Curved metal drawer pull that hangs from metal bolts.

BAIL HANDLE A type of handle that rises over the top of the vessel, like a bucket handle, instead of being fixed and parallel to the sides.

BAIN, ALEXANDER Scottish inventor of the electric CLOCK, patented in 1843.

BAKELITE An early form of plastic, invented by L.H. Baekeland in 1913, and used for industrial and domestic objects, including ART DECO sculpture. *See also* PLASTIQUE.

BAKER BAYONET Common in the early 19thC and made to fit the Baker rifle, a sword-cum-bayonet with a knuckle guard.

BAKEWELL GLASS Wares made at the Pittsburgh Flint Glass Manufactury, established c.1800. The firm was the first American producer of fine lead GLASS, and was noted for luxury TABLEWARE and CHANDELIERS, and pressed glass.

BAKHMETEV GLASS Russian (Moscow) firm, founded in the late 18thC.

BAKHTIARI Southern Iranian nomads producing red, brown, and blue RUGS of cotton and wool, with floral motifs, often in squares.

BALANCE In CLOCK mechanisms, a device used to control and counteract the force of the MAINSPRING.

BALANCE SPRING Developed c.1675, a spring acting on the balance wheel in a WATCH mechanism to control the oscillations of the MAINSPRING.

BALD HEAD BISQUE doll's head with a solid crown.

BALEEN Whalebone, used in the 18th and 19thC for buttons, and also carved into ornaments by sailors.

BALL, TOMPKINS & BLACK An American, New-York based silversmith and jeweller, established in 1839. They made SILVER hollow ware, chased and decorated in the ROCOCO STYLE. The firm became Black, Starr & Frost in 1876.

BALL, WILLIAM (active c.1755–69) English, Liverpool-based PORCELAIN maker who produced DELFTWARE and elaborate ROCOCO sauceboats.

BALL-AND-CLAW FOOT Introduced c.1720, a popular style for feet on CHAIRS and other FURNITURE. It depicts a taloned bird or animal foot clasping a ball, and was usually used on a CABRIOLE LEG.

BALL BACK A country-made CHAIR with wooden balls held between rails in the back. Made in East Anglia, England, and sometimes called a SUFFOLK CHAIR.

BALL CLOCK A CLOCK in which the oscillations of the MAINSPRING are controlled by the backward-and-forward movement of a steel ball in a see-saw. Also used of rare clocks driven by heavy metal balls.

BALL FOOT Orb-shaped style used for the feet of CHESTS OF DRAWERS.

BALL JOINT Joint used on the limbs of a DOLL that enables them to swivel in all directions. Some BISQUE-head dolls have eight ball-jointed or floating-ball-jointed bodies. In the latter case, the limbs slide over unattached joints.

BALL KNOP Ball-shape on the stem of wineglasses, used from the 18thC.

BALLOON BACK Victorian DINING CHAIR with a rounded back.

BALLOON CLOCK A late 18th and early 19thC MANTEL CLOCK with a balloon-shaped case, curving inward below the dial.

BALL STOPPER On early GLASS bottles, a glass ball in a retaining cage. The ball falls out to allow for pouring when the bottle is tilted, and falls back to seal the neck when the vessel is stood upright.

BALTIMORE GLASS Items of GLASS from one of several factories in Baltimore, Maryland, USA. Types include "Amelung" glass, and Baltimore flint glass, especially pressed glass, patterned with a fig shape.

BALTIMORE SILVER Early 19thC American SILVER bearing the assay mark of Baltimore.

BALUCHI From the Afghan/Iranian border region, a nomadic tribe producing dark blue and rust-red RUGS with floral motifs.

BALUSTER Derived from Renaissance architecture, a vase-shaped form with a bulbous base, narrow waist, and flared neck. Commonly used on SILVER, CERAMICS, and DRINKING GLASSES, and found on VASES, JUGS, TEAPOTS, FINIALS, and the stems of CANDLESTICKS and drinking vessels. Also refers to shaped turning used as the centre column or legs of a TABLE. Various designs were achieved, a familiar one being the vase shape used in the 17thC.

BALUSTER GLASS Popular from *c.*1690 to *c.*1720, a wineglass based on the baluster. These glasses are heavy and symmetrical in form, with conical or domed, folded feet and distinctive stems with one or more KNOPS, after the style of Baroque furniture. DIAMOND-POINT ENGRAVING was preferred on Anglo-Dutch glass, because the SODA GLASS used was too fragile to be decorated by WHEEL-ENGRAVING. Engraved decoration is rare on the bowl of an English glass. On a "true baluster" stem, the widest part of a lower KNOP is nearer the base, and there is a cushion knop. Knops on early balusters are plain, but in the early 18thC more elaborate forms developed; the "egg" and "cylinder" forms are the most valuable. Early 18thC English baluster glasses often had bowls with heavy solid bases, and this adds to the weight of the object. Glasses with thick-walled, shallow bowls designed to hold a small quantity of alcohol were popular with publicans when drinking with their customers. Known as "illusion" glasses – because the bowl appears to be full – they were made in the 18thC and 19thC. Many heavy glasses were melted down after the imposition of the 1745 Excise Tax, and are hence rare today.

BALUSTER STEM A late 17thC DRINKING GLASS with a swelling stem. It is "true" if the thicker swelling is beneath, "inverted" if above.

Airtwist glass with a BALUSTER stem, *c.*1740.

Late-18thC mahogany BANJO
BAROMETER.

BALUSTER VASE A VASE shaped like an architectural BALUSTER, with a bulbous body and long neck.

BALUSTROID A taller, lighter form of BALUSTER.

BAMBOO FURNITURE Lightwieght conservatory and garden FURNITURE made from bamboo, a giant tropical grass. Bamboo furniture was popular in the Regency period, when it was used to furnish CHINOISERIE interiors. Beech was often carved in imitation of bamboo from the late 18thC onward. Bamboo furniture with Oriental-style LACQUER tops became popular in the Edwardian period, and large numbers of small TABLES were made in Japan for the Western market. Bamboo TEA TABLES with folding trays and lacquer tops decorated in traditional colours are typical of the type of furniture made at the beginning of the 20thC; however, few have survived in good condition.

BAMBOO TURNING Furniture legs turned to simulate bamboo. Made in the Chinese taste during the late 18thC and Regency period.

BANDING Contrasting strips of VENEER laid around the edge of drawer fronts and the tops of tables and case furniture to decorative effect. Depending on the way in which the grain of the wood runs, banding is referred to as straight banding, CROSSBANDING (with the grain at right angles to the main veneer), feather, or herringbone banding.

BAND SWORD Ornamental SWORDS, with curved scimitar blades and cruciform hilts, issued to drummers and military bandsmen from c.1768.

BANISTER BACK A CHAIR with vertical, split banisters in the back.

BANJO BAROMETER A wheel-type barometer, so-called because of its shape. Weights floating on the surface of the mercury and linked to pulleys convert linear movements to turn a pointer around a circular dial.

BANJO CLOCK Popular form of late 18th to mid-19thC PENDULUM CLOCK resembling an upturned banjo on a pedestal base. *See* WILLARD CLOCKS.

BANKER Old term for a bench.

BANQUETTE Long STOOL, with high scrolling ends and a caned seat.

BANTAM WORK Type of LACQUERWORK that has incised designs instead of the more usual, raised designs. It originated in the Java province of Bantam in the 17thC, and is also known as CUT WORK.

BAR BACK Descriptive of a CHAIR with the top rail formed as a bar.

BARBIE Introduced in 1959 by the American firm Mattel, the "Barbie" DOLL epitomizes the image of the post-war American dream: she is glamorous, wealthy, and attractive. Original Barbies had a slightly Oriental look, with pale complexions. During the 1960s, the skin tone became darker, reflecting the fashion for suntans. Early dolls wore ponytails, but, by 1961, Barbie's hairstyle developed into a bouffant "bubble" cut. Titian and brunette Barbies are rarer than blondes, and more valuable. Barbie's success was due to the range and quality of her outfits, including handbags and shoes, and miniature furniture wardrobes were made especially to house them. Dolls made between 1959 and 1969 (the "Couture Period") had clothes inspired by haute-couture houses such as Balenciaga, Dior, and Givenchy; these dolls are very collectable. Some garments are worth more than the doll. Among the rarest outfits are "Gay Parisienne" and "American Stewardess". Various friends were created for Barbie, including "Stacey", "Skooter", and "Ken". The last was first produced in 1963. Barbie's friends are worth less than Barbie, but they are rarer, and are hence becoming more sought after. An original Mattel box can double the value of any Barbie doll, while mint condition is vital in a recent example. If a Barbie has holes in the feet for a stand, she is one of the first dolls made – this feature was phased out by 1961. All genuine Barbies are marked, with the maker's mark usually located on Barbie's bottom, or on the back of a shoulder. Look for the Barbie label on the clothes, because they may have been swapped with clothes for other makes of doll of the same size. Dolls are sometimes tampered with – look out for holes in the feet that have been drilled but have not have acquired the grime of age.

BARBIZET-PALISSY Late 19thC POTTERY produced at Barbizet, near Paris, France, in imitation of 16thC Palissy ware.

BARBOTINE Painting on POTTERY using coloured KAOLIN pastes. The technique was invented in 1865 by Ernest CHAPLET.

BARGUEÑO (Vargueño) Spanish CABINET with a fall front enclosing drawers.

BARKER WARE Items made from the mid-19thC at the British, Yorkshire-based firm of Samuel Barker.

BARLEY-SUGAR TWIST Spiral-turned pillars popular on CHAIRS and TABLES in the late 17thC.

BARLOW SISTERS Artists employed by the DOULTON pottery in the 1870s, and famous for their animal designs on the company's decorated tablewares.

BARNSLEYS Two brothers, Ernest (1864–1962) and Sidney (1865–1962), who founded the Cotswold Arts and Crafts Movement with Ernest GIMSON. Their FURNITURE designs were inspired by rural woodworking techniques.

BAROGRAPH A late-18thC barometer that measures air pressure with a vacuum chamber linked to a rib, which draws a graph on a revolving drum.

BAROMETER, PORTABLE So-called because instead of being wall mounted, this instrument was free standing – mounted on a wooden pillar with three brass feet. It was used in the late 17th and early 18thC.

BAROQUE STYLE A heavy, highly ornamental late-17thC style, principally in Italy. It was originally a derogatory term, derived from the Italian *barroco*, or "misshapen pearl". Baroque FURNITURE and other items are decorated with heavy carving, often including figural sculpture and curving shapes. The style prevailed throughout Continental Europe in the late 17th and early 18thC. Key designers include Daniel MAROT in Holland and England, Andrea Brustolon in Venice, and Jean Le Pautre in France.

BARR, G. From Bolton, England, an 18thC maker of Yorkshire-style CLOCKS.

BARRAUD & LUND English, London-based company active from the mid-19thC, and specializing in electric CLOCKS.

BARREL The part of a CLOCK mechanism that contains the MAINSPRING, around which the spring driving the train is wound.

BARTHOLOMEW BABIES Rare, carved, wooden DOLLS produced for sale at English fairs (originally for the St Bartholomew Fair at Smithfield in 1721).

BARUM WARE ART POTTERY produced in Barnstaple, Devon, England from *c*.1879. Usually made with red clay and a shiny blue-and-green glaze.

BASALTES An unglazed black STONEWARE developed in the 1760s by WEDGWOOD. It was produced at the Etruria factory, which specialized in ornamental wares. Wedgwood made a range of library busts of both Classical and contemporary figures. Modern reproductions are called basalt wares.

BASKET A hollow SILVER vessel for serving sweetmeats, bread, fruit, or cake. The earliest 18thC examples were oval, with pierced-and-chased sides simulating wickerwork; they had flat bases, often decorated with coats of arms. Toward the end of the Neo-classical period, baskets were oval or boat-shaped on raised feet, and decorated with applied Classical ornament, with reeded borders or beaded work around the rim. Pierced work was a favoured technique. Some of the finest 18thC baskets were made by Paul de LAMERIE, William Plummer, and Burradge DAVENPORT (3). Until the 1720s, a handle was placed at each end of the basket, but by the mid-18thC, hinged swing handles in the centre had become standard. The body of an early basket was constructed from a single piece of SILVER, which was hammered up to form a bowl; cast ornament, a cast foot, and a handle were then added. With increased mass production from the 1770s, baskets were made from thin sheets of stamped silver, which resulted in poorer-quality, lighter, easily damaged designs. In the late 18thC, silver was drawn into wires and used imaginatively to simulate the open lattice weave of a basket. Early baskets should be marked underneath. Decorative motifs often provide clues as to the basket's intended use – for example, sheaves of wheat for bread or bunches of grapes for fruit. Reproductions of 18thC baskets, especially Neo-classical boat shapes, were popular in the 19thC. Look for the marks on baskets along the rim, where the handle meets the body. On examples with pierced decoration, the marks are often lost in the pierced work. Handles should always be at least partly marked. *See also* NEO-CLASSICAL STYLE.

BASKET HILT Perforated hilt (covering the hand) at the end of a SWORD.

BASKET-TOP CLOCK CLOCK with a dome-shaped case, usually of metal.

BASKET WEAVE Low-relief motif simulating woven twigs or reeds.

BAS RELIEF (Low relief) A slightly raised, carved, or sculpted design.

BASSANO WARE POTTERY produced near Venice, Italy, from the 15thC. The firm later specialized in PORCELAIN imitations of Chinese wares.

BASSET TABLE Small TABLE for playing bassette, a card game.

BASSETT-LOWKE Producers of clockwork locomotives and scale models from *c.*1910. The firm made one of the best-known early models of live steam, the "Black Prince" locomotive, which was available in three gauges. The most admired train of the inter-war period was the "Flying Scotsman". BING, CARETTE, and Trix all supplied locomotives to Bassett-Lowke. Look out for hand-built locomotives and pre-1914 trains, which are often unmarked. Bing/Greenly models made mostly pre-World War I for Bassett-Lowke are also desirable. Bassett-Lowke continued to make trains until 1969.

BATEMAN & CO. An English family-run silverware firm. Hester Bateman (1708–94) expanded her husband's business following his death in 1760, and was one of the first manufacturers to establish a fully mechanized workshop in London. Although a vast quantity of SILVER from the Bateman factory survives, much is of thin gauge and poorly made.

BATH METAL Made from the late 17thC as a substitute for gold, an alloy of 32 parts copper to 39 zinc.

BATON In JEWELLERY, a large stone cut into a rectangular shape.

Whitefriars, "Drunken Bricklayer" vase by GEOFFREY BAXTER, 1967.

BAT PRINTING An early -19thC printing technique, which involved using flexible glue bats instead of transfer paper as a way of transferring a design from an engraved copper plate to a POTTERY or PORCELAIN body.

BAT'S-WING FLUTING Graduated GADROONING that radiates from a fixed point, and somewhat resembles the outline of a bat's wing.

BATTEN Thin strip of wood.

BATTERSEA ENAMEL PORCELAIN trinkets, such as SNUFF-BOXES, decorated with enamel from the British, London-based firm founded in the mid-18thC.

BATTERY METAL Earliest form of English brass, made in the 16thC and named after a noted manufacturer, the Mineral & Battery Works of London.

BATTING American term for wadding.

BAUDOUINE, CHARLES A. (1808–95) An American, New-York-based cabinet-maker, he made vast quanties of parlour FURNITURE, using ROSEWOOD and a particular laminating process, in the ROCOCO Revival style.

BAUHAUS German artistic style, inspired by new industrial materials, such as stainless steel, with the emphasis on cubic, unadorned shapes. The term was coined by the architect Walter gropius, who became director of the Weimar school of Arts and Crafts in 1919, and renamed it the Bauhaus.

BAXTER, GEOFFREY (active 1954–80) Designer at the British WHITEFRIARS glassworks. He designed the "Drunken Bricklayer" vase, which was made from 1967 to *c*.1977, and came in two sizes and several colours.

BAYLEY & UPJOHN Late -18th and early -19thC English, London-based makers of the regulator CLOCK.

BAYONET Short blade attached to the muzzle of a FIREARM. The first bayonet (PLUG BAYONET), made in the mid-17thC, was simply a dagger plugged into the barrel of a musket after it had been discharged. In the late 17thC, the French invented the SOCKET BAYONET, which allowed the weapon to be fired while the bayonet was fixed to the musket. The socket bayonet was used until the late 19thC, when it was replaced by the SPRING-LOADED BAYONET.

BAYONET FITTING Method of attaching a cover to a body by means of two locking lugs that are slotted into a flange and rotated.

"BEADED" PATTERN FLATWARE embellished with a continuous border of beaded decoration; it was especially popular in the Victorian period.

BEADING A decorative border of compact beads, either cast and applied, or embossed. Also a term used for moulding – either a small, plain, half- or quarter-round, wooden moulding, or moulding in the form of a string of beads.

BEADWORK Decoration on material using GLASS beads of different colours.

BEAKER A drinking vessel without a handle, stem, or foot. The basic cylindrical form has changed little since the 15thC. Most 16th and early 17thC beakers are plain, with bands of ARABESQUES, stylized flowers, or foliage; later 17thC examples feature embossed-and-chased flowers and leaves, often with engraved initials or armorials. From the 17thC, particularly in Continental Europe, beakers were sometimes produced in groups, known as "nesting" sets, where the individual vessels fitted into one another for storage. In the 18thC, it was common for beakers to be made in pairs. Complete sets are most valuable; a pair will be worth more than twice the value of a single vessel. Vessels in novelty forms were a popular concept in the Victorian and Edwardian periods; examples include little beakers resembling sewing thimbles and used to measure "thimblefuls" of liquor.

BEAR-BABY Rare toy made in 1914 by Louis S. Schiffer, based in New York, USA. One half is a BISQUE-head DOLL; the other side is a TEDDY BEAR.

BEARER *See* LOPER.

BEAR JUG English STONEWARE JUGS made in the 18thC in the shape of a bear. They were first made in Derby and Staffordshire, but were widely copied.

BEATLES MEMORABILIA Items owned by or marketed for the music group The Beatles, pioneers of the pop music that epitomized the sounds of the 1960s. They have a unique place in the history of pop music: no previous group had enjoyed such enormous and lasting success. Almost any object associated with the group is of interest to collectors. The wide range of Beatles merchandise made during the 1960s and '70s reflects the group's phenomenal popularity. Among the diverse Beatles objects that come up for sale are furnishings, jewellery, clothing, games, books, wigs, and even confectionary. Drawings by John Lennon, who also wrote and illustrated two books, are among the most desirable Beatles memorabilia, and can fetch high prices. Look out for handwritten lyrics to famous songs; autographed and handwritten letters; autographed photographs (these are often faked, so beware); artwork for record sleeves; and animation cels from *Yellow Submarine*. *See also* CELEBRITY DOLLS and ROCK AND POP EPHEMERA.

BEAUTY SPOT Applied beauty marks typical on late-17thC dolls. Pretending to have a "mole" to offset a beautiful complexion began as a way to cover up smallpox scars. Beauty spots became fashionable at the French Court in the

1960s record player decorated with a BEATLES design.

17thC, and reached England when Charles I married Henrietta Maria in 1625. They were painted onto dolls, but in reality were made of black silk impregnated with adhesive, and came in a variety of shapes, such as half-moons, stars, hearts, and cupids. Different meanings were conveyed by the position in which patches were fixed: stars at the corner of the mouth, for example, are particularly suggestive. The larger beauty spots were called "assassins" for their supposedly devastating effect. *See also* PATCHBOX.

BEAUVAIS WARE Religious figures and tableware produced at Beauvais, France, from the late 14thC.

BEAVER (Bevor) The front part of a helmet, hinged at the top so that the face guard could be raised or lowered.

Large, French BÉBÉ doll marked "SFBJ Paris", c.1890 (*see* p.387).

BÉBÉ Modelled on a child of eight to 12 years of age, a DOLL of short, chubby build and with childlike features such as large eyes. Until the 19thC, dolls were modelled and dressed as adults. However, after the English, London-based dollmaker Henry PIEROTTI created "Royal Model Babies" representing the children of Queen Victoria, it was realized that children prefer to play with dolls that resemble themselves. In 1855, leading Parisian dollmaker Pierre François JUMEAU was the first to make a bébé, and rival firms such as BRU copied him. Bébés took the form of idealized young girls, with BISQUE heads, real hair, either wool or mohair wigs, large (usually glass) eyes, and delicately painted facial details. Their bodies were jointed by a ball that was fixed to the limbs, and they were made in varying materials – but with noticeably chubby limbs and gently rounded stomachs. At first, their mouths were closed, and their wrists were fixed. The use of articulated wrists and open mouths on bébés came later. The heyday of the bébé occurred between the 1860s and '90s. In the late 19thC, small firms sprang up, especially in porcelain-making areas such as LIMOGES, where dolls' heads and whole dolls were made between 1897 and 1925. However, their quality is poor, and the colouring of some is too pink. Besides GAULTIER and ROHMER, the small firms MAISON HURET and RABERY & DELPHIEU made bébés. Prices depend on maker, condition, quality, and certain details. The earlier dolls with pale, flawless BISQUE heads are the most valuable, especially if they have their original clothes. *See also* ETHNIC DOLL.

BED (1) Traditional piece of FURNITURE used for sleeping on. Elaborate early beds have solid headboards and two pillars supporting deep, carved friezes and ceilings called "testers", hence the term "tester bed". Opulent draperies were drawn to enclose the occupants, protecting them from draughty bedchambers. A popular variation from the late 17thC, the "half-tester" bed, has no foot posts, although the tester still covers most of the bed. On later versions, the tester covers only half of the bed. Early beds have heavy bedposts that are often elaborately turned and carved. As the centuries progressed, posts became more slender and elegant. Until the introduction of sprung mattresses in the 19thC, mattresses were usually stuffed with straw and supported on wooden lathes or ropes. "Half-headed bedsteads", with no testers and low headboards, were found in the homes of the less wealthy from Elizabethan times. The rails of the bedstead were pierced to take rope supports that held rudimentary stuffed or woven mattresses. Wooden beds continued to be made in the 19thC and beyond. MAHOGANY was commonly used, but PINE and even PAPIER-MÂCHÉ were also popular, as were beds with padded, upholstered headboards. Beds in the 19thC style of the AESTHETIC MOVEMENT increase in value when signed or attributed to a maker, such as the American designer Bruce Talbert. Eary beds are rare: they are small by today's standards, and are almost impossible to find unaltered – although there is a plethora of "made-up" beds put together with wood taken from other pieces of furniture. Early American beds, while following English and Continental European styles, were made larger from the start, so they are less likely to have been rebuilt. Tubular brass beds were made from 1820 onward. As metal-casting techniques improved, cast-iron beds became popular. Less-expensive beds were also made from steel tubing plated in brass. The prices of all metal beds tend to be lower than those of wooden beds, although many of them have survived unaltered. Today, antique beds are usually fitted with modern sprung mattresses that sit on top of the original bed rails (supports). Before you buy an antique bed, measure it to ensure that it is big enough for your needs. Many "double" beds measure about 1.21m (4ft) wide by 1.82m (6ft) long and are rather small by modern standards. Take into account the cost of having a mattress specially made. Also consider the cost of a QUILT or coverlet, and hangings if you are buying a bed with a tester.

BED (2) The part of a drop-leaf table top that does not hinge.

BEDROOM SUITE Several items of FURNITURE designed to be used together in a bedroom, usually a double BED or a pair of single beds, a WARDROBE, a DRESSING TABLE, and a pair of BEDSIDE CABINETS or TABLES. Suites made before plumbing was standard in middle-class homes in the mid-19thC may also have washstands. Most suites date from the early-Victorian period onward. You can often buy a whole suite for the same price that you would pay for two or three pieces separately. The most popular items in a suite are pairs of small bedside cabinets, followed by CHESTS OF DRAWERS and dressing tables. Bedroom suites that have survived with their original painted decoration are worth looking out for, as are those with a well-documented provenance.

BEDSIDE CABINET (bedside cupboard, night table) A small CABINET designed to stand near or next to a bed. They are sometimes fitted with washstands and can be found with drawers, tambour slides or tray tops with carrying handles. English cabinets tend to have ceramic or brass casters; wooden casters can be found on French bedside cabinets.

BEDSTEAD Of a BED, the framework supporting the bedding.

BED STEP Two or three solid steps for climbing into a high BED; sometimes they doubled as a COMMODE and had small cupboards for chamber pots.

BEECH A brownish white wood with a flecked grain, beech (*Fagus sylvatica*) is strong but prone to woodworm and rot. It was used in a solid form on COUNTRY FURNITURE from the 17thC onward, as well as for the frames of upholstered FURNITURE, because it does not split when tacked. It was also popular in the 18th and 19thC as a base for painted furniture. It is easy to carve, and almost all French CHAIR frames are made from it. Beech has been used for kitchen utensils, as well as for the handles of tools and brushes.

BEEHIVE CLOCK From New England, USA, a mid-19thC MANTEL CLOCK with a case shaped like a Gothic arch. So-called for its resemblance to a beehive.

BEHRENS, PETER (1868–1940) German designer of everything from GLASS to stationery. He founded the Vereinigte Werkstätten in Munich, but later rejected ART NOUVEAU to create a new, simplified, Classical style.

BEILBY GLASS Wares made by the Beilby family. William (1740–1819) and his sister Mary (1749–97) were celebrated practitioners of painting and enamelling on GLASS, especially ARMORIALS and ROCOCO ornamentation. William experimented with white enamels on plain glass. In the early 1760s, he set up a workshop in Newcastle, England, decorating DRINKING GLASSES, TUMBLERS, and DECANTERS. Delicately painted, white-enamel designs of landscapes, hunting scenes, Classical ruins, and vines are typical of the Beilbys; their armorial GOBLETS with coloured-enamel, heraldic decoration are more rare.

BEINGLAS Made in Bohemia in the late 18thC, GLASS of "milky" appearance created with the inclusion of bone ash.

BELLARMINE Named after Cardinal Roberto Bellarmino (1542–1621), who sought to outlaw alcoholic beverages, a bulbous, narrow-necked German STONEWARE jug, with a spout in the form of a grotesque human face. A brown, mottled glaze, known as "tiger skin", is characteristic of these jugs. The base should have an impressed oval mark like a thumbprint where the piece was removed from the wheel. *See also* POTTERY, GERMAN.

BELLEEK Established in 1863 by David McBirney and Robert Williams Armstrong in County Fermanagh, Northern Ireland, Belleek specialized in producing a thin, high-quality, white PORCELAIN using a glazed PARIAN body. Warm and creamy in appearance, Belleek resembled the texture and translucence of seashells, and the factory began making wares in the forms of shells decorated with iridescent glaze, as well as finely woven BASKETS.

Late-19thC, BELLEEK, porcelain 13-piece cabaret set.

Baskets from the 19thC are three-stranded; after *c.*1900 four strands were used. Belleek is popular in the USA, and many workers from the Irish factory emigrated and set up rival establishments there – their products are termed "American Belleek". The factory is still in production, and the same designs are still produced. The fineness of Belleek makes it vulnerable to damage, and hairline cracks can devastate value. The mark with "BELLEEK" in black was used until 1891, after which a second mark was used, adding the word "IRELAND" to the name. More modern marks are in green or gold.

BELLE ÉPOQUE Translated from French, it means "beautiful period" and relates to the lavish styles of the late 19thC to World War I.

BELLE VUE TABLEWARE made in Hull, England, in the 19thC.

BELLEVUE An 18thC FAIENCE from a French firm at Meurthe on the Moselle.

BELLFLOWER Hanging flower bud of three or five petals carved or inlaid one below the other, usually on a TABLE or the leg of a CHAIR. *See also* GARYA HUSK.

"BELLFLOWER" PATTERN A floral-inspired design used by BOSTON & SANDWICH GLASS CO. in the USA. The design was later made in non-flint (non-lead) GLASS by others. Several variations were made, mostly in clear glass, but on rare occasions in different colours. Flint glass is more costly than non flint.

BELL SUNDIAL French 18thC SUNDIAL with a lens to focus sunlight at noon onto a thread; it burned and released a hammer, which struck a bell or gong.

BELL TOYS Made in the USA, popular toys that include a bell, which is operated when pushed or pulled on wheels. TINPLATE was used from the late 19thC; cast iron from the the early 20thC

BELL WARE Red STONEWARE made by Samuel Bell, in Newcastle-under-Lyme, England, in the mid-18thC. Also refers to the products of the Scottish, Glasgow-based factory of J. & M.P. Bell in the latter half of the 19thC.

BELPER WARE English STONEWARE made in the 19thC by BOURNE & SON, whose first factory was at Belper, Derbyshire.

BELTER, JOHN HENRY (1804–63) American, New York-based furniture-maker known for ROCOCO-style seat FURNITURE for the parlour or living room. He used laminated ROSEWOOD bent into elaborate shapes.

BELUCHISTAN From the 19thC, small RUGS made for export, originally used as PRAYER RUGS and horse blankets. They are made of goat and camel hair, and are dark-red to brown, with geometric motifs.

Gebruder Heubach bisque-head character baby on a composition, BENT-LIMB body, c.1910.

BENEMAN, JEAN GUILLAUME (active *c.*1784–1804) German-born cabinet-maker who worked in Paris, France, in the late 18thC. He made a large amount of FURNITURE for Queen Marie Antoinette and the French Court.

BENNETT POTTERY American, Ohio-based pottery founded in 1839 by James Bennet. It made practical, inexpensive POTTERY at first, then PARIAN ware.

BENNINGTON American pottery established in the early 19thC, making red EARTHENWARE and STONEWARE vessels, PARIAN wares, and dark-brown, mottled, ROCKINGHAM-type wares.

BENT-LIMB DOLL A covered, five-piece, jointed body made only to sit, with limbs fixed in the seated position. Bent-limb COMPOSITION bodies were used on various babies and characters between 1910 and 1939.

BÉRAIN ROCOCO-style ornamentation on French FAIENCE. It was originally blue and white, later polychrome, with a narrative scene in an ornate frame.

BERGAMA Weaving centre in Turkey noted for making PRAYER RUGS in bright colours with geometric patterns.

BERGÈRE Made in France *c.*1725, an ARMCHAIR with a concave back, wood frame, and solid, upholstered or caned sides, often with a deep, low seat. French, 18thC versions are luxurious and expensive – *bergères* made in England in the mid-19thC are more affordable. French, 18thC *bergères* have CANE woven sides and backs; cane was not often used in England until *c.*1800. French chair frames were always made of beech, either left plain, gilded, or painted. English, 19thC examples vary in quality; look for ones with quality carving such as deep GADROONING and PATERA on the legs. *See also* ARMCHAIR, BUTTON-BACK; ARMCHAIR, WINGED; and EASY CHAIR.

BERGNER, CARL (active1890-1909) German dollmaker based in Sonneberg who made DOLLS with two or three faces. He used a BISQUE head on a PAPIER-MÂCHÉ SHOULDER-PLATE attached to COMPOSITION lower limbs. Using strings in the side of the body, the crying face can be changed to a smiling face.

BERLIN PORCELAIN Founded in 1752 by W.K. Wegely, this was the first PORCELAIN factory in Berlin, Germany; it closed five years later. Wegely made a range of figures based on MEISSEN models. In 1761, King Frederick the Great established a second factory, which survives to the present day. It made a series called "The Cries of Berlin", modelled by the Meyer brothers. Berlin porcelain of the 18thC is rare – more common, 19thC pieces are exquisitely decorated with detailed panels on solid coloured grounds, but these wares are easily confused with porcelain made around the same time in Vienna and Paris. Topographical and city views were a speciality of Berlin and Viennese porcelain decorators from the early 19thC. The scenes are often named, and are among the most finely detailed of those produced in Europe. Earlier examples have rectilinear or formal borders. They can be found on PLATES and cabinet cups and saucers, and occasionally on small decorative items. The Berlin factory also produced quantities of porcelain plaques, many of which were independently decorated with copies of well-known paintings by artists such as Jean-Antoine Watteau and Bartolomé Murillo. Berlin porcelain is widely available at a range of prices, depending on size, subject, and decorative appeal. Berlin marks include a sceptre on early pieces; from 1832 an orb appears, and sometimes the letters "KPM" either in underglaze blue or red or impressed are also found.

BERLIN FAIENCE Products of several 18thC factories in the Berlin region, including DELFTWARE and VASES of unusual shape and bold blue decoration.

BERLIN TINWARE Made in Berlin, Connecticut, USA, in the mid-18thC, household wares made from TINPLATE, often JAPANNED.

BERLIN WOOLWORK **panel, c.1840.**

BERLIN WOOLWORK Amateur embroidery using coloured wools on a canvas grid. Berlin woolwork pictures were made in large numbers in the mid-19thC. Subjects vary enormously, from famous paintings to portraits of the royal family. Pictures of birds and dogs are always popular.

BERRY SPOON A utensil for serving fruit. Most berry spoons are made in pairs or sets of four and six, and are sold in velvet-lined cases. Embossed fruit is typical Victorian decoration.

BERTOIA, HARRY (b.1915) American sculpture and FURNITURE designer known for his modern, organic forms, using tubular steel and wire mesh.

BESSARABIAN From the Romanian/Russian border region, CARPETS that are characterized by naturalistic designs.

BESWICK English POTTERY-making company founded in the late 19thC by James Beswick; it was taken over by his son John in 1920, and sold to ROYAL DOULTON in 1969. Since the 1920s, it has established a reputation for its range of daring, decorative VASES and BOWLS designed by Albert Hallam; Colin Melbourne added to this mordern look by producing an "Art" range in 1956. Beswick is also known for its china animals. Among the most sought-after figures are Beatrix Potter subjects, Alice in Wonderland figures, and Snow White and the Seven Dwarfs, produced between1954 and 67; Beswick also made Winnie the Pooh figures. Horses are particular popular with collectors, and, from the 1950s onward, the firm employed highly skilled modellers to produce their designs. Pieces can be dated from the mark and model.

A BETTY BOOP **telephone, early 1990s.**

BETTY BOOP A 1930s cartoon character and the inspiration for much collectable paraphernlia. In 1932 Joseph Kallus, president of the Cameo Doll Co., designed the Betty Boop DOLL (along with "Baby Bo Kaye" and "Little Annie Rooney"), which has an over-sized SWIVEL HEAD with moulded, knobbly hair and painted features, with large, round eyes. The jointed body, which might be wooden or COMPOSITION, was moulded as a bathing suit.

BEVEL Slope cut at the edge of a flat surface and usually associated with plate glass used in MIRRORS.

BEZEL Metal rim to the GLASS covering a CLOCK or WATCH face.

BIANCHI Working in Ipswich, England, in the early 19thC, a noted maker of BANJO BAROMETERS, often incorporating CLOCKS and thermometers.

BIANCO SOPRA BIANCO White-glaze patterns painted over a greyish-white background. Typical of 16thC MAIOLICA and 18thC DELFTWARE.

BIBLIOTHÈQUE-BASSE A type of low, French CUPBOARD fitted with shelves for storing books.

BIDDERY Imported from India in the 19thC, cheap METAL wares made of a copper, lead, and tin alloy.

BIDEFORD The most prolific of several Devon potteries producing wares in England for export to the American colonies. Items were typically white glazed with SGRAFFITO ornament revealing a red BODY.

BIEDERMEIER STYLE A bourgeois style found mostly in FURNITURE, but also in GLASS and CERAMICS, made in Germany, Austria, and Scandinavia from c.1820 to 1830. The furniture was produced from pale-coloured woods such as BIRCH, CHERRY, and MAPLE, which often contrasted with an EBONY inlay, and it has a strong architectural appearance, based on simple, symmetrical Classical principles. The glassware is characterized by the quality and range of its colours. Beware: there are many modern imports.

BIEMAN, DOMINIK (1800–57) A Bohemian GLASS engraver, specializing ing in scenes and portraits in Vienna and Prague.

BIFURCATED DROP Type of late 17thC drop handle, which divides into two branches at the end.

BIGGIN A small, cylindrical SILVER COFFEE-POT, with a cotton sleeve to hold the coffee grains, and sometimes with a stand and spirit lamp. It is said to resemble the shape of a "biggin", or nightcap, hence its name.

BIJOUTERIE TABLE Small TABLE with a top formed as a glazed display case.

BILBOHITT Named after the port of Bilbao, a Spanish broadsword with two large plate guards curving toward the POMMEL.

BILDERBOGE German cut-out paper TOYS.

BILLINGSLEY PORCELAIN painted by the British flower artist William Billingsley (1758–1828), who worked for DERBY and elsewhere, and founded NANTGARW.

BILSTON ENAMEL Door knobs, finger plates, BOXES, and trinkets of painted enamel on copper, made in Bilston, Staffordshire, England, in the late 18thC.

BIM-BAM Name imitating the two-toned strike of a popular early 20thC German-made MANTEL CLOCK.

BIMBELOTERIE French term for antique TOYS, literally, "playthings".

BIMETALLIC BALANCE A brass-and-steel instrument with different rates of expansion and contraction, so that the oscillations in a CLOCK mechanism remain constant despite changes in air temperature.

BINDESBØLL, THORVALD (1846–1908) Danish painter, designer, and potter, known for his simple, bold, ART NOUVEAU forms.

BING ARTIST'S DOLLS Company based in Nuremberg, Germany, making fine character DOLLS in the 1920s and '30s.

BING, SAMUEL (Siegfried; 1838–1905) Native of Hamburg, Germany, who, in Paris, France, in 1885 opened a shop specializing in Japanese art. He re-opened it in 1895 to promote the new decorative arts of Europe, and called it "La Maison de L'Art Nouveau", from which the term ART NOUVEAU is derived.

BING TOYS A German manufacturer of TINPLATE TOYS and TEDDY BEARS, the Gebrüder Bing ("Bing brothers") of Nüremberg began making tin kitchenware in 1865, then enamelled toys in 1890. They added teddy bears to their output before World War I. Bing bears are often dressed in colourful outfits made of felt and silk. They are noted for their mechanical abilities, such as walking, and their small facial features. In some instances, they have identity tags fixed to the ear. Before 1919, these tags bore the letters G.B.N. (Gebrüder Bing, Nuremberg); afterward, B.W. (Bing Werke).

BIRCH A pale, whitish-yellow, indigenous wood with a close grain, birch (*Betula alba*) was used for COUNTRY FURNITURE from the 17thC onward, but few early examples survive. It is seen in a solid form, or as a VENEER on

Austro-German BIEDERMEIER furniture,1800-1930. The best birch is called "Satin birch" and was occasionally used as a veneer in the late 18thC. From *c.*1850 to 1900, it was commonly used as a lining for work boxes. Figured birch can be mistaken for SATINWOOD when used on the fronts of CHESTS.

BIRDCAGE SUPPORT Found under the top of some TABLES, a small hinged mechanism, which enables them to revolve as well as tip up.

BIRDCAGE CLOCK An 18thC novelty CLOCK in the shape of a birdcage, with a hidden clock mechanism and a singing "bird" instead of a strike.

BIRD'S EYE Marking of small spots associated with MAPLE wood.

BIRMINGHAM DRIBBLER Early toy locomotive powered by steam, heated by methylated spirits, and so-called because of its propensity to leak. It was mass-produced in Birmingham from *c.*1870.

BIRMINGHAM SILVER English SILVER assayed in the Birmingham office, founded in 1773, largely due to the influence of the local manufacturer Matthew BOULTON. In 1773, there were more than 2,000 firms in the city specializing in small silverware including BUCKLES, CADDY SPOONS, VINAIGRETTES, and BOTTLE LABELS. The town mark for Birmingham is an upright anchor. It is usually shown with the lion rampant, a date letter, duty mark (the sovereign's head), and maker's mark. Before 1773, Birmingham silver was stamped with the wheatsheaf and dagger assay mark of Chester, or the leopard's head of London.

BIRNKRUG Pear-shaped drinking vessels from Germany or The Netherlands.

BISCUIT Unglazed POTTERY or PORCELAIN, fired only once. *See also* BISQUE.

BISCUIT WARE Any unglazed POTTERY, but specifically unglazed figure groups first made in France in the mid-18thC, and copied elsewhere.

BISMUTH Metal used as a strengthening agent in PEWTER and other alloys.

BISQUE French term for BISCUIT, or unglazed POTTERY or PORCELAIN.

BISQUE DOLL A DOLL with a head made from unglazed, tinted PORCELAIN. The head or SHOULDER-PLATE is cast in a mould and fired, then cleaned, sanded, and painted to give a skin colour. The facial details are painted on, then the head is fired again. Hands and feet might also be BISQUE. The first examples were produced in Germany in the 1850s, but the market was soon dominated by the French. Bisque-headed dolls with jointed wood or KID bodies were made to look as realistic as possible and have wigs attached to a cardboard or cork PATE. Elaborate construction allowed them to adopt numerous poses, and their wardrobes were lavish. The dolls were popular in France and Germany from the mid-19th to the 20thC for top-quality FASHION DOLLS, girl dolls, BÉBÉS, and CHARACTER DOLLS. The finest French bisques, made by the leading makers such as JUMEAU, BRU JEUNE, GAULTIER, and STEINER, were expensive status symbols when they were first made. The price of bisque dolls for the collector depends on the maker, condition, and quality, and on details such as the rarity of the mould number, as well as the type of mouth, eyes, and body. Many bisque dolls have COMPOSITION limbs, and bodies that are prone to damage. Slight wear is generally acceptable, and the dolls should only be repainted as a last resort.

BIZARRE A highly colourful range of ART DECO tableware designed by Clarice CLIFF and produced by A.J. Wilkinson Ltd in the 1930s.

BLACK, STARR & FROST *See* BALL, TOMPKINS & BLACK.

BLACKAMOOR A three-dimensional negro figure, often depicted as a page boy, perhaps as a support for a table top.

BLACK FIGURE Invented in ancient Greece 700 BC, a POTTERY-decoration technique in which figures from myth and legend are painted in black silhouette on a red-brown background. It was much imitated in the 19thC. *See also* RED FIGURE.

BLACK FOREST CLOCK A simple CLOCK with a wooden movement made in the 18th and 19thC by country craftsmen. The case is often mildly Gothic in form, and the dial may be painted with rustic scenes.

BLACK GLAZE A dense, glossy glaze used on 18thC English EARTHENWARE; it is often dark brown rather than true black.

BLACKJACK Used in the 17thC, a leather tankard or flask, usually with a SILVER rim and APPLIED DECORATION.

BLACK MAMMY In the form of a negress, a fabric DOLL designed by Martha Jenks Chase of Panstucket, Rhode Island, USA, between 1921 and 1925.

BLACK MARBLE CLOCK A French MANTEL CLOCK with a case made of or faced with black marble, and mass-produced in the 19thC. Less-expensive versions used slate instead of marble.

BLACK WALNUT Variety of WALNUT, which is also known as red walnut or Virginian walnut, because it comes from that part of the USA. It was also grown in England, and used mainly during the William and Mary and Queen

Claric Cliff, *Crocus* pattern "BIZARRE" jug, 1930s.

Guanyin with acolytes, 1662–1722.

Anne periods. It is a dark, red-brown colour, and never displays any burr figuring. It was used both in a solid form and as a VENEER on English and American furniture from *c.*1730.

BLACKWARE Iron-rich type of ancient Chinese POTTERY.

BLADED KNOP A KNOP with a concave curve, culminating in a sharp edge.

BLADE SIGHT Thin, vertical, leaf-shaped sight at the front of a gun barrel.

BLANC DE CHINE French term for "Chinese white" that refers to fine Chinese PORCELAIN from Fukien, with a pure white glaze and notably decorated with figures in swirling drapery. It was exported to Europe in the 17thC, and widely imitated in the 18thC.

BLANC FIXE White decoration on a greyish, bluish, or yellow background, typical of TIN-GLAZED EARTHENWARE.

BLEEDING KNIFE Medical instrument used for blood letting. The finest examples are those with a letting cup for catching the blood.

BLEU CELESTE A sky-blue enamel ground colour developed in the French Vincennes factory in 1752; associated with SÈVRES and Vincennes PORCELAIN.

BLEU PERSAN French for "Persian blue". TIN-GLAZED wares with blue decoration painted on a greyish-white or yellow ground in imitation of Middle-Eastern, medieval POTTERY.

BLIND FRET Fretwork either glued to, or carved upon, a solid surface and therefore unable to be seen through.

BLIND FRONT Another term for a BLOCK FRONT.

BLINKING-EYE CLOCK A CLOCK with a dial in the shape of a human face with "eyes" linked to the movement – they blink alternately in time with the tick. Originally made in Germany in the 16thC, clocks of this type were widely produced in Europe and the USA in the 18th and 19thC.

BLISTER In wood, marking that is thought to resemble a blister. It is usually associated with MAPLE, but also found in CEDAR, POPLAR, PINE, and MAHOGANY.

BLOCK FOOT On FURNITURE, a foot formed as a solid block.

BLOCK FRONT On a CABINET, the thick, solid, unglazed doors that allow for a recessed centre section. Also known as a BLIND FRONT.

BLOND(E) BISQUE BISQUE-head DOLLS tinted pink to resemble flesh tones.

BLOTTER A letter-writing implement used to absorb ink and prevent it from smudging. Ink was slow to dry on oily vellum, so in the 18thC poor-quality uncoated paper was used for blotting alongside powder or POUNCE; however, it was not until the early 1840s that it was sold specifically as "blotting paper". Absorbent paper is wrapped around the wooden base of the blotter, then tucked under the detachable silver top. Blotters are popular with collectors, although condition is vital.

BLOWING The technique of producing GLASS vessels by blowing a molten mass of glass, or GATHER, through a blowpipe or blowing iron, either freehand or into a mould.

BLOWN MOULDED Method of mass-producing GLASS to standard shapes, where molten glass is blown into a mould.

BLUDGEON A mid-19thC, American, short-barrelled pistol, shaped like a small metal club.

BLUE AND WHITE CERAMICS decorated with cobalt blue enamel on a white background in imitation of Chinese wares.

BLUE-AND-WHITE KITCHENWARE *See* CORNISH WARE.

BLUE-AND-WHITE TRANSFER-PRINTED WARES Inexpensively made CERAMICS decorated with underglaze-blue transfer prints taken from engraved copper plates and that needed only one firing. Different copper plates had to be created for each different size and form produced, and sometimes designs are oddly adapted to fit more unusual shapes. The earliest pieces were inspired by Chinese ceramics; the famous "WILLOW" pattern was a pastiche of Oriental design produced by numerous English manufacturers. The heyday of blue-and-white transfer wares was the late 18th to the mid-19thC, and pieces made within this period tend to be most sought after. Numerous makers in England produced blue-and-white wares, and while most collectors do not collect by factory, pieces by SPODE and Rogers, the main makers, are particularly sought after. DINNER and TEA SERVICES were made in large numbers, so PLATES far outnumber other pieces. A huge range of shapes is available, from foot baths to washstand sets, platters, drainers, and tureens. Unusual patterns can have a bearing on value; many were taken from fashionable engravings such as topographical views of foreign scenes. Among the most popular are Spode's "Indian Sporting", based on engravings after the firm's leading decorator, Henry Daniel. "Caramanian" – a series of views of Turkey – is also sought after. Other subjects to look out for include: eye-catching animals – the "Durham

**Bristol Delftware *Adam and Eve*
BLUE-DASH CHARGER, c.1740.**

Ox" is a favourite – arctic scenery, and views of Oxford and Cambridge colleges. Much Staffordshire EARTHENWARE was intended for export to the USA, and these pieces showed American views. Later versions tend to be of inferior quality, and are less sought after. Modern reproductions are easily identifiable, but beware of a "Dr Syntax" series made in the 1920s and based on 18thC Rowlandson prints – these are not as old as they may look. Marks add to value, especially with a piece by a small maker; however, unless made by one of the larger factories with a retail shop, most pieces are not marked.

BLUE-DASH CHARGER DELFTWARE dish decorated with a border of broad, blue brush strokes. Commemorative CHARGERS featured portraits of monarchs, popular members of the royal family, or military leaders, such as Charles I and II, William and Mary, Queen Anne, and George I, II, and III. Value depends on the rarity of the piece and the complexity of the background. One of the simplest backgrounds is a design of sponged trees.

BLUE GLASS Colour obtained by the inclusion of cobalt. It was popular in Renaissance Venice, Italy, and revived in Bristol, England, in the 18thC.

BLUEING A decorative heat treatment applied to metal that also protects it from rust. The colour can range from blue to black.

BLUNDERBUSS A heavy, short handgun with a flaring barrel designed to scatter a large quantity of shot at short range.

BLUNT, EDWARD & GEORGE American company that made various SCIENTIFIC INSTRUMENTS, including COMPASSES and BAROMETERS.

BOARDED FURNITURE Simple, early FURNITURE, constructed entirely of shaped boards held together by nails or pegs.

BOAT BED American BED in the Empire style, shaped like a gondola.

BOAT-SHELL HILT A heart-shaped SWORD guard, split on the upturned side to accommodate the forward quillon.

BOB Weight at the end of a CLOCK pendulum.

BOBBIN (1) A thin, bone or wooden spool or reel, used to hold thread for making bobbin lace. There are many types of lace bobbins, with a wide range of decoration. The most common bobbin has at its base a spangle, usually of nine glass beads threaded on brass wire. Price depends on the quality of the beads, particularly the larger central one. The value is enhanced if the spangle includes coins, medals, unusual buttons, or carved shell. Inscriptions on the shaft add human interest and value: look out particularly for dates, names of the owner and village, records of a betrothal, marriage, birth, or death, cryptograms, and political slogans. Most collectable of all are bobbins inscribed with the name and execution date of a murderer by a relative of the victim. Hollow bobbins, which contain miniature bobbins, balls, or "church-window" apertures are more valuable than plain bobbins. A complete set of bobbins with one to six PEWTER rings named after Henry VIII's wives are sought after. Damage decreases value, although 19thC hybrid bobbins spliced or dowelled from different parts are collectable.

BOBBIN (2) In the shape of a bobbin or reel. In FURNITURE this is usually a turned element resembling a row of connected spheres.

BOBBIN TURNING Popular during the 17thC, a style of turning in the form of bobbins, one on top of another.

BOCAGE French for "small wood", a background of trees, foliage, and flowers on 18thC figure groups, used to decorate the supporting plinths.

BOCCARO Unglazed, red and brown STONEWARE, made in the late 17th and early 18thC in imitation of similar Chinese imports.

BOCH FRÈRES CERAMICS firm established in Luxembourg in 1767, and known for its ART DECO pottery made in the 1920s and '30s.

BODY The material from which a piece of POTTERY or PORCELAIN is made (the word paste is also used for porcelain), excluding the glaze.

BOHEMIAN GLASS Used to describe RUBY GLASS first produced in the late 17thC in Bohemia, and high-quality engraved GLASS produced in that region over four centuries.

BOHEMIAN WEIGHT A type of PAPERWEIGHT, made in the 19th through to the early 20thC, and often engraved on the base. The design is made by cutting through the thin layer of coloured GLASS to expose the clear glass underneath. The top and sides are faceted.

BOHM, AUGUST (1812–90) One of the most accomplished Bohemian engravers of GLASS in the BIEDERMEIER style, Bohm is known to have worked at the STOURBRIDGE glass factories in England.

BOIS DURCI Wood-based substance made from fine sawdust and blood. It can be easily moulded and was used for ornamental decoration.

BOKHARA Wool and jute RUGS in red, ornamented with repeated octagonal "flowers". They were made by tribes of the Iranian/Soviet border region.

One of a pair of late-19thC, BOHEMIAN GLASS vases.

BOKHARA WORK QUILTS and coverlets embroidered with colourful floral patterns from the Bokhara region, in the southern part of the former USSR, in the 18th and 19thC.

BOLECTION Descriptive of a shape of OGEE section used as a drawer front or as a projecting door surround.

BOLOGNA Centre of POTTERY production in Italy from the 15thC. Noted for large basins and JUGS with applied decoration, produced up to the 18thC.

BOMBÉ A swelling or bulbous curving shape favoured particularly in Continental Europe for COMMODES and other types of case furniture.

BONBONNIÈRE A small BOX, usually of PORCELAIN but also made in SILVER, decorated with a whimsical scene and used to contain small sweetmeats or breath-fresheners. The term also applies to a bowl made to hold sweetmeats.

BONE CHINA A type of English HARD-PASTE PORCELAIN first made *c*.1794, supposedly by Josiah SPODE at Stoke-on-Trent, using a large proportion of calcified bone, or bone ash. Bone china is the most commonly found type of PORCELAIN made in England after *c*.1820 and was produced by Spode, DERBY, FLIGHT & BARR, ROCKINGHAM, COALPORT, MINTON, and others. The body of objects made from bone china is pure white in appearance.

BONE GLASS "Milky" glass made with added bone ash.

Cup and saucer from a Coalport, BONE CHINA, 15-piece tea set, early 19thC.

BONHEUR DU JOUR Designed for a lady's drawing room, a small writing cabinet of delicate proportions with a raised back comprising a CABINET or shelves. It originated in France *c*.1760, and was popular in the 19thC in France and England. *See also* WRITING FURNITURE.

BONNET CHEST A CHEST that appears to be a DRESSER base or a double chest. However, the top two rows of drawers are false, and the hinged top opens to give plenty of room for storing hats (hence the name).

BONNET HEAD An American DOLL wearing a hat or bonnet moulded as an integral part of the head. Also known as a bonnet doll.

BONNET TOP American term for a BROKEN PEDIMENT.

BONNIN & MORRIS The first American PORCELAIN firm, founded in Philadelphia in 1769 by British-born Gousse Bonnin and Philadelphian Antony Morris. The factory made dinner- and teaware in underglaze blue with polychrome decoration, but survived for only two years. Bonnin & Morris pieces are rare and expensive. They may be marked with a letter "P".

BOOK, SILVER-MOUNTED A leather book fitted with a SILVER cover. Books or bibles with silver clasps of 17th and 18thC Dutch or German origin are rare and valuable, but many 19thC silver-mounted books are affordable and popular. Check the condition, because silver is fragile.

BOOKCASE First introduced in the 17thC and perfected in the 18thC, a large item of FURNITURE for storing books in grand libraries and reading-rooms in wealthy homes. PINE bookcases made in the 18thC were painted to fit in with the décor of the room. As books became more affordable, a wide variety of smaller bookcases was made. The innovative revolving bookcase became popular in the 1820s, and was refined by the Victorians and Edwardians. Bookcases with glazed tops were made from the 18thC, and the delicacy and intricacy of the glazing bars add to their decorative appeal. Those with hexagonal, wavy, or arched designs are more sought after and valuable than those of a simple, rectangular configuration. Before choosing a bookcase, make sure that it is not a WARDROBE that has had its upper doors glazed – a common alteration in the 19thC. The top, glazed section of an 18thC bookcase is usually narrower than the base. Early bookcases tend to have small individual panes of glass puttied into the glazing bars. On both later Victorian and modern versions, the GLASS is more likely to be made from a single sheet; the glazing bars then sit on the surface of this glass. Gothic Revival bookcases from the 1840s, with glazed doors and fitted with adjustable shelves, are especially desirable. On bookcases with open doors, the joint on the corners of the door frame can help with dating – those with a 90-degree joint were popular during the late 18thC.

BOOK STAND A stand for books with open, often adjustable shelves. Sometimes the base has a drawer or a CUPBOARD, and the top shelf is often edged with a brass gallery. It is one of a number of smaller pieces that were made for libraries from the mid-18thC. A telescopic stem adds to its value.

BOOT-BUTTON EYES Used on early German TEDDY BEARS, black, button eyes made from metal or wood, and stitched to the head or attached by wires or hooks. Also known as SHOE-BUTTON EYES.

BOOTLEGGER Also known as a bootleg pistol, an American percussion pistol with the striking hammer under the barrel. Used by New England smugglers.

BORDEAUX Centre of FAIENCE and PORCELAIN manufacture from the 18thC. Wares are characterized by polychrome designs in the Spanish style.

BORDSHALI-KAZAK Caucasian CARPETS essentially of red and blue, but with patterns, medallions, flowers, and figures in many other colours.

BORE Internal diameter of the barrel of a FIREARM.

Victorian, flame-mahogany BOOKCASE over a three-drawer base, *c*.1890.

BORLOU Turkish CARPETS with stylized patterns on a red or blue ground. They are floppy, and not densely woven.

BORRELL, HENRY London clockmaker (active 1795–1840), and specializing in CLOCKS and WATCHES, often with Turkish numerals, for export.

BOSOM BOTTLE Small, decorative, GLASS or SILVER BOTTLE worn as a pendant and often used to contain perfume.

BOSTON & SANDWICH GLASS CO. American GLASS producer, so closely associated with pressed-glass manufacture that much American pressed glass is called "Sandwich glass". The firm produced wares in the "Bellflower" pattern. Although better known for its press-moulded glass, it also made PAPERWEIGHTS, between 1852 and 1888, specializing in floral designs, especially poinsettias, wheat-flowers, and roses, as well as MILLEFIORI patterns that incorporated canes with silhouettes of wildlife, such as bees, rabbits, and eagles. Boston & Sandwich weights can be distinguished by the fact that they are not very heavy, and the quality of the clear glass and lampwork.

BOSTON GLASS Products of 19thC glassworks in Boston and Cambridge, Massachuesetts, USA, including the Boston Porcelain & Glass Co. and American Flint Glass Works. Noted for early pressed GLASS and silvered glass.

BOSTON ROCKER (1) An American ROCKING CHAIR with a tall spindle back and a seat that curves up at the front and down at the back.

BOSTON ROCKER (2) Rocking horse consisting just of the horse's head and a seat mounted on curved rockers.

BOTEH In CARPETS, a decorative motif similar to the European "paisley" pattern, essentially a leaf-form with a curled or hooked tip. A small *boteh* is known as a *boteh-miri*.

BÖTTGER Early products of the MEISSEN factory named after J.F. Böttger, its supervisor *c.*1710 -1720. The glazes are bubbly, and decoration is in low relief.

BOTTLE Vessels first used for storing and transporting perfumes, oils, and wine. From the 1stC AD the principal method of GLASS bottle manufacture was free-blowing. The earliest complete examples surviving in any number are from the mid-17thC, particularly from England, where a distinctive dark-green, almost black, bottle glass was developed. All bottles dating from the mid-17thC are rare, and, if in good condition, can command high prices. Around the neck, they often have applied rings, used to attach stoppers. "Shaft-and-globe" bottles were exported on a large scale to Continental Europe; they feature bulbous bodies with tapering necks, and kicks, or

19thC BOSTON ROCKER, stained black.

indentations, in the bases. The shape can also be found in CERAMIC and leather bottles of the period. An irregular shape indicates that the bottle was free-blown – later examples were mould-blown for ease of stacking and to standardize capacity, and are sometimes also decorated. The shaft-and-globe design was later replaced by more globular shapes, and, by the late 18thC, by the tall, narrow, cylindrical form with a relatively short neck that is most familiar in bottles manufactured today. Coral-covered, 18thC, Dutch bottles have often been found by divers in the West Indies and in Surinam, where they were used as ballast but discarded before the return voyage. It is unwise to remove the build-up of coral, because this will damage the bottle.

BOTTLE COLLAR A variation on the BOTTLE LABEL, the bottle collar, or ring, became popular during the Regency period (c.1790–1820). Many bottle collars were gilded and decorated with scrolls, putti, such drink-related motifs such as grapes and vine leaves. A set of three or four labels is valuable.

BOTTLE CRADLE A late-Victorian invention designed to hold an open bottle of wine during the meal. They were produced in numerous variations, including those with winding mechanisms; most were made in silver plate and were embellished with flowers, fruits, and vines.

BOTTLE GLASS Cheap GLASS that has been made of impure materials, typically brown or green in colour.

BOTTLE LABEL Used to identify a bottle's contents, the earliest wine labels (known as "bottle tickets") were handwritten on parchment. These were replaced in the 1740s by SILVER labels, which were suspended around the necks of the bottles on chains, with the name of the wine or spirit engraved or pierced. They were stamped from sheets of silver in great numbers during the Victorian period, and often made in sets of six or ten. Designs include escutcheon, oval, and crescent shapes, as well as masks, shells, scrolls, anchors, and vine leaves. Labels made for DECANTERS are larger and more lavishly decorated with scrolls or foliage. More than 1000 names have been recorded – labels featuring obscure names such as "Rhenish", "Orange", and "Shrub" are more valuable than those with common titles such as "Sherry", "Port", or "Madeira". Labels for homemade wines or rare dessert wines often bear amusing titles, and are collectable. Early labels are rare and demand high prices, as do provincial labels from Scotland or Ireland. Specialist makers such as Sandylands Drinkwater and Margaret Binley are sought after, as are heavier cast Regency labels by Paul STORR or Benjamin Smith.

BOTTLE TAG *See* BOTTLE LABEL.

BOUCHERON, FRÉDÉRIC (1830–1902) Founder of the French JEWELLERY firm and leading ART NOUVEAU designer, especially for American clients.

BOUCHERON, LOUIS The son of FRÉDÉRIC BOUCHERON and head of the Boucheron JEWELLERY firm following his father's death in 1902. Louis made the business famous for its ART DECO designs after World War I.

BOULE DE SAVON GLASS Or "soap-bubble" GLASS, so-called because of the rainbow hues visible when this type of glass catches the light.

BOULLE, ANDRÉ (1642–1732) French artist and bronze worker after whom the process of BOULLE MARQUETRY is named. He did not invent the technique, but perfected it, and became chief cabinet-maker to Louix XIV.

BOULLE MARQUETRY Sometimes referred to as *buhl*, a technique perfected in France by André-Charles BOULLE in the late 17thC, in which MARQUETRY is made by cutting a pattern from thin sheets of brass overlaid on red or coloured TORTOISESHELL or horn. It became popular in England in the early 18thC. Before buying, check that the brass is not lifting, because it can be costly to repair. Note: to take tortoiseshell out of the EU you need a licence.

BOULTON, MATTHEW (1728–1809) A well-known English maker of SILVER. His ORMOLU mounts were of the finest quality, and were made at his factory at Soho, near Birmingham. *See also* BIRMINGHAM SILVER.

BOURDALOU Used by 18thC French ladies, a portable chamber pot that resembled a SAUCEBOAT.

BOURG-LA-REINE French PORCELAIN and FAIENCE produced 1774-1806.

BOURNE & SON In Derby, England, a 19thC factory that made STONEWARE.

19thC blue-and-white "semi-china" BOURDALOU.

BOVEY TRACEY POTTERY *See* WEMYSS WARE.

BOW FACTORY Arguably the earliest of the English PORCELAIN factories, founded in 1744 by Thomas Frye, an Irish painter, and Edward Heylyn, a GLASS merchant, at Stratford Langthorne in the East End of London. It was called "New Canton" and in its heyday employed hundreds of workmen producing wares for a wide market. Until its closure in 1775 – when it was acquired by W. Duesbury, the owner of the DERBY porcelain factory – Bow continued to produce huge quantities of blue-and-white porcelain in the Chinese style, Japanese-inspired coloured wares, and a range of figures based on those of MEISSEN. Early Chinese-influenced polychrome work includes paeony and chrysanthemum flower decorations, and the wares were decorated in FAMILLE ROSE colours. The earliest wares have a greyish body, but, by 1754, a good ivory tone was often achieved. On wares after 1760, the colours appear dull and dirty. One of the features on the domestic blue-and-white wares produced by Bow is a handle finished with a heart-shaped terminal – a feature unique to Bow. Blue-and-white wares are divided into three periods, which coincide roughly with changes in the appearance of the wares. In the early period (1749–54), wares were often thickly potted, and the glaze can be blue/green in pools. Many wares were painted in a pale, clear, royal blue, which sometimes blurs. Some well-potted wares, often marked with an incised "R", were also produced, as were "in-the-white" wares with applied decoration. In the middle period (1755–65), the firm used a darker underglaze blue. The wares were more thinly potted but heavy, and the body was more porous and prone to staining. Painter's numerals were used on the base, and occasionally inside the foot-rings. In the late period (1765–76), the translucency was poor, and there was a marked deterioration in quality. Bow figures were simply modelled, with a warm glaze and slight discolouration. Later Bow figures are identifiable by the tall, raised, ROCOCO, scroll bases and extensive BOCAGE. The factory's extensive output means that there is plenty available, and values tend to be lower than for CHELSEA. Various incised marks were used, but wares are often unmarked. The most common mark on figures is a red anchor and dagger.

BOW FRONT Convex form on CHESTS OF DRAWERS from the late 18thC.

BOWIE KNIFE A heavy, sheath KNIFE with a long, curved blade that was double edged near the point. Named after the Texas pioneer Colonel James Bowie (1799–1836), it was carried as a weapon.

BOWLS, GLASS Vessels that have been widely used over the centuries as luxury objects intended to display the skills of the glassmaker; only since the late 18thC have bowls been widely produced as functional tableware. The invention of glassblowing in the 1stC AD revolutionized the production of bowls, because they could then be formed by blowing a GATHER to the desired shape, attaching a PONTIL ROD, and expanding the PARAISON outwards. These bowls were often decorated with simple, vertical ribbing, and strengthened with plain, moulded feet. Similar wares were produced throughout the medieval period for the wealthy classes. In Venice, the addition of a stem and foot to a shallow bowl transformed it into a TAZZA. Medieval bowls of POTASH GLASS made in central Europe are generally small and slightly green-tinted, often with simple moulded decoration, though fine FILIGRANA and LATTICINIO items were produced in 16thC Venice. Bowls made in and before the 18thC are diverse in shape, style, and decoration. With the invention of LEAD CRYSTAL, engraving and cutting became more popular methods of decoration in the 18thC and 19thC. In the early 18thC, lead glass was still novel and costly, so large items such as PUNCHBOWLS would have been treasured, and only used on special occasions. Irish, cut-glass pieces with distinctive boats, turnover rims, or kettle-drum shapes are valuable and sought after. Boat shapes are associated in particular with Irish cut-glass bowls from c.1780 to the 1830s. In the late 18thC, the emergence of the complete glass table service led to the development of bowls for specialized uses, such as WINEGLASS COOLERS, FINGER BOWLS, and CADDY BOWLS. New developments in glass technology in the late 18thC and early 19thC meant that glass tableware was affordable to a wider section of society. After the repeal of the Excise Tax in 1845, English glassmakers returned to producing large, elaborately decorated glass bowls. Check for signs of wear on the base – this indicates that the piece is genuine.

BOWLS, SILVER In contrast to the BASKET, this type of hollow ware does not have a handle. Bowls have long been made in a great variety of decorative forms and designs for many different purposes. Their decorative and functional appeal ensures that they remain popular among collectors today.

BOX *See* BOXWOOD.

BOXES, DECORATIVE Small containers made in a huge range of shapes and sizes – some of the most exquisite examples were produced in the 18thC to contain snuff, patches, or tobacco. The highest-quality boxes were often made from gold or SILVER, perhaps decorated with precious stones, but others were made from less-expensive metals. The wide variety of decorative silver boxes intended for the DRESSING TABLE (to hold beauty products, toiletries, and pharmaceutical items) forms an important collecting area, with pieces more valuable as a matching set. Many of these items show imagination of form, decoration, and usage. Enamelled and PORCELAIN boxes are also popular, some of the most attractive being made in the shape of birds or animals. BILSTON (Staffordshire), Birmingham, and BATTERSEA led the field in producing English ENAMEL boxes during the 18thC. Lids of 19thC LACQUER boxes were often decorated with a copy of a well-known Old Master – erotic subjects were very popular – and many boxes of this type were made in Germany. TORTOISESHELL was often used for making small boxes in the 18th and 19thC. Price is usually determined by quality and the type of materials used. In general, boxes made from wood or PAPIER-MÂCHÉ are more widely available and affordable. Chipped enamel reduces value. *See also* PATCH BOX, POWDER BOX, SNUFFBOX, and TUNBRIDGE WARE.

BOXLOCK Flintlock in which the mechanism is held within the gun breech.

BOX SEAT Seat that rises to provide storage space within.

BOX STOOL STOOL with a rising seat that hides a storage space below.

BOX TABLE Table with a rising top that reveals a storage space within.

BOXWOOD A hard, light-coloured wood, with a fine, close grain, boxwood (*Buxus sempervirens*) was used in the 16th and 17thC for INLAY turning. It was used in the 18thC for inlay and, from 1770 to 1820, for stringing.

Mid-18thC, elm settle of tiny proportions (1m/42in), with a BOX SEAT.

BOYS AND CROWNS Found on the cresting rails of some 17thC CHAIRS, carved ornament depicting a crown supported by two flying, naked boys.

BOYTON, CHARLES & SON A family-run SILVER firm established in 1825 by Charles Boyton. Two different Charles Boytons were important to the firm: the original Boyton, and his great grandson, a celebrated ART DECO designer. Following the ARTS AND CRAFTS tradition, the work of the great grandson was enhanced by CHASING and hand-hammering. The firm made ordinary silver FLATWARE until it began producing Art Deco silver. It became known as C. Boyton & Son Ltd in 1904 – the company failed in the 1930s, but the name continued until 1977.

BRACKET Small length of wood used to strengthen the joint between the leg and supporting rails of a CHAIR.

BRACKET CLOCK A 17thC, spring-driven CLOCK, which was set high up on a bracket because of the length of the weights. Nowadays the term refers to all clocks with a short pendulum and spring-driven mechanism. They are sometimes called MANTEL CLOCKS or TABLE CLOCKS. Bracket clocks were made from *c*.1660, the earliest with square, brass dials, and EBONY-, WALNUT-, or even OLIVEWOOD-veneered cases; by the early 18thC, arched dials were more common. A bracket clock made in the Regency period usually has a convex dial signed by its maker, simple hands made from brass or blued steel, and a MAHOGANY or ROSEWOOD case. The most common British bracket clocks had mahogany-veneered cases. Large numbers were made in the late 18th and early 19thC, mainly in London. Most mahogany clocks are larger than earlier ebony or walnut examples. Most originally had VERGE ESCAPEMENTS; many of these were converted to ANCHOR ESCAPEMENTS. French, 19thC clocks made in a variety of shapes are also common. Many of these incorporate lavish decoration. The value of a clock is greatly increased if it is signed by a famous maker such as Thomas TOMPION, the KNIBB brothers, and Edward EAST.

BRACKET FOOT An 18thC flat, diagonally shaped foot for case furniture.

BRACKET LAMP A LAMP, (often an OIL LAMP), of brass or iron with an integral bracket, designed to be fixed to a wall or partition.

BRACKET LOBES Flat-topped, projecting motif used as a moulding on PLATES and other TABLEWARE.

BRADFORD PEWTER Copying English forms, American PEWTER wares made by Cornelius Bradford in Philadelphia in the latter half of the 18thC.

BRADWELL WOOD Late 17thC, English, Staffordshire-based pottery making red STONEWARE teapots and cups in imitation of contemporary Chinese imports.

Brass, Arts and Crafts BRACKET LAMP, 1890–1900.

BRAGANZA FOOT A type of foot found on FURNITURE with an otherwise straight leg. It bends outward a little at the bottom, similar to a hockey stick.

BRAMELD Family that acquired the ROCKINGHAM factory in Yorkshire, England, in the early 19thC. Makers of BONE CHINA with rich decoration.

BRAMPTON English POTTERY-making centre near Chesterfield, Derbyshire. Noted for utilitarian, brown STONEWARE, some with internal green glazing.

BRANDER, W. Early to mid-18thC, major gunsmith in London England.

BRANDER, W.B. Leading gunsmith in London, England, from the late 18th to early 19thC

BRANDER & POTTS Major early 19thC gunsmith in London, England.

BRANDISTOCK A pole weapon, with, concealed in the haft, retractable spikes, which swing out when the safety catch is released.

BRANDY BOWL Used from the 17thC, a shallow but wide SILVER BOWL with handles, for warming and serving brandy, usually with a shallow ladle.

Early-19thC, travelling flintock pistol by BRANDER & POTTS.

BRANDY SAUCEPAN Also known as a "pipkin", a small saucepan used for warming brandy or mulling wine. Most have bowls that bulge at the bottom, with lips for pouring, wooden or ivory handles at right angles to the pouring lips, and usually SILVER covers (rarely still found with the saucepan).

BRANDY TUMBLER Wide, squat, glass BEAKER made with straight sides from the 17thC; later examples were often etched or engraved.

BRANGWYN, FRANK (1867–1943) English artist who was apprenticed to MORRIS & co. and specialized in ART NOUVEAU FURNITURE and TEXTILE design.

BRAS DE CHEMINÉE Produced from the 17thC, wall-mounted candle holders made in gilded wood or metal with several branches.

BRASS A metal alloy of copper and zinc (and sometimes other metals in small quantities), made since antiquity for household objects and ornaments, FURNITURE legs, knobs and handles, and often used as an INLAY. Old brass objects often reflect the decorative styles of SILVER objects from the same period. Pieces marked with makers' stamps command a premium. Most modern copies are lighter in weight than genuinely old ones. Look for signs of wear and tear consistent with age: the undersides of objects should be covered with a fine PATINA of scratches, and edges of plates and hollow wares should be worn smooth.

BRATINA Originally from Imperial Russia, a richly decorated, frequently enamelled-and-jewelled, drinking or loving cup of silver or gold.

BREAK In FIREARMS, the point at which the barrel block hinges open, so that bullets or cartridges can be loaded into the breech, or the points at which the gun components can be dismantled for cleaning and casing.

BREAKER Trade name for a piece of FURNITURE worth more as raw materials.

BREAKFAST TABLE An informal TILT-TOP TABLE with a central pedestal and feet supporting the table top. It is usually oval or circular, and smaller than a DINING TABLE. A narrow APRON and heavy, downswept legs were popular in the 1820s. Original, 18thC tables rarely have CROSSBANDING, so any such embellishment may have been added at a later date, or it may indicate a reproduction. At the beginning of the early 20thC, when large houses were divided into smaller living areas, the demand for bigger dining tables diminished; dealers often rounded the corners of sections from large pedestal tables to make them into two or more breakfast tables. Look under the top to make sure that there are finger stains around the edge of the table – a sign that the table has not been made from a cut-down dining table. Reproductions tend to be smaller, with thinner tops and legs, and do not have the depth of PATINA that you would see in a period example.

BREAKFRONT BOOKCASES or SIDEBOARDS with a prominent centre section that protrudes forward from the line of the side sections.

BREATH MOTIVATED Toys that move or make a noise when blown.

BREECH-LOADING Any FIREARM loaded through the breech of the barrel, the end closest to the user, as opposed to down the barrel.

BREGUET Family of well-known, French, Paris-based clockmakers. Abraham, one of the greatest in his field, was active from 1770 to 1810; Louis from 1830 to 70; and Louise A. from 1800 to 33.

BRETBY ART POTTERY English firm founded in Woodsville, Derbyshire, in 1883; it became Tooth & Co. in 1887, and closed in 1920. The firm made ranges with Oriental subjects and in the ART NOUVEAU style, with simulated copper and metal, and jewelled ornaments.

BREVETÉ The French word for "patented", it was stamped on dolls as evidence of patent or registration. Often abbreviated to "B.T.E." or "Bte".

BREWSTER CHAIR A 17thC, American ARMCHAIR with turned spindles and posts, and a RUSH SEAT.

BRIANCHON A lustrous glaze, like MOTHER-OF-PEARL, invented by J.J.H. Brianchon, and characteristic of late-19thC BELLEEK wares, especially ornamented PARIAN wares cast in the form of seashells.

BRIDLE JOINT A joint used to set a table leg into the top frame.

BRIGADER Danish manufacturer of toy soldiers since 1946.

BRIGHT-CUT ENGRAVING Faceted engraving used to decorate SILVER, popular in the late 18thC, especially for NEO-CLASSICAL-STYLE ornament. It is identical in execution to ENGRAVING, but the design is carved at an angle with a burnished steel chisel, creating facets on the surface of the metal that reflect the light at different angles and add a sparkle to the decoration. The facets are easily worn away by polishing, and this is detrimental to the value.

BRILLIANT A precious stone cut with 58 facets: 33 above the girdle, 25 below.

BRILLIANT-CUT GLASS Type of rich, all-over, complex cutting, combining patterns such as "hobnail", "star", and "strawberry diamond", and found on lead glassware. First shown at the Philadelphia Centennial Exhibition in 1876, the style was widely copied by pressed-glass makers in the USA and Europe. Most American, brilliant-cut GLASS dates from c.1880 to 1915. Glass of this type should be heavy, with sharply defined cutting, and signs of wear on the base. Some pieces are signed with acid-etched factory marks.

BRIOLETTE A pear-shaped, faceted jewel, often pierced to hang as a pendant.

BRISLINGTON DELFTWARE made in Bristol, England c.1650-c.1750.

BRISTOL BLUE Rich, blue GLASS, coloured using cobalt oxide.

Early-19thC, BRISTOL BLUE, glass cologne bottle with gilt frame and cover.

BRISTOL GLASS Blue, green, and "amethyst" GLASS, including DRINKING GLASSES, DECANTERS, and FINGER BOWLS, made in Britain from the late 18thC to the mid-19thC. Although Bristol was an important glassmaking centre, coloured glass was made at many other British glassworks at this period. Coloured drinking glasses, where the bowls, stems, and feet were all made with tinted glass, were popular in England from c.1790; they usually have a drawn-trumpet (or drawn-funnel or "tulip") bowl, with a plain or knopped stem. Green glass was popular in the Victorian era. A rounded bowl is typical of later 19thC Bristol glass. Most coloured drinking glasses are green; amethyst is rare, and blue is scarce and valuable. Victorian drinking glasses with coloured bowls and clear stems are not considered to be Bristol glass.

BRISTOL PENNY TOYS Cheap, wheeled, wooden TOYS sold by English street vendors. They were made in Bristol from c.1800 and in London from 1850.

BRISTOL PORCELAIN SOFT-PASTE PORCELAIN was first discovered at Bristol, England, by Benjamin Lund, *c*.1749, with a formula that included soaprock from Cornwall. Bristol PORCELAIN from *c*.1749 to 1752 is rare, but examples sometimes show the relief-moulded marks "Bristol" or "Bristoll". Pieces are mostly UNDERGLAZE-BLUE ware, with CHINOISERIE decoration. The glaze had a tendency to pool and bubble, and the blue often looks watery, where it has run in the firing. In 1752, the Bristol moulds were sold to WORCESTER, and it is difficult to differentiate late Lund's Bristol from early Worcester. William Cookworthy transferred his PLYMOUTH factory to Bristol in 1770, and, from *c*.1770 to 1781, Bristol porcelain had a body with a tendency to slight tears and firing cracks. Early wares are hard to differentiate from those by Plymouth, because both show the same firing imperfections, such as smoky ivory glaze and wreathing in the body. RICHARD CHAMPION took over in 1773. Toward the mid- and late 1770s, the dominant decorative style was NEO-CLASSICAL, with particular reliance on delicate swags and scattered flowers. Later pieces showed small imperfections in enamel and potting. Later Bristol colours are sharp, and gilding is of an excellent quality.

BRISTOL POTTERY Tin-glazed EARTHERNWARE such as blue-dash CHARGERS made at one of the many potteries in the Bristol area, in southwest England, from the late 17thC. Also, the orginal name of Pountney & Co., which made tableware for the home and for hotels – and Weymss ware from 1904.

BRITAIN, WILLIAM LTD Leading English manufacturer of toy soldiers and other figures and vehicles from 1893, established by William Britain (1828–1906). The firm's hollow-cast technique, developed by Britain's son William, led, from 1900, to a wider range of more realistic figures, which were lighter and less expensive to produce. Soldiers made before 1912 are marked "William Britain"; those made after 1912, "Britain's Ltd".

BRITANNIA METAL An alloy of TIN with some antimony (a metallic-looking element) and copper added. It was first developed in the late 18thC and used in the 19thC as a substitute for PEWTER. Britannia metal is a poor-quality alloy that perishes easily. In the second half of the 19thC it was often electroplated to make inexpensive tableware marked "EPBM" (electroplated Britannia metal). Worn or damaged items can rarely be replated or repaired.

BRITANNIA METAL, **bachelor's coffee pot, 1860.**

BRITANNIA STANDARD Used from 1697 to 1720, a high SILVER standard, in which an object contains 95.8 per cent of pure silver. During the English Civil War, silver was melted down and converted to coinage to pay troops. After the Restoration of Charles II in 1660, the demand for silver was so great that coins were melted down. This practice was made illegal in 1697, and the higher Britannia standard was introduced. Silver produced in the Britannia standard period is brighter in colour than STERLING SILVER, and of a better quality. The hallmarks were changed to signify that this new

Venetian, Schiavona BROADSWORD, c.1650.

standard was in effect. The sterling lion was replaced by the figure of Britannia, and the profile of a lion's head was erased (torn off at the neck). Makers were also required to register new marks, showing the first two letters of their surnames.

BRITISH NATIONAL DOLLS LTD A London-based, DOLL-making firm, specializing in new-born "babies" that produced sounds. The noise was emitted through the holes of a voice box in the back of the baby when the doll was tilted back. The mark is on the back of the head.

BRITISH PLATE Nickel alloy made in the mid-19thC. Objects in British plate are often "hallmarked" in an attempt to pass them off as SILVER.

BROADHURST *See* Kathie WINKLE.

BROADSWORD From the 16thC onward, a SWORD with a flat, double-edged blade, often used with a small-sword or rapier.

BROKEN CORNERS A rectangular shape or decoration in which the corners do not extend to their natural point but are cut short and rounded.

BROKEN PEDIMENT Triangular superstructure, in which the central part is absent and often filled with a carved motif. Found on FURNITURE, notably BOOKCASES, and known as broken arch, goose neck, scroll top, and swan neck.

BROKEN SET An incomplete set of matching CHAIRS.

BRONZE A bright alloy of copper and a small amount of TIN, with zinc and lead sometimes added; it develops a brown or dull-green PATINA with time. Easily cast, it has been used from antiquity, especially for figurines and statues. To determine if an object is made from bronze scratch the metal underneath – a yellow colour means that the piece is made from bronze; a silvery tone indicates spelter. The patination of a bronze is fundamental to its appeal. Never polish a bronze, or you will seriously reduce its value.

BRONZES D'AMEUBLEMENT French term used to describe gilt or patinated mounts for FURNITURE. *See also* ORMOLU.

BROOKLYN GLASS Products of American factories based in Brooklyn, New York, in the 18th and 19thC, especially the Brooklyn Flint Glass Co., which specialized in cut GLASS and moved to Corning *c.*1870.

BROUWER POTTERY (Also Middle Lane Pottery) American, New-York based producer of ART POTTERY, 1894–1947, founded by Theophilus Brouwer. The simple BOWLS and vessels had vibrant, rich, iridescent glazes.

BROWNFIELD Mid-19thC pottery from the Albion Works, at Cobridge, England. The firm made BONE-CHINA figures, basketwork dishes, and PLATES printed with the caricatures of Phiz (the illustrator of Charles Dickens' works).

BROWNHILLS Based in Staffordshire and founded *c*.1760, an English POTTERY firm specializing in TRANSFER-PRINTED, SALT-GLAZED WARES.

BROWN OAK A sought-after variety of OAK, which is a deep, reddish-brown, caused by the pigment from a fungus that penetrates the whole tree.

BRU JEUNE & CIE Active from 1866 to 99, a leading French dollmaker, noted for DOLLS in elaborate, contemporary costumes. Bru made BISQUE-headed dolls using various types of body until 1883. Initially, the heads were supplied by other firms, such as Barrois and JUMEAU. The bodies were made from KID, and early BÉBÉS had wooden lower legs. Before 1880, arms were on a wire armature and had bisque forearms. From 1880, arms became articulated, with upper arms made from wood covered in kid, and a BALL JOINT at the elbow. From the early 1880s, heads were attached by metal wing-nuts and springs. Especially fine dolls made by Bru are known as "circle-and-dot" dolls, so-called because of the circle and dot marks found on the back of the head. These rare dolls usually have distinctive open/closed mouths with a hint of teeth. Bru produced innovative bébés: "Bru Téteur", patented in 1879, could suck from a bottle, initially by squeezing a rubber bulb in the head, then by pressing an external ivory knob, and lastly by turning a wing-nut to exert pressure. "Bébé Gourmand" could be fed morsels of food, which were then carried through a tube in the hollow body to an opening in the foot. Bru experimented with smiling dolls and dolls that could laugh and cry; two-faced dolls developed from the latter. In 1883, the firm began producing Oriental and black dolls, with fired red lips. They are rare, and there are many fakes. Bru was Jumeau's biggest rival until 1899, when both joined an association (the S.F.B.J.) to compete against German makers. Bru Jeune was sold in 1883 to Henri Chevrot, who concentrated on making top-quality dolls, and experimented with rubber and "swimming" dolls. After a decline in the 1880s, Bru was taken over by Chevrot's friend, Paul Eugène Girard, who made novel, less-expensive dolls. He produced a doll with a COMPOSITION and wood body that can walk, talk, and blow kisses. The voice-box is activated by the legs moving, to cry "Mama". The jointed right arm is worked to blow kisses by a pull string from the waist. The painting on the face is less refined than earlier Bru bébés. The open mouth with upper teeth and the heavy, dark, feather eyebrows are also typical of Girard. A "BRU Jne" stamp can be found on the head and shoulders of early bébés. A stamp may also be found on original shoes, and a brown and beige paper label on the body. Girard used the mark "Bru Jne R".

BRUNSTROM PEWTER Made by one of two pewterers of that name in late 18thC Philadelphia, USA.

White, semi-glazed jug with mistletoe design by BROWNFIELD, 1881.

BRUNSWICK American, New Jersey-based, POTTERY firm, producing DELFTWARE and ROCOCO figure groups in the 18thC.

BRUSHING SLIDE Found in some CHESTS OF DRAWERS, a wooden slide that pulls forward to provide a large working surface.

BRUSSELS CARPETS A generic term for CARPETS of moquette-wool and linen, brushed to resemble silk. They were made from the 16thC, although not necessarily in Brussels.

BUCKET A container made of MAHOGANY with copper or brass banding. A bucket with a gap down one side was used in the 18th and 19thC to carry plates; without the gap, it was used for carrying logs, coal, and peat.

BUCKLE Fasteners that were first used on shoes instead of shoelaces in England in the 17thC; in the 18thC they were commonly used to anchor neckbands and sashes as well as to fasten shoes and knee breeches. In the late 19th and early 20thC, intricate, ART NOUVEAU buckles, with trailing scrolls, stylized boat patterns, and lily pads, often with coloured enamelling, provided decorative embellishment to ladies' belts. Make sure that both parts of the buckle are hallmarked. Buckles produced by well-known makers such as TIFFANY & CO., LIBERTY, and Omar RAMSDEN are highly sought after, and, if signed, they should fetch a handsome premium.

BUCKLER Small, round shield used to ward off the blows of an adversary.

BUDDHA KNOP spoons with a knop or finial in the form of an eastern deity, perhaps Buddha. They were made in the 17thC, and associated with Raleigh Clapham, an English silversmith who marked his work with the initials "R.C".

BUEN RETIRO Factory founded in 1760 near Madrid. It made POTTERY for the Spanish court, and was noted for ROCOCO figure groups by Giuseppe Gricci.

"BUFFALO WILLOW" PATTERN American PLATES depicting a child on a buffalo in the style of the "WILLOW" PATTERN.

BUFFET Term applied to structures that have more than one tier, with or without enclosed sections. *See also* COURT CUPBOARD, LIVERY CUPBOARD, and PRESS CUPBOARD.

BUGATTI, CARLO (1855–1940) Italian designer of bizarre, ART NOUVEAU FURNITURE made of parchment, and an interior decorator. His son, Ettore, designed and manufactured the famous Bugatti racing car.

BUHL An old-English interpretation of BOULLE.

BULB The bulging swelling found on some 17thC legs and supports, more correctly known as a PORTUGUESE SWELL.

BULB BOWL Small Oriental POTTERY bowl, with three feet, for growing bulbs.

BULLOCK, EDMUND English clockmaker, active in Shropshire in the 18thC.

BULL'S EYE Used in CABINETS, clear glass with a large central GATHER.

BUN FOOT Similar to a BALL FOOT but with the rounded shape slightly flattened. Common on late -17thC case FURNITURE.

BUNYAN, ROBERT English clockmaker, active in Lincoln in the late 18thC.

BUREAU First made in the 1680s, a sloping, fall-fronted writing desk with drawers. The top is a steeper version of the 17thC writing box and has a hinged flat that folds up when not in use, while the base is a chest of drawers. Early bureaux were often made in two parts, with the join concealed by moulding. The upper part, fitted with pigeonholes and drawers, often had a secret compartment. Bureaux were made in quantity from the 18thC, generally from OAK, WALNUT, or MAHOGANY, and were sometimes decorated with LACQUER or MARQUETRY. They were often combined with BOOKCASES and CABINETS to become BUREAU BOOKCASES or BUREAU CABINETS. These were intended as much to display the wealth of their owner as for any practical purpose. Many bureaux have a strong, architectural, feel and were designed to co-ordinate with the architecture of the room in which they stood. Signs of quality include stylish interiors, perhaps with arched or stepped compartments or marquetry, a concealed writing well, and figured VENEERS. With the accession of a Dutch king to the English throne in 1689, many Dutch craftsmen came to England, bringing their cabinet-making techniques with them. Most Dutch bureaux are large by comparison with their English counterparts. Size affects value: a bureau under 0.92m (3ft) wide is desirable because it will fit more easily into today's smaller rooms. When you open a bureau, always pull out one or, preferably, both lopers (supports), and examine the hinges to ensure that they are in good condition. *See also* WRITING FURNITURE.

BUREAU À CYLINDER *See* CYLINDER-TOP DESK.

BUREAU BOOKCASE First made in the 18thC, a BUREAU with a glazed bookcase fitted above it. The best Georgian bureau bookcases are often larger than those of earlier and later periods, measuring 2.34m (7ft 8in) high, by 0.99m (3ft 3in) wide. The style of the pediment can help to date a piece. The top part is typically slightly narrower than the base, and there is usually a lip moulding concealing the join. If the sides of the top and bottom are flush, this might imply a MARRIAGE, or that the piece has been reduced in

Mahogany BUREAU bookcase, George III (1760–1820).

Victorian, inlaid walnut BUREAU DE DAME.

size. Look at the sides to make sure that the grain and colour of the wood are similar at the top and bottom, and that there are no signs of tampering. Looking at the back of the piece can be misleading – the two parts do not always match. The upper part may be panelled, because it is visible through the glazing, whereas the back of the base was intended to be unseen and therefore often made from unfinished flat boards. Many bureau bookcases have 13 panels of glass in each door. The shelves are usually adjustable and supported by pegs. Examine the shelves carefully – if the piece has been cut down, the shelves will have been trimmed too.

BUREAU CABINET A BUREAU with a solid-doored or mirrored cabinet above it, often containing fitted CUPBOARDS and drawers. *See also* WRITING FURNITURE.

BUREAU DE DAME Meaning "lady's desk" in French, a delicate writing desk, supported by slender CABRIOLE LEGS and with one or two external drawers. Popular in Continental Europe in the late 19th and early 20thC.

BUREAU PLAT French WRITING TABLE with a flat top and drawers in the frieze.

BUREAU-TOILETTE A piece of FURNITURE that combines the functions of a DRESSING TABLE and a WRITING TABLE.

BURGONET Originally a Burgundian steel cap worn by pikemen, but in the 17thC, a cavalry helmet with a crested crown, peak, and hinged chin pieces.

BURL The marking in wood of a knot or protruding growth, which displays beautifully patterned grainings when cut as a VENEER.

BURLAP American term for hessian.

BURLEIGH WARE POTTERY by the firm Burgess & Leigh, established 1851. From the late 1880s, the company produced a wide range of EARTHENWARE, including cottage and NOVELTY WARE. Hand-painted jugs in quirky designs, with handles in the form of animals were extremely popular when launched in the 1930s. Jugs from the "Sporting" range are sought after.

BURMESE GLASS An opaque, heat-sensitive GLASS.

BURNISHING Method of polishing metals by rubbing the surface with a hard, smooth tool, such as agate, to create a lustre.

BURR Another name for BURL.

BURSA Northern Turkish PRAYER RUGS with a short PILE, of silk or cotton, and predominantly blue, red, and ivory in colour.

BUSBY A late-19thC tall, military fur cap. A plume and a bag are suspended from the top, hanging over the right side of the face.

BUST HEAD American term for SHOULDER-HEAD.

BUTLER'S TRAY A small TABLE with a detachable top that rests on a stand. It can be used as an OCCASIONAL TABLE, and for carrying food and crockery to and from the kitchen. Few stands are found complete with their original trays.

BUTT The rear-end of a gun, placed against the shoulder while firing.

BUTTER DISH Popular from the late 18thC until *c.*1850, a vessel used for serving butter at the DINING TABLE. They usually have stands (except with later, American butter dishes), perhaps for ice to keep the butter cool.

BUTTERFIELD, MICHAEL (d.1724) Noted, 18thC, British maker of pocket SUNDIALS. The name was used on similar instruments well into the 19thC.

BUTTERFLY GATE Type of table-leaf support that comprises a shaped flap board, which swings out from the main frame to support the leaf.

BUTTERFLY JOINT Butterfly-shaped joint for joining two pieces end to end.

BUTTERFLY TABLE DROP-LEAF TABLE with leaves supported by BUTTERFLY GATES.

BUTTERFLY WING A TABLE with shaped leaves similar to the wings of a butterfly. Usually applied to PEMBROKE TABLES.

BUTT HINGE Common CABINET hinge, with only a thin strip of metal visible.

BUTTON BACK Upholstered seat FURNITURE where the back has been adorned with fabric-covered buttons. *See also* ARMCHAIR, BUTTON-BACK.

BUTTON HOOK Metal hooks, sometimes with ornate SILVER or IVORY handles, used between *c.*1840 and *c.*1920 for fastening the buttons of boots and spats.

BYE-LO American DOLLS designed by Grace Storey Putnam in 1922, and dubbed "million-dollar babies" because of the overwhelming demand for them. "Bye-Los" were based on a newborn child with half-closed eyes and creased limbs, and made in different materials, from life-size to miniature examples, with varying features. All-bisque Bye-Los are marked "Copr Grace S. Putnam, Germany" on the body, and are numbered according to size. A typical Kestner miniature has painted eyes and hair, jointed limbs, and a splayed body.

BYRNE, MICHAEL Leading, mid-18thC English gunsmith.

Late-Regency, single-rope-back
(CABLE MOULDED), carver chair, 1830.

White, stoneware CACHEPOT and
stand, unmarked, but probably by
Chetham and Woolley, c.1810.

CABARET A complete TEA SERVICE in PORCELAIN and consisting of TEAPOT, MILK JUG, SUGAR BOWL, cups, saucers, and TRAY. Another name for a TÊTE-À-TÊTE.

CABBAGE WARE First made at WORCESTER, tableware of green PORCELAIN with cabbage-leaf decoration in low relief.

CABINET Originally the name given to a small room, but, by the 17thC, a term applied to a small decorative CUPBOARD with drawers and compartments. Cabinets were made in the 17th and 18thC specifically to store precious curiosities. They were symbols of prestige, produced only by the most skilled craftsmen, hence the term "cabinet-maker". Most cabinets are strongly architectural in appearance. All 17th and 18thC examples are expensive. However, purpose-built cabinets made in the late 19th and 20thC can be found for modest sums. Legs on cabinets have often been replaced.

CABINET FURNITURE HANDLES, ESCUTCHEONS, and hinges for FURNITURE.

CABLE MOULDING A decorative MOULDING of twisted rope used during the REGENCY period on some chair backs and columns. Such chairs are known as ROPE BACKS or TRAFALGAR CHAIRS, because this moulding was a tribute to the British Admiral Lord Nelson's victories at sea.

CABLE TWIST On a QUILT, a pattern imitating the curves of a rope cable.

CABOCHON (1) Motif with a domed or ball shape surrounded by leaves.

CABOCHON (2) GEM cut into a dome shape, popular in 19thC JEWELLERY.

CABRIOLE LEG The outwardly curving, S-shaped leg popular on FURNITURE from the late 17thC. It had CLUB, PAD, PAW, BALL-AND-CLAW, or SCROLL feet.

CACHEMIRE Pattern, copied from Chinese models, of closely spaced and interlaced flowers in many colours. Typical of vases from DELFT.

CACHEPOT Holder for a flower pot. Similar to but smaller than a JARDINIÈRE.

CADDY BOWL A type of GLASS bowl found in an 18th and early 19thC CADDY. It was thought that such bowls, now often separated from the box, were used for blending the tea, but today it is accepted that they were used for serving sugar. A tall, straight-sided shape, with a small rudimentary foot is typical. Most are of clear glass, but coloured pieces are also found. Check for chips and cracks around the rim and foot, and look for scratches inside the bowl caused by sugar crystals or spoons. *See also* CADDY SPOON.

CADDY SPOON A short-handled spoon small enough to fit inside caddies, used for measuring tea. They were made from *c*.1770, when caddies no longer had caps for measuring tea. Birmingham was the main centre of British caddy-spoon production. Look for spoons decorated with tea-leaf shapes or plantation scenes. Most were stamped or raised from a thin sheet of silver, and are fragile. Check for splits in the bowl and damaged handles – repairs lower the value. *See also* CADDY BOWL and CADDY, TEA.

CADDY, TEA A container, usually in SILVER (but sometimes PORCELAIN), and housed in a wooden box for storing tea, which was imported in chests and sold loose. Each box, decorated with exotic VENEERS, usually had two caddies that sat either side of a glass bowl, called a CADDY BOWL. The term "caddy", used from the 1770s, is derived from the word *kati*, a Malay standard weight of tea. Tea was once so expensive that it was drunk only in the wealthiest homes, and the caddies for storing this precious commodity were intended as objects for display as much as for storage. Most early caddies were small, reflecting the high cost of tea. Some had locks to protect their contents from dishonest servants. Tea caddies resembling Chinese PORCELAIN tea bottles had sliding bases or tops for filling the caddy, and pull-off, rounded caps that were used to measure the tea. Caddies were sometimes marked with the initials "G" and "B" to distinguish between the two types of tea available to European drinkers: unfermented green tea or the less-expensive, fermented black variety. Many caddies were fitted with lead liners to keep the tea fresh, but few liners survive. From the 1730s, box, BOMBÉ, or vase shapes chased with ROCOCO or CHINOISERIE decoration were typical. In the 1770s, caddies were no longer fitted into boxes but were made lockable. NEO-CLASSICAL drum and oval forms were in vogue in the 1770s and '80s, and, in the Victorian period of the 19thC, novelty forms were popular. Caddies were mass-produced at this time, but the quality of these pieces was inconsistent. By the late 19thC, most caddies were made without locks, because tea had become less expensive. Caddies are keenly collected, and sets command a premium. On silver caddies look for high-quality decoration, unworn condition, and 18thCdate marks – 19thC caddies are usually less valuable. The bodies and lids of caddies should have a full set of matching HALLMARKS, although early - 18thC pieces with detachable lids are often unmarked on the cap. *See also* CADDY BOWL and CADDY SPOON.

CAFÉ-AU-LAIT POT A French COFFEE POT, with a small lip and a side handle. They were made in pairs, with one pot for coffee and the other for hot milk.

CAILLOUTÉ Derived from the French word for "pebble", GILDING applied in a series of dotted patterns.

CAKE BASKET Used from the late 16thC to serve fruit, bread, and sweetmeats, a SILVER or SILVER-GILT dish, often two-handled, with sides pierced in a variety of patterns. Early examples are circular, and those from the 18thC are oval.

CALAMANDER Imported from Sri Lanka, calamander (*Diospyros quaesita*) is a reddish- brown hardwood used as a VENEER and for CROSSBANDING in the REGENCY period. It was also employed on small boxes.

CALCEDONIO Marble effect in GLASS in imitation of precious minerals.

CALENDAR CLOCK A CLOCK with separate openings in the dial showing the day and month and, more rarely, the year.

CALIVER In use in the 16thC, an early MUSKET, with a short barrel and matchlock mechanism. It is fired from the shoulder.

CALLOT Grotesque figure group, usually in PORCELAIN but also in metal and GLASS, after the etchings of French caricaturist Jacques Callot (1592–1635).

CALYX Decorative motif of leaves enclosing a bud.

CAMAIEU Monochrome PORCELAIN decoration resembling ancient shell cameos, using different tones of the same colour.

CAMBRIAN WORKS In Swansea, Wales, a factory noted for POTTERY painted by floral artist William BILLINGSLEY in the early 19thC.

CAMEL BACK A CHAIR or SOFA with a back that curves in a similar fashion to the hump of a dromedary.

CAMEO (1) Design carved in relief, usually on a SEMI-PRECIOUS STONE, and often with a contrasting background.

CAMEO (2) In FURNITURE, the oval-shaped back of a SETTEE.

CAMEO GLASS Carved GLASS with two or more different-coloured layers, so that the design stands out in relief. An outer layer of cased or flashed glass, usually opaque white, is cut back to reveal a contrasting colour underneath. The ancient Roman technique was revived in the 19thC, after the PORTLAND VASE (1stC BC–AD 1stC) was brought to England. Cameo glass is found on decorative wares such as VASES and SCENT BOTTLES, because the technique was too expensive to decorate large suites of glass tableware. The work involved in carving cameo glass was so detailed that if the engraver made a small error the piece was often abandoned. The best-known English exponents were John Northwood (1836–1902), and George Woodall (1850–1925). The fashion for cameo glass spread from England to France, where factories such as BACCARAT and the ST LOUIS GLASSWORKS produced fine, hand-carved pieces. As the demand for this style of glass grew, short cuts were introduced to make it more affordable. Known as *faux* or commercial cameos, such pieces were acid-cut, and can be distinguished from hand-carved pieces in several ways. The top layers of *faux* cameo are thinner than those on true cameo glass, the definition between each of the layers is not as sharp, the edges of the decoration are softer, and the background appears matt and slightly rough to the touch. Cameo glass is one of the more expensive types of 19thC coloured glass. At the turn of the century, French glass artists, notably Fmile GALLÉ, created innovatory cameo glass in the ART NOUVEAU and ART DECO styles. Incomplete, cameo-glass items, such as vases, are widely available, although of lesser value. Always check on pieces with a pattern around the neck that the carved design is complete – on some damaged pieces, the rim has been ground down to remove chips and cracks.

CAMEO PARIAN Mid-19thC PORCELAIN imitating CAMEO GLASS, originally with white-paste decoration on a blue ground, but later in other colours.

CAMERA A mechanical instrument for creating photographs. The earliest, commercially manufactured cameras were produced from *c.*1841, and used the DAGUERREOTYPE process, developed in France by L.J.M. Daguerre in 1837. However, each daguerreotype image was unique, and it was not until Henry Fox Talbot's invention of the calotype that multiple copies could be produced from one exposure. The invention by George EASTMAN of the dry plate in 1879 led to the mass production of cameras, but handmade MAHOGANY and BRASS pieces are the most desirable. The more functional roll cameras of 1888 to 1920 lack the aesthetic appeal of contemporary plate cameras, but fetch reasonable prices in good condition. Among the most intriguing of cameras are the novelty, detective, and spy cameras produced towards the end of the 19thC, as the photographic process became more refined. Cameras in the form of books, watches, rings, and packets of cigarettes may have been made more as curiosities than for any real espionage, but are nonetheless popular with collectors, and can fetch high prices. The period between 1920 and 1940 was one of greatest technical innovation, when technical features were quickly superseded. A camera's age is not necessarily reflected in its value – the rarity and quality of a particular model are often more important than when it was made. Look out for milestone cameras that incorporate unusual technical innovations, and rare models by Ernst Leitz (Leica), Zeiss, Contax, and Rollei. The first examples of post-war innovations in camera technology should be of interest to collectors in the future. *See also* CAMERA, JAPANESE.

CAMEO GLASS **vase by Gallé,** *c.*1900.

CAMERA, JAPANESE Mass-produced cameras made in Japan after World War II. They came into favour as a result of photojournalists covering the Korean War and recognizing the superior quality of Japanese lenses. Today, rare and limited-edition models by companies such as Nikon or Canon can fetch high prices, although this is dependent on quality and condition.

CAMERA LUCIDA A prismatic device used from the early 19thC by artists to project an image onto a sheet of paper to trace an outline.

CAMERA OBSCURA Boxlike instrument containing lenses that project an image onto a black surface. Used from the late 17thC as an artist's aid.

CAMPAIGN BUTTON First designed in 1896, a badge produced during American presidential elections promoting a candidate or party slogan.

CAMPAIGN FURNITRE Items of FURNITURE designed to be dismantled or folded flat for travelling, even to the battlefield (as in the case of a campaign bed). The campaign chest – a CHEST OF DRAWERS with BRASS protective mounts designed for officers on army manoeuvres – could be separated into two parts, and was made from the late 18thC onward. Campaign chests often contain hidden surprises, such as folding tables and sets of four chairs.

CAMPANA VASE A vase shape resembling an inverted bell.

CAMP CANTEEN Set of boxed CUTLERY and accoutrements such as pepper- and SALT-CELLARS designed for travellers. The box often has retractable or folding legs, so that it can serve as a table.

CAMPHOR Light, yellowish-brown wood from the East Indies. It has a distinctive smell, and is used mainly for making trunks and boxes.

CAMPAIGN **armchair attributable to Ross & Co., mid- to late 19thC.**

CAMPHOR GLASS White or semi-opaque American PRESSED GLASS.

CANAPÉ The French word for a SOFA.

CANARY Canary-yellow background on early 19thC RESIST-LUSTRE pottery.

CANDELABRUM A table CANDLESTICK with two or more branches for holding lights. They were first made in the mid-17thC, but most surviving examples date from the late 18thC and 19thC. SILVER candelabra mirror the styles of contemporary candlesticks, and were made in pairs. Early candelabra had two branches, but those made at the end of the 18thC, when the main meal was taken after dark and more light was required, had three. Some of the most exceptional ROCOCO candelabra were produced in France in the first half of the 18thC. Massive, elaborate, SILVER-GILT examples were made during the REGENCY period, usually as part of lavish table CENTREPIECES. In the 19thC, it became fashionable to make candelabra with five or more branches. It was common for candelabra to be produced in SHEFFIELD PLATE as part of a matching set with more valuable silver candlesticks. Because they were of better quality and more valuable than candlesticks, silver candelabra did not suffer the same harsh wear or damage, and many found on the market today are in good condition. Sometimes candelabra were altered according to changing fashions, and many were converted to OIL LAMPS (and later, electrical lamps), when oil and electrical lighting were introduced. GLASS candelabra were produced from the mid-18thC, and copied BRASS and silver models. During the 19thC, glass candelabra became increasingly elaborate, with numerous branches and candle holders ornamented with LUSTRES. Coloured glass was especially popular. Spears, crescents, or "pineapples" often embellish the top of the stem. Each detachable part – the nozzle, stem, and branches – should be in the same style and decoration, and bear an identical maker's mark. Always check carefully for missing branches (indicated by holes in a brass plate at the top of the stem), lustres, and shades. On candelabra with many branches, check that all the nozzles are present, because missing ones are detrimental to the value.

CANDLE BOX Square or cylindrical box of metal or wood for storing candles. Also, a lidded compartment within a CHEST for the same purpose.

CANDLE SLIDE A small, wooden slide designed to carry a candlestick.

CANDLE SNUFFER See SNUFFER.

CANDLESTAND A portable stand for a CANDLESTICK, CANDELABRUM, or lamp. Also known as a GUÉRIDON or torch.

CANDLESTICK An object for holding a candle. The basic form is a base, vertical stem (or column), nozzle, and, on most examples, a drip pan. On some candlesticks, above the nozzles, there are ledges that feature as drip pans, designed to catch dripping wax; others have trays between the stem and the base to catch drips. The drip pan at the base of the stem became smaller and was absorbed as a decorative feature. The socket (or SCONCE) is the cylindrical holder into which the candle fits. Most early candlesticks, made of light, thin, hammered, sheet metal, and hollow, were designed with large bases to counterbalance their instability, and were 13cm (5in) tall at most; decoration was limited to an engraved ARMORIAL or embossed trailing flowers. By the 1680s, skilled HUGUENOT craftsmen were casting candlesticks in solid SILVER. Candlesticks became heavier, taller, and more ornate, and could stand on small bases. In the early 18thC, plain candlesticks came into fashion but by the 1730s, they had spool-shaped sconces and richer ornamentation of pleated or lobed forms. Detachable nozzles were typical

Early-19thC, mahogany CANDLE BOX with a dummy drawer front.

Bow CANDLESTICK **with a youth against a tree, on a rococo scrollwork base, c.1770.**

from the 1740s. The nozzle fits into the socket to hold the candle and stop the wax dripping inside the stem. Lavish ROCOCO candlesticks were made in the mid-18thC. Few North American candlesticks were made prior to 1760. In the 1770s, mechanization led to "loaded" candlesticks stamped from rolled sheet silver, with the bases weighted for stability; vast numbers of loaded candlesticks were produced in Sheffield and Birmingham. A large quantity of loaded sheet silver, SHEFFIELD PLATE, or cast silver examples were produced, either in the plain baluster style on a circular foot, or in the form of a Corinthian column on a square plinth. Toward the end of the 18thC the NEO-CLASSICAL STYLE brought about changes in candlestick design, including the use of square bases, Corinthian-column stems with urn-shaped nozzles, and restrained CLASSICAL ornament such as GADROONING, SWAGS, BEADING, REEDING, and stylized foliage. In the REGENCY period, candlesticks became more ornate, with lavish scrolls and foliage applied to the bases, around the sockets, and at the tops of the stems. From c.1820, many 17th and 18thC styles were revived, with the Rococo taste popular. Unlike earlier cast examples, most revival candlesticks were made of loaded sheet silver. Figural candlesticks, in the form of rustic figures of shepherds, caryatids, or knights in armour were fashionable during the 19thC. In the late 19thC, British and North American silversmiths produced handmade wares in the simple designs of the ARTS AND CRAFTS MOVEMENT. Candlesticks made in the 20thC encompass a host of styles, including ART NOUVEAU and ART DECO. Most candlesticks were made in pairs or larger sets, and collectors should expect to pay more than double for a pair of candlesticks than for two singles. To form a true "pair", candlesticks must be the work of one maker and produced at the same date. Cast silver examples are more desirable than loaded ones. Any detachable part should match the main body in style, date, and maker's mark. Sheet candlesticks are marked in a line above the base, cast ones are marked in the well or under each corner. GLASS candlesticks were made in the medieval period, but only with the invention of brilliant, clear, lead crystal did they become more common. The patterns of early lead-crystal candlesticks were copied from BRASS and silver models, with elegant, plain, knopped BALUSTER STEMS. Throughout the 18thC, English glass candlesticks featured stems with decoration following that of contemporary DRINKING GLASSES, such as AIR-TWIST STEMS and OPAQUE-TWIST STEMS. *See also* CHAMBERSTICK, TAPERSTICK, and WAXJACK.

CANDY A cord that holds the sides of a RUG in place and prevents fraying.

CANE A rod of GLASS drawn out by the glassblower for use as decoration.

CANEWARE Of pale buff colour, a range of ovenproof STONEWARE produced by Josiah WEDGWOOD in the late 18th and early 19thC.

CANOPY Hanging or over-hanging covering associated with a BED.

CANTAGALLI Firm founded in Florence, Italy, by Ulysse Cantagalline. It was one of the most prolific producers of late-19thC MAIOLICA, specializing in reproductions of Renaissance wares. Pieces are marked with a cockerel.

CANTARO Mediterranean GLASS drinking vessel, made in the 18thC, with a wide spout for filling and a smaller one for pouring.

CANTED CORNER A CHAMFERED or BEVELLED corner used as a decorative feature on 18thC CASE FURNITURE.

CANTEEN A set of cased SILVER tableware or CUTLERY. Also, an URN, likewise of SILVER, with a tap at the base for dispensing the contents.

CANTERBURY First made in 1803, a small, portable music stand, with partitions for holding sheet music. They were named by Thomas SHERATON after the Archbishop of Canterbury, the first person to order one from him. Canterburies are popular, and hold their value well. The proportions can give important clues as to the date. Earlier examples were larger, but lighter than later ones. Check for signs of tampering – look for original crossbars and supports, and original castors on the feet. A DRAWER is a definite bonus.

CANTON PORCELAIN Elaborately decorated and gilded Chinese wares made in the Canton (Guangzhou) district for export to the West in the 18thC.

CAPACITY MARKS Marks on TANKARDS in PEWTER that were used in taverns. Required by law after 1826, such marks aid with dating and provenance.

CAPACITY MUG Any vessel marked to hold a specific quantity of liquid. Used from the 17thC to measure beer and other liquors.

CAPE COD GLASS Pressed-and-cut GLASS made by the American Cape Cod Glass Co. in the second half of the 19thC.

CAPODIMONTE Italian SOFT-PASTE PORCELAIN factory, established in 1743 at Capodimonte, Naples, and noted for the figure groups carved by Giuseppe Gricci. When Naples fell under Spanish rule, the Capodimonte factory moved to BUEN RETIRO in Spain, but returned to Naples in the late 18thC. NEO-CLASSICAL decoration, inspired by the local archeological excavations at Herculaneum and Pompeii on the Bay of Naples, was popular on Neapolitan PORCELAIN of the late 18thC. An angular, scrolled handle is characteristic of the Capodimone factory, and it can be found on COFFEE POTS, cups, and other similar wares. The factory copied MEISSEN figures by J.J. KÄNDLER, and although their re-interpretation in soft-paste porcelain did not have the same crisp details as a Meissen original, it is worth more. Capodimonte use a fleur-de-lis mark, usually in UNDERGLAZE BLUE or gold. *See also* PORCELAIN, ITALIAN.

Fine, Salisbury, James I CAQUETEUSE jointed armchair, 1580–1630.

CAPSTAN All or part of an object in the shape of a ship's capstan or a domestic cotton reel. Usually refers to SALT-CELLARS, FINIALS, or feet on a piece of SILVER.

CAPSTAN TABLE Another name for a DRUM TABLE.

CAPUCHINE STONEWARE vessel that, when inverted, resembles the hood of a Capuchine, or Franciscan, friar. First made in Nottingham, England, c.1700.

CAQUETEUSE CHAIR with a tall back and splayed arms to accommodate the full dresses of ladies in the late 16thC. Also known as a GOSSIP'S CHAIR.

CARAFE GLASS vessel with a bulbous body and tall, narrow neck for water, wine, or liquor. Examples made in the 18thC are engraved and made for table use, while 19thC examples designed for bedroom use are often plainer, and have beakers that sit over the neck and double as stoppers.

CARBINE Cavalry MUSKET, similar in most respects to infantry FIREARMS, but lighter and lacking a BAYONET.

CARBUNCLE A garnet cut into a dome shape.

CARCASS (Carcase) The solid, inner frame, or chassis, that forms the body of a piece of CASE FURNITURE, such as a CHEST OF DRAWERS or WARDROBE.

CARCASS FURNITURE General term for FURNITURE used for storage purposes, as distinct from TABLES and seating furniture.

CARD CASE A small object for storing visiting cards. First made in the 1820s, card cases were made of valuable materials such as SILVER and intricately decorated to reflect the status of the owner. Most early examples were oblong and made of SILVER GILT, usually with pierced or FILIGREE decoration on both sides, and sharply angled corners to fit the shape of the cards. The main centre of manufacture in Britain was Birmingham. The peak period for production, 1840–60, coincided with the burgeoning fashion for travel by rail. Many card cases found today feature architectural scenes and views of British landmarks. Known as CASTLE-TOPS and made as souvenirs, card cases of this type are very collectable. A concertina-style interior made of silk-covered cardboard is a good example of the inventive type of interior in some card cases; others, intended to hold money or stamps, featured clips for security. In the late 19thC, many card cases were made in the Far East to satisfy the European taste for Oriental wares. They incorporated such exotic materials as IVORY, TORTOISESHELL, MOTHER-OF-PEARL, and LACQUER, and were lined with ivory or silk. Following the invasion of Japanese territorial waters by the US Navy in 1853, ivory card cases decorated with SHIBAYAMA became popular, and these cases are sought after today. The value of a card case will be reduced if the piece is in poor condition, so avoid dented examples and those with weak or damaged hinges. Check tortoiseshell cases carefully, because the tortoiseshell is typically delicate, and tends to deteriorate over time.

CARDER, FREDERICK (1864–1963) English-born glassmaker who worked at STEVENS & WILLIAMS before moving to the USA, where he was artistic director of STEUBEN GLASSWORKS in Corning, New York from 1903 to 1933. He was responsible for introducing AURENE GLASS. *See also* GLASS.

CARDEW, MICHAEL (1901–83) English art potter, taught by Bernard LEACH and inspired by Oriental PORCELAIN. He worked at the Winchcombe Pottery in Cheltenham from 1926 to 1939.

CARD TABLE *Demi-lune* (half-moon-shaped) or rectangular table with a folding top and baize-covered inside, first made for cards and other games *c*.1700. A concertina action, where the back legs of the table pull out, allows the legs to support the top when unfolded. Projecting, circular corners of the table are stands for candles to illuminate cards and chips during play. Numerous tables were made for card-playing in the 18thC in a variety of woods, and even PAPIER-MÂCHÉ. By the early 19thC, card tables with central supports (and no legs to disturb the players) were popular. *See also* GAMES TABLE.

CARETTE A manufacturer, active 1886–1917, of TINPLATE toys, including cars, boats, and trains. The firm was established in Germany by a Frenchman, and produced railway stock for BASSETT-LOWKE. Several companies bought their tooling, so pre-World War I Carette parts can be found on post-war trains.

CARLIN, MARTIN (d.1785) French cabinet-maker active in the late 18thC. He was commissioned by royalty, and worked mainly with LACQUER and SÈVRES porcelain plaques, which he incorporated into his FURNITURE.

CARLTON HOUSE DESK A grand, D-shaped WRITING TABLE, surmounted by a curved bank of DRAWERS and compartments. It was so-called because the first one was believed to have been designed for the house of the same name of the Prince Regent (later George IV). This desk was popular toward the end of the 18thC, and again at the end of the 19thC. *See also* WRITING FURNITURE.

CARLTON WARE Items produced by WILTSHAW & ROBINSON LTD of the Carlton Works, based in Stoke-on-Trent, England. The company was founded in 1890, and renamed Carlton Ware Ltd in 1957. The pottery enjoyed a heyday of popularity during the 1920s and '30s, when it produced a huge range of decorative items and tablewares; geometric designs, moulded tablewares, novelty items, and lustre decoration are particular specialities. Decorative items painted in distinctive, abstract designs with bright colours (more common on early pieces), and lustre wares in the Oriental style are among the most

Sheraton revival, demi-lune CARD TABLE, late 19thC–early 20thC.

sought-after items. Objects advertising the drinks manufacturer Guinness have a cult following, but watch out for modern fakes. Some early marks feature the initials of Wiltshaw & Robinson, as well as the name Carlton Ware.

CARNIVAL GLASS An inexpensive, PRESS-MOULDED, or MOULD-BLOWN type of GLASS, with a shimmering, iridescent finish made by spraying the hot glass with metallic salts, in the style of luxury ART GLASS by TIFFANY. It was made in North America from the 1890s to the 1920s by firms such as the Imperial Glass Co. at Bellaire, Ohio, and Harry Northwood at Indiana, Pennsylvania. Brightly coloured examples were exported to Britain between the two world wars.

CAROLEAN FURNITURE made during the reign of Charles I (1625–49).

CARPET A woven textile for covering floors. There is no hard and fast rule as to when a RUG becomes a carpet, or vice versa, but as a general guide, when the size of the piece is more than 2.6m (8ft 6in) long by c.1.7m (5ft 6in) wide then the term "carpet" will apply; under this size, the object is a rug. The majority of carpets are categorized according to the tribe who produced them or their place of origin; distinctive patterns, motifs, colours, and weaves are characteristic of each type. *See also* RUGS, CAUCASIAN AND TURKISH; RUGS, CHINESE; RUGS, EUROPEAN; RUGS, INDIAN; and RUGS, PERSIAN.

CARRARA Fine, white marble quarried in Tuscany, Italy. Also refers to STONEWARE by DOULTON, and 19thC English PARIAN ware made to imitate the appearance of white marble and popular for decorative objects.

CARRIAGE CLOCK A small portable CLOCK with a carrying handle – hence the name – and fitted with a device to ensure that the jolts common in coach travel would not interfere with the oscillations of the BALANCE SPRING. One of the earliest types of travelling clock, carriage clocks usually have BRASS cases; many came with leather travelling cases. Nearly all carriage clocks were made in France during the 19thC and the early years of the 20thC, although a few were produced in England. Carriage clocks are among the least expensive antique clocks available. Engraved-case carriage clocks are more valuable than plain ones. Look for elaborate, detailed decoration that covers as much of the case as possible. Clocks with smaller subsidiary dials are also desirable. Some clocks have dials showing the seconds or the days of the week, but the most common subsidiary dial is an alarm. Some carriage clocks have "repeat" buttons on the top of the case – when the button is pressed, the clock repeats the last hour struck. Typical features on a French carriage clock are: a white enamel dial, black numerals, stamped mark or signature on the BACKPLATE, an eight-day, spring-driven movement with a going barrel (a drum containing the MAINSPRING), BEVELLED glass panels, and blued-steel hands. Signs of quality are a case in either engraved metal, panelled CLOISONNÉ, or PORCELAIN, and subsidiary dials. Firms and makers to look out for include Auguste (active from 1840,

Exceptional and rare, gorge cased, striking and repeating CARRIAGE CLOCK, c.1870.

French), Abraham-Louis BREGUET (1747–1823, French), Achille and Louis Brocot (active 19thC, French), Dejardin (active 19thC, French), Pierre and Alfred Drocourt (1860–89, French), Frodsham family (19th/20thC, English), Paul GARNIER (1801–1869, French), JAPY FRÈRES (1772–early 20thC, French), F.A. Margaine (c.1870–1912, French), E. Maurice (active 1880s, French), James McCabe (19thC, English), and Soldano (c.1855–80, French).

CARTEL CLOCK An 18thC, French WALL CLOCK in the shape of a shield. Often with a gilded bronze case, and elaborately ornamented in the ROCOCO style.

CARTER, STABLER & ADAMS *See* POOLE POTTERY.

CARTONNIER Item of FURNITURE that usually stood at one end of a WRITING TABLE and was intended to hold papers. Also known as a SERRE-PAPIER.

CARTOPHILIST A collector of cigarette cards. Often includes those who are interested in postcards, greetings cards, and other ephemera.

CARTOUCHE Decorative feature resembling a scroll of parchment with curled edges, usually surrounding an inscription, coat-of-arms, or pictorial decoration. In SILVER it is normally engraved, embossed, or cast.

CARVED DECORATION Decoration cut into wood. One of the most popular ways of decorating FURNITURE, and widely used throughout the centuries. The fineness of the detail depends on the grain of the wood, but also on the expertise of the carver. OAK is difficult to carve. Carving on WALNUT and MAHOGANY is typically finer and more intricate. In the 17th and 18thC, the effect of intricate, pierced carving was lightened by under-cutting, with the back of the design angled inward. On late 19th- to early-20thC copies of earlier carving there is little or no under-cutting, and the overall effect is heavier. Carving is not always contemporary with the piece; in the late Victorian and Edwardian periods (1860–1901 and 1901–1910 respectively), early, plain furniture, especially oak, was often "improved" with later carving. Pieces adorned with later carving are less desirable than those with original decoration.

CARVER A DINING CHAIR with arms.

CARYATID An upright, carved female figure (although sometimes the term is used for a male figure) of ancient Greek origin. Sometimes used as supports on cabinet bases.

CASED GLASS An ancient technique, revived in the 19thC, in which one layer of GLASS, often coloured, is sandwiched between two plain-glass layers; on some examples this is reversed, with plain glass between two coloured layers. The outer layer is engraved to decorative effect.

CASE FURNITURE Items of FURNITURE made to hold and store objects, such as CHESTS, COFFERS, CUPBOARDS, and CHESTS OF DRAWERS.

CASEIN A type of plastic patented in 1900, and employed in imitation of horn and TORTOISESHELL.

CASE OF SWORDS Two SWORDS that clip together and fit into a single scabbard. They are sometimes made as duelling rapiers.

CASING A technique in which a clear-GLASS layer is fused over a coloured-glass body. The term is interchangeable with OVERLAY.

CASSANDRE, ADOLPHE J.M. (1901–68) French designer of posters. He designed the poster for the liner *Normandie* – one of the most valuable posters of the ART DECO period.

CASSAPANCA Italian SETTLE with a CHEST under the seat.

CASSEL Short-lived, German PORCELAIN factory, active from 1766 to 1788. It is noted for blue-painted coffee and tea sets.

CASSONE Italian CHEST used for general storage of linen and clothes.

CASTELLATO Meaning "little castle", a popular motif in European PORCELAIN painting in the latter half of the 18thC.

CASTELLI MAIOLICA from the Abruzzi region of Italy. It is noted for delicate landscapes painted by members of the Grue family.

CASTER A cylindrical vessel with a pierced cover for dispensing seasonings and so-called because it "casts" its contents over the food. Casters were first made in the second half of the 17thC. Early SILVER ones had straight sides. BALUSTER casters were made from *c*.1705, becoming taller throughout the 18thC. Sometimes called a sugar sifter or dredger, the lighthouse-shaped sugar caster was popular in the late 17thC. The popularity of the caster waned in the late 18thC, but, in the 19thC, the Victorians were fond of novelty forms such as animal-shaped examples. Casters were made in pairs or sets of three (one large caster for sugar and two smaller ones for dry mustard and pepper); although single casters are desirable, complete sets are more highly prized. For maximum value the FINIAL on top of the caster should be in good condition, and unrestored. Good engraving of a coat-of-arms adds to the value if contemporary with the piece. Silver that has been re-engraved will be thin, and you can feel this by pressing the surface. Check that the inside cover has not been repaired, and that the piercing is undamaged. The top may be attached to the base by a BAYONET FITTING. Check that it fits the base snugly.

Armorial albarello, probably CASTELLI, 1701.

CAST GLASS GLASS cast in a mould.

CASTING BOTTLE A small, 18thC, SILVER container with pierced sides. They held perfume-soaked sponges, and hung from chains as air fresheners.

CASTING, GLASS A technique for forming GLASS, in which molten glass is poured into a mould and allowed to cool, before the mould is broken away. A perfect cast is difficult to produce, especially for large objects, because the outer layers of the glass cool more rapidly than the inside. The cast must be cooled slowly in an annealing furnace to prevent stresses inside the material.

CASTING, SILVER A method of forming intricate shapes in SILVER, which cannot be successfully raised from sheet silver. To cast the component, silver is melted, poured into a mould fashioned in the desired shape, and cooled. Once the component has solidified, it is removed from the mould, finished by hand, polished, and soldered onto the object. It is likely that many cast components, which often conform to standard patterns, were supplied by specialist workshops that mass-produced them for a number of silversmiths. Cast objects are heavier and more solid than their raised counterparts, and their undersides or insides are left quite rough. *See also* LOST-WAX CASTING.

CAST-IRON TOY Toys were produced in cast iron from the 1880s to *c*.1910, and were especially popular in North America. Novelty MONEY BOXES were particularly favoured, but manufacturers also made horse-drawn toys, automotive toys, cap guns, bell toys, and other novelties. Among the main producers were J. & E. Stevens, Arcade Manufacturing Co., DENT HARDWARE CO., and the Gong Bell Manufacturing Co. Look for cast-iron toys with good paintwork. Repairs are acceptable, if properly carried out.

CASTLEFORD An English pottery established near Leeds *c*.1790, and noted for glossy, white porcellaneous STONEWARE.

CASTLE-TOP A CARD CASE that features decoration of famous landmarks, such as scenes of well-known monuments, cathedrals, or stately homes. Typical British landmarks include Windsor Castle, St Paul's Cathedral, and Warwick Castle. The earliest castle-tops featured a scene on both sides; later ones usually have a scene on one side only. The central panel with a scenic view was stamped in relief from a steel die and inset into the body of the case, with a chased or engraved decorative border surrounding it. SNUFF-BOXES were also made as castle-tops, as were VINAIGRETTES, from the 1830s. Those with more detail, hand-finishing, and rare examples – such as views of Buckingham Palace – are sought after.

CASTLE, WENDELL (b.1932) An American designer known for creating FURNITURE in unusual, sculptural forms, using wood and fibreglass.

Victorian, CASTLE-TOP card case, decorated with a view of Windsor Castle, 1855.

CASTOR (Caster) A small wheel made of wood, china, BRASS, or leather, and attached to the legs of FURNITURE. Made since the 16thC, they can be plain or in shapes such as a lion's paw. Leather was used around metal casters in the 18thC; some 19thC Victorian castors were made of PORCELAIN.

CAST SPOON A cast, rather than hammered-and-drawn, highly ornate spoon from the mid-18thC. The bowl, stem, and FINIAL are all decorated.

CAUDLE CUP The American term for a PORRINGER.

CAUGHLEY Prolific English POTTERY manufacturer, established at Caughley, near Broseley, in Shropshire, c.1750–99. The firm began producing PORCELAIN after it was taken over by Thomas Turner in 1772. In 1775, Robert Hancock, formerly of WORCESTER, joined Caughley and introduced TRANSFER-PRINTING in UNDERGLAZE BLUE. Caughley porcelain is made using soaprock, and may have a greyish tinge. From the 1780s, gilding is characteristic of the factory, which also printed dense CHINOISERIE such as the "WILLOW" PATTERN on their wares. Caughley is often confused with Worcester, as the two firms have many patterns in common. Howver, hatched crescents never appear on Caughley; they were purely a Worcester mark. Caughley marked their wares with a "C" (similar to Worcester), or the word "Salopian" or "S".

CAULDRON SALT Popular from the 1730s, a circular, three-footed SALT-CELLAR in the shape of a cauldron. Many examples, especially those made between 1750–80, were inexpensively and lightly constructed, and are prone to damage.

CAUSEUSE From the French verb *causer* ("to chat"), a large CHAIR or small SOFA intended to seat two people.

CAVETTO A quarter-round, concave MOULDING.

CEDAR From North America, as well as the West Indies and Honduras, cedar (*Juniperus virginiana*) is a hard, durable, reddish, aromatic, worm-resistant wood, used between c.1770 and 1820 for DRAWER linings on quality FURNITURE and storage CHESTS. While the wood is not particularly strong, it is noted for having a high resistance to decay and insects.

CELADON **dish, with biscuit fish, from the Northern Sung Dynasty,** AD**960–1127.**

CELADON A distinctive, olive-green Chinese STONEWARE, first produced in the northwest region of China in Henan and Shaanxi during the SUNG dynasty (960–1279). After this time, Longquan (in Zhejiang) became the main centre of production, and wares (known as southern celadon) were made in a soft, blue-green colour. Bowls are the most common examples of northern Chinese celadon; they typically have a conical form and moulded, floral decoration. If the decoration is carved or figural, the value increases. Modern Korean imitations of southern celadon are similar to the originals.

CELEBRITY DOLL A DOLL made to look like a famous person, such as a film star or musician. The first examples were made to portray pre-World War II stars of the silver screen. Sometimes, one celebrity was portrayed by different makers in different materials. "Shirley Temple", the most popular celebrity doll made, was first produced in 1934 by the American IDEAL TOY & NOVELTY CO. Early dolls mostly had jointed, COMPOSITION, toddler bodies, brown glass SLEEPING EYES, and open mouths with teeth. Some examples have eyes of enamelled tin, but the best are those with glass FLIRTY EYES. Ideal also produced Shirley Temple babies. The film star and singer Deanna Durbin was another Ideal favourite. Her doll is less common than Shirley Temple's, and it commands higher prices in the USA than in Britain. Many North American manufacturers made vinyl, plastic, and porcelain figurines of The Beatles. The most sought after were made in 1964 by Carmascot, with composition heads and real hair. The heads of "Bobb'n Beatles" dolls move on a spring. Look out for a mark on the head or shoulder-plate and body of a Shirley Temple doll, and a badge bearing a photograph of Shirley Temple. The most sought-after Shirley Temples are the Ideal composition dolls, with their original box. Vinyl is less desirable.

CELERY VASE A VASE intended to hold celery to be eaten with cheese at the end of a meal. Celery vases were made in England from *c*.1800 until the 20thC, and in North America in the 19thC. They have wide, flared, stemmed forms, and were usually made in clear GLASS.

CELLAR *See* SALT-CELLAR.

CELLARET A lidded container on legs used from the 18thC onward for storing wine and keeping it cool. The interior is often divided into sections for individual bottles. Cellarets usually have locking lids and are sometimes lead-lined, with a plug in the base to drain away melted ice. They were sometimes incorporated into a deep, lead-lined DRAWER in SIDEBOARDS. By the end of the 18thC, the terms "cellaret" and "WINE COOLER" were interchangeable. Sarcophagus-shaped cellarets from the early 19thC are desirable. Stands for cellarets are prone to damage and often replaced, but a replaced stand reduces the value of the piece quite considerably. To determine whether a stand is a replacement, look for a difference between the colour of that and the top.

"CELLINI" PATTERN A Renaissance-inspired pattern found on wine EWERS wine jugs, and CLARET JUGS in the 19thC. Characteristics of this ornament include masks, foliage, STRAPWORK, beasts, and fruit, and a CARYATID handle.

CELLULOID The trade name for pyroxylin, an early, flammable form of plastic invented in North America in 1869 by the Hyatt Brothers. It was originally used for making billiard balls, and, later, in the production of DOLLS

An Ideal composition CELEBRITY DOLL of Deanna Durbin, *c*.1930s.

and various household objects. It was superseded by cellulose acetate or "nonflammable celluloid" in 1926.

CELLULOID DOLL A doll made from CELLULOID. The German Rheinische Gummi und Celluloid Fabrik Co. of Bavaria used celluloid as early as 1873, and other manufacturers soon followed suit, because celluloid was less expensive than BISQUE. Leading makers in Germany and France include KESTNER & CO., KÄMMER & REINHARDT, and JUMEAU. Celluloid dolls were also made in England, although in smaller numbers, and in North America by firms such as E.I. Horsman and Averill. The dolls were modelled both as babies and children, and have glossy sheens on the face. Kammer & Reinhardt dolls have either SWIVEL HEADS on celluloid or COMPOSITION bodies, or SHOULDER-HEADS attached to soft bodies with celluloid lower limbs. The hair may be moulded and painted or a wig, but only better-quality dolls have GLASS eyes. Where lower limbs may be visible beneath clothing, they are celluloid. A KID body is typical with a shoulder-head. Celluloid dolls are accessible to most collectors, because so many were produced. However, celluloid is flammable, and easily cracked and dented, and likely to fade when exposed to light, so the condition of a celluloid doll is important to its value. Kestner character dolls are sought after, as are dolls with glass eyes or with original clothes, preferably made between 1910 and 1915. Poorly defined fingers and toes are characteristic of less valuable dolls.

CELLULOID TOY A child's toy made from CELLULOID. They are keenly collected, although they are less expensive than TINPLATE toys of a similar date. Toys made from celluloid are flammable, and prone to denting and cracking. Celluloid is almost impossible to restore, so avoid damaged toys.

CEMETERY RUG A small Turkish PRAYER RUG, with a design of cypress trees and tomblike buildings. *See also* RUG.

CENTENNIAL An American term referring to high-quality, reproduction, CHIPPENDALE-style FURNITURE made for the 100th anniversary of the signing of the Declaration of Independence in 1776. Also used to refer to items made to celebrate the centennial in 1876.

Neo-Classical table CENTREPIECE by Joseph Scammel of London, 1795.

CENTREPIECE A large, richly decorated piece of tableware, intended to reflect the wealth and status of its owner. In the REGENCY period, heavy stands with scroll feet and female CARYATID figures supporting the central bowl were popular. In the early 19thC, ornamental CENTREPIECES with central bowls for candied fruits and sweetmeats, either made of solid SILVER or pierced, and with glass liners, replaced ÉPERGNES as the focal point of the DINING TABLE. Because centrepieces were so valuable, many were fitted in wooden boxes with baize linings to protect them when not in use. Decorative centrepieces were often used as presentation items, especially during the Regency period.

Some 19thC centrepieces were made in quirky shapes, such as a sledge, which was characteristic of the Victorian penchant for novelty forms. By the second half of the 19thC, the form of centrepieces changed, mainly due to ELKINGTON & CO., which pioneered a method of electroplating that made it possible to produce elaborate silver items more affordably. By the end of the 19thC, centrepieces had become smaller and less elaborate, and some featured large central vases for flowers and three smaller bud vases. If glass bowls are later replacements, or chipped or cracked, this reduces the value. On centrepieces made of SHEFFIELD PLATE make sure that on areas that have been frequently polished, such as ornate scrolled feet, the plate has not worn off, leaving the copper base (revealed as pink) showing through.

CENTRE TABLE A table designed to stand in the centre, or other open part, of a room, and hence fashioned to look attractive when viewed from any angle. Centre tables are similar in form to SOFA TABLES, but without the flaps at each end. The position of the STRETCHER on a centre table can give an indication of date. A high stretcher points to an early date of *c*.1790, while a decade later stretchers were lower, or had been replaced by central pedestals.

CERAMICS The materials from which ceramics are made are divided into three families: POTTERY, made from EARTHENWARE; STONEWARE, a fine, water-resistant body created by firing clays at high temperatures; and PORCELAIN, a mixture of china clay and PETUNTSE (hard paste), or crushed glass or quartz and white clay (soft paste). GLAZES are used to make a porous body watertight, and for decoration, and may be translucent, opaque, or coloured. LEAD GLAZES, TIN GLAZES, and SALT GLAZES are used on pottery. Glazes on porcelain vary according to the factory. Porcelain is highly prized by collectors, and is more expensive than pottery. Understanding the materials or techniques used in the manufacture of a piece of ceramic can help in identifying its origin, date, and value. The main factors to assess are material, glaze, and decoration. Copies and imitations of earlier ceramic styles have been made throughout the centuries. Most early imitations were intended to show admiration for earlier designs. Deliberate faking with the intention to mislead began during the 18thC, with the decoration of SÈVRES porcelain blanks by independent decorators who marked them as if they were genuine Sèvres wares. *See also* COMMEMORATIVE CERAMICS.

CERAMICS, 20THC A rapidly growing collecting area, POTTERY and PORCELAIN manufactured in the 20thC by makers such as CARLTON, Susie COOPER, and POOLE POTTERY now have a well-established following. This category encompasses pieces by leading designers and studio potters, as well as a plethora of commercially produced wares that reflect the prevailing taste of the day. Large pieces designed or made by well-established designers tend to be the most striking wares available, and attract the highest prices. However, there is a rich hunting ground of more affordable, smaller

Art Deco, Beswick faun, No.369,
c.1930s (20THC CERAMICS).

designer-made pieces, as well as stylish wares by lesser manufacturers. The geometric forms that typify the ART DECO styles of the 1920s and '30s are very popular, and pieces in dramatic shapes or with interesting designs are often worth more than less-stylish pieces by the same designer. Ornamental figurines are also popular, and among the most sought after are those by DOULTON, WADE, and BESWICK.

CERAMICS, CARE OF Unless restored, HARD-PASTE PORCELAIN and high-fired STONEWARE may be safely washed by hand in mild soapy water and rinsed off well before being left to air-dry. However, unglazed ceramics, which are porous, should not be exposed to water, because this causes discoloration; clean them by dusting only. Low-fired EARTHENWARE and other SOFT-PASTE PORCELAIN and BONE CHINA may also be discoloured and damaged by washing, but can be wiped gently with a damp cloth. Do not secure loose lids to the main bodies with adhesive tape or adhesive paste, as these can damage any original gilding and enamel. When picking up objects with lids, always remove the lid first, without using the KNOP, which is vulnerable to damage. Lift hollow objects by supporting the body gently using two hands; do not pick up pieces by their handles, which may be weak through use. Try to avoid touching gilding, which is easily rubbed and worn through handling.

CERAMICS, CHINESE Almost every major development in POTTERY and PORCELAIN occurred in China, and throughout the centuries Chinese ceramics have exerted a profound influence over those made in the Far East, Middle East, and Europe. The earliest wares evolved between c.3000 and 1500 BC. These were made as unglazed funerary objects and were simply decorated with earth pigments. During the Shang dynasty (1700–1027 BC), pottery became more refined, and shapes were based on contemporary metal vessels. LEAD and FELDSPATHIC GLAZES were not developed until the Han dynasty (206 BC– AD 220), when high-fired STONEWARE was made. Outside influences from central Asia gradually infiltrated China, altering the appearance of ceramics, and Chinese wares began to spread throughout the Middle East carried by Arab traders. Potters rediscovered white clay, which led to the development of porcelain. Considering the age and importance of these early ceramics, they are available at modest prices. *See also* PORCELAIN, CHINESE; POTTERY, CHINESE; and STONEWARE, CHINESE.

CERAMICS, ISLAMIC Richly diverse, Islamic POTTERY has influenced the development of ceramics in the West. The Islamic world spanned from Spain in the West to the Indus Valley in the East, and craftsmen in this vast area were responsible for a huge range of decorative traditions and potting techniques. The first main centres included Mesopotamia, where TIN-GLAZED EARTHENWARE and LUSTRE DECORATION were developed and refined between the 8th and 13thC. From the Middle Ages until the 15thC, Persian centres in Kashan and Rayy (now Iran) were pre-eminent; they made lustre pottery, elaborately decorated with calligraphic designs or naturalistic patterns. In the 16th and 17thC, Meshed and Kirman in Persia produced BLUE-AND-WHITE wares that rivalled Chinese porcelain. Designs were based on those of the late MING DYNASTY in China and on transitional porcelain, but some Persian examples are outlined in black. Among the most famous examples of Islamic pottery are wares made by Turkish potters around Iznik, and later at Kutahya. Few pieces of Islamic pottery are marked, and attributions are based on the decoration and pottery bodies known to have been made in each area. Iznik pottery is the most popular of all types of Islamic ceramics among European collectors. *See also* POTTERY, IZNIK.

CHAD VALLEY CO. LTD Founded in Birmingham in 1823, a British manufacturer that began making TEDDY BEARS, SOFT TOYS, and DOLLS *c.*1920. Chad Valley took over CHILTERN in 1967, and itself was taken over by Palitoy in 1978. Early bears were made of luxuriant MOHAIR, usually gold coloured and with soft KAPOK-stuffed limbs. Bodies were large (sometimes with a hump), with short, fat limbs, and were noted for their softness (especially bodies filled entirely with kapok). Feet, on some models covered in felt, were small, and snouts were defined with horizontally stitched noses. Eyes were of amber-and-black GLASS attached by wires. EXCELSIOR, which is harder than kapok, was used for the heads. In later bears, the ears are placed flat on the heads, rather than at an angle, and the bulbous noses are stitched on vertically instead of horizontally, while arms are longer and more curved than on earlier bears. A desirable range was made in rainbow colours. Early bears were labelled on the foot "Hygenic toys, made in England by the Chad Valley Co., Ltd". The label was printed or embroidered in black or red. Metal identity buttons were also used, usually inserted into the right ear, and labels were stitched into side seams. From 1938 to 1953, a square label with a royal crest was stitched to the foot confirming that Chad Valley were "Toy Makers to H.M. the Queen" (the wife of King George VI). Chad Valley also produced soft toys such as "Bonzo" (from 1927), the bull-terrier pup originally featured in a cartoon in the *Daily Sketch*, as well as his girlfriend "Oolo"; the latter, made in the 1930s, is worth more. In terms of dolls, Chad Valley specialized in designs by Mabel Lucie ATTWELL, "Snow White" dolls, and PORTRAIT DOLLS of royal children such as the English princesses Elizabeth and Margaret. The firm had a reputation for making well-crafted dolls with high-quality PLUSH, velvet, felt, stockinette, and other fabrics. Most 1920s and '30s dolls are marked "Hygienic Toys Made in England by Chad Valley Toy Company Ltd". After 1938, some dolls were labelled "Toy Makers to H.M. The Queen," which changed to "...the Queen Mother" after the coronation in 1953. All Chad Valley records and catalogues were destroyed, so dating is not always easy.

CHAD VALLEY, **mohair bear in mint condition, c.1935**

CHAFFERS, RICHARD & PARTNERS English, Liverpool-based, pottery firm, active *c.*1754–65. It made EARTHENWARE that was based on WORCESTER forms and resembled BONE CHINA. *See also* CHRISTIAN, PHILIP; and POTTERY.

CHAFING DISH Used from the mid-17thC, a SILVER vessel for keeping plates warm. It has a charcoal brazier or spirit lamp in the base, and supports above.

CHAIN FUSEE Developed *c*.1800, a FUSEE with a chain. Prior to this, the fusee was connected to the MAINSPRING barrel in a CLOCK mechanism by gut, whose expansion or contraction jeopardized the clock's accuracy.

CHAIN MAIL Armour of interlocking metal rings used until the 17thC.

CHAIR A seat with a back made for a single person; it may or may not have arms. Seating once reflected social status, and, in the Middle Ages, often only the head of a household had a chair, while everyone else sat on benches or STOOLS. The finest antique chairs – those made in the 18thC or earlier – can be valuable. The first chairs were simply constructed like stools, with planks of wood at the back, which sometimes had carved decoration. It was not until the 17thC that chairs were elaborately turned and carved. Some incorporated inlaid MARQUETRY decoration. Chairs of the Carolean period (1625–49) are usually of WALNUT, OAK, or stained BEECH, with caned seats, BARLEY-SUGAR TWISTS, and tall backs. During the 17thC, chairs were made with upholstered seats, and some had spiral turnings or elaborate carving with SCROLLS and leaves. In the second half of the 17thC, walnut replaced oak as the most popular wood, and chairs were often elaborately carved with scrolls on STRETCHERS and legs. The CABRIOLE LEG dominated the early 18thC. MAHOGANY chairs became popular during the 18thC, and chair styles reflected designs published by leading designers such as Thomas CHIPPENDALE, George HEPPLEWHITE, and Thomas SHERATON. Pattern-books of their designs were circulated nationwide to local cabinet-makers, who reproduced them, often in simplified form. Nowadays, when a chair is described as "Chippendale", "Hepplewhite", or "Sheraton" it usually means that it is based on one of their patterns. SABRE LEGS are associated with the REGENCY period, when chairs were usually mahogany or ROSEWOOD, and of ornate design. French EMPIRE STYLES continued to be an influence (especially on chairs made in North America). In the 19thC, VICTORIAN designs were sturdy and ornate, while in the early 20thC, the Edwardians returned to the elegance of the late 18thC, although typically with slightly narrower chairs. After World War I, designers rediscovered the early 18thC, mixing QUEEN ANNE and later GEORGIAN or Chippendale styles in an eclectic muddle. The changing styles of chair backs, legs, and feet can help collectors to date chairs. However, as most styles were repeated in later periods, the style of a chair is only a guide to its age, not proof of its authenticity. Early chair seat frames had blocks glued to their corners. By 1700, frames were given open corner braces, usually glued or nailed from one seat rail to the other, leaving an open triangle between the brace and leg. From *c*.1850, the Victorians returned to an improved version of the 17thC idea, using a filled block or bracket that was glued and screwed. Victorian repairers often replaced the open Georgian bracket with the block

Mid-Georgian, walnut dining CHAIR, with scroll-top roll and cabriole legs, 18thC.

system, leaving the marks of the earlier construction. The shape of corner blocks provides a clue as to when a chair was made. Victorian blocks are usually convex, while 20thC ones tend to be larger and concave. Examine each chair carefully for signs of genuine wear and the PATINA of age. If the colour of one part looks different, it may have been replaced. Thick brown varnish indicates that a chair is trying to be made to look older than it is. *See also* ARMCHAIR; COUNTRY CHAIR; DINING CHAIR; FURNITURE; FURNITURE, 20THC; FURNITURE, ALTERATION OF; FURNITURE, CARE OF; GONDOLA CHAIR; HALL CHAIR; LADDER BACK; ROCKING CHAIR; TABLE-CHAIR; and WINDSOR CHAIR.

CHAIR-BACK SETTEE A distinct type of SETTEE with a back that looks like two or more chairs joined together.

CHAIR-TABLE *See* TABLE-CHAIR.

CHAISE-LONGUE From the French for "long chair", an upholstered day-bed with an elongated seat, which allowed the sitter to recline horizontally. They were often made in mirror-image pairs (with the headrests at opposite ends), but are now usually sold singly. Their elegance ensures that they are still in keen demand, although they are not always particularly comfortable.

CHALCEDONY A translucent SEMI-PRECIOUS STONE with a waxy appearance. Much used in antiquity for SEALS and stamps.

CHALET-STYLE CLOCK First made *c.*1850, a German, Black Forest, CUCKOO CLOCK in the form of a mountain chalet.

CHALKWARE Painted ornaments and figure groups made of plaster of Paris in imitation of PORCELAIN.

CHAMBER CLOCK A small 15th and 16thC iron CLOCK that was a scaled-down version of the TURRET CLOCK. Sometimes refers to any domestic clock.

CHAMBERLAIN PORCELAIN PORCELAIN decorated from 1751 to 1783 by Robert Chamberlain at the British manufacturer WORCESTER, and porcelain by the firm of Chamberlain & Son, which he founded in Worcester in 1786.

CHAMBERSTICK A small CANDLESTICK with a short stem and saucerlike base for lighting the way to the bedchamber at night. Chambersticks were made in large sets for each member of the household. The central socket for the candle is mounted in a circular dish, often decorated with REEDING, shells, BEADING, or GADROONED motifs, and designed to catch the hot dripping wax. Early chambersticks have long, flat handles, but few survive. More common are later ones, with ring or scroll handles, introduced in the 1720s; some designs had sockets for conical extinguishers or pierced slots to hold scissor-action SNUFFERS. Chambersticks were made in large numbers in SILVER and SHEFFIELD PLATE from the 1770s. Those in Sheffield plate tend to be light, and of poorer quality than silver ones. A simple gadrooned border was a common decorative motif from the mid-18th to the early 19thC, and decoration was usually stamped and applied rather than cast. All detachable parts of the chamberstick should bear the same HALLMARKS as the main body.

CHAMFER A BEVELLED edge.

CHAMPAGNE GLASS Originally an 18thC DRINKING GLASS with a bowl in the shape of a cyma, or DOUBLE OGEE. Today's simple, hemispherical bowl was introduced in the mid-19thC.

CHAMPION, RICHARD Founder of a late 18thC PORCELAIN factory, noted for its clear, colourful glazes, in Bristol, England. *See also* BRISTOL PORCELAIN.

CHAMPLEVÉ ENAMELLING in which a glass paste is applied to a hollowed-out design, fired, and ground smooth. *See also* CLOISONNÉ.

CHANDELIER An ornamental hanging light, composed typically of a central shaft and a variable number of arms or branches, each fitted with a candle-nozzle and a drip-pan, and decorated with CUT-GLASS drops. British GLASS chandeliers were made from the early 18thC. They were affordable only to wealthy households because of the high costs of hand-cutting each drop. Highly elaborate glass chandeliers have been made in MURANO since the 18thC. In France, BACCARAT produced EMPIRE-STYLE chandeliers in the 19thC. BRASS chandeliers with GLASS decoration are also popular. *See also* VENETIAN GLASS.

CHANNEL MOULDING A uniform, grooved design usually seen on early FURNITURE in OAK.

CHANTILLY A French SOFT-PASTE-PORCELAIN manufacturer, active in the 18thC, and patronized by Louis-Henri of Bourbon, Prince of Condé. Most of the factory's wares (including JARDINIÈRES, TEAPOTS, jugs, PLATES, and figures) reflect the prince's taste for Japanese KAKIEMON and Chinese FAMILLE-VERTE porcelain. The firm used TIN GLAZE until the 1750s, perhaps to hide defects in the clay and to improve the surface, so wares often have an opaque appearance. To compete with VINCENNES, a transparent LEAD GLAZE was introduced in the 1750s. Many floral designs were produced between 1755–and 1780, often in one colour, such as the "Chantilly sprig", which was copied by other factories, including CAUGHLEY. Chantilly's style was imitated in the 19thC by SAMSON – and sometimes the original Samson marks have been removed. However, Samson used HARD-PASTE PORCELAIN, and pieces look harder and shinier than true, soft-paste ones. Chantilly's mark was a hunting horn, in iron red, black, and UNDERGLAZE BLUE.

CHAPE Originally the metal tip of a scabbard, then the term for the buckle by which it was attached to a belt.

CHAPLET, ERNEST (1836–1909) French potter inspired by the artist Paul Gauguin and Oriental CERAMICS. Known for BARBOTINE wares and FLAMBÉ glazes, some unique to him, because he destroyed the formulae before his death.

CHAPTER RING The part of a CLOCK face on which the hours are inscribed. It is usually separate from the DIAL plate.

CHARACTER DOLL Introduced in the early 20thC, mainly in Germany, a DOLL with a realistic expression, such as a smiling, crying, laughing, or even frowning face. They are much sought after because of the range of styles. Early KÄMMER & REINHARDT and the rarer SIMON & HALBIG dolls are the most expensive. Those by KESTNER and Armand MARSEILLE are less rare. Cost is influenced by the quality of decoration, body style, and condition. Pale BISQUE is preferred. Over-simplified facial details reduce value, as will a bent-limb body.

CHARACTER JUG Widely made in EARTHENWARE in the 18th and 19thC, a jug, and sometimes a MUG, depicting a popular character such as a politician, general, or actor. DOULTON produced huge quantities from the 1930s onward.

CHARACTER TOY CO. A major American maker of TEDDY BEARS. Founded in Connecticut, the company copied the STEIFF idea of putting identification in the ear, although it used a label instead of a button. In the 1930s, production shifted from the long, narrow body of early designs to shorter, rounder bears, with larger feet and paws, heavier limbs, and no hump. By the 1940s, the bears were more unrealistic, with cheeky expressions and stylized limbs. Most were fully jointed, with large, cupped ears, pointed snout, glass eyes, and felt pads.

CHARGER A large, flat, circular or oval plate or dish, used for serving the main meat dish, or as a buffet dish on the SIDEBOARD.

CHARLEVILLE MUSKET An early American gun, used in the Revolution (1775–83) and copied from French prototypes.

CHARMES, SIMON DE A HUGUENOT maker of fine CLOCKS. He worked in London, England, from 1700 to 1710.

CHARPAY A RUG approximately 1.2m (4ft) long.

CHARPENTIER, ALEXANDRE (1856–1909) French ART NOUVEAU artist, sculptor, and designer of FURNITURE, CERAMICS, METALWORK, and leatherware.

CHASED SILVER *See* CHASING.

Royal Doulton, protoype CHARACTER JUG of a baseball player, modelled by David Briggs, 1970.

CHASE, MARTHA JENKS From Pawtucket, Rhode Island, an American dollmaker who produced mask-faced stockinette DOLLS with white sateen or cotton bodies, initially for her children. The dolls' success led to the founding in the 1880s of the Chase Stockinette Doll Company, which operated until 1925. Chase dolls have oil-painted features, such as bright eyes and hair, applied ears, and thick upper lashes. Early bodies have seams at the knees, hips, elbows, and shoulders; later ones have joints only at the shoulders and hips. Some dolls bear paper labels; others are stamped on the left leg or arm.

CHASING Popular in the late 17th and mid-18thC, the skilled art of hammering metal to create relief decoration. The metal is displaced (but not removed) into the decorative pattern with a chasing tool – a blunt or ball-pointed chisel or punch. The impression of the chased pattern can often be seen on the reverse or underside of the piece. Chasing is also referred to as "FLAT-CHASING". The most common decorative motifs included flowers, foliage, and scrolls of various types, and during the Victorian period (1837–1901) the plain surfaces of earlier silver items were often lavishly chased. With SILVER chased at the time of manufacture, HALLMARKS were added after the piece had been decorated, and any later decoration was superimposed on the hallmarks. Paul de LAMERIE and Aymé Videau are among the 18thC silversmiths celebrated for the quality of their chasing. *See also* EMBOSSING.

CHÂTELAINE Worn by men and women on a belt or girdle, an ornamental clasp from which several small objects for household use were hung on short chains. The earliest English examples date from the 17thC, and were usually intended to hold SEALS and WATCHES. It later became the fashion to use them for holding all sorts of objects, from scissors, keys, and POMANDERS to tape measures, thimbles, and bodkin cases. Examples still complete with original attachments are desirable, but the individual items may be collectable in their own right. An original case increases the price.

CHATIRONNÉ On PORCELAIN, floral decoration with the outlines drawn in black, in imitatation of Oriental motifs.

CHAUFFEUSE A low, fireside CHAIR.

CHELSEA FACTORY English PORCELAIN factory founded *c.*1745 in London by Nicholas Sprigmont, a French HUGUENOT silversmith. Chelsea catered for the luxury market, and many of its inventive pieces reflect fashionable, SILVER shapes. Chelsea wares are divided into groups according to the four marks used during the life of the factory: the "Triangle" period (1745–49) is characterized by small, often white pieces and silver shapes; the "Raised Anchor" period (1749–52) produced small MEISSEN-style wares with a slightly opaque glaze; the "Red Anchor" period (1752–57) is associated with highly refined wares in Meissen and KAKIEMON styles, and the porcelain is typically

One of a pair of CHELSEA porcelain figures, c.1765.

greenish in hue; and the "Gold Anchor" period (1759–69), when wares were made with sumptuous decoration and in the florid SÈVRES style. During this last period, Chelsea often used a deep-blue ground, but claret grounds were also popular. Because the GLAZES were often patchy, GILDING was used to hide a fault. The most sought-after pieces are those of the Red Anchor period, such as the "Hans Sloane" wares decorated with botanical specimens. Chelsea botanical plates can be distinguished from those by other factories, because the flowers take up almost the entire surface of the plate, and the specimens are often painted on a larger scale than the flowers. The body of Chelsea porcelain often has imperfections, and some of the insects and floral sprays in the decoration probably disguise small blemishes. The British Ambassador in Saxony borrowed figure models for Chelsea to copy, but the limitations of SOFT-PASTE PORCELAIN meant that the dramatic Meissen poses were impossible to achieve. Chelsea figures of the later 18thC became more elaborate, and usually stood on bases richly applied with floral BOCAGES. The costumes were heavily decorated, and painted with pastel colours. The firm was taken over by the DERBY PORCELAIN WORKS in 1769, and closed in 1784. Chelsea has a huge following, and pieces copied from Meissen can fetch more than the originals. The French firm of SAMSON made 19thC animal tureens imitating those by Chelsea. Fake red and gold anchor marks are usually larger than the genuine examples.

CHELSEA KERAMIC ART WORKS Based in Massachusetts, a North American, late-19thC producer of ART POTTERY. Their GLAZES have a crackled appearance, made to resemble Oriental high-fired crackled glazes; black was used to emphasize the crackling. Renamed Denham Pottery in 1943.

CHENGHUA (Ch'eng Hua) Chinese MING DYNASTY emperor, 1488–1505.

CHEQUER INLAY Dark and light wood squares inlaid alternately as on a chessboard, but forming a strip of INLAY.

CHÉRET, JULES (1836–1932) The father of the modern poster, a French artist responsible for the design of more than a thousand examples.

CHERRY A hard, close-grained wood with a warm, reddish colour, cherry (*Prunus cerasus/P. avium*) was occasionally used for INLAY in the 17thC, and in a solid form in mid-18thC, American furniture in the CHIPPENDALE and QUEEN ANNE STYLES. It was used in France from *c.*1750 for provincial pieces.

CHESAPEAKE POTTERY American manufacturer of PARIAN ware, MAJOLICA, and "Calvert" ware (green or blue items decorated with bands),1880-1924.

CHEST A simple, large box with a lid constructed from planks of wood and used for storage. Most early chests were made from solid OAK or WALNUT, and had carved decoration or painted embellishment. Early chests used for storing

A poster for Job cigarette papers, by JULES CHÉRET, **1895**.

grain are called "arks"; they have rounded lids that can be removed and reversed for kneading dough. The Yorkshire surname "Arkwright" was given to the makers of this type of chest. During the 18thC, a wider variety of chests was made, not only in terms of the wood used, but also the shapes. Examples with walnut VENEERS were made early in the century, followed by MAHOGANY chests (those with SERPENTINE shapes are especially valuable). There are also striking CHESTS-ON-STANDS and CHESTS-ON-CHESTS. The most expensive, distant cousins of the humble chest are American HIGHBOYS and lavish English COMMODES. *See also* BONNET CHEST and COFFER.

CHESTERFIELD A large, overstuffed, sprung and upholstered SOFA, usually buttoned. They were popular in the late 19thC.

CHESTNUT A type of wood that ranges in tone from light to dark brown. Used in the 18thC for French provincial FURNITURE made in a solid form.

CHEST OF DRAWERS A frame containing a set of DRAWERS; it developed from the plain CHEST, as drawer space at the expense of the box became fashionable. Solid MAHOGANY and mahogany VENEER were used to make chests from *c*.1730 onward. Mahogany chests of drawers are more common than WALNUT ones, so are less expensive. A veneer can add to the value of a chest, even if it is in poor condition. Features such as brushing slides, CANTED (angled) CORNERS, STRINGING, and finely figured wood also add to a piece's value. The most sought-after chests are handsome, 18thC, SERPENTINE versions. CHESTS OF DRAWERS with BOW FRONTS were popular throughout much of the 19thC. Chests of drawers were made to stand against walls, and their backs and undersides are usually made from rough unpolished boards. Plainer, mahogany chests, functional storage for bedrooms in the 18th, 19th, and early 20thC, are among the most readily available examples. PINE was used to make chests of drawers for servants and poorer households from *c*.1750. Most old pine chests were originally scumble-painted, but they are usually sold stripped today. To find one with its original paint is a bonus – look out for a soft colour. A chest-of-drawers has many of the elements found in other types of furniture – drawers, feet, and HANDLES – and examining one carefully can teach you a great deal. Locks can help to date a piece: drawers in the 17th, 18th, and 19thC were always fitted with locks, either made from good-quality steel or, on a better-quality chest, brass. Before you buy a chest of drawers, pull out the drawers and examine the sides carefully – their construction can tell you when the chest was made. During the 17th and 18thC, DOVETAIL JOINTS on drawers were cut by hand. Size has an important bearing on the price of all chests of drawers, and smaller ones are most desirable. Sometimes larger chests have been reduced in size to make them more valuable or convenient. Tell-tale signs are feet that are disproportionate with the chest, or a marked difference in the depth of the two long drawers, suggesting that there may once have been another drawer. The feet on chests of drawers are prone to wear and are often replaced, so check the colour and grain of each one. If the replaced feet are in keeping with the style of the chest and correctly proportioned, the value of the piece may not be greatly affected. Check drawers inside and out for marks. Finer chests from pre-1780 might have OAK linings, while less-refined drawers have pine linings, which became increasingly common after 1780. On 17th and early 18thC drawers, the grain of the bottom usually runs from front to back; after *c*.1750 it usually runs widthways. To determine whether the handles have been replaced look for shadows and extra holes where the original handles once were. Retain replaced handles if they are within keeping of the style, because newer ones will leave even more marks. *See also* CAMPAIGN CHEST, CHEST-ON-CHEST, CHEST-ON-STAND, and WELLINGTON CHEST.

CHEST-ON-CHEST (TALLBOY in the USA) Two CHESTS OF DRAWERS, one on top of the other, popular from the 1720s. Look out for chests-on-chests with concave, inlaid sunbursts – a decorative feature that can add hugely to the value. On some, the lower part has a top DRAWER that opens at 90 degrees, enclosing small drawers and a writing surface. A slightly rounded top edge of the sides of the drawers is typical of early 18thC FURNITURE in WALNUT.

CHEST-ON-STAND (HIGHBOY in the USA) A CHEST OF DRAWERS fitted on top of a stand. They were popular in England from the 1660s to 1720s, when they were replaced by CHESTS-ON-CHESTS. Chests on-stands are not as capacious as chests-on-chests, but they are more elegant. Few have survived with their original stands intact. They are often seen with replacement bun feet and no legs, giving them an odd, dumpy appearance. The chest usually has short DRAWERS at the top and in the stand, and graduated long drawers in between. Look for examples with attractive graining and elaborate APRONS.

CHEVAL MIRROR A large, free-standing, toilet MIRROR in a frame. The mirror can be pivoted and is adjustable within the frame. "Cheval" means horse in French, and the name given to the mirror refers to its four supporting legs. It had become popular by the 19thC, when large plates of glass could be cast.

George III, mahognay-framed oval CHEVAL toilet mirror, 1760–1820.

CHEVAL SCREEN A type of FIRESCREEN comprising two uprights each on two legs, and enclosing a decorative panel.

CHEVERET A small WRITING TABLE of delicate proportions, often with a raised back, containing small DRAWERS and a shelf.

CHI Chinese symbol of immortality portrayed on CARPETS and CERAMICS as a cloud or sponge-like shape.

CH'IEN LUNG Chinese, 18thC PORCELAIN imitating various non-ceramic materials such as horn, LACQUER, wood, and jade.

Chinese, CHIEN WARE **tea bowl from the Sung dynasty, 1960–1279.**

CHIEN WARE With a deep, red-to-brown HARE'S-FUR glaze, Chinese STONEWARE made in the Fukien province during the SUNG DYNASTY, and used for tea-ceremony vessels.

CHIFFONIER A French term, meaning a small CABINET for storing everyday bric a brac. Two types were made in England: those with cupboard doors below and stepped shelves above, and those with flat tops that often had bookshelves on each side of the central doors. *See also* SIDE CABINET.

CHIHULY, DALE (1941–) One of the most influential and acclaimed North American GLASS artists. He experiments with complex, blown, organic forms and brilliant colours. His one-of-a-kind studio pieces command high prices.

CHILDREN'S FURNITURE Small-scale FURNITURE for children to use, as distinct from the more valuable miniature toy furniture. From *c*.1800 onward, a huge variety of CHAIRS were made for children, including complex designs with multiple uses, such as high chairs that could be separated to make chairs and play tables. Items including CHESTS, cots, cradles, BEDS, BUREAUX, and BOOKCASES were also produced, but they are less common, and hence command high prices. Many extant pieces of children's furniture were produced in the late Victorian and Edwardian periods (1860–1901 and 1901–10 respectively) for less-affluent homes. Because children's furniture follows the same stylistic changes as full-sized pieces, it can usually be dated in the same way. Sometimes the proportions of pieces produced for children are not as well drawn as those of the full-sized and miniature versions. Quality children's furniture of the 17th and 18thC is much scarcer than the equivalent full-sized pieces, and it is keenly collected.

CH'ILIN A mythical Chinese animal – the symbol of goodness – with a dragon's head, the body of a deer, and a lion's tail. The motif appears on Oriental CARPETS.

CHILTERN TOYS English toy factory established by Bavarian-born Leon Rees, dollmaker since 1912, in Chesham, Buckinghamshire. One of Rees's first TEDDY BEARS was a "Master Teddy", which featured as a *Daily Mail* character in *The Teddy Tail League*. In 1920, the firm of H.G. Stone teamed up with Leon Rees as H.G. Stone & Co. In 1924, the company was registered as Chiltern Toys, after the name of the Buckinghamshire factory where the bears were produced. Noted for the rare, 1922 "Baby Teddy", Chiltern Toys was quickly established as a leading manufacturer. Chiltern bears are renowned for their soft, mohair PLUSH, which has a long pile and is of the finest quality. In top condition, this can greatly increase the bear's value. Other features include the shaved muzzle, amber and black eyes, stitched nose with upward stitching at either end, long, curving arms, and wide feet with velvet pads that are reinforced with cardboard. The 1930s "Winter

Skater" has arms wired to make them stand away from the body to hold a hand muff. Chiltern produced one of the few teddies made during World War II, a bear dressed as a Home Guard Sergeant; it is non-jointed, which was cheaper to make than a jointed version. From 1960 onward, Chiltern bears had black, moulded, plastic noses. The company produced bears until 1967, when it was taken over by CHAD VALLEY. Bears were marked "Chiltern Chad Valley" from 1967 to 1978. Unshorn faces and narrow, soft, velvet feet with no reinforcements are typical of later bears, although some have canvas feet. On the feet or in side seams of Chiltern bears, there will be a label reading: "Chiltern Hygienic Toys made in England".

CHIME Of CLOCKS, where the hours and quarters are sounded on more than one bell, as distinct from a strike.

CHIMERA Carved animal decoration found during the REGENCY period.

CHINA A general term for PORCELAIN, derived from "China wares" imported into Europe from the 16thC. In 19thC England, it came to mean almost any porcelain-like ceramic.

CHINA CABINET A CABINET made for the display of CHINA and PORCELAIN.

CHINA CLAY A fine, white clay also known as KAOLIN, which is mixed with PETUNTSE to form true, HARD-PASTE PORCELAIN.

CHINA DOLL A DOLL with a ceramic head. After the secret of making PORCELAIN was discovered in Europe in 1709, porcelain factories were established in the dollmaking centre of Thuringia, Germany, and china dolls were an obvious progression. Their SHOULDER-HEADS were made from glazed, HARD-PASTE PORCELAIN, which had a shiny finish, unlike that of BISQUE dolls, and they were attached to the rest of the body by glue, nails, or stitches through specially made holes. From the 1840s to the end of the 19thC, these dolls were produced in huge numbers. Many famous porcelain factories including ROYAL COPENHAGEN and MEISSEN, made dolls, although pieces were rarely marked. On German dolls, features were painted on and fired. Fewer French dolls were made, but they were more refined, sometimes with SWIVEL HEADS, glass eyes, and real hair. Dolls with dark-brown rather than black hair in elaborate, deeply moulded styles adorned with lustre ornaments are the most sought after. A typical German doll has a white face with red cheeks, black hair, and blue eyes. A red, rosebud mouth also indicates that she is German. Early dolls are the most elegant, with red lines on the eyelids and possibly pink-tinted faces. Some delicate examples made 1845 - 1860, known as "Biedermeier chinas", have bald heads with black spots on top covered by curled plaits of real hair. A doll based on Empress Eugenie, the wife of Napoleon III, is one of the finest German examples. China dolls modelled on the British Queen Victoria were also popular. Less common French dolls have closed, smiling mouths – unlike those of their German contemporaries. Look out for oddly shaped, cotton bodies, which may indicate that a doll has been homemade – possible because china heads could be bought separately. Commercial firms used a wide range of body materials, but generally painted legs with black boots and fancy garters. Before 1860, all shoes were flat. If bodies and clothes have been replaced, the doll's value will be reduced. Dolls made in the late 19thC are less desirable. Known as "lowbrows" in contrast with earlier "highbrows", their hair sits lower on the forehead, and is black (sometimes blonde), short, and centre-parted with curls at the back and sides.

CHIN DYNASTY The period in Chinese history from AD 1115 to 1260.

CHINÉ MANNER Technique patented for DOULTON that involved pressing lace onto a wet clay surface and finishing with hand colouring and gilding. Vast quantities were made in the late 19th and early 20thC.

CHINESE DYNASTIES The divisions in Chinese history marked by the reigns of ruling families and, therein, by individual emperors. They are: SHANG YIN c.1532–1027 BC; Western Zhou (Chou) 1027–770 BC; Spring and Autumn Annals 770–480 BC; Warring States 484–221 BC; Qin (CH'IN) 221–206 BC; Western Han 206 BC–AD 24; Eastern Han 25–220; Three Kingdoms 221–265; Six Dynasties 265–589; WEI 386–557; SUI 589–617; T'ANG (Tang) 618–906; Five Dynasties 907–960; LIAO 907–1125; SUNG 960–1280; CHIN 1115–1260; YUAN 1280–1368; MING 1368–1644; and qing (CH'ING) 1644–1916.

CHINESE EXPORT WARES Ceramic items made in China specifically for export, often in European designs. Large-scale export began shortly after the arrival of the Portuguese in China in 1517. Thousands of pieces went to Lisbon as ballast in ships laden with spices, lacquer, silks, and other luxury items. Throughout the 17thC, the Dutch monopolized the trade with China and Japan, but the English dominated the export of PORCELAIN in the 18thC. The early export wares made in the MING period were decorated with panels filled with repeating flowers, animals, birds, or figures – this distinctive decoration is known as KRAAK-PORSELEIN. Early export goods are sometimes indistinguishable from those made for the home market, and it was not until the 17thC that the Dutch began requesting European shapes such as mustard pots, cuspidors (spittoons), COFFEE POTS, and narrow-necked jugs. Another popular palette for export wares was known as FAMILLE VERTE, formed of translucent colours; this replaced the old WUCAI PALETTE. From c.1718 onward, porcelain in the FAMILLE-ROSE palette was decorated using colours to which white had been added to make them opaque; pink is not necessarily the dominant shade. By the 18thC, there was a thriving demand for ARMORIAL porcelain. The trade in Chinese export porcelain waned, as European porcelain factories and CREAMWARE production became more

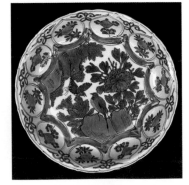

Chinese, Kraak-porcelain saucer dish, 1573–1619 (CHINESE EXPORT WARE).

competitive in the late 1700s. After 1735, instead of wares being potted and enamelled before being shipped to Canton (Guangzhou) for export, they were sent from the potteries "in the white" (undecorated), when they were less fragile; enamelling shops were set up in the Canton area to adorn them, and vast quantities of decorative "Canton" wares were made in the 19th and 20thC. Canton porcelain of the 19thC is usually crammed with figures and detail, with pink, turquoise, and gilding predominant. Marks on Chinese export porcelain include tripods, lozenges, lotus and artemisia leaves, and earlier reign marks. Much export porcelain is readily available at modest sums.

CHINESE IMARI Produced from the early 18thC, Chinese imitations of Japanese blue, red, and gold painted IMARI wares.

CH'ING DYNASTY From 1644 to 1912, the period during which much decorated Chinese PORCELAIN was exported to Europe.

CHINKIN-BORI Japanese LACQUERWARE in which the design is engraved in hairlines and filled with gold or coloured lacquer.

Early-18thC, CHINESE IMARI ecuelle and cover.

CHINOISERIE European interpretation of Oriental-style decoration used on different objects, including PORCELAIN, FURNITURE, and garden architecture, in the 17th and mid-18thC. The decoration features Chinese-style motifs, such as landscapes, pagodas, stunted trees, exotic birds, monsters, and figures. SILVER decorated with Chinoiserie is rare and collectable.

CHINTAMANI Oriental CARPET motif consisting of three balls arranged in a triangular form, the symbol of the Buddha.

CHINTZWARE Tableware decorated with all-over floral patterns, and one of many affordable ranges manufactured for everyday use by such factories as Crown Ducal, *Royal Winton*, James Kent, Grimwades Ltd, and MIDWINTER in the 1920s and '30s. The condition of the transfer pattern is crucial: clean-looking, clear, crisp patterns ensure maximum value, while fading, scratches, obvious join lines, or inserts of other patterns will detract from value.

CHIPARUS, DIMITRI Romanian-born sculptor working in Paris in the 1920s. Noted for painted bronze and ivory figures in exotic dance poses.

CHIP CARVING Associated mainly with OAK, simple carved decoration in which the surface has been lightly cut or chipped away.

CHIPPENDALE, THOMAS (1718–79) One of the most influential FURNITURE designers of his age. In 1749 Chippendale set up business as a cabinet-maker in London. He was a master of proportion, using a ROCOCO style embellished with delicate and intricate carving, and the quality of his designs and workmanship set new standards in furniture production. In 1754, Chippendale published a book of designs called *The Gentleman and Cabinet-Maker's Director*. It was printed in several editions and sold in England and North America to cabinet-makers and wealthy patrons, many of whom copied his designs. Chippendale did not sign his work, so only a few pieces of furniture can be attributed to him. Many of his CHAIR designs featured pierced SPLATS, carved with scrolling foliage and incorporating GOTHIC elements. Ribbons and CHINOISERIE details were also popular motifs.

CHOCOLATE GLASS A North American, coloured GLASS invented by the Indiana Tumbler and Goblet Co., also known for its "Holly Amber" glass.

CHOCOLATE POT Used to serve hot chocolate, a vessel similar in shape to a COFFEE POT but with a lip rather than a spout. Chocolate was introduced to Europe in the late 17thC via trading routes to the West Indies. Often drunk in coffee houses, chocolate was tiresome to prepare and enjoyed only briefly as a favoured drink in fashionable society. Chocolate pots are recorded from the 1650s, but few made before 1700 survive. They mirror the styles and forms of coffee pots, but have hinged FINIALS, which allowed swizzle-sticks or MOLINETS to be inserted to stir the chocolate. Hinged finials were easily mislaid, and some were attached to the pots with SILVER chains. Chocolate pots are less often found in Britain than in Continental Europe, and they were rarely made in Britain after 1750, when the drink was no longer fashionable. Many were converted into coffee pots. Chocolate pots made before the 1730s had tapering, cylindrical forms and were made of heavy-gauge silver, with seams down the handle side; they featured cast-and-applied foot rims, straight or curving spouts, and hinged, domed covers with finials. By the 1730s, flat lids were more typical, with domed lids popular again by *c*.1800. Decoration is limited to engraved ARMORIALS or cut-card work around the handle. Most handles are of FRUITWOOD or IVORY. COMPOSITION handles are later replacements, but these do not always lower the value of the pot. Earlier pots are more desirable than the later pieces of the 1740s. Some chocolate pots were produced in sets with matching stands and burners, and all parts of the set should bear the same HALLMARKS.

CHONGZHEN (Ch'ing Cheng) Chinese MING DYNASTY emperor, 1628–44.

CHOSROES Celebrated, much-copied, 6thC Persian RUG.

CHRISTIAN, PHILIP British PORCELAIN manufacturer, who acquired Richard CHAFFERS' Liverpool factory in 1765, and continued making wares based on WORCESTER prototypes until 1776.

CHROME DYE The dye now used in modern CARPET production. It is more colourfast and less likely to run than ANILINE DYE.

CHROMOLITHOGRAPH A coloured print taken from etched and polished stone. Invented in 1796, it enabled a finer range of tints and shades to be achieved than metal plates.

CHRONOMETER A timepiece of great accuracy, often marked with seconds or fractions of seconds, and made for scientific research or navigation.

CHRYSELEPHATINE Material known for its use in ART DECO sculpture. Originally a combination of GOLD and IVORY, in sculpture of that type it was usually a combination of BRONZE (or sometimes another metal) and IVORY.

CHURCH WARDEN Fashionable from c.1750, a clay tobacco pipe with a long stem, up to 60cm (24in).

CIDER GLASS A late, 18thC DRINKING GLASS, similar to an ALE GLASS, but decorated with apple motifs.

CIGAR CASE Either a portable carrying case that could fit inside a pocket, or a box for storing cigars at home. One type with a pull-off cap held a small bundle of cheroots or cigars; made in great numbers in the mid-19thC, they were embellished in a variety of decorative techniques, from embossed hunting scenes to enamelled and elegantly engraved designs. A torpedo-shaped case was intended to hold a single cigar; holders for two or three cigars were also made. Cases with elegant decoration are highly prized. Fine-quality,SILVER cigar boxes for the table or desk should have wooden or solid-silver bases. Less-valuable types are lined in the base with pieces of leather that are "loaded" and lined with cedar to keep the contents fresh.

CIGAR CUTTER A device for trimming cigars. The cigar is inserted into the opening on the central pole, which has a metal cutter inside that snips off the end of the cigar when the top section is pressed down. The base serves as an ashtray and receptacle for clippings. If there is a tubular container attached to the back, it is intended for holding bundles of matches. Cigar cutters in the form of CHAMBERSTICKS were popular from the late 19thC. The pan is intended for collecting ashes, spent matches, and cuttings, while the nozzle holds a candle, and the attached tubular cutter trims cigars.

CIGARETTE CARD A card supplied by a tobacco company with a pack of cigarettes. Cards became an important component in the battle for markets, and technically accomplished cards, with good colour and gilding, were produced as customer-loyalty incentives. The first cards were produced by Ogden's, Wills, Carreras, Gallahers, Churchman, and John Player. The golden age for cigarette cards begins with the introduction of colour printing in 1885 and ends c.1918, after which time cards were printed in such quantity as to have little value. Between 1885 and 1902, many small

WILL'S CIGARETTES.

NAPOLEON.

Will's CIGARETTE CARD of Napoleon, issued to commemorate the centenary of the Battle of Waterloo, 1914.

tobacco companies issued cards, which are keenly collected for their rarity: those by MacDonald, Alberge and Bromet, Taddy, and Ainsworth are among the most valuable. Certain pre-1902 subjects are particularly popular, notably monarchs, sporting figures, military heroes (particularly of the Boer War), ships, and contemporary celebrities. Some 1918–40 cards are sought after because they refer to contemporary events or fashions. Of these, Edward VIII coronation cards, and portraits of 1920s and '30s beauties and actresses are most popular. Because collectors enjoy building up their own sets, a rare individual card in good condition can have significant value. Albums were introduced *c*.1930; complete ones fetch a premium if in mint condition.

CIGARETTE CASE A portable carrying case or box for storing cigarettes, produced in great numbers in the late 19thC. Early cases are small, as cigarettes made before *c*.1900 did not have filters. Many portable cases are oblong, with rounded sides and corners, and are slim or curved to fit inside pockets. Enamelled cigarette cases featuring battle scenes, aircraft, and animals are the most sought after by collectors, but those decorated with erotic scenes achieve the highest prices. After World War I, cigarette-smoking became fashionable among the wealthy, and elaborate SILVER cases were made for ladies to carry on special occasions. Some examples came with a matching VESTA CASE. Fine-quality, silver cigarette boxes for the table or desk, with sprung handles, had wooden or solid-silver bases, whereas less-valuable examples are lined with leather. These boxes are often converted to velvet-lined jewellery boxes. Late -19th and early -20thC cigarette cases do not fit modern cigarettes, and unless the cases are jewelled or made of an especially valuable material, they are not especially popular nowadays.

CINQUEDEA A 15th and 16thC DAGGER or shortsword, so-called because the blade measures five fingers (*cinque diti* in Italian) in length.

CIRCULAR MOVEMENT A CLOCK movement contained within a circular plate. A feature of French clocks after the early 19thC.

CIRCUMFERENTOR Predecessor of the THEODOLITE, a surveying instrument consisting of several sights mounted over a compass and a brass circle marked with degrees of a circle. Used from the early 17thC.

CIRE PERDUE French for "lost wax", a method of moulding metal. *See also* WAX CASTING.

CIZHOU WARE STONEWARE produced in China, mainly in the northern provinces of Henan, Hebei, and Shaanxi. Pieces are often highly decorative, characteristically adorned with painted, incised, or punched designs. These proved to be inspirational in the 20thC for modern studio potters such as Bernard LEACH. *See also* STONEWARE, CHINESE.

CLAIR DU LUNE French for "moonlight", a type of Chinese PORCELAIN with a pale-blue GLAZE. Also used for opalescent, sapphire-tinted GLASS.

CLARET JUG A JUG or EWER made in SILVER from the 19thC and used for serving claret. Often indistinguishable from a standard EWER. *See also* JUG, WINE.

CLARKE, ARUNDELL Patron and retailer of FURNITURE in the ART DECO and MODERNIST styles in England (London) in the 1920s and '30s.

CLASSICAL Any style that relates to or copies ancient Greek or Roman art and architecture.

CLAW-AND-BALL FOOT *See* BALL-AND-CLAW FOOT.

CLAW BEAKER A late Roman and Saxon BEAKER in GLASS (often coloured), with hook-shaped PRUNTS projecting from the body. Rare, medieval, German, glass examples are also known. The style was revived in Germany by the Ehrenfeld Glassworks near Cologne from 1879.

CLAY, HENRY British maker of FURNITURE and, in the 18thC, the originator of PAPIER-MÂCHÉ furniture.

CLAYMORE Used by Scottish Highlanders up to the 18thC, a large double-edged broadsword, with quillons angled toward the point. *See also* SWORD.

CLAY WARE Objects, especially TRAYS, cups, and boxes, produced in the late 18thC by the Birmingham factory of Henry CLAY. The wares were made from sheet paper and glue, and often gaily painted.

CLEAT A strip of wood used to secure the end of two planks, for example on the tops of trestle and REFECTORY TABLES. The grain on the small strip runs at a right angle to the planks.

CLEMENTS, WILLIAM Noted clockmaker, active in the late 17thC and specializing in ANCHOR ESCAPEMENTS. *See also* CLOCK.

CLERMONT-FERRAND French town that was briefly the centre of FAIENCE production in the mid-18thC. Their products are now rare.

CLEWS, JAMES AND RALPH English, Staffordshire-based potters making wares decorated by TRANSFER-PRINTING for export to the USA in the early 19thC.

CLICHY French maker specializing in cheap export GLASS, but renowned for PAPERWEIGHTS. The factory was founded in Paris, but moved to Clichy-la-Garenne c.1840. One of the most distinctive patterns features white staves

Royal Worcester, ivory ground CLARET JUG, 1884.

alternating with a single colour. The central motif consists of a cluster of MILLEFIORI rods in a star pattern. Clichy weights can often be identified by a characteristic rose, and are also sometimes marked with initials.

CLIFF, CLARICE (1899–1972) One of the most prolific and innovative British potters of the 1920s, whose brightly coloured wares with their streamlined modern shapes have become synonymous with ART DECO. Cliff worked for A.J. WILKINSON Ltd, a Staffordshire pottery at Newport, where she introduced a range of hand-painted pottery called "Hand Painted Bizarre by Clarice Cliff". By 1930, the success of her designs led to her appointment as art director. She drew on a range of sources as inspiration for her patterns. Floral and foliate ones include "Crocus", "Autumn", "Alpine", "Capri", and "Latona". Landscape provides the theme for "Secrets", while textile design inspired "Blue Chintz" and "Appliqué". Cliff produced such a plethora of shapes and designs, including her "Bizarre" and "Fantasque" ranges, that sales are now devoted exclusively to her wares. Value is determined by the rarity of the design. Small objects and items in the "Crocus" pattern are the most affordable. Dramatic, futuristic shapes are a keynote of Cliff's pottery. All genuine wares were handpainted, and brushstrokes should be visible in the coloured enamels. A warm, yellow "honey glaze" gives the background an ivory colour that is seen on many Cliff wares, and the decoration is often outlined in black. Desirable designs include "Age of Jazz" figures (a limited range of cut-out silhouette figures painted on both sides); wall masks; "Inspiration" pieces (now rare); the "Circus" series (designed by Dame Laura KNIGHT); Graham Sutherland designs; and Frank Brangwyn circular plaques. Most pieces are marked with a printed mark and a facsimile signature. Condition is important to value, and restoration can be difficult to spot. Check spouts and handles for signs of chipping, and run a finger around rims and bases to see if they are intact. There are many reproductions and fakes on the market, but these can usually be distinguished by their inferior colour and design. Some fakes have photographically copied marks, which usually have a fuzzy appearance. If collecting one of Cliff's common designs, it is usually possible to build up a set by buying individual pieces.

18thC, Chinese, export charger with CLOBBERED decoration.

CLOBBERING The technique of applying coloured enamel GLAZES over blue-and-white underglaze colours; or on old TIN-GLAZED EARTHENWARE, re-decoration, or additional decoration, in polychrome GLAZES to enhance the value of a piece. Practised as early as the 17thC in The Netherlands.

CLOCK Made since the 17thC, a mechanical instrument for keeping time. Sometimes described as "mechanical pictures", clocks can be appreciated both for their visual appeal and their technical mastery. Most are easy to date and identify, because the vast majority were signed by their maker on the DIAL and movement, and records of most makers have survived thanks to the control of the governing body, the Clockmakers

Company, founded in 1631. Value depends on the maker, movement, case, and condition, but a clock's visual appeal lies in its case, which usually reflects the FURNITURE style of the period. Cases are rarely signed, and little is known about this aspect of the trade. There are three key elements that you should assess before buying a clock; the mechanism (or movement), the dial, and the case. The movement consists of a system of brass-and-steel wheels and gears known as the train, usually housed between two brass plates. The ESCAPEMENT controls the speed at which a clock runs. Weight-driven and spring-driven clocks usually have a PENDULUM, which swings in a regular arc and controls the clock's speed. The dial, or face of the clock, is attached to the movement by a number of brass "feet". There may be a strike/silent lever that controls the striking mechanism and can be used to turn it off without affecting its running. The case houses the movement and dial. Most clocks are signed, but a signature is not always a guarantee that the clock was made by the maker whose signature it bears; clocks made in the 19thC may be signed by the retailer rather than the maker. Genuine signatures are found in the following places: until 1690, along the bottom of the dial plate; from 1690 to 1720, on the CHAPTER RING; after 1720, on the chapter ring, on the boss in the arch, or on a separately applied plaque. Most clocks can be repaired, but restoring a "bargain" can be expensive and it is often cheaper to buy a clock that has been properly overhauled and restored to working order by a skilled maker. Despite their popularity, clocks are available at a wide range of prices. Plain CARRIAGE CLOCKS are the least expensive type, followed by simple BRACKET CLOCKS; late -19thC LONGCASE CLOCKS are the most expensive. Most maintenance should be left to a specialist, although wooden cases can be lightly dusted and, occasionally, lightly waxed. Brass and silvered dials are protected by lacquer and should never be polished or placed in contact with water or detergent. Any cleaning and oiling of a clock's movement should be carried out with great care by a specialist. A SPRING-DRIVEN clock with a short pendulum can be carried from one room to another, but it should be held upright; for long-distance journeys, secure or remove the pendulum. Longcase clocks should be dismantled before being moved.

CLOCK CASE A box used to house the DIAL and movement of a CLOCK and often made by a different craftsman to the movement itself. Knowledge of case materials and styles is useful in dating a clock and in assessing its value. In Britain and North America, wooden cases were popular. Metal cases, or those combining materials are more likely to be Continental European. Wooden cases were introduced in the 17thC, and many are covered with thin VENEERS of wood. The most commonly used woods are EBONY, WALNUT, MAHOGANY, and ROSEWOOD. Wooden cases are sometimes decorated with inlaid MARQUETRY, LACQUER, applied metal mounts, INLAY in BRASS (especially on rosewood cases), or a combination of TORTOISESHELL and brass (BOULLE work). Brass is the most common metal used in metal cases – all CARRIAGE

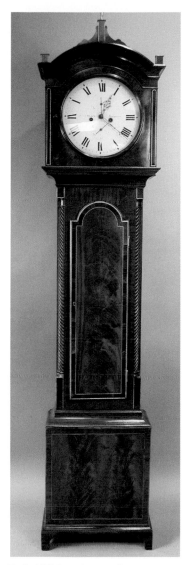

Early-19thC, mahogany longcase CLOCK by John Black, Aberdeen.

CLOCKS are brass-cased. Old brass is uneven and shows marks left by the casting process, while modern, rolled brass is of uniform thickness. Brass cases may be engraved or decorated with enamel colours.

CLOCK GARNITURE For the mantelpiece, a set of ornaments comprising a CLOCK and matching VASE or CANDELABRUM. They are often highly ornate.

CLOCK HAND Indicator used on a CLOCK to point at numbers to indicate the time. Early clocks have only one hand (for hours), but most made after *c*.1660 have minute and hour hands. Seconds hands are usually shown on a subsidiary dial. Hands are usually made from blued steel, although gilded brass is found from *c*.1790. Until *c*.1740, the hour hand was elaborate, while the minute hand was longer and plainer. Replacement hands are acceptable if they are in the right style.

CLODION, CLAUDE MICHEL (1738–1814) French designer who made figure groups in TERRACOTTA, PEWTER, BRONZE, and, for SÈVRES, PORCELAIN. He is noted especially for mildly erotic scenes.

CLOISONNÉ ENAMELLING Floral ENAMEL decoration with divisions in the design separated by lines of fine brass wire. The technique was used by Byzantine and Celtic craftsmen, and is still used by Chinese craftsmen today. The design is outlined by soldering metal strips onto a metal base to create a network of compartments, known as "cells", or *cloisons*. These are filled in with coloured enamels, but the tops of the metal strips are left exposed. The piece is fired and then polished smooth.

CLOSE BAND On an Oriental CARPET, a motif resembling strands of seaweed.

CLOSED MOUTH On a DOLL, a term referring to a mouth with lips close together. Dolls with open mouths were expensive when introduced *c*.1900, but nowadays examples with closed mouths are more valuable.

CLOSE-HELMET A helmet made to cover the neck as well as the head, and with a visor hinged at the temples.

CLOSE STOOL (Close chair) Rectangular or drum-shaped boxed STOOL or CHAIR, designed to house a chamber pot and used for sanitary purposes.

CLOTHES PRESS A CUPBOARD with shelves. Those with double doors, open shelves, and low CHESTS OF DRAWERS are usually made from MAHOGANY, and date from the GEORGIAN period. In smaller country houses, these cupboards stored the clothes of the whole family. By the late 19thC, old clothes presses were used to store linen rather than clothing. *See also* WARDROBE.

18thC oak CLOTHES PRESS.

CLOTHING, VINTAGE Old clothing collected for display or for wearing. Pre-1830 clothing is scarce, garments made 1830 to 1900 are more numerous, and early 20thC clothing is still common. Within these period divisions, value is related to condition, quality, decoration, and colour, but a famous former owner or a desirable couturier's label can raise the value considerably. Elaborately trimmed, decorated, or embroidered pieces are sought after, and floral, embroidered waistcoats, evening gowns, christening robes, and country smocks are all popular. Black is an unpopular colour among collectors, and the large quantity of 19thC mourning garments rarely fetch as much as equivalent items in other colours. Colour should be bright, consistent, and not faded by sunlight. Couturiers began labelling their work *c.*1861, but labels were frequently removed. Look out for unlabelled garments whose worth may have gone unrecognized. Many dresses were designed as an ensemble with matching accessories. Shoes, veils, hats, handbags, gloves, stockings, and prayer books to accompany a dress add value. Prices can be surprisingly high for apparently insignificant garments if there is a keen specialist market; examples include garters, corsets, underwear, nightdresses, and servants' clothing, as well as theatrical costume and fancy dress. Condition is critical. Beware of items that have been treated, cleaned, or repaired, although ancient repairs and alterations can add interest to a piece.

CLOWES, JAMES Noted, late -17thC English maker of CLOCKS.

CLUB FOOT Virtually the same as PAD FOOT.

"CLUTHA" GLASS ART GLASS made from 1885 by the Scottish firm of Couper Ltd, following the designs of Christopher DRESSER. Inspired by ancient glass, it is greenish, opaque, and has bubbles and deliberate "flaws".

"CLUTHRA" GLASS A trademark used by the North American STEUBEN GLASSWORKS for a type of ART GLASS developed by Frederick CARDER in 1920. It has a milky appearance, with blotches of opacity and rows of air bubbles.

CMIELOW From the early 1950s, a maker of extravagantly shaped, BONE-CHINA tableware and ornaments, with sparse decoration, often limited to hand-applied SGRAFITTO lines. Pastel colours, such as pink and grey, were mixed, and rich turquoises and glossy black contrasted with the bright, white body.

COACHING CLOCK A large WATCH with a swivel handle for suspending in a coach or carriage, as on a CARRIAGE CLOCK.

COACHING TABLE A popular mid- to late -19thC TABLE, so-called because it could be folded flat and carried on the side of coaches for use on picnic stops, although its uses were not restricted to this. They were made from solid MAHOGANY, and had little decoration. Examine the hinge on the flap to

Chiffon glass beaded evening dress, 1920s (CLOTHING, VINTAGE)

105

make sure that it is in good condition. Check that the top and base belong together by looking underneath for any signs of tampering. Make sure that the legs and any stretchers are sound. *See also* BUTLER'S TRAY.

COADE STONE Artificial stone invented by Mrs Eleanor Coade *c*.1769. Frostproof and difficult to distinguish from real stone, it was used for casting garden statuary and architectural ornament in the late 18th and early 19thC.

COAL BOX Made from the mid-19thC, a box to contain coal. Most were produced in brass-bound hardwood, with a drop front and detachable lining, and they were usually made in pairs to stand either side of the hearth. Some examples double as fireside seats.

COALBROOKDALE Name used for PORCELAIN wares made by the COALPORT FACTORY and decorated in the ROCOCO style with elaborate floral decoration and SCROLLS. Wares of this kind, which were fashionable in the 1830s, were similar to pieces made in Dresden, Germany, and this led to them being known as "English Dresden style".

COALBROOKDALE IRON CO. The leading manufacturer in Britain of cast-iron garden furniture during the 19thC, Coalbrookdale of Ironbridge, Shropshire, made a range of ornately cast benches, tables, and chairs. Many of the designs popularized at the GREAT EXHIBITION of 1851 were based on naturalistic forms such as nasturtiums, ivy, horse-chestnut leaves, ferns, and oak leaves. Coalbrookdale seats were listed in the company's catalogue.

COALPORT, porcelain scent bottle encrusted with flowers, c.1840.

COALPORT FACTORY Founded by John Rose at Coalport, Shropshire, a British manufacturer of fine ornamental wares and domestic pieces, such as tea and dinner services. The firm is noted for the translucent, FELDSPATHIC wares produced from 1820, and the delicate colours of its figure groups. The varied tastes of the day are mirrored in the changing styles of the factory's output. Coalport mimicked styles first made by MEISSEN, DRESDEN, and SÈVRES, with coloured grounds, eccentric shapes, and generous decoration. The factory is famous for flower-encrusted pieces made in the 1830s, known as COALBROOKDALE. From the turn of the century until the 1920s, Coalport had success with jewelled PORCELAIN, a distinctive, decorative technique made by placing beads of turquoise enamel on a gilded or coloured ground. These pieces are widely collected. Coalport allowed artists to sign pieces in the late 19th and 20thC. Among the best-known decorators are Edward Ball and Percy Simpson, who painted landscapes. John Randall was a specialist in exotic bird subjects, and Frederick Chivers specialized in still life. Coalport was also a major supplier of white porcelain to independent china painters, and many wares carry decoration that was executed outside the Coalport factory. Wares are often marked "AD 1750", which is the date that the company was founded, not the date of production.

COAL VASE A tall and often ornate metal vessel for the storage of coal. They were usually made in pairs to stand either side of the hearth.

COASTER Made of SILVER, often with feet (and sometimes wheels or castors), a small TRAY into which a bottle or DECANTER fits, so that it can be slid down a table. Early coasters were known as "stands" or "slides"; the term "coaster" dates from 1887. Wine coasters were made in great numbers from the mid-18thC. Most have silver, galleried sides and rounded, wooden bases, which may be inlaid with crested silver discs or bosses for engraving, and have baize linings underneath to protect FURNITURE from scratches. Many coasters made from the 1780s were embellished with NEO-CLASSICAL ornament, such as BEADED or REEDED borders, urn motifs, and leaf patterns. Some SILVER-GILT wine coasters with heavy cast sides and engraved bases of silver were made in the REGENCY period. Silver-plated wine coasters decorated with grapes and vines were made by ELKINGTON & CO., and silver-gilt versions with gilded bases were popularized by RUNDELL, BRIDGE & RUNDELL. Smaller coasters were designed to hold DRINKING GLASSES. These typically have glass bases with cut decoration, which allows air to escape and stops wet coasters sticking to WINEGLASSES. If a coaster has a wooden base, check the condition of the wood to see if it has shrunk. The condition of the wood does not greatly affect the value – worn or split wood can be replaced – but it does give an indication of how much the coaster has been used. All coasters were manufactured in pairs or in sets, and a pair or set is more valuable than a single one.

One of a pair of George III, silver COASTERS, with fret tracery and turned wooden base, 1765.

COASTER TROLLEY A 19thC design in which two wine COASTERS are linked together to hold wine DECANTERS; wheels and a handle were used to pull the decanters along DINING TABLES. ELKINGTON & CO. made SILVER-PLATE examples in the 1850s, but large, elaborate examples were made earlier than this by such well-known silversmiths as Paul STORR and Benjamin Smith. Variations on this design include double-decanter coasters on single wooden bases, and the "JOLLY BOAT": a coaster trolley in the shape of a rowing boat.

COBALT The mineral oxide used to give colour to blue GLASS. The term also describes glass of that colour.

COBB, JOHN (d.1778) English cabinet-maker who worked with William VILE.

COCHINEAL Bright red CARPET dye derived from Central American insects.

COCK (1) In a WATCH mechanism, the BRACKET attached to the plate that supports one end of the BALANCE SPRING.

COCK (2) In early FIREARMS, the metal jaw that clasped the flint or pyrites used to spark the powder. Later, the spring-tensioned arm used to hold the firing agent. To cock means to set the tension ready for firing.

COCK BEADING Curved strip of moulding often applied to DRAWER edges.

COCK METAL Copper-and-lead alloy, resembling PEWTER in appearance and used for inexpensive domestic wares in the 19thC.

COCK'S HEAD HINGE A twin-plate hinge with FINIALS shaped like a cock's head. It is usually found on FURNITURE dating pre-1650.

COCKTAIL GLASS A DRINKING GLASS for cocktails. During the "Jazz Age" of the 1920s and '30s, drinking became socially acceptable, and cocktail shakers and glasses were made in large quantities. Look for ART DECO cocktail glasses with wide, flared rims and that rely on dramatic shapes and colour rather than intricate ornate decoration (as on earlier glasses) for appeal.

Silver COFFEE POT with a raised foot and chased floral design, 1765.

COFFEE POT Made in various shapes, a SILVER vessel for mixing and serving coffee; some examples have filters for the grounds. Since coffee became fashionable in the late 17thC, large numbers of pots for serving it have been made. The earliest were produced in the 1650s, but few survive from before 1700. They resemble Turkish wine jugs (with lips rather than spouts), but the TEAPOT form, with a handle opposite the spout and a cover, soon became more popular. A tapering cylindrical form is characteristic of coffee pots made before the 1730s. The BALUSTER shape, with a tucked-in base and tall, domed cover was a favoured shape from the 1740s. Rims were often decorated with GADROONING, while flat-chased bands of ROCOCO ornamentation were added around the top and bottom of the body. The pear shape with a drop bottom was a popular form from the 1760s. Gadrooned borders on the feet are also characteristic of coffee pots of this period. From *c.*1800, most examples were made as part of matching TEA SERVICES. The weight, colour, and original decoration determine value, as will the name of an accomplished maker. The shapes of coffee pots can help with dating; however, many 18thC styles were repeated in the 19th and 20thC, so check the HALLMARKS on the base to tell whether the piece is a later reproduction. Lids should also be marked. Look for coffee pots by Paul de LAMERIE, BATEMAN & co., the Barnards, the FOX FAMILY, GARRARD., and Paul STORR. Many coffee pots have become worn, so before you buy one examine it carefully for damage, which can be expensive to restore. Examine handle sockets and hinges for signs of wear, and check to see if a coat-of-arms has been erased, which leaves the silver thin and reduces the value. During the 19thC, covered TANKARDS were sometimes converted into coffee pots. Converted pots are illegal unless the additions are marked.

COFFER A travelling trunk that is banded with metalwork, and covered with leather or other material. Also a term used to describe CHESTS of various kinds. Coffers were used for storing and transporting goods, but also served as seats or SIDE TABLES. They are difficult to date – while some joiners adopted new means of construction, others clung to traditional techniques. The basic coffer construction, using six planks (at the top, bottom, front, back, and sides), held together with wooden dowels or nails, dates from 1600 or earlier. Later, a framed construction connected with MORTISE-AND-TENON joints was employed. By the mid-17thC, some coffers had DRAWERS at their bases to make it easier to find items at the bottom; coffers of this type, sometimes called "MULE CHESTS", evolved into CHESTS OF DRAWERS. Most coffers have iron hinges and locks, and were made from solid OAK or WALNUT, with carved or painted decoration, although some plain 17th and 18thC coffers are on the market. In the late 19th and early 20thC, early coffers were sometimes recarved. Original carving adds to value; be suspicious of any carving that seems regular and stiff – it could have been added in the 19thC. Dates on chests can be misleading. Pieces were often inscribed with an earlier date, or a coffer given as a marriage gift was carved with initials and a date (of the marriage) years after it was made. Before buying a coffer, make sure that the hinges are in good condition and the locks are original; inside, check to see that the wood is dry and has not been tampered with. Also ensure that the legs have not been replaced. If the coffer is of framed construction, the legs and the sides of the frame should be made as a single piece.

COFFIN STOOL The name given to a joined STOOL, especially one with a storage area under the seat, although strictly speaking it applies only to a stool used as a coffin bier.

COGSWELL, JOHN (active 1769–82) Boston-based, American cabinet-maker known for his AMERICAN CHIPPENDALE-style FURNITURE in MAHOGANY.

COIN GLASS A GOBLET with a coin in the KNOP of the STEM. They were made as a commemorative custom from the late 17thC onward, and often faked.

COLICHEMARDE An 18thC, leaf-shaped small-sword that is wide at the hilt and rapier-like at the point. Used for both cutting and thrusting.

COLINET, CLAIRE JEANNE ROBERTE Belgian-born artist who worked in France and produced ART DECO figures based on mythology and dance.

COLLECTOR'S CABINET *See* SPECIMEN CHEST.

COLLIER (COLLYER), BENJAMIN English clockmaker, active 1693–1730.

COLLIER REVOLVER An early 19thC American firearm produced by Elisha Collier. Predecessor of the COLT REVOLVER.

COLLINOT Decoration on PORCELAIN resembling CLOISONNÉ. Produced by the Collinot factory in Paris, France, in the late 19thC.

COLONIAL Term used to describe American FURNITURE, SILVER, metalware, and textiles (as well as architecture and paintings) made prior to *c.*1680, when the North American colonies were under Dutch and English rule. At the time there were few inhabitants, and most items were either brought from Europe by the settlers, or imported. Furniture produced in the colonies (typically CHESTS, PRESS CUPBOARDS, and seating) was usually simple and functional, and made of OAK and other indigenous woods. Silver was crafted by skilled HUGUENOTS who settled in the colonies in the late 17thC.

COLONNA, EDWARD, (KNOWN AS EUGÈNE) (1862–1948) French artist who supplied the MAISON DE L'ART NOUVEAU, the Parisian shop of Samuel BING, and clients in North America, with FURNITURE, JEWELLERY, POTTERY, textiles, and ART GLASS.

COLOURED GLASS *See* GLASS, COLOURED.

COLOUR-TWIST STEM A coloured air twist in a wineglass stem. One or more rods of coloured or white glass are embedded within a clear-glass GATHER, and pulled and twisted to form a spiralling pattern. Inspired by 16thC, Venetian, LATTICINIO glass, this decoration is associated with STEMS on mid-18thC, English DRINKING GLASSES. Opaque-white stems are sometimes described as "cotton" twists; red and green are the colours most often found, while blue, purple, canary yellow, and other intense colours are rarely seen, and are hence sought after, as are twists of more than one colour. *See also* AIR-TWIST STEM, COMPOUND-TWIST STEM, MIXED-TWIST STEM, and OPAQUE-TWIST STEM.

COLOURWAY The main colour combinations found on items such as CERAMICS or fabrics. An object in an unusual colourway may be worth more than one in a common colourway.

COLT REVOLVER Invented by Samuel Colt of Hartford, Connecticut, an American, mid-19thC, percussion pistol, with an automatically revolving chamber. *See also* COLLIER REVOLVER.

COLUMBO, JOE An Italian FURNITURE designer, noted for his elegant use of plastics, as on "Elda", an extravagantly upholstered lounge chair, designed for the manufacturers Comfort in 1963.

COMB BACK Descriptive of a COUNTRY CHAIR with a TOP RAIL and back shaped somewhat like a comb. *See also* CHAIR and WINDSOR CHAIR.

COMBED DECORATION A type of GLASS decoration in which coloured trails are "combed" into featherlike patterns with a pointed instrument and then MARVERED to roll them into the surface. This technique was first used on ancient Egyptian, core-formed vessels. *See also* TRAILING.

COMBING On EARTHENWARE, a pattern of wavy, parallel lines created by incising the surface, or drawing a pattern in SLIP, with a comb. A common motif on 17thC SLIPWARE.

COMFIT BASKET Used for serving sweetmeats and crystallized fruits from the late 18thC, a TRAY in SILVER with pierced sides. Smaller than a CAKE BASKET.

COMMANDO KNIFE Issued to commandos from the early 1940s, a short, dagger-shaped knife with a crossguard and razor-sharp edge.

COMMEDIA DELL'ARTE Used to refer to characters from traditional Italian theatre of the same name, notably HARLEQUIN, Columbine, Scaramouche, and Pantaloon. These characters were popular as PORCELAIN figures, and were modelled by many factories in a variety of poses. Their value depends on the quality and their condition, rather than the subject.

COMMEMORATIVE CERAMICS Any ceramic item produced to mark a historical event such as a royal wedding, death, coronation, or jubilee, as well as wars, elections, and strikes. Collectors often concentrate on a particular theme or character. Ceramic commemoratives that predate the coronation of Queen Victoria are rare and valuable. Commemoratives of obscure events are less sought after than those marking more significant ones. However, huge numbers of MUGS were made for the Diamond Jubilee of Queen Victoria in 1897, so look for those that are well detailed, because these will be most desirable. Most commemoratives date from the mid-19thC, when improved methods of TRANSFER-PRINTING allowed potters to make souvenirs inexpensively. Vast quantities of royal souvenirs were made in the 20thC, and values are low unless the piece is unusual or by a top maker; examples of these include cartoon mugs, with ear-shaped handles, designed by Mark Boxer to mark the 1981 wedding of Prince Charles and Lady Diana Spencer.

COMMODE (1) A grand CHEST popular in Continental Europe and often of semicircular, SERPENTINE, or BOMBÉ shape, incorporating CUPBOARDS or DRAWERS, or both. Expensive and elaborate, these chests originated in France in the early 18thC ("commode" is French for "convenient"). The design was first adapted in England by Thomas CHIPPENDALE in the mid-18thC. French commodes usually have tops made from loose marble slabs. In England, marble was not used until the Victorian period (1837–1901), when copies of French examples were made with the marble tops held in place by metal galleries. They were luxury items made from costly materials, so you are unlikely to find a "bargain" commode today. The quality of the painting can effect the value, so look for fluid painting.

COMMODE (2) Used from the 19thC, a small CUPBOARD made for a chamber pot. They were known as "night tables" by the Georgians, but the prudish

Chippendale-period COMMODE without seat, c.1760.

Victorians dubbed them "commodes". They have been altered more than any other form of FURNITURE, and are rarely found as originally made. On many examples, the lower parts have been converted to incorporate CUPBOARDS or DRAWERS, but this does not affect prices unduly.

COMMON FURNITURE BEETLE Another name for WOODWORM.

COMPAGNIE DESSIN PORCELAIN made to the orders of the Compagnie des Indes, and exported from China in the 18th and 19thC.

COMPASS An instrument for orientating oneself by reference to magnetic fields. The most valuable compasses are ornate examples of the late 17th to early 19thC, often made of GOLD, SILVER, SILVER GILT, or IVORY. The best ones are finely engraved with the latitudes of important cities on the lid. Less-decorative, 19thC compasses, liquid compasses, and later card compasses can be bought inexpensively, and are likely to appreciate in value.

COMPENDIARIO Made at Faenza, Italy, in the 16thC, MAIOLICA with a white GLAZE and restrained decoration, often in only one or two additional colours.

COMPENDIUM TABLE GAMES TABLE housing a variety of game boards and playing accessories.

Mauchline-ware COMPASS with a view of the White House, Washington, c.1870.

COMPENSATED PENDULUM A PENDULUM of iron and steel (and, rarely, with a mercury well) to compensate for variations in length caused by changes in temperature. Keeps the duration of each oscillation constant on a CLOCK.

COMPORT *See* TAZZA.

COMPOSITE SET Term given to a collection of CHAIRS that are similar but not a true set. Also called a "HARLEQUIN" set.

COMPOSITE-STEM GLASS Produced from the third quarter of the 18thC, a wineglass with a STEM that combines a variety of elements, including plain, BALUSTER, and twist designs. Most of the twist elements in these so-called "composite" stems are air twists. Opaque examples combined with KNOPS and plain sections are more rare. *See also* AIR-TWIST STEM and OPAQUE-TWIST STEM.

COMPOSITIERA A small TRAY and matching sets of two or more SILVER vessels with lids and spoons. They contained different types of spice, sauce, or food to be mixed on the plate according to taste.

COMPOSITION Used for making DOLLS and MIRROR frames, an inexpensive substance made from cloth, size, wood, wood-pulp, plaster of Paris, glue, and sawdust. On dolls, it was a less-expensive alternative to BISQUE.

COMPOSITION DOLL A DOLL with a COMPOSITION head made from the late-19thC until World War II, in Europe and North America. Before 1914, the cold-press method of construction was used, although the disadvantage of this was that the top layer peeled away in time. This fault was rectified by the hot-press method, in which heat was applied during the moulding process. North American designers were more adventurous with composition than those in other countries, and based dolls on cartoon figures such as BETTY BOOP and SKIPPY, advertising characters, and contemporary celebrities. These are more sought after than European composition dolls. Many dolls created as advertising novelties became collectable. English manufacturers were not as keen on composition, but nonetheless produced a number of popular dolls such as the "Bisto Kids", from a gravy advertisement. In general, the more novel the doll, the more desirable it will be. Idealized rather than exaggerated features were preferred by German makers in the first half of the 20thC. The face should be as similar to that of a baby as possible. Due to the huge variety of composition dolls produced, there are no easy rules for identification – the most effective method is familiarity with the type. Look carefully at small details. Composition dolls usually have a seam running down the side of the head. They are difficult to clean without damaging their varnish. Bisque-headed dolls with composition bodies are more desirable than dolls with the head and body both made from composition. *See also* HUG-ME-KIDDIE and TOPSY.

COMPOSITION FIGURE Manufactured from *c*.1904, a toy soldier made of a COMPOSITION mixture on a wire skeleton and with a plasterlike appearance.

COMPOUND TWIST STEM In a STEM on a wineglass, any air twist made of multiple spirals. *See also* AIR-TWIST STEM.

CONCERTINA ACTION Descriptive of the way in which the frame of some CARD TABLES and GAMES TABLES extends to support the fold-over top. The back half of the frame is hinged in two sections, and opens out for support.

CONDIMENT ACCESSORIES The range of small SILVER items associated with the flavouring of food expanded significantly in the 18thC. These items included a number of novel forms, such as CRUETS. Other traditional shapes, such as pepper CASTERS, were refined according to the latest fashions. Under the influence of the French court, dining customs had become more elaborate by this time, and small, utilitarian accessories became an essential part of the table setting. Such pieces were made in great numbers in a variety of decorative styles, and today comprise an important collecting area. In the late 19thC, it became fashionable to set each place at the table with small individual condiment holders or sets. A set may comprise pots for pepper, salt, and mustard, with two matching spoons. These sets, which were sometimes equipped with GLASS liners, were often fitted in leather presentation

Circular, silvergilt cruet, by the widow of Edward Aldridge Senior, London, 1766 (CONDIMENT ACCESSORIES).

boxes, and were given as wedding gifts. Fine-quality, 20thC condiment sets signed by a renowned craftsman are desirable, especially if in the original cases. Sets in good condition are rare. Hand-crafted examples may have a family crest, monogram, or ARMORIAL incorporated into the design. The emblems cannot be easily removed, and they detract from the value. *See also* MUSTARD-POT, PEPPER BOX, SALTCELLAR, and SOY FRAME.

CONDIMENT POT A small SILVER pot, often with a GLASS or ceramic lining, for holding salt, pepper, mustard, and other condiments.

CONFIDANTE Of French origin, a large SOFA on which the ends are formed as separate seats facing diagonally outwards.

CONSOLE TABLE First produced *c*.1720, a rectangular TABLE made to stand against a wall, with only two legs or a carved base at the front. Some examples have SERPENTINE fronts, many are ornate in the Italianate manner with decoration of SWAGS, garlands, and PUTTI, and most were made in pairs. With no supporting back legs, console tables were fixed to walls in entrance halls or grand salons, often with MIRRORS above them. They are found in GILTWOOD or JAPANNING, and often have marble tops. The most desirable examples come in pairs, with the original marble tops in good condition, and with attractive carving. Outspread eagle bases are also sought after.

CONSTRUCTIVISM One of the styles of the 1920s developed in reaction to ART NOUVEAU, and associated principally with the Dutch DE STIJL movement.

CONSULAR WATCH The successor to the PAIR-CASED WATCH from the early 19thC. It has a glazed bezel, and a MOVEMENT hinged to the backcase.

CONTINENTAL Term referring to European countries excluding Britain.

CONVERSATION SEAT A large circular upholstered seat that is divided into segments. Made during the 19thC, it is more decorative than practical.

COOPER, J. Leading English gunsmith, active in the mid-19thC.

COOPER, J.M. Leading North American gunsmith, active in the mid-19thC.

COOPER, SUSIE (1902–95) One of the most influential, British CERAMICS designers of her generation, Cooper produced a wide range of commercial wares. After working for A.E. GRAY Ltd, she set up her own company in 1929. Early output concentrated on EARTHENWARES, often handpainted; fine BONE CHINA was produced after World War II. Wares are categorized according to their shape and the pattern with which they are decorated, such as the "Kestrel" shape. Other popular shapes include "Curlew", "Jay",

Early-1930s, SUSIE COOPER beaker, hand painted in a geoemtric design with silver lustre.

and "Wren". Decoration is wide ranging, with floral designs, transfer prints, incised decoration, and geometric patterns all used. In 1961, the firm of Susie Cooper merged with R.H. & S.L. Plant, which was taken over by WEDGWOOD in 1966. Wedgwood reissued some of Cooper's early designs such as "Pink Fern", "Polka Dot", and "Yellow Daisy". The most sought-after pieces are early handpainted wares and LUSTREWARES, and services have risen enormously in popularity in recent years. Most pieces are marked with facsimile signatures, and can be dated both by mark and by serial number. Pieces made while Cooper was working at A.E. Gray's may bear both the company name and the designer's initials.

COOPERED JOINT A curved, timber joint, as found on WINE COOLERS.

COPELAND & GARRETT British wares produced by SPODE after the firm was acquired by William Copeland and T. Garrett in the early 19thC.

COPENHAGEN A PORCELAIN works founded *c*.1750, and known for its "Flora Danica" range, decorated with Danish flowers. *See also* ROYAL COPENHAGEN.

COPER, HANS A studio potter who worked with Lucie RIE. Unusual shapes with little decoration are a hallmark of Coper's vases. A pale, finely textured surface, and contrasting, brownish-black interior is also characteristic of his work. Pieces are marked with an impressed "HC" cipher resembling a potter's wheel on its side. *See also* STUDIO CERAMICS.

CORDIAL GLASS Smaller version of a wineglass, with a thick STEM, heavy foot, and small bowl. It evolved in the 17thC for strong drinks.

CORALENE First used by the American MOUNT WASHINGTON GLASS CO., applied GLASS decoration made to resemble coral. Also found on European glass.

CORE-FORMING Technique of producing a GLASS vessel by shaping trails of molten glass over a core – usually moulded into the required shape from mud or clay and fixed to a metal rod – and fusing them together in a furnace; the core is carved or acid-etched out when cool. The rod is then reheated and rolled (MARVERED) on a flat surface to make walls of even thickness. Threads of differently coloured glass were often trailed over the surface, and combed into contrasting featherlike patterns. After the rim, handle, and feet were added, the object was cooled, the metal rod removed, and the core scraped out. Prior to the invention of glassblowing in the 1st century AD, most small, hollow vessels such as bottles, flasks, and vases were produced by core-forming.

CORGI **No.206 Hillman Husky, 1956–61.**

CORGI Firm established in Swansea, Wales, in 1948 by Mettoy. The range of DIECAST TOYS, made from German dies, was intended to emulate the success of DINKY. As many extras as possible were packed into each toy, including

Dutch, silver, pocket CORKSCREW with sheaf, c.1850.

plastic windows and spring suspension (added in 1959). From 1963, vehicles with opening doors and bonnets, and folding seats were made. One of its most popular cars is the James Bond Aston Martin; the "Batmobile" of the 1960s was also successful. The firm was taken over by Mattel in 1992.

CORK GLASS Early, hand-cut FLINT GLASS, made in the late 18th and early 19thC by two factories in Cork, Ireland.

CORKSCREW Originally called a "steele worme" or bottle screw, a device for removing a cork from a bottle. They come in a variety of forms and designs, some with additional attachments for multiple use, such as button hooks or tobacco tampers. SILVER corkscrews are often decorated with engraved or chased decoration, and those in novelty forms, such as fish, are popular. Corkscrews were sometimes part of a set, including a matching bottle-cap lifter for removing metal caps. Corkscrews have an enthusiastic following among collectors, and those with fitted cases are much sought after.

CORN CHEST A CHEST made for storing corn and, probably, other grains. Some were made with small DRAWERS and shallow backs.

CORNER CHAIR Designed to fit neatly into a corner, a CHAIR of squarish appearance with two side legs, one back leg, and one central front leg. Also called a "writing chair" or "roundabout".

CORNISH WARE Produced by T.G. GREEN & Co. Ltd. and dating to the 1920s, kitchen accessories decorated with a striped design. It was extremely popular in Britain in the 1950s, and the blue-and-white version is still favoured today. On authentic pieces the blue areas are always in relief, and the white areas recessed.

CORNUCOPIA Meaning "horn of plenty", a cone-shaped, fruit-filled BASKET, often used as a motif. EARTHENWARE cornicopia were made for attaching to walls and holding flowers. WHIELDON-TYPE and SALT-GLAZE versions are desirable.

COROMANDEL (1) A dark, figured wood, almost black in parts, with pale yellow striations. Used as a VENEER for refined FURNITURE of the REGENCY period.

COROMANDEL (2) Oriental, carved LACQUER work, used especially to create pictorial folding screens. So-called because Coromandel, in Bengal, was the principal export port in the 17th and 18thC.

CORRECTION CHAIR A tall, high-backed CHAIR on which children were taught to sit correctly.

CORRIDOR CARPET A long thin RUG, or runner.

CORRIDOR STOOL Made throughout the 19thC, a long STOOL with raised ends and never upholstered. Also known as a "ROUT STOOL".

CORSET BACK A 19thC, North American CHAIR with a waisted back.

COTTAGE CLOCK General term for small, 19thC, North American, New England-made, MANTEL CLOCK with a wooden case.

COTTON TWIST A pattern of fine, white spirals in the STEM of a wineglass.

COTYLEDON A motif of stylized, cup-shaped leaves, sprouting from a bud.

COUCH An old term for a DAY BED.

COUNTER A structure resembling a TABLE but with a compartment below. So-called because the top was used for reckoning accounts with counters.

COUNTER BOX Often of SILVER, but also of wood or ivory, a box used from the 17thC for storing gaming counters or tokens.

COUNTERSINK The cutting of a BEVELLED hole to accommodate and conceal the head of a screw.

COUNTRY CHAIR A rustic CHAIR made in a remote rural area, and developed independently from chairs by the top designers. Country chairs are made of solid wood from indigenous trees such as ASH, BEECH, ELM, OAK, and YEW. The wood used can have a bearing on the price. Chairs made entirely or partly from yew are rare and sought after, while beech is more common. Dating can be difficult, because designs changed little between the 18th and early 20thC, although examining the PATINA of the wood and the decorative details can help. If a chair combines decoration typical of different periods, always date it by the latest decorative detail. Most country chairs vary more due to where, rather than when, they were made. Elaborately arched SPLATS on oak chairs are typical of British chairs made in South Yorkshire and Derbyshire. BOBBIN TURNING on the front STRETCHER can date a chair to the late 17thC. The number of chairs in a set can affect the price. A set of six can be worth almost one-third more than a set of five, while a single chair may be worth only one-tenth of the value of a set of six. *See also* LADDER BACK and WINDSOR CHAIR.

COUNTRY FURNITURE Term to describe FURNITURE made by provincial craftsmen, especially pieces in ELM, FRUITWOOD, OAK, and PINE.

COUNTWHEEL STRIKE Consisting of a wheel with notches on the rim, a mechanism for controlling the number of strikes that mark the hours in a CLOCK movement. The lever (or detent) continues to strike until it catches in a notch.

COUPER LTD Scottish, Glasgow-based maker of "CLUTHA" GLASS, from 1885.

COUP PERDU Meaning "lost beat" in French, a CLOCK with a PENDULUM that beats every half-second, but a seconds hand that moves every second.

COURONNE DE FEU Meaning "fire crown" in French, an iron CANDLESTICK with two or more branches.

COURT CUPBOARD A two- or three-tiered, open structure used to display plates and other finery. The earliest "cup board" evolved from a board or shelf used for storing cups or drinking vessels. Court cupboards were made of solid wood, usually OAK, and not veneered. Look carefully at pre-1700 CUPBOARDS to make sure that there are genuine signs of age – imitations were produced in the late Victorian period (1860–1901), made up from early wood or wainscoting. On Victorian copies (or later pieces) the carving is often more complex than on early ones. *See also* PRESS CUPBOARD.

COURTHOUSE STEPS A version of the "Log Cabin" PATCHWORK block in which dark and light strips are placed on opposite sides of the centre square.

COUTY, EDMÉ (d.1917) A French designer who worked for the SÈVRES factory, but also designed TAPESTRIES and FURNITURE in the ART NOUVEAU style.

COW CREAMER Produced from mid-18thC, a cow-shaped PORCELAIN, or SILVER boat or jug used for holding cream; its "tail" serves as a handle, and its "mouth" as a spout. Cow creamers were the speciality of John Schuppe (active 1753–73), a silversmith of Dutch origin working in London, England. The surfaces of these naively modelled jugs are either plain or tooled to resemble the texture of animal hair; a few examples are found in SILVER GILT. Made of thin-gauge SILVER and subjected to heavy use, many creamers have been damaged, despite the beaded or reeded wires often applied to strengthen the rims. *See also* JUG, CREAM AND MILK.

COZZI FACTORY *See* PORCELAIN, ITALIAN.

CRABSTOCK On a TEAPOT, spouts and HANDLES modelled as knotted apple tree branches. Popular in the 18thC.

CRACKLE *See* CRAZING.

CRACKLE GLAZE On glazed CERAMICS, patterns of fine cracks, deliberately induced for decorative effect. *See also* CRAZING.

CRAFTSMAN STYLE Similar to the British ARTS AND CRAFTS MOVEMENT and spanning the period from the 1890s to *c.*1920, a North American style in which FURNITURE, CERAMICS, and other objects were well crafted but simply formed and decorated.

CRAFTS REVIVAL A movement that began in North America in the 1950s and advocated traditional craftsmanship, using natural materials. The arrival of European refugee artists after World War II contributed to the revival.

CRAILSHEIM From an 18thC factory near Württemburg, Germany, FAIENCE noted for its bright and colourful, floral decoration.

CRAZING A fine network of cracks on certain glazed surfaces. It is sometimes used as a decorative effect and sometimes the result of ageing. Particularly common on the faces of COMPOSITION DOLLS and WAX DOLLS.

CRAZY PATCHWORK In quilting, randomly shaped patches in a variety of fabrics stitched together, with the seams covered with embroidery stitches.

CREAM JUG *See* JUG, CREAM AND MILK.

CREAM PAIL A bucket-shaped vessel with a swing handle, used for clotted cream, and popular from the mid-18thC. In the 1770s, cream pails were often pierced with trelliswork and embossed with Chinese pastoral scenes or views of the English countryside *See also* PIGGIN.

CREAMWARE A refined, cream-coloured EARTHENWARE with a transparent LEAD GLAZE. First introduced in the 1740s, it was produced by British potters in Staffordshire, Leeds, Liverpool, Bristol, Derby, and Swansea, and decorated with moulded decoration, painted enamels, or TRANSFER-PRINTING Its most successful manufacturer was Josiah WEDGWOOD, who called it QUEENSWARE. Chintz patterns were popular on pieces made *c.*1770; other handpainted flowers, castles, and cottages are also common. Creamware decorated with transfer-prints or decorated in low relief with political personalities of the day were popular from the late 18th to mid-19thC. Value depends on the rarity of the subject. Look for red and black enamelling by Robinson & Rhodes; wares marked "Wedgwood"; pierced wares that may be marked "Leeds Pottery"; and moulded pieces such as CRUETS and CENTREPIECES. Few creamwares are marked. *See also* STAFFORDSHIRE POTTERIES.

CREAMWARE **milk jug and cover, possibly by Wedgwood, *c.*1765.**

CREDENZA An Italian word originally referring to 16thC SIDEBOARDS. The Victorians used it to refer to a type of SIDE CABINET with glazed or solid doors, made to display collections. Credenzas are often ornate and decorative. VENEERS in WALNUT, original GLASS, gilt mounts, and INLAY are all desirable.

CREIL Late 18th and 19thC FAIENCE from the French factory of the same name. It often imitates English forms and types of decoration.

CRENELLATED POTTERY vessels with a pie-crust or wavy rim.

CRESSENT, CHARLES (1685–1768) French cabinet-maker employed by royalty in the first half of the 18thC.

CREST On a coat-of-arms, a heraldic device used to denote ownership.

CRESTED CHINA POTTERY manufactured as seaside souvenirs and decorated with colourful heraldic crests. First made by GOSS, by 1880 it was also produced (until *c*.1930) by firms across the United Kingdom and in Germany in vast quantities. Some German pieces are marked "GEMMA".

CRESTING Carved decoration on the highest part of a piece of FURNITURE.

CRESTING RAIL On a CHAIR the TOP RAIL that joins the UPRIGHTS of the back.

CRICKET STOOL Term used in the 17thC to describe a small footstool. Both three-legged and four-legged STOOLS were known as "crickets".

CRICKET TABLE A country-made, three-legged TABLE with a round top.

CRIMPING A pattern of small, parallel ridges created by pinching clay.

CRESTED Arcadian-ware "Cheshire Cat", c.1903–33.

CRINOLINE STRETCHER A curved STRETCHER on an early WINDSOR CHAIR.

CRISTALLO First developed in the mid-15thC by the MURANO glassmaker Angelo Barovier, a refined, colourless SODA GLASS, made with soda from the ashes of the barilla plant. It led to the use of fanciful decoration, such as the serpent-shaped stems found on VENETIAN GLASS and FAÇON-DE-VENISE goblets.

CRIZZLING A fine network of small cracks on the surface of GLASS due to an excess of alkali, which creates fissures, in the batch. Such "diseased" glass continues to deteriorate, as the process causing crizzling cannot be reversed.

CROCK A salt-glazed STONEWARE made in the eastern states of the USA in the 19th and early 20thC. Look for vessels in cobalt blue by William E. Warner and examples from Hubbell & Chesebro.

CROCKET Commonly seen on GOTHIC-style FURNITURE, a stylized, protruding, carved leaf or flower motif of architectural origin.

CROFT Designed especially for the library, a small filing cabinet comprising numerous small DRAWERS and a writing surface .

CROMWELLIAN CHAIR A 16th and 17thC, leather-upholstered CHAIR.

CROOKED DRESSER An L-shaped DRESSER designed to fit into a corner.

CROSSBANDING A veneered edge at right-angles to the main VENEER. Often found on the edges of DRAWERS, it became increasingly refined in the 18thC.

CROSSBILL A GLASS vessel with two interlaced necks.

CROSS STRETCHER Either a curved or a straight X-shaped STRETCHER.

CROUCH WARE English salt-glazed STONEWARE produced at Burslem in Staffordshire during the 17thC. *See also* STAFFORDSHIRE POTTERIES.

CROWN DERBY Strictly, wares by Derby Crown Porcelain Co. (est. *c*.1877) in Britain, but sometimes used of 18thC products by the Derby Porcelain Manufactory, which used a crown as its mark. *See also* ROYAL CROWN DERBY.

CROWN DEVON Introduced in 1913 by FIELDING & CO., of Staffordshire, a range of British POTTERY influenced by ART NOUVEAU and, later, ART DECO. They made a prolific range of moulded EARTHENWARE tableware, salad wares, novelties, and figures. VASES, dishes, and wall plaques in innovative shapes, with handpainted decoration, from florals to fantasy landscapes, are sought after.

Mahogany, Sheraton-period, open armchair with CROSS STRETCHER, *c*.1795.

CROWN GLASS Early cabinet GLASS made by the process of blowing, and then flattened by spinning.

CRUET Originally, a small GLASS vessel for serving oil and vinegar at table; later, the collective term for a SILVER frame holding an assortment of silver and glass CASTERS and bottles containing condiments, introduced to England from France in the late 17thC. Early examples were designed to hold oil and vinegar only, while larger stands, common by the 1720s, also held salt, pepper, and mustard. Cruet bottles were similar in style to glass DECANTERS in the late 18th and early 19thC. Always check that the gilding has not been worn. Collectors should check that the stands, bottle covers, and casters are all matching and fully hallmarked. *See also* CONDIMENT ACCESSORIES, SOY FRAME, and WARWICK CRUET.

CRYSTAL Brilliant clear GLASS, resembling rock crystal, developed in Venice, Italy, in the mid-15thC when it was named CRISTALLO.

CRYSTALLIZED WARE The name given to the 19thC technique of decorating TINPLATE by coating it with clear varnish and painting on top.

CRYSTELLO-CERAMIC Developed in 18thC France, the technique of enclosing a ceramic ornament in GLASS.

C-SCROLL A HANDLE shape, resembling the letter C. Also, a carved motif.

CUCKOO CLOCK First made *c*.1730, a CLOCK with an automaton in the form of a cuckoo, whose call announces the hours.

CUENCA On early Spanish POTTERY, a decorative technique achieved by stamping the vessel to leave a raised outline, then glazing the area within, thus keeping different glazes from running into each other.

CUP AND COVER Bulbous form of carved decoration resembling an acorn, and found on Elizabethan and early 17thC FURNITURE.

CUPBOARD The term "cupboard" evolved from a board or shelf used for storing drinking vessels. The earliest type was the COURT CUPBOARD, which had two or three open shelves. From the mid-17thC, enclosed cupboards were known as PRESS CUPBOARDS. By the late 18thC, doors were hinged on the inside. On earlier 18thC and provincial cupboards the hinges are on the outside.

CUPID'S BOW Shaped like a bow, the TOP RAIL of a CHIPPENDALE-style CHAIR.

CUP PLATE A vessel to hold tea- or coffee cups without HANDLES. Early North American, clear and coloured PRESSED-GLASS versions were made from the 1830s. Those with commemorative designs or patriotic emblems are valuable.

19thC, walnut, secretaire cabinet with a moulded cornice over a CUSHION DRAWER.

CUSHION DRAWER A convex-fronted DRAWER, often disguised as a piece of MOULDING near the top of a CHEST-ON-STAND, ESCRITOIRE, or a similar item.

CUSHION STOOL A 16th and 17thC, joined STOOL, with an upholstered top.

CUSP The point at which two curves meet, descriptive of the shaped corners of some tabletops. Also, the faceted KNOP on the STEM of a wineglass.

CUSTARD GLASS A creamy-coloured, opaque, uranium GLASS.

CUT-AND-ENGRAVED DECORATION A combination of cutting and engraving techniques found on American glassware. *See also* GLASS.

CUT-CARD WORK Developed in the late 17thC, a decorative shape cut from a thin sheet or card of SILVER, and soldered to the body of the vessel.

CUT DECORATION A GLASS-decoration technique in which facets are cut into glass to emphasize its refractive qualities. The earliest patterns were shallow surface cuts made by hand, but, by *c*.1830, mechanized wheel cutting became the norm. The fashion for heavily cut glass reached its peak during the late 18thC and early 19thC in England and Ireland, where LEAD CRYSTAL – the most suitable type for cutting – was invented. The object was held above the wheel to create facets or deep grooves, which were polished to create a sparkling surface. A variety of complex cutting patterns, such as strawberry and relief diamonds, developed during the REGENCY period, but, from the 1820s and '30s, simpler, flat-cut, vertical facets were more fashionable. In the 1840s, bold, simple designs, often incorporating a GOTHIC arch framing heavy-cut diamonds, were in vogue. Cut glass can be identified in several ways, notably by its sharply faceted decoration, a lack of mould lines along the inside, and irregular thickness. Look for flaws in the METAL and slight irregularities in shape that show that a piece is handmade. Collectable cut-glass objects include sweetmeat dishes, fruit bowls and CANDLESTICKS.

CUT GLASS GLASS embellished with CUT DECORATION It was revived in Bohemia in the 17thC and was common until superseded by PRESSED GLASS.

CUTLASS A short, single-edged SWORD with a flat, wide, slightly curved blade. The standard British naval sword in the 18thC.

CUTLERY *See* FLATWARE.

CUTLERY BOX Usually of MAHOGANY, or covered with leather, velvet, SHAGREEN, or wood VENEERS with SILVER trims, an ornamental box for holding a set of silver cutlery. They came into fashion in the reign of George II (1727–60). Often designed as a pair to stand at each end of a SIDEBOARD, they were typically of square form, with sloping BOMBÉ fronts.

CUTLERY STAND Small stand with compartments for holding cutlery and plates. Also called a "SUPPER CANTERBURY".

CUT WORK *See* BANTAM WORK.

CYLINDER-TOP DESK A DESK or BUREAU with a rounded or cylindrical shutter to enclose the interior working area. *See also* TAMBOUR.

CYMA Double-curved MOULDING. "Cyma recta" is concave above and convex below; "cyma reversa" is the opposite. Also known as OGEE and reverse-ogee moulding, it was popular with late, 18thC cabinet-makers.

"CYMRIC" SILVER The tradename used by LIBERTY & CO. for a range of silverware designed by Archibald KNOX, and introduced in 1899. Inspired by Celtic art, it was embellished with swirling, interlaced tendrils and CABOCHON-enamel decoration, and hammered in low relief with a lily-pad motif.

CYPHER Used on PORCELAIN in the mid- to late 19thC, an impressed or painted mark giving the year of manufacture. Factories had individual marks.

CYST The swelling at the base of a GLASS bowl.

Bohemian, engraved, glass goblet on a CUT petal-base, 19thC.

D

DAGGER Any short-edged and pointed weapon with a cross hilt, used for thrusting and stabbing.

DAGHESTAN RUG-making region on the western shores of the Caspian Sea.

DAGUERROTYPE Early form of photograph, using metal containing a high proportion of silver, coated with light-sensitive iodine, and developed with mercury vapour. The earliest commercially manufactured camera used the daguerreotype process, developed in France by L.J.M. Daguerre in 1837. Daguerreotypes look like mirrors – the image is formed on silvered metal, usually protected behind sealed glass. Despite their relative rarity, portrait groups can still be found. An interesting view or a known sitter adds to value.

DAIMYO Japanese nobleman. During the Edo period (1614–1867) they sponsored or retained master craftsmen with whose objects their names are sometimes associated.

DAISHO A pair of Samurai SWORDS: one long (dai) sword is called the katana; the other short (sho), the wakisashi.

DAISY PATTERN TOYS TINPLATE toys made from 1815 with cast-iron wheels. So-called because of the pattern made by the spokes.

DAKIN, R. AND CO. A large, North American producer of SOFT TOYS and TEDDY BEARS. The firm began by importing hand-crafted toys from Japan. In 1957, a shipment of Japanese toy trains had velveteen soft toys as packing material, and the founder's son, Roger, thought them attractive enough to sell. Within a few years, Dakin were selling nothing else. In 1966, most members of the Dakin family were killed in a plane crash, but the firm continued producing TEDDY BEARS. They set high safety standards – no toxic materials are used in production and stress tests ensure that eyes are secure.

DAMASCENE INLAY of GOLD or SILVER onto another metal such as steel. It is named after Damascus, from which fine examples derive.

DAMASCENING A type of SWORD decoration of inlaid GOLD or SILVER. True damascening involves hammering metal into V-shaped grooves, while counterfeit damascening is laid onto a cross-hatched surface, is shallower, and easily worn away.

DAMASCUS BARREL In FIREARMS, a barrel ornamented with spiral bands of iron, originally from Damascus. Also known as a twist barrel.

DAMASCUS RUG A brightly coloured, angora-wool RUG made in Africa, Spain, and Turkey. So-called because they were exported through Damascus.

DANCING JACK Flat, cardboard or wooden DOLLS with limbs joined by string. Some examples are mounted on frames.

DANEL & CIE A French DOLL factory at Montreuil-sous-Bois, founded by Danel – a former director of JUMEAU, who left that firm amid much acrimony in 1889 – and Guepratte. Jumeau won a lawsuit against Danel for enticing Jumeau workers to join him, borrowing moulds and other equipment, and taking heads and bodies. The "Paris Bébé" mark is registered by Danel & Cie, who used a picture of the Eiffel Tower as their trademark. The firm began to specialize in black dolls before being taken over by Jumeau in 1896.

DAOGUNG (Tao Kuang) Chinese CH'ING dynasty emperor, 1821–50.

DATE APERTURE On the face of a CLOCK, an opening showing the day of the month.

DAUMENGLAS A traditional, German, cylindrical or barrel shaped BEAKER.

DAUM FRÈRES (Daum Brothers) An important glassworks established in 1878 in Nancy, France, by Jean Daum. His sons, Auguste (1853–1909) and Antonin (1864–1930), contemporaries of Emile GALLÉ, joined him, and turned to ART-GLASS production in 1889. They specialized in ART NOUVEAU and ART DECO designs in CAMEO, etched, and PÂTE-DE-VERRE glass, and in MARTELÉ glass, resembling beaten metal. Daum glass is made in a wide range of styles, and is often similar to that made by Gallé. It can usually be identified by a gilt signature "DAUM NANCY" on the black enamel on the underside.

DAVENPORT (1) Popular in the REGENCY period, a small, free-standing WRITING TABLE, with a sloped top above a case of real or false DRAWERS. It was named after Captain Davenport, for whom the first one was made, by GILLOWS, in the late 18thC. There are two types: early ones are plain and have upper sections that pull forward to provide a writing surface over the user's knees. By c.1840, many had recessed cases and desirable "piano-rise" tops, so-called because of the curved shape of the top of the writing surface. They are sometimes known as "harlequin davenports" because they have stationery compartments that push down into the main carcase and pop up at the release of a button. Later ones are elaborate, typifying the VICTORIAN STYLE. Expect to pay more for good-quality woods, such as BURR WALNUT, SATINWOOD, or ROSEWOOD. A SERPENTINE front and CABRIOLE LEGS add value.

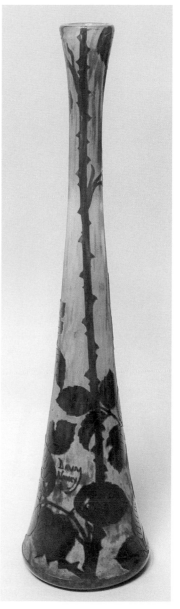

DAUM, frosted, cameo, glass vase, c.1910.

125

DAVENPORT (2) American term for a DAY-BED or reclining SOFA with a headrest.

DAVENPORT (3) Successful British factory, established at Longport, Staffordshire, in 1794 by John Davenport. The firm made EARTHENWARE, BASALTES, CREAMWARE, BONE CHINA, and even GLASS throughout the 19thC, until its closure in 1887. Davenport produced extensive DINNER SERVICES using PORCELAIN and other, less-expensive materials. The factory has no particularly distinctive style, but is recognized for decoration of high quality, and was noted from 1820 for fine botanical wares and IMARI-style decoration. Pieces were usually marked with a name and pattern number, which help with dating. Davenport patented a technique for making thinly potted porcelain plaques, many of which were sold to independent decorators. Although popular with collectors and often of equally fine quality, pieces by this firm tend to fetch lower prices than those by WORCESTER, SWANSEA, or ROCKINGHAM. Among the most affordable pieces to look out for are BLUE-AND-WHITE printed plates. Davenport was marked with a crown between c.1870 and 1886; the words "Davenport Longport" also appear in some marks.

DAVID AND GOLIATH First published in the 1930s, a PATCHWORK block pattern for a QUILT, based on a 10 x 10 grid of squares.

DAVIDSON, JOSEPH Leading English gunsmith, active in the early 19thC.

DAVIDSON, PETER WYLER (d.1933) English ART NOUVEAU designer of JEWELLERY.

DAY-BED (DAVENPORT in the USA.) A couch with one sloped end to support the sitter's head and back while reclined. Made from the 16th until the mid-18thC, they were either upholstered or caned and sometimes have six or eight legs.

DAY, ROBIN (b.1915) English FURNITURE designer best known for his "Polyprop" stacking chair, with a seat made of moulded polypropylene supported by a bent tubular frame. The British firm of Hille commissioned Day to design modern furniture for the 1949 British Industrial Fair. Day's wife, Lucienne, (b.1917), is renowned for her textiles designs.

DEADBEAT ESCAPEMENT Invented c.1715, it eliminates the recoil of the ESCAPE WHEEL on a CLOCK, as the pallets catch in its teeth, thus improving accuracy.

Hillestack chair by ROBIN DAY, in beech with cherry-laminate bent plywood, 1954.

DEAN'S RAG BOOK CO. LTD Based in London, a British firm established by Samuel Dean in 1905 to print rag books, DOLLS, and TEDDY BEARS. The first dolls were printed on material to be made up at home. Moulded, felt dolls were made from 1920 onward, including "Princess", "Smart Set", "Frilly", and "Sunshine" dolls. Children's illustrators, such as Hilda Cowham, were employed to design several of the dolls. The "Evripose" line was introduced in 1923. Printed shoes and socks are characteristic features. As well as their Evripose bears, Dean's was noted for bears of unusual colours, and for novelties such as bears on wheels. Earlier teddies have heads that are more angular and ears that are more rounded than some later editions. "Bertie" is the archetypal English bear; made in 1938 (and now fairly common), he is jointed, shaggy, yellow, and stuffed with KAPOK. Dean's bears may be labelled on the foot or have silver buttons fixed, as on STEIFF bears. Dean's merged with Dean's Childsplay Toys and with Gwentoys, whose factory was in Gwent, Wales, in 1972. One of Dean's chief designers was Silvia Wilgoss, who was inspired by the bears at London Zoo to create a 1950s teddy that sits like a real bear. It has painted black glass eyes with a black rubber surround, black rubber nose and lips, large ears, a hunched back, long arms, and legs with beige rubber paws and claws. Dean's also produced SOFT TOYS, and "Dean's Rag Book Band", which includes white rabbits, gold-plush teddy bears, and rubber-faced monkeys playing instruments, is a rare and sought-after group. The monkeys are dressed in band-player's outfits, and all have instruments. Dean's started making soft toys of characters in children's literature such as Peter Rabbit from the Beatrix Potter books. "Tatters" (a hospital pup with an upraised, bandaged paw) was issued in 1928. "Dismal Desmond" (first manufactured as a pitiful-looking Dalmatian in 1923) was supplemented in 1933 by "Cheerful Desmond". The most valuable characters are "Bonzo", "Dismal Desmond", "Bambi", and "Peter Rabbit". The popularity of new arrivals and births at London Zoo led to the creation of toys such as a white polar bear mother and cub in the 1950s. Dean's original trademark showed a terrier and a bulldog tugging at either side of one of the company's rag books. After the 1930s, laws required more information to be provided on labels, so the picture was dropped to make room for more text. Many Dean's dolls have oval stamps with their trademark, sometimes inscribed "Hygienic A1 toys, made in England, Dean's Rag Book Co. Ltd".

DEAN'S RAG BOOK Ivy (mother) and Brumas (baby) polar bear set, 1950s.

DECANTER Originally, a vessel used to store wines such as port and Madeira, which have been decanted from another vessel to remove the sediment. However, "decanter" is now used more broadly to describe any type of tall, stoppered GLASS vessel for storing and serving drinks. In England, dark-green SEAL BOTTLES were made from the mid-17thC. Decanters in colourless LEAD CRSTAL were first made at the beginning of the 18thC. Styles altered considerably over the years – early-18thC forms are tall and tapering, sometimes decorated with simple engraving of motifs such as FESTOONS and fruiting vines, while heavily cut bulbous, ovoid shapes, with shorter necks with applied moulded rings for ease of handling, are associated with the REGENCY period. Initially decanters were provided with corks – it was not until the 1750s that glass stoppers were introduced. Like decanters, stoppers were produced in a variety of styles throughout the 18th and 19thC, from the faceted disc, lozenge, and bull's-eye shapes to flat-mushroom and faceted-ball ones. Coloured decanters first appeared in blue BRISTOL GLASS at the end of the 18thC, but became more popular in the Victorian era (1837–1901) for serving the white wines fashionable at that time. Decanters were often decorated with engraved or gilded labels describing their contents. Some examples have applied NECK RINGS, which make them easier to handle. Creating a decanter of standard capacity and shape involved blowing the GATHER of molten glass into a coasterlike mould. In the late 18th and early 19thC, some moulds, particularly Irish ones, featured the name of the manufacturer, which was incorporated into the base. Such pieces are rare. Today, many collectors look for matching pairs or sets of decanters. The decoration on the body and stopper should always match, showing that the two pieces were made at the same time and that the stopper is not a replacement. The ground texture of the stopper peg should be matched by that inside the neck of the decanter. Signs of wear on the base of the decanter are a good indication that the piece is genuine. All lead-crystal decanters should show signs of wear on the base, and have a clear ring when tapped. *See also* GLASS, CARE OF.

DECANTER, AMERICAN A decanter made in the USA, mainly from the 19th and early 20thC, in a wide variety of colours and styles. While some early American glass decanters copy English CUT-GLASS styles, many are narrower and more bottlelike in shape, perhaps inspired by the vast quantities of plain and practical glass bottles used for storing wine and spirits in the newly established communities of the Midwest. MOULD-BLOWING and, especially, PRESS MOULDING were the most popular methods for making inexpensive yet decorative decanters, with often elaborate patterns created as integral parts of the body. More luxurious decanters were made at the end of the 19thC, and include coloured items with naturalistic decoration in SILVER overlay. Decanters and jugs in an ART DECO, geometric style, many with matching DRINKING GLASSES, were produced in the 1930s.

DECANTER, BOHEMIAN A DECANTER made in central Europe. Early ones were made as part of travelling sets. The bottles usually had screw tops, and were designed to fit snugly into travelling boxes. Any expensive, gilded decoration would have been confined to the shoulders and neck, the only parts visible when the decanter was tucked into its travelling box. These boxes could hold several decanters – sometimes up to eight – but only two glasses, so that the wealthy traveller and his companion had a selection of warming drinks for the journey. During the early 19thC, a fashion for English crystal swept across Europe, and Bohemian glass factories lost no time in producing copies of the more popular styles. These imitations were made in SODA GLASS, and thus were often lighter than the originals, but the cutting is usually more ornate, in accordance with Bohemian taste. August BOHM – who is known to have worked at the STOURBRIDGE glass factories in England – is one of the most accomplished Bohemian glass engravers from the BIEDERMEIER period.

DECANTER, ENGLISH Made in the first two decades of the 18thC, the earliest English DECANTERS in LEAD CRYSTAL followed the style of contemporary

BOHEMIAN DECANTER with engraved roundels and strapwork, c.1890.

dark-green SEAL BOTTLES, and often had projecting rims at the top to attach corks on strings to be used as stoppers. Glass stoppers replaced the corks in the mid-18thC. Forms of decanter evolved rapidly throughout the 18thC, gradually becoming taller and more elegant until the 1770s and '80s. Often made in pairs, the "taper" decanter, named for its shape, was popular from the late 1760s. It was often left undecorated to show the colour of the wine and the brilliant clarity of the GLASS. The "Indian-club" shape, with a bulbous body, appeared in the 1770s. These decanters were usually engraved with floral motifs or fruiting vines. The ovoid shape and target stopper are characteristic of REGENCY decanters. In the 18th and early 19thC, decanters in BRISTOL GLASS were used for serving spirits, as their gilded labels – usually "rum", "brandy", and "hollands" (gin) – suggest. Blue is the colour most commonly found; amethyst decanters are more rare. Cutting is scarcely found on decanters made before the 1760s. In contrast to the restrained styles of English decanters from the first half of the 18thC, later GEORGIAN and VICTORIAN decanters feature greater use of cut, engraved, and mould-blown decoration, dictated by the fashion for richer ornament. In this period, deep-cutting on both English and Irish glass was fashionable, and the finest decanters were embellished all over with relief panels, or strawberry diamond-cut patterns, horizontal-cut bands, and vertical fluting. PILLAR-CUTTING was popular between 1820 and 1840. Decanter shapes became heavier, with wide and stout bodies and shorter necks. Coloured decanters became more popular from the 1830s, along with the fashion for hock and other German white wines. Mid-19thC decanters were produced in a broad range of styles, and are still widely available today. The lingering influence of heavy, Regency styles can be seen in the continued use of NECK RINGS and cutting – much less fashionable after the GREAT EXHIBITION – but the Victorian fascination with the past is evident in such features as spire-shaped stoppers inspired by the contemporary interest in medieval GOTHIC art. Decoration varied from engraved and acid-etched patterns to more complex, coloured OVERLAY, especially on the tall narrow decanters in the style of hock bottles. However, in the second half of the 19thC, there was a reaction against ornate decoration led by the critic John Ruskin (1819–1900), leading to the development of simpler, plainer forms. Between 1850 and 1900 the shaft-and-globe shape of decanter, with a long neck and rounded body, was popular. Engraving was the preferred form of decoration, and the overall effect is much lighter than earlier styles. By the late 19thC, decanters were produced as part of large, matching table services. Many elaborate services were made in England during the late 19thC for wealthy Americans. Manufacturers in STOURBRIDGE maintained their reputation as the leaders in the production of luxury glass decanters and other tableware, and were known for their use of ROCK CRYSTAL and INTAGLIO engraving on their best, top-of-the-range pieces. SILVER mounts, which were first used on CLARET JUGS in the 1860s, are also a distinctive feature of decanters made from the 1880s until the beginning of World War I in 1914. The Regency style was revived

Set of ENGLISH spirit DECANTERS in a plated frame, c.1880.

in the 1880s and the 1930s – a slightly clumsy form, and bright, rather than grey, tone of the glass will mark a decanter as a copy. Originals have more concave lines to the shoulders, are not rounded around the bases, and never feature "hat"-shaped stoppers. Copies from the 1930s can also be identified by neck rings that are moulded out of the body rather than made separately.

DECANTER, FRENCH The fashion for using DECANTERS to serve wine at the DINING-TABLE was adopted in France at the beginning of the 19thC. This trend coincided with the new enthusiasm in France for English LEAD CRYSTAL. Many French and Belgian glass factories employed itinerant English and Irish workers, and the decanters produced there were influenced by the Anglo-Irish styles, with their elegant forms and high-quality craftsmanship. Later in the century, the passion for all things English was followed by an essentially "French" style, with the emphasis on colour (usually blue), gilding, and, occasionally, enamelled decoration; those with ENAMELLING are rare. French decanters are considerably larger or smaller than their English counterparts; the latter commonly hold a standard measure of two imperial pints (just over one litre), while some French decanters can hold a magnum.

DECEPTION TABLE A small TABLE similar to a PEMBROKE TABLE but containing a secret compartment, which is revealed, on close inspection, by a flap hanging downward and outward.

DECOEUR, EMILE (1876–1953) French artist potter, specializing during the 1920s in relatively simple, plain STONEWARE.

DÉCOR À LA CORNE Design on mid-18thC French FAIENCE consisting of CORNUCOPIA, birds, flowers, and insects.

DÉCOR À LA GUIRLANDE Design on 18thC French FAIENCE (usually on plate rims) of garlands of flowers, often enclosing a mythological scene.

DÉCOR BOIS Often found on wares from the French NIDERVILLER factory, PORCELAIN decoration painted to simulate wood.

DÉCORCHEMENT, FRANÇOIS EMILE (1880–1971) French glassmaker, specializing in ART DECO vases and *objets d'art* in PÂTE-DE-VERRE. *See also* GLASS.

DEDHAM POTTERY In Dedham, Massachusetts, an American factory that made ART POTTERY from *c.*1900, with inspiration provided by Oriental CERAMICS and French art pottery. Hugh Robertson, the founder, developed a variety of decorative effects, including FLAMBÉ and "volcanic" glazes, and a dragon's-blood finish, as well as crackle glazes decorated with blue-and-white borders of various animals marching clockwise. They used a blue stamp reading "Dedham Pottery" above a rabbit enclosed in a square frame as a mark.

DEHUA An alternative spelling of Te Hua, the region in the southern Chinese province of Fukien. The area is famous for its BLANC-DE-CHINE white-glazed PORCELAIN.

DELANDER, DANIEL Active in the late 17th and early 18thC, a noted English, London-based, maker of CLOCKS.

DELFTWARE TIN-GLAZED EARTHENWARE made either in England (delftware, with a lower-case "d") or in Holland (Delft ware, with a capital "D"). English delftware is rarely marked, and can be confused with Dutch Delft ware, which is less valuable. *See also* DELFT WARE, DUTCH and DELFTWARE, ENGLISH.

DELFT WARE, DUTCH TIN-GLAZED EARTHENWARE, first produced in the Netherlands – mainly in the town of Delft – at the beginning of the 16thC by immigrant Italian potters. By the mid-17thC, as Dutch Delft POTTERY flourished, the brewing industry declined, and many potteries were set up in disused breweries, hence there are potteries with names such as The Three Barrels, The Two Ships, and The Claw. Approximately 33 factories flourished in the region around Delft, producing a wide range of ornamental and everyday objects. BLUE AND WHITE was the dominant palette, and the vast majority of wares were influenced by Chinese porcelain imported to Dutch ports. However, by the 17thC, the designs were based on Dutch landscapes. The Dutch Delft potters first produced GARNITURES in the 17thC, and they were prolific makers of tiles and plaques. Most pieces were painted in blue and white or polychrome, and price depends on the quality of decoration and detail. Unusual forms include tulips, pagodas, and cows. Dutch Delft bears a strong resemblance to English wares of a similar date. Dutch pieces may be identified by their ambitious forms and brush work, and by pinholes in a greyish body. They were also often marked. Condition can have an enormous bearing on price – because tin-glazed earthenware is soft, some chipping is to be expected, but more serious damage reduces value. Later copies of earlier styles often carry fake marks of famous factories such as APK and PAK, so these marks should not be relied upon for identification. *See also* DELFTWARE and DELFTWARE, ENGLISH.

DUTCH DELFT WARE **fluted dish, painted in polychrome, late 17th–18thC.**

DELFTWARE, ENGLISH TIN-GLAZED EARTHENWARE made in England from the mid-16th to the late-18thC. London, with factories in Southwark and Lambeth, was the most important early centre of English delftware, and after *c*.1650 centres were established in Bristol, Brislington, Liverpool, Glasgow, and Dublin. English delftware is characterized by its simple forms and colourful decoration, and primitive designs of figures, animals, and floral subjects, influenced by Chinese PORCELAIN. They were mainly painted in blue, white, yellow, green, and manganese. The "farmyard" series – plates decorated with various birds and domestic animals, including peacocks, cockerels, and hounds – is popular. Painted decoration became increasingly

Art pottery plaque in imitation of DELLA ROBBIA, by Hannah Jones of Birkenhead, c.1900.

sophisticated in the 18thC. Delicately painted landscape, with figures are typical of the mid-18thC, and can be seen on VASES, plates, dishes, and other wares. Among the most sought-after pieces are BLUE-DASH CHARGERS. Unusual and decorative forms to look out for include barbers' bowls, PUZZLE JUGS, POSSET JUGS, shoes, apothecaries' pill slabs, and flower bricks. Unlike most CERAMICS, prices for early delft are not too adversely affected by damage, because pieces are so scarce. Chips are acceptable. Although often dated, items are not usually marked. Blue-and-white pieces are common, but polychrome examples are also found, and are more valuable. English wares bare a resemblance to Dutch Delft of similar date. English delftware can be identified by a simpler form, fine body, and simple, painted, decoration work. *See also* DELFTWARE and DELFT WARE, DUTCH.

DELLA ROBBIA The Florentine Renaissance sculptor who invented the technique of applying vitreous GLAZE to TERRACOTTA. Some English ART POTTERY made at Birkenhead in the late 19thC imitates his work.

DEMI LUNE A half-round D-shape, commonly used for tabletops on CARD TABLES, particularly *c.*1780.

DE MORGAN, WILLIAM FREND (1839–1917) One of the most important British figures in the ARTS AND CRAFT MOVEMENT, de Morgan was employed as a designer by William MORRIS before he established a pottery works in London's Chelsea (1871) and, later, in Fulham (1888–1907). De Morgan specialized in producing tiles in a wide range of styles and patterns, many of which were produced for fireplace surrounds. His lustre wares (pottery with an iridescent surface produced using metallic pigments, usually silver or copper) were inspired by Islamic and Hispano-Moresque ceramics, and he was famed for his ruby lustre. A range of triple-lustre glazes known as "Moonlight" and "Sunset suite" are the most complex and valuable of all de Morgan's lustre wares. He also made distinctive "Persian" wares with stylized floral decoration, based on Turkish pottery designs. Full-masted galleons and stylized fish were favourite motifs. Among the leading decorators he employed were Fred and Charles Passenger and Joe Juster, all of whom frequently signed pieces with their initials rather than with the de Morgan mark. De Morgan's highly decorative wares can fetch high sums, according to size and choice of decoration. An impressed or painted mark with the name of the company is usually found on the pieces, frequently in conjunction with a motif such as an abbey, a tulip, or a rose. The motifs relate to the period and the location of the various factory sites established by de Morgan.

WILLIAM DE MORGAN, rare, covered vase decorated by Joe Juster, c.1888.

DENBY English STONEWARE made by BOURNE & SON, at Denby, Derbyshire, in the 19thC, and also known as Bourne POTTERY. The firm is known for its 20thC, utlitarian kitchen wares, especially the fireproof ranges.

D-ENDED TABLE An adaptable DINING-TABLE that comes in several sections. The "D"-shaped ends can be used as SIDE TABLES.

DENT HARDWARE CO. Founded in 1895 at Fullerton, Pennsylvania, an American manufacturer of CAST-IRON TOYS and hardware. The firm made an outstanding range of cast-iron toy vehicles in the 1920s and '30s.

DEP An abbreviation of the French *déposé* or the German *deponirt,* indicating a registered patent. Found on French and German DOLLS.

DEPRESSION GLASS Inexpensive, mechanically produced GLASS tableware with shallow glass patterns made in the USA in the 1930s and '40s. Many American glassmakers survived the depression of the 1930s by producing automatically PRESSED GLASS at prices to tempt even the poorest. Huge amounts of matching cheap tableware were made, and these are now collected for their historical value and contemporary look. Most of these pieces were manufactured in coloured or translucent glass, but some clear and opaque examples may also be found. Much depression glass is angular in style. As with any inexpensive pieces, good condition is essential.

DEPTHED Term used of CLOCK mechanisms mounted with the aid of a depthing tool, so that the wheels and pinions are correctly meshed and run true, hence making them more accurate and less susceptible to wear.

DERBEND A RUG from DAGHESTAN on the Caspian Sea.

DERBEND **rug, c.1910.**

DERBY PORCELAIN WORKS An important English PORCELAIN factory, founded in 1750, and known in its early days as "new Dresden", because it specialized in producing figures in the style of MEISSEN. Few wares survive from Derby's early years, because the paste used had a tendency to split. Judging by what has survived, Derby aimed for the upper echelons of the CERAMICS market: most pieces are elaborate, and would have been expensive. The factory is well known for its teaware, decorative VASES, and other ornamental pieces. Early designs are of fine quality and attract the highest prices, while later pieces are often less detailed, but still decorative. Derby's huge variety of figures reflects different styles, ranging from elaborately sculpted ROCOCO subjects to simply modelled, NEO-CLASSICAL figures. Derby's earliest figures are known as "dry-edge" figures because of the characteristic dry appearance of the edge of the base; many of these pieces were made in the white. Crisp, fine modelling is a feature of most early figures. White pieces are nearly always less valuable than similar-shaped, enamelled ones. In contrast to the stiffer style of the mid-18thC CLASSICAL figures, which had plain square bases in keeping with the taste for simplicity, late-18thC Classical subjects were treated in Rococo style, with elaborate pierced bases. They were intended for vitrines (display cases), so the backs were far less

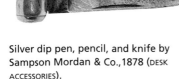

detailed, or left plain, than earlier examples, which were made to be viewed in the round. Derby took over the CHELSEA concern in 1769, and for a period it is difficult to distinguish between the products of the two firms, because similar models were used and the pastes can appear the same. Various marks were used in the early 1750–70 period. After the factory merged with Chelsea in 1770, marking was more consistent – usually crowned "D"s or crossed batons. Some of Derby's ornamental wares were copied by the French firm of SAMSON. *See also* ROYAL CROWN DERBY.

DERBYSHIRE CHAIR Another name for a YORKSHIRE CHAIR.

DERBYSHIRE POTTERIES A group of British potteries, including DENBY, in Derbyshire. Wares are similar to those made by the STAFFORDSHIRE POTTERIES.

DERRINGER Small, inexpensive, pocket pistol invented by Henry Deringer (with one "r") of Philadelphia, North America, *c.*1825, and produced in great quantity by many gunsmiths. Those made by Deringer's firm, stamped PHILADEL DERINGER on the lock plate, are eagerly sought after.

DESIGN AND INDUSTRIES ASSOCIATION The organization established in Britain in 1915 by Ambrose HEAL and others to promote high quality in mass-produced FURNITURE. It promoted simple but elegant designs, inspired by the ARTS AND CRAFTS work of Ernest GIMSON and the BARNSLEYS.

DESIGN REGISTRATION MARK *See* REGISTRATION MARK.

DESK A piece of WRITING FURNITURE generally comprising a base that includes DRAWERS, with a work area above. *See also* BUREAU, DAVENPORT, KNEEHOLE DESK, PEDESTAL DESK, ROLL-TOP DESK, and WRITING FURNITURE.

DESK ACCESSORIES A vast assortment of fine writing accessories, which offer limitless opportunities for assembling a varied, affordable collection. As sophisticated methods of communication developed from the late 18thC, including the establishment of the "penny" post and the use of envelopes, and as letter-writing and the keeping of journals came into vogue, the fashion for practical yet decorative desk furnishings resulted in the production of an abundance of writing equipment. The WRITING DESK of a Victorian gentleman or lady contained a variety of useful items, the most widely collected of which are PAPERWEIGHTS. Decorative INKSTANDS in SILVER, produced with matching accessories, and INKWELLS are also sought after. Pens, including dip pens, fountain pens, ballpoint pens, and pencils, which were produced in quantity, have become increasingly sought after among collectors since the mid-1980s. Portable writing sets intended for travel, such as penners, blotters, STAMP HOLDERS, letter openers, SEALS engraved with crests or monograms, brushes, and wipes for cleaning pens, paper knives,

Silver dip pen, pencil, and knife by Sampson Mordan & Co.,1878 (DESK ACCESSORIES).

and rulers are among the diverse, miscellaneous writing accessories available. Such pieces must be in good condition to retain their value. These items can be easily repaired and restored, and can therefore still be used and enjoyed today. *See also* PEN, DIP and PEN, FOUNTAIN.

DESK SET A writing set comprising an INKWELL, paper holder, dip pen, and desk seal, originally fitted in a lined case. *See also* PEN, DIP.

DESSERT STAND Used from the 17thC onward, a shallow SILVER dish on a short pedestal.

DE STIJL Dutch artistic movement founded *c*.1917 in reaction to ART NOUVEAU and associated with the abstract painter Piet Mondrian. De Stijl FURNITURE is decorated with bold, rectangular blocks in primary colours.

DEUDDARN (Deudarn) A Welsh variety of the PRESS CUPBOARD with two tiers. The full name is *cwpwrdd deuddarn*.

DEUTSCHE BLUMEN Meaning "German flowers", a term to describe realistically painted flowers, derived from prints and noted for their subtle shading and botanical accuracy. Used as a popular decorative motif on 18thC POTTERY and PORCELAIN by MEISSEN and other manufacturers.

DEVLIN, STUART Australian-born designer, based in London, England, since 1965. Made Goldsmith and Jeweller to Queen Elizabeth II in 1982.

DEVON POTTERIES A handful of small potteries that established in Devon, south west England, in the mid- to late 19thC, encouraged by the discovery of deposits of high-quality red clay suitable for making fine TERRACOTTA wares and a burgeoning tourist industry with a growing demand for souvenirs. In 1869 the Watcombe Terracotta Company began producing painted wares and unglazed terracotta pieces decorated with turquoise borders and glazed interiors. Their wares included religious subjects, portrait busts, and CLASSICAL subjects and figural groups. The Torquay Terracotta Company made figurative subjects, painted wares, and CERAMICS in the style of the AESTHETIC MOVEMENT, and these are among the most expensive Devon pottery pieces; the company also made unglazed terracotta figures in the late 19thC. Another South Devon pottery was Aller Vale, which made wares such as jugs and teapots decorated with incised mottoes, as well as now-obsolete items such as plaques for resting curling tongs. They used pixies as a decorative motif, which proved popular with tourists. The Aller Vale pottery was one of the most prolific of the Devon potteries, and it later merged with Watcombe. In North Devon, near Fremington, Edwin Beer Fishley produced pottery simply decorated with coloured SLIPS or incised designs. Another important pottery, located at Barnstaple, was C. H. Brannam, which became well known for its "ROYAL BARUM" WARE. The use of incised decoration with coloured slips is typical of the Brannam pottery. The company's reputation grew in the 1880s, when it began selling through LIBERTY in London; later pieces are more elaborately coloured and varied. Decorators include James Dewdney and William Leonard Baron; the latter eventually set up his own pottery in Barnstaple. The marks most commonly found on Devon pottery include: "Aller Vale" as an impressed name or incised hand-written signature; "Torquay Terracotta Co", either the initials or name in full; and "Watcombe", usually a printed mark.

DHURRI An Indian flat RUG without a PILE.

DIAGHILEV DANCER Popular motif in ART DECO statuary. A figure based on the revolutionary ballets choreographed by the Russian Sergei Diaghilev in the 1920s and '30s.

DIAGONAL BAROMETER An instrument with a tube set at a slant so that the mercury moves further than it would in a vertical column as pressure changes, enabling more accurate readings. Examples dating from the 18thC are often ornate.

DIAL The front plate of a CLOCK mechanism to which the CHAPTER RING is attached, or on which the numerals are painted. There are four main types of dial: brass; painted metal; painted wooden; and enamelled metal. Brass dials are the earliest type and were used on LANTERN CLOCKS, BRACKET CLOCKS, and LONGCASE CLOCKS, each with the hours engraved on a separate chapter ring. Painted metal dials can be found on most clocks after *c*.1800; they became more elaborate in the 19thC. Painted wooden dials are found on British dial clocks, TAVERN CLOCKS, and Continental European clocks. If authentic, the wood should show signs of cracking caused by temperature changes. Enamelled-metal dials are common on CARRIAGE CLOCKS and other types of French clocks. They are made out of enamel that has been fired on top of a thin copper sheet. Clocks with replaced dials are much less desirable than those with original ones.

DIAMOND-CUT GLASS that has been cut into facets in imitation of diamonds, or lozenge shapes.

Victorian drinking glass with DIAMOND-CUT ovals and one panel engraved with a spider's web and oak leaves.

DIAMOND-POINT ENGRAVING Line-drawing made on a GLASS surface using a stylus tipped with a tiny diamond nib or metal point. Designs comprising a series of dots rather than lines using this type of tool are called STIPPLE ENGRAVING. The technique was popularized by FAÇON-DE-VENISE glassmakers in the 16thC, and by Bohemian and Dutch craftsmen in the 17th and 18thC. It was also used in Britain in the late 16thC. It is less laborious and requires less skill than WHEEL ENGRAVING, so designs are rarely as detailed, and were sometimes executed freehand by talented amateurs rather than special engravers. The overall effect is much more linear than wheel engraving, and the incised areas are shallower. Because the use of styluses required only light pressure on the body of the glass, this method of engraving is suitable for brittle SODA GLASS.

DIAPER Surface decoration composed of repeated diamonds or squares, often carved in low relief.

DIE-CAST TOY First produced in France *c.*1910, a toy made by hollow casting. In Britain, DINKY TOYS, part of the MECCANO Co., dominated the market for die-cast toys from the 1930s to 1960s. In the 1950s, Mettoy's CORGI range began to grow, dominating the market by the 1960s and '70s. Complete sets of die-cast toys are desirable, especially when complete with the original packaging. Even a battered box can add to a toy's value.

Russian DIE-CAST Moscovich 412, *c.*1960s.

DIEPPER MODEL Made by sailors in the late 18thC, an IVORY (or sometimes wood) model ship, usually encased in a GLASS dome.

DIE-SINKING Method of making a metal object by hammering sheet metal into a mould to produce two identical halves, which are then soldered together. The hollow is often filled with lead or PEWTER.

DIE-STAMPING A method of decorating sheet SILVER or other SHEET METALS by pressing solid metal moulds together on either side of the sheet metal by means either of punches or drop hammers. The dies were originally made by craftsmen known as "die sinkers". With the advent of machine production in the late 18thC, the process became an especially fast and efficient way of reproducing a design or object. It was also an inexpensive technique, encouraging manufacturers to mass-produce whole objects such as toys, spoons and forks cost effectively, as well as elaborate decorative surfaces. Used extensively throughout the 19thC, die-stamping was also a favoured method for manufacturing handles and feet in SHEFFIELD PLATE. These components were stamped in halves, filled with lead, and then applied to the object. The metal is stretched through the die-stamping technique, so it may be thin and vulnerable to wear. Sometimes holes may be present, especially on objects featuring relief decoration.

DINGYAO Dating from the SUNG and YUAN DYNASTIES, Northern Chinese POTTERY characterized by carved or moulded floral decoration, covered with rich ivory-coloured GLAZES with pale-green or brown patches.

DINING ACCESSORIES Items made for the formal DINING-TABLE, which was the centre of social activity in the 17th and 18thC. Notable implements include meat skewers, which were first made in SILVER from the mid-18thC,

19thC, mahogany DINING CHAIR in Hepplewhite shield-back style.

when it was fashionable for the hostess to carve meat at the table; MARROW scoops for extracting marrow jelly from bones; GRAPE SCISSORS for selecting grapes from a bunch; EGG FRAMES for serving eggs; and TOAST RACKS. Dish rings, card holders, HONEY SKEPS, and STRAWBERRY DISHES are just some of the other items in this diverse range. When extensive, mechanized production was introduced in the 19thC, a great assortment of dining silver was made in vast quantities, making miscellaneous items such as these widely available to the collector today. *See also* CONDIMENT ACCESSORIES and DINNER SERVICES.

DINING-CHAIR From after 1700, one of a set of CHAIRS used specifically for sitting at a DINING-TABLE. Early-18thC WALNUT dining-chairs have restrained carving, and their elegant shapes make them pleasing to the eye. From the mid-18thC onward, fashions for seating were established by the patterns engraved in the books of the leading furniture designers such as Thomas CHIPPENDALE, George HEPPLEWHITE, and Thomas SHERATON, whose designs were widely copied. Hepplewhite's shield-back chair was one of his most popular designs, while Sheraton introduced square-backed chairs of light proportions. Decorative motifs drawn from CLASSICAL antiquity are characteristic of chairs made in late-18thC England, after designs by Hepplewhite. On such a chair look for detailed carving on the back SPLAT – a sign of quality – original STRETCHERS, and drop-in seats, which are easier to re-upholster than the fitted variety. A curved TOP RAIL and outswept back legs reflect the influence of ancient Greek seating, and can be found in chairs made between 1810 and 1840. Look for ones with circular, tapering, reeded legs, or outward curving SABRE LEGS; chairs of lesser quality have simpler legs. Sets of six chairs with two matching armchairs are desirable. Salon suites comprising six side chairs with matching SETTEES and ARMCHAIRS originated in Europe and were popular in England from *c*.1850 to 1910. It is rare to find these in sets of more than six, or with arms. BALLOON BACKS with CABRIOLE LEGS are more sought after than those with straight legs. WALNUT and ROSEWOOD, followed by MAHOGANY, are the most desirable woods; stained BEECH is less valuable. Chair seats became narrower at the end of the 19thC, as the demand grew for chairs that would fit into smaller rooms. Mahogany remained the wood that was commonly used for formal dining chairs, but walnut and rosewood were also used to produce quality sets. GILLOW – a leading 19thC furniture-maker – favoured OAK. Old decorative forms were interpreted in new ways in art nouveau CHAIRS made in the early 20thC. Tapering forms and elongated proportions are characteristic of the ART NOUVEAU style. Choose chairs from this period with sculptural and unusual designs, chairs more akin to a design by a well-known designer such as Charles Rennie MACKINTOSH, Charles VOYSEY, or Arthur MACKMURDO, and chairs with original upholstery (although this does not always add value). In England, the chair designs of Sheraton and Hepplewhite became fashionable again in the late 19thC. The proportions in later versions tend to be less generous than on early ones, with thinner arms, legs, and splats. STRINGING, popular in the Edwardian era (1901–1910), but rare in the 18thC, is found on better-quality chairs, often made of East Indian SATINWOOD. Look for ones with sturdy proportions – some have spindly appearances. There is nothing wrong with buying a reproduction of this period if you recognize it as such. On an original chair the wood will have a mellow hue with signs of wear, the splat will be attached by a separate shoe, the back leg will curve gently outward, the seat will have a generous width, and the chair will feel heavy when the seat is removed. On a reproduction there will be a dull, even tone, the splat will fit directly into the back rail, the back leg is often exaggeratedly outswept, and the frame will be made from light hardwood, so it will have a heavy seat to compensate. Dining-chairs are subjected to considerable wear and tear because they are sat on and moved around over the years. For this reason, it is important to take the condition of a set or individual chair into account before buying. To test the chair stand in front of it, gently put your knee on the seat and press the back – it should feel firm, with no "give". If you buy rickety chairs, have them re-glued before using them to avoid accidents. Armchairs from a set of dining-chairs should be wider than the matching side chairs, so be suspicious if they are the same width – an original armchair should be up to 5cm (2in) wider. Some side chairs have later arms added to make the set more valuable. Prices for dining-chairs are affected by quality and age, and by the number of chairs in the set – the larger the set the more expensive each chair becomes. *See also* PINE KITCHEN FURNITURE.

DINING-TABLE A table used at meal times. During the 16thC, the OAK stretcher table, or REFECTORY TABLE, was the most common type. Tables in the 17thC were made from planks, often held together with cleats. Look carefully on plank tops for unexplained marks (nail holes) that might indicate that the wood came from floorboards. Ingenious extending tables, including GATELEG TABLES and DROP-LEAF TABLES, were made by cabinet-makers in the REGENCY period, and, in the 19thC, Victorian manufacturers quickly capitalized on these earlier designs. The "Cumberland-action" table stored extra leaves and legs within a deep apron under the top. Robert Jupe, an innovative maker of FURNITURE, patented a capstan (rotating) circular extending table in 1836; when the top was twisted, the segmented top opened, allowing the extra pieces to slot in. Other dining-tables were extended with winding handles and telescopic sliders. Circular tables have become especially fashionable. The elaborateness of the supports can affect price; the best have heavily carved pedestals or legs. Make sure that the opening mechanism works well. Most 19thC dining-tables have tops made from solid MAHOGANY, some with veneered friezes (the band that supports the top); solid oak was a less common alternative. Veneered tops are often found on reproduction tables. On large tables the grain usually runs widthways. Look at the wood on the top – an attractively grained top is a definite plus, and will increase the price. Do not dismiss tables that have marked tops – if the wood has not been damaged it can probably be restored. Do not forget to sit down at the table to make sure it feels a comfortable height, and the legs do not get in the way of yours. Most measure a standard 74cm (29in) high. If the table is lower, it may have been reduced, and will be uncomfortable. If the frieze is deep, the table may be awkward for a tall person to sit at, especially if the overhang of the top is skimpy. Look for the following: signs of wear on the legs and top (scratches and marks are a sign of age and to be expected); legs of more or less the same colour (if one is noticeably different it might be a later replacement); and flaps that match the rest of the table (those used only occasionally may not have faded as much as the rest of the table, but their figuring should be similar). Sometimes there is a marriage of the top to a different base, so look carefully under the top for holes or colour changes that could indicate where a different base was once attached. Many of the classic tables designed in the 18th and early 19thC are still reproduced today. A copy made a few decades ago and subjected to some wear can mislead inexperienced collectors. Reproduction tables are smaller and lighter, and the PATINA of the wood lacks the depth and richness that you would expect to see on the genuine article.

DINKY TOYS Die-cast model cars and other vehicles produced by MECCANO. The first pocket-sized vehicles were issued in 1933, and marketed as "Modelled Miniatures" to go with accessories the firm was making for model railway sets. The diecast models became known as "Dinky toys" in April 1934. Products were made in sets or series. The 24 series of saloon cars, with a stylish design and attractive colours, typifies early Dinky toys. Pre-war production included a fine range of delivery vans in the 28 and 280 series. One of the most valuable Dinky toys is a "Bentalls" van, produced as a promotion for the department store of the same name. Other Dinky vans bore advertisements for products such as Hartley's jam and Bisto gravy. The transfers should be original and in good condition. Old models were re-issued after World War II, using an improved alloy that was less prone to fatigue, but the colours on the new versions were more drab. In 1947, Dinky introduced a "Supertoy" range of larger vehicles, and the 40 series of saloon cars. The latter each had their own range of colours such as grey, black, pale blue, green, and red – a model found in an unusual colour is desirable. The series' golden age was 1958–64, when new models were introduced, including commerical vehicles such as a BBC television van, and buses. Dinky Toys were taken over by Airfix in 1971. *See also* DIE-CAST TOYS.

Some pieces from a 19thC, Masons Patent Ironstone part DINNER SERVICE.

DINNER SERVICES The amount of items for the DINING-TABLE is vast, from the most basic of dining items such as PLATES and FLATWARE to elaborate dishes for serving food at the table. It includes magnificent CENTREPIECES designed as vehicles for show and sometimes made as presentation gifts, multi-purpose BASKETS and bowls, CRUETS and CONDIMENT ACCESSORIES, and an unclassifiable collection of miscellaneous items from meat skewers to menu-card holders. In the late 17thC, complete dinner services, which included matching plates, cutlery, and serving dishes, were introduced to Britain from France. By the mid-18thC, the custom of dining on a grand scale demanded large, luxurious dinner services, most of which consisted of six dozen meat plates, two dozen soup plates, and a variety of attendant serving dishes made en suite. Silver was a popular material for dinner services. In the early 19thC, many complete services were commissioned by wealthy families from such leading makers as Paul STORR, Benjamin Smith, and Philip RUNDELL. From the mid-19thC, increased mechanization meant that silver items could be mass-produced far more cost effectively than before, so a great amount of dining silver was produced at this time. It was common practice in the 19thC to alter plates by removing old borders, which were either worn or out of fashion, and applying new, more elaborate ones. Re-bordered plates are best avoided, because any alteration or later decoration reduces the value. *See also* DINING ACCESSORIES, SERVING DISH, SAUCEBOAT, and TUREEN.

DINNER WAGON A set of open rectangular shelves or trays-on-casters for transporting food into the dining-room. Also known as a "running footman".

DIORAMA Realistic scenes recreating famous battles using hand-painted toy soldiers on a fixed base.

DIPLOMATIC SWORD Worn to show rank, a SWORD with no cutting edge.

DIRECTOIRE (Directory) A style in France in the last decade of the 18thC. It used NEO-CLASSICAL motifs, but combined with forms based on bold curves.

DIRK The small, pointed DAGGER of a Scottish Highlander (carried strapped to the calf) or of a naval midshipman.

DISBROWE, NICHOLAS (1612/13–1683) The earliest-known American maker of FURNITURE, and one of the first settlers in Connecticut.

DISC BOX A MUSICAL BOX that used a disc instead of a cylinder to play music. They were popular, especially in the USA, from 1885 until superseded by the PHONOGRAPH. The Symphonion and Polyphon were marketed in Europe, while the Regina was sold in the USA. Collectors look for rarity, technical innovation, and the availability of discs for playing on a model. Pieces attracting high prices include coin-operated boxes, multiple-disc players, automatic disc changers, and orchestrations with percussion and bells.

Regina-style DISC BOX, No.33245, Rahway, New Jersey, 1898.

DISC JOINT A joint made of discs of cardboard held in place by a metal pin. Used to articulate SOFT TOYS and TEDDY BEARS.

DISHED Term used to describe the shallow depressions in GAMES TABLES used for holding counters or money. Also known as "guinea pockets".

DISH-HILT Saucer-shaped sword guard introduced *c.*1625.

DISH RING Sometimes erroneously called a "potato" ring, a ring used to raise a hot dish off the surface of a polished wooden table – an Irish speciality from the mid-18thC. The finest versions were pierced and embossed with ROCOCO ornament of birds, farm animals, rustic figures, foliage, architecture, and sometimes an engraved coat-of-arms. Many dish rings were made in the early 20thC, but these are less sought after than their 18thC counterparts. Most dish rings are fitted with blue-glass liners, which also enable the piece to be used to hold fruit or flowers. Examples made in Ireland in the 18thC, and provincial Irish examples (even later ones) are valuable.

DISNEYANA Any toy or other memorabilia associated with the characters and films of Walt Disney. The earliest toys from the 1930s representing Disney characters, including "Mickey Mouse", were produced by German toy manufacturers such as Distler. The most sought-after Disney toys include "Mickey and Minnie on a motorcyle" by TIPP & CO., "Mickey the Musical Mouse" by Nifty, "Mickey the Drummer" by Nifty, and "Donald Duck" with a long bill. A toy made under special licence is more desirable than an unauthorized version. Films by Walt Disney have also led to the production of a wealth of SOFT TOYS. The most desirable of these include the friends of Christopher Robin in the stories of WINNIE-THE-POOH by A.A. Milne. "Pooh Bear" is the favourite, but "Piglet" and "Eeyore" are also sought after.

DISPLAY CABINET A CUPBOARD with large glazed panels. CABINETS designed specifically for displaying objects only became common in the latter part of the 19thC – cabinets made in the 18thC were probably intended as BOOKCASES. Simple, heavy glazing bars are typical of the early 18thC. When purchasing, keep in mind that glazing bars with hexagonal, wavy, or arched designs are more sought after and add more value than those of a simple, rectangular configuration. CROSSBANDING on a display cabinet is often thought to be a later feature, but it was popular on provincial pieces made in Scotland and the north of England *c.*1800. Mirror backs, which enabled the viewer to see both sides of the object being displayed and also increased the light in the room, were popular on display cabinets made from *c.*1850 onward. ART NOUVEAU cabinets were mass-produced in the 1920s; however, they are becoming difficult to find in good original condition, and are probably sound investments for the future. Many Continental European and 20thC English display cabinets include panels of SERPENTINE glass, but, before investing in one, make sure that none of the glass panels is chipped, as this can be expensive to replace.

Advertising papier-mâché DISPLAY PIECE figure, *c.*1910.

DISPLAY PIECES Advertising figures made of stout card or (more rarely) metal or plaster. Tobacco-store Indians, Highlanders, and negros are among the earliest and most collectable examples.

DISPLAY TABLE A small TABLE with a hinged GLASS top, used to display precious ornaments. Known in France as a VITRINE. Many were made in the late 19th and early 20thC. Decorative woods – usually veneered and then sometimes painted – were used. Display tables with an elegant shape and CABRIOLE LEGS reflect quality. Check that there are no chips or cracks in the glass, because this could be expensive to replace. Attractive decoration – whether painted, gilt metal, MARQUETRY, or GILTWOOD – is desirable.

DISTRESSED A term used to describe FURNITURE in need of obvious repair.

DISTRESSING The deliberate superficial damaging of FURNITURE in order to make it appear aged. Possibly carried out by a faker.

DIXON, JAMES & SONS British, Sheffield-based, SILVER firm established in 1806 and known as James Dixon & Sons from 1835. They produced CANDLESTICKS in the style of the ARTS AND CRAFTS MOVEMENT in the early 20thC. Their wares are marked "J.D&S" with numerals representing pattern numbers, and in some cases a trumpet trademark.

DOBUTSU Japanese name for objects carved in the shape of real animals, as opposed to mythical ones (KAIBUTSU).

DOCCIA In Florence, Italy, a mid-18thC PORCELAIN factory producing white and painted figures and MAIOLICA. *See also* PORCELAIN, ITALIAN.

DOCKYARD MODEL Perfect, scaled-down model of a ship, produced as a prototype by dockyards from the late 17th to the late 19thC.

DOG LOCK On a FLINTLOCK, a type of safety-catch, so-called because the head of the lever holding the flint resembled a dog's head.

DOGNOSE SPOON Derived from the TREFID SPOON in the early 18thC but no longer cleft, so that the terminal is one continuous TREFOIL shape, with a pronounced central lobe. Said to resemble the head and snout of a hound.

DOG OF FO A mythical Chinese animal, resembling a lion-spaniel, the guardian spirit of the temple of Buddha (Fo).

DOGWOOD Whitish-yellow wood used in INLAY and MARQUETRY in the 18thC.

DOLL A child's toy that imitates the human form. Most dolls are categorized by the material from which the head is made (often different from that of the body), such as wood, WAX, PARIAN, BISQUE, and COMPOSITION. The earliest dolls were carved from wood, and were made in forest regions throughout Europe in the 17thC. The important WOODEN DOLLS date from the 18thC,

DOCCIA **teapot and cover, c.1770.**

All-bisque Kewpie DOLL, with shield label: "Kewpie Germany", c.1915.

when they were well carved and dressed. The 19thC marked a vast expansion in the doll trade, as other materials replaced wood. PAPIER-MÂCHÉ was widely used as an inexpensive alternative, and POURED WAX, WAX-OVER-COMPOSITION and wax-over-papier-mâché were good substitutes, as were china and parian. These led to the enormous boom in French doll manufacturing, first with the FASHION DOLLS. In the second half of the 19thC new bisque-headed dolls were made to look realistic. Elaborate construction allowed them to adopt numerous poses, and their wardrobes were lavish. They were outdone only by the French BÉBÉ, pioneered by dollmaker Pierre François JUMEAU. It is often difficult to distinguish between a bébé and a French FASHION DOLL, except for the length of their similarly extravagant dresses. German dollmakers, whose supremacy had been ousted in the 19thC by the French, began producing quality pieces at lower prices. By the 1890s, huge numbers of German bisque dolls were flooding the market, sparking the French factories to establish the S.F.B.J. By the end of the 19thC, demand was growing for more realistic-looking dolls. KÄMMER & REINHARDT were the first to make a character baby, the KAISER BABY, which looked too unattractive to be popular. However, lifelike CHARACTER DOLLS were produced by Germany's top manufacturers until 1930, most notably J.D. KESTNER, Armand MARSEILLE, SIMON & HALBIG, and Gebrüder HEUBACH. Bisque versions of two American, cartoon-inspired dolls, GOOGLY DOLLS and KEWPIE DOLLS, were made in huge quantities in the 1920s for the American market. Meanwhile, the creation of the GOLLIWOG also sparked a demand for FABRIC DOLLS and RAG DOLLS. STEIFF were among the major makers, along with LENCI, who made designer dolls. New materials such as CELLULOID, followed by plastic and VINYL, offered great potential – and the American makers took the lead during World War II. BARBIE, the American VINYL DOLL created in 1959, is the most successful doll ever made. Among the most valuable dolls are carved, wooden examples made in Britain in the 18thC and French bisque-head dolls made during the 19thC. Doll head types include: SHOULDER-HEAD, OPEN HEAD, SOCKET HEAD, SWIVEL HEAD, and SOLID-DOMED HEAD. Some dolls were of the FLANGE NECK type. Because many dolls' heads are hand-painted, examine the attention to detail, the artistry of the expression, and also the skill in shading. Painted eyes were used on dolls made from all materials. INTAGLIO EYES were a development of painted eyes; other types of eyes include FIXED EYES, PAPERWEIGHT EYES, SLEEPING EYES, FLIRTY EYES, and GOOGLY EYES. The earliest dolls had closed mouths. Open-closed mouths with the lips slightly apart but the paste uncut appear on early BISQUE dolls made by BRU, and on German characters. An open mouth with teeth was first used in c.1900. "WATERMELON" or closed, smiling mouths drawn as thin lines added to the charm of "Googlies" and "Kewpies". Today, closed-mouthed dolls are more sought after than those with open mouths. Some early WOODEN DOLLS had carved ears, although many had none. Most French fashion and some better-quality German dolls had pierced ears and earrings. Ceramic dolls usually had ears moulded with the head, and some larger bébés had applied ears. The body of a doll is all-important in assessing origin, history, and value, and the range is enormous. Bisque, shoulder-headed, fashion dolls often had gusseted KID bodies with wide hips and shoulders to suit period dress. Forearms were sometimes bisque, and TENON JOINTS were used at the shoulders, elbows, and knees. Early French bébés with bisque heads and jointed bodies had their limb parts connected by means of a ball, which was fixed to one of the limbs. Some bisque-head dolls have eight ball-jointed or floating-ball-jointed bodies. In 1833, an American patented the NE PLUS ULTRA body with a bisque shoulder-head, composition or leather arms, and jointed knees and elbows. On this piece, the body, unusually, forms part of the thigh. Five-piece, bent-limb composition bodies were used on various babies and characters between 1910 and 1939. From 1920, German composition bodies were made with FLAPPER LEGS, with the knee joints set higher than on earlier dolls. A knowledge of different body types is thus invaluable in identifying a particular doll and in spotting "wrong" replaced limbs. Carefully fashioned hands and feet often give a clue as to quality, although they are probably the most likely parts to have been replaced. Most dolls had painted or moulded-and-painted hair until the mid-19thC, when wigs of human hair and MOHAIR were common. Hairstyles can provide valuable clues to dating on parian and CHINA DOLLS; wigs on other dolls may have been replaced. The more elaborate the hairstyle, the more valuable the doll. Hats, feathers, snoods, jewellery, plaits, colour, and lustre, all moulded and fired, add extra value. Similarly with painted hair, the more decorative or appropriate to the character, the better. Real hair or mohair wigs are of less consequence because they have often been damaged by combing and handling. Synthetic, rooted hair suffers too, but good condition matters to the value. In Barbie's case, an original hairstyle is an important bonus. The less restoration a doll undergoes the better. Bad restoration can cause irreversible damage and reduce the value. Clothes may add to the value of any doll. Some had elaborate wardrobes, and those in their original costumes command a premium. Outfits and hairstyles that reflect the fashions at the time of production are particularly collectable. However, do not ignore badly dressed or even naked dolls – just buy it a new outfit. If a doll and its outfits came in an original box or trunk, retain the packaging, even if it is slightly damaged, because it will add to the value. Newer dolls made from hard plastic and vinyl must be in an excellent condition to be collectable. *See also* BISQUE DOLL, CELLULOID DOLL, and IVORY DOLL.

DOLL, CARE OF The care of a doll is mainly dependent on the materials from which it is made. Clean BISQUE heads by washing them with cotton wool dipped in pure soap and water. It is vital to keep the water away from the eyes, because it can remove or loosen eyelashes and even the eyes themselves. COMPOSITION bodies should not be washed, because this will damage varnish and cause loss of colour and shine. The heads on CHINA DOLLS and PARIAN DOLLS can be washed with a damp cloth. KID or leather

Late-19thC wax doll with a cloth body.

bodies cannot be cleaned and are better left alone, although leaking sawdust can be patched with old kid gloves. Dolls with damaged cloth bodies can be patched using old fabric. Never try to wash a WOODEN DOLL, because this will remove the protective GESSO and varnish. Wax dolls and also WAX-OVER-COMPOSITION DOLLS and PAPIER-MÂCHÉ DOLLS require some specialist restoration. Although they are often cracked, these cracks are best left alone. POURED-WAX DOLLS can be restored, but there are only a few specialists in this field. Fabric dolls are difficult to clean, and even "washable" types should not be washed, as this could ruin them. Bodies can be carefully patched and re-stitched, and moth holes, which are common on felt dolls, can be mended. If the face of a fabric doll is damaged, it is better left alone – you may damage it further by attempting restoration. Never break into an unopened packet with a doll or doll's clothes because doing so could halve their value. Treat wigs carefully. They often seem sparse, but where there is enough hair it should be teased out. A hat or bonnet can disguise stringy hair. Early fashion dolls with original hair should not be tampered with, but replacement wigs made from mohair or real hair are available for German and French child dolls. Keep the original wigs and clothing you replace, and label them for future reference. SLEEPING EYES that are not working can be reset by an expert, and teeth can be replaced. Fingers on COMPOSITION bodies often need to be replaced, and this should not detract from the doll's value.

DOLL ACCESSORIES The production of items for DOLLS was such a large industry that there was a whole range of accessory manufacturers working in the Passage Choiseul area of Paris, France, including doll milliners, cobblers, corsetmakers, and glovemakers. Specialist shops sold miniature fans, jewellery, underwear, and a host of other minute objects, while various publications such as *La Poupée Modèle* advised girls on the latest doll fashions, and included patterns for making clothes at home. FASHION DOLLS came equipped with trunks full of other outfits and accessories, and if the trunks and their contents are still with the doll, they add hugely to its value. Dolls' wardrobes are sometimes sold separately, so if you have a doll without its original clothes, it may be worth hunting for period replacements. A relatively small outlay on the right garments can increase a doll's value. Trunks of tiny clothes need special care. Watch out for moths, and layer clothes with acid-free tissue.

DOMINICK & HAFF American, New York-based firm of silversmiths, established in 1872 by Blanchard Dominick and Leroy Haff. Produced VINAIGRETTES and other small items, and high-quality silver-plated wares.

DON WARES EARTHENWARE, and occasionally BONE CHINA, with painted decoration produced in Yorkshire, northern England in the 19thC.

DONYATT English, Somerset, maker of yellow-glazed SLIPWARE in the 17thC.

Victorian, silver-lidded, cut-glass biscuit jar by DOMINICK & HAFF, 1899.

DOOLITTLE, ISAAC American, Connecticut, clockmaker, active 1742–90.

DORFLINGER, CHRISTIAN (1828–1915) The founder of the Greenpoint Glassworks, established in 1860 in Brooklyn, New York, as well as two other GLASS firms. The German-born glassworker introduced European advances in cutting techniques and the making of LEAD CRYSTAL to his American firms.

DORMANT Another name for a TRESTLE.

DOROTHEENTHAL Founded in the early 18thC, a German FAIENCE factory that produced brightly coloured wares decorated with leaves and STRAPWORK.

DORST, JULIUS Active at Sonneburg from 1865 to the early 20thC, a German maker of wooden DOLLS.

DORUYE Reversible CARPET with a different design on each face.

DOS-À-DOS Meaning "back-to-back" in French and used of a CERAMIC group in which two identical figures face in opposite directions.

DOSSER Old term for the headboard of a BED.

DOT MEISSEN PORCELAIN made by MEISSEN in the late 18thC, marked with a dot between crossed swords. The late 18thC is generally considered to be the period in which much of the finest Meissen was produced.

DOUBLE ACTION A FIREARM that may either be cocked manually, or automatically (self-cocking), when the trigger is depressed.

DOUBLE "D" A moulding in the form of one capital "D" above another one.

DOUBLE-OGEE BOWL Bowl of a DRINKING GLASS with two S-curves, one large one above another. Found on pre-19thC CHAMPAGNE GLASSES.

DOUBLER Made from the 17thC, a PEWTER bowl with a wide, slanted rim.

DOUBLE WEDDING RING A pieced block design making a pattern of interlocking circles across the surface of a QUILT.

DOUCAI Chinese for "contrasting colour", enamel decoration introduced under the reign of the MING Emperor Chenghua (1465–87).

Shallow, 18thC, Chinese soup plate decorated in DOUCAI style.

DOULTON English pottery established in Lambeth, London, in 1815, to produce household wares, and one of the most prolific and innovative manufacturers of the 19th and 20thC. Doulton's success was due to the

Marks on the base of a DOULTON Jadeware figure of cockatoos, showing "HN" (for Harry Nixon) and "Noke" (for C.J. Noke), 1920s.

entrepreneurial spirit of Henry Doulton, who took over the running of the company in 1854. The factory produced utilitarian STONEWARE, such as water filters until 1862, when decorative items designed by students from the nearby Lambeth School of Art began to be produced. Over the following decades, Doulton established a line in decorated stoneware, and employed numerous designers, including the BARLOW SISTERS in the 1870s. In 1882, Doulton took over a second factory in Burslem, STAFFORDSHIRE, where PORCELAIN and earthenware tablewares were produced. The factory became "ROYAL DOULTON" in 1901, and the Burslem factory is still in production; the Lambeth factory closed in 1956. Doulton's stoneware was influenced by 16th and 17thC designs and often features incised or applied and hand-carved decoration. Motifs such as BEADED borders are typical, as is a restrained palette in shades of blue and brown. Another popular method of decoration was known as CHINÉ MANNER, which was patented for Doulton. Chinese ceramics were the inspiration behind Royal Doulton's "Song" ware, which came in a choice of subjects, such as exotic birds and indifferent colours. A number of Doulton's designers became prominent: George Tinworth specialized in speciality modelling, religious plaques, and groups of frogs and mice, as well as imp musicians; his work is marked with "GT" and "Doulton". Hannah Barlow was known for her incised decoration and animal subjects, with deer a recurring theme in her work; she used "BHB" and "Doulton" to mark her work. Florence Barlow produced incised bird subjects, and used "FEB" and "Doulton" to mark her designs. Frank Butler was known for bold shapes, decorated with natural forms; his work is marked with "FAB" and "Doulton". Harry Nixon was responsible for "Song", "Chang", and FLAMBÉ wares. He generally placed his mark "H Nixon" on the side of a piece. Mark V. Marshall, who also worked with the MARTIN BROTHERS, is known for well-modelled stoneware, and he marked his pieces with "MVM". Eliza Simmance produced high-quality, ART NOUVEAU designs, and used a simple "ES" to mark her pieces. Doulton is also renowned for its figures. Although a few were made at the end of the 19th C by C.J. Noke, the vast majority were produced in the Burslem factory at some time between the 1920s and the present day. These are popular with collectors in both Britain and the USA, and they were produced in an enormous range of subjects. Figures are identifiable thanks to the marks and names on their bases. Each bears a series number and the prefix "HN". The factory records are also helpful, because they state how long every design was produced. Pretty ladies in elegant dresses became one of the firm's specialities, as did bathing belles, figures in historic dress, animals, dancers, jesters, and street vendors. Value depends on the rarity of the model and on the subject, and rare colour variations also command a premium. One of the more elaborately decorated Doulton figures is the "Modern Piper" (1925–38). Based on the *Pied Piper of Hamelin*, the piece is marked "HN 756". It commands a high value, which reflects the decorative appeal of the subject, and the fact that the design was made for a relatively short time. Lesley

Harradine designed the rare and sought-after figure entitled "Scotties", marked "HN 1281" and made between1928 and 1938. A naked figure entitled "The Bather" was produced in the 1920s and '30s in several versions. In the 1930s, a similar figure was introduced, dressed in a swimming costume, and the clothed figure is more valuable than the naked one. Another of Doulton's most successful 20thC products, CHARACTER JUGS continue the tradition of TOBY JUGS of the 18th and 19thC, and were produced in huge quantities from the late 1930s onward. Character jugs were often made in four different sizes ranging from large, small, and miniature, to tiny. Subjects include famous personalities of the past and present. Dick Turpin, Old King Cole, Winston Churchill, and Francis Drake have been represented in this way. The handles of Doulton character jugs are often modelled to reflect the subject. For example, the "Gondolier" (1964–69) has a handle modelled as a Venetian gondola. Rarity rather than date has the biggest impact on value. The "Alfred Hitchcock" character jug is recent in date (1995), but an example with a pink shower curtain handle (a feature from the film *Psycho*) is rare and more valuable than later, more common versions with blue curtains. As with figures, jugs are marked and well documented. They are invariably named on the piece, they often also bear the initials of the artist, plus the full factory mark (generally impressed, printed, or painted), a date showing when the design was introduced, and a "D" series number.

Rare, Royal DOULTON, character jug of Francis Drake, No.D6115, 1940–1.

DOUNE PISTOL Decorative pistol without a trigger guard and made in the 18thC in the town of the same name in Scotland. They were standard issue to soldiers of the Black Watch infantry regiment. *See also* FIREARMO.

DOUTER Scissorlike implement for snuffing out a candle flame. *See also* SNUFFERO.

DOVETAIL JOINT Often found on the corner of DRAWERS, the triangular joint that slots together. From the early 18thC, joints were dovetailed and glued. The earliest drawers have three coarse dovetails; later drawers usually have four or five finer ones. By *c.*1700, influenced by Dutch craftsmen, dovetails became finer and more sophisticated. As the 18thC progressed, dovetails on top-quality pieces became finer still, while on country pieces of a similar date they may be relatively crude. By the 20thC, with the spread of electricity, the more sophisticated workshops were using machinery to produce dovetails. Machine-cut dovetails are easy to identify because the prongs are the same size as the insets, and because there is never a scribing line – on hand-cut dovetails, a line made by the cabinet-maker along the outer side of the drawer that marked the depth to which he had to cut.

DOWEL Small, round, wooden peg used to hold early MORTISE AND TENON joints in place. Also known as a "trennell" (treenail).

DOZAR A CARPET of two ZARS in length, ie. about 1.8m (6ft).

DRAGON CARPET Old Caucasian CARPET decorated with heraldic dragons.

DRAGON-LUNG (Dragon-loang) Male dragon symbol on a Chinese CARPET.

DRAKE FOOT Another name for DUCK FOOT.

DRAM CUP Two-handled SILVER cup. Smaller than, but similar to, a PORRINGER.

DRAM GLASS A short-stemmed GLASS for strong liquor. It has a small bowl on a heavy foot.

DRAWER Originally known as a TILL, a lidless box within a framework from which it can be drawn. Early drawers were crudely made, often nailed together with a groove on each side to allow the drawer to slide. Until the 18thC, they ran on runners set into the carcass. Some drawers ran on the dust boards and had no runners. From the Queen Anne period (1702–14) the runners were placed under the drawer at the sides and ran on bearers placed on the inside of the carcass. From c.1790, drawers were strengthened by baseboards running from side to side with a central rib. When looking at any piece with drawers, always pull each one out and examine the DOVETAIL JOINTS. Check drawers inside and out for marks, such as holes or the outline of an old HANDLE shape, where different handles might once have been fixed. Original handles can help date a piece. *See also* FURNITURE.

DRAWER STOP Fixed within a carcass, a small block of wood that mates with another block on the underside of a drawer to prevent the latter from being pushed in too far.

DRAW-LEAF TABLE Another name for a WITHDRAWING TABLE.

DRAWN-TRUMPET BOWL The most common BOWL shape found on 18thC, plain-stem DRINKING GLASSES. The bowl and stem were made from the same GATHER of GLASS, while the foot was added separately. Glasses with other bowl shapes were made in three parts. If there is a heavy-folded foot, the glass was made before the 1745 Excise Act, when a tax was imposed on glassmakers.

Green DRAWN-TRUMPET-BOWL **wine glass, c.1790.**

DREAM BABY First made in 1924, the most popular Armand MARSEILLE baby doll. "Dream Babies" were produced in vast quantities, from life-size to very small, but quality varies. Those with open mouths are marked "351"; those with closed mouths, "341". Some have soft, stuffed bodies with a squeaker, plus soft, thickly stuffed legs, and COMPOSITION hands. Others have five-piece, bent-limb, composition bodies. A closed mouth, bent-limb composition body, and small size is preferable. Avoid ruddy, orange BISQUE. Some soft-bodied Dream Babies have celluloid hands, and, if damaged, they are impossible to restore. The value is reduced, if the body has been replaced.

DRESDEN POTTERY AND PORCELAIN An important centre of FAIENCE production, noted for large jars and pots. During the 19th and early 20thC, the area surrounding the city of Dresden became a major German centre of PORCELAIN manufacture, with numerous factories producing ornamental and tea and dinner services in the style of MEISSEN and SÈVRES. Carl Thieme was one of the major makers in the area. Dresden porcelain is available at a range of prices, depending on the size, subject, and decorative appeal of a piece.

DRESSEL, CUNO & OTTO The oldest-known German dollmaking firm, founded in 1700. It became Cuno & Otto Dressel in 1873, until its closure in 1945. The company had several factories in the Sonneberg area, and began making heads for BISQUE DOLLS in the 1870s, although it also bought heads from other firms. Dressel also produced COMPOSITION DOLLS and WAX DOLLS.

DRESSER A piece of FURNITURE on which food was dressed. Some appear as a sideboard-type base and are known as LOW DRESSERS, while others have a rack, or superstructure of shelves above, and are called HIGH DRESSERS. Dressers were made from the 17thC onward, and could be found in the dining-rooms and kitchens of more modest homes throughout the 19thC. As with most COUNTRY FURNITURE, styles changed little over time, but were influenced by the region where the dresser was made, hence it is often easier to tell the place of origin of a dresser than the date of manufacture. Dressers vary in price according to the style; those made from simple pine during the 19thC, or later, are most likely to be affordable; early ones, especially those made of OAK, are more expensive. Early (i.e. those made pre-c.1800) dressers have some recognizable features, including: simple, joined construction; rather crude construction; and at least three DRAWERS across the base – if there are two the piece may have been reduced in size. Not all dressers had racks, so beware of pieces where there is a MARRIAGE of a base and rack that did not originally belong together. Compare the colour and PATINA of wood on both parts – the colour of rack and base should be similar to that of the dresser. Make sure that the outline of the rack on the base also matches the rack.

DRESSER, DR CHRISTOPHER (1834–1904) An English POTTERY and GLASS designer inspired by Japanese art and the AESTHETIC MOVEMENT. He worked for TIFFANY as well as the pottery firms of Ault, Linthorpe, and PILKINGTON. Probably one of the most influential designers of the Victorian period (1837–1901), Dresser was a modern industrial designer who stressed function, economy of materials, and minimal decoration, which served mainly to strengthen a piece. Practical points, such as an insulated finial and handles on a soup tureen to make it easier to use without burning the hands, formed the cornerstone of Dresser's design ethos of simplicity and purity of form. His designs are usually stamped with his name or monogram, and often include a REGISTRATION MARK.

DRESSING MIRROR *See* DRESSING-TABLE MIRROR.

Ault propeller vase by CHRISTOPHER DRESSER, c.1930s.

Victorian, rosewood toilet box containing DRESSING-TABLE ACCESSORIES, 1870s.

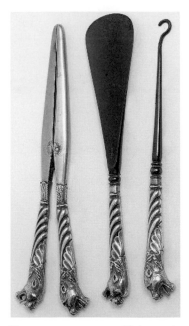

Silver DRESSING-TABLE SET, with leopard-head handles: glove stretcher, shoe horn, and button hook, c.1930.

DRESSING-TABLE A small TABLE with compartments to store ladies' and gentlemen's toiletry accessories in the bedroom or dressing-room. Dressing-tables of the 18thC or earlier are rare. Early examples were covered with rich tablecloths, on which DRESSING-TABLE ACCESSORIES could be arranged. Many of them are multi-purpose, and include writing slides and deep drawers that held washbasins, which can make even a plain table more valuable. A gallery along the top of a plain table suggests that it was used as a dressing-table, even if it does not have a MIRROR. To make tables of this kind into more saleable desks, superstructures such as mirrors and galleries are sometimes removed, and their tops are lined in leather. Plugged holes are evidence of this type of alteration. Prices for early-20thC FURNITURE can be modest, and well-designed pieces with labels from well-known retailers such as LIBERTY or HEAL & SON are probably good investments for the future. *See also* DUCHESSO.

DRESSING-TABLE ACCESSORIES Toiletry items kept at the dressing-table. The status of the lady of the house was often reflected by SILVER made to adorn the dressing-table – essential articles include toilet boxes for powders, soaps, and lotions, bottles for perfume and cologne, comb and hairbrush sets, clothes brushes, and tiny boxes for pills and patches. These pieces were produced in silver and SILVER GILT, sometimes with enamelled decoration or featuring exotic materials such as TORTOISESHELL and MOTHER-OF-PEARL. By the 19thC, silver accessories were made in sets. Also designed to adorn the dressing-table, silver frames for MIRRORS and pictures are enduringly collectable, largely, as with much dressing-table silver, because many of them can still be used and enjoyed. Made in a range of eye-catching styles, toilet mirrors, heart-shaped mirrors, and double picture frames are especially sought after by collectors. *See also* BOXES, DECORATIVE; DRESSING-TABLE SET; GENTLEMEN'S TOILETRY; PATCH BOX; and SCENT BOTTLE.

DRESSING-TABLE MIRROR A MIRROR on a stand, intended to sit on CHESTS-OF-DRAWERS and on DRESSING-TABLES. Shield-shaped mirrors are typical of the late 18thC designs of Thomas SHERATON and George HEPPLEWHITE.

DRESSING-TABLE SET SILVER or SILVER-GILT accessories made together as a set for the DRESSING-TABLE. Initially the preserve of the privileged, for whom fine examples with ornate chased, engraved, or embossed ornament were produced, by *c.*1830, dressing-table sets were also made in simpler forms, aimed at a wider clientele and considered the zenith of gentility by the rising middle classes. The essential accessories of a dressing-table set were a hand mirror and hairbrushes, backed with silver, but perfume bottles or flasks with silver mounts, clothes brushes, combs, shoehorns, button hooks, and even boudoir timepieces were often also included. Larger sets may also have contained eye-baths, jewel caskets, pomade jars, and drinking cups, and some elaborate examples featured secret compartments. From the late 19thC, sets were also produced for men, typically with elegant, simply decorated silver accessories, such as flasks to hold cologne. By the 1830s, these sets were sometimes fitted in lockable wooden travelling cases, intended specifically for use on the road. Travelling cases usually came with outer canvas covers to protect the exotic wood or leather from wear and tear. Dressing-table silver by a celebrated maker such as Bernard Instone commands a high price. These sets are made of high-quality, heavy-gauge silver, and show close attention to detail, for example through the use of elaborate decoration. It is important to check that all the pieces in a set are by the same maker and that they match. Prices vary according to the number of items in a set, the extent of the decoration, and the condition. Watch out for damage to the enamel, and check that an engraved monogram has not been removed, leaving the silver thin. Sets in good condition, fitted in pretty lined boxes, will be the most highly priced.

DRGN Emblem of the German Toy Federation and the mark found on early German, mass-produced toy locomotives and other items from *c.*1890.

DRINKING GLASS Drinking vessels made from GLASS since at least ancient Roman times – mould-blown conical beakers with relief decoration from the late 1stC AD were excavated at Pompeii and Herculaneum, in Italy. In the Middle Ages, designs became more varied, especially on vessels made in German-speaking areas, and were often decorated with PRUNTS and TRAILING. Venetian goblets from the 16th and 17thC, with FILIGRANA and LATTICINIO bowls or tooled "wings" of coloured glass ornamenting the stem, are among the most sophisticated produced. Before the late 17thC, few drinking glasses were produced in England; instead, most domestic glass was imported from the Netherlands and Venice. With the development of LEAD CRYSTAL by George Ravenscroft in 1675, English styles of drinking glass began to emerge. During the 18thC, large numbers of drinking glasses were made in many different styles. Bowls of 18thC drinking glasses are small, owing to the potency of alcoholic drinks of the time. Value depends on the rarity of the decoration, as well as the shape of the bowl, stem, and foot. The decoration, such as air and opaque twists and faceting, focused on the stem, which often had a KNOP or a series of knops, made by compressing the hot glass rod of the stem during manufacture. Some glasses have domed feet, a feature that is characteristic of many early glasses, while others have conical feet. In the 19thC, demand for complete table services resulted in the development of different shapes of drinking glass for red and white wine, champagne, dessert wines, and liqueurs, often made in matching sets. Bowl shapes include round funnel, bucket, wasted bucket, conical, bell, ogee, and trumpet. Greater use was made of colouring, engraving, and etching to produce a variety of designs. Check the edge of the rim for unevenness, as this may mean a chip has been ground down. Signs of age include: a conical or funnel bowl; a foot that is wider than the rim; flaws in the glass; a slightly irregular body indicating that the piece was handmade; a bumpy PONTIL

18thC wine glass, with ogee bowl, and opaque-twist stem with swollen centre knop (DRINKING GLASS).

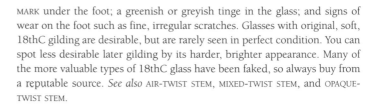

MARK under the foot; a greenish or greyish tinge in the glass; and signs of wear on the foot such as fine, irregular scratches. Glasses with original, soft, 18thC gilding are desirable, but are rarely seen in perfect condition. You can spot less desirable later gilding by its harder, brighter appearance. Many of the more valuable types of 18thC glass have been faked, so always buy from a reputable source. *See also* AIR-TWIST STEM, MIXED-TWIST STEM, and OPAQUE-TWIST STEM.

DRINKING GLASS, AMERICAN Often inspired by European luxury tableware, a broad variety of TUMBLERS, GOBLETS, and other drinking vessels in unusual coloured and OPALESCENT GLASS, as well as fine cut and engraved glasses, was manufactured in North America during the 19th and early 20thC. American pieces were originally made from FLINT GLASS – a perfect medium for pressed glass – and although flint (lead) was not used from the 19thC, the name remained. The majority of American glasses that survive today are made from non-flint (non-lead) material, creating a lighter and less brilliant finish than those made with flint. Matching drinking glasses formed part of a larger table service, or were produced in pairs or sets with DECANTERS and JUGS as wedding gifts or presentation pieces. Forms are similar to styles made in Europe, but the range of colours and decorative motifs is distinctively American. The rapid expansion in the production of PRESSED GLASS in the USA in the first half of the 19thC resulted in a plethora of named patterns, often used by several manufacturers. Pressed glass can be identified by the smooth interior, whereas on mould-blown glass the pattern on the exterior can be discerned on the inside. Opalescent glass was often used for pressed-glass wares in the USA, from the 1830s onward.

DRINKING GLASS, BELGIAN *See* DRINKING GLASS, DUTCH.

DRINKING GLASS, BOHEMIAN An important glassmaking centre from the 15thC, Bohemia, the area adjoining Bavaria and Silesia, now part of the Czech Republic, pioneered the formula for a colourless, easy-to-cut GLASS, which incorporated lime derived from chalk or limestone. By the late 16thC, the use of this lime glass, which facilitated the perfection of WHEEL ENGRAVING, had spread to other glass centres on the European continent. The making of engraved glass has traditionally been a Bohemian speciality, with vessels sculpturally cut in relief or engraved in INTAGLIO, or a combination of both. Popular subjects for engraving on early Bohemian glass include coats-of-arms, portraits of princes, the ages of man, the seasons, Classical mythology, and courtly life. From the end of the 17thC, Bohemian salesmen carried their products around the world. Their glassware was decorated to order, because the salesmen were also skilled engravers who filled the demand for this coveted commodity on the spot. Bohemian glass produced during the early 19thC was technically some of the best ever made. There was an enormous amount of experimentation in colours and types of glass, as well as great

Ruby BOHEMIAN DRINKING GLASS, with engraved panels revealed in amber, c.1870.

skill in the decoration. Much of the glass was never intended to be used, but made as cabinet pieces designed to show off the wealth and taste of the owner. Enamelled wares from the early 19thC feature landscapes, floral designs, and portraits. During the BIEDERMEIER period in the mid-19thC, many glassmaking factories were established throughout Bohemia. The emerging middle class preferred a lighter, more intimate style, and the Biedermeier glassmakers answered this demand with the use of finely detailed decoration and subtle new colours. FLASHING, if it incorporated a contrasting colour, could be cut through to produce a pattern that is not unlike the CAMEO GLASS made by the ancient Romans. This technique was popular with the Bohemian glassmakers of the Biedermeier period. In the 1830s, the Bohemian glassmaker Josef Riedel created glass with a yellow colour by adding uranium to the batch. Toward the mid-19thC, skill in design and decoration overtook taste to some extent, and a number of the items became over elaborate; however, even today these pieces have their admirers. A large wine set would comprise a JUG or DECANTER and six, eight, or more wineglasses (possibly of differing colours). By the early 20thC, glassware made in Bohemia had developed into an interesting and highly innovative product, surpassing the fine quality but lacklustre style of the early 19thC. Spearheaded by the FAÇON-DE-VENISE factory of J. & L. LOBMEYR, many new styles were produced, beginning with the BAROQUE revival and spanning the influential periods of ART NOUVEAU (or JUGENDSTIL) to ART DECO. Many glasshouses were opened in Bohemia between 1900 and the 1920s. Among the most prominent and successful of these factories were those at Haida and Karlsbad, where the glassmaker Ludwig MOSER (1833–1916) made glass portraits in the style of Dominik BIEMANN, who had worked during the first half of the 19thC. Traditional Bohemian designs continued to be produced into the 20thC, but the copies hardly matched the elegant proportions of the originals, and the workmanship rarely equalled the superb quality found in early Bohemian glassware. Scrolling arabesque foliage and geometric ornamentation can sometimes be found on Bohemian glassware produced for export to the Ottoman Empire.

DRINKING GLASS, DUTCH Quality GLASS made in the Netherlands for several hundred years, which reflects a variety of imported styles that were often improved upon. By the early 17thC, there was a sizeable group of emigrant Venetian glassmakers working in the region. Antwerp, in particular, attracted many of the finest Venetian workmen. At first, they produced high-quality copies of popular VENETIAN GLASS, but a style loosely based on the Venetian style began to emerge, known as FAÇON DE VENISE (in the Venetian manner). Vessels were often made of thin SODA GLASS, and decorated with FILIGRANA or ornate embellishments such as "winged" glasses. The most accomplished of early *façon-de-Venise* pieces are often difficult to distinguish from original Venetian work. The flute form is a shape typically found in the Netherlands. By the late 17thC, the powerful glassmaking influence of Venice

Dutch DRINKING (wine) GLASS with round funnel bowl, and red and white bands over white gauze, c.1755–75.

Rare ENGLISH DRINKING (wine) GLASS, with pan-topped bowl and a central air-twist cable encircled by twin opaque white threads, c.1760.

had begun to wane. English glass began to be imported into the Netherlands in the early years of the 18thC, and Dutch glass produced from this period emulates popular English styles, with knopped stems and AIR-TWIST STEMS and enamel-twist designs. While glassmakers from the Netherlands did not excel in the design of GLASS itself, they were masters at engraving it. In this part of the world the art of DIAMOND-POINT ENGRAVING was advanced, and it developed more swiftly there than in other countries. Diamond-point engraving was supplanted at the end of the 17thC by WHEEL ENGRAVING, which was fashionable in the glass centres of Bohemia and Silesia. Because its superior refractive power and soft nature was well-suited for work on the wheel, English LEAD CRYSTAL was often favoured by Dutch engravers. Glasses may have been made in England and engraved in the Netherlands, but it is now thought possible that they are all Dutch. By the mid-18thC, the technique of STIPPLE ENGRAVING with the diamond point was adopted; this rendered variations of light and shade with great delicacy. Glasses were engraved with popular subjects to celebrate marriages, friendship, battles, leisure pursuits, and politics. *See also* NEWCASTLE GLASS.

DRINKING GLASS, ENGLISH With the development of LEAD CRYSTAL by George Ravenscroft in 1675 (before most glass was imported from the Netherlands and Venice), distinctively English styles of DRINKING GLASS began to emerge, the earliest of which is the BALUSTER style. The familiar elements of modern wineglasses – bowl, STEM, and foot – evolved, as seen in the great variety of English drinking glasses made in lead crystal from the 18thC. Among the most recognizable is the JACOBITE GLASS. With the accession of the German Elector George of Hanover as King George I of England in 1714, new Continental European styles were introduced into English glass. On drinking glasses, a distinctive mould-blown stem with a hollow centre – originating in Silesia – was popular for a relatively short period (c.1710–30). Like baluster glasses, Silesian-stemmed glasses were rarely decorated. Glasses with plain stems first appeared in England c.1720, and were produced throughout the 18thC; they were much less expensive than earlier baluster- or Silesian-stem pieces, so they were more affordable for the middle-class market. Glasses with plain stems were intended for everyday domestic use, and thus the quality of decoration is often poorer than that found on more expensive glasses with elaborate stems. Engravings of flowers and fruiting vines – reflecting the use of the glass for wine – are common subjects on plain-stem glasses. In 1745, the British government introduced an Excise Act levying a heavy tax on glassmakers. Thereafter, producers attempted to reduce the overall weight of their wares, and features such as folded feet and KNOPS became less common. The AIR-TWIST STEM developed as a way of making drinking glasses lighter while still maintaining a decorative element. The Excise Act of 1745 taxed only clear, lead-crystal glass, so from the 1760s to the 1780s glassmakers began to use opaque white or coloured glass as a form of decoration on the stems of glasses that would minimize the amount of tax paid. Few OPAQUE-TWIST STEMS were made after 1777, when an Excise Act raised a tax on coloured glass. The faceted stem – in which glass was cut away from the stem in decorative patterns to reduce its weight – was developed as an alternative. With the introduction of the REGENCY style, the fashion for heavier, more solid forms brought about a dramatic change in the style of English drinking glasses in the late18th and early 19thC. The bowls of glasses became much wider and larger, and the stems shorter, while bowls rather than stems became the main focus of decoration. The type of drinking glass most associated with this period and style is the RUMMER, a large-bowled drinking GOBLET. In the 1820s and '30s the fashion for heavy, all-over cutting in deep relief on drinking glasses began to decline, and simpler, broad-flute cutting became popular. This form of decoration was much less expensive and labour-intensive than deep-relief cutting, reflecting the new wider market for reasonably priced and practical glass tableware among the growing middle classes. Different forms of drinking glass were developed for white wine, champagne, red wine, and liqueurs. In 1845, the punitive Excise Tax on glass was repealed, and British glass manufacturers experimented with new techniques and innovative designs. High-quality cased glass and flashed glass in the Bohemian style, for example, was produced by the leading manufacturers George BACCHUS and W.H., B. & J. Richardson, both of Birmingham, J.F. Christy of London, and STEVENS & WILLIAMS of STOURBRIDGE, one of the main English, glassmaking centres. The new fashion for drinking glasses that combined coloured bowls with clear stems replaced the earlier "BRISTOL" glass examples, which were made entirely in one colour. Such glasses were probably made for white wines. Green and "cranberry" are the most common colours, while amethyst, yellow, and blue are more rare. Engraved and etched Victorian drinking glasses are representative of the new fashion for lighter decoration, in the mid- to late 19thC, replacing the heavier, more solid styles that were popular in the early part of that century. With the fashion for high-quality, engraved tableware during the mid-19thC, a number of Bohemian master engravers came to work for English glass manufacturers. Among the leading exponents were Paul Oppitz, who worked for W.T. Copeland in London, and Frederick Kny and William Fritsche, who were employed by Thomas WEBB of Stourbridge and specialized in rock-crystal engraving.

DRINKING GLASS, GERMAN

GLASS has been made continuously in the Rhine district since the days of the Roman Empire, and the tradition spread to central Europe during the Middle Ages. Glassmaking centres were established in the wooded forests and mountainous regions dividing Bohemia from Bavaria, Saxony, and Silesia. These areas had easy access to the necessary raw materials, such as wood for fuel, and minerals for the manufacture of the GLASS itself. Early German glass should not be confused with the high-quality glass produced in southern Germany or Bohemia. The early glass is of a type known as WALDGLAS or "forest glass", and is coloured

GERMAN **gilded pewter champagne glass by Orvit, c.1905.**

One of a pair of late-19thC VENETIAN goblets in blue, white, and aventurine, with moulded hollow knops.

in various shades of pale green, with occasional touches of clear or dark blue. The shapes and types of these early German glass vessels are fairly primitive, but nonetheless distinctive. Popular forms, such as the ROEMER, have even survived to the present day. By the 14thC, the German glassmaking industry had really begun to develop. Nuremberg was a significant centre for glassware decoration from the 16thC onward, specializing in enamelling in SCHWARZLOT and shallow WHEEL ENGRAVING. Many of the most accomplished glass cutters had originally practised their art engraving rock crystal and gemstones. HUMPEN were among the most distinctive items of enamelled glassware produced in 17thC Germany. Potsdam was another area famed for decorated glass. Although later German DRINKING GLASSES tend to follow earlier, established forms, they also reflect a variety of recent technical advances that had been made and, owing to this, are usually made of new materials. The most important innovation of this period was the SPA GLASS. Traditional vessels, such as Roemer and Humpen, continued to be produced, although they were frequently painted with spurious dates and crests. The union of the individual German states into one country in the late 19thC encouraged a desire to reinvent German history. This trend gave birth to the highly popular HISTORISMUS GLASS, made in large quantities. The new fashion for coloured and enamelled glass eventually led to a decline in the glass-cutting industry.

DRINKING GLASS, VENETIAN From the beginning of the 16thC, GLASS made in Venice, Italy, where lightness and elegance of form were highly prized in glassware, set the standard for glassmakers in the whole of Europe. Owing to Venice's superior trading position, its authoritarian government, and its guild structure, early VENETIAN GLASS (1500–1800) was widely exported, although the secrets of its production were jealously guarded. The Venetian glassmaking industry was based on the island of MURANO in order to limit the risk of fire on the mainland, and the fine CRISTALLO GLASS made there, along with coloured glass and highly prized vessels emulating precious stones, such as onyx, agate, and CHALCEDONY, was the envy of Europe. The fragility and thinness of Venetian glass made wheel-cutting and WHEEL ENGRAVING virtually impossible. DRINKING GLASSES with moulded LION-MASK stems were common products of both Venice and FAÇON DE VENISE glasshouses throughout Europe. As the attribute of St Mark and the symbol of the city of Venice, the lion mask was a popular decorative motif for Venetian glassware, ornamenting hollow-blown stems or moulded in relief on PRUNTS. By the late 17thC, the supremacy of the Venetian glass industry had begun to decline, largely through the extreme fragility of the glass and its increasing role as a merely decorative novelty. While the popular taste for artistically decorated glassware continued to grow, the overall demand was for a more serviceable and robust type of glass, which was much more successfully produced by the competitive glassworks in both England and Bohemia. By the mid-18thC, the status of the celebrated Venetian glassmaking industry had suffered a dramatic decline. Yet, with the end of the Austrian occupation in 1866, the reputation of Venice as an important glass centre was restored, as makers rediscovered the decorative techniques and intricate Venetian patterns of glass recipes from the 16thC. A key figure in this revival was Antonio Salviati, who established the VENICE AND MURANO GLASS CO., which produced mainly tableware based on Venetian glass styles from the 16th and 17thC.

DRINKING VESSEL, SILVER Drinking vessels in SILVER have always been made in large numbers. Over the centuries their basic design has changed little, and in general they do not feature the elaborate decoration seen on more prestigious dining plate. Among the earliest drinking vessels are BEAKERS, with only a few surviving from the 15thC. TANKARDS date from the mid-16thC, and are mostly plain, although some 19thC Victorian examples are elaborately decorated in revival styles. GOBLETS were also made from the mid-16thC. MUGS, which are one handled but lidless, date from the mid-17thC. PORRINGERS are two-handled vessels made in the late 17thC. Cups are difficult to define, as presentation cups and drinking vessels made for special occasions are often given the name regardless of their forms. In theory a cup has two or more handles, but this is disproved by the most basic form – the TUMBLER CUP – and by the elaborate cups designed for wagers. In the 18thC, when tea and coffee were more popularly drunk than beer, many mugs and tankards were given as christening presents. Today drinking vessels are popularly collected, although heavy use has left many damaged, which makes it vital to look for pieces without wear or damage, such as split rims or cracked handles.

SILVER DRINKING VESSEL: **a George IV christening mug, the body chased with matted fluting, 1826.**

DRINKS TABLE Used for serving drinks, a small TABLE usually dating from the late Victorian and Edwardian periods (c.1860 to 1910). It was popular in more affluent households because it could be moved about easily from room to room and locked away from thirsty servants. On some examples there are compartments that open to reveal a selection of DRINKING GLASSES and DECANTERS in a locking TANTALUS.

DRINKS TROLLEY Used for serving drinks, a trolley usually dating from c.1890 to 1910. It would have been perfect for wheeling drinks into the garden. Look for one with a top that is a removable, glass-lined tray, and with glass shelves below. Glass is more practical than wood in the event of a spillage.

D.R.M.R. (Deutsches Reichsgebrauchsmunster) The German term for the official governmental roll of registered patents.

DROP The short, blunt support that links the handle to the bowl of a spoon. A later development of the RAT TAIL.

DROP HANDLE A hanging, tear-drop-shaped brass HANDLE, either solid or hollow, and attached to the DRAWER by SNAPES. Commonly seen on late-17th and early-18thC FURNITURE.

Sicilian, maiolica, wet DRUG JAR, 1708.

DROP-IN SEAT An upholstered seat supported within the frame of a CHAIR, but not attached to it.

DROP-LEAF TABLE An early-18thC refinement of the GATELEG TABLE, a table with "leaves" or ends that can be raised to extend the table, or lowered to be put away when not in use. The table has four legs – two fixed to opposite corners of the central panel and two that hinge out to support the side flaps. Elegant CABRIOLE LEGS and simple PAD FEET are typical of this style of table. By the mid-19thC, a much smaller version with deep rectangular flaps – known as a SUTHERLAND TABLE – had become popular. Most drop-leaf tables can seat no more than six people comfortably, so their relatively small size makes them suitable for dining-rooms in today's smaller houses – and hence desirable. Always check the flaps and hinges, which might be made from wooden rule joints or from metal, for damage. The flaps are quite heavy, and it is easy for the hinges to break, causing the flaps to drop and split. Look for tabletops that are solid rather than those with a VENEER. The grain of the wood on the flaps and the centre should run parallel to the hinges. Drop-leaf tables dating from the 18thC are usually MAHOGANY. Country drop-leaves are found in OAK, ELM, or FRUITWOOD.

DRUG JAR A TIN-GLAZED EARTHENWARE vessel made for storing drugs. They are divided into two main types: one has a spout and was meant to hold wet drugs; the other, with a straighter form and no spout, and known as an ALBARELLO, was for dry drugs. They were made both for display and storage, and often had colourful decoration. Jars with blue decoration on white backgrounds can be dated by the design around the CARTOUCHE. Angel designs were common from 1650 to 1700, birds from 1700 to 1780, and cherubs thereafter. All early examples are collectable.

DRUM CLOCK A type of early portable CLOCK that was made in the shape of a drum or cannister, with the dial and movement arranged horizontally, rather than vertically.

DRUM TABLE First made c.1800, a type of circular TABLE with a central pedestal support and a frieze that contains DRAWERS. It is also known as a CAPSTAN TABLE.

DRUNKARD'S PATH Pieced block design in a QUILT, in which curved patches are joined to form a pattern of staggered waves. It was possibly named by women of the Temperance Movement, for whom it was a favourite pattern when made in the blue-and-white colours that were emblematic of the Movement.

DRY EDGE An unglazed area found on a ceramic vessel, such as along the rim of a piece.

DRY-PLATE CAMERA A mechanical device for making photographs, invented by George EASTMAN in 1879 and produced even after the roll camera was invented in 1888. It was usually constructed by cabinet-makers from MAHOGANY and BRASS.

DUBLIN DELFTWARE Made by the Irish Delft Ware Manufactory, mid-18thC, TIN-GLAZED EARTHENWARE with blue or purplish decoration.

DUCHÉ American POTTERY produced by the Duché family in Philadelphia, Charleston, and Savannah during the early 18thC. They principally made STONEWARE and REDWARE, but also produced some PORCELAIN.

DUCHESNE CLOCK Early-18thC musical CLOCKS made in England by the French clockmaker Claude Duchesne.

DUCHESS A term used to describe a type of large DRESSING-TABLE that was manufactured in the Victorian period (1837–1901) with a variety of DRAWERS, a raised and mirrored back, and a footboard.

DUCHESSE A type of long seat formed out of two BERGÈRE chairs facing each other and joined by a STOOL in the middle. It became popular in France during the reign of Louis XV. A "Duchesse brisée" is a duchesse "broken" in two sections; others come in three sections with stools. Copies were made in large numbers c.1900.

DUCK FOOT The American term for a three-toed CLUB FOOT, which is found particularly in FURNITURE from the Delaware region. It is also known as a DRAKE FOOT and WEB FOOT.

DUCK'S EGG PORCELAIN with a delicate, translucent, bluey-green colour produced briefly in the early 19thC at SWANSEA, in Wales.

DUDSON English EARTHENWARE decorated with inlaid mosaic, made by James Dudson, in Hanley, Staffordshire, in the late 19thC.

DUELLING PISTOLS Known from the mid-17thC onward, pistols made in matched pairs of exactly the same weight and balance for settling disputes. FLINTLOCK pistols were superseded by faster PERCUSSION-LOCK pistols in the early 19thC. Boxed pairs with all their accoutrements are highly prized.

DUESBURY English PORCELAIN decorated in the studio of William Duesbury (1725–86), especially the products of the CHELSEA FACTORY and the DERBY PORCELAIN WORKS, which he co-founded.

DUET STOOL Piano stool for two people. Used when playing a duet.

19thC, flintock DUELLING PISTOL by Rosser, with diamond-carved walnut stock.

Irish, mahogany, three-tier DUMB
WAITER with hoof feet, c.1790.

DUFRÈNE, MAURICE (1876–1925) French designer of ART NOUVEAU book bindings, FURNITURE, JEWELLERY, textiles, and wallpaper. Toward the end of his career, he became a leading exponent of Modernist design based on industrial materials.

DUMB WAITER A type of DINING-ROOM stand produced with either two or three circular, revolving trays. Some examples are particularly elaborate, with special compartments for bottles, plates, and other objects associated with the dining-room. Made from *c*.1750 onward, dumb waiters were used for displaying food when the servants had been dismissed and the gentlemen tucked into their port.

DUMMY BOARD A painted, two-dimensional, cut-out figure or animal. They were possibly originally made as FIRESCREENS, but were eventually used chiefly for decorative purposes.

DUMMY DRAWER A false DRAWER front that looks like a drawer.

DUMP Heavy GLASS object, such as a PAPERWEIGHT or door stopper. Often dome-shaped and decorated with air bubbles.

DUNAND, JEAN (1877–1942) Swiss sculptor who first produced beaten metal vases in the ART NOUVEAU style, before adapting his designs to the more geometric shapes of ART DECO.

DUNLAP, JOHN (1746–92) Based in New Hampshire, an American craftsman who made plain FURNITURE using MAPLE. He worked with his brother Samuel Dunlap (1752–1830), and their more celebrated pieces incorporate elaborate CABRIOLE LEGS, aprons, and SCROLLS. If similar furniture from New Hampshire cannot be attributed to a craftsman, it may be referred to as "Dunlap School".

DU PACQUIER PORCELAIN from the VIENNA FACTORY, especially CHINOISERIE wares produced in the early 18thC.

DURLACH Late 18thC FAIENCE made in Germany, especially CHINOISERIE wares decorated with celadon-green, orange, and cobalt blue.

DUSSACK Medieval short-sword with a straight, single-edged blade.

DUST BOARD A board found between DRAWERS as part of the carcass in some CHESTS OF DRAWERS.

DUST CHAMFER The CHAMFERRED bottom edge of a panel frame enabling dust to be more easily cleaned away.

DUST MOULD (1) The MOULDING that is applied to cover the gap where two doors meet.

DUST MOULD (2) A strip of quarter-round moulding found along the inside lengths of a DRAWER. Introduced in the early 19thC.

DUTCH DELFTWARE *See* DELFT WARE, DUTCH.

DUTCH DROP A type of DROP HANDLE similarly shaped to the head of an axe.

DUTCH PEG DOLL Type of crudely carved WOODEN DOLL. The term "Dutch" probably stems from "Deutsch" (meaning "German"), because they were chiefly made in Germany and Austria. *See also* GRÖDNERTAL DOLL.

DUTCH STRIKE A CLOCK that gives advance warning by striking the next hour half an hour before on a smaller bell with a higher note. Such a feature is common on German as well as Dutch clocks.

DUTY DODGER A HALLMARK removed from a small piece of assayed SILVER and applied to another, larger piece. In the 18thC, and especially after 1720 when duty on silver was increased, the practice was widespread in Britain. It involved transposing hallmarks from damaged or redundant pieces of silver, particularly those from the late 17thC, into newly made items of silver to avoid paying the high duty, or tax, that had been levied on wrought plate. High-quality, small pieces of silver were also sent to the assay office for marking, dodgers then removed the marks and inserted them into unassayed larger objects, which could mean considerable savings, as the duty payable was determined partly by weight. *See also* ASSAY MARK.

DUTY MARK A mark found on SILVER. To help offset the staggering costs of the American War of Independence (1775–83), increased duty was imposed on British silver. A new mark, featuring the monarch's head in profile within an ESCUTCHEON, was introduced in 1784 as proof that duty had been paid to the government at the time of assay. The heads of successive reigning sovereigns appeared on English silver until the duty was abolished in 1890. *See also* HALLMARK.

DWERRIHOUSE & CARTER Based in London and active in the early 19thC, English makers of CLOCKS with SHERATON- and EMPIRE-style cases.

D.W.T. Abbreviation for "penny weight" – the smallest weight in the TROY system of weighing GOLD, SILVER, and PRECIOUS STONES.

DYOTTVILLE Early-19thC GLASS made in Philadelphia by the American firm of Thomas W. Dyott and decorated with masonic and patriotic emblems.

E

EAMES, CHARLES (1907–78) American FURNITURE designer who used moulded plywood to form chairs in streamline form. Most of his furniture was made by the American firm Herman Miller; some of his designs such as a lounge chair (design "670") and ottoman (design "671"), first made in 1956, are still produced today.

EARNSHAW, THOMAS (1749–1829) An English maker of CLOCKS and WATCHES, he developed the spring-detent ESCAPEMENT, and simplified the production of the CHRONOMETER, so that it could be made commercially.

EARTHENWARE Clay objects fired at a temperature of less than 2200°F (1200°C). The BODY is porous unless covered with a GLAZE, and it may be white, buff, brown, red, or grey, depending on the clay.

EAST, EDWARD English clockmaker, active in London in the mid-17thC.

EASTERN HAN Period in Chinese history, AD 25–220, in which POTTERY and STONEWARE were produced. Tomb figures of servants and buildings were typical.

EASTLAKE, CHARLES LOCKE (1836–1906) Designer and exponent of "modern GOTHIC", involving a return to old values and simpler shapes. His book *Hints on Household Taste* (1868) was influential both in Britain and the USA, giving rise to the so-called "Eastlake style".

EAST LIVERPOOL A 19thC EARTHENWARE factory in Ohio. One of the first to develop ROCKINGHAM WARE in the USA.

EASTMAN, GEORGE (1854–92) An American manufacturer of CAMERAS and founder of the Eastman Kodak Co. in 1892. He developed the dry-plate process, and produced the popular "Box Brownie", launched in 1900.

EASY CHAIR An American CHAIR, like a BERGÈRE, made *c*.1820-1840. It has rounded TOP RAILS of wood that continue down the arms to form hand holds.

ÉBÉNISTE French term for a cabinet-maker. Used since the 17thC, when EBONY was employed as a VENEER.

EBERLEIN, JOHANN FRIEDRICH (1696–1749) A German sculptor at MEISSEN between 1735 and 1749. His works include CLASSICAL and allegorical figures.

EAMES chair for Herman Miller, in oak-faced plywood, designed in 1945 and manufactured between 1949 and 1958.

EBONIZED Wood stained and painted black to resemble EBONY.

EBONY A dense, almost-black, fine-grained wood from tropical climates, ebony (*Diospyros*) was used as a contrasting INLAY in MARQUETRY on CABINETS and MIRRORS in the 17thC, and favoured in the REGENCY period. Its black tone was copied in English and French, EBONIZED (*bois-noircie*), 19thC pieces.

ECKENFÖRDE Short-lived FAIENCE factory in Schleswig-Holstein, Germany. Founded in the mid-18thC, it was renowned for its lively decoration.

ÉCUELLE A 17thC SILVER (or sometimes CERAMIC) vessel for serving soup. It has a shallow, two-handled circular bowl, a domed cover, and often a stand.

EDEN TOY INC. An American toy firm noted for a number of character animals, including PADDINGTON BEAR and Beatrix Potter's PETER RABBIT.

EDGED WEAPON *See* SWORD AND OTHER EDGED WEAPONS.

EDICT OF NANTES *See* HUGUENOT.

EDO The era in Japanese history from 1615 to 1867, when Tokyo (Edo) was the capital of the country. The arts flourished during this period, notably PORCELAIN from 1661 to 1673 and LACQUERING and NETSUKE from 1716 to 1736.

EDWARDIAN Pieces made during the reign of Edward VII (1901–10).

EDWARDS GLASS GLASS manufactured by the father and son, both Benjamin Edwards, in Belfast, Northern Ireland, in the late 18th and early 19thC.

EDWARDS STONEWARE Products of the Dale Hall pottery, founded at Burslem, Staffordshire, England, in the mid-19thC.

EFFANBEE TOY CO. *See* SKIPPY.

EGERMANN, FRIEDRICH (1777–1864) The Bohemian glassmaker who patented LITHYALIN GLASS, and found new ways to stain glass red and yellow.

EGGEBRECHT FAIENCE produced by MEISSEN in the late 17thC.

EGG FRAME A CRUET for serving eggs at the table from the early 18thC until *c.*1900. Egg frames have detachable cups and spoons, often decorated with PARCEL GILDING to protect the SILVER from staining caused by the sulphur in eggs. Some versions had SALT-CELLARS. In the early 19thC, individual frames were made combining one or two egg cups with salt and pepper pots and a small toast rack.

Charles X, giltwood, French brometer with an EGLOMISÉ-painted dial, c.1825.

EGGSHELL PORCELAIN Thin, tough PORCELAIN with a MOTHER-OF-PEARL lustre made at BELLEEK, but also by STAFFORDSHIRE POTTERIES, in the late 19thC.

EGLOMISÉ Painting on GLASS on CLOCK faces. The reverse side of the glass is covered in GOLD or SILVER leaf, which is then engraved and painted black.

EGYPTIAN BLACKWARE Alternative name for BASALTES.

EIGHT-DAY MOVEMENT On a CLOCK, a movement that runs for eight days.

EISEROT *See* SCHWARZLOT.

ELASTOLIN German manufacturer of COMPOSITION toy soldiers and zoo figures, between 1904 and 1955.

ELBOW Part of the arm of a CHAIR.

ELDER Whitish wood, occasionally used for INLAY.

ELECTION POTTERY PLATES and MUGS made from the mid-18thC, notably in Bristol, England, promoting a parliamentary candidate or celebrating a victory.

ELECTRIC BRIGHT EYE Made from *c*.1909, a TEDDY BEAR with eyes that light up when a paw is shaken.

ELECTROPLATE Used from *c*.1840, a technique in which a base metal is covered with a thin layer of pure SILVER by electro-deposition. The base metal was initially copper, but later nickel was used, hence "EPNS" (electro-plated nickel silver), and sometimes both. Electroplate has a harsher, whiter appearance than STERLING SILVER or SHEFFIELD PLATE, and is often marked by its maker. Apart from pieces by an eminent maker, such as ELKINGTON, electroplate is less collectable than other silver. It is also susceptible to wear – pieces can be replated, but this creates an undesirably bright appearance. Avoid over-polishing it, because this will wear away the thin layer of silver.

ELECTROTYPE A non-metallic object, such as a flower or leaf, coated with GOLD or SILVER using electrical and chemical methods.

ELECTRUM An alloy of copper, zinc, and nickel, used for household wares since the 19thC.

ELEPHANT'S FOOTPRINT Alternative name for the GUL in Oriental CARPETS.

ELERS REDWARE Early STONEWARE, made by the Dutch Elers brothers in Staffordshire, England, before 1700.

ELFE, THOMAS (1719–1775) English-born cabinet-maker based in Charleston, South Carolina, North America. He produced high-quality FURNITURE in the CHIPPENDALE style and made distinctive use of FRETWORK.

ELIZABETHAN The period during the reign of Elizabeth I, 1558–1603.

ELKINGTON & CO. English firm, founded *c.*1830 in Birmingham. It patented ELECTROPLATE in 1840, thus revolutionizing the production of affordable SILVER PLATE. Its mark is an abbreviation of the name. In 1963, GARRARD merged with MAPPIN & WEBB and ELKINGTON to form British Silverware Ltd.

ELLICOTT, JOHN A noted English clockmaker, active in the mid-18thC.

ELLIOT REPEATER American Civil War pepperbox pistol made in New York.

ELLIS DOLL A 19thC American DOLL with a painted wooden head, body, and limbs, made by Joel Ellis of Springfield, Vermont. It had complex joints that enabled the doll to be manipulated into many positions.

ELM English elm (*Ulmus procera*) is a medium-brown, coarsely grained, water-resistant wood that looks similar to OAK but is softer. It was used for COUNTRY CHAIRS, especially for the seats of WINDSOR CHAIRS in the 18thC, and for large country pieces in the 19thC. WYCH ELM has a greenish cast and an attractive grain. Elm is rarely used for FURNITURE in the USA.

ELTON WARE ART POTTERY made in the late 19th and early 20thC by Sir Edmund Elton (1846–1920). Active from 1880, Elton produced wares noted for multi-colours and novel shapes, which he signed "Elton".

EMAIL OMBRANT Developed in France in the mid-19thC, a POTTERY design in relief overlaid by a transparent GLAZE. Creats a *chiaroscuro* effect.

EMBOSSED SILVER Vessels with relief ornament applied by EMBOSSING.

EMBOSSING Also known as "REPOUSSÉ" work, a technique that involves hammering a piece of METAL from the back with decorative punches or dies to create a relief pattern. Detail and definition are added by CHASING on the front of the design. Continental European, 17thC, Baroque silver was often decorated with embossed flower and fruit motifs. By the 19thC, embossing had fallen out of fashion, in favour of faster, cheaper DIE-STAMPING.

EMBROIDERY Fabric decorated with stitches, sometimes incorporating beads and precious stones. The finer the stitching and the brighter the colours, the more desirable a piece will be. Silk embroideries are more valuable than those sewn in wool. Because 19thC textiles are abundant,

George II, gentleman's gold pocket watch by Frederick Seydell, with EMBOSSED outer case, 1733.

avoid badly damaged pieces, unless they are particularly unusual. *See also* BERLIN WOOLWORK; RAISED WORK; SAMPLER; and TEXTILES, CARE OF.

EMPIRE STYLE The French equivalent of the REGENCY STYLE; synonymous in France with the reign of Napoleon between 1804 and 1815. Only simple lines and minimal ornament were used. MARQUETRY and carving were replaced by metal MOUNTS, often in the form of either swans, military motifs – such as wreaths, eagles, and trophies – or bees. Leading FURNITURE designers included Charles Percier and Pierre-François Fontaine.

ENAMEL (1) Colours made from GLASS, applied to METAL, CERAMICS, or GLASS in paste form, then fired for decorative effect.

ENAMEL (2) In CERAMICS, the practice of applying a second GLAZE over a first and refiring, also known as OVERGLAZE enamel. Made by adding metallic oxide to molten GLASS and reducing the cooled mixture, which, when combined with an oily medium, could be painted over the glaze and fused to it by firing. The range of colours was larger than with UNDERGLAZE colours.

ENAMELLING, GLASS Techniques for apply coloured ENAMELS, or coloured GLASS ground to a powder, to a vessel; popular on VENETIAN GLASS from the late 15thC, and in England from the mid-18thC. The best-known English enamellers were the BEILBY family. There are two types of enamelling: cold enamelling and fire enamelling. Cold enamelling, also known as cold painting, involves painting LACQUER and oils the reverse of the glass, which is not fired. This technique has the disadvantage that the enamelling wears off easily, and hence was used on inexpensive items. In fire enamelling, the enamel, comprising finely ground glass mixed with metallic oxides in an oily medium, was painted on the surface of the glass, which was then fired in a low-temperature kiln to fuse the colours to the object. This is the most permanent and usual form of enamelling. Transparent black, brown and red enamels, known as SCHWARZLOT, were popular from the mid-17th to the mid-18thC on German and Bohemian glass. *See also* HAUSMALER.

Krenit, ENAMELWARE, salad bowl, designed by Herbert Krenchel, 1955.

ENAMELLING, SILVER A process that involves applying a paste or oil-based mixture of metallic oxides to make a GLAZE. When fired, the glaze fuses onto the surface of the object, creating a colourful decorative effect. In the Victorian and Edwardian periods (1837–1901 and 1901–10 respectively) the technique was popular for decorating small silver objects, such as VESTA CASES, CARD CASES, CIGARETTE CASES, CLOCKS, and SCENT BOTTLES, which were often embellished with inlaid, painted enamel plaques. Enamelling is easily chipped, which will lower the value.

ENAMELWARE Metalwares given a coating of powdered GLASS and fired to create a hard smooth surface. *See also* ENAMELLING, SILVER.

EN CAMAÏEU VERT A type of scattered, floral decoration painted in green. Used on German pottery from the Wiesbaden factory.

ENCAUSTIC On CERAMICS, engraved patterns filled with a coloured SLIP. Used on wall and floor tiles in the Middle Ages, and revived in the 19thC.

ENCOIGNURE French marble-top corner CUPBOARD with ORMOLU mounts.

ENCRUSTED Of GLASS, applied decoration, often of metal, mineral, or stone.

ENCRUSTING Engraved SILVER or GOLD ornament on a SWORD. It protrudes from the surface in contrast to DAMASCENING, which is inlaid.

END-OF-DAY GLASS Small GLASS ornaments made of scraps left at the end of a day's work. They were mass-produced as novelties from the late 19thC.

END STANDARDS The UPRIGHTS that support a tabletop at either end.

ENGHALSKRUG Type of narrow-necked jug with bulbous body. Popular in Germany and the Netherlands from the mid-17th to the mid-18thC.

ENGINE-TURNING Introduced during the late 18thC, a technique in which machine-driven lathes carve lines into the surface of SILVER, creating a textured effect. The most common designs are waves, rosettes, and braids.

ENGLISH DELFTWARE *See* DELFTWARE, ENGLISH.

ENGLISH DIAL A type of 19thC WALL CLOCK with a painted sheet-iron DIAL, ANCHOR ESCAPEMENT, and PENDULUM. Often hung in public places such as railway stations.

ENGLISH PATCHWORK Technique in PATCHWORK in which the fabric patches are basted over paper templates before being stitched to each other.

ENGLISH PLATE American term for SHEFFIELD PLATE.

ENGRAVING, GLASS Techniques used to add patterns and scenes to GLASS objects. There are four types of engraving: DIAMOND-POINT ENGRAVING, WHEEL ENGRAVING, STIPPLE ENGRAVING, and ACID ENGRAVING. Plain, early GLASS may have been decorated with later engraving to make it seem more valuable. To check that decoration is authentic, drop a white handkerchief in the glass – old engraving will look dark and grey, new engraving white and powdery.

ENGRAVING, PRINT A printing technique in which a copper plate is incised with a design; ink is applied to the plate, which is used to make a print.

19thC, Minton, ENCAUSTIC bread board designed by Pugin, inscribed "waste not, want not."

ENGRAVING, SILVER A technique that involves cutting a decorative pattern into SILVER by removing metal from the surface with a sharp tool called a "burin" or "graver". The style of the work provides a valuable clue as to whether the engraving was done at the time of manufacture or added at a later date. Some of the finest engraving was produced in Continental Europe, particularly during the 17th and early-18thC in the Netherlands and Germany. Engraving was most commonly used for CRESTS, ARMORIALS, initials, and inscriptions, and was suited to large items with generous surface areas; on many items the engraving is featured within a decorative CARTOUCHE. An engraved coat-of-arms is sometimes removed (polished out or erased), and replaced with a new one when silver changes hands, leaving the metal thin and weak. A coat-of-arms that has been re-engraved or added at a later date will be more sharply defined than earlier engraving. *See also* BRIGHT-CUT ENGRAVING.

ENNECY CARPETS decorated with cruciform motifs and used as door hangings.

ENTRÉE DISH SILVER dish and cover, sometimes with a stand and spirit lamp. New dining fashions – introduced in France in the late 17thC – whereby diners served themselves at the table, necessitated the creation of these dishes, which were made in pairs or sets and used to keep food warm. They are usually shallow, with flat bottoms or four feet and handled domed covers, which were sometimes detachable and used as separate dishes. Before 1800, entrée dishes were of oval, circular, or navette (boat) form, with simple border decoration of GADROONING; in the 19thC, oblong or cushion shapes were favoured. Many later examples have elaborate handles, perhaps cast as crests, vegetables, or fruits. From the early 19thC, the bases of entrée dishes were often made of SILVER PLATE, and filled with boiling water or a bar of heated iron to keep the food warm. Sometimes the bases have insulated wooden feet to protect the TABLE or SIDEBOARD from the heat. In the mid-19thC, it became fashionable to serve food from a sideboard, so fewer entrée dishes were made. In the 1870s and '80s, NEOCLASSICAL-STYLE, oval examples, with BEADED, SCROLL, or reed-and-ribbon borders, were popular. The value of a piece is determined by the quality of the design, or the decorative techniques employed by individual makers. Heavy weight usually indicates a better piece, but watch out for dishes in OLD SHEFFIELD PLATE with lead-filled bases. Avoid damaged or worn examples, and look for dishes with original, well-fitting covers. Bases and covers were often scratched with a number or mark to indicate which base matched which cover. *See also* VEGETABLE DISH.

ENVELOPE TABLE From the EDWARDIAN period, a CARD TABLE with a top comprising four hinged segments that open out to reveal baize playing surfaces.

Rosewood and inlay ENVELOPE TABLE, c.1880.

E.P.B.M. (Electroplated Britannia Metal) BRITANNIA METAL, originally developed as a SILVER substitute, and used widely from *c*.1840 as a base metal for ELECTROPLATE. It was often stamped with these initials.

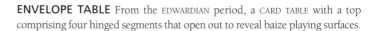

ÉPERGNE An elaborate CENTREPIECE with several decorative, GLASS or SILVER sections attached to or slotted into a metal frame. They are one of the many items of large, richly decorated tableware intended to reflect the wealth and status of their owner. *Épergnes* were first used at the French court in the late 17thC. Comprising a single stand with a central basket surrounded by small bowls, they were introduced to England *c.*1715, and popular in the mid-18thC. Early examples featured candle sockets that could be exchanged for smaller baskets. Some *épergnes* could be simplified by removing the top layer of branches and using the bowls for "bon-bon" dishes (for sweets) and the larger central dish as a fruit basket. Holes that were left when the detachable scroll branches and baskets were removed for cleaning were disguised with silver caps, usually in the form of flowers. By the 1740s, *épergnes* were associated with the dessert course and used to hold fruits, candied fruits, and sweetmeats. Always check that an *épergne* is complete – holes in the base or holder indicate missing parts. Delicate branches, feet, and pierced decoration are prone to damage, so check for repairs. The body and central basket should be fully HALLMARKED, with other parts stamped with a maker's mark and lion passant.

E.P.N.S. (Electroplated nickel silver) *See* ELECTROPLATE.

ENTRELAC From the French for "to interlace", a Celtic-inspired, interweaving, tendril decoration, often used in JEWELLERY, especially pieces by ARTS AND CRAFTS designers. It was also used on ART NOUVEAU metalware.

ENTY, JOHN Leading English gunsmith, active in the early to mid-19thC.

EQUATION CLOCK A CLOCK with a MECHANISM and DIAL that shows the difference between mean time and solar time. The dial has two hands: one pointing to the day of the month, the other indicating how far solar time is behind or ahead of mechanical time.

ERFURT In Thuringia, Germany, a factory founded in the early 18thC and specializing in brightly coloured TANKARDS in FAIENCE with PEWTER lids.

ERSARI From Turkestan, a dark-red-and-blue CARPET with large GULS.

ESCAPEMENT On a CLOCK, part of a clockwork mechanism that controls the driving force of the spring, checking and releasing it by pallets, which engage and disengage in the teeth of the escape wheel. In a balance-wheel escapement, the oscillating balance wheel releases on the vertical bar the two pallets or "flags", which engage the toothed wheel. The VERGE ESCAPEMENT is similar but has a short PENDULUM. Verge or balance-wheel escapements were used on LANTERN CLOCKS until *c.*1670. In the ANCHOR ESCAPEMENT, the anchor engages with the teeth of the escape wheel. This type was first used in LONGCASE CLOCKS from *c.*1670, and is standard for them and BRACKET CLOCKS.

Silver and enamel pendant with ENTRELAC, designed by Archibald Knox for Liberty & Co., and manufactured by Murrle Bennet & Co. Ltd, *c.*1905.

Charles Schneider, acid-ETCHED "Le Verre Français" cameo glass, c.1925.

ESCRITOIRE French for a type of WRITING TABLE, usually of WALNUT, and with a large cabinet that has a front that drops down for use as a writing surface. The interior is normally fitted with small drawers and compartments.

ESCUTCHEON Any applied metal plate, but especially an ornamented one around a keyhole, or a plate bearing a maker's name on a CLOCK face.

ESHERICK, WHARTON (1887–1980) American craftsman who made free-form FURNITURE, in which flowing, modern, sculptural forms were applied to functional designs using traditional woodworking methods.

ÉTAGÈRE A stand with open shelves, used in the dining-room to display bowls of food and, like the WHATNOT (a similar design to the *étagère*, but with slimmer, smaller shelves), popular in the late 18thC. Some examples feature collapsing mechanisms that allow them to be folded flat into TABLES. Victorian *étagères* with fret-cut decoration are highly sought after. *See also* DUMB WAITER.

ETCHED GLASS GLASS that has been treated with hydrofluoric acid to give it a matt or frosted finish. High-relief etching is known as deep-etched. Layers of multi-coloured glass were often treated in this way to make CAMEO GLASS. The technique was favoured by ART NOUVEAU and ART DECO makers.

ETCHING Printing technique in which a copper plate is coated with wax, into which a design is scratched, inked, and printed.

ETHNIC DOLL Oriental and black DOLLS, first produced by BRU JEUNE in 1883 with fired red lips. Other firms, including GAULTIER, JUMEAU, and SIMON & HALBIG, produced mulatto and negro dolls for the 1878 and 1889 Paris International Exhibitions. Fakes have lips painted red after firing, or lips that are the same brownish colour as the face tint. SIMON & HALBIG were probably the most prolific German makers of mulatto or brown dolls, and were specialists in Oriental girl dolls, whose value is increased by an original exotic costume. Dolls with negroid features and unusual mould numbers, such as 130, are among the most valuable of all BISQUE dolls.

ETRUSCAN MAIOLICA English and American, lead-glazed EARTHENWARE made in the 19thC and so-called for its resemblance to Tuscan MAIOLICA.

ETRUSCAN STYLE Style of decoration based on ancient Greek and Roman ornamentation. Associated with the work of Robert ADAM. *See also* CLASSICAL.

ÉTUI A small, decorative, SILVER case fitted with a variety of tiny personal items, including SEWING ACCESSORIES and novelties. It provided ready access to items deemed crucial to running a household, such as scissors, needles, tweezers, thimbles, bodkins, and pencils. Gentlemen's *étuis,* used by men when travelling, contained tiny steel forks, knives, and ear-picks, folding steel scissors with SILVER handles, and silver spoons. Often hung from CHÂTELAINES, these cases were made in a range of shapes and often decorated with ENAMELS and GILDING. If a piece is in good condition, complete with its original contents, has decorative elements such as FILIGREE work, and is dated from the early 19thC, it will be collectable.

EVERTED CERAMIC or GLASS rim form, in which the edge is turned over to create a double thickness.

EWER Large jug with a lip. Often part of a set including a basin.

EWER, WINE A large jug with a tall, deep, lipped bowl, a stemmed base, handle, and sometimes a lid; they were often made of SILVER, but were also produced in GLASS and PORCELAIN. Some ewers were cast and of excellent quality, and these are more desirable than other lighter examples that were stamped. The Renaissance-inspired "Cellini" pattern was the most popular design in the 19thC. Some ewers were made with a set of matching wine goblets, and the full set would fetch a high price; however, a ewer would still be desirable on its own. Glass ewers with silver mounts were popular from the 1850s until *c.*1900, and were often made in pairs in fitted boxes, and given as presentation pieces or wedding presents. Numerous makers followed this style, but ewers by Christopher DRESSER are prized. *See also* JUG, WINE.

EXCELSIOR Soft mixture of long, thin, wood shavings. Often employed as stuffing for TEDDY BEARS.

"EXCELSIOR" PATTERN In the GOTHIC STYLE, an American GLASS pattern attributed to firms including the BOSTON & SANDWICH GLASS CO. Clear-glass examples are common, while those in coloured and opalescent glass are rare.

EXCISE MARK Required after 1824 on British PEWTER vessels in which liquor was sold to a specific measure. These marks usually combined a crown, a local emblem, and letters or numbers indicating the date and person doing the test.

EXETER CARPET Hand-knotted, English CARPET produced in the mid-18thC in Exeter by the Swiss maker Claude Passavant.

EXOTIC WOOD An unusual, often expensive wood such as ZEBRAWOOD, PARTRIDGE WOOD, and SNAKEWOOD.

EXPORT WARE Chinese ceramic objects made for the European market. They were often in Western shapes but were decorated with traditional Chinese designs. *See also* POTTERY AND PORCELAIN, CHINESE.

Engraved claret jug or WINE EWER by R. Martin & E. Hall, London, 1871.

F

FABERGÉ, PETER CARL (1846–1920) Russian jeweller known for GEM-encrusted Fabergé eggs; he also made other ornaments in GOLD, SILVER, and precious stones in the ART NOUVEAU style. Under his direction the Fabergé firm in St Petersburg, Russia, became one of the world's most renowned jewellers. Designs are marked "KF" or "K. Fabergé" in Cyrillic letters.

FABERGÉ gold, ruby, and diamond brooch, c.1900.

FABRIC DOLL A DOLL with a moulded fabric head and stuffed fabric body, painted or stitched facial features, and hair made from wood, cotton, or MOHAIR, or painted on. Being fabric, few have survived the rigours of playtime or ravaging of moths, and the first significant examples date only from the second half of the 19thC. There was a strong domestic, RAG DOLL tradition in North America, where homemade versions were created out of scraps of material by early European settlers in the 17thCas playthings for their children. The first American patent for a fabric doll was taken out in 1873. Commercial production in North America began in the mid-19thC with Izannah Walker and Martha Jenks CHASE, followed by J.B. Sheppard & Co. of Philadelphia with their "Philadelphia" babies, but it did not take off there in an important way until the early 20thC. In Europe, mass production of printed, cut-out fabric dolls began after fabric colour printing developed c.1830. High-quality fabric dolls were manufactured from the mid-19thC by makers including Madame Montanari, PIEROTTI, and John Edwards. The top German producers were Margarete STEIFF and Käthe KRUSE, whose dolls were modelled, like BYE-LOS, on newborn babies. In Italy, LENCI made elegant dolls for adults. Many British dolls were inspired by characters in children's literature, such as the babies by Mabel Lucie ATTWELL. The British royal family was also frequently portrayed by dollmakers. Early dolls' heads were moulded from calico, with three, hand-stitched PATE seams. Hair and features were painted with oils. After 1929, dolls have one pate seam. From 1935, some heads were made of magnesite (a plaster substitute). Hollow SWIVEL HEADS of covered cardboard were introduced after World War II, but these were superseded from 1950 by heads made of CELLULOID and plastic. Today the price of fabric dolls varies widely. The most expensive are those by Martha Jenks Chase, Izannah Walker, Käthe Kruse, and Steiff, plus 1920s and '30s Lenci. Those by English makers such as Norah WELLINGS, CHAD VALLEY, J.K. FARNELL, and DEAN'S are usually much more affordable. Fabric dolls with expressive features, in good condition, and with elaborate clothes with original labels are the most desirable. Few examples made prior to the late-19thC are available. Restoration is difficult, and many fabric dolls cannot be washed, so condition is important.

FACETED Found on SILVER and GLASS items, a decorative surface cut into sharp-edged planes in a criss-cross pattern to reflect the light.

FACETING Technique used to decorate curved GLASS surfaces by grinding to make flat, geometric sections.

FACET-STEM GLASS A DRINKING GLASS that has a stem in which GLASS is cut away from it to form a decorative pattern and to reduce its weight; it was developed to avoid punitive taxes imposed on coloured enamel glass in 1777. Popular from *c*.1780 to *c*.1810, facet-stem glasses feature three main patterns of faceting: diamond, created by cutting diagonally across the stem; hexagonal, made by cutting down and across the stem at an angle; and flat-cut, formed by slicing downward from the bottom of the bowl to the foot. Simple, flat-cut facets were used on inexpensive types of drinking glass for a tavern or for everyday home use. Complex facet-cutting of diamond or hexagonal patterns was used on expensive drinking glasses, because these techniques required more dexterity and skill. The hexagonal style of faceted stem is less common than the diamond-cut facet variety, because more glass was removed, so the stem was weaker. Examples with one KNOP are rare; those with more than one knop are practically unknown. Until *c*.1770, the conical folded foot was popular, but the flat foot is typical of facet-stemmed glasses of the late 18thC. Sometimes the foot of the glass is faceted, but rarely the bowl, which is often engraved with motifs of fruiting vines, CHINOISERIE, and egg-and-dart ornament. Copies of facet-stemmed glasses were made by STEVENS & WILLIAMS and the WHITEFRIARS glassworks in the early 20thC, and are still available today. They can be distinguished from the 18thC originals by their heavier weight, thicker stems, flatter and thinner feet, and brighter colour. If the facets are irregularly shaped, the piece was cut by hand. The introduction of new, mechanical, grinding techniques during the late 18th and early 19thC means that on most facet-stemmed glasses the PONTIL MARK will be ground out.

FAÇON DE VENISE Meaning "in the Venetian manner", glassware imitating that from Venice, Italy. By the 16thC, Antwerp had become the most important glassmaking centre in the Netherlands, attracting highly skilled workmen from Venice. Venetian-style glass was made in vast quantities to meet the growing demand created by local patrons, who sought to publicize their wealth and status with displays of glassware in this celebrated style. *See also* DRINKING GLASS, BELGIAN AND DUTCH; DRINKING GLASS, VENETIAN; and MURANO.

FAIENCE TIN-GLAZED EARTHENWARE named after the town of Faenza in Italy, but actually used to describe products made anywhere, particularly in France and Germany, except for Italy, where the same wares are called "MAIOLICA". Frankfurt was the leading German centre for the production of faience from the latter half of the 17thC. *See also* FRENCH FAIENCE.

FAÇON-DE-VENISE glass, by Bonhomme, Liège, from the second half of the 17thC.

FAIENCE-FINE Cream-coloured EARTHENWARE produced by 19thC French factories to imitate English CREAMWARE. Sometimes used to denote high-quality FAIENCE. *See also* FRENCH FAIENCE.

FAIRINGS Cheap, mould-made PORCELAIN figure groups made in the 19th and 20thC, especially in Germany, and often humorous or sentimental. They are so-called because they were sold, or given as prizes, at fairs.

FAIRYLAND LUSTRE *See* MAKEIG-JONES, Daisy.

FAKE A piece deliberately made or altered to give the impression that it is older than it really is. Some items were made as faithful reproductions, but have been passed on by third parties as antique or original. In recent years, increasing numbers of fakes have appeared in shops and auction rooms, and some are so carefully made that even the most expert eye can be fooled. FURNITURE fakes made from new timber are easy to identify, because the wood does not have the PATINA one would expect. Some fakes are made from old wood, and these can be more difficult to identify. Beware of any piece being sold as 18thC or earlier if it has circular saw marks. These mean the wood was cut after *c.*1800, when circular saws were first used. Always take time to examine a piece carefully, in good light, and try to build up your experience through hands-on contact with as much furniture as possible. Many reproductions are artificially distressed to give the appearance of age, but on close inspection it should become clear that the wear is unrealistically evenly distributed. A genuine antique would look most battered around the base and feet. Painted decoration can fool even seasoned collectors. Generally, the faker will decorate the front of a CHEST or BOX and leave the sides a solid colour – something the more careful 18th- or 19thC decorator would not do. *See also* FURNITURE, ALTERATION OF and MARRIAGE.

FALCHION Curved broadSWORD with the cutting edge on the convex side.

FALL FRONT Hinged flap of a DESK that pulls down to make a writing surface.

FALLING-BALL CLOCK Of spherical form, a CLOCK hung from a chain linked to the mechanism, so that the clock's weight provides the driving force. The hours are marked on a moving band around the circumference.

FALSE EDGE On a SWORD, the back edge that has been sharpened for some of its length rather than remaining blunt.

FALSTAFF JUG A TOBY JUG made in the form of Shakespeare's drunkard.

FAMILLE JAUNE Meaning "yellow family", a Chinese PORCELAIN vessel in which yellow is the predominant GROUND colour.

FAMILLE NOIRE Meaning "black family", Chinese PORCELAIN in which black is the predominant GROUND colour.

FAMILLE ROSE Meaning "pink family", PORCELAIN decorated with opaque pink enamel. Despite the term, pink is not necessarily the dominant shade. *Famille-rose* wares were first made *c.*1718; the style was much copied in the 19thC, particularly by the French firm of SAMSON. Crackling in the enamel colours is a good sign that the piece is authentic.

FAMILLE VERTE Meaning "green family", PORCELAIN dominated by a bright, apple green. It was used to decorate export wares from the KANGXI period (1662–1722). *See also* CHINESE EXPORT WARES.

FANCY BACK A spoon with decoration on the back of the bowl.

FAN PATTERN Term describing the back of a CHAIR with ribs spread to resemble a half-opened fan.

FANTASIE VÖGEL Colourful, often imaginary, birds ("*Vögel*" is German for birds), painted on porcelain by MEISSEN and widely copied elsewhere.

FANTASQUE Name of a colourful range of household china designed by Clarice CLIFF, and manufactured in the 1930s by A.J. WILKINSON Ltd.

FARIS, WILLIAM American clockmaker, active in Philadelphia, 1755–90.

FARMER'S WATCH A WATCH mass-produced in the 19thC and so-called because the DIAL was painted with rural scenes.

FARNELL, J.K. & CO. A British toymaking firm (1871–1968) that initially produced SOFT TOYS at the Alpha Works, London. It was founded by Agnes Farnell, who claims to have invented the TEDDY BEAR, because the firm produced rabbit-skin animal toys from at least 1897. Angled ears and large, amber glass eyes are typical of soft toys from this maker. The firm supplied teddy bears to the London department store Harrods in the 1920s. By 1925, artist Chloe Preston was designing dolls for Farnell in modern materials. In 1930, Farnell introduced the "Alpha" range of dolls – one of their most popular – and placed a label on the foot reading "Farnell's Alpha Toys made in England". The firm's FABRIC DOLLS have five-piece bodies, with wide hips and rather crudely formed torsos. Although the factory was bombed in 1940, production continued. Alpha bears have large feet and short legs. The early ones were made using long mohair PLUSH; later ones (from the end of World War II) were made using a synthetic fibre, and jointed. Farnell's Alpha also made soft toys, including rabbits, dogs, foxes, birds, and monkeys. The last are not as popular as other animals, and this is reflected in the value they fetch. *See also* WINNIE-THE-POOH.

Chinese Kangxi FAMILLE VERTE vase, 1662–1722.

Bisque FASHION DOLL with French kid,
gusset-jointed body, c.1870.

FARTHINGALE CHAIR Misnomer for a joined-and-upholstered CHAIR, so-called because of the belief that the design was influenced by the wide "farthingale" dress, which it could accommodate.

FASHION DOLL An early French DOLL (usually with a BISQUE head) that resembled a fashionable lady and came with a wardrobe of elaborate clothes. Also known as "PARISIENNE" DOLLS, fashion dolls were made between 1860 and 1890. Bodies came in various styles and materials, and construction was elaborate to allow the dolls to adopt the most natural poses. They often had gusseted KID bodies with wide hips and shoulders to suit period dress. Forearms were sometimes bisque, and tenon joints were used at the shoulders, elbows, and knees. The dolls' complexions were realistically tinted, and their glass eyes and real-hair wigs added to their naturalistic appearance. Look for large, almond-shaped eyes with blue spiral glass – the white thread running through the iris gives an impression of depth. GAULTIER and BRU JEUNE were two important 19thC firms to produce fashion dolls. Expensive examples were bought for children as a symbol of their parents' wealth and status. They also helped a young girl to develop a fashion-sense, and improve her sewing skills by adding clothes to a doll's large wardrobe. Identification of a doll's original clothes can be difficult, because the original owner may have added to her outfits – the best guide is usually to examine the fit. Adult dolls are distinguishable from BÉBÉS by their thin waists. Dolls with SWIVEL NECKS are worth double those with rigid necks. Fashion dolls are mostly attributed by type, because few were marked, although the name of the shop or maker is occasionally found under the kid on the SHOULDER-PLATE. Firing lines and other PORCELAIN defects may reduce a doll's value, although much may depend on where the problem is and if the defect makes the doll less attractive. Raised pink spots are not uncommon. Wire inside the kid body, allowing limbs to move, may create rust marks. *See also* DOLL ACCESSORIES.

FATAMID POTTERY Islamic and Christian POTTERY made in Egypt under the Fatamid dynasty, AD 969–1171, and often in the form of birds, animals, and human figures.

FAUSSE-MONTRE Literally "false-watch". An 18thC dummy worn at one end of a watch-chain to balance the weight of the real WATCH at the other end.

FAUTEUIL A French or French-style upholstered ARMCHAIR.

FAUX BOIS French term for wood painted to resemble a more exotic timber.

FAVRILE GLASS A type of GLASS treated with metallic oxides to create a shimmering, iridescent surface reminiscent of that found on long-buried, ancient Roman glass. It was associated with TIFFANY, who patented the glass in 1894. Most "Favrile" glass was used for decorative items, such as VASES, but

Tiffany also made useful wares (now collectable), such as SALT-CELLARS, from this glass. Tiffany used a range of marks, which should be checked carefully to avoid fakes. Etched signatures for Favrile glass include "L.C.T", "L.C. Tiffany – Favrile", "Louis C. Tiffany – Favrile", or a variation of these.

FEATHERBANDING Around the edge of a surface, strips of VENEER cut diagonally to the main veneer. Also called HERRINGBONE.

FEATHER-EDGE A bright-cut pattern of small lines around the FINIALS of silver CUTLERY from the late 18thC.

FEDERAL STYLE American FURNITURE made between 1785 and 1830 in the NEO-CLASSICAL STYLE, but influenced by British taste, and on a slightly grander scale. There are varieties in regional styles, and MAPLE was commonly used.

FELDSPAR Form of PORCELAIN patented by the second Josiah SPODE (1754–1827) containing the crushed mineral feldspar. It was popular from 1800, especially for export to countries that taxed imported, true porcelains.

FELDSPATHIC GLAZE A hard and glassy, high-temperature GLAZE, based on using the mineral FELDSPAR.

FENG-HUANG Half-dragon, half-phoenix motif on Chinese CARPETS.

FERAGHAN A CARPET from central Iran with a strong cotton warp visible on the underside, dense short PILE, and HERATI MOTIFS on a red or blue ground.

FERGANA CARPET From Kirghiz, central Turkestan, a predominantly red, often rather loosely woven, CARPET.

FERNWARE Wooden boxes, FIRESCREENS, and other objects with fern fronds applied, then varnished. More rarely, a fern pattern stencilled onto the surface. Produced by William Smith of Mauchline, Ayrshire, Scotland, 1900–9.

FEDERAL-STYLE, **stained pine night stand, 1786–1810.**

FERRARA MAIOLICA made in the Italian town of Ferrara in the 16thC. It is difficult to distinguish from maiolica from Faenza.

FERRYBRIDGE A British pottery firm, founded in the 19thC by William Tomlinson and Ralph WEDGWOOD in Yorkshire, and specializing in EARTHENWARE and STONEWARE.

FESTIVAL OF BRITAIN A series of exhibitions and displays organized across Britian in 1951. New designs, exciting scientific developments, and modern architecture were shown alongside displays on Britain's history. Everything in the exhibition was specially commissioned and designed in the new "comtemporary" style, with a huge number of painters, sculptors, and designers producing work. This vision of the future especially appealed to young people, who wanted the look for their own homes, and although it took some years to filter into shops, the style was set for the next decade. There is an enormous selection of souvenirs from the Festival.

FESTOON Characteristic of the BAROQUE STYLE, a motif consisting of a garland of flowers or ribbons in a horseshoe shape, with a dip in the middle.

FIDDLEBACK A grain of mahogany VENEER, resembling the back of a violin.

"FIDDLE" PATTERN Used in British FLATWARE from c.1820 and so-called because the shape of the handle resembles that of a violin.

FIELD The central area of a RUG or CARPET within the frame or borders.

FIELDED PANEL A raised central panel bordered by a BEVELLED edge.

FIELDING & CO. British, Staffordshire-based, POTTERY manufacturer, which made ART NOUVEAU-style CROWN DEVON wares from 1913.

FIGURING The different grains and patterns found in wood.

FILIGRANA Italian, meaning "thread-grained"(FILIGREE in English), used to describe variations of a decorative style that incorporates threads of (usually opaque-white) glass inside a clear-glass body in a variety of lattice patterns, It is also known as LATTICINIO. The fine threads have to be cut, flattened, joined together, and shaped into the vessel, which is heated at high temperatures to form intricate designs, including VETRO A FILI and *vetri a reticello*. Such popular patterns were produced until the 18thC. *See also* GLASS.

French, FILIGREE card case in silver gilt, c.1875.

FILIGREE A type of SILVER or GOLD openwork decoration made by twisting or plaiting fine wires into intricate decorative patterns of geometric or foliate ornament, and soldering the wires together. Filigree decoration is made separately and applied unsupported as an openwork border – for example on JEWELLERY – or by being soldered onto a flat metal plate on such items as boxes or buttons. It was popular in Continental Europe in the 17thC, while in Britain it was only used to a small degree in the late 17thC, and again during the 19thC, when revival styles were the rage. Objects with filigree decoration are often delicate, and the technique was usually used in the production of small items such as CADDY SPOONS, CARD CASES, and PILL BOXES. However, filigree has also been used with particular success to produce large items of silver, for example CANDLESTICKS, INKSTANDS, and caskets.

FILLET A thin strip of wood.

FILM MEMORABILIA Collecting category consisting of objects that reflect the glamour of the movies, from the nostalgic old films of Hollywood's golden age of the early 20thC, to the high-tech special effects films of the late 20th and early 21stC. The main types of collectable film memorabilia are costumes, props, autographs, POSTERS, and photographs; however, almost anything associated with a particular film or star can be collectable. Even recently reproduced photographs of key stars such as Marlene Dietrich are desirable, because to many collectors a classic image of the star is more important than the age of the photograph. Props associated with the key actors of cult movies attract the highest prices, especially if rarely available. The best film props are well-made, sophisticated pieces, such as Darth Vader's helmet from the *Star Wars* films. The key is to look for a particular object that conjures up the essence of a particular star. More affordable types of film memorabilia include posters, photographs, autographs, and publicity stills. Among the most desirable posters are those from classic films of the 1950s and '60s. Autographs on photos are often not genuine, because many stars allowed their secretaries to sign photographs on their behalf. Sometimes the negative of the photograph was signed, thus some photographs are stamped with signatures. Clapperboards are among the least expensive memorabilia. Look for boards from popular films and printed with the name of the production and the director. *See also* CELEBRITY DOLL.

Promotional poster for the classic 1972 film *Raging Bull*, signed by Robert de Niro and Martin Scorsese, 1980 (FILM MEMORABILIA).

FIN DE SIÈCLE Prevalent at the end of the 19thC in Europe, a decorative style that used BAROQUE, ROCOCO, and ART NOUVEAU motifs on highly ornate objects, with the implication that the art was decadent or gross.

FINE-LINE On GLASS, a matt background or infill of close-set incised lines.

FINGER BOWL A type of bowl filled with water to be used for rinsing the fingers between courses. Finger bowls are similar in form to WINEGLASS COOLERS, but they do not have the pouring lips. *See also* BOWLS, GLASS.

FINGER JOINT Wooden hinge mechanism of the supporting leg or bracket of a FOLDOVER or DROP-LEAF TABLE. Also known as a knuckle joint.

FINIAL (1) Spirelike ornament used to finish a vertical projection. Carved in many forms, from human and animal figures to columns or obelisks.

FINIAL (2) On SILVER spoons, the ornamented piece at the opposite end of the shaft to the bowl.

FIORA Working in Nottingham, England, in the early 19thC, a notable maker of BANJO BAROMETERS with SHERATON-style inlaid cases.

FIRANGI Indian SWORD with an imported European blade.

FIREARM A weapon such as a pistol or rifle that discharges a projectile after the ignition of gunpowder. Most antique firearms fall into one of two categories: FLINTLOCKS, which use a flint to make a spark and ignite the charge; or PERCUSSION LOCKS, in which a metal cap containing a small explosive charge is ignited by the stroke of the hammer. Although most antique weapons are never used, the "feel" of a firearm is an important factor to consider when buying. Pieces that feel top-heavy and uncomfortable in the firing position are least desirable. On early rifles, look for features that reflect quality such as fine engraving on the lock plate, a maker's mark, and elaborately inlaid stock decorated with stag horn, SILVER wire, and MOTHER-OF-PEARL. In cased sets of pistols, such as DUELLING PISTOLS, always check that all the pieces are from the original group.

FIRECATS Similar to ANDIRONS or FIREDOGS, but with many legs. They are so-called because if dropped they will always land on their feet.

FIRECLAY WARE Large URNS and VASES produced in the 19thC by Bell of Glasgow as an alternative to the BASALTES of WEDGWOOD. They are decorated with CLASSICAL scenes and are overglazed with black ENAMEL.

FIRE CRACK In a PORCELAIN body, a crack that appears during firing.

FIREDOGS Alternative name for ANDIRONS. Sometimes used to describe smaller, unadorned examples.

FIRE GILDING An early technique of gilding copper or other metals by painting with an amalgam of GOLD and mercury, and heating until the mercury vaporizes.

FIRE IRONS Collective name for a matching set of tools – tongs, a shovel, brush, poker, and sometimes a fork – for stoking and cleaning a fireplace. Brass examples from the 18th and 19thC are often highly decorative, and were made to match the fender.

FIRE POLISHING A technique employed to make PRESSED GLASS resemble CUT GLASS. Involves reheating to polish the surface and remove the mould seam. *See also* GLASS.

FIRESCREEN A portable SCREEN, usually with a wooden frame, made during the 17th and 18thC to protect ladies near a roaring fire. (Without such protection, wax-based cosmetics would melt and drip down ladies' faces.) Firescreens were made from a range of materials, including MAHOGANY and simulated BAMBOO. Some examples have tapestry panels. Modern central heating and smaller rooms mean that they are no longer of practical use, but they are still attractive in front of fireplaces. *See also* POLESCREEN.

Victorian rosewood FIRESCREEN with carved decoration and an embroidered tapestry panel.

FIRING GLASS With a solid, heavy base and STEM, a DRINKING GLASS made from the 17thC for banging on the table in approval or applause, or at a toast.

FISH-HEAD PORCELAIN ornaments in the form – often naturalistic – of a fish's head. Made by various English factories in the late 18th and 19thC.

FISHING MEMORABILIA Items connected with fishing. Instruments such as reels, rods, and tackle, and trophies incorporating a caught fish are among collectable pieces. Early reels were finely made from materials such as BRASS, IVORENE (an IVORY substitute) and ebonite (simulated EBONY); examples with makers' marks are desirable. Finely engineered reels made from the early 19thC onward are popular. Reels made by Hardy Bros of Alnwick are keenly collected. Other notable makers are Charles Farlow, S. Allcock, Alfred Illingworth, P.D. Malloch, and Ogden Smith. Reels in mint condition are rare, but those with damaged or replaced parts or that have their owner's name scratched on them (unless he is famous) are best avoided. Reels with makers' marks are more valuable. Fish trophies of the late 19th and early 20thC, in cases with BOW FRONTS and mounted by expert taxidermists (such as J. Cooper & Sons) fetch good prices, but avoid trophies in poor condition.

FISH KNIFE AND FORK Designed for eating fish, a knife with a wider blade and fork with shorter TINES than standard. Both IVORY and MOTHER-OF-PEARL were often used for the handles of fish knives and forks, and these should always be examined for signs of weakness or damage through regular use.

FISH PLATTER Elongated oval platters made to hold fish; especially long ones were made for salmon. They were more popular in Continental Europe than Britain, and can be fairly easily found and affordable today.

FISH SLICE SILVER or plated utensil with a broad flat blade, and often with pierced or engraved ornament. Designed from the 18thC for serving fish.

FISH TAIL Decorative carving resembling the tail of a fish. It is typically found on the cresting rail of a CHAIR with a BANISTER BACK.

FITZHUGH Possibly named after a merchant or importer, a pattern of flowers, insects, and fruits in UNDERGLAZE BLUE on PORCELAIN from Nanking. *See also* NANKIN.

FITZROY BAROMETER Mass-produced barometer introduced *c.*1870 and named after Admiral Fitzroy, the first weather-forecaster, whose predictions were published in *The Times*. The oblong case has printed charts and guidance notes pasted onto it. Some have "storm glasses" to measure static electricity.

FIVE DYNASTIES Period in Chinese history AD 907–960.

Pewter-lidded FLAGON, with wriggle work and the initials and date within a heart, 1832.

FIXED EYES On a DOLL, glass eyes that do not move and are usually dark with no pupil. Used on 18thC wooden and 19thC wax and PAPIER-MÂCHÉ dolls.

FLAGG, JAMES MONTGOMERY (1877–1960) The American illustrator responsible for the "I Want You" recruitment poster featuring Uncle Sam. His work appeared on the cover of *Life* magazine and on film posters.

FLAGON Larger version of a TANKARD, with a flat bottom, slightly tapering sides, a handle, and thumbpiece, and, often, a hinged PEWTER lid. Usually made of TIN- OR SALT-GLAZED STONEWARE.

FLAG SEAT A seat woven with rush.

FLAIL Weapon consisting of a spiked ball head attached by a chain to a staff.

FLAMBÉ A deep red GLAZE used by ART NOUVEAU and ART DECO potters in imitation of the SANG-DE-BOEUF (bull's blood) colour of Chinese PORCELAIN.

FLAMBEAU A FINIAL carved to resemble flames. *See also* AUGER FLAME.

FLAMBOYANT BLADE A type of blade with a wavy or undulating edge.

FLAME FIGURING A VENEER cut to enhance the grain of the wood, and resembling flames.

FLANDERS BABY An alternative name for 19thC DOLLS that were imported from Eastern Europe.

FLANDERS FURNITURE The general name given to panelled FURNITURE imported from, or via, Flanders, in the Netherlands, in the early 16thC.

FLANGE NECK On a DOLL, a head with a ridge at the base of neck with two holes, so that the head could be sewn onto the body. Used mainly on soft-bodied dolls such as the "DREAM BABY".

FLAPPER LEGS On a DOLL, legs with the knee joints set noticeably high. From 1920, German COMPOSITION bodies were made with flapper legs.

FLASHING GLASS-decoration technique that involves dipping a glass vessel into a GATHER of another colour, leaving a thin surface layer to be engraved. It was frequently used as a less expensive alternative to CASED GLASS.

FLATBACK A figurative POTTERY group designed to stand against a wall or on a mantelpiece and hence not decorated on the reverse. First made *c*.1840, mostly in Staffordshire, England, flatbacks were usually formed by

PRESS MOULDING, and made in vast numbers in a huge variety of subjects, from royal personalities, naval and military heroes, and politicians to criminals, theatrical personalities, and animals. *See also* STAFFORDSHIRE FIGURES.

FLAT CARPET A CARPET without a PILE such as a DHURRI or KILIM.

FLAT-CHASING Hammered ornament in low-relief on a flat SILVER surface, leaving an impression of the punched pattern on the back. *See also* CHASING.

FLATS Two-dimensional toy soldiers cast in lead or tin alloy by German, Nuremberg-based, toymakers from the 16thC. Widely exported in the 18th and 19thC. *See also* SEMI-FLATS and SOLIDS.

FLATWARE (1) Collective name for all flat and shallow tableware, such as PLATES and SALVERS.

FLATWARE (2) A term referring to forks, spoons, and serving utensils. Before the custom of setting a table with flatware was introduced in the 17thC, spoons and knives were personal possessions. Spoons, used since pre-Roman times, survive in great quantities, and are collectable. By far the most personal of all pieces of SILVER from medieval times, they were given as baptism presents, and were carried throughout life. Being "born with a silver spoon in your mouth" carried great social significance, because wealth and status determined the quality of one's spoon. Food was eaten with a spoon until the 16thC, when the fork – until then used only for desserts and sweetmeats – became popular in Continental Europe. Fashions from France influenced flatware styles from the mid-17thC, with new styles including TREFID SPOONS. The fashion for eating with a fork was adopted by the court of Charles II while in exile in France, and brought to England after the Restoration in 1660. The earliest English dining forks date from the mid-17thC, and had two or three TINES. They were set following the French custom with the open "bowl" facing the table, which is why original engraving usually appears on the stem back. Early forks in good condition are rare, especially dessert forks. Beware of fakes created by soldering modern forks onto the stems of old spoons. Four-pronged forks were introduced in the 1720s and were commonplace from the 1760s. From the early 18thC, sets of matching spoons, forks, and knives were made in a vast range of patterns. The "HANOVERIAN" PATTERN was the first one used for matching flatware; it evolved into the "OLD ENGLISH" PATTERN in the 1760s. From the late 18thC, flatware was produced in services in a variety of patterns, and elaborate SILVER-GILT dessert services became fashionable, in keeping with the trend for lavish dining customs. Of major influence on flatware design and production was the launch, from the 1770s, of mechanized silver manufacturing, notably in Sheffield, which became the main centre for cutlery production in England. The most popular late-18th

FLATWARE with Bohemian *millefiori* handles, c.1850.

and early-19thC flatware designs include the "FIDDLE" PATTERN and the lavishly decorated "KING'S" and "QUEEN'S" PATTERNS. Other items of flatware include FISH SLICES and pretty boxed sets of matching coffee spoons. Serving spoons, which are of medium to large size (length 33–38cm/13–15in) were first used in the mid-17thC, but they became more commonplace from the 1700s. The date of a piece of flatware affects its price. Complete services, which usually comprise settings for 12 of tablespoons, table forks, dessert spoons, dessert forks, and teaspoons, are rare, and so may seem prohibitively expensive, but odd numbers of spoons and forks in the most common patterns, such as Old English, Fiddle, or Hanoverian, are easy to find, making it often far less costly to build up a service piecemeal. Flatware services do not usually include knives, which often had thin metal blades that quickly became worn. Badly worn flatware is difficult to restore; most collectors prefer reproductions, which are more robust. Sets of serving utensils may be found fitted in silk- or velvet-lined boxes, and, if in good condition, these fetch high prices. Small spoons for stirring tea or coffee are worth little individually, even if by a well-known designer. However, if they are in a finely presented, labelled box, their value increases considerably. Whereas in England the same pattern could be used by many makers, in the USA, patterns were patented, and used only by one manufacturer. The date when the pattern was patented is often stamped on the back of the stem. Part services by a major firm such as TIFFANY can usually be added to in order to build up a complete service; however, this is often difficult with flatware by more minor makers.

FLEISCHMANN, ADOLF Active from the mid-19thC to 1930, a German maker of DOLLS in PAPIER-MÂCHÉ.

FLEMISH SCROLL A curving, double-scrolled, X-shaped STRETCHER found on British FURNITURE of the William and Mary period (1689–1702).

FLEURS CHATIRONÉES On PORCELAIN, flower painting characterized by bold, black outlines.

FLEURS DES INDES Meaning "flowers of India", decoration on PORCELAIN imitating Oriental flower painting, especially of lotus and peony blossoms.

FLEURS FINES Meaning "fine flowers", flower painting on PORCELAIN characterized by subtle shading and botanical accuracy.

FLIGHT & BARR PORCELAIN made by WORCESTER in the years 1792–1804, when BONE CHINA was first introduced, and the GLAZES were slightly less translucent – with a yellow tinge – than those of the preceding period.

FLINT GLASS Strictly speaking, GLASS made from powdered flint, but used generally of any strong, brilliant glass.

FLINTLOCK The firing mechanism used for FIREARMS from the 17thC, until superseded by the PERCUSSION LOCK in the early 19thC. A flint held in the cock strikes a steel to create a spark, which primes the powder in the pan.

FLIP GLASS Produced in GLASS, a BEAKER, usually straight-sided, for making or serving flip (fortified and heated wine mixed with sugar and beaten egg).

FLIRTY EYES American term for eyes that open, close, and move from side to side, when a doll's head is tilted. They were made of GLASS, and typically found on early 20thC CHARACTER DOLLS. *See also* DOLL.

FLOATING JOINT On a DOLL, a loose or "floating" ball over which the limbs slide for mobility.

FLORAL CARPET A decorative, rather than functional CARPET, characterized by floral motifs. Made in industrial centres, rather than by nomads.

FLORENCE MAIOLICA Early-15thC TIN-GLAZED EARTHENWARE from Tuscany, Italy. Predominantly green in colour.

FLORIAN WARE Produced by the British potter William MOORCROFT, wares with decoration made by "drawing" onto the pot with thin lines of clay, rather like icing a cake, and then applying colours in between the lines.

FLÖRSHEIM From Flörsheim, late-18thC, German FAIENCE noted for brightly coloured, floral decorations.

FLOWERED GLASS ornamented with floral engravings in the 18thC.

FLUTE GLASS Evolved in the Netherlands in the 17thC, a GLASS with an exaggerated tall narrow bowl.

FLUTING Concave, parallel furrows repeated in vertical lines. Used to decorate the legs of CHAIRS, and on SILVER.

FLUX An alkaline substance added to the GLASS batch to aid the fusion of the ingredients.

FLY BRACKET Small, hinged support for the flap of a TABLE.

FLYING GEESE PATCHWORK pattern in which right-angled triangles are arranged to resemble the flight-formation of a skein of geese.

FLYING STRETCHER Typically found on early DINING-TABLES in OAK, a STRETCHER spanning the single supporting leg at either end.

Moorcroft Macintyre FLORIAN-WARE yellow-tulip-design vase, c.1900.

FLY LEG A leg without STRETCHERS and that swings out to support a TABLE leaf.

FO Motif of a lion with a flowing mane, found on Chinese Buddhist CARPETS.

FOIBLE On a SWORD, the part – from the mid-point of the blade to the tip – that is weakest and most likely to break in battle.

FOLDED FOOT Of wineglasses, the edge of the foot folded under to give extra strength and thickness. Common before the mid-18thC.

FOLDOVER Descriptive of card, gaming, and certain tea TABLES, which have tops that fold over onto themselves when not in use.

FOLEY The name of a British, Staffordshire-based, pottery established by H. Wileman in 1860, and acquired by E. Brain in 1880. Famous for its INTARSIA polychromatic wares, it was renamed SHELLEY POTTERY LTD in 1925, and became known for its ART DECO services.

FOLIOT Found in early CLOCKS, a simple form of balance, consisting of a bar and suspended weights, designed to counteract the thrust of the wheel against the pallets.

FONTANGE An elaborate, ribboned-and-wired head-dress, named after Mademoiselle de Fontange, one of the mistresses of Louis XIV of France in the 1690s. On one occasion, following his attentions, her hair was in disarray, so she tied it up in a topknot with one of her garters. The next day, all the ladies at Court adopted the fashion, even improving upon it – thus the style spread. WOODEN DOLLS with this head-dress have SWIVEL HEADS. *See also* DOLL.

FOREST GLASS An unremarkable, poor-quality SODA GLASS made in small provincial glassworks in France, from the early 17thC until the 19thC.

FORGERY *See* FAKE.

FORM A long bench seat with no back.

FORM WATCH Any WATCH of an unusual decorative form – for example, shaped like a skull, animal, musical instrument, or crucifix. Popular in the 16th and 17thC as novelties.

FORTE The strongest part of a SWORD's blade, from the mid-point to the hilt.

FORTIN'S BAROMETER An instrument with a device such as a moving scale or a cistern that can be raised and lowered to overcome errors due to the fluctuating volume of mercury in the tube.

FOUR-COLOURED WATCH A WATCH with a case decorated with gold INLAY tinted with alloys to make four colours; pure gold, blue, white, and green. Common in the late 18thC in France.

FOUR-HEADED DOLL Set produced by KESTNER comprising a DOLL with a socket body and detachable, interchangeable heads.

FOUR-POSTER BED Bedstead with four tall posts supporting a TESTER.

FOX FAMILY British, London-based, family firm of silversmiths, including George (d.1910), Charles, and Thomas Fox. Established c.1801, the firm is reputed for its high-quality, decorative VICTORIAN wares.

FOX-HEAD Small, 18thC vessels in the form of a fox head, often in CERAMIC (e.g. sauce or CREAM JUGS) but also in GLASS and SILVER (e.g. STIRRUP CUPS).

FOXING Term referring to brown spots of discoloration found on paper in old books and on old prints.

FRAME QUILT Style of British PATCHWORK quilt in which a central square is surrounded by a series of borders. *See also* QUILT.

FRANKENTHAL PORCELAIN FACTORY In Bavaria, Germany, a leading 18thC factory, known for its pieces in the ROCOCO style. Noted for symbolical and mythological figure groups, which are often high quality, albeit with rather stiff poses. Features found on Frankenthal figures are large hands, doll-like faces, arched edges to bases, and tufts of green moss. The shallow, rounded bases often have slim, ROCOCO scrolls broadly washed in GILDING. Key modellers are Johan Friedrich Lück, J.W. Lanz, and Conrad Linck. Pieces were marked with the intials "CT" in UNDERGLAZE BLUE, and sometimes numbers were used to show the year of production.

FRANKLIN CLOCK Early American, weight-driven CLOCK said to be based on Benjamin Franklin's design. Also the name of a clock with a wooden movement, made in the early 19thC by Silas Hoadley of Connecticut.

FREE-BLOWING Technique for shaping a GLASS vessel without the aid of a mould, by blowing and spinning it. Often regarded as the most significant development in glassmaking, free-blowing was invented in the late 1stC BC in the Middle East under Roman rule. It was the most common method of forming glass until automated pressing was introduced in the 19thC. Free-blowing was usually carried out by a team comprising a master craftsman (the gaffer), responsible for forming and working the object, and a number of assistants (the servitors). The process requires great skill and dexterity, and involves using a basic tool – a hollow metal pipe (blowing iron) about 1.2m

(4ft) long, with a mouthpiece at one end. The other end of the pipe is dipped into a crucible containing molten glass in the furnace to collect a "GATHER" or small amount of molten glass. The gather is rolled against a paddle or metal plate to cool it slightly, and the gaffer blows into the pipe to expand the gather into a bubble (PARAISON). The finished object is created by alternately blowing the glass and reheating it in a special furnace, called a "glory hole", to restore its malleability, while tools such as shears, tongs (pucellas), and pincers are used to refine the form, and to manipulate additional applied gathers into HANDLES, feet, STEMS, and rims. This finishing is often carried out in a "glassmaker's chair" – a bench to which horizontal arms are attached. The iron is rolled along these arms to keep the gather in an even shape, and the gaffer may also swing the rod to and fro for the same reason. To create DRINKING GLASSES, dishes, bowls, and other vessels, the paraison is transferred while still hot to a solid iron called a PONTIL ROD that is applied opposite the blowpipe; the last is then removed with the waste glass. The open end is drawn out and fashioned into the required shape. After forming, the object is cooled to room temperature – known as ANNEALING – in a lehr. When the pontil is cracked off, a "PONTIL MARK" is often visible: on glass made before the 19thC the pontil was simply snapped off, leaving a rough surface, but later the mark was machine-polished or ground out. Free-blown wares have slight striations on the surface, where the object was formed and tooled by hand.

FREEDOM BOX A small box engraved on one side with the arms of a city, and on the other with a dedication. In the 18th and 19thC, they were presented when a person was granted the freedom of a city in recognition of his or her service to the public. Most freedom boxes were small – about 7cm (2¾in) in diameter – and made in SILVER; however, some fine examples were also made in GOLD. It is rare to find freedom boxes complete with the original papers granting the freedom of a city, but if the latter is present it will add to the value. Provincial examples, particularly Irish ones, are collectable.

FREEHAND FEATHERS Traditional quilting pattern of feathers marked on the QUILT top without the use of templates or stencils.

FREE MACHINE-QUILTING The production of a QUILT with the feed-dogs of the sewing machine disengaged.

FREEMAN, JOHN Leading English gunsmith, active in the mid-18thC.

FREMINGTON Inexpensive EARTHENWARE made at Fremington, Devon, England, in the latter half of the 19thC. *See also* DEVON POTTERIES.

FRENCH FAIENCE TIN-GLAZED EARTHENWARE from France. Early examples look similar to POTTERY made in Italy, because Italian potters migrated to the French towns of Rouen and Lyons early in the 16thC, bringing with them their native style. Identifiably French faience was produced in the leading centre of Nevers by the 17thC, and styles show the dual influences of Baroque and Chinese design. As the century waned, Rouen superseded Nevers as the most important French centre. In the 18thC, potters moved away from the use of hot, high-fired colours to PETIT FEU ENAMELS, with a more refined, delicate palette. Other important centres of French pottery included the towns of STRASBOURG, SCEAUX, MARSEILLES, and MOUSTIERS. Milk-white, near-perfect GLAZES and botanical painting of the highest order are characteristic of Strasbourg 18thC pottery. In the Marseilles region, 11 factories flourished, included the celebrated VEUVE PERRIN. Pottery decorators were encouraged to attend drawing academies, and a free, spontaneous style of decoration is typical of Marseilles pottery. Toward the end of the 19thC, French pottery returned to earlier styles of the 17th and 18thC, and there were few new developments, although French CREAMWARE called FAIENCE FINE was made in response to competition from the English company WEDGWOOD. Present-day value is based on the size and decorative appeal of the individual item. Among the most valuable pieces are large, early objects such as cisterns and VASES. Pieces made in the 19thC in earlier styles are often highly decorative and available for modest sums. Copies of French faience made in the 19thC are sometimes identifiable by their stiffly painted decoration. Many pieces of French faience are marked with the initials of the maker or with a cipher, which is characteristically painted by hand.

18thC FRENCH-FAIENCE cruet stand from Strasbourg, modelled as a galleon.

FRENCH JOINT On a DOLL, a limb with a ball attached that then fits into the body.

FRENCH LOCK A common FLINTLOCK firing mechanism, developed in France in the early 17thC. It has a notched tumbler, which acts as the sear catch.

FRENCH PLATE A copper plate with SILVER applied as a thin sheet of foil, and either heated or burnished.

FRENCH POLISH Process of applying SHELLAC onto a wood surface, leaving a high-gloss finish. It involved stripping away an old varnish, filling the grain with a chalky substance, and repolishing; with use, the chalk shows through the varnish. In the late 19th and early 20thC, the demand for a high-gloss finish led to much 18thC FURNITURE being French polished. Furniture of this type needs regular stripping back, which, if done too often, will wear away the wood or VENEER. However, a good professional restorer will be able to renew finishes and recreate PATINAS.

FRENCH STOOL Another name for a window seat.

FRETWORK Intricate carved decoration that may be pierced or blind, and is used as a border, or to form a gallery. *See also* BLIND FRET and OPEN FRET.

Derby FRILL VASE, applied with twin mask heads, flowers, and foliage, c.1765.

FRIEND PETZ Early name for German-made TEDDY BEARS.

FRIESLAND CLOCK An 18thC Dutch BRACKET CLOCK with an ornate BRASS or gilt OPENWORK case.

FRIEZE (1) An ornamental band of carved or painted decoration.

FRIEZE (2) A horizontal band of wood that supports a tabletop or desktop, or the cornice on a piece of CASE FURNITURE. On a TABLE or DESK, a DRAWER is sometimes incorporated. Friezes are also applied to horizontal elements found on SILVER and CERAMICS.

FRIGGER A novelty object made of GLASS in the shape of a walking stick, cane, or rolling pin.

FRILL VASE A VASE with pierced sides that was meant for holding pot pourri. The form was made in Britain by DERBY and other factories, and the French SAMSON factory produced copies in the 19thC. Large applied flowers are typical of Derby; flowers by CHELSEA (also in Britain) are more delicate.

FRIT PORCELAIN SOFT-PASTE PORCELAIN containing ground glass. One of the CERAMIC types developed in the search for true PORCELAIN.

FRITWARE Islamic POTTERY made from a silica-rich clay, which, when fired, forms a semi-translucent BODY with a glassy appearance.

FRIZZEN Striking plate of a FLINTLOCK, just above the pan, designed to create a spark when struck with the flint. Also known as the frizzle, or steel.

FROG'S LEGS Flat, splayed legs found on soft-bodied, German baby DOLLS, particularly those made by Armand MARSEILLE.

FROMANTEEL CLOCK Fine-quality, early English PENDULUM CLOCKS made by a Dutch family working in London in the 17th and early 18thC.

FROSTED GLASS Type of GLASS with a surface pattern resembling frost patterns. Common on PRESSED-GLASS vessels for serving cold confections.

FROSTED SILVER On SILVER, matt decoration achieved by etching the surface with mild sulphuric acid, engraving multiple small lines, or hatching.

FROTHINGHAM, BENJAMIN (1734–1809) Massachusetts cabinet-maker who made quality American CASE FURNITURE in the style of Thomas CHIPPENDALE.

FROZEN CHARLIE Male version of a "FROZEN CHARLOTTE".

FROZEN CHARLOTTE A 19thC CHINA DOLL, so-called because the head and limbs do not move.

FRUIT BASKET Used for serving fruit, a SILVER container with a handle and FRETWORK sides.

FRUIT KNIFE First made *c*.1780, a folding knife used for peeling fruit, and popular on picnics. Many examples have SILVER blades and ornate handles of IVORY, horn, MOTHER-OF-PEARL, or TORTOISESHELL.

FRUITWOOD Wood of a fruit tree, such as an apple, pear, or cherry tree.

FU A Chinese bat motif, found on CARPETS and PORCELAIN. Considered to be a symbol of good fortune.

FUDDLING CUP An EARTHENWARE vessel consisting of several linked cups. Anyone challenged to empty one of the cups was forced to drain them all.

FUKUGAWA Japanese PORCELAIN company based in ARITA. It was founded in 1689, but only 19thC products are common.

FULDA Factory at Hessen that produced some of Germany's best FAIENCE in the mid-18thC. In the late 18thC it began making MEISSEN-style PORCELAIN.

FULHAM English pottery, based in London and noted for fine, early-18thC, salt-glazed figures modelled by John Dwight, as well as early STONEWARES.

FULLER Groove running down the centre of the blade of a SWORD or DAGGER.

FULL STOCKED Any FIREARM in which the fore-end of the stock extends the length of the barrel.

FULPER POTTERY CO. Founded in 1815 in New Jersey, this American firm made STONEWARE and utilitarian EARTHENWARE before moving to ART POTTERY. William Hill Fulper made moulded or hand-thrown stoneware in CLASSICAL and Oriental forms, and used a variety of GLAZES. Fulper pottery lamps, patented in 1912, have ceramic bases and shades fitted with slag GLASS inserts. Fulper is usually marked with an impressed name; pieces with vertical letters are earlier than horizontal ones. A circular mark with the date 1805 is sometimes seen.

FUMÉ GLASS with a smoky appearance.

FUNDAME Japanese, matt-gold decoration as opposed to bright gold, or KINJI.

FUNNEL *See* WINE FUNNEL.

Very rare, salt-glazed, stoneware flask from FULHAM pottery, *c*.1835.

FURNITURE Functional objects, including storage and seating pieces. Early furniture was made from solid-wood planks that were nailed together, whereas later, a framework joined by MORTISE-AND-TENON joints, held in place by wooden dowel pegs or "trenails", and filled with panels became popular. This method is found on COFFERS, SETTLES, and CHESTS OF DRAWERS made before 1700. The vertical boards that become the legs are called STILES; the horizontal members are RAILS. The technique of decorating furniture by applying VENEERS was developed in the late 17thC. From the latter part of the 17thC onward, DOVETAIL JOINTS were used in CASE FURNITURE such as CHESTS OF DRAWERS and CUPBOARDS. Dowel pegs were used less in the 18thC, as glues improved. By 1800, PINE was used increasingly, and dovetails were less sophisticated. Until the late 18thC, when the circular saw was introduced, all wood was sawed by hand, leaving straight saw marks. After *c*.1800, circular marks may be visible on unfinished wood. It was not until electricity was widespread in the early 20thC that machine-made dovetails prevailed. In the 18thC, on most English DRAWER bottoms, the grain runs from back to front. Many feet styles were revived and reproduced in later periods, so this is no guarantee of age. Feet may have rotted and been replaced. Replacement feet will not reduce the value, if their style is consistent with the piece. Having casters that are original to a piece is always desirable. HANDLES and locks can help with dating. Replacements are acceptable if they are in keeping with the style of the piece. A rich, mellow colour, the PATINA, is important on any piece of furniture. *See also* FURNITURE, 20THC; NAIL; and SCREW.

FURNITURE, 20THC New manufacturing techniques and materials led to changes in FURNITURE design in the 20thC. Many leading designers, such as Marcel Breuer, Ludwig MIES VAN DER ROHE, and LE CORBUSIER, produced tailor-made furniture for new homes, where space was at a premium, so folding and stacking furniture was prominent. Much 20thC furniture was mass-produced. Novel, inexpensive materials such as tubular steel and moulded plywood were used in streamlined forms, with minimal decoration. From the 1950s, the availability of plastics and fibreglass allowed designers to create biomorphic shapes and organic designs. Look out for innovative designs attributed to recognized designers such as those listed above and Alvar AALTO (Finland), Harry BERTOIA (USA), Charles EAMES (USA), Arne Jacobsen (Denmark), and Pierre Paulin (France). Original upholstery is always desirable, although re-upholstering by the original manufacturer will not affect value.

"ABCD" chair by Pierre Paulin, which comes with matching sofa, *c*.1965 (20THC FURNITURE).

FURNITURE, ALTERATION OF Much FURNITURE has been altered. Typical alterations include large DINING-TABLES made into smaller BREAKFAST TABLES, POLESCREENS made into small wine tables, and TALLBOYS divided into two CHESTS. At the top end of the market, an altered piece will be less desirable than one in original condition, but among the more functional, less exclusive pieces a practical alteration may have little bearing on price. A COMMODE made into a bedside table will not be worth much less than one with all its fittings. Another common alteration by the Victorians and Edwardians (1837–1901 and 1901–10 respectively) was later decoration. CROSSBANDING, often in SATINWOOD, and INLAY were added to plain MAHOGANY pieces, while plain COFFERS in OAK were jazzed up with carved decoration. These alterations have little bearing on price. Some alterations made furniture more comfortable; 18thC, oval-backed, upholstered chairs were fitted with spring-upholstered seats in the 19th or 20thC. Value will not be affected unless the springs alter the profile of the chair. More problematic are alterations to enhance the value of a piece – for example, a CUPBOARD that has been fitted with glazed doors or a large DRESSER that has been cut down to a smaller size. A piece that looks too heavy on top, or has legs that are too big or small may be a MARRIAGE. Freshly cut surfaces, repositioned handles, and plugged holes are signs of alteration, and pieces changed in such a way are less desirable than their genuine counterparts.

FURNITURE, CARE OF Excessive heat and intense sunlight are the two main factors that can cause damage to FURNITURE. Central heating and double-glazing creates hot, airless rooms without humidity, causing VENEERS to split and planks to warp, especially if a piece is near a radiator. A humidifier will alleviate this problem, but damp conditions may cause wood to rot. Although gentle daylight helps to give wood an attractive, soft PATINA, excessive sunlight dries the wood and can cause cracks and damage to veneers. Do not place furniture in direct sunlight – diffuse the light with a blind. Patination is an all-important factor, especially on English pieces of furniture, and pieces should be repolished only as a last resort, and then by a professional. Avoid FRENCH POLISH. Polish antique furniture sparingly (once a year is almost too much), using a bee's-wax polish. Never use a silicone spray, which dries the wood. Dust your pieces regularly, but with care, especially items decorated with veneering and INLAY. If small sections of veneer or inlay break off or come out, repair them immediately, or rough edges will be left that flick up when dusted. To repair such pieces, clean out any old glue first and use a wood glue, not a modern adhesive. *See also* WOODWORM.

FURNIVAL IRONSTONE Painted and relief-decorated tablewares made in quantity by T. Furnival & Sons of Cobridge, Britain, from the mid-19thC.

FÜRSTENBERG German PORCELAIN factory, founded in the mid-18thC, and noted for plaques and CERAMIC pictures for hanging on walls.

FUSEE Invented in the 18thC, a cone-shaped drum linked to the spring barrel to ensure constant timekeeping on a CLOCK.

FU TS'ANG LUNG Chinese dragon symbol found on CARPETS and PORCELAIN.

FYFOT A motif of a reversed swastika, found on Indian CARPETS.

G

GABBEH A sought-after domestic RUG from south Persia. They are coarsely woven, with thick, chunky wool, bright colours, and bold designs.

GADROONING Consisting of a series of raised, convex curves, a pattern found on the rims and handles of 18thC SILVER, and carved in FURNITURE.

GAILLARD, LUCIEN (1862–1933) French silversmith and jeweller, and member of the Paris school of craftsmen. *See also* JEWELLERY and SILVER.

GAINSBOROUGH CHAIR Open ARMCHAIR of rectangular appearance made in England in the 18thC. Also known as a "HOGARTH CHAIR".

GALENA Powdered lead sulphide used by medieval potters as a GLAZE, ranging from almost colourless to rich yellow.

GALL The source of black or dark-brown dye used in Oriental CARPETS.

GALLÉ, EMILE (1846–1904) One of the leading French exponents of the ART NOUVEAU style, and founder of a talented circle of designers based around Nancy. In the 1880s, he began both experimenting with new GLASS techniques, and designed delicate FURNITURE embellished with MARQUETRY. Gallé established his own factory for ART GLASS in 1867. In 1889, he developed CAMEO GLASS; in 1897, MARQUETRIE DE VERRE. The firm made vases, lamps, and tableware, and clear-enamelled items showed Islamic and Venetian influences. Gallé was best known for hand-carved CAMEO GLASS and etched glass. Most wares are high quality and individually decorated. Gallé also produced a commercial line of acid-etched cameo for the popular market. Later, machine-made versions of Gallé glass pieces are less valuable than handmade ones, and are identifiable because the carving is not as deeply cut. Wares by Gallé are usually marked with a cameo or incise-carved signatures. If there is a star after the signature, the piece was made during the first three years after Gallé's death, between 1904 and 1907. Fake pieces of cameo glass marked "Gallé" are recognizable by stiff, lifeless decoration. The features characteristic of most Gallé furniture include a strong, sculptural quality, inventive design, FRUITWOOD marquetry, stylized, floral decorative motifs, and a signature. Furniture marked "GALLÉ" that lacks the originality of earlier designs and is less inventive in its use of INLAY may have been made by Gallé's firm after his death. Although collectable, such pieces are less valuable than pieces made in his lifetime.

GALLERY A brass or wood, open, decorative, raised edging to a flat surface.

GALTUK A CARPET from the Arak region of northern Iran.

GAMBOGES A bright yellow colour, named after the resin from which it is derived, and used in RUGS and textiles.

GAMES TABLE A TABLE with compartments and a specially designed tabletop on which to play games such as backgammon, chess, and tric-trac (a variation of backgammon). Tric-trac tables often resemble PEMBROKE or SOFA TABLES, but have removable panels that conceal wells that are divided in two. Various woods were used, as well as PAPIER-MÂCHÉ. Inlaid MOTHER-OF-PEARL was sometimes used to create chess boards. *See also* CARD TABLE.

GARDE DU VIN A CELLARET designed en suite with a SIDEBOARD.

GARDEN CARPET From western Iran, a CARPET featuring a garden scene.

GARDNER, FRANCIS English founder of a mid-18thC PORCELAIN factory near Moscow, Russia. *See also* GARDNER FACTORY.

GARDNER FACTORY Russian PORCELAIN factory established in 1776 by Francis GARDNER. It flourished until the 1880s, when it was taken over by the KUZNETSOV FACTORY. Gardner was famed for figures in regional costumes, and often used matt unglazed surfaces in sombre colours, especially blue.

GARDEN FURNITURE Benches, seats, and TABLES for use out of doors. Purpose-built garden FURNITURE was made, for the most part, from the Victorian era (1837–1901) onward. The most expensive examples are made from marble or stone. Furniture of this type became popular in the 19thC, when tourists in Italy bought it as a souvenir; later, as demand grew, it was exported for sale to other countries. Stone seats and benches were carved from local materials by stonemasons throughout Europe. COADE STONE, an early type of reconstituted stone made since the 18thC, is valuable. Look for Carrara marble statuary, stone benches, and early types of reconstituted stone. Avoid modern stone or cement. Just because a piece looks weathered, it does not necessarily mean that it is old – the moss-clad look may be achieved in a matter of weeks if a modern piece of stone is painted with sour milk. Garden furniture changed dramatically after the improvement of iron casting, which was pioneered by the COALBROOKDALE IRON CO. in the 1840s. Cast-iron seating was fitted with metal, PINE, or OAK slatted seats. The slats may be replaced, and this is a common alteration that does not greatly affect value. The rising value of cast-iron furniture has led to many reproductions, including 1990s' replicas of 1860s' Coalbrookdale designs. Some copies include the date of the "original", but seek expert advice if you are in doubt.

Early-20thC, French, Kingwood kidney-shaped side table with a brass GALLERY and inlaid decoration.

Paul GARNIER **carriage clock, c.1840.**

Signs of authenticity include crisp casting, a registration or kite stamp (this may be indistinct, even on a genuine piece), and a foundry mark. Among the more affordable garden furniture is a wide range of attractive, bent-wire metal pieces produced in France in the early 20thC. The French used flat, curving strips of metal to form sprung supports on the back and seat of the chairs, creating metal furniture that was more comfortable than most. When purchasing any type of metal furniture, make sure that the wire is strong – the welding is vulnerable to damage from rust. Metal garden furniture will last longer if it is repainted regularly, and this does not reduce the value of less-expensive pieces. *See also* BAMBOO FURNITURE and WICKER FURNITURE.

GARNIER French clockmaking family, including (Jean-)Paul, active from 1825.

GARNISH A set of SILVER, PEWTER, or PORCELAIN tableware.

GARNITURE A group of PORCELAIN figures or ornaments, such as a set of three or more VASES of matching and complementary form, intended to stand on a mantelpiece or on the top of a CABINET. The group may include a CLOCK.

GARRARD A dominant name in the SILVER trade since the 18thC, with Robert Garrard I and his son Robert Garrard II particularly influential. Due mainly to the direction of the latter, the family firm was appointed Goldsmith to the British Crown in 1830 and, in 1843, Crown Jewellers. They used "RG" under a crown as their mark between 1822 and 1900, but wares made since 1900 feature the initials "RG" only. In 1963, Garrard & Co. merged with MAPPIN & WEBB and ELKINGTON & CO. to form British Silverware Ltd.

GARYA HUSK A stylized flower such as a wheat husk or bluebell used as carved or inlaid decoration. It is usually associated with furniture in the styles of George HEPPLEWHITE and Robert ADAM.

GATELEG TABLE A type of 17th and 18thC DROP-LEAF TABLE with leaves supported by legs with STRETCHERS (called gates), which swing out from the main frame. Ideal for less-formal occasions or smaller houses, gateleg tables were first fashionable in the mid-17thC; some early versions had legs halved vertically to form supports. The standard design has four fixed legs that are connected by stretchers, with pull-out gates that extend to support the flaps on either side. Larger tables sometimes have two pull-out gates on each side. Most gateleg tables are large enough to seat no more than six people comfortably; the most expensive ones seat six or more. Check the flaps and hinges for damage. The hinges might be made from wooden RULE JOINTS or from metal. The flaps are heavy, and it is easy for the hinges to break, causing the flaps to drop and split. Look for tabletops that are solid rather than finished with a VENEER. The grain of the wood on the flaps and the centre should run parallel to the hinges. OAK or a combination of oak and

ELM are usual for early gatelegs. Signs of a 20thC reproduction piece include thin tops and stretchers, a high contrast in the grain on the top but no depth to the PATINA, and a moulded top edge (earlier gatelegs had square-cut edges). *See also* DINING-TABLE and DROP-LEAF TABLE.

GATE, SIMON (1883–1945) Swedish designer of GLASS tableware, engraved glass, and cut-glass VASES that exploited the optical qualities of clear glass. His work was shown at the Stockholm Exhibition of 1930.

GATHER The mass of molten GLASS attached to the end of a blowpipe or PONTIL ROD before a glass vessel is formed. *See also* FREE-BLOWING.

GATLING GUN Early machine gun named after its mid-19thC inventor.

GAUDREAU, ANTOINE (d.1751) French cabinet-maker patronized by royalty in the early 18thC.

"GAUDY DUTCH" Cheap, colourful, hand-decorated PEARLWARE, imitating DERBY and WORCESTER "IMARI" patterns. Made by 19thC, English Staffordshire potters for export to the USA, and popular with Pennsylvanian Germans.

GAULTIER DOLL A BISQUE-head DOLL made by François Gaultier (1860–99) on a variety of bodies: gusseted KID, GUTTA-PERCHA (latex), and articulated wood or metal padded with KAPOK and covered with stockinette. Late 19thC Gaultier dolls had narrow waists and wide shoulders and hips – an ideal shape for showing off their bustled dresses to best advantage. Gaultier FASHION DOLLS and BÉBÉS are recognizable by the slightly smiling mouths and well-defined upper lips. Gaultier bébés, noted for the size and quality of their fixed glass "paperweight" or bulbous eyes, often had small pointed chins, pierced ears, and chubby cheeks. Pre-1885, lightly arched eyebrows are thin; on later dolls they are dark and glossy. A typical 1870 Gaultier doll has a closed mouth, real hair over a cork PATE, and a SWIVEL HEAD. Hats were important to achieve the chic look of PARISIENNE DOLLS. Separately stitched fingers and toes are more desirable than "mitten" hands and feet stitched in one block. A closed mouth and large size increase the value. Gaultier marked most of its fashion dolls on the shoulder and/or back of the crown of the head. It is important when checking a doll to be sure that the head and body belong together. Many Gaultier heads were sold to other firms who attached their own bodies. GESLAND, a French firm that specialized in doll repairs and spare parts, used Gaultier heads, but its dolls are not marked on the BISQUE except for maybe a number denoting the size.

GEMS Stone found in JEWELLERY and sometimes used to adorn metal and GOLD objects. Precious stones include diamonds, rubies, pearls, sapphires, and emeralds; semi-precious stones, include amethyst and peridot. Precious stones are more valuable than semi-precious ones. Other factors that affect value include the clarity and cut of the stone, and its size and colour. Ornamental gems are hardstones such as agate, coral, lapis lazuli, onyx, and turquoise.

GENDJE A brightly coloured, Caucasian RUG with linear decoration.

GENTLEMEN'S TOILETRY A toilet set, first used in the 19thC when it became fashionable for men to scent themselves with cologne. Such sets are smaller and not as elaborate as those for women, and for personal use (often for when travelling) rather than show. They varied from a single GLASS cologne flask contained in a SILVER case, to several flasks housed in a leather box. EDWARDIAN toilet sets for men often also held silver accessories, such as brushes, shaving items, and perhaps also curling tongs for the moustache. *See also* DRESSING-TABLE SET.

GEORGIAN STYLE Strictly, the period from 1760 to 1800, but often used to cover the reigns of the three British King Georges (1714–1830), which are subdivided into Hanoverian (1714–60), Late Georgian (1760–1800), and Regency (1800–30). It encompasses the ROCOCO, NEO-CLASSICAL, and REGENCY styles and, collectively, forms a period in which the leading designers, such as William KENT, Thomas CHIPPENDALE, and Thomas HOPE, had a powerful impact on FURNITURE through their design books.

GERA Late-18thC, German, Thuringia-based, PORCELAIN factory, imitating wares by MEISSEN.

GERMAN METAL Nickel or tin-based alloy intended to imitate SILVER.

GERMAN SILVER White metal alloy, composed of nickel, copper, and zinc, and used in the 19thC for SILVER PLATE in preference to copper, which showed through where the SILVER coating became worn through constant use.

GESLAND On a DOLL, a body made from articulated wood or metal, padded with KAPOK, and covered in stockinette. Also, a doll-repair company.

GESSO Plaster-like substance applied in thick layers to an inexpensive secondary timber before carving, gilding, and painting.

GHASHOGHDOUN Small carpet bag used by nomadic peoples for transporting clothes and household utensils. *See also* RUG.

GHIORDES KNOT Characteristic of the Caucasus and Turkey, a CARPET-making knot formed by passing the yarn over two threads, turning them under, and bringing the ends up through the space between. Also known as a Turkish or symmetric knot. *See also* SEHNA CARPETS and SENNEH KNOT.

GHIORDES RUG From the Turkish town of the same name, a small, high-quality RUG in wool or silk with a dense, highly ornate pattern.

GHOUM From the Teheran (Qum) region of Iran, a CARPET decorated with rows of multi-coloured motifs.

GIBBONS, GRINLING (1648–1721) Famous for his naturalistic wood-carving adorning house interiors as well as FURNITURE, Gibbon was appointed master-carver to King George I of England in 1714.

GIEN French 19thC FAIENCE imitating earlier styles. Sometimes decorated with TRANSFER-PRINTING.

GILBODY, SAMUEL (*active* 1753–61) English potter, whose Liverpool-based factory produced blue and iron-red wares with a silky glaze.

GILDING, CERAMIC GOLD applied to CERAMICS by mixing it with oil, mercury, or honey and refiring the piece at a lower temperature; or by applying cold, liquid gold. Mercury gilding was popular in Continental Europe, and looks bright and shiny; honey gilding was used in England from *c.*1750, and is slightly dull in appearance; oil gilding was used on STAFFORDSHIRE POTTERY and early English PORCELAIN, and pieces finished in this way are vulnerable to wear.

GILDING, FURNITURE Decorative finish made by covering a base with a layer of GOLD leaf or powdered gold. On a carved softwood frame (usually BEECH) there are four stages: first, the wood is sealed and made smooth with a layer of GESSO; secondly, a red- or yellow-coloured layer of clay bole is applied to give depth and richness to the gilding; thirdly, the gold leaf is applied with a brush and glued in place with size (boiled linseed and turpentine); finally, the desired shine is created by burnishing (rubbing) the surface with an agate (an impure form of quartz). Other methods achieve slightly different results; water gilding, where the gold leaf is applied to the clay bole with a gilder's sable tip, gives a brighter finish. In the USA, almost any piece is imperfect if regilded. Good new gilding is difficult to achieve because it can look too harsh; it should always be undertaken by a qualified expert.

GILDING, GLASS GOLD applied to GLASS by one of several methods. Gilding is sometimes combined with coloured enamels, and is often applied to an engraved surface to protect the gold from wear. Honey gilding involves painting on a mix of ground gold leaf and honey, and firing it at a low temperature to fix the gold. Mercury gilding, also used on SILVER, is a similar process, using gold combined with mercury, which burns off when the object is fired, leaving a film of gold. However, this method is no longer used because of the toxicity of the mercury fumes. Cold gilding is a less durable method, because the gold leaf is mixed with oil and applied to the surface but not fired, so it can easily flake off.

GIEN, faience ewer painted with renaissance-style decoration, 19thC.

GILES, JAMES (1718–80) One of the most notable English GLASS decorators working in the 1760s and early 1770s. As well as glass drinking wares, SCENT BOTTLES, VASES, and DECANTERS, the Giles workshop decorated PORCELAIN from WORCESTER and other English factories. Designs are gilded or enamelled, and characterized by delicately painted exotic birds, CHINOISERIE, floral sprays, and CLASSICAL motifs such as husks and FESTOONS.

GILLILAND GLASS made in the 18thC by the American firm of John L. Gilliland & Co., which later became the Brooklyn Flint Glass Co.

GILLINDER, JAMES & SONS American glassworks founded in Philadelphia by William Gillander, active from 1860 to the1930s. The firm manufactured the popular "Westward Ho" pattern, consisting of buffalo, elk, and Native Americans.

GILLOWS Prominent FURNITURE workshop founded in Lancaster *c.*1727 by the English cabinet-maker Robert Gillow (1704–72). It produced tasteful, well-made furniture in the 19thC. George HEPPLEWHITE was apprentice here.

GILTWOOD Wood that has been gilded but without an application of GESSO.

GIMSON, ERNEST (1864–1920) Founder, together with the BARNSLEYS, of the Cotswold Arts and Crafts workshops, based in Gloucestershire. He was a leading member of the Cotswold School, known for its plain wood finishes. Gimson designed simple but elegant rustic FURNITURE associated with the ARTS AND CRAFTS MOVEMENT.

GIN BOTTLE STONEWARE jar or flask often modelled in the 19thC with the caricature of a political figure.

GINGER JAR Tall, richly engraved, lidded SILVER vessel, used from the 17thC. It is so-called because of its shape, which is similar to Oriental vessels used for storing crystallized ginger.

GINORI Early MAIOLICA made by the Ginori family in Doccia, Italy. Also refers to 19thC reproductions of older forms.

GIRANDOLE (1) An elaborate MIRROR with a CANDELABRUM or SCONCE attached. From the mid-17thC, they were made to hang on the wall.

GIRANDOLE (2) A pendant or a pair of earrings with a larger central GEM surrounded by clusters of smaller ones, suspended in a chandelier-like fashion. They were popular in France and Spain in the 18thC.

GIRANDOLE CLOCK Early 19thC BANJO CLOCK of especially ornate appearance, with applied gilt SCROLLS, eagles, and other decoration.

GIRL IN A SWING An English, London-based, PORCELAIN factory that made similar wares to CHELSEA, and is known after its most famous figure, the "Girl in a Swing". It has now been identified as Charles Gouyn's factory, which was active from *c*.1749 to 1759.

GIUSTINIANI Family of 18thC MAIOLICA makers based in Naples, Italy.

GLASGOW DELFTWARE Mid-18thC, tin-glazed wares made by London (Lambeth) potters, who founded a factory in Glasgow, Scotland.

GLASGOW SCHOOL Originally the name of Scotland's Glasgow School of Art at which Charles Rennie MACKINTOSH studied in the 1880s, and whose new buildings he designed in the 1890s. Now used to describe the simplified linear form of ART NOUVEAU, which was developed by Mackintosh and his followers and highly influential on Continental European work of the period.

GLASGOW-SCHOOL, copper tray with repoussé and hammered peacocks within pear trees, c.1900.

GLASS A transparent or translucent substance made by fusing silica, derived from sand, quartz, or flint, with an alkaline in the form of sodium carbonate (soda) derived from plants, or potassium carbonate (potash) obtained from burnt beechwood, oak, or bracken, at high temperature. This combination of ingredients – the basic materials of glassmaking – is known as a "batch". Lime, from chalk or limestone, is usually added as a stabilizer, while small amounts of other ingredients, such as lead or borax, will affect the physical properties of the glass, such as its brilliance. When molten, glass is described as "METAL", and it is this that is drawn, blown, or shaped by the glassmaker. There are three main types of glass: SODA GLASS, POTASH GLASS, and lead glass (LEAD CRYSTAL). Various methods have been used for forming glass objects: the most familiar type is FREE-BLOWING, but molten glass can also be cast like metal or shaped in a mould, or, for small, hollow vessels, wound round a core. Throughout history, glass has been made in an infinite range of styles, forms, and colours, from simple, disposable bottles to elaborate, cut-glass vessels, and mirrors. The earliest glass objects – including bottles and flasks made in ancient Egypt – were generally small, heavy, and irregular in shape, owing to the fact that the core-forming method used was impractical for large objects. The invention of free-blowing and MOULD-BLOWING by the ancient Romans enabled the production of larger vessels, few of which have survived today. It was not until the development in the mid-15thC of CRISTALLO that fanciful decoration was widely used. Some decorative techniques, such as cutting, only became possible after the invention of heavy and brilliant lead crystal in England in the 17thC. Techniques such as engraving and cutting were practised to the highest degree of skill in northern and central Europe from the 17thC. Decoration was also applied to the surface of glass by trailing, combing and milling, enamelling, and gilding. Developments in both chemical and glass technology during the Industrial Revolution of the 19thC enabled a much broader range

Art Nouveau GLASS vase overlaid in silver flowers and sinous tendrils, probably American, c.1900.

of glassware to be produced, including the emergence of new types of glassware, such as BUTTER DISHES, JUGS, wineglass coolers, and FINGER BOWLS. Bohemian and, later, American craftsmen were the leading exponents of coloured glass. Today, glass is one of the most affordable types of antique available. Decoration added onto glass can add substantially to the value of a piece, such as the layering of clear and coloured glass through casing and overlay, and the insertion of coloured-glass rods in a section of clear glass to produce a variety of ornamental twisting or interlaced patterns. The colourful glass produced in the 19thC is becoming increasingly popular with some collectors. Items marked by famous makers can be expensive, but unmarked glass from the 19thC is still available at reasonable prices, and 19thC table glass can sometimes be less expensive than modern equivalents. Antique DRINKING GLASSES are collectable, and copies and fakes of many of the more expensive types abound. In the 19thC, Victorian glassmakers made imitations of 18thC glass, and many fakes have been produced in the 20thC. These are often discernible by considering three key issues: colour, manufacturing method, and proportions. With the colour, the distinctive tint caused by impurities may not be present in reproductions. In terms of manufacturing methods, note that hand-blown glass usually has a PONTIL MARK; it may also have striations of ripples in the glass, and a rim of uneven thickness. Later, machine-made glass does not have these imperfections. Regarding proportions, glass has varied in style and proportions throughout the centuries. On old glasses the foot is usually as wide as the bowl, or slightly wider. The wrong proportions may indicate a fake. Genuine ancient Roman glass has a metallic lustre inside the glass, not just the outside, and is also light in weight compared to modern pieces. Fakes of CAMEO GLASS made in 19thC France and England may be hand-finished, but the cutting is rarely as intricate or detailed as on earlier pieces, while the colours are brighter and more "chemical" in appearance. In Germany, reproductions of 15th and 16thC forms, such as ROEMER, were made in the 1870s; the 19thC versions often had over-elaborate decoration, with excessively bright enamelling. Watch out for fake signatures on ART NOUVEAU glass, especially pieces by GALLÉ and TIFFANY, and on 19thC English ART GLASS in the styles of Thomas WEBB & Sons and STEVENS & WILLIAMS. Marks or signatures on antique glass are rare, so hands-on experience is one of the most immediate ways of acquainting yourself with the styles of different manufacturers or decorators. Suites of glass tableware – sets of DECANTERS, bowls, and glasses in different sizes – though produced only from the early 19thC, are rare, often because they were divided among family members. To form a large collection it is useful to focus on a particular theme, for example a certain glassmaking area, period, colour, or decoration. Popular areas include 18thC drinking glasses, which are characterized by a wide range of decorative stems, 19thC Bohemian glass, or scent bottles. Somewhat rarer and more expensive are early PAPERWEIGHTS, American and French art glass, and 15th and 16thC glass. Increasing public interest in 20thC design has meant that post-war, sculptural glass and more practical domesticware such as PYREX dishes are collectable. These are among the most affordable types of glass available today. Avoid buying damaged pieces, which are always less desirable than those in good condition. Examine items carefully to check for cracks and chips, which are often not immediately visible. *See also* ACID-ENGRAVING; CASTING; COLOUR TWISTS; CORE-FORMING; COMBED DECORATION; CUT GLASS; ENAMELLING; ENGRAVING; FLASHING; GILDING; GLASS, 20THC; GLASS, CARE OF; GLASS, COLOURED; LAMPWORK; LATTICINIO; LATTIMO; OVERLAY GLASS; POTASH GLASS; PRESSED GLASS; PRESS MOULDING; PRUNT; STAINING; TABLEWARE, GLASS; and TRAILING.

GLASS, 20THC The value of a piece of 20thC glassware is dependent on its maker or designer. Look for wares in the ART DECO style produced by French designers and manufacturers, such as Emile GALLÉ and René LALIQUE, and TIFFANY and STEUBEN GLASSWORKS in the USA. French glassmakers used angular forms, geometric, enamelled decoration, and dramatic colour combinations. Glass was increasingly used to make a plethora of decorative VASES and new electric lamps, and designers produced objects as diverse as car mascots, JEWELLERY, and SCENT BOTTLES. All named glass of the Art Deco period is collected, and the best pieces are expensive; wares by Lalique are especially collectable. Scandinavian designers, led by the Finns Aino and Alvar AALTO, who designed elegant and functional tableware in a new MODERNIST style, focused on a typically Art Deco contrast of clear and black glass, often engraved with stylized motifs that influenced leading designers, such as Keith MURRAY in Britain. In Austria, the faceted, monochromatic designs of Josef HOFFMANN led the trend toward chunky forms. These stylistic elements were adapted and incorporated into a huge range of tableware, of varying quality, especially the DECANTERS, cocktail glasses and shakers, and DRINKING GLASSES that flooded onto the market as manufacturers sought to capitalize on the new hedonistic lifestyle that Art Deco epitomized. Most decanters were accompanied by sets of six glasses. Few sets have survived intact, and individual glasses, especially stylish ones with a strong Art Deco feel and in excellent condition, are a good starting point for collectors. Art Deco tumblers were small and decorative sculpture rather than practical pieces of tableware – they held little and often had uncomfortable, chunky forms. In Sweden, designers and manufacturers such as ORREFORS and KOSTA were making affordable tableware and a range of engraved glass that was shown at the Stockholm Exhibition of 1930, and in 1931 toured Britain, where it influenced leading designers. In Austria, the designers of the WIENER WERKSTÄTTE also experimented with new forms. Some English glassmakers established firms to make a range of luxury CUT GLASS to compete with the inexpensive glassware that was flooding in from Czechoslovakia. New companies sprang up that concentrated on cased and coloured glass, such as MONART and GRAY-STAN. In the USA, luxury glass made for the top end of the market was matched in the 1920s and '30s by vast quantities of cheap, mechanically mass-produced wares known as DEPRESSION

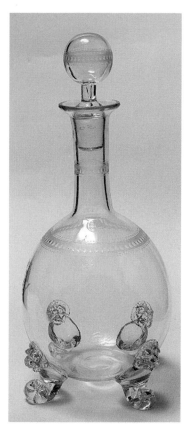

GLASS **decanter by Thomas Webb with unusual lion mask prunts above the feet, c.1880.**

GLASS. The Organic Design in Home Furniture Exhibition, held in New York in 1940, was the showcase for the fluid shapes that became known as the "New Look". This stylistic movement offered relief from the austerity of the early post-war years. In the 1940s and '50s, the Scandinavians and Italians interpreted the "New Look" most successfully, with Nils Landberg's work for Orrefors, Per Lutken's designs for the Danish Holmegaards Glassworks, Tapio WIRKKALA at Ittala in Finland, and a range of lively coloured glass from Italian manufacturers. The Scandinavian designers continued the tradition of restrained, minimalist lines. British glassmakers were initially slow to respond to the "New Look", but came to the fore with the STUDIO GLASS movement that had begun in the USA in the 1960s. Scandinavian and Italian glass, especially by well-known designers, is an established collecting area. Sculptural pieces by renowned makers may be the "antiques" of tomorrow. *See also* ART GLASS.

GLASS, CARE OF Glass tableware was designed to be functional, and 19th and 20thC pieces are suitable for everyday domestic use. However, items of rare and valuable glass from the 16thC and 17thC often require specialist attention, because they are sometimes chemically unstable. Take care when handling or displaying PAPERWEIGHTS; if knocked, they can "bruise" (but not crack) inside, causing permanent damage and reducing their value. Do not leave vases filled with water for long because the water will corrode the surface, leaving a cloudy appearance. It is safe to use DECANTERS or CLARET JUGS for dinner parties, but do not store wine or alcohol in them, because alcohol will leave stains. Lead will also leach out from LEAD CRYSTAL into liquid stored in decanters, albeit slowly, over many years and in small amounts. Most glass can be cleaned simply by using warm, soapy water and a soft cloth, fine brush, or sponge. Avoid hot water because this can lead to thermal shock. Always handle the object with care when cleaning to avoid breaking handles, rims, and feet. Large hollow vessels such as decanters or jugs should be cleaned with a bottle brush; use bleach to remove stubborn wine or alcohol stains. However, an object such as a decanter or vase with a cloudy appearance on the inside needs to be cleaned by a specialist. Never use bleach or detergent on enamelled or gilded glass, because this risks damaging the delicate paint or layer of gold. Abrasive cleaners should be avoided, because they leave fine scratches on the surface. After cleaning, the glass object should always be rinsed, then dried with a soft cloth, gently but thoroughly to prevent water stains. Decanters, vases, and jugs can be dried by being left upside down in a dry, warm atmosphere. Decanter stoppers should always be dried thoroughly, or they may become jammed in the top of the decanter. Do not put glass on a cold or hot surface directly after washing, because this may cause thermal shock. Never put antique glass or any other good glass in a dishwasher; the detergents can cause lead crystal to cloud and will leave spots or rings on SODA GLASS, and some detergents may abrade the surface. Do not let candles burn too far down glass CANDLESTICKS

Thomas Webb, yellow cameo GLASS bottle with silver flip top, *c.*1880.

and candelabra, or the candle stub can be difficult to remove. If this happens, do not take it out with a knife or other sharp implement, as this will scratch the glass – instead pour warm water around the top of the rim, and the wax will soften, making it easy to dislodge.

GLASS, COLOURED Owing to impurities in a batch of GLASS, coloured glass has sometimes been produced accidentally. However, most items of coloured glass are produced intentionally by adding metallic oxides to the batch; these dissolve and disperse throughout the liquid glass. Different metals produce different colours, but the shade varies according to the amount of metallic oxide used and other additives in the batch. Blue is the easiest colour to achieve, while yellow and orange are the most complex. It can be difficult to match green glass, even in pieces made at the same time in one glasshouse, because the tone varies from yellowish green to a deep, rich emerald or olive green. Coloured glass has also been used to imitate hardstones, for example mosaic glass, invented by the ancient Romans and made by arranging thin slices of fused-glass rods of different colours in a mould. Coloured DRINKING GLASSES (and DECANTERS) were produced in small quantities in England during the 18thC. However, many 18thC styles were copied in the late 19th and early 20thC, and some later versions are so convincing that even experienced collectors can be confused. Most of the coloured glass you are likely to come across dates from after *c.*1800, when many lavishly decorated glass objects were made in Britain, Continental Europe, and the USA. Look for pieces marked by the workshops of Thomas WEBB & Sons, W.H.B. & J. Richardson, and STEVENS & WILLIAMS; larger pieces; unusual shapes (particularly for ornamental pieces); multiple layers of glass; and high-quality design (NEO-CLASSICAL figures are especially desirable). *See also* CAMEO GLASS; GOLDRUBINGLAS; LITHYALIN GLASS; OPALINE GLASS; and ZWISCHENGOLDGLAS.

GLASS PASTE A coloured or clear GLASS, often faceted, used in JEWELLERY as a cheap substitute for precious and semi-precious stones. *See also* GEMS.

GLASTONBURY CHAIR Name given to a type of X-frame CHAIR with "elbowed" arms, which link the chair seat to the top of the back.

GLATIGNY French PORCELAIN workshop, established in the 1890s and noted for its ART NOUVEAU designs.

GLAZE Glassy coating applied to the BISCUIT BODY of POTTERY and PORCELAIN, and fired to make it non-porous; it can be translucent, opaque, or coloured. HARD-PASTE PORCELAIN was given a FELDSPAR GLAZE, which fused with the body when fired. On SOFT-PASTE PORCELAIN the glaze tends to pool in the crevices. There are many different types of glaze, each with its own distinctive characteristics, but the main ones are: LEAD GLAZE, SALT GLAZE, and TIN GLAZE.

Green-glass-bead and GLASS PASTE Dior necklace, 1930s.

GOEBELS, hand-coloured figure of a lady with a fan, 1930s.

GLOBAL CLOCK A CLOCK of spherical shape, with a moving band marked with the hours around the circumference, rather than hands and a DIAL.

GOBLET A 16thC SILVER, CERAMIC, or GLASS drinking vessel, with a semi-ovoid bowl, STEM, foot, and lid. Silver goblets declined from the late 17thC until the late 18thC, when glass vessels were more popular. In the 18thC, it was common for goblets to be made in pairs. In the 18thC, NEO-CLASSICAL period, wine goblets were made in silver; minimally decorated vase-shaped ones are notable.

GOEBELS German pottery known for its 20thC novelty range. They made strikingly designed face masks and 1930s figures, which are now collectable.

GOFUM DOLLS Japanese 19thC DOLLS with cloth bodies and faces made from a paste of crushed shell, and usually with a squeak.

GOGGINGEN In Bavaria, Germany, a FAIENCE factory founded in the mid-18thC, and noted for richly coloured flower designs and CHINOISERIE.

GOLD A dense but malleable bright yellow element used to make JEWELLERY and plating (on vessels and other items). In Britain, a legal standard for gold items was established in the early 14thC. Commercial gold is an alloy in which fine gold is mixed with silver and copper (and often other metals) to increase its strength. The proportion of fine gold to alloy metals is measured (assayed) to establish its quality. This has to reach a legal standard before it can be hallmarked. Quality is measured by the "carat", which is a ¼th part of the weight of the object being assayed. A 22 carat piece has 22 parts of fine gold to 2 parts of alloy metals. An 18 carat piece has 18 parts of fine gold to 6 parts of alloy metals. A 9 carat piece has 9 parts of fine gold to 15 parts of alloy metals. The legal gold standards in Great Britain and North Ireland are as follows: 1477–1575, 18 carats; 1575–1798, 22 carats; 1798–1854, 22 and 18 carats; 1854–1932, 22, 18, 15, 12, and 9 carats; and 1932–present, 22, 18, 14, and 9 carats. In the Republic of Ireland the current standards are: 22, 20 (rare), 18, 14, and 9 carats. The marks are made up of the maker's mark, the standard mark, an ASSAY office mark, and a date letter. From 1842, imported pieces were assayed and hallmarked; from 1876, the HALLMARK included a stamped "F". After 1904, each assay office was allocated a special "office" mark for foreign items. This replaced the normal office mark. Few other countries have systems of marking gold wares as reliable as British hallmarks.

GOLD GLASS *See* ZWISCHENGOLDGLAS.

GOLD LUSTRE Metallic GOLD oxide used by 19th and 20thC art potters to give a red-to-coppery gold sheen to their wares.

GOLD PLATED Metal item coated with a layer of GOLD, often by ELECTROPLATING.

GOLDRUBINGLAS (Gold-ruby glass) A ruby-coloured GLASS made in the 17thC by adding gold chloride to the batch. It was often decorated with gilding and engraving, and was produced in Nuremberg and Augsburg, Germany.

GOLDSCHEIDER PORCELAIN factory established in Vienna, Austria, in 1886, and famous for ART NOUVEAU vases and ART DECO figures.

GOLDSMITHS AND SILVERSMITHS CO., LTD A British company, established in the 1890s, and noted for its ART NOUVEAU designs for tableware, photograph frames, CLOCKS, and other objects.

GOLDSTONE GLASS with a golden lustre from the inclusion of copper oxide.

GOLF MEMORABILIA Clubs, balls, and other memorabilia linked with the sport of golf. Pre-19thC golfing collectables are rare, but examples have survived from the late 17thC. Early hand-crafted clubs had names rather than numbers. Before *c.*1850, clubs had long, slender heads, but, by the 1880s, the head, had become shorter with thicker necks. Value depends on rarity, age, quality, and condition. Wood and iron clubs were made until the 1930s. Look out for: clubs marked by one of the great makers such as Auchterlonie, Andrew Forgan, Jack Morris, or Philp; feathery golf balls (made from hand-stitched leather stuffed with dampened goose down); and pottery commemorating golfing events or personalities, especially if made by premier British factories such as SPODE and DOULTON.

GOLLIWOG A fabric DOLL based on a character with a black face, big smile, staring, white-rimmed eyes, and fuzzy hair, and traditionally dressed in blue top coat, stand-up collar, bow tie, and red or striped trousers. Florence Upton, born to English parents in New York in 1873, illustrated *The Adventures of Two Dutch Dolls and a Golliwogg* (1895) with a black RAG-DOLL character. Gollies went out of fashion due to their political incorrectness, but have enjoyed a comeback since the 100th anniversary of their creation in 1895. Many companies produced them, but the best to look out for are by STEIFF. Robertson's, a jam and preserve manufacturer, adopted the figure as its symbol in 1910. In 1928, they introduced enamel "Golly" brooches, which could be sent for in return for buying its products. Halted in 1939, because metal was required for the war effort, the scheme was relaunched in 1945. The Robertson's Golly also appeared in felt, cut-out form.

GOMBRON Persian blue-and-white POTTERY imported in quantity to Britain in the 17th and 18thC. *See also* BLUE AND WHITE.

GONDOLA CHAIR A REGENCY-style CHAIR with legs that flare out and a broad curved top, much like a Greek "KLISMOS" chair. Gondola chairs were often EBONIZED and, later, stripped.

GOOGLY DOLL A CHARACTER DOLL with distinctive features including a roguish expression, large "googly" eyes, and an impish smile. "Googlies" were inspired by the drawings of Grace Gebbie Drayton, an American illustrator and artist who created the Campbell Kids. The first Googlies with BISQUE heads were marketed in 1911, and produced for 20 years by various major German factories, including KÄMMER & REINHARDT, KESTNER, and Armand MARSEILLE. Typical Googly characteristics are: round, sideways glancing eyes, short, slanting eyebrows high on the brow, a WATERMELON-type mouth, and a snub nose that is tiny compared to the huge eyes. These DOLLS came in a wide assortment of costumes. The more detail is visible, the higher the value.

GOOGLY EYES On a DOLL, disproportionately large, round eyes that glance sideways. Originally seen on GOOGLY DOLLS designed by Grace Grebbie Drayton.

GOOSE NECK *See* BROKEN PEDIMENT.

GORGELET An Oriental drinking vessel with spouts or jets. Made for export from the 17thC.

GORHAM MANUFACTURING CO. American firm established in 1818 in Rhode Island. In the late 19thC, they made innovative SILVER objects decorated with other metals, including copper, nickel, and brass, with the copper frequently appearing reddish and the brass appearing soft. The technique of combining mixed metals was used for naturalistic ART NOUVEAU-style silver and distinctive, Japanese-influenced designs. From 1868, the firm marked its wares with a date letter or symbol and the firm's trademark.

GOSS Various wares made in the 19thC by W.H. Goss in Stoke-on-Trent. This English firm was principally known for CRESTED CHINA souvenirs for popular holiday resorts, but it also produced PARIAN wares and jewel-inlaid PORCELAIN. Goss pieces were well made. The Arcadian and CARLTON works in England and other factories in Germany made similar crested pieces, but none could rival Goss for quality. The most sought-after pieces are "Goss cottages", which represent the homes of national figures of interest such as Anne Hathaway, Lloyd George, Charles Dickens, and other landmarks. Apart from heraldic ceramics and model buildings, this firm also produced a keenly collected range of decorative figures, some based on famous sculptures. World War I pieces from Barmouth, decorated with the flags of Britain's allies, are among the more desirable examples. Other sought-after pieces include lighthouses (and other buildings) and animals. Genuine Goss china should have a printed mark with a hawk. Beware of fake cottages produced with spurious hand-painted Goss marks.

GOSS DOLL Rare BISQUE dolls produced in England by the firm of William Henry GOSS during World War I, when German imports were stopped.

GOSSIP'S CHAIR Another name for a CAQUETEUSE.

GOSTELOWE, JONATHAN (1744–1806) Skilful American cabinet-maker who produced CHIPPENDALE-style furniture of outstanding quality.

GOTHA PORCELAIN produced in Thuringia, Germany, from the mid-18thC.

GOTHIC Decoration in the style of Gothic architecture, featuring such motifs as pinnacles, CROCKETS, and TREFOILS. The style was revived from the 1820s in Europe, and from the 1840s in North America.

GOTHIC CLOCK Iron CLOCKS, made in Germany in the 15th and 16thC, in the shape of a tower with four pillars, an arched canopy, and pinnacles. Sometimes also used of 19thC clocks with GOTHIC ornament or steeples.

GOTZKOWSKY Repeated pattern of flowers set in panels, named after the originating artist at the MEISSEN porcelain factory.

GOULD, CHRISTOPHER Noted English maker of 17thC LONGCASE CLOCKS.

GOÛT GREC From the French "Greek taste", the term used in France in the 1760s to describe the early NEO-CLASSICAL style, with emphasis on geometric forms and decoration based on the ancient architecture of Greece. Motifs include VOLUTES, bay-leaf swags, VITRUVIAN SCROLLS, PALMETTES, and GUILLOCHES. It is also known as LOUIS XVI STYLE.

GOUTHIÈRE, PIERRE (1732–1813) A leading French cabinet-maker who was employed by royalty and the nobility, but died in poverty.

GNOMON Shadow-casting element of a SUNDIAL, often a rod and a triangular pointer, sometimes made in the form of a bird.

GRAHAM, GEORGE Eminent English clockmaker, active 1695–1720.

GRAIN The general arrangement of the fibres in wood, and the direction in which they run. Also known as "figure".

GRAINGER WORCESTER BONE CHINA from Thomas Grainger's factory, based in Worcester in the early 19thC. Noted for PARIAN-ware, leaf-form JUGS.

GRAMOPHONE Patented in 1887 by Emile Berliner, an instrument that reproduces recorded sound, which is amplified by a horn. It differs from Edison's PHONOGRAPH in that it plays a disc, not a cylinder. It developed rapidly over the next three decades, and successive innovations can be dated by the patent number. All pre-1920 models are sought after.

GRAINGER, **Lee & Co.** WORCESTER porcelain teapot, cover, and stand, c.1812–20.

Pair of George IV silver GRAPE SCISSORS by John Bridge, London, 1824.

GRANDE SONNERIE A CLOCK that strikes the quarter followed by a repetition of the hour, usually on different bells, dating from the late 17thC.

GRANDFATHER CLOCK *See* LONGCASE CLOCK.

GRAND FEU ENAMELS Named after the French for "great fire", high-temperature colours – cobalt blue, manganese purple, iron red, copper green, and antimony yellow – used in FAIENCE and MAIOLICA decoration.

GRANDMOTHER CLOCK A LONGCASE CLOCK under 1.8m (6ft) in height.

GRAND RAPIDS FURNITURE Mid-19thC, American centre of FURNITURE production in Michigan. Although 49 factories were operating in Grand Rapids in 1908, few survived the 1920s' Great Depression. Mass-produced, modern designs contributed to the revival of the industry in the late 1930s.

GRAND TOUR European, but especially British, practice from the late 16thC and throughout the 18thC of sending young gentlemen to visit major cities in Europe, often ending after one or two years in Italy. Intended to educate the men, the tour led to the collecting of antiquities, and inspired NEO-CLASSICISM.

GRANITE MARBLED Invented in the 18thC by WEDGWOOD and widely copied, a purplish lead GLAZE sprayed onto EARTHENWARE to imitate marble.

GRANITEWARE EARTHENWARE covered with cream-coloured GLAZES that contain numerous blue to black flecks and spots, resembling granite.

GRANULATION Small specks of metal soldered onto SILVER or GOLD metalwork to decorative effect. It is often polished to create sparkle.

GRAPE SCISSORS Scissors with inset steel blades used for cutting grapes from a bunch. The earliest ones from the late 18thC are simple and elegant, while REGENCY examples and those made in the VICTORIAN period (1837–1901) are lavishly decorated with trailing vines. Some were made as part of large dessert sets. Those found with their original cases are especially desirable. Check for damaged pivots and loose mechanisms, which are costly to repair.

GRAVEYARD RUG A Turkish PRAYER RUG with a design of cypress trees and small, tomb-like buildings.

GRAVITY CLOCK A CLOCK suspended from a chain or ratchet and powered by its own weight.

GRAVY POT SILVER or silver-plated vessel with a central well for gravy and an outer compartment for hot water to keep the pot warm. *See also* ARGYLL.

GRAY, A.E. LTD British, Stoke-on-Trent-based pottery established in 1907. The firm employed notable designers, including Susie COOPER, and is renowned for its imaginative patterns and hand-painting. Beautifully painted, floral designs, LUSTREWARE, and pieces signed by well-known decorators are desirable.

GRAY, EILEEN (1879–1976) Irish designer working in Paris, France. Made lacquerwork FURNITURE influenced by MODERNIST movements and ethnic art.

GRAY-STAN A small English (1926–36) glasshouse that produced transparent coloured GLASS and pastel-shaded, coloured and cased glass.

GREAT EXHIBITION, THE Held in London, England, in 1851, the first major international exhibition. It gave manufacturers around the world a chance to show off their products, and promoted new technology.

GREEK KEY A geometrical decoration of straight and right-angled lines somewhat resembling a maze. Also known as "Grecian key".

GREENER, HENRY & CO. A British, Sunderland-based glassworks established in 1858. Known for LACY GLASS and PRESSED GLASS.

GREEN GLASS An alternative name for BOTTLE GLASS. Green is the natural colour of glass made from unpurified silica, which contains iron oxide.

GREEN-GLAZED WARES POTTERY with a translucent, green GLAZE invented by WEDGWOOD in the mid-18thC. Typical of CABBAGE WARES

GREEN, T.G. & CO. English, 20thC pottery, best known for its CORNISH WARE, although its gingham and spotted patterns are now classics. Its "Gayday" range from the 1960s used strong geometric shapes to form repeat patterns.

GREENWARES Products of the English, Yorkshire-based, Don pottery when under the ownership of John Green in the early 19thC. *See also* DON WARES.

GREINER, LUDWIG Active in Philadelphia, USA, a 19thC manufacturer of dolls' heads in PAPIER-MÂCHÉ. *See also* DOLL.

GRETTON, CHARLES Clockmaker active in the late 17th and early 18thC.

GRIDIRON PENDULUM One made of several rods of steel or iron linked to rods of brass; the differences in the rates of expansion and contraction between the two metals cancel each other out, keeping the length constant.

GRIFFEN, SMITH & HILL A Pennsylvanian factory founded in 1880, and a major American producer of ETRUSCAN MAJOLICA. Wares are marked "GSH".

T.G. GREEN **Cornish-Ware tea caddy, c.1980s.**

Flight Worcester porcelain plate with a central panel painted in GRISAILLE, showing the figure of Hope, by John Pennington, c.1790–92.

GRISAILLE Using shades of grey, black, and white, monochrome decoration used on wood, CERAMICS, GLASS, and stone objects in the 18thC.

GRISWOLD, A.B. & CO. North American gunsmith, active in the 19thC.

GRÖDNERTAL DOLL A type of DOLL made in Grödnertal, Austria, a major centre for WOODEN DOLLS in the 19thC, along with regions in Germany. Grödnertal dolls are also known as DUTCH PEG DOLLS and "PENNY WOODENS". Features include limbs of carved-and-turned wood, with heads occasionally of BONE CHINA, wax, or PAPIER-MÂCHÉ. Some pre-1840 dolls have swivel waists. Hands are spade-like, and any visible limbs are painted white. Their gessoed-and-varnished faces yellow with age. The shoes may be real or painted. Pedlar dolls, usually with baskets or trays of miniature wares and wearing red cloaks, were common in the 19thC. Many characters were produced, including clerics, shopkeepers, schoolmasters, and gentlemen. The English firm of Dryad craft suppliers in London made similar wooden dolls in the 1960s, but the arm and knee joints on their versions were fixed with strips of metal slotted into the wood, and held with nails.

GROSZBREITENBACH Founded in the late 18thC in Thuringia, Germany, a PORCELAIN factory known for its imitations of MEISSEN.

GROTESQUE Any fanciful ornament composed of distorted faces, mythical animals (satyrs, sphinxes, etc.), and fantastical fruit and flower forms.

GROUND The background area of a single colour onto which further enamelled decoration or gilding may be applied.

GROWLER Inside a TEDDY BEAR, a voice-box device that produces a growl or roar. Voice boxes with papered bellows were introduced in 1905. In 1908, these were replaced with automatic ones, and, in 1912, voice boxes were inserted. The growling ability does not add to a bear's value, because growlers were common.

GRUBER, JACQUES (b.1870) Working in Paris and Nancy, an important French designer of FURNITURE and JEWELLERY in the ART NOUVEAU style.

GRUEBY American, Boston-based pottery, established in 1894 by William H. Grueby and specializing in architectural tiles and VASES ornamented with floral or geometric designs. Grueby used matt GLAZES in green, yellow ochre, and brown, and crisp applied decorations in the form of leaves and buds.

GUANGXU (Kuang Hsu) Chinese CH'ING dynasty emperor, 1875–1908.

GUAN YAO Chinese for "imperial ware", used to refer to PORCELAIN with blue or grey crackle glaze. Made in the SUNG DYNASTY, and much copied in the 18thC.

GUANYIN Alternative spelling of Kuan yin. *See also* KUAN.

GUARD On an Oriental CARPET, part of the border motif, specifically the narrow outer band running parallel to the main one.

GUBBIO A centre of MAIOLICA production in Umbria, Italy, during the RENAISSANCE. Noted for the gold and ruby lustre decoration of Giorgio Andreoli.

GUÉRIDON A small French TABLE, usually in the form of a column or pedestal with a tray top, and used to hold a candlestick. *See also* OCCASIONAL TABLE.

GUILD SILVER Ceremonial SILVER vessels bearing the insignia of a trade guild.

GUILLOCHE Decorative motif inspired by CLASSICAL antiquity, and formed from a continuous, interlaced, figure-of-eight pattern.

GUILLOCHÉ ENAMELLING SILVER that is engraved or engine-turned then covered with a layer of translucent enamel, which allows the decorative design to shine through to shimmering effect.

GUL Persian for "flower". In Oriental CARPETS, a common motif based on a stylized geometric rose. Each nomadic tribe had its own identifying version.

GULESTAN In Oriental CARPET design, a rose-garden pattern.

GUL-HENNA A motif (often all-over) of henna flowers on a Persian CARPET.

GUND MANUFACTURING CO. American firm founded in Connecticut in 1898 by the German emigré Adolph Gund. It began to produce TEDDY BEARS, for which it is known, in the mid-1920s, when the firm moved to New York. The first bears produced by Gund were made with silk PLUSH.

GUN METAL Alloy of copper and tin used for making gun stocks, but also for casting CANDLESTICKS, furniture ornaments, and other items in the 19thC.

GÜNTHERMANN German, machine-pressed, TINPLATE toymaker, founded in 1877. The firm was known for the quirky humour and detail of its toys, which ranged from ragtime dancing couples to painted frogs.

GURI SCROLL patterns carved into alternative layers of red and black LACQUER.

GUSSETED On a DOLL, a cloth or KID body with insets to allow movement.

GUTTA-PERCHA Synthetic, rubber-like material used for the bodies and heads of DOLLS in the late 19thC.

Tin plate and clockwork bus by GUNTHERMANN, with printed decoration, 1920.

H

HADLEY CHEST Made in New England at the turn of the 17thC, a distinctive American dower CHEST, with carving of vines and leaves on the front.

HADLEY WARE Late-l9thC POTTERY established by James Hadley, and noted for ART NOUVEAU vases. It was later taken over by ROYAL WORCESTER.

HAFNER WARE Produced in Germany and Central Europe from the 13thC, lead-glazed POTTERY and tiles, some with relief-moulded designs.

HAGUENEAU Near Strasbourg, France, a FAIENCE factory noted for floral painting in the late 18thC.

HAGUE PORCELAIN Made briefly at The Hague in the Netherlands in the late 18thC, PORCELAIN, sometimes with gilded decoration on a blue ground.

HAHUKO Period of Japanese history AD 672–685.

HAIGH, THOMAS (fl.1771–79) British cabinet-maker who was a partner of Thomas CHIPPENDALE.

HAIRY-PAW FOOT On FURNITURE, a foot carved to resemble a furry paw.

HALF-DOLL Or "PINCUSHION FIGURE". Popular from the early 20thC, a tiny DOLL for mounting on a pincushion or other accessory from a lady's boudoir.

HALF-HUNTER A WATCH with a hinged front cover with a central, glass-covered aperture, so that the dial is visible when the cover is closed.

HALF-STOCKED FIREARM with a stock only part way down the barrel.

HALF TESTER A BED canopy that covers the bedhead. *See also* TESTER.

HALL CHAIR Strong, but plain and un-upholstered CHAIR used in a hall to accommodate messengers and callers in outdoor clothing. Such chairs had to impress important callers, so were often carved with crests or coats-of-arms.

HALLIFAX BAROMETER An early-18thC. English barometer designed by John Hallifax of Barnsley. The first barometer with a dial, it is the predecessor of the WHEEL BAROMETER and similar in appearance to a LONGCASE CLOCK.

19thC, gothic oak HALL CHAIR.

HALLMARK The mark stamped on SILVER or GOLD objects when passed at assay (a test for quality). Marks were applied to both the main body and any detachable parts of an object. English hallmarks were introduced in 1300 by Edward I to reduce fraud. The Worshipful Company of Goldsmiths was given permission to enforce assay laws from the Goldsmiths' Hall (hence the name "hallmark") in London. Assay offices were set up across the country. There are four main marks on silver: the sterling guarantee; the town mark; the date letter; and the maker's mark. Silver that is at least 92.5 per cent silver is STERLING SILVER. All silver objects of sterling quality were stamped with a leopard's head from 1300. By 1478, the leopard had a crown; from 1544, the sterling mark changed to a lion passant, shown walking to the left (after this date the leopard's head was used as London's town mark). Between 1697 and 1720, a higher standard of silver, known as BRITANNIA STANDARD, was introduced. Marks showing the town of assay were added by the end of the 15thC. Marking with a date letter, using a letter (from 20 in the alphabet) that changed each year, was introduced in 1478 in London, and later in other parts of England. The letters usually follow an alphabetical sequence, but the dates they indicate are unique to each assay office. The letters are contained within a shield. Marks to show the identity of the maker were used from the 14thC. The earliest were pictorial symbols, but, from the late 17thC, marks began to incorporate the silversmiths' initials. Outside London, a number of smaller towns marked their own silver. Provincial marking was haphazard and inconsistent, and pieces featuring rare or unusual provincial marks are prized among collectors. Birmingham was an important centre for silver production in the late 18thC. An assay office was opened there in 1773, with the town mark designated by an anchor. Although marking systems were established in Scotland, Ireland, and Continental Europe, their standards for silver varied. The marking system introduced into Ireland in the 17thC was arbitrary, and Irish silver does not always bear complete marks. The crowned harp was Dublin's town mark from 1637 and 1730, and, in 1731, the figure of Hibernia was added. In 1638 date letters were introduced for Irish silver. Marks on Scottish silver were introduced in the mid-15thC. The town mark of Edinburgh, instituted in 1485, is a castle with three towers. In 1759, a thistle replaced the assay master's mark in Edinburgh. Marks were employed on silver made in Continental Europe to signify quality or periods when duty was payable. Town marks were frequently used. There is no official marking system in the USA, and the only assay office operated in Baltimore between 1814 and 1830. However, most makers stamped their silver with abbreviated or full maker or company names, and these may include the pattern number and the standard of silver used. Emblems were used by many makers. The shape of the enclosure around the mark can help to establish where or when an item was made. A shield, quatrefoil, TREFOIL, or heart was used in the late 17thC; an oval or circle in the early 18thC; CARTOUCHES in the mid-18thC; rectangles by 1800; and banners, lunettes, and INTAGLIOS by the early 19thC. Some firms used their

Oak HALL-PORTER'S CHAIR with two side drawers, c.1760.

own date marks, or stamped wares with the weight of the piece in ounces. Fake marks that have been added, or "let in", to a piece are often incorrectly placed and may look distorted; if they have been made by recasting a genuine piece, there may be small granulations visible in the outline. Marks are sometimes taken from low-value objects and inserted into larger, more valuable ones. Breathing on transposed marks should reveal a faint outline around the marks where they were soldered in. *See also* ASSAY MARK, DUTY DODGER, DUTY MARKS, and IMPORT MARKS.

HALL-PORTER'S CHAIR An ARMCHAIR with the back and sides extended upward to form a canopy. Designed for the draughty hallways and corridors of large houses and mansions. Also known as a WATCHMAN'S CHAIR.

HALL RIFLE Breech-loading, FLINTLOCK gun invented in the early 19thC by John Hancock Hall of Maine and used by the American army.

HAMADA, SHOJI (1894–1978) Japanese studio potter, whose work, typified by plain forms and strong use of GLAZES, has provided inspiration for British, Japanese, and American potters. He helped Bernard LEACH establish his pottery, where Shoji worked 1920-3. Hamada set up his own pottery in Japan in 1930.

HAMADAN The centre of the local CARPET industry in a region in western Iran. Products are often made of cotton or wool with a central medallion.

HAMBURG WARE Made in the 17thC, FAIENCE jugs often bearing the coat-of-arms of Hamburg, Germany. The exact location of the factory is unknown.

HAMMERING Method of beating out SILVER, GOLD, or PEWTER to form a vessel without using heat. It usually leaves a regular pattern of hollows.

HAMMONTON North American, New Jersey-based glassworks, established in the early 19thC, and noted for high-quality flasks.

HAN In Chinese history, the period 206 BC–AD 220, usually divided into two periods: Western Han, 206 BC–AD 24, and Eastern Han, AD 25–220.

HANAP A large GOBLET with a lid but no handles. Usually made of SILVER, but sometimes also found in STONEWARE with silver mountings.

HANAU FAIENCE factory founded by Dutch settlers in Germany in the mid-17thC, and noted for JUGS decorated with BAROQUE flower-and-bird patterns.

HANCOCK, S. & SONS British firm (1857–1937) noted for its hand-painted tableware. TOAST RACKS in EARTHENWARE from the "Ivory Ware" range, jam pots, and "tea-for-two" sets are popular items among collectors.

HANCOCK, WILLIAM (1794–*c*.1860) Boston-based, American furniture-maker thought to be responsible for the American rocker (ROCKING CHAIR). He made quality REGENCY-style FURNITURE and, after 1830, parlour furniture.

HAND COOLER A glass "egg", often decorated like a PAPERWEIGHT and said to be used for keeping the hands cool at balls and assemblies.

HANDKERCHIEF TABLE With a triangular top and a single, triangular leaf, a TABLE that fits into a corner when closed and forms a square when opened.

HANDLE Used on FURNITURE to open drawers and doors. Handle styles can help with dating. From *c*.1690 they were secured by POMMELS and nuts. Old pommels were hand-cast in single pieces of BRASS, with the thread only halfway up the shank. Modern pommels are made from brass heads with steel shanks, and the thread running the length of the shank. The nuts used in the 18thC were circular and irregular; modern nuts are regular and hexagonal. Check furniture for holes or the outline of an old handle shape. Replaced handles are common, and this is not too detrimental to value if they are in keeping with the rest of the piece. It is best not to polish handles.

HANDWERCK, HEINRICH Active during the late 19th and early 20thC, German makers of DOLLS in BISQUE.

HANLEY One of five (with Burslem, Stoke-on-Trent, Tunstall, and Longton) CERAMICS-producing towns in the STAFFORDSHIRE POTTERIES, England.

HANOVERIAN Period from 1714 to 1760, covering the reigns of George I (1714–27) and George II (1727–60), monarchs of the House of Hanover.

"HANOVERIAN" PATTERN SPOON Early, simple, GEORGIAN spoon with a a long bowl and a central spine running up the face of the handle.

HANSEN-JACOBSEN, NIELS (b.1861) Danish ART NOUVEAU ceramicist.

HARD METAL Highest quality of PEWTER, made with a high proportion of tin with bismuth as a hardening agent. Produced from *c*.1700.

HARD-PASTE PORCELAIN True PORCELAIN made from KAOLIN (china clay) and PETUNTSE (china stone). The object is fired, then dipped in GLAZE, then refined. The china stone bonds the particles of clay together and gives translucency. The firing takes place at a high temperature, and the finished object appears to have the consistency of GLASS. The first hard-paste porcelain was made in China in the 9thC AD. In Europe, the MEISSEN factory began making porcelain in the early 18thC. Chips in hard-paste porcelain look glassy; chips in SOFT-PASTE PORCELAIN look floury, like fine pastry.

HANDWERCK **doll with bisque head and sleeping glass eyes, on a double-jointed composition body,** *c*.1910.

Longton Hall porcelain figure of HARLEQUIN (which came with a figure of Columbine), c.1754–57.

HARDSTONE *See* GEM.

HARE'S FUR Oriental GLAZE in which the mineral inclusions form extremely fine lines, usually in black on red or brown.

HARLAAM In the Netherlands, a town that made TIN-GLAZED EARTHENWARE before Delft. It was the first place to produce the BLUE-AND-WHITE, Chinese-style decoration characteristic of early DELFTWARE.

HARLEQUIN (1) In Italian COMMEDIA DELL'ARTE, a character distinguished by his colourful, diamond-pattern tunic and often partnered by Columbine.

HARLEQUIN (2) CHAIRS of similar design but not a proper set. Also known as a composite set.

HARLEQUIN TABLE Combined CARD TABLE and tea table with a series of folding tops. Also known as a TRIPLE-TOP TABLE. *See also* TABLE.

HARRACHOVE GLASSWORKS Founded in 1712 in northern Bohemia, a GLASS company known for its high-quality wares. In 1887, it was acquired by Josef Riedel, whose family developed "Annagrün" and "Annagelb" glass in the 1840s. Riedel made luxury decorated pieces. *See also* DECANTER, BOHEMIAN.

HARSHANG Oriental CARPET motif of a flower with an outline like a crab.

HARVEY, AGNES Associated with the GLASGOW SCHOOL, a British designer of ART NOUVEAU metal and enamel JEWELLERY.

HATCHLI A CARPET design based on a cross, especially one that divides the field into QUADRANTS.

HAUFENBECHER Usually of PEWTER or SILVER, a set of cups, designed to fit one inside the other. Made in Germany from the late 16thC.

HAUNCH POT Baluster-shaped 16th and 17thC TANKARD in PEWTER or SILVER.

HAUSMALER Meaning "home painter", used to refer to an independent painter of German PORCELAIN blanks (most often with reference to MEISSEN).

HAVILAND PORCELAIN firm established in France in 1842 by the American David Haviland, and acquired by Ernest Chaplet in 1885. In 1892, David's son Theodore set up a new firm of the same name specializing in ART DECO wares.

HAVILAND-LIMOGES ART POTTERY made at the factory of Charles HAVILAND in Limoges, France, in the late 19thC.

HAWKES, THOMAS G. A North American, New York-based, GLASS firm, whose high-quality, cut-and-engraved decoration was a trademark of its luxury tableware. Less-expensive imitations were made by PRESS MOULDING.

HEAL & SON A family-based, FURNITURE-retailing business, established in London in 1810 by John Harris Heal. His great grandson, Ambrose Heal (1872–1959), was a patron of 20thC design and was instrumental in promoting new designs in the store. It became an important retailer of furniture, metalware, and other objects in the ARTS AND CRAFTS style.

HEATHCOTE WARES English EARTHENWARE and BONE CHINA decorated with blue, transfer-printed scenes at an early-19thC Staffordshire (Fenton) pottery.

HECKERT, FRITZ An enameller and gilder from Bohemia who set up a glass-decorating works in 1866, and a GLASS firm in 1889. He is known for enamelling HUMPEN and for "Drahtglas", in which glass is blown into wire mesh.

HEIAN The period of Japanese history AD 794–1185.

HEINRICHSEN German, Nuremberg, maker of toy soldiers 1870–1920.

HEINRICHSEN SCALE An alternative name for the Nuremberg scale, the standard size of German-made toy soldiers. Sizes are 30mm (1⅛in) for infantry, 40mm (1⅔in) for cavalry.

HELIOGRAPH Early form of photographic print, in which a metal plate is coated with light-sensitive chemicals, which can be used to make a portrait or engraving. It was contemporary with the DAGUERREOTYPE, but less efficient.

HENDERSON WARES Products, especially STONEWARE and TOBY JUGS, made in David Henderson's factory, established in the 19thC in Jersey City, USA.

HENNELLS FAMILY A London-based family of silversmiths spanning five generations and manufacturing novelty CONDIMENT POTS and SALT-CELLARS.

HENRI DEUX A term (sometimes "Henry II") for rare, 16thC, French EARTHENWARE with coloured-clay INLAY, and their 19thC reproductions.

HEPPLEWHITE, GEORGE (d.1786) English cabinet-maker identified with the post-CHIPPENDALE period. In *The Cabinet-Maker's and Upholsterer's Guide* (1788), he published detailed designs, styles, and patterns, which were copied and adapted in Europe and North America. His designs reflect a simpler version of the NEO-CLASSICAL STYLE. Although Hepplewhite is best known for CHAIRS with shield and oval backs, and SIDEBOARDS with concave corners, his work influenced a wide variety of furniture.

Open-mouth HERMANN bear called Zotty, c.1950.

HERAT Made from the 16th to 18thC in a region in Afghanistan, a type of CARPET whose design gave its name to the HERATI MOTIF.

HERATI MOTIF Rosette within a diamond, often used in all-over patterns.

HEREKE Turkish town noted for fine silk RUGS with a close-clipped PILE.

HEREZ Northwestern Iranian CARPET-making centre, noted for large pieces with angular patterns on a red field.

HERMAN MILLER INC. Founded in Michigan, USA in 1905, and known for post-war FURNITURE. Among the firm's most noted designers are Charles EAMES, Ray Eames, Isamu Noguchi, and Verner Panton. *See also* FURNITURE, 20THC.

HERMANN German TEDDY BEAR firm, established in 1907 by Johann Hermann near Sonneberg, then the world centre of toymaking. The family-run firm relocated in 1948 to Hirschaid near Bamberg, where the name was changed to Gebrüder Hermann. Hermann bears are completely jointed and made of the best-quality PLUSH IN MOHAIR. Bears produced until 1929 have identity tags with the letters "BEHA". The identity tag "BEHA" was changed in 1930 to "Marke BEHA Teddy", then to "Hermann Teddy" ("Teddy" is always underlined), between 1940 and 1951. Since 1952, Hermann bears have borne tags and medallions stating "Hermann Teddy Original". Limited editions of replica bears and new designs include their "Nostalgic bear" range. Limited editions of new designs are collectable as long as than 5,000 are made.

HERRINGBONE Another name for FEATHERBANDING.

HERTER BROTHERS Leading North American, New York-based FURNITURE firm, active from the 1850s to 1905. Their designs were influenced by the AESTHETIC style and the work of Charles Locke EASTLAKE, with characteristics including intricate INLAY using exotic woods.

HEUBACH, ERNST Based in Koppelsdorf, this German dollmaker produced inexpensive girl dolls, babies, and CHARACTER DOLLS between 1887 and 1930. Highly coloured cheeks are an immediate clue to a Heubach DOLL. Black dolls had grass skirts, necklaces, bracelets, and earrings. The firm used a horseshoe mark. Do not confuse these dolls with those made by Gebrüder HEUBACH.

HEUBACH, GEBRÜDER German firm founded originally to make PORCELAIN by the Heubach brothers in 1820 in Thuringia. By 1905, it was making whole dolls. Distinctive, usually pink, BISQUE heads with exaggerated expressions are its strong point. (In comparison, the bodies are crudely modelled.) Look for realistic INTAGLIO EYES, moulded with an indented pupil and iris and then painted, often with a white dot added to the iris. Gebrüder Heubach was also known for PIANO BABIES, all-bisque figurines of babies intended for display on a piano, hence the name. Most Gebrüder Heubach dolls bear the firm's rising sun mark or "Heubach" incorporated into a square. Fakes have been made from old Gebrüder Heubach moulds, and these can be recognized by their size, which is slightly smaller than that of the originals.

HEYDE German, Dresden-based manufacturer of flat and solid toy soldiers, between 1870 and 1944. The firm is best known its large display groups, including an oasis set with Arabs and camels. Its figures were often imported into Britain before similar types in that country became successful.

HICKORY An American wood that is similar to ASH but a little darker in colour. It turns well and is strong without being heavy.

HIGGS, WILLIAM The first known English dollmaker, thought to have begun making wooden-jointed "babies" in London in the late-17thC. *See also* DOLLS.

HIGHBOY American term for CHEST-ON-STAND. The top is usually heightened by FINIALS on North American examples.

HIGH DRESSER A DRESSER with a rack (a structure consisting of shelves). Many high dressers started life without racks, which were added later, either taken from other dressers or made up of old wood. If the alteration is sympathetic and was done some time ago, it can be difficult to detect, and does not greatly affect the value. Nearly all early high dressers were made of OAK, although ELM was occasionally used for boards. Examples with parts made from YEW are valuable. Some of the most expensive dressers are those with CABRIOLE LEGS (usually from the mid-18thC). In southern England, racks on dressers were usually open, but the boarded back was popular on WELSH DRESSERS. When choosing a high dresser, look on the top and base for matching decorative motifs, which show that the two parts belong together. Inspect the top for signs that the piece has been used – for example, there may be knife marks or scratches from pots – and look for plenty of encrusted dirt in the grooves and corners (a sign of authenticity). *See also* LOW DRESSER

HIGH STANDARD SILVER SILVER that contains a higher proportion of pure metal than STERLING SILVER ie. better than 92.5 parts per 100 of pure silver.

HIGH-TEMPERATURE COLOURS (GRAND FEU ENAMELS) Colours that can withstand firing to a high temperature of 2,200–2,400°F (1,200– 1,300°C), used in Spain, Italy, France, the Netherlands, Germany, and England on CERAMICS. They were available in a limited palette: cobalt blue, manganese/purple, copper green, antimony yellow, and ochre.

HILL, MATTHEW Late-18thC English maker of ACT OF PARLIAMENT CLOCKS.

HIPPED Term used to describe a CABRIOLE LEG, which continues at the top above the SEAT RAIL. Usually found on better-quality FURNITURE only.

HIRADO Japanese PORCELAIN with figure and landscape painting in blue on a white body, often depicting boys at play. It was made exclusively for the Lords of Hirado, near ARITA, in the mid-18th to mid-19thC.

HIRAME Irregular GOLD or SILVER inclusions in Japanese LACQUERWORK.

HISTORISMUS GLASS A central European GLASS that copied old Venetian and traditional German glass forms from the 15th and 16thC, following the unification of Germany in 1871. These wares are pale, yellowish green or amber, and were made in large quantities. They can be identified by elaborate decoration in garish enamels, false dates, and fictitious coats-of-arms.

HITCHCOCK, LAMBERT (1795–1856) Connecticut-based, North American FURNITURE-maker, known for his rush-seated, birch or maple "Hitchcock" CHAIR, introduced in the 1820s. Look for his mark on early chairs.

HOBBS, BROCKUNIER & CO. Founded in 1863, a firm specializing in AMBERINA and PEACHBLOW coloured, PRESSED GLASS. It was one of the largest North American glassworks at the time of its closure in 1891.

HOCHSCHNITT A type of high-relief decoration on late-17thC, German GLASS. *See also* TIEFSCHNITT.

HÖCHST FACTORY German, mid-18thC, PORCELAIN factory, which made figures of children with sweet, plump faces. The simple grassy mound bases have brown streaks, and the figures were on creamy bodies, decorated with pale yellow, pink, and blue details. J.P. Melchior, Johann Friedrick Lück, and Laurentius Russinger are modellers who produced works for the factory.

HOCK GLASS A GLASS for drinking white wines from the Hoch Rhein area of Germany, with a pale green or golden bowl on a long, clear, glass stem.

HOCK LEG A CABRIOLE LEG with a broken line to the inner curve of the knee.

HOFFMANN, JOSEF (1870–1956) Pupil of Otto Wagner in Vienna and a founder of the WIENER WERKSTÄTTE (est. 1903). As a designer, he bridged the transition from ART NOUVEAU to ART DECO, reviving an appreciation of square and rectangular forms in FURNITURE. He also designed PORCELAIN and GLASS.

HOGARTH CHAIR Another name for a GAINSBOROUGH CHAIR.

HO HO BIRD The phoenix bird that is occasionally used as decoration.

HOLITSCH Mid-18thC FAIENCE and CREAMWARE from Hungary.

HOLLAND AND GREEN A late-19thC factory in Longton, Staffordshire, England. Noted for brightly coloured GLAZES and fine STONEWARE.

HOLLINSHEAD & KIRKHAM Known as H & K, a British pottery that made tableware, VASES (popular, especially if large, with collectors), plates, CANDLESTICKS, and boxes, c.1870–1956. Their hand-painted wares have a high gloss, and decoration includes fruit, flowers, and geometric patterns.

HOLLOW-CAST FIGURES Toy soldiers with a hollow core. They were made by a process invented by W. Britain Ltd, c.1893. *See also* CAST-IRON TOY

HOLLOW-COLUMN CLOCK Early-19thC CLOCK in which the weights are concealed in hollow columns that appear to be part of the case.

HOLLOW CUT Pattern of concave forms, especially on GLASS.

HOLLOW STEM A type of 18thC wineglass with a hollow in the upper stem for collecting wine sediment.

HOLSTER PISTOLS Short-barrelled pistols made in pairs in the 18thC for horse riders, and housed in leather holsters at the front of the saddle.

HOLT-HOWARD CO. In the USA, a Connecticut-based CERAMICS firm, which made whimiscal kitchenware such as cat cruets as well as other novelties 1948–90. The firm is known for its "Pixiware" range, made from 1958 to the early 1960s. Many pieces are dated on the bases and have "HH" marks.

"HOMEMAKER" CERAMICS pattern made for the British high-street chain Woolworths between 1955–70. Enid Seeney's design featured contemporary objects such as furniture by Robin DAY, on a background of freely drawn lines.

HONEY SKEP Designed to imitate early, dome-shaped beehives made of horizontal coils of tied straw, honey skeps were made mainly of honey-coloured SILVER GILT during the reign of George III (1760–1820) to hold glass honey pots. They had matching saucer stands, and are often engraved on the side with a flying "bee".

HONGWU (Hung Wu) Chinese MING DYNASTY emperor, AD 1368–98.

HOOD The structure of a LONGCASE CLOCK containing the movement and dial. In old CLOCKS it lifts off; hinged front doors were a 19thC innovation.

HOOP BACK Back of a WINDSOR-type CHAIR with a TOP RAIL bent like a hoop.

Ridgeways HOMEMAKER-pattern teapot, c.1950.

HORNBY **train set, complete in its original box, 1950.**

HOPE CHEST American term for a dower CHEST. *See also* HADLEY CHEST.

HOPE, THOMAS (1770–1831) British FURNITURE designer, architect, and scholar, whose designs were both formal and CLASSICAL.

HOP GLASS DRINKING GLASS, especially an ALE GLASS, with hop vine decoration.

HORNBY Makers of clockwork and electric locomotives from *c*.1920, best known for the "Dublo" range introduced in 1938. Electric train sets were manufactured from 1926. Clockwork trains were made as alternatives to electric ones, but production halted in 1941. Pre-World War II trains have horizontal hooks and eye couplings of blued steel. The post-war Peco coupling has vertical bent hooks. Of the post-war production, sets in the Southern Railways livery are the most popular with collectors. Hornby products were packed in sturdy, printed cardboard boxes, which add considerably to value.

HORNSEA British pottery founded in 1949, when it mostly produced small giftware items such as TOBY JUGS. Later, the firm made a range of wares, many in the modern designs of John Clappison.

HÖROLDT (HEROLD), JOHANN GREGOR *See* MEISSEN.

HOURGLASS CLOCK Early-19thC American MANTEL CLOCK, with a case in the shape of an hourglass.

HOWARD CLOCK A BANJO CLOCK manufactured in the mid-19thC by Edward Howard, later by the American Waltham Watch Co.

HUBBARD, ELBERT GREEN (1856–1915) Founder of the ROYCROFTERS (1895–1938), a community of craftsmen who followed the principles of the ARTS AND CRAFTS MOVEMENT. The group made simple MISSION-STYLE furniture and metalwork as well as leatherwork.

HUBERTUSBERG Founded by Frederick II of Saxony, a factory producing fine EARTHENWARE in the late 18th and 19thC.

HUBLEY MANUFACTORING CO. American CAST-IRON TOY maker, active 1894–1940s. Popular lines include fire-engines, wagons, and circus trains.

HUGHES IRONSTONE Based at Brownhills, Staffordshire, a 19thC British firm making POTTERY by Thomas Hughes in quantity for export to the USA.

HUGUENOT French Protestant refugees who settled in England and the Netherlands following the Revocation of the Edict of Nantes in 1685, an edict that had given them a degree of civil and religious freedom. Many were skilled silversmiths, weavers, furniture-makers, and clockmakers, and introduced French styles into the decorative arts of England and Holland.

HUG-ME-KIDDIE A cheap, GOOGLY-EYED DOLL produced in 1912 by Leon Rees, a Bavarian toymaker in London. They were crudely made and dressed as both boys and girls. The heads are COMPOSITION, the body is made of pink felt, and the hands are stubby. The eyes move around when operated by a lever. The value increases with the "naughtiness" of the expression.

HUMMEL Small PORCELAIN figurines made from 1935 by the German GOEBEL factory. The designs of these rural children were created by Sister Maria Innocentia (Berta Hummel), a Franciscan nun. Many originals are still produced.

HUMPEN Tall, cylindrical German or Swiss beer GLASS made from the mid-16thC to the 18thC. They were often decorated with elaborate, colourful enamelling, featuring armorial bearings, figures, and animals or local scenes.

HUNTER WATCH with a solid hinged cover protecting the glass over the DIAL. This cover has to be opened in order to read the time. *See also* HALF-HUNTER.

HUNTING CUP Also known as a STIRRUP CUP, a small SILVER cup often in the shape of a foxhead. Used from the late 18thC for drinking before hunting.

HUNTLEY & PALMERS British, Berkshire-based biscuit manufacturer, whose early 20thC tin boxes are now collected.

HURDALS VERK GLASS from the Norwegian factory of that name, operating in the late 18th and early 19thC.

HUSK FINIAL At the end of a spoon, a FINIAL resembling a wheat husk, a popular mid-18thC motif. See also BELLFLOWER and GARYA HUSK.

HUTCH American term for DRESSER.

HYACINTH-BULB VASE In GLASS, a VASE designed to grow a hyacinth bulb, which sits in the cup-shaped top while its roots grow down into the water. They were made in quantity during the 19th and early 20thC. Coloured vases that conceal the roots are more popular than clear ones.

HYALITH GLASS Black GLASS wares, usually gilded, developed by the Count von Buquoy in 1819, in Nove Hrady, Bohemia. They were inspired by the BASALTES made by WEDGWOOD and used for VASES and bowls.

HYLTON Active in Sunderland, England, in the late 18th and early 19thC, one of the first factories to make transfer-printed EARTHENWARE and LUSTREWARE.

HUMMEL **figure entitled "Chick Girl", c.1960–72.**

I

ICE GLASS Developed in Venice, Italy, and Liège, Belgium, in the 16thC, GLASS with the appearance of cracked ice, achieved by a sudden drop in temperature in the furnace, or by sprinkling broken glass onto the surface of the hot vessel.

IDEAL NOVELTY & TOY CO. American, New York-based firm responsible for producing perhaps the first TEDDY BEAR, established by inventor Morris Michtom. The business started when, in honour of President Theodore Roosevelt's refusal to shoot a cub on a bear hunt, Michtom's wife made a soft, jointed bear and displayed it in the window of her sweet shop. Michtom was given the President's permission to call it "Teddy". Unmarked, early Ideal bears can often be identified by their large, barrel-shaped bodies, often with small, pointed humps at the backs of the neck. They are wider than German bears of the same date, and are referred to by Americans as "football-shaped". Most early Ideal bears were made in short, gold or beige MOHAIR PLUSH, with matching pointed, felt paws. The bears were jointed at the hips and shoulders. The heads were triangular, the snouts were pointed with D-shaped noses made of twill, and the mouths were stitched. Earlier bears often had SHOE-BUTTON EYES and shorn fur around the muzzles; later bears had glass eyes and longer fur. By the 1930s, Ideal were also producing other types of bear, including a black-and-white panda. Because early Ideal bears are desirable, fakes are being produced. Be suspicious of bears with no sign of wear, and those with uneven seams or thickly stitched, unworn noses. *See also* TEDDY BEAR, AMERICAN.

IGA WARE From the 17thC, Japanese STONEWARE vases with a matt surface.

ILLUSION GLASS A DRINKING GLASS designed to be used by somebody proposing a series of toasts, or the landlord of an inn, who would have wanted to avoid drinking too much alcohol. The glass has a smaller capacity than it seems, because the walls of the bowl are thick, leaving only a shallow depression for liquid at the top. These glasses were produced in England from the early 18thC. Earlier examples have smaller bowls and longer stems than later ones.

ILMENAN German PORCELAIN factory established in the late 18thC.

IMARI Exported through the Japanese port of Imari – hence the name – a type of PORCELAIN with opulent decoration inspired by brocade designs. Imari is one of the most common types of Japanese porcelain. The pieces were painted with dark, UNDERGLAZE BLUE decoration, glazed, and fired, then

IMARI jar and lid, c.1860.

enamelled with colours, gilded, and fired again. Most wares were in dark blue and iron-red, with gilding and a black outline; shades of greenish-yellow, turquoise, and manganese are also found. Floral designs or landscapes are often set in shaped panels against the underglaze blue. Some pieces have figural KNOPS. Large display wares are sought after. Pieces in pairs and garnitures command premium prices. Condition is crucial to value, but damage can be restored. Imari is unmarked, or may have an impressed stamp. Chinese potters made imitation Imari from the early 18thC, and European versions were made in the Netherlands, Germany, Italy (Venice), and Britain. These copies are valuable in their own right. *See also* POTTERY AND PORCELAIN, JAPANESE.

"IMARI" PATTERN Flower-basket pattern in red, blue, and gold, copied from Japanese wares, and popular on European PORCELAIN of the 18thC.

IMPASTO Paint applied so thickly to MAIOLICA or FAIENCE that it creates a pattern in low relief.

IMPERIAL PORCELAIN FACTORY Russia's foremost PORCELAIN factory, established *c.*1748 in St Petersburg, the town after which it was originally named. It became the Imperial Porcelain Factory in 1763, and is still in production. Early wares reflected the style of MEISSEN, but under imperial patronage the factory began making more ambitious pieces. Wares of the early 19thC are distinctive, with detailed pictorial decoration, including copies of famous oil paintings and Russian peasant figures, and extravagant gilding. Gilded wreath decoration is unique to St Petersburg. After the 1917 Revolution, the factory was taken over by the State and produced innovative, angular, Constructivist designs, which are sought after. Subject matter reflected the country's new political ideals, such as factory scenes and workers, and a Constructivist palette was made of reds, black, and grey. St Petersburg porcelain is marked with a crown and, in Roman letters, the initials of the emperor or empress of the period.

IMPERIAL YELLOW Distinctive yellow ENAMEL, developed by Chinese imperial potters in the 15thC and reserved for the imperial household.

IMPORT MARK The Customs Act of 1842 made it illegal to import GOLD or SILVER wares into Britain and Ireland unless they had been assayed at a British office. From 1867, silver articles produced outside Britain were assigned a distinctive mark of foreign origin – the letter "F" within an oval escutcheon – in addition to the standard British HALLMARKS. From 1904 until 1973, all imported silver had to be marked with its relevant standard in decimal: .958 for Britannia silver and .925 for sterling silver. *See also* ASSAY MARK.

IMPRESSED A MARK or decoration that is stamped or indented into the surface of POTTERY. On a DOLL it can be found on the head or SHOULDER-PLATE.

IMPERIAL PORCELAIN **soup plate from the service of Emperor Paul I, late 18thC.**

IMPROVED Term used to describe an object, such as an item of SILVER, given additional decoration some time after its original manufacture.

INCE & MAYHEW Well-reputed, British FURNITURE firm run by the partners William Ince (1759–1803) and John Mayhew (c.1736–1811), whose wares incorporated GOTHIC or Chinese styles. Their pattern-book, *The Universal System of Household Furniture,* contained more than 300 designs.

INCISED A MARK or decoration that is cut or scratched into the surface.

INCISED LAQUER *See* BANTAM WORK.

INCLUSION Within the body of a GLASS vessel, particles that are either deliberately introduced for decorative effect, or by accident (i.e. a flaw).

INDESTRUCTIBLES DOLLS made of plastics or resin from the mid-19thC. They were less liable to damage than dolls with ceramic heads.

INDIANISCHE BLUMEN German for "Indian flowers". Refers to painting on PORCELAIN in the Oriental style, especially on mid-18th MEISSEN and HÖCHST.

"INDIA"-PATTERN BAYONET Standard BAYONET originally made for the British army in India, then used in the Napoleonic Wars (1799–1815).

"IN FRONT OF THE KILN" Phrase used to describe applied decoration added by hand to a hot GLASS object.

INKSTAND A TRAY and its accessories used for writing. Few inkstands were made before the late 17thC. The earliest examples are in the form of rectangular caskets, with inkpots (with small holes in the rim to hold quill pens), wafer pots (for wax disks for sealing letters), and pounce pots for sand or pounce, which was sprinkled on parchment paper to prevent the ink from spreading. By the 18thC, most inkstands consisted of rectangular silver trays on four feet, usually with inkpots and pounce pots, plus a TAPERSTICK or small handbell. Early inkstands were known by the name "standish", after their upwardly curved or dished sides. Most early examples are plain, except for moulded scroll-and-shell or beaded rims and fancy feet. Early, 18thC inkstands are well made, and more valuable than later ones. Inkpots were often fitted with ceramic or lead liners, but these are often lost, as are the bells and covers. Inkstands gained popularity from the 18thC, when they were made of SILVER, SHEFFIELD PLATE, and sometimes PEWTER. Silver-mounted, GLASS ink bottles were introduced in the mid-18thC as cheaper alternatives to all-silver ones. Mechanization in the 1770s sparked a surge in the popularity of items that could be mass-produced from a small amount of silver. Most inkstands from the 18thC were in the form of footed trays, usually with troughs for pens and perhaps a bell, WAXJACK, or taperstick. Complete sets in top condition are desirable. Edwardian inkstands were produced using an economy of silver, with light, flimsy, machine-stamped borders. By this date, many 18thC writing accoutrements, such as pounce pots and sealing wax, no longer formed sets with inkstands. Novelty examples in the form of figures or animals were popular at this time. Watch out for unmarked fittings (such as SNUFFERS, lids, and guard rails for glass bottles), because they may be replacements. Many inkstands bear inscriptions, coats of arms, or armorials, which can provide clues to the identities of the original owners, DESK ACESSORIES, and add to the value. *See also* POUNCE BOX.

INKWELL Vessels mostly made in SILVER, or in GLASS with a matching TRAY for containing ink. Few silver inkwells survive from before the mid-17thC, and, until the 18thC, they were usually portable. Some inkwells were made in sets, or contained within penners. Silver inkwells were produced in a variety of imaginative and decorative designs, often in combination with other materials. Some were made as special commissions, and were intended for display only. Novelty inkwells are popular. A silver inkwell in the shape of a ship's CAPSTAN (over which a tie-up rope was thrown) was a common form, and popular from the 1880s until the 1920s, and remains in great demand among collectors today. Many examples were made as parts of boxed sets, sometimes with a matching CANDLESTICK. Many "capstan" inkwells had elaborate lids or hinged covers with channels to hold dip pens, and glass liners inside to facilitate cleaning. Glass inkwells were made from the mid-18thC, with detachable silver or BRASS covers, and were often set on silver or silver-plated trays with pierced partitions for holding the pots in place. Some are decorated with cutting, usually around or under the base, so that spilt ink did not catch in the decoration. Glass inkwells were often carried in travelling sets or fitted into cases, and any gilded decoration is on the shoulders of the pots, the only part visible. Inkwells were mostly made in pairs, but are rarely found as such today.

INLAY FURNITURE decoration in which a shape is gouged out of a wooden surface, and pieces of contrasting woods or other materials such as bone, HORN, IVORY, metal, or MOTHER-OF-PEARL are inserted. It was used on English and Continental European furniture from the 17thC onward. In the USA, it was used in New England betweem 1760 and 1790. After 1790, ornamental inlays became popular. *See also* BANDING and MARQUETRY.

INNER STRIPE On a CARPET, part of the border design. A narrow band between the FIELD and the main border.

INRO A small, Japanese, compartmented medicine-box, worn on the belt (OBI) and attached by the NETSUKE, or toggle.

INSERTED HAIR Hair, either real or artificial, set into the scalp of wax DOLLS.

Lacquer INRO with ojime bead on thread, 19thC.

INTAGLIO Incised GEMstone, often set in a ring. Used in antiquity and during the Renaissance as a seal.

INTAGLIO EYES Painted eyes with concave pupils and irises on a DOLL. The eyes are carved out of the head and highlighted with white.

INTAGLIO GLASS A technique originating in late-17thC Germany and Bohemia, in which the GLASS surface is INCISED to varying depths to create three-dimensional effects. In the late 19thC, the use of Bohemian master engravers by English firms led to the fashion for intaglio engraving in Britain.

INTARSIA Inlaid pieces of different-coloured woods to form a picture.

IPEK Turkish word for silk, used of CARPETS.

IRIDESCENT GLASS A type of GLASS made using metal oxides to produce a lustrous surface that changes colours depending on the light's reflection. J. & L. LOBMEYR and Thomas WEBB & Sons were among the first firms to make iridescent glass in the 19thC. Later, it was favoured by ART NOUVEAU and ART DECO art glassmakers such as TIFFANY.

IRISH CHAIN In quilting, a PATCHWORK block pattern built up from diagonally arranged squares. *See also* QUILTS.

IRISH GLASS GLASS made in Ireland from the 18thC. It can be identified by its greyish tinge, shallow, DIAMOND-CUT decoration and (often) lopsided shape.

IRON CLOCK Earliest form of domestic CLOCK, made in Germany from the 15thC, often in the form of a church tower, with four pillars.

IRONSTONE A robust, white EARTHENWARE, containing ground glassy slag (a by-product of iron smelting). Still produced today, it was patented in 1813 by Charles James Mason, an English, Staffordshire-based potter, as "Mason's ironstone". It is a successful material for dinner services, because it holds the heat well and is hardwearing. Ironstone was also referred to as "granite china" and "opaque china". Pieces are usually decorated in colourful, pseudo-Oriental patterns, and shapes are often inventive. Apart from services, ironstone was also used for ornamental VASES, JARDINIÈRES, WINE COOLERS, jugs, teapots, miniature wares, garden seats, and card racks. Mason's ironstone has an impressed mark, and changes in details can help with dating. Other makers of similar materials are: SPODE, DAVENPORT, MINTON, WEDGWOOD, and RIDGWAY.

Large, Mason's IRONSTONE vase with pseudo-oriental decoration, 19thC.

ISFAHAN In the late-16th and 17thC the site in Persia of the royal CARPET manufactory, noted for rich silk rugs often incorporating gold and silver. Since 1900, it has made rugs with floral designs and central medallions.

ISLEWORTH Variously used of BONE CHINA from a Liverpool factory producing wares from *c*.1800; and of colourful FLATWARES made at Isleworth, Middlesex, England, in the 19thC.

ISLIM On Persian CARPETS, a floral design with serpentine foliage trails.

ISNIK WARE Made in Isnik, Western Anatolia, Ottoman-Turkish 13th–19thC POTTERY painted with blue, floral and geometric designs on white grounds.

ISPARTA Name for Sparta CARPETS made in Smyrna (now Izmir, Turkey), but so-called to distinguish higher-quality products from inferior Smyrna products.

ISTORIATO Mythological, historical, or biblical scenes used to decorate PLATES, DISHES, and other MAIOLICA wares. From *c*.1520 potters in URBINO, Italy, began producing these decorative maiolica wares, which were treated like canvasses and entirely covered with narrative scenes (*istoriato* means "story"). The predominant shades of ochre and yellow are typical of early pieces; later, the palette became brighter and more varied. Factors affecting value include date, quality of the painting, a signature, and condition. Copies of *istoriato* dishes were made in the 19thC. *See also* POTTERY, ITALIAN.

IVES, JOSEPH American, Brooklyn-based clockmaker, active 1820–30.

IVORENE A simulated IVORY, usually made from plastic.

IVORIDE Early and rare form of plastic made from 1868, simulating IVORY.

IVORY White, fine-grained dentine derived from the tusks of elephants and narwhales, used in Europe in the Middle Ages for carving religious groups, by sailors to make scrimshaws, and for mass-produced, ornamental objects in the Far East. Old ivory has a mellow PATINA, which can be faked.

IVORY DOLL Made in China and the Far East, a DOLL with a carved IVORY head, typically exquisitely carved and dressed. Increasing trade with the Orient in the 18thC made the dolls popular in Europe. Ivory stains with age and may crack, but these factors do not necessarily detract from the value.

IVORY PORCELAIN Development of the 19thC, similar to PARIAN, but ivory coloured in BISCUIT form.

IVORY-TINTED EARTHENWARE with an ivory coloured, glaze, developed in Britain by William Copeland at SPODE in the 19thC.

IVRENE A slightly iridescent, ivory-coloured translucent ART GLASS developed by Frederick CARDER at STEUBEN GLASSWORKS in America in the 1920s.

J

JACKFIELD Black-glazed, sometimes moulded and gilded, tableware and figures developed in Jackfield, Shropshire, England, in the mid-18thC .

JACKIE THE JUBILEE BEAR A bear cub with short, fat back legs and a chunky body, designed by Steiff in 1953 to commemorate 50 years of the firm's bear production. The most obvious identifying marks are the pink stitch showing on the top of the dark thread of the nose, and a small, dark-shaded area in the MOHAIR plush on the tummy, representing the navel. The bear was made in three heights: nearly 18cm (7in), 23cm (9in) and 33cm (13in) tall – in either beige or brown. Brown is a rare colour.

JACOB-DESMALTER, FRANÇOIS HONORÉ (1770–1841) Son of Georges JACOB. Apart from its numerous CLASSICAL motifs, his work is notable for its inserts, mainly of BRONZE but also of MOTHER-OF-PEARL and PORCELAIN.

JACOBEAN Period between 1603 and 1625, spanning the reign of James I;, The term is sometimes used to cover the period 1603 to the Restoration of 1666, because Jacobean styles continued long after the death of James I.

JACOB, GEORGES (1739–1814) The leading French ÉBÉNISTE, or cabinet-maker, of the years immediately before the French Revolution of 1789–99. He specialized in CHAIRS, and worked in a NEO-CLASSICAL STYLE, with some influence from England – for example, he used MAHOGANY.

JACOBITE BLADE Basket-hilt SWORD etched with inscriptions or symbols in support of the Jacobite cause. They were mostly made in Germany for export to Scotland in the early 18thC.

JACOBITE GLASS Made in the 18thC, a wine- or ALE GLASS engraved with Jacobite motifs, such as roses, doves, oak leaves, mottoes, and hymns, to show allegiance to the Old Pretender (James Edward Stuart), and the Young Pretender (Charles Edward Stuart), considered by supporters as the rightful claimants to the English and Scottish thrones. Jacobite glasses are collectable, but can be expensive. Genuine examples date to between 1746 and 1788. Countless later copies and forgeries exist. *See also* DRINKING GLASS.

JACOBS, CARL A leading Danish designer, he created the "Jason" CHAIR, which was designed to stack easily, and was produced commercially by Kandya Ltd in the 1950s.

JACOBITE wine glass, with bowl engraved with rose and single bud, c.1760.

JAMBIYAH Arab DAGGER with a sharply curved blade, bending almost at right angles from the hilt.

JAMESON, GEORGE Early-19thC maker of CLOCKS and CHRONOMETERS.

JANINA A stylized pattern with a central leaf and two circular fruits either side. Found in the borders of Turkish CARPETS.

JAPANESE STYLE *See* AESTHETIC MOVEMENT.

JAPANNING Popular in the 17thC, the European imitation of Chinese and Japanese LACQUER. Black was the most common colour; red is rarer.

JAPONAISERIE Designs based on Japanese forms and decorative motifs.

JAPY FRÈRES French manufacturer of CLOCKS and watches, *c*.1770–1936.

JARDINIÈRE Stand with a lead or zinc lining for containing indoor plants.

JASPER WARE Unglazed STONEWARE introduced *c*.1767 by Josiah WEDGWOOD. It was originally decorated with SLIP, but later with high-relief decoration, medallions, and pictorial scenes, and became one of the firm's most popular products, with manufacture continuing through the 19thC and later. Many designs were based on drawings by artists of the day and inspired by antiquity. Cutting of the applied CAMEO design should be crisp and refined, with a slight translucence in the shallow areas. Jasper ware was made in colours from green, yellow, lilac, claret, and black and white, to, most commonly, blue. Early blue wares are far more distinctive in colour than 20thC versions, being either a deep purplish-blue, or a strong slate-blue – not today's pale "Wedgwood" blue.

JAUNE JONQUILLE French for "daffodil yellow", a light-yellow ground used sparingly by SÈVRES in the 1750s.

JELLY GLASS First made in the 18thC, a cone-shaped dessert vessel with a short stem, often with two handles and a matching saucer.

JELLY MOULD Ceramic form made in many shapes and sizes from the mid-18thC to *c*.1830. After 1830, they were also produced in metal; from 1935, GLASS versions were made. Sets and unusual forms are collectable.

JENKINS, HENRY Maker of ASTRONOMICAL CLOCKS in the late 18thC.

JENNENS & BETTRIDGE WARE Early,-19thC, PAPIER-MÂCHÉ items, notably FURNITURE. Much English, papier-mâché furniture was made in Birmingham; Jennens & Bettridge were also active in London.

JELLY GLASS **with gadrooned base and folded rim, c.1710.**

Sèvres porcelain, ormolu-mounted vase, with gilt and JEWELLED DECORATION, c.1860.

JENSEN, GEORG (1866–1935) Danish silversmith and jeweller whose designs are still made by the Jensen factory. His workshop was established in 1904 in Copenhagen, and he collaborated with other Danish artists, notably Johan Rohde, to produce robust work for international sale throughout the 1920s. Pieces made by well-known designers who worked for Jensen, such as C.F. Hallberg or H. Nielsen, add a premium, and their stamped initials are incorporated with the Jensen marks. Check for English import marks to help date the piece. Jensen's early production from the 1920s is rare and more sought after by collectors than that from the 1960s and '70s.

JERSEY GLASS Early American PRESSED GLASS from the Jersey Glass Co., founded in the early 19thC, and from other factories in the same locality.

JESUIT CHINA Decorated with New Testament scenes, PORCELAIN made in China in the 17th and early 18thC to the order of Jesuit missionaries.

JET Petrified wood, usually from Whitby in Yorkshire, England. It was used to make MOURNING JEWELLERY in Victorian times.

JETWARE English, 19thC, black-glazed EARTHENWARE made in Staffordshire.

JEWELLED DECORATION Method of inlaid ceramic decoration created by placing drops of coloured ENAMEL over gilding, creating a rich, gemlike effect. It was first used by SÈVRES in the late 18thC, and was popular with English factories, such as COPELAND, MINTON, and WORCESTER in the 19thC.

JEWELLERY, COSTUME Items of jewellery in inexpensive materials. It was first produced in the 20thC, when new materials and techniques made it possible to mass-produce items and sell them at modest prices. Without the restraint of gemstones, and using materials such as BRASS, BAKELITE, and GLASS, designers created elaborate designs inspired by the styles of the times and major events, such as the discovery of Tutankhamen's tomb in the early 1920s. During the 1920s and '30s many designers, including René LALIQUE, Jean DUNAND, Marcel Boucher, Hattie Carnegie, Corocraft, Miriam Haskell, Hobé, Mazer & Co., Joseff, and Trifari, made quality pieces. Popular post-war designers to look for include Dior, Yves Saint Laurent, Kenneth Jay Lane, and Butler & Wilson.

JEWELLERY, FINE Decorative objects, such as bracelets, earrings, necklaces, and rings, worn for personal adornment. The most valuable pieces are made with precious gemstones and with GOLD, SILVER, or platinum settings. Jewellery made with SEMI-PRECIOUS STONES can also be valuable. Pre-World War II jewellery is now so popular that many inexpensive modern copies are manufactured. To avoid mistakes, learn how to recognize the stones, stringing, and setting methods appropriate to the period. Value depends on age, condition, the value of the materials, and current fashions. Unique or handmade pieces fetch more than mass-produced ones, and a famous previous owner can affect the value. Gold, silver, and platinum are usually marked, which aids authentication. Diamond jewellery has an intrinsic as well as antique value. Do not rely on the glass-scratch test for diamonds, because there are other, less-valuable stones that produce a similar effect. Good-sized diamonds fetch more than small ones or off-cuts, and BRILLIANT-CUT designs are preferred to ROSE-CUT ones, which have fewer facets. The value of CAMEOS depends on the material and the skill of the carving. Cameos of semi-precious stone are worth more than shell cameos, and coral cameos are particularly desirable. Necklaces of strung coral are common. *See also* GEMS, MEMENTO MORI JEWELLERY and MOURNING JEWELLERY.

JIAJIAN (Chia Ching) Chinese MING DYNASTY emperor, 1522–66.

JIAN YAO Noted for its HARE'S-FUR GLAZE, POTTERY made in the Jian (Chien) region of Fukien province, China, during the SUNG DYNASTY.

JIAQING (Chia Ch'ing) Chinese CH'ING DYNASTY emperor, 1796–1820.

JINGLING JOHNNY TOY consisting of a frame and small bells that jingle.

JOEL, BETTY (1896–1984) Scottish-born, London-based designer of FURNITURE in the ART DECO style, using laminated wood.

JOHNSON, MASON & TAYLOR American, 19thC maker of RAG DOLLS.

JOHNSON, THOMAS (fl.1756–58) British designer and carver best known for his MIRRORS and CONSOLE TABLES in the ROCOCO and Chinese styles.

JOINED FURNITURE made by a joiner. Two common types of join are DOVETAIL JOINTS and MORTISE-AND-TENON JOINTS.

JOINT Where two pieces of wood are attached to each other in construction.

JOINTED TODDLER German DOLL with a wood or COMPOSITION body, and pronounced side-hip joints and tummy. CHARACTER DOLLS of this type were made after 1910.

JOLLY BOAT Boat-shaped COASTER on wheels for circulating wine or liquor.

JONES, GEORGE & SONS English, Stoke-on-Trent-based pottery, 1861–1951, known for MAJOLICA, often in whimsical forms, such as animal-shaped TUREENS, with crisp moulding and a colourful, glossy glaze (a cobalt-blue ground is desirable). Also made PÂTE-SUR-PÂTE and PARIAN wares.

Schoenau & Hoffmeister, bisque-headed JOINTED TODDLER, *c*.1915–20.

Bohemian-green, enamelled glass jug, *c.*1900 (CENTRAL EUROPEAN JUG).

JOSHAGAN Central Iranian CARPETS decorated with flowers, each framed by diamonds, on a rich red or blue ground.

JUFTI Double knot in CARPET production. The yarn wraps around four threads of the warp instead of two, resulting in a less-dense PILE.

JUG, CENTRAL EUROPEAN The earliest GLASS jugs made in central Europe during the 16th and 17thC, often with SILVER, SILVER-GILT, or GOLD MOUNTS and hinged lids, were intended as luxury items for display, or to be exchanged as diplomatic or court gifts. These jugs, made with large, bulbous bodies, elegantly curving handles, and rudimentary feet, were derived from examples in silver, because glass was then a luxury commodity as expensive as precious metal. In the 18thC, jugs from central Europe were made of POTASH GLASS. A formalized pattern of scrolls and flowers is characteristic of central European glass engraving from 1750 to 1800. Fine-quality, clear-glass jugs embellished with sophisticated engraving – a speciality of central European, especially Bohemian, glassmaking – were made in the 18thC and 19thC. The handle is a good indication of date; before the late 19thC it was applied at the neck and drawn down onto the body. Jugs were produced in LITHYALIN GLASS, as well as in the style of HISTORISMUS GLASS. Bohemian, 19thC jugs can be identified by the high standard of their enamelling and engraving. During the early 19thC, glass-enamelling workshops were established by Samuel Mohn (1762–1815) in Leipzig and Dresden, and by Anton Kothgasser (1769–1851) in Vienna. Some of the most prominent 19thC glass engravers were Bohemian, including Dominik BIEMANN (1800–57), August BOHM (1812–90), and the Sachr and Pohl families. Many engravers worked all over Europe and the USA.

JUG, CREAM AND MILK Vessel used to serve cream or milk, and made from the early 18thC as a result of the popularity of tea. The earliest form of cream jug was plain and pear-shaped or ovoid, with a low foot rim and an applied handle and lip. Some jugs had hinged lids and wooden handles for serving hot milk, which, before *c.*1720, was often taken with tea. Pear-shaped jugs were common until the 1770s, but later, 18thC examples had three cast feet, in the form of shells, scrolls, or pads, rather than low foot rims. Other mid-18thC vessels for holding cream include COW CREAMERS and cream boats – the latter being a smaller version of a SAUCEBOAT, which was sometimes lavishly decorated with cast-and-chased ROCOCO shells, scrolls, and foliage. With the onset of the NEO-CLASSICAL syle, cream jugs were made in the shape of tapering urns, and in vase form, with high loop handles and pedestal feet, sometimes on square plinths. From the 1790s, most cream jugs were made as parts of TEA SERVICES. CHARACTER JUGS were made in considerable numbers in the late 19thC, particularly in Germany and the Netherlands. They were popular, although impractical and poorly produced. Made of thin-gauge silver and subjected to heavy use, many jugs have been damaged, despite the beaded or reeded wires applied to strengthen the rims. Forgeries and conversions of pitcher-style cream jugs are found, made by adding a lip to a christening mug, or a lip and handle to the body of a sugar, salt, or pepper caster. Check for splitting in the rim, and repairs around the handle joints. Also look to see that the foot has not been pushed into the body of the jug. *See also* CREAM PAIL; JUG, SILVER; and PIGGIN.

JUG, ENGLISH AND IRISH WINE Before the early 19thC, GLASS and wine were both expensive commodities. From early in the Victorian era (1837–1901), wine jugs were increasingly made as part of table services, or with GOBLETS as presentation sets. Clear-glass jugs were intended for claret and red wines, to show off the colour of the wine, while coloured-glass pieces were used for white wines and champagne. Most 19thC jugs follow the style of contemporary DECANTERS, but have handles and pouring lips. Unlike later pieces, early jugs came without stoppers. If there is a slight ridge inside the neck, and if the neck is narrower than a thumb's width, there should be a stopper. Shapes developed from simple lines to more ornate and heavy forms later in the century. In the late 18th and early 19thC, glass manufacture expanded rapidly in Ireland – many leading English glassmakers emigrated their due to the heavy taxes on glass in England. Irish glasshouses are associated with CUT GLASS, particularly pieces combining different patterns of cutting, such as STAR-CUTTING on the base, a STEP-CUT neck, and a DIAMOND-CUT body – characteristic of good Irish, Regency glass. Good-quality, Regency jugs are valuable today, because many were damaged through handling, with chips or cracks in the rims and broken handles. Tapping the handle lightly may indicate whether a piece has been damaged – it should ring if in perfect condition. A taller, elongated body and high-looped handle date a jug to the mid-19thC, when the cutting and engraving were lighter in style than on Regency pieces. The handle was first applied at the top of the body and then drawn down, as shown by the thickness of the handle just below the rim. With the popularity of the Grecian style in the 1870s, jugs were often produced in shapes derived from ancient vases. Most were engraved with simple GREEK-KEY patterns, but the best examples, largely produced for the international exhibitions of the time, feature linear, engraved or etched designs adapted from Greek sculpture or pottery. Gift sets were often given as presentation pieces, and are described on manufacturers' lists as sets for serving lemonade or champagne. *See also* GLASS, CARE OF and JUG, GLASS.

JUG, GLASS A GLASS vessel with a handle and spout for pouring liquids and known from ancient Roman times, when it was intended for religious rituals. In the 15th and 16thC some elaborate jugs and EWERS with globular bodies, often embellished with hinged lids and thumbpieces in precious metals, were created as luxury items for display or exchange as diplomatic gifts. It was not until the early 19thC, when technical advances permitted the production of reasonably priced glass TABLEWARE, that practical, utilitarian glass jugs were introduced. A variety of shapes can be found, including globular, conical,

Liverpool (Seth Pennington), porcelain cream boat, painted with polychrome floral sprays, *c.*1785.

Victorian, etched, glass and chased-silver-plated and panel gilt claret JUG by Elkington & Co.

ovoid, and cylindrical, sometimes with a stopper. Jugs were made for serving both wine and water (the latter type usually have wider necks that were suitable for frequent refilling) and for display. In the 19thC, fine-quality jugs were made across Europe and the USA, and featured elaborate enamelling, cutting, engraving, and coloured-glass decoration. Glass CLARET JUGS from this period were also made with fine silver or plated mounts and handles. Jugs with matching pairs of goblets were popular in the Victorian era as wedding gifts and as part of larger table services. In contrast to these luxury pieces – and more affordable today – are the more practical, sturdy jugs made of bottle glass in provincial English factories, and the colourful, pressed-glass pitchers produced in the early 20thC by English and American manufacturers, often with matching sets of DRINKING GLASSES. Jugs in pristine condition are rarer today than DECANTERS, because the handles and pouring lips were vulnerable. When buying glass jugs, always check for damage around the lip and where the handle joins the body. The inside of the vessel, if heavily used, may be cloudy from water damage. *See also* JUG, WATER; JUG, WINE.

JUG, SILVER Made from the 16thC, a vessel for serving liquids such as beer, wine, water, milk, or cream, or for shaving. Earlier jugs occasionally had hinged lids. Marks should be on the base or body, near the handle, or under the spout. Lidded jugs should bear a full set of marks on the body, and a maker's mark and "lion passant" only on the lid – a full set of marks on the lid means that the piece was probably once a tankard (commonly converted into jugs in the 19thC). Beware of soldering around the spout, as this could indicate a less-valuable conversion. To be legal, a conversion must have later marks on any parts that were added. *See also* HALLMARK; JUG, CREAM AND MILK.

JUG, WATER GLASS vessels for serving water were introduced *c*.1800, when there was increasing demand for sets of glass TABLEWARE. Before this, water and beer were served in POTTERY jugs. In the early 19thC, changes in dining etiquette, as well as improvements in water quality and the introduction of mass-produced glassware, meant that water jugs were seen in middle-class homes. PILLAR-CUTTING around the body was popular in the 1820s. In the Victorian era (1837–1901) there were many styles, from expensive, engraved pieces to sturdier, plain, or simply etched jugs for bars and taverns. Heavy cutting on a jug is characteristic of Georgian jugs, while curvaceously shaped bodies, handles, and pouring rims, and scrolling forms on the rim can date jugs to the mid-19thC, when there was a preference for lighter engraving. Coloured-glass jugs were mass-produced in the 19thC; some examples have coloured bodies and clear handles. On jugs made before *c*.1870, the handle was attached just under the rim and drawn down; on pieces after this date, it is fitted further down and drawn upward. Simply decorated, straight-sided jugs were made by the thousand from the 1870s until 1914, and are still easy to find. Some were engraved, but the engraving lacks the depth of cutting and detail found on more costly pieces. They were made mainly for bars and hotels.

JUG, WINE Intended to hold wine or beer, these large jugs came into use with the Restoration in 1660. Some early examples have covers, but lidded jugs made after the 1730s are rare. Most 18thC jugs are baluster-shaped and, until the reign of George II (1727–60), had plain bodies. Harp-shaped handles were popular until the 1750s, when the S-scroll form became more fashionable. Many jugs were commissioned by the nobility from top-quality Huguenot makers. The ROCOCO era led to the production of more elaborate designs. SILVER wine jugs with vine motifs came into fashion *c*.1830. Early examples are made of solid silver; later versions are made of glass with silver mounts. From the 1820s until the early 20thC, silversmiths adopted a variety of highly innovative, ornamental styles. CLASSICAL, medieval, and naturalistic forms were all Victorian favourites, and many silver wares were produced in NEO-CLASSICAL STYLE. The Renaissance-inspired "CELLINI" PATTERN was the most popular design for claret and wine jugs in the 19thC. A jug from this period may have an insulated wooden handle so that it could also be used to hold hot liquids. Collectors should look out for early 18thC TANKARDS that have had spouts added, or plain, pear-shaped jugs that have lost their covers and had the hinges removed. *See also* EWER, WINE.

JUGENDSTIL German, ART NOUVEAU style, named after the magazine *Jugend*, which was published from 1896 in Munich. Characteristically, the style transforms plant shapes into sensual, but limpid, abstractions.

JULEP A type of BEAKER, made in America during the late 18th and early 19thC. They were usually in SILVER and had straight sides, sometimes tapering to the base. Many were awarded as prizes or trophies.

JUMEAU Leading French doll-making firm (1842–99), which made high-quality DOLLS, famed for their elegant clothes, and distinguished by their pale-coloured, BISQUE heads and large, glass eyes. Pierre François Jumeau was the founder, but handed over the reins to his son Emile in 1875; from this point, dolls bearing Emile's mark were referred to as "E.J.s". The birth of the BÉBÉ was pioneered by Pierre, and, in one year alone in the 1880s, the firm sold an extraordinary 85,000 of these dolls. Portrait bébés, supposedly modelled on real children, were introduced in 1870. Bébés were given blue eyes with long lashes then highlighted with black eyeliner. The "Jumeau Triste", or long-faced bébé, is especially sought after. Most early dolls have Jumeau marks on the heads, then on the bodies, after Jumeau won a gold medal at the 1878 Paris Exposition Universelle. The rarest is marked with an "A". Later Jumeau dolls may have red ticks on their heads.

JUN WARE Produced in central Henan, China, these pieces (often shallow DISHES) have wedge-shaped foot rims, and are glazed in shades of blue, sometimes with splashes of purple and, more rarely, CELADON-like green. The glaze often dribbles.

German, JUGENDSTIL, electroplated jewellery box, *c*.1900.

K

KABISTAN Caucasian CARPETS decorated with birds and animals.

KAGAMIBUTA A NETSUKE that incorporates metalwork.

KAGI The Japanese term for keys and other small items worn on a cord suspended from the waist sash (OBI) of a kimono.

KAIBUTSU Japanese objects carved in the shape of mythical animals.

KAISER BABY A DOLL supposedly modelled on the German Emperor (Wilhelm II) as a baby, including his crippled hand, by KÄMMER & REINHARDT. The doll has one arm bent inwards and the hand held up, which was unpopular at the time. Legs and toes are modelled with an accentuated big toe. The earliest Kaisers have multi-jointed bodies, but most are the five-piece, bent-limb type. The mould No. 100 was used. Brown-eyed Kaisers are rare.

KAKIEMON WARE Named after a 17thC, Japanese pottery family, Kakiemon PORCELAIN is recognizable by its palette of iron-red, deep sky-blue, turquoise, yellow, aubergine/manganese, and black, and its style of decoration. The sparse, asymmetric decoration is delicate, and allows much of the white PORCELAIN to show. Kakiemon ware was copied in 18thC Europe by MEISSEN, CHELSEA, CHANTILLY, and many other factories. *See also* POTTERY AND PORCELAIN, JAPANESE.

KAMAKURA Period of Japanese history between 1185 and 1333.

KÄMMER & REINHARDT A doll-making firm (1886–1940) founded in Waltershausen, Germany, by designer and modelmaker Ernst Kämmer and entrepreneur Franz Reinhardt. Their fine-quality, innovative DOLLS often had mohair wigs. Despite Kämmer's death in 1901, the company was successful, and, in 1909, it was the first firm to produce a CHARACTER DOLL. One of their dolls was known as a KAISER BABY. Kämmer & Reinhardt dolls were made with moulds, and the mould numbers are used to identify the dolls. Certain moulds were interchangeable as girls or boys, depending on the dress and painting of the face. Mould No.s 117 and 117/A, dating from 1911, are favourites; these dolls have closed, slightly smiling mouths, glass eyes, and six-ball-jointed, wood-and-composition bodies. Do not confuse dolls of mould No.s 117 and 117/A with the No. 117N doll, which is worth much less. The 117N was made from 1919, and has a much rounder face, an open mouth, upper teeth, and "flirting" eyes. The rarest mould numbers such as 106 (of

18thC, Japanese KAKIEMON saucer.

which only 50 are thought to have been made), 107, and 108 are valuable; other rarities are 102, 103, 104, and 105. Look for the manufacturer's stamp on the back of the neck or head under the hairline. Pre-World War I character dolls are most wanted. The firm merged with SIMON & HALBIG in 1919.

KÄNDLER, JOHANN JOACHIM (1706–75) MEISSEN modeller, 1733–75.

KANGXI (K'ang Hsi) Chinese CH'ING Dynasty emperor, 1662–1722.

KAOLIN (china clay) A fine, white, granite clay used in HARD-PASTE PORCELAIN.

KAPOK Lightweight, silky fibre from the seed pods of the tropical kapok tree. Used to stuff TEDDY BEARS, especially in England and Germany in the 1920s.

KARABAGH CARPETS from the southern Caucasus. They are often Persian in style, with some influenced by French floral, rather than geometric, patterns.

KARATSU POTTERY decorated with pale-coloured glazes, and made by Korean craftsmen working in Kyushu, Japan, in the 16th and 17thC.

KAS Large WARDROBE with a heavy cornice and arched panels separated by twisted columns. Usually on ball feet.

KASHAN Centre in Southern Iran, noted for its RUGS with central medallions.

KASHGAI Woven by Iranian nomadic tribes, RUGS notable for their springy lustrous texture and finely detailed, rectilinear designs.

KASHMIR The northern Indian centre of silk and wool CARPET manufacture.

KASTRUPZ Danish, Copenhagen-based, late-18thC, FAIENCE factory.

KAST-STEL Set of five DELFTWARE vases – three baluster shaped and two straight sided – used to decorate CUPBOARD cornices in the late 17th and 18thC.

KATABORI NETSUKE on which all of the surfaces are carved.

KATAR Indian DAGGER with a sharply pointed blade and bar POMMEL.

KAYSER, ENGELBERT (1840–1911) Chief German exponent of the ART NOUVEAU style in PEWTER. His range may be called "Kayserzinn" pewter.

KAZAK A Caucasian RUG with bold geometric patterns and long, fine-quality wool. They are often named according to their distinctive designs, such as "pinwheel", "karachov", "fachralo", and "bordjalou".

"Kayserzinn" pewter liquor bottle designed by Hugo Leven, employed in ENGELBERT KAYSER's studio, Germany, c.1900.

KEENE GLASS Glassware from one of two factories operating in Keene, New Hampshire, USA, in the 19thC.

KELIM A flat-woven RUG with no knots and no PILE, and traditionally made entirely from wool. Modern reproduction kelims have bright colours and a coarse weave. Old rugs are finely woven and softly coloured. Also the flat woven fringe that finishes the ends of a pile carpet. *See also* RUG, PERSIAN.

KELLINGHUSEN Made in Schleswig Holstein, Germany, from the late 17th to 19thC, EARTHENWARE and FAIENCE, with bright floral designs.

KELSTERBACH PORCELAIN figures made in the 18thC by former MEISSEN potters, and imitating that factory's style.

KENAREH Runner or side CARPET, made to flank the main central carpet.

KENDI Japanese ceramic vessel originally to hold purified water. Export *kendi* were used as *hookah* bases. *See also* POTTERY AND PORCELAIN, JAPANESE.

KENNEDY Late-19thC factory in Burslem, Staffordshire, England. It is noted for PORCELAIN decorated with impressed scenes.

KENTUCKY RIFLE Early, often ornately decorated rifle with a long barrel, developed in Colonial America from European prototypes. *See also* FIREARMS

KERMANSHAH West Iranian centre of multi-coloured CARPET production.

KESTNER & CO. Doll-making firm founded by Johannes Daniel Kestner in Waltershaüsen, Germany, in the early 19thC. Under his grandson Adolph, the firm made child DOLLS with BISQUE heads on jointed COMPOSITION bodies in the 1880s. Kestner manufactured the heads and bodies themselves. From 1910, Kestner made CHARACTER DOLLS in the "200" series of marks. The most famous of these was Hilda; introduced in 1914, she was created under different mould numbers, with real or painted hair. Kestner also made Oriental babies with widely spaced, crescent- or almond-shaped eyes, and open mouths with teeth. Like all Kestner babies, they are chubby with fat tummies; some have solid, domed heads with moulded hair. Oriental baby boys are rarer than girls. Kestner dolls were popular in the USA. *See also* CELLULOID DOLL.

KETTLE *See* TEA KETTLE.

KETTLE STAND Small galleried TABLE used while taking tea.

KEW BLAS From Massachusetts, USA, late-19thC ART GLASS made of MILK GLASS, overlaid by etched, coloured GLASS, and topped with clear glass.

George III, figured, mahogany and boxwood inlaid KETTLE STAND, *c*.1785.

KEWPIE DOLL Cupid-like (hence "Kewpie") baby DOLLS with topknots; supposedly the guardian angels of children. The dolls were the inspiration of American illustrator Rose O'Neill. Designed under her supervision by Joseph Kallus, the first BISQUE Kewpies were made by KESTNER in 1913. They were also produced in other materials, but bisque is the most sought after. Most have pedestal legs, jointed arms, starfish-shaped hands, "wings" that are just visible below the ears, and the Rose O'Neill signature on the foot. A circular label may be attached to the doll's back or on its front. It may be heart-shaped or there may be no label at all, just the signature on the foot. Watch out for Japanese Kewpies with labels such as "Nippon" or "Foreign".

KHANDAR Indian long-sword with a double-edged blade and long POMMEL.

KHANJAR Indian DAGGER with a curved blade, and handle often of precious material such as IVORY or jade.

KHILIN On Oriental CARPETS, the motif of a stylized deer.

KHORASSAN Northeast Iranian CARPETS decorated with the *herati* motif.

KHOTAN Chinese-influenced CARPETS from Central Asia, by Siankiang.

KIAN SUNG DYNASTY, Chinese CERAMICS from Kiangsi, with resist designs.

KICK Indentation in the base of a GLASS vessel.

KID Soft leather used for the bodies of DOLLS in the late 19thC.

KIDDERMINSTER CARPET-weaving centre in the English Midlands since the early 17thC. Motifs are based on Flemish tapestries.

KIEL FAIENCE made in Schleswig-Holstein, Germany, in the late 18thC. Noted for its lively, floral decoration on an almost pure white ground.

KINDJAL Also known as a kindjhal, a Caucasian double-edged shortsword or DAGGER, with broad blade and no quillons.

KING'S LYNN GLASS wineglasses and TUMBLERS made in the 18thC, and decorated with a series of horizontal grooves around the bowl.

"KING'S" PATTERN On FLATWARE, a pattern with waisted sides, featuring a scallop shell and anthemion motifs. Popular during the REGENCY period.

KINGWOOD Also known as violet wood, a coarse-grained, yellowish-brown, Brazilian wood, with dark stripes and varying in hardness. Kingwood

KIT-KAT GLASS on folded foot, c.1730.

(*Dalbergia*) was used in France from the early 18thC to *c*.1780 for quality parquetry. Side panels and drawers were often QUARTER-VENEERED with grains radiating from the centre. In England, it was sparingly used in the 17th and late 18thC, when it was known as "Prince's wood", and was popular in the Victorian period (1837–1901) for LOUIS XV REVIVAL-STYLE furniture.

KINJI Japanese for a bright gold finish (FUNDAME is a matt gold finish).

KINRANDE Japanese PORCELAIN with gilt decoration over deep colour glazes.

KIRIGANE Japanese for "cut metal". Refers to small geometric shapes cut out of gold foil and inlaid in LACQUER.

KIRK, S. & SON American SILVER company founded in 1815 in Baltimore, Maryland, by Samuel Kirk and John Smith. The latter left the company in 1821, and after 1846 Kirk was joined by his sons. The firm made elegant silver in the ROCOCO taste, but are best known for introducing their REPOUSSÉ technique to the USA, and for creating silver embossed with floral, CHINOISERIE, or architectural ornament. In 1979, the firm merged with the Stieff Co.

KIRMAN Fine, densely woven CARPETS of cotton and wool from southeast Iran. They are decorated with floral designs around a central medallion.

KIST Name used for a CHEST or COFFER, especially in the north of England.

KIT-CAT GLASS (Or Kit-kat glass.) A balustroid GLASS with a trumpet bowl. They are so-called because they are depicted in portraits of members of the Kit-Kat Club, an early-18thC, political and literary association.

KITCHEN FURNITURE *See* PINE KITCHEN FURNITURE.

KITSCH Following the deprivation of the years during World War II, there was a movement in the 1950s to accessorize the home with all manner of colourful, decorative items, including VASES and FIGURES. Interior accessories featured prominently on tableware designs, as on the "HOMEMAKER" pattern.

KLEY & HAHN German maker of early-20thC DOLLS with BISQUE heads.

KLING, C.F. German maker of glazed-PORCELAIN dolls from the mid-19thC.

KLISMOS CHAIR made during the REGENCY period. It had concave tapering legs and a curved back, based on a traditional Greek chair.

KLOSTER-VEILSDORF German (Thuringian) factory, founded in the 18thC. It made PORCELAIN in imitation of MEISSEN, before developing its own style.

KNEE The curved top, often carved, of a CABRIOLE LEG.

KNEEHOLE DESK A WRITING TABLE with three drawers across the top and three down each pedestal; between the pedestals there was a recessed cupboard for storing boots and shoes. Kneehole desks were developed as FURNITURE for a gentleman's bed or dressing room and had a writing surface and DRESSING-TABLE combined. Because of their small size and elegant proportions, such desks remain in demand, which has led to fakes and conversions. Check the inner sides of the pedestals for a VENEER that does not match the rest of the piece. Also look inside the carcass around the drawer opening for lack of wear to the kneehole side. A kneehole desk with drawers on one side only is almost certainly a converted Victorian WASHSTAND.

KNIBB Family of clockmakers based in Oxford and London, England, from the late 17thC onward. John, active *c*.1680, made fine LONGCASE CLOCKS.

KNICKERBOCKER TOY CO. American TEDDY BEAR manufacturer, whose bears have particularly heavy, triangular heads, large, rounded ears and snouts, and long torsos. Look in a front-centre seam for a label that reads "Knickerbocker Toy Co. New York".

KNIFE-BOX A wooden box with the interiors fitted for holding CUTLERY. Typically, there would have been a pair of matching knife-boxes, one placed on either end of a SIDEBOARD. Wooden URNS with lids were also fitted for cutlery in the 18thC; these have often been converted to hold stationery.

KNIGHT, DAME LAURA (1877–1970) A British CERAMICS designer much commissioned by Clarice CLIFF. She specialized in patterns featuring circus and ballet themes. "Circus" pieces are extremely rare.

KNOB HANDLE Wooden handles found on much late-Victorian furniture.

KNOLE SETTEE First made in the early 17thC, an upholstered SETTEE that can be reclined by means of ratchets.

KNOLL ASSOCIATES Founded in 1938 by Hans G. Knoll, a FURNITURE firm linked with some of the most prominent 20thC designers, including Harry BERTOIA, Ludwig MIES VAN DE ROHE, and Eero SAARINEN.

KNOP (1) The decorative, hollow, or solid bulge on the stem of a drinking glass or candlestick, usually placed at the mid-point.

KNOP (2) On covers and lids, the decorative knob often serving as a handle.

KNOP (3) In furniture, a swelling on an upright member.

KNOPPED SPOON A spoon with a decorative FINIAL or seal-top at the end of the stem. *See also* APOSTLE SPOON and SEAL SPOON.

KNOT Threads that form the WEFT of a CARPET and loop through the WARP to form the PILE. The quality of a RUG is reflected by the fineness of the knots, which are measured according to their number per square decimetre (15 sq in). A coarse rug may have only 400 knots per square decimetre, whereas a fine one may have many thousands. The knots are tied over the warps of the rug by hand, then cut to the correct length. Each row of knots is separated by one or more lines of weft beaten into place with a metal comb. Two main types of knot are used: the Turkish (symmetric, or Ghiordes) type, used in Turkey and by tribal groups in Persia and central Asia; and the Persian (asymmetric, or Senneh) knot, used in Iran and by some central Asian groups.

KNOWLES, TAYLOR & KNOWLES CO. (1870–1929) American CERAMICS factory in East Liverpool, Ohio. Noted for its thin, translucent "Lotus Ware".

KNOX, ARCHIBALD (1864–1933) British designer of SILVER and PEWTER items, and known for his wares made for the London firm of LIBERTY in the late 19th and early 20thC. He had a distinctive Celtic-inspired style, influenced by the ARTS AND CRAFTS MOVEMENT and used the naturalistic motifs and sinewy lines typical of the ART NOUVEAU style. Celtic-inspired silver items are known by the trade name "CYMRIC"; those made of pewter, "TUDRIC".

KOREAN CERAMICS CELADON STONEWARE, reflecting the influence of Chinese POTTERY, ranks among Korean potters' finest achievements, and enjoyed a golden age from 1150–1250. Korean potters were the only makers of early celadon with inlaid decoration, filled with white or black slips. Other celadon wares were decorated with moulded, stamped, or carved designs. "Punch'ong" ware is similar to celadon, but more elaborately decorated with stamped,white slip designs. Favourite motifs include bamboo, dragons, peony flowers, birds, landscapes and roundels. Korean potters produced porcelain from the 11thC onward, and it is identifiable by its idiosyncratic imperfections. PORCELAIN objects for the scholar's table, such as brush droppers, brush holders, and censers, were produced in Korea in the 18th and 19thC. Some pieces are adorned casually with some sort of pierced decoration, which was popular in the late Yi dynasty (16th–19thC).

KORNILOV Early, 19thC PORCELAIN factory in St Petersburg, Russia. It made high-quality. coloured, gilded wares and, later, mass-produced export items.

KOSTA GLASS From the Swedish glassworks, founded in the mid-18thC, and noted for CHANDELIERS. Kosta became an important producer of ART GLASS in the 20thC, and employed notable designers such as Monica Morales-Schildt (b.1908) and Vicke Lindstrand (1904–83).

1970s cased, blue, KOSTA GLASS vase by Monica Morales-Schildt.

KOVSCH Popular until the mid-18thC, a one-handled, boat-shaped Russian vessel used for ladling out wine and spirits.

KRAAK-PORSELEIN (Kraak porcelain) PORCELAIN raided from Portuguese carracks (ships), which carried early Chinese export ware made in the MING dynasty in the 16th and 17thC. The wares were often decorated with panels filled with flowers, animals, birds, or figures, and were exported to Europe.

KREUSSEN Bavarian centre of German STONEWARE production since the 17thC. Noted for TANKARDS with applied decoration in relief.

KRUSE, KÄTHE (1910–68) A German maker of safe, unbreakable, washable DOLLS that were attractive to children, and are still produced. The first examples were made in 1909 by KÄMMER & REINHARDT, but, unhappy with the quality, Kruse began making them in her own workshop at Bad Kosen by 1912; by 1945, she had her own factory, at Donauwörth, and production continued there. Earlier dolls had navels, wide hips, and five seams to the legs to create a realistic shape. Narrow-hipped bodies came in from 1930. Käthe Kruse dolls were always marked on the left foot with a signature and number. The first dolls had labels on their wrists, while from 1928 labels were placed around the neck. Modern dolls have the name and number on one foot, but there is also a label with the shield trademark around the neck.

KUAN SUNG dynasty Chinese CELADON ware, of greyer colour than usual.

KULA Nomadic RUGS from western Turkey, made only in wool.

KUNGSHOLM Swedish glassworks, operating from the late 17th to the early 19thC, and noted for elaborate imitations of Venetian and German GLASS.

KÜNNERSBERG Reputed German, Bavaria-based maker of FAIENCE, noted for COFFEE-POTS decorated with hunting and sporting scenes, and for figures in the French ROCOCO style.

One of a pair of late-19thC KUTANI vases, decorated with warriors.

KUTANI Made in the 17thC and revived in the 19thC, Japanese PORCELAIN painted with blue-and-white underglaze motifs. Similar to ARITA ware.

KU YUEH HSUAN Chinese CH'ING DYNASTY enamelled CAMEO GLASS, named after a noted craftsman, and imitating contemporary European techniques.

KUZNETSOV FACTORY Russia's biggest PORCELAIN manufacturer at the turn of the 19thC. It made a range of wares for the home and export market.

KWAART A clear, lead glaze used over a tin glaze in DELFTWARE to provide the hard, glossy finish.

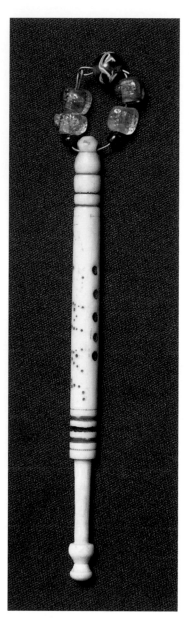

Mid-19thC, Midlands bone LACE BOBBIN enscribed "Jane".

LABURNUM A yellowish-brown wood with darker brown streaks. It was used as a VENEER, and is particularly attractive when cut as an OYSTER VENEER.

LAC BURGAUTÉ Chinese LACQUER wares inlaid with MOTHER-OF-PEARL, and imported to the West in quantity from the late 16thC.

LACCHE Italian term for painted or lacquered furniture. *See also* LACQUER.

LACE BOBBIN *See* BOBBIN.

LACE GLASS Speciality of glassmakers in Venice, Italy. They formed a lacelike pattern of fine, coloured, or plain-glass threads, which was then enclosed between two layers of GLASS to form the body of the vessel.

LACEWORK Lace dipped in SLIP, then applied to PORCELAIN, and burned away in firing, leaving a lacy pattern.

LACLOCHE FRÈRES Parisian jewellers noted for their ART DECO designs.

LACQUER A decorative, impermeable finish applied to FURNITURE and other objects, used in Asia (especially in Japan) from the 6thC onward. The furniture is coated with successive layers of resin from the lac tree. This forms a shiny surface, which is then decorated with GOLD leaf or inlaid with powders, SHELL, and other decorative items. Lacquer was fashionable in the Western world in the mid- to late-17thC, and the demand inspired European JAPANNING. Red, blue, green, and yellow lacquer are rarer than black.

LACQUERWARE Oriental objects carved in wood and coated with LACQUER. Chinese lacqerware is inferior to that from Japan, because of the inclusion of glues from animal bones, and the repetitiveness of the formalized designs. Oriental LACQUER panels were often incorporated into European furniture.

LACY GLASS Developed *c*.1830 by Deming Jarves of the BOSTON & SANDWICH GLASS CO., USA, a type of pressed glass with a surface pattern of stippled dots, made to resemble lace. It has decorative patterns of moulded foliage, flowers, scrolls, or rosettes and was used on cups, PLATES, JUGS, BOWLS, and TRAYS.

LADDER BACK A COUNTRY CHAIR with a back made from a series of horizontal bars between the two vertical uprights. *See also* COUNTRY FURNITURE.

LADIK In central Anatolia, a village renowned for its fine-quality PRAYER RUGS, which are usually decorated with a niche and stylized tulips. *See also* RUGS, CAUCASIAN AND TURKISH; RUGS, PERSIAN.

LADLE SERVING SPOON, with a deep bowl and long handle, and made in SILVER. They were often made to match TUREENS or BOWLS and used for serving punch, warmed brandy, soups, and other liquids.

LAFAYETTE WARE GLASS bottles and flasks, but also CERAMICS, made to celebrate the visit of the French Marquis de Lafayette to the USA in 1824.

LALIQUE, RENÉ (1860–1945) Leading French ART NOUVEAU and ART DECO JEWELLERY and GLASS designer, famous for his SCENT BOTTLES. He founded his own workshop in Paris in 1885, and his prolific output included car mascots, CLOCKS, lighting, jewellery, FURNITURE, and figurines. He usually worked with frosted-white OPALESCENT GLASS, and rarely used colour. For decoration he preferred naturalistic motifs, including fish, animals, flowers, leaves, and fruit. After his death, his son, Marc, continued the business as "Cristal Lalique", and modern pieces are marked "Lalique, France". All types of glass made by René Lalique during the Art Deco period are highly collectable. His distinctive glassware was also much imitated, so before buying something that you think is genuine, check the following: the form should be inventive yet heavy; on opalescent-glass items, the effect should be more noticeable on high-relief areas, and less on thin walls; and the piece should be marked "R Lalique", possibly with "France" and a model number.

LAMBETH Variously: the London factory producing DELFTWARE in the early 17th and 18thC; the factory in the same area established in the 19thC and producing STONE- and EARTHENWARE; and a range of DOULTON wares imitating early Italian MAIOLICA and produced in the late 19thC.

LAMBREQUIN Ornate patterns resembling, or derived from, LACEWORK. They were used as decorative motifs on CERAMICS, especially French 17th and 18thC FAIENCE and PORCELAIN, and on wood and metal wares.

LAMERIE, PAUL DE (1688–1751) Probably the most important 18thC London maker of SILVER, de Lamerie was born in Holland, of Huguenot descent. In 1689, he moved to London, where he became apprentice to the Huguenot silversmith Pierre Platel. His clients included royalty, and his most famous pieces were lavishly decorated. His early work was in the understated QUEEN-ANNE STYLE, but, by the 1730s, he was the most lauded exponent of the ROCOCO STYLE. His work includes innovative design and unsurpassed craftsmanship. De Lamerie registered several marks, which include the letters "PL" with a crown above them.

LAMP First produced in OLD SHEFFIELD PLATE in the late 18thC, portable lamps were used by travellers, or to enable late-night reading by industrious students. One rare example, made in the Victorian period (1837–1901), in SILVER, has a gilded interior to spread the light efficiently, and a flap that folds over to protect the GLASS. The top hinges open to make lighting a candle easy. A trio of crescent-shaped feet provide the stand with stability.

LAMP CLOCK Either a timepiece in which the hours are marked on a GLASS reservoir, and the time is indicated by the falling level of oil as it is consumed by a lighted wick; or a lamp with a clockwork mechanism that pumps the oil from a reservoir to the wick.

LAMPWORK GLASS that is blown or manipulated from clear or coloured RODS over a blow lamp or torch. The ornate "wings" of 15th and 16thC Venetian (and FAÇON-DE-VENISE) GOBLETS were made by manipulating rods and cylinders of clear or coloured glass over an open flame or "lamp". Intricate and detailed, small NAILSEA glass models of ships, which were often made by itinerant glassworkers to be sold at country fairs, are a tour de force of the art of lampwork. Models with turned wooden bases and protective glass domes are preferable. Damaged pieces are virtually impossible to repair.

LANCASTER GLASS Coloured-GLASS JUGS, BOTTLES, and flasks made by the American, New York-based, Lancaster Glassworks, founded in the mid-18thC.

LANE DELPH An 18thC English, Staffordshire-based pottery, noted for its green-glazed wares. Josiah WEDGWOOD worked at Lane Delph, and later sent his early CREAMWARE there for glazing.

LANGE LIJSEN *See* LONG ELIZA.

LANGET On a SWORD or SABRE, a quillon, or crosspiece, which forms one continuous item with the knuckle guard.

LANG YAO Chinese name for SANG-DE-BOEUF, or ox-blood glaze, so-called for its rich red-brown colour.

LANTERN CLOCK Made from *c.*1600, a weight-driven WALL CLOCK in the form of a latern, often with brass fretwork, and with only an hour hand.

LANTERN, PORTABLE A small, robust OIL LAMP designed to be carried by night watchmen. It was made from the early 19thC of brass or copper, sometimes with a lens but often with plain-glass sides.

LAP DOVETAIL (Rabbet dovetail) DOVETAIL JOINT with the end grain showing on one side, and the other side left for veneering. *See also* THROUGH DOVETAIL.

LAPIS LAZULI An artificial stone or paste made by grinding silicates of bright, ultramarine blue, much used since ancient times as a hardstone for decorating jewellery. It can be recognized by the golden flecks of pyrite.

LAP JOINT (Rabbet joint) With SILVER, the technique used to join a spoon finial to the stem by cutting each piece in opposing L-shapes.

LAPPED EDGE Of SHEFFIELD PLATE, the sheet SILVER turned over the edge or lip of the vessel to disguise the copper core, or an extra band of silver applied to the edge and fused to achieve the same effect. *See also* SHEET METAL.

LAPPET Small projection or spur found at the top of some FURNITURE legs.

LARCH Soft wood with a colour that ranges from yellowish white to reddish brown. It was occasionally used as a carcass wood, but tends to warp.

LA ROCHELLE Late-18th and 19thC French FAIENCE factory, producing wares decorated with historical and commemorative scenes and CHINOISERIE.

LATTICINIO (*Latticino*) A glassmaking technique in which a variety of interlacing patterns of LATTIMO threads are embedded in a clear-glass body to form a "lacy" pattern. Simple patterns of straight or spiral threads are called *vetri a filigrana* or *vetri a filato*, while complex, mesh-like patterns are *vetri a reticello*. The method is also known as FILIGRANA. *Latticinio* wares of the 19thC can be distinguished from the Venetian originals by the use of lead rather than SODA GLASS, the complexity of decoration, and the wider range of colours.

LATTIMO Meaning "milk glass" in Italian, a slightly translucent, opaque GLASS developed in Italy in the 15thC as a PORCELAIN substitute, and made by adding bone ash or tin oxide to the batch. A similar glass was made in Germany, the Netherlands, Bohemia, and England in the 18thC. Pure *lattimo* is rare; it was often mixed with clear glass in Italy from the early 16thC to form LATTICINIO.

LAUB-UND-BANDELWERK German for "foliage and scrollwork", a late-17thC motif featuring interwoven leaves and bands, first used on Baroque pieces in France. It was used in Germany in the 18thC on FURNITURE, GLASS, metalwork, and other materials.

LAVA GLASS Or "volcanic glass", an iridescent-gold ART GLASS with a textured surface resembling dripping lava. Patented by TIFFANY in the late 19thC.

LAVA WARE Purplish-blue GLASS wares of the late 19thC made using iron slag.

LAY METAL The cheapest form of PEWTER, made of three parts tin to one of lead. It was used for the most utilitarian objects, such as chamber pots.

Early Meissen bowl with painted panels within a gilt and iron-red LAUB-UND-BANDELWERK motif, c.1725.

Mahogany LAZY SUSAN, late 19th/ early 20thC.

LAZY SUSAN Another name for a DUMB WAITER.

LEACH, BERNARD (1887–1979) Leading figure in the revival of British, post-war STUDIO CERAMICS. After a visit to Japan where he met the potter shoji HAMADA, Leach, with Hamada, established a factory at St Ives, England, in 1920, where he influenced and inspired a generation of student potters. Leach was influenced by traditional SLIPWARE techniques in the vein of Thomas TOFT, and some of his work reflects this fascination. His work is thickly potted and simple in form. Leach usually marked his work "BL".

LEAD CRYSTAL (Lead glass) GLASS containing lead oxide, which lends extra strength and brilliance. The dominance of the English glass industry in the 18th and early 19thC was the result of the invention of lead-oxide glass by the English glassmaker George RAVENSCROFT in 1673. The addition of red lead (lead oxide) to the batch increased the working life of the glass and its density, making it more brilliant: hence the common term "lead crystal". It is soft but also strong, making it ideal for decorating by cutting and engraving. Lead crystal is sometimes described as "FLINT GLASS", because the earliest examples were made with silica derived from English flints rather than imported Venetian pebbles. It has a distinctive grey tone, and is heavier than SODA GLASS.

LEAD GLAZE The earliest form of glaze, used by early medieval potters. It was also employed on most European EARTHENWARES, including CREAMWARE and PEARLWARE, as well as Chinese Tang ware, to seal the porous body. The glaze is transparent and looks shiny, and may be coloured with metal oxides.

LEAD STATUARY Garden statuary cast in lead, a cheaper alternative to stone, and superseded in the 18thC by COADE STONE.

LEAD TOYS A type of toy, especially soldiers, made from lead during the late 19thC. Firms in Germany, France, and Britain made high-quality solid and HOLLOW-CAST lead toy soldiers. Lead was also used for a variety of cheap toys and early "DINKY" vehicles. Lead is easily damaged, and toys made from them should be kept away from damp, acidic conditions.

LE BOURGEOYS Leading French gunsmith, active in the early 17thC.

LE CORBUSIER (Charles Edouard Jeanneret, 1887–1965) French architect and one of France's most important 20thC furniture designers. He began working with Charlotte Perriand in the 1920s, in the Modernist style. Along with Pierre Jeanneret, they designed such classics as "Le Grand Comfort", which was was originally made by THONET Frères, Paris, and later by Heidi Weber (1959) and the firm Cassina (1965).

LE CREUSOT Late-18th to early 19thC French GLASS made near SÈVRES.

LEEDS English city in Yorkshire, where EARTHENWARE, notably CREAMWARE, often with interlaced and "lacy" OPENWORK handles, was made from the 18thC.

LEG, FURNITURE Vertical elements used to raise furniture off the ground. The variety of legs (and feet) found on TABLES, CHAIRS, and other FURNITURE can help to date a piece. However, many styles were revived and reproduced in later periods, so the style of a leg is no guarantee of age – also take into account the appearance of the wood when dating.

LEHMANN Toy-making firm founded in 1881, producing a fine range of lithographed and painted, TINPLATE figures, which were sold in most European countries and the USA. The firm made numerous animals, many of them based on African animals. Their TOY vehicles were often based only loosely on actual vehicles. Lehmann toys made over a long period are less valuable than those with a shorter production run.

LEHN WARE Turned-and-handpainted wooden BOXES made in the 19thC by Joseph Lehn of Lancaster County, Pennsylvania, USA.

LELEU, JEAN (1729–1807) French cabinet-maker, taught by J.F. OEBEN.

LEMON-SQUEEZER FOOT A distinctive style of foot found on Irish REGENCY cut-glass BOWLS. They have square bases and high-domed, cut shapes, and are moulded on the underside with ribbing to catch the light.

LENCI An Italian company founded in 1908 by Enrico di Scavini, who produced the first so-called "art dolls", made to appeal to anyone over the age of five. Many were designed by leading Italian artists. Made of moulded felt with jointed bodies, the DOLLS had expressive faces, often with sideways-glancing, painted eyes. (Those with glass eyes are worth more.) Lenci made elaborate designs for dolls dressed in national costume, and patchwork was favoured by the designers, because it gave them the chance to experiment with colour. Organdie, a delicate, translucent form of muslin, was used to produce extravagant puff sleeves, trains, and frills. Features that help to identify a Lenci doll are two white dots painted in the eyes (sometimes imitated by Norah WELLINGS) and the colour of the lower lip, which is paler than the upper one. Separately stitched outer fingers and two inner fingers joined together is also an indication of a Lenci doll, as is a zig-zagged seam at the back of the head. The jointing of the hips on a Lenci doll is more sophisticated than on copies, which "bolt" the leg to the torso by a nail. The most desirable dolls were made between 1920 and 1941. All but a few early dolls are marked. 1920s and '30s dolls were stamped in black or purple on the foot, and 1930s dolls had model numbers, which started at 100, on their labels. Cardboard tags were introduced in 1938. Some early dolls have PEWTER buttons marked "Lenci" on their clothes. From 1925–50, ribbons with the company name were sewn into Lenci garments.

LENCI **felt doll in good condition, c.1930.**

Matchbox Moko-LESNEY No.7 milkfloat, 1954.

LENOX PORCELAIN CO. American, New Jersey-based, factory, founded in 1889 and still in production today, specializing in BELLEEK.

LENZBURG Town in Switzerland producing French-style FAIENCE in the mid-18thC, and enamelled stoves in the 19thC.

LÉONARD, AGATHON (1841–1923) French, ART NOUVEAU sculptor who created the gilt-bronze series "Le jeu de l'écharpe", inspired by the dancer Löie Fuller, whose movements were regarded as the epitome of fluidity.

LEPAGE Leading French gunsmith, active in Paris in the mid-19thC.

LES ISLETTES In the Lorraine region of France, a factory manufacturing traditional FAIENCE wares in the late 18th and 19thC.

LESNEY British toy-making company founded in 1947, with their first DIECAST TOYS appearing the following year. Their most successful line was the MATCHBOX range of affordable, pocket-sized toys, created in 1953 by Jack Odell. Lesney was taken over by the Hong Kong firm Universal Holdings in 1982.

LEVER ESCAPEMENT Mid-18thC modification to the ANCHOR ESCAPEMENT that made portable CLOCKS and watches possible. The pallets that restrain the escape wheel are positioned at either end of a lever, which see-saws on a central pivot when rocked by a pin attached to the balance wheel.

LIAO DYNASTY Period in Chinese history AD 907–1125.

LIBBEY GLASS Cut and pressed GLASS wares from the factory established in the late 19thC in Toledo, Ohio, USA.

LIBERTY & CO. Founded by Arthur Lasenby Liberty (1843–1917) in 1875, and based in London's Regent Street, this English retail firm still sells FURNITURE, fabrics, and metalware. In reaction against the poor-quality wares mass-produced during the Victorian period (1837–1901), they became exponents of the ARTS AND CRAFTS MOVEMENT. The firm commissioned pieces that were exclusive to the store from well-known artists, including Archibald KNOX, and by 1900, it was famed as a world leader in the Arts and Crafts style. Furniture made for the firm is usually marked with a Liberty's label, which will add value to a well-designed piece. Metal wares feature a Liberty & Co. mark and the range name beneath, such as "CYMRIC" or "TUDRIC", but not the designer's name.

LIBERTY GLASS American CUT and PRESSED GLASS wares made in New Jersey and the Mid West in the late 19thC.

LIBRARY CHAIR Another name for a READING CHAIR.

LIBRARY STEPS A set of steps used as an aid when reaching books on a high shelf. There are two main types: fixed steps, which may have a handrail, or folding steps, which usually form or fit into another piece of FURNITURE.

LIBRARY TABLE A rectangular TABLE with frieze drawers, end supports, and a central stretcher. Library tables tend to be grand – the most elaborate versions have hinged tops for showing maps and prints. They also usually have leather tops; original leather tops are often scuffed and worn, but avoid having them recoloured and repolished if possible.

LIGHTER First used in the 19thC to light a gentleman's cigar or cigarette, a device that contains spirit oil and a nozzle for a wick. Early versions were usually designed to stand on tables. Dragon-shaped table lighters were often found in late-VICTORIAN-STYLE regimental silver. They were made, usually in pairs, for handing around the table.

LIGHTHOUSE CLOCK Rare, early-19thC MANTEL CLOCK in the form of a lighthouse, with the dial enclosed in the glass lantern.

LIGNUM VITAE Exceptionally dense wood that is dark brown with black streaks. Imported from the West Indies and used both solid and as a VENEER.

LILIHAN CARPETS from the Hamadan region of Western Iran. They were decorated with stylized flowers in bold colours.

LILLE French factory producing, from the late 17thC, DELFTWARE, decorated with CHINOISERIE and BAROQUE-STYLE figures.

LILLIPUT RANGE Figures made by W. BRITAIN Ltd to match the scale of "OO" and "HO" model railway gauges.

LIMBACH In Thuringia, Germany, a factory founded in the late 18thC, which produced close imitations of MEISSEN figures.

LIME Whitish wood that is excellent for carving.

LIME GLASS GLASS containing powdered limestone for both strength and brilliance. It is lighter than LEAD CRYSTAL, and was used from the mid-19thC.

LIMOGES Used to refer to late-18thC PORCELAIN in the SÈVRES style, 19thC wares imitating medieval LIMOGES enamel work, and, in the USA, imported French, or domestically produced, French-style porcelain.

LIMOGES ENAMEL Enamelled copper from the central French town. It was made from the early Middle Ages to the present day.

LINDBERG, STIG (1916–82) Influential designer who worked at the Scandinavian Gustavsberg factories, and created decorations that were copied all over Europe. He began to make his mark with elastic shapes and organic decoration, and used stripes, figures, and leaf patterns. Hourglass VASES and curling-leaf-form BOWLS are typical of his work in the 1950s.

LINE INLAY American term for STRINGING.

LINEN CHEST A hybrid COFFER/CHEST OF DRAWERS with either nine or twelve drawers and sometimes a lift-up top (in which case the drawers may be false).

LINENFOLD Carved decoration that resembles folded linen.

LINEN PRESS Used for storing clothes and linen, a CUPBOARD containing sliding shelves and raised above a series of drawers.

LINER Inner sleeve of a vessel, made of SILVER, PLATE, or GLASS.

LINES BROTHERS Makers of mass-produced, clockwork locomotives and other toys from *c.*1910.

LING ZHI Floral motif first found on 16thC, Chinese PORCELAIN.

LIONEL CORPORATION Major American producer of electric toy trains, founded in New York in 1901. Many models in the "O" gauge range had operating whistles, and chimneys that could produce steam. Lionel were also noted for their line-side features, such as stations that lit up.

LION MASK Carved decoration shaped a lion's head, such as the LION OF ST MARK. Also, a type of BRASS, ringed handle in the form of a lion's head.

LION OF ST MARK The symbol of Venice, Italy. Motif on Venetian glassware.

LION SÉJANT A seated lion used as a KNOP motif on SPOONS from the 16thC.

LION'S-PAW FOOT A foot carved to resemble a lion's paw. The form was popular for early 19thC CASTERS.

LIQUOR TOT A DRINKING VESSEL in pierced SILVER with cut-glass liners, usually made in boxed sets of six. They were popular in the late-19th and early 20thC, and often came with matching, silver-mounted DECANTERS. A single liquor tot is worth little, but a set of six with its decanter is desirable.

LISBON Portuguese MAIOLICA, not necessarily produced in Lisbon. It was made from the early 17thC, with Chinese-influenced designs painted in blue.

LI SHUI Chinese name for CELADON wares from the SUNG DYNASTY.

LIT DE REPOS Early French DAY-BED, which later developed into the SOFA.

LIT EN BATEAU French BED with a canopy above and curtains around it.

LITHYALIN GLASS Coloured GLASS patented in 1829 by the Bohemian maker Friedrich Egermann. Its marbled appearance imitates natural AGATE.

LIVERPOOL Mid-18thC POTTERY centre in England. Samuel Gilbody's Factory, c.1754–61, made an attractive, sometimes blurred, greyish UNDERGLAZE BLUE, and some designs were enamelled in iron red. Their heavily potted early wares can be confused with BOW. Richard CHAFFERS & Partners, c.1754–65, conducted an EARTHENWARE manufactory in Liverpool in the 1740s. Its early phosphatic wares have a greyish body, while the later steatitic wares are whiter. The potting was based on WORCESTER shapes. Philip Christian, c.1765–76, took over Richard Chaffers' factory, but in 1776 CHRISTIAN sold his interest and ceased manufacturing. The William Ball factory, c.1755–69, made many shapes, such as TEAWARES, with decoration that resembled DELFT. The paste has small turning tears that show up as lighter flecks when held to the light. Their polychrome wares are rare; elaborate SAUCEBOATS in the ROCOCO STYLE were a speciality. William Reid, c.1755–61, made a crude, semi-opaque body. The glaze was opacified by the use of tin. The wares were mainly blue and white. Reid went bankrupt in 1761, and his factory was occupied by William Ball. The majority of the output by James, John, and Seth Pennington, c.1769–1799, was blue and white. Some collectable ship-painted, dated jugs and BOWLS were made in the 1770s and '80s, when a dark underglaze blue was used. The glaze is sometimes tinted bluish-grey. Their TRANSFER PRINTS were smudgy in appearance. Thomas Wolfe & Co., c.1795–1800, took over one of the Pennington family's factories. Unlike the other Liverpool factories, most of their output was decorated in polychrome. Some of the wares are well potted and attractively painted.

Rare LIVERPOOL (John Pennington) spoon tray with a "Tudor Rose", c.1785.

LIVERY CUPBOARD Three-tiered structure similar to a COURT CUPBOARD. However, the centre tier has an enclosed compartment, often with CANTED sides.

LLOYD LOOM FURNITURE The brainchild of the American Marshall B. Lloyd, FURNITURE made from BENTWOOD frames covered in a machine-made, twisted paper fibre reinforced with metal wire. Lloyd Loom furniture is simple to identify – a genuine piece contains metal wires within the upright strands, so a magnet will stick to it. A huge range of furniture was made, including TABLES, linen baskets, DRESSING TABLES, and CHESTS. All Lloyd Loom was marked with a label that varied according to the date of manufacture; many of the pieces were also date stamped. Labels are usually attached to the frame of seating, or to the underside of items. The Lusty company held the franchise to produce Lloyd Loom furniture in England.

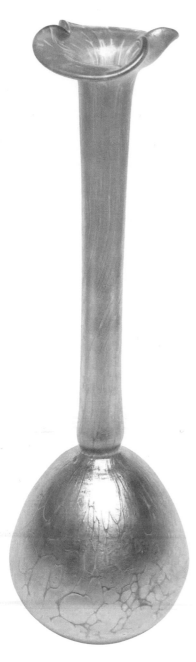

LOETZ solifleur vase, c.1900.

LOBMEYR, J. & L. A distinguished, Austrian-based glassworks founded by Josef Lobmeyr in 1822, and the leading maker of fine-quality GLASS in a variety of exotic and historical styles in 19thC central Europe. Among their wares, they produced GOBLETS with enamelled decoration combining Islamic script and RENAISSANCE motifs. The FAÇON-DE-VENISE factory was known for HOCHSCHNITT and TIEFSCHNITT, as well as for enamelled and IRIDESCENT GLASS, and it spearheaded many new styles in Bohemian glass, from the BAROQUE revival to ART NOUVEAU (or JUGENDSTIL) and ART DECO.

LOCK Mechanical piece on FURNITURE to secure a drawer or door. Early locks are made of wrought iron and held in place with iron nails. From the 18thC, locks were steel or brass and secured with steel screws.

LOCKE, JOSEPH A glassmaker who worked for the English firm of W. H., B. & J. Richardson, near Stourbridge in the Midlands. He emigrated to the USA in 1882, and began working at the NEW ENGLAND GLASS CO., where he invented methods for colouring and etching GLASS, including AMBERINA GLASS.

LOCKING PLATE Alternative name for the COUNTWHEEL, which controls the number of times a CLOCK strikes on the hour.

LOCKPLATE Plate that protects a keyhole.

LOETZ Austrian glassmakers based at Klöstermühle, Bohemia. They first produced IRIDESCENT GLASS in 1873.

LOG CABIN On a QUILT, a PATCHWORK block in which strips are sewn round a central square, with dark strips on two sides and light strips on the other two.

LONGCASE CLOCK (Tallcase clock; grandfather clock) First made *c.*1660 in England, a tall CLOCK with a case containing weights or a pendulum, and a hood housing a dial and movement. Most longcase clocks were made in Britain from the late 17th to 19thC, although lesser numbers were produced in Europe and the USA. The standard longcase clock runs for eight days and has an ANCHOR ESCAPEMENT. As with most types of clock, value is dependent on the quality of the case, movement, and dial, and on the identity of the maker. Originally square, DIAL faces developed arches in *c.*1720. Most longcase clocks have brass dials or painted ones. Brass dials have applied CHAPTER RINGS (the band with the numerals) and decorative SPANDRELS (corners). Some of the earliest longcase clocks were decorated with walnut VENEER over an oak carcass. CROSS-BANDING add to the value. Floral MARQUETRY was popular on longcase clocks from 1680 to 1710. Earlier examples have small panels of marquetry inset in the veneer but are otherwise similar to WALNUT longcase clocks; later ones are more lavishly decorated. MAHOGANY was used to make longcase clocks from the mid-18th until the early 19thC. The trunk, or centre section of the case, had a door that opened to allow you to adjust the pendulum and fit the weights. The style of the PEDIMENT can give an indication of the age of the clock. FINIALS are easily damaged, and replacements, though acceptable, are less desirable. If a clock has an unusual or attractively painted dial, or an elaborate marquetry or lacquered case, it is more desirable. Size can have a bearing on price – smaller longcases are usually more expensive than larger ones, as they will fit in modern homes. London makers of longcase clocks are usually particularly sought after, especially Thomas MUDGE Sr., William Dutton, and John Holmes.

LONG ELIZA Slender, female figures on Chinese PORCELAIN and copied on Dutch and English blue-painted porcelain. Also known as "Lange Lijsen".

LONGQING (Lung Chinq) Chinese MING Dynasty emperor, 1567–1572.

LONGTON HALL Founded by William Jenkinson, 1749–60, the first porcelain factory in Staffordshire, England. Their earliest pieces are the "Snowman" figures and some BLUE-AND-WHITE wares. Copies of Chinese FAMILLE-ROSE designs, TUREENS, and pot-pourri vases are also among the varied output. Moulded patterns using floral and vegetable motifs were a speciality of the factory. All products are collectable, although not especially refined.

LOPER Slide of wood that pulls out to support the fall front of a BUREAU when open; also known as a BEARER.

LORENZL, JOSEF (1892–1950) ART DECO sculptor who produced figures in BRONZE, CERAMICS, and IVORY. His work is recognizable by the long limbs and slender, almost androgynous figures in atheletic poses. His ceramic figures, designed for the Austrian firm GOLDSCHEIDER, are keenly sought after.

LOST-WAX CASTING Technique, also known as CIRE PERDUE, in which a wax model is encased in plaster or clay. The wax is then heated and poured out ("lost") to make room for molten SILVER or GLASS. Once the object has cooled, the mould is broken away. *See also* PÂTE-DE-CRISTAL AND PÂTE-DE-VERRE.

LOTUS WARE Made by the Knowles factory, East Liverpool, Ohio, USA, in the late-19th and 20thC, thin-bodied PORCELAIN with a MOTHER-OF-PEARL sheen.

LOUIS XIV STYLE The growth of the BAROQUE STYLE, as seen in Versailles, synonymous with the reign of Louis XIV, king of France 1643–1715.

LOUIS XV STYLE French, high ROCOCO STYLE, with curving shapes and asymmetrical forms, and synonymous with the reign of Louis XV, king of France 1715–74. CHINOISERIE and Oriental motifs were popular. Leading cabinet-makers include Jean-François OEBEN and Charles CRESSENT.

Art deco bronze figure of a dancer by JOSEF LORENZL, *c*.1930.

LOUIS XVI STYLE (GOÛT GREC) In France, the NEO-CLASSICAL STYLE partially overlapped the reign of Louis XVI, king of France 1774–93. Lines became straighter and more rectilinear. Upholstered CHAIRS had padded, oval backs and straight, tapered, and fluted legs. Giltwood and painted furniture was popular, as were MARQUETRY, exotic woods, LACQUER, PIETRE DURE, and figurative bronze mounts. Leading cabinet-makers included Georges JACOB, with makers such as Jean-François OEBEN and Jean-Henri RIESENER working in the ROCOCO and neo-classical styles, as well as in the intermediate "transitional" style, when Rococo curves started to straighten.

Early-19thC, oak LOWBOY with three drawers and a fret-cut centre, on square chamfered legs.

LOWBOY Name now given to a small dressing-table, usually with either a single frieze drawer or a small, central, shallow drawer, flanked on either side by a deep drawer. They have been made from c.1700 to 1750 for writing or dressing, and the table usually has stretcher-less cabriole legs. The top drawer fronts are often dummies applied to a single drawer. Lowboys were made from oak, walnut, or mahogany. Look for ones with decorative details such as ogee arches or friezes; RE-ENTRANT CORNERS (shaped corners on top); tops with moulded edges; and outlines of overlapping drawer fronts on the carcass.

LOW DRESSER A rack-less DRESSER used in the kitchen or dining-room for storage in provincial houses from the late 18thC. Low dressers from the 17thC are the rarest examples. Prices are boosted by decorative details such as friezes, inlaid or carved decoration, and a mellow colour. BALUSTER legs from the 17thC predate CABRIOLE LEGS used in the 18thC. With the introduction of cabriole legs, the central legs and STRETCHERS were no longer used. The inside of the drawers should look dry, with no signs of staining or tampering. Pull out the drawer and check that the wood is all of a similar colour, and that the DOVETAIL JOINTS were coarsely hand-cut.

LOWESTOFT An English PORCELAIN manufacturer (in production 1757 until 1799), Lowestoft made CHINOISERIE PORCELAIN and also figures and animals, notably dogs. The firm used a phosphatic body for its figures, and this often has a greenish tinge, suffering over time from brown, rustlike discolouration. They usually marked their pieces with crossed swords, although a crescent similar to that of WORCESTER is also sometimes used. Also refers to Chinese export wares imported through the port at Lowestoft, and re-exported to the USA.

LOW RELIEF Another name for BAS RELIEF.

LOZENGE Carved decoration of diamond shape but with a horizontal axis.

LUCOTTE French maker of solid toy soldiers, 1790–1900. The heads and bodies were casted separately – the head has a plug on the base to fit into the body. Accessories were soldered on later. Figures were larger than the 54mm (2in) standard. C.B.G. MIGNOT took over the Lucotte name in 1825.

LUDWIGSBURG FACTORY German PORCELAIN manufacturer established in the mid-18thC, which made stiffly posed figures with faces that had long, bridgeless noses and doll-like features. They used a subdued, pastel palette and smoky, greyish glaze. Interlaced "C"s with a coronet or a staghorn were used as their mark, with three in a shield or one separate.

LUND'S BRISTOL *See* BRISTOL PORCELAIN.

LUNETTE A motif using repeats of crescent-shaped or semi-circular areas, either left plain or decorated. Popular in the JACOBEAN and VICTORIAN periods.

LUNÉVILLE In the Lorraine district of France, a factory producing FAIENCE-FINE from the late 18thC. *See also* FAIENCE.

LUNG CH'UAN SUNG DYNASTY CELADON, with a blue-green glaze.

LUSTRE A cut-glass drop or rod hung from the SCONCE of a CANDELABRUM to increase the volume of light reflected.

LUSTRE DECORATION (Lustreware) A decorative glaze made from metallic oxides that create a lustre, or metallic sheen. First used in European pottery in the 13thC in Spain, it enjoyed a revival of interest in Britain in the 19thC. Lustre colours depend on the metal oxides used, and on the colour of the body beneath. Pink or purple lustre, are created using a mixture of gold and copper oxides on top of a white body. If gold lustre is applied to a dark body, it creates a bronze colour, while silver is made from platinum oxides. Lustre glazes are applied to pieces after glazing and firing, and are refired at a lower temperature. It is limited to bands or reserves, applied all over, or streaked using a "splash" technique. WEDGWOOD introduced a mottled range called "Moonlight Lustre". Lustre was often used with stencil-printed decoration, and is often seen on jugs, teapots, MUGS, and chamber pots. Such objects were made in many potteries in England in Staffordshire and Sunderland, and in Wales and Scotland. Pink lustre was often applied to the rims of white-bodied, commemorative wares in the early 19thC.

Copper-LUSTRE jug with flower decoration, *c.*1850.

LYONS French POTTERY centre, known for early tin-glazed wares similar to Italian MAIOLICA, items of BLUE AND WHITE, and yellow-painted decoration.

LYRE Descriptive of FURNITURE components – particularly some CHAIR backs and TABLE supports – that are shaped like the musical instrument.

LYRE CLOCK Early-19thC American CLOCK in a shape similar to that of a lyre.

M

MACDONALD, FRANCES (1874–1921) Also called Frances MacNair, a Scottish artist of the GLASGOW SCHOOL. Known for enamel- and metalwork.

MACDONALD, MARGARET (1865–1933) Scottish artist and designer of the GLASGOW SCHOOL; married to Charles Rennie MACKINTOSH.

MACKINTOSH, CHARLES RENNIE (1868–1928) Scottish architect and designer during the ARTS AND CRAFTS period, he originally produced graphic work and REPOUSSÉ metalwork in conventional ART NOUVEAU style, but, from the 1890s, developed a distinctive, simplified style with clean lines. His work was highly influential on Viennese furniture and architecture.

MACINTYRE, JAMES & CO. (*c*.1847–1913) English pottery, which made utilitarian wares, in Burslem, Staffordshire. William MOORCROFT worked there.

MACKMURDO, ARTHUR H. (1851–1942) One of the fathers of the ART NOUVEAU style. In 1882 he founded the Century Guild of Craftsmen, whose magazine, *The Hobby Horse*, was published from 1884.

MACULATED Spotted or stained, usually used of books, prints, or textiles.

MADAME ALEXANDER *See* ALEXANDER DOLL CO.

MADELEY SOFT-PASTE PORCELAIN made by Thomas Randell in Shropshire, England, in the early 19thC.

MAGDEBURG German city known for its brightly coloured, 18thC FAIENCE.

MAGIC LANTERN Machine with a lamp and lenses for projecting an image onto a glass or photographic slide; also known as a magascope.

MAGNUM Large GLASS for wine and spirits, or a BOTTLE holding two quarts.

MAHAL Western Iranian CARPETS, loosely woven, but characteristically soft, and decorated with floral and geometrical motifs.

MAHOGANY A rich, golden-brown- or red-brown-coloured wood, mahogany (*Swietenia*) became popular in England *c*.1730. There are several different types – San Dominguan, Cuban (also known as Spanish), and

Mahogany and brass MAGIC LANTERN, c.1910.

Honduran are the most common. Cuban mahogany is the rarest type and was chiefly used before *c.*1750. Its darker tone is seen only on expensive pieces. Mahogany was popular in the 18thC because it is easy to carve, resistant to woodworm, and fairly stable. It was used both as a VENEER and in a solid form. In some of the poorer rural areas, OAK and ELM were stained with ox blood to resemble mahogany; RED WALNUT has also been used as a substitute. Continental European mahogany was usually from Haiti, and has a distinctive grain. It was popular in France during the EMPIRE period, and was also used from the late 18thC in Germany and Denmark.

"MAINE" PATTERN American glassware design of scrolling vine leaves, with a simple pattern of beading between the panels. The beading was also used to create lettering on English, mould-pressed GLASS.

MAINSPRING In FIREARMS, the powerful spring that forces the COCK to strike the steel or the hammer to strike the firing pin.

MAIOLICA TIN-GLAZED EARTHENWARE from Spain and Italy, produced since the 14thC. Spanish maiolica is noted for its shiny, metallic, LUSTRE decoration. Maiolica developed in Italy in the 15thC, in the important centres of deruta and GUBBIO. The earliest pieces were adorned with primitive designs and a limited palette, but gradually decoration became increasingly sophisticated. By the 16thC, castel durante, URBINO, and SIENA emerged as leading areas of production, and a fully developed type of maiolica, known as the "beautiful style", evolved. In most Italian maiolica, the colours predominating are blue, yellow, orange, black, and green. If a wider range of colours is used, this may indicate that the piece is of higher quality or a later date. Do not expect to find early maiolica in perfect condition; chips and cracks are common, and pieces are valuable despite damage. Many honest copies, marked by makers such as DOCCIA, Molaroni, Maiolica Artistica Pesarese, and Bruno Buratti, were made in the 19thC; these are collectable, but less valuable than earlier originals. The CANTAGALLI factory produced imitations of early Italian POTTERY and marked them with a cockerel. *See also* POTTERY, ITALIAN.

MAISON CARDEILHAC French company established in 1804 to produce SILVER CUTLERY and FLATWARE. It became famous under Ernest Cardeilhac (1851–1904) for ART NOUVEAU designs in GOLD and SILVER.

MAISON HURET French dollmaker (1850–1920), based in Montmartre, Paris. The firm is known for jointed DOLLS and socket swivel heads, patented in 1858. A double chin, closed mouth, and painted eyes indicate an early BÉBÉ.

MAJOLICA A richly enamelled STONEWARE developed by MINTON during the 19thC, and inspired loosely by the Italian MAIOLICA of DELLA ROBBIA, and the 16thC pottery of Frenchman Bernard Palissy. It was produced in England,

Pair of 19thC Italian MAIOLICA circular plaques, decorated with dancing figures and washerwomen.

French Art Nouveau-period rosewood marquetry cabinet by LOUIS MAJORELLE.

Europe, and the USA from the mid-19thC. Majolica was modelled in relief, and decorated with pigments added to the body itself or, more usually, to the glaze. The manufacturer's ability to control the glaze during firing was critical, and, on poor-quality examples, the colours bled together to disastrous effect. Top factories in addition to Minton were George JONES, and WEDGWOOD, but many other large firms including ROYAL WORCESTER and COPELAND made majolica, as did small manufacturers such as Holdcroft and BROWNFIELD. Novelty domestic wares such as game tureens and strawberry sets were typical of the tablewares made in the 19thC. Big names command a premium, as do pieces made in the USA, although their quality is inferior to English examples. Small, unusual pieces are also highly coveted by collectors. Unmarked majolica, or items by less well-known makers can still attract high prices if the design is strong. Although majolica is prone to chipping and flaking, many pieces are bought for their decorative appeal, so value is less affected by damage than is usually the case with antiques, and restoration is common. Some unmarked pieces have had fake marks added with an etched "Minton" to boost their value. Modern reproductions are usually easily identifiable by their light potting and less well-defined modelling.

MAJORELLE, LOUIS (1859–1926) French FURNITURE designer and the leading ART NOUVEAU furniture supplier in France by 1900.

MAKEIG-JONES, DAISY (1881–1945) A chief designer at WEDGWOOD in England in the 1920s, Makeig-Jones designed the range known as "Fairyland lustre", a variegated, dark-coloured ground, printed with colours and gilding depicting imaginary landscapes and fantastic figures. Some of the rarer designs can attract high prices. Makeig-Jones also created less elaborate, more modestly priced ranges of lustreware such as "Dragon lustre" and "Butterfly lustre".

MALACHITE GLASS A coloured GLASS, so-called because its pattern imitates the veining of the stone.

MALAGA WORK Hispano-Moresque EARTHENWARES with a gold LUSTRE. They were produced in Valencia, Spain, from the 14thC.

MALING British EARTHENWARE manufacturer, established 1762. Known for the surface decoration, especially the hand-painted and tube-lined detail, on its 20thC pieces. Also renowned for its range of LUSTREware.

MAMLUK Polychrome POTTERY made in Egypt and Syria in the 13th and 15thC, and exported to Europe for the storage of spices and medicines.

MANARDI MAIOLICA TIN-GLAZED EARTHENWARE made by the Manardi brothers in Italy in the 16th and 17thC. Pieces were decorated with fine landscape paintings and flowers on a pearly white ground.

MANDARIN CHINA Ornate Chinese PORCELAIN exported to Europe in the late 18thC, with painted figures framed in red, pink, and gold panels.

MANGANESE Mineral used to make purple-brown pigments.

MANJU NETSUKE of round flat shape, carved in relief.

MANTEL CLOCK A CLOCK with feet, designed to stand on the mantelpiece.

MANTUA Early-19thC coloured GLASS from Mantua, Ohio, USA.

MANX FOOT Chair or table foot that appears as a flat-soled shoe with a heel.

MAPLE Pale-yellow wood with a close grain that is subject to a variety of markings. It is good for turning but was used mainly as a VENEER.

MAPPIN & WEBB British silverware and jewellery firm, founded in 1774 by Jonathan Mappin. The firm used "MN & WB" as their mark on 20thC wares. In 1963, GARRARD & Co. merged with Mappin & Webb and ELKINGTON & Co. to form British Silverware Ltd. *See also* SILVER.

MARIEBURG Swedish factory founded in 1758, and noted for fine figures in TIN-GLAZED EARTHENWARE, imitating PORCELAIN.

MARINER'S COMPASS In quilting, a PATCHWORK block pattern, in which long triangles radiate from the centre, resembling compass points.

MARINOT, MAURICE (1882–1960) A French GLASS designer, 1922–37. Created remarkable effects by catching air bubbles between layers of glass.

MARK *See* MARKS, CERAMIC; HALLMARK; ASSAY MARK.

MARKHAM, MARKWICK Noted London clockmaker, active 1720–60.

MÄRKLIN German TINPLATE toy firm founded by Theodor Märklin, which began producing clockwork train sets in 1859. DIECASTS with crisp details were made from 1935, concentrating on German vehicles such as Mercedes-Benz, Volkswagen, and Porches. The early 1900s marked the first golden age of Märklin trains, when the products were increasingly realistic and had a distinctive heavy style with a thick, lacquered finish. Märklin made a range of rolling stock and accessories, from ornate station buildings to signals and lamps. The firm introduced a standardized system of gauges in 1891, and made a number of Gauge III locomotives; from c.1910, they made smaller Gauge I and "0" Gauge models in response to a growing demand for them. Märklin's locomotives were powered by clockwork, steam, or electricity. In

One of a pait of MAPPIN & WEBB, Art Deco, silver candlesticks designed by Harold Stabler, 1934.

1933, the firm produced a range of six- and eight-couple trains based on contemporary locomotives worldwide; the black-and-green versions of the British London and North Eastern Railway "Cock o' the North", produced 1935–7, are popular. In 1948, the firm changed the scale to "HO" Gauge. Some of the most sought-after diecast sets of the early 1950s include diesel or electric "Triebwagen" (express railcar units), such as the ST 800.

MARKS, CERAMIC Identification marks providing useful information about a piece. Many factories such as SÈVRES, CHELSEA, and DERBY changed their marks, and these changes can help to date an item. Marks commonly include a factory mark such as a symbol (Chelsea uses an anchor); initials, monograms, and letters, such as the letter "Z" used by ZÜRICH; or the name of the factory written as a word or signature. Marks are hand-painted in UNDERGLAZE or OVERGLAZE enamels, incised by hand, impressed with a stamp, or printed. Other marks on ceramics may refer to the individuals involved in production: the designer, decorator, modeller, and gilder. There may also be a pattern serial number, which gives useful information if the factory's records have survived. Printed marks were used by most major English factories of the 19thC. Small changes in the pattern or wording can help with dating: from *c.*1820, marks with a royal coat of arms began to be seen; from *c.*1896, marks included the word "England" or other country names, following the McKinley Tariff Act of 1891; 20thC marks bear the words "Made in England" or "Bone china". "Limited" or "Ltd." tend to denote a date after 1861 – but they became much more common after 1885. The word "Royal" in a firm's name tends to be late 19thC. An impressed "Trade Mark" can be assumed to be after 1862. A diamond registration mark was used on English ceramics 1842–83; letters and numbers in the corners of the diamond refer to the date of manufacture. After 1883, "Rd No" (the registered number), followed by the number itself, was used. Marks cannot always be taken at face value. In Chinese CERAMICS, pieces were frequently marked with earlier reign marks as a sign of respect for the skill of earlier potters. The celebrated MEISSEN mark of crossed swords was imitated by numerous factories throughout Europe; WORCESTER's crescent mark was also used by BOW; and numerous other factories capitalized on the popularity of successful factories by copying designs and imitating marks. *See also* HALLMARK and ASSAY MARK

MARLBOROUGH LEG Used on furniture in the 18thC, the tapering leg of square section with a collar above a BLOCK FOOT.

MAROT, DANIEL (1663–1752) Huguenot craftsman and designer who produced fine furniture in the LOUIS XIV STYLE for royal households.

MARQUETERIE DE VERRE This MARQUETRY-in-glass technique, developed by Emile GALLÉ, involves setting pieces of semi-molten, coloured GLASS into the body of a glass vessel while the latter is still soft. Many pieces cracked in the process, and examples are now rare. Most are signed by the artist.

Chelsea anchor MARK painted in red, 1752–56.

MARQUETRY A refinement of the INLAY technique that involves cutting shapes into VENEER. Marquetry decoration first became popular in England in the late 17thC. Marquetry that includes bone or MOTHER-OF-PEARL is desirable, as are designs with birds and insects. BOULLE furniture of the late 17thC uses a marquetry of BRASS and TORTOISESHELL. Marquetry on WALNUT fetches more than that on MAHOGANY; and the last is more valuable than marquetry on OAK. Some pieces have marquetry panels added later. If a panel appears slightly lower than the surrounding wood, be suspicious. A genuine piece will have raised ridges of either glue or grain, which can be detected by the fingertips.

MARQUISE Jewel cut into a pointed-oval shape, used in brooches and rings.

MARRIAGE A piece made from two or more parts that did not start life together, often found in FURNITURE and SILVER. The married parts may be of a similar period, or one part may be later. A common marriage is that of a small, 18thC BUREAU with a BOOKCASE on top. DRESSERS with racks, and tops and bottoms of tables are other examples. Look at the overall appearance of a piece to identify a marriage – the proportions usually look wrong. On a dresser or BUREAU BOOKCASE, look closely at the sides: the wood should be of approximately the same grain and colour on both parts. Also look for similar mouldings, details, and hardware on the top and bottom. The boards on the back of the top and base should be the same if they originate from the same place. Look underneath tables for unexplained holes, clues to replaced tops. On silver, check the HALLMARKS. Marriages are usually less desirable than pieces in their original condition. *See also* FAKE, FURNITURE ALTERATION OF and REPRODUCTION.

MARRIAGE CHEST Another name for a dower chest. *See also* CHEST

MARROW SCOOP A mid-18thC, SILVER implement with a long narrow channelled end for extracting the marrow from meat bones (roasted marrow bones were popular snacks in England from the 17thC until the mid-19thC). There is sometimes a second channel of a different width.

MARROW SPOON A type of SPOON with a conventional bowl at one end for eating stew and a thin scoop at the other end for extracting the marrow when the bones were brought to the table. *See also* DINING ACCESSORIES

MARSEILLE, ARMAND (1865–1940) Russian-born dollmaker who ran a German PORCELAIN factory in Thuringia, then bought a toy factory where, with his son Armand Junior, he was making BISQUE heads by 1890. They supplied other companies with heads from 1900 to 1930. They were prolific, but are not noted for quality, and their dolls are less expensive than other German character dolls. The "DREAM BABY" was the most popular Armand Marseille baby DOLL. Black babies were made from the Dream Baby mould. Colouring varies, from

MARTIN BROTHERS **ewer moulded on either side with grotesque smiling faces, 1903.**

black painted to coffee-coloured fired bisque; the last is more desirable. If in doubt, scratch the surface somewhere hidden, and paint will come away, leaving a white mark. Armand Marseille made only one type of yellow-tinted baby doll, and the modelling is less lifelike than on Oriental babies by other firms. However, they are still collectable. Some bodies are cloth; some are composition. Armand Marseille created a few extremely refined dolls, which are highly valued. Look out for Armand Marseille marks, such as a mould number or the name of the style, for identification rather than dating. Elaborate original clothes can make a basic doll more valuable. Look for original paint on the face and hands because repainting reduces the value.

MARSEILLES French CERAMICS centre noted for colourful FAIENCE from the second half of the 17thC.

MARTELÉ Form of faceted GLASS, made to resemble hammered metal, invented by DAUM FRÈRES and used for their ART NOUVEAU glass.

MARTIN BROTHERS (1) English, London-based, studio pottery, active 1873–1914 and run by the Martin brothers: Robert Wallace, Charles Douglas, Walter Frazer, and Edwin Bruce. Robert Wallace, fascinated by grotesque gargoyles, was responsible for the introduction of the "bird jars"; known as "Wally" birds, the jars were in the form of birds with removable heads, and are among the company's most distinctive, individual wares. The quirky features on the jars were often based on people the brothers knew. The company also made jugs and mugs with faces on each side, plus VASES, some in the form of naturalistic gourds, jugs, and other ornamental pieces. Fish in an underwater setting can be seen decorating tiles and vases. Pieces are usually incised "R W Martin Bros, London & Southall" and dated. Early pieces may be signed "Martin". Fakes are usually identifiable by their lack of subtlety in decoration and modelling. They have sometimes been made by taking a mould from an original piece, hence the marks are also moulded.

MARTIN BROTHERS (2) Mid-18thC, French furniture-makers, who, in 1730, developed *vernis martin*, a substitute for Oriental lacquer.

MARTIN, EDMUND Late-18thC maker of LONGCASE CLOCKS in London.

MARVERING A glass-making technique in which hot threads of softened GLASS are rolled over a flat table (a marver) to smooth and fuse the glass.

MARX, LOUIS & CO. Toy firm established in 1919 in the USA and known for TINPLATE and CHARACTER TOYS.

"MARY GREGORY" GLASS Late-19thC GLASS wares decorated in white enamel with scenes of children at play. It was made at the BOSTON & SANDWICH

CLASS CO. in Massachusetts, USA, and in Europe. Wares in this style are made in yellow, "Cranberry", dark green, and "Amethyst" glass.

MARYLAND POTTERY STONEWARE and EARTHENWARE made in Baltimore, USA, from c.1800. The BENNETT FACTORY is the best-known producer.

MASON'S IRONSTONE Factory that made wares of ironstone, a heavy EARTHENWARE substance, first patented in 1813 by Charles James Mason. Wares are marked with an impressed mark. The details of these marks changed over time. If the word "Improved" appears, it means that the piece was made after c.1840. Mason's was taken over by Ashworth's in 1859.

MASSACHUSETTS CLOCK Early-19thC WALL CLOCK associated with the WILLARD family of Massachusetts, USA. The case containing the movement sits on top of a box housing the weights or pendulum.

MASSY Clockmakers, active mid-17th to early 18thC, in London, England.

MATCHBOX TOYS DIECAST TOYS of scaled-down road and construction vehicles, made by the firm of LESNEY from 1953. The toys are so-called because they were sold in matchbox-sized packages. From 1950–59 the name "Moko" appears alongside Lesney on these toys.

MATCHLOCK Earliest form of firing mechanism on firearms invented in the 14thC. The serpentine holds a match (cord saturated with saltpetre); it pivots when the trigger is depressed, bringing the lit match into contact with the powder.

MATTING A technique in which a compact pattern of tiny dots is made in SILVER to render a surface dull. It was popular in England and Germany in the mid-17thC. Matting was used to produce background decoration to give an impression of depth, and is also known as matted silver.

Scottish, MAUCHLINE-WARE, tartan and pen-work snuff box, c.1880.

MAUCHLINE WARE Souvenir or commemorative BOXES, needle cases, NAPKIN HOLDERS, and eggs made of varnished and tartan-patterned, TRANSFER-PRINTED wood, made by A. & A, Smith in Mauchline, Ayrshire (later in Birmingham, England), from c.1820 to the 1930s.

MAYHEW, THOMAS *See* INCE & MAYHEW.

MAZARINE (1) Rich, blue colour, characteristic of SÈVRES PORCELAIN; also a background colour on English SOFT-PASTE PORCELAIN and BONE CHINA.

MAZARINE (2) A pierced insert, fitted into a SERVING DISH and used to drain the juices from meat or fish. A variety of patterns were pierced, including scrolls, stars, flowers, and geometric designs. Popular in the mid-18thC.

MAZLAGHAN Persian CARPETS characterized by the zig-zag edge to their FIELD.

MCLAUGHLIN, MARY LOUISE (1849–1939) Prominent in AMERICAN ART POTTERY, McLaughlin decorated EARTHENWARE by UNDERGLAZE painting in coloured slip. She designed for ROOKWOOD POTTERY, and her "Losanti" range, made 1900–4, is collectable.

MEAD GLASS A GLASS with a cup-shaped bowl used for mead or champagne. Moulding at the bottom of the bowl hid the sediment in the alcohol.

MEAKIN, ALFRED Manufacturer of affordable dinnerware in the 1950s. Among the traditional floral patterns are some patterns with lively cacti and everyday scenes, often cartoonlike in style. The hand-painted ranges with checks or plaids, spots, and stripes are particularly collectable.

MEAKIN, J. & G. English, Staffordshire-based, CERAMICS firm that produced Meakin ironstone and exported it in quantity to the USA in the early- to mid-19thC. In 1964, it launched the "Studio" shape, such as a COFFEE-POT in a tall cylindrical form with a chunky, easy-to-grip lid, made in a huge variety of patterns. The firm took over MIDWINTER in 1968, and their designer Jessie Tait made designs for Meakin. Meakin became part of WEDGWOOD in 1970.

MEAT DISH Also platters or "meat flats", a serving dish for presenting meat, made in sizes from 22.5cm (9in), with 30cm (12in) being common. The majority were made in OLD SHEFFIELD PLATE or ELECTROPLATE, and had wells to collect the juices from the meat. In the early 19thC, dome-shaped covers with loop handles were popular – these were placed over the meat to keep it hot at the table. Meat-dish covers are often in poor condition and require considerable storage space, which means that in general they are not practical. Graduated sets fetch a premium. *See also* SERVING DISH.

1970s MECCANO model of the Countess Tank Locomotive.

MECCANO Parent of DINKY TOYS, and manufacturer of constructional toys consisting of metal strips and plates held together with nuts and bults – first launched in 1907. The "Constructer Set" ranges included cars and aircraft. Complete boxed sets with all the tools and instructions are sought after.

MECHANICAL BANK Any MONEY BOX that has moving parts activated when a coin is dropped into it. Cast-iron models are popular in the USA.

MEDAL A piece of metal with a stamped design, usually to acknowledge an achievement. Military medals are collectable; before buying, check the history of the soldier and regiment concerned to ensure he was entitled to it.

MEDICAL INSTRUMENTS Utensils used for surgical or other medical procedures. The value of sterilization, discovered by Lister in 1872, spelt an end to instruments that could not be boiled, so most collectors are interested in the IVORY- or wood-handled instruments of the 18th and early 19thC. Complete sets of bleeding knives, and surgical instruments in their original cases fetch the best prices. Other collectable instruments include scarifiers, stethoscopes, trephines, douches, artificial limbs, and false teeth.

MEDICINE CHEST Used by itinerant medics from the 17thC, usually with compartments, labelled bottles, spoons, and balances. Chests with their original contents are collectable, especially if they have poison compartments.

MEEKS, JOSEPH & SONS American, New York-based furniture-maker, active 1797– 1868. Renowned for its early-19thC EMPIRE-style FURNITURE.

MEIGH POTTERY Mid-19thC POTTERY by the Meigh family in Staffordshire, England. Best known for Charles Meigh's GOTHIC-style STONEWARE jugs.

MEIJI Period in Japanese history between 1868 and 1912, when the nation's art was influenced by contact with the West, and much was made for export.

MEI P'ING Chinese for "cherry blossom", this refers to a tall VASE, with high shoulders, small neck, and narrow mouth. Used to display flowering branches.

MEISSEN Founded in 1710, the first factory in Europe to make true HARD-PASTE PORCELAIN, after J.F. BÖTTGER discovered its secret. Meissen is known for the high quality of its products. The earliest wares included a RED STONEWARE called JASPERWARE and porcelain decorated in the Oriental style. In 1720 the factory was joined by J.G. Herold, a skilful chemist and painter, who developed a new range of colours. Painted decoration became more European in style, and modelling became increasingly important. Coloured grounds were introduced in the later 1720s. A turquoise ground reflects the colour of Chinese CELADON; other colours include yellow, claret, and dark blue. Monochrome decoration was fashionable in the mid-18thC; puce was popular in the ROCOCO period. Meissen began to concentrate on producing figures from c.1730, following the arrival of the sculptor Johann Joachim KÄNDLER. Before long, Kändler's figures were more popular than Meissen tablewares. Meissen's figures are made from white paste, perhaps with a slight grey tinge; the figures were modelled separately from the bases, which are covered with flowers and leaves. The faces are severely modelled but subtly coloured, and the painting is detailed, using bold or pastel shades. As other porcelain factories opened throughout Europe, they began making figures in the style of Meissen – some of them even using the Meissen mark of crossed swords. In the early 19thC, Meissen produced elaborately decorated and gilded pieces in the prevailing EMPIRE STYLE. Painted decoration became increasingly elaborate, with the surface treated as a canvas and adorned with romantic topographical views or Classical subjects. Forms

MEISSEN **figure of a girl playing the flute by J.J. Kandler, c.1750.**

became more complex, and, by the end of the 19thC, decoration often featured a confusion of styles – a typical figurative group might contain elements of the NEO-CLASSICAL STYLE mixed with the rustic naturalism of the Rococo. In the 19thC, the factory also concentrated on repetitions of 18thC designs, such as hunting scenes, and this revivalist trend continued until the 1920s, when designers such as Paul Scheurich, who specialized in figures with elongated limbs and decadent poses in the ART DECO style, and von Lowenich, began to produce imaginative, modern pieces. Meissen's crossed swords are the most commonly faked mark, and were copied by WORCESTER, MINTON, BOW, and DERBY – among others. The "KPM" mark is only used on grand, early (pre-1740) pieces. Marks on 19th and 20thC figures are usually bigger than those on 18thC ones. On pieces produced between the two world wars the blades of the swords are curved. *See also* PORCELAIN, EUROPEAN.

MELBOURNE, COLIN (b.1928) A CERAMICS designer known for his strong sculptural style, Melbourne produced many figural items for the BESWICK and MIDWINTER potteries. He also made a range of small VASES for Midwinter, and a huge selection of shapes and decorations for Beswick. He collaborated with CROWN DEVON to produce the classic "Memphis" range.

MELON BULB *See* PORTUGUESE SWELL.

MEMENTO MORI JEWELLERY Latin for "remember that you must die", jewellery with motifs of death, such as skeletons, skull and crossbones, and coffins, worn by men and women in the 16thC as a reminder of the transience of life. By the 17thC, it commemorated the death of a specific person.

MEMENTO MORI SPOON A late-16th and 17thC spoon, especially of Scottish origin, with a disc FINIAL engraved with a skull, and often with a motto associated with death on the handle.

MENNECY French SOFT-PASTE PORCELAIN manufacturer, established in the mid-18thC outside Paris. The factory was noted for novelty items such as SNUFFBOXES, walking-stick heads, and figures. Mennecy's stiff, puppet-like figures were naively modelled and painted in soft, washed-out colours, with the predominant use of pastel blue, irregularly streaked pink, and yellow. The faces on the figures often lack detail. Subjects include peasants, traders, and foreigners, which are usually most valuable. The initials "DV" for Duc de Villeroy, the patron of Mennecy, were used, sometimes with a crown.

MENU-CARD HOLDER Small decorative holders for menu cards were used at formal dinners from the late 19thC. Many examples feature enamel plaques, decorated with sporting motifs, animals, game birds, or vintage cars. Most menu-card holders are disc shaped; cased sets are desirable. Place-card holders are smaller than those for menu cards. *See also* DINING ACCESSORIES

MENUISIER Old French name for a craftsman who made FURNITURE from plain or carved wood, as distinct from veneered items.

MERCURY TWIST AIR TWIST of silvery colour or particular brightness.

MERRYMAN PLATES Sets of six to eight DELFTWARE plates with humorous verses and scenes from marital life. Popular in England in the late 17thC.

MERRYTHOUGHT LTD TEDDY-BEAR firm founded in Shropshire, England, in 1930 by W.G. Holmes and G.H. Laxton, with a number of ex-employees from CHAD VALLEY. Merrythought bears are confused with those by Chad Valley because the chief designer until 1949 was Florence Atwood, who had gained experience working with Norah WELLINGS at Chad Valley. Merrythought made traditional bears and novelties such as sitting bear cubs. Large, round ears spaced widely apart, and joined claws are typical of this maker. A celluloid button, placed initially in the ear, later on the back, was used to avoid confusion with STEIFF bears. Introduced in 1957, "Cheeky", made in several sizes and versions, was one of the firm's most popular designs. Merrythought bears have muzzles made of velvet, with noses stitched vertically; their ears, which are large and attached to the side, of the heads, have bells sewn inside them; their eyes, made from amber and black plastic, are big and set low on the muzzle; their mouths are stitched in wide smiles; and their paws and feet are large, with claws stitched across the plush into the felt. The bottom of one foot should be labelled, "Merrythought Ironbridge Shropshire Made in England Regd. Design". Be suspicious of old labels appearing on new pads.

MESHED Northeast Iranian centre of CARPET production, noted for the use of deep pink. Wares usually have a central medallion and flower motifs.

METAL The body of a GLASS item. The colour and texture of the metal change according to the ingredients used in production.

METROPOLITAN SLIPWARE Lead-glazed SLIPWARE, often bearing Puritan mottoes, from an untraced, 17thC, English, London-based POTTERY.

METTOY CO. LTD Toy firm founded by Philip Ullman in Northampton, England, in 1936, and known for its lithographed TINPLATE vehicles and aircraft.

MEUBLE À HAUTEUR D'APPUI A low French CUPBOARD or BOOKCASE.

MEZZA-MAIOLICA White-slipped EARTHENWARE with SGRAFFITO decoration, made in Italy from the 14th to 17thC; dabs of green and orange may feature.

MEZZOTINT Print made from engraved copper or steel plates that have been treated in order to achieve subtle tonal gradations.

Blue METTOY van marked "FLY BY BOAC" (the British Overseas Airways Corporation), 1953.

MICROSCOPE SCIENTIFIC INSTRUMENT for the close inspection of minute objects. After 1745, microscopes were produced in quantity, and usually made of brass mounted on a box base with a drawer. Cuff, Adams, Martin, Dollond, and Cary are notable makers. The Culpeper-type with S-shaped legs is valuable. Compound and binocular microscopes made in the 19thC were a great technical improvement on their predecessors. The finest examples were made by Abrahams, Aransberg, Beck, Lealand, Leitz, Powell, Ross, and Zeiss. Cased models with accessories have the highest value.

MIDWINTER One of the larger POTTERY firms in Stoke-on-Trent, England, founded in 1910. "Springtime", one of the most collectable CHINTZWARE patterns, was made by Midwinter. Influenced by American west-coast potteries, the firm launched the "Stylecraft" shape in 1953. The use of designer Jessie TAIT, with Hugh Casson and Terence Conran, gave the factory a lead over its competitors. Midwinter launched the "Fine" shape in 1962, which dictated the trends for the next decade. Psychedelic-inspired patterns such as "Spanish Garden" began the "flower-power" pottery craze in the late 1960s. Biscuit barrels and sugar sifters with chrome accessories are rare; the "Mediterranean" and "Diagonal" patterns were sold for short periods only, so these are collectable.

MIES VAN DER ROHE, LUDWIG (1886–1969) German MODERNIST architect and FURNITURE designer who emigrated to Illinois, USA, in 1938. He designed tubular steel, cantilevered furniture and is known for his 1929 "Barcelona" chair.

MIGNOT Established in 1830, French manufacturer of solid-cast toy soldiers and other solid, flat, and hollow figures. *See also* CAST-IRON TOY.

MIHRAB A niche with a pointed arch; the motif distinguishes a PRAYER RUG from other types of rugs. *See also* RUG, PERSIAN.

MILA (Mela, Mili) Turkish PRAYER RUG, typically with a MIHRAB and Tree of Life on a terracotta ground with a yellow border.

MILAN Italian MAIOLICA centre in the 18thC. Noted for CHINOISERIE flatware.

MILDNER Late 18thC Bohemian glassware. Designs are double walled with internal decoration in GOLD, SILVER, or ENAMEL. *See also* GLASS.

MILDNER, JOHANN JOSEF (1763–1808) Austrian glassmaker, whose wares feature medallion panels and borders decorated on the inner side in gold leaf and red LACQUER, inserted into cut-out spaces. He revived the method of making sandwich gold glass, or ZWISCHENGOLDGLAS. *See also* GLASS.

MILITARY CHEST CHEST OF DRAWERS designed for travelling. It has no protruding parts and metal mounts to protect the corners.

Rare, handpainted, MIGNOT lead figure of Cardinal Richelieu, *c.*1950.

MILK GLASS ("Milchglass") An opaque-white GLASS made by adding tin oxide to the batch. Inspired by Venetian LATTIMO glass, it was revived by Bohemian glassmakers, who applied enamel designs and used it for pressed glass in the 19thC. American glassmakers made it in the late 19thC until World War I.

MILK JUG *See* JUG, CREAM AND MILK.

MILLEFIORI Often found in PAPERWEIGHTS, a GLASS pattern resembling "a thousand flowers" (hence its Italian name). It is made of densely packed sections of coloured-glass RODS, or CANES, set into a base of clear glass, and sealed with a GATHER of molten glass. This technique was used in 15thC Venice, but the finest *millefiori* paperweights were made for around 30 years in the mid-19thC by French factories, especially BACCARAT, CLICHY, and ST LOUIS.

MILLS, NATHANIEL English, Birmingham-based silversmith who entered his first mark in 1825. He is especially celebrated for his production of CASTLE-TOP card cases and VINAIGRETTES, and the majority of his production dates to the third quarter of the 19thC. One of his marks is "NM".

MING DYNASTY Period in Chinese history from 1368 to 1644.

MING POTTERY AND PORCELAIN Chinese CERAMICS from the Ming period (1368–1644). Pieces can be identified by a thick, bluish glaze suffused with bubbles, a tendency to reddish oxidization, and knife marks on the tallish foot-rim. Ming patterns were often repeated during the CH'ING period (1644–1916). *See also* POTTERY AND PORCELAIN, CHINESE.

MINIATURE FURNITURE Small replicas of full-size pieces, produced as children's playthings. The exterior quality of a piece is often similar to that of a full-sized version, but the interior is far less refined. With many items of miniature FURNITURE the proportions may be different than on their larger counterparts – for example, the top drawer in a miniature CHEST may be deeper than on a full-sized version. Miniatures are often erroneously called apprentice pieces; some may have been made as samples. Salesmen's samples are generally smaller and more elaborate than furniture that has been made for the nursery.

MINSTER JUG Popular form in STONEWARE, decorated with figures of the Apostles under GOTHIC canopies, modelled in high relief; all in imitation of the original, patented by MEIGH POTTERY in the latter half of the 19thC.

MINTON FACTORY Founded by Thomas Minton (1765–1836) in 1798, at Stoke-on-Trent, England, the Minton factory was one of the biggest 19thC producers of every type of CERAMICS, ranging from humble EARTHENWARE to fine BONE CHINA. As well as ornamental pieces, Minton also produced dinner,

MINTONS "Secessionist"-ware vase, decorated with stylized rui heads, c.1905.

dessert, and tea services. After 1850, the company made elaborate MAJOLICA pieces and, in 1870, it set up the Minton Art Pottery Studio in London as a training academy for young designers. Minton's greatest period spans from the mid- to late 19thC. Among its finest wares are pieces made using the PÂTE-SUR-PÂTE technique. Japanese styles also influenced the factory c.1870–80; many patterns were based on Japanese porcelain, including CLOISONNÉ, using brilliant, turquoise enamels and gilding to simulate the effect of the copper wires that divide the panels in true *cloisonné*. Minton pioneered the use of innovative design in the late 19thC. The ART NOUVEAU style was reflected in its "Secessionist" wares, designed by John Wadsworth and Leon Solon, and identifiable by their unusual shapes and simple decoration. Top examples of the sophisticated PÂTE-SUR-PÂTE technique rank among the firm's most valuable products today. Printed tiles designed by leading artists, such as John Moyr Smith, and many other less elaborate pieces can be found for modest sums. Nearly all Minton is marked, with the name "MINTON" or, after c.1873, "MINTONS". Pre-1914 pieces often have a date code mark.

MINTONS English, Staffordshire-based CERAMICS firm, founded in 1793 and known for its 1920s and '30s NOVELTY WARE such as the "Apple" jam pot.

MIQUELET LOCK Early form of flintlock firing mechanism, developed in the Mediterranean in the early 17thC. *See also* FIREARM.

MIR Persian RUG with an all-over, palm-leaf pattern. Originally made in the village of Mirabad.

MIRA (Miri) Palm-leaf motif used to decorate Oriental CARPETS.

MIRROR Object with a reflective surface; examples range from grand, 18thC GILTWOOD designs to mirrors made with SILVER frames and small dressing-table mirrors that can cost less than modern reproductions. Early glass, or "Vauxhall Plate" as it was known, was not made in big sheets, so large mirrors often had two or more pieces of mirrored glass butted together. A difference in tone in one of the panels of glass implies that it is a replacement. The shape of the mirror can suggest its original use – a wide rectangular mirror might have been made to hang above a fireplace. On a Georgian, carved, GILTWOOD mirror, the back of the carved decoration was tapered inwards (undercut), so that the decoration appeared lighter when viewed from the front or side. Few later copies have such attention to detail. Some mirrors are decorated with giltwood PRINCE-OF-WALES FEATHERS – fakes of this style abound, and prices have been kept low. The carving on a fake will be crudely undercut, seeming flat and somewhat naive, with a darker, more even appearance. Convex mirrors first became fashionable in the early 19thC, and were also popular from the 1880s to the 1920s. Late-17th and 18thC silver-framed mirrors are rare; most found today are small, and date from the 1880s onward. Produced in a host of styles and forms, they are popular, being both decorative and functional. On most examples, the silver has been stamped from a sheet, meaning that it is thin and easily damaged. Better-quality pieces are cast. High-quality, silver-framed mirrors are rare and sought after. The largest examples command the highest prices, with heart-shaped mirrors favoured. Those in good condition, with fine-quality, bevelled glass and ornate decoration are valuable. In general, the smaller the mirror, the later it was produced. Less-expensive mirrors, in COMPOSITION, were made from the Victorian period (1837–1901) onward. Composition frames remain much less expensive than giltwood versions, and you should not buy damaged ones. During the late 19th and early 20thC, other less-expensive mirrors were made from wooden frames covered with velvet, and decorated with die-stamped silver. These are often badly worn and can be difficult to clean, but are still sought after. Make sure that the mirror you buy is not a picture frame that has had a glass plate inserted. It is important to buy a mirror that has not been restored, so check carefully to see that all parts of the mirror are original. Remove the mount and ensure that the original glass with its bevelled edge is still in place, even if it has been permanently discoloured or spotted. Replaced wooden backing and new velvet or leather covering will reduce the value. An accumulation of dirt is difficult to simulate and is a reassuring sign of age. Whenever possible, try to buy a mirror with its original glass. If the glass is unacceptably murky, it is preferable to have it re-silvered rather than replace it completely. If the glass is cracked, and you do have to replace it, try to find glass of an appropriate thickness. Bear in mind that heavy Victorian glass, especially when bevelled, looks incongruous on a Georgian mirror. A simple test with a coin can give you an idea of the age of the glass – Georgian glass is thin, therefore the reflection of the coin appears quite close, and the bevelling should be shallow, while the cutting may be slightly uneven. By the mid-19thC, glass was made thicker, so the reflection of the coin would be further away; the bevelling was also cut at a more acute angle, with no variation in cutting. On modern, imitation "antique" glass, made in Italy, the impurities are regular, and the closeness of the coin's reflection shows the glass to be even thinner than that made in the 18thC. *See also* CHEVAL MIRROR, DRESSING-TABLE MIRROR, GIRANDOLE, TOILET MIRROR, and VENETIAN MIRROR.

Early Georgian (18thC) giltwood MIRROR.

MIRROR CLOCK From New England, USA, a 19thC CLOCK with a MIRROR.

MIRROR STAND Adjustable looking-glass on a pole with a tripod base.

MIRZAPUR Town in India producing white CARPETS, often with a fluffy pile.

MISSION STYLE Now referred to as American Arts and Crafts, American FURNITURE and decorative arts produced in the ARTS AND CRAFTS period in a plain, simple style, reminiscent of early American Mission churches.

MITRE CUT A deep, V-shaped cut.

MITRE JOINT Right-angled joint, where two surfaces are fitted together, each cut at a 45° angle.

MITTEN HANDS (mitten feet) On DOLLS, hands or feet in a block shape, with no separate fingers and toes.

MIXED METALS SILVER objects that have been decorated with other metals, including COPPER, NICKEL, and BRASS, with the copper appearing reddish, and the brass appearing soft. In the late 19thC, the American firms of TIFFANY & CO. and GORHAM MANUFACTURING CO. produced innovative wares using this technique, especially in the ART NOUVEAU style, and using Japanese-influenced designs. The mixed-metal technique was also used on more utilitarian items, such as TEA SERVICES. While British designs are hallmarked, in the USA and Continental Europe wares made of mixed metals are clearly marked "sterling silver and other metals". Objects of this type should be cleaned carefully, as the patina is delicate and can be stripped easily.

MIXED-TWIST STEM On DRINKING GLASSES, a decorative stem featuring an AIR TWIST and an OPAQUE TWIST. Most mixed-twist stems feature a white-opaque twist with an air twist; stems in which an air and colour twist are combined are more rare. Mixed twists with combinations of different colours and types of twist are the most sought-after type of 18thC, English, twist-stem drinking glasses. Copies of such glasses were made from the mid-19thC; these are larger than the 18thC originals.

MOCHAWARE Decoration on early-19thC EARTHENWARE imitating Mocha stone, a CHALCEDONY that often has inclusions of fossil ferns and mosses; dabs of colour are applied to wet slip so that the colour spreads.

T.G. Green MOCHAWARE mug, 1910–20.

MODEL HOME FARM Scale figures made by W. BRITAIN Ltd from 1923.

MODELLED MINIATURES Model cars produced by MECCANO LTD in 1933; in April 1934 the range was extended and the name changed to DINKY TOYS.

MODERNIST Arising after World War I, this influential stylistic movement emphasized the functional. Its designers preferred modern materials, such as plastic and steel, and were influenced by Cubist art.

MOHAIR Long, lustrous, and dirt-resistant hair from the Angora goat, native to Asia Minor. Generally used for DOLLS' hair and TEDDY BEARS.

MOKO POTTERY Inexpensive form of MOCHAWARE, with colour splashed or spattered onto the body before firing.

MOKUME Japanese LACQUERWARE made to imitate wood grain.

MOLINET A stick used to mix and stir chocolate in a CHOCOLATE-POT before it is poured into cups. The *molinet*, usually made of precious hardwood with silver-mounted ornaments, was inserted into a hole, which was usually concealed by a flap or decorative, hinged FINIAL in the cover of the pot.

MOMOYAMA A period of Japanese history, 1573–1615, during which Korean potters based at Kyushu introduced glazing techniques.

MON Japanese, heraldic emblem indicating the owner's status or family.

MONART GLASS A clear, heavy GLASS streaked with black, scarlet, and other colours typical of the ART DECO period.

MONCRIEFF'S GLASSWORKS Firm founded *c.*1922 in Scotland by John Moncrieff in order to make decorative GLASS wares, and now known for PAPERWEIGHTS. MONART GLASS was developed at Moncrieff in 1924 by Paul YSART and his father Salvador. Their contemporary ART GLASS is called "Monax".

MONDSCHEINGLAS Meaning "MOONSHINE GLASS" in German, a type of blue, semi-opaque GLASS developed by Emile GALLÉ in the late 19thC.

MONEY BOX *See* MECHANICAL BANK.

MONKEY ORCHESTRA Figures of monkeys playing musical instruments, first produced at MEISSEN, and later much copied.

MONOPODIUM (1) A table support comprising a solid-looking three- or four-sided pillar, usually on paw feet, mainly found on DRUM and RENT TABLES.

MONOPODIUM (2) FURNITURE leg carved as an animal's limb with a paw, and usually found on CONSOLE or PIER TABLES.

MONTEITH Large BOWL with a shallow, scalloped rim, made from the 1680s, and used for cooling wineglasses. The glasses were hung by their stems on the scalloped, or notched rims, and the bowls of the glasses cooled in iced water. Some examples were made with detachable, crenellated collars, and this allowed them to be used as PUNCHBOWLS. Many early monteiths were decorated with fluted panels on the body for added strength, had cast, lion-mask handles, applied, beaded foot rims, and engraved coats of arms. Few were made after the 1730s, although they enjoyed a revival in France in the late 18th and early 19thC. Reproductions from the late Victorian period (late 19thC) were made to emulate monteiths from the early 18thC. In the late 19th and early 20thC, reproductions were popular wedding presents.

Meissen porcelain MONKEY ORCHESTRA figure, *c.*1860.

Unusual, 17thC MONTELUPO MAIOLICA dish, painted with a woman holding a heart pierced with an arrow.

One of a pair of MOORCROFT Macintyre Aurelian-ware vases, c.1904.

MONTELUPO MAIOLICA TIN-GLAZED EARTHENWARE produced in Tuscany, Italy, in the 15th to 17thC and characterized by bold painting. *See also* MAIOLICA.

MONTEREAU French factory producing EARTHENWARE and FAIENCE in the 18th and 19thC.

MONTH CLOCK A CLOCK that will run for 32 days without rewinding.

MONTMORENCY Curved, single-edged blade with one shallow and one narrow FULLER on each face.

MONTPELLIER From the 16thC, this southern French city was a centre of FAIENCE production, noted for its late-16th and 17thC pharmaceutical jars.

MOONSHINE GLASS Or MONDSCHEINGLAS; blue, semi-opaque glass developed by Emile GALLÉ in the late 19thC.

MOONWORK The part of some CLOCK mechanisms that drives a display showing the phases of the moon.

MOORCROFT, WILLIAM (1872–1945) A British, Staffordshire-born-and-trained potter who began designing for the firm of MACINTYRE, JAMES & CO. in 1898, and worked there until 1913. Moorcroft is best known for his use of slip-trailing decorations called FLORIAN WARE. Most of his early designs combine ART NOUVEAU naturalism, in which flowers, mushrooms, or landscapes often form part of the design, with shapes influenced by Eastern, and later, Classical ceramics. Inspired by Iznik and Persian ceramics, Moorcroft's "Persian pattern" is slightly more finely detailed than "Persian" ware by DE MORGAN, and is highly decorative and popular with collectors. Moorcroft supplied wares to LIBERTY, who often sold pieces with PEWTER mounts; many of his designs were also sent abroad. In 1913, Moorcroft set up his own factory and introduced new designs. It is known for colourful vases with floral designs and its "Florian" and "Aurelian" wares. Moorcroft's son, Walter, joined the firm in 1935, and produced mainly floral designs. Value depends on the rarity of the design and the form. The factory still continues to make a range of innovative designs. Moorcroft marks vary; "W Moorcroft Des" or "WM des" are often found on Florian ware from the Macintyre period. Pieces produced in Moorcroft's own factory were usually marked "MOORCROFT BURSLEM", impressed with either "WM" or "W. Moorcroft".

MOORE, BERNARD Founder of an ART POTTERY based in Longton, Staffordshire, England, c.1900, and specializing in unusual glaze effects.

MOORFIELDS English CARPETS handmade in London, England, in the latter half of the 18thC; some were designed by Robert ADAM.

MOORISH FURNITURE FURNITURE made in a Moorish style, featuring elaborate turning and derived from Musharabyeh panelling (used for Oriental screens). Large quantities were produced throughout the Middle East (especially in Cairo) for export to the West in the late 19thC.

MOQUETTE Wool, linen, or cotton cloth treated to resemble silk or velvet. Often used in modern CARPET production instead of true knotting to give the appearance of a PILE, and for upholstery materials.

MORGAN, SAMPSON & CO. English, London-based firm, named after Sampson Morgan (1790–1843), and famed for its pens, pencils, and novelty and character wares. It entered its first mark in the 1820s, and traded until 1941. From the late 19thC the firm made VESTA CASES decorated with finely enamelled soldiers representing different regiments; these are highly prized.

MORGAN, WILLIAM FREND DE *See* DE MORGAN, WILLIAM FREND.

MORRIS, WILLIAM (1834–96) Regarded as the progenitor of the ARTS AND CRAFTS MOVEMENT, British, London-born Morris advocated a return to craftsman-made FURNITURE of simple design, unspoiled by stains or similar preparations. The company Morris, Marshall, and Faulkner (later Morris & Co.) was founded in 1861 to produce wallpaper, stained glass, chintz CARPETS, and tapestries. The origins of Morris's influential style can be traced to medieval GOTHIC, but his organic flowers and bird motifs encouraged later artists to seek inspiration for their designs in nature.

MORTISE AND TENON A joint used in FURNITURE. The mortise is a cavity, into which the shaped tenon fits and is held in place by dowels or pegs.

MORTISE LOCK A lock set into the edge of the door and hidden from view.

MORTLAKE (1) In southwest London, England, a long-established factory producing household STONEWARE, DELFTWARE, and EARTHENWARE.

MORTLAKE (2) ART POTTERY studio established c.1900 in southwest London, England, and specializing in glaze effects.

MORTUARY CHAIR From Yorkshire in England, a CHAIR with a carved, bearded head on its back, supposedly representing the decapitated Charles I.

MORTUARY SWORD A 17thC, straight-bladed longsword with a shell-and-basket hilt, so-called because the hilt is carved with the head of Charles I.

MOSAIC PATCHWORK Quilting technique in which the QUILT top is made by fitting together geometric shapes as in MARQUETRY or floor tiling.

Brown-stoneware, MORTLAKE jug, moulded with "VR" monogram and inscribed "Well played '60' not out", c.1897.

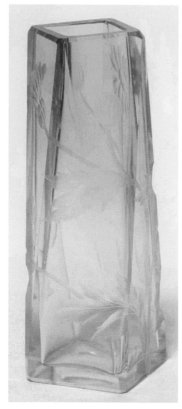

LUDWIG MOSER cut-glass vase, c.1900.

MOSER, KOLOMANN (1868–1918) Austrian graphic artist and influential figure in the Viennese ARTS AND CRAFTS MOVEMENT; one of the founders of the Viennese SECESSION in 1897 and of the WIENER WERKSTÄTTE in 1901.

MOSER, LUDWIG (1833–1916) German glassmaker who, in Karlsbad in 1857, founded a factory that manufactured engraved glass and later iridescent glass imitating "Favrile" by TIFFANY.

MOTE SPOON Or mote skimmer; a small spoon with a pierced bowl used to skim floating tea leaves and tea dust (motes) off the surface of a cup of tea. This late-17thC invention formed part of a TEA SERVICE. "Picture" or "fancy-back" mote spoons, with stamped designs on the backs of the bowls, are desirable. Mote spoons are often found in fitted cases with tea caddies and teaspoons.

MOTHER-OF-PEARL Slices of shell often used for decorative INLAY.

MOTSCHMANN-TYPE A china DOLL named after a PAPIER-MÂCHÉ doll with a voice-box, marked Charles Motschmann, dated 1857, and found in a German museum. They have porcelain SHOULDER-HEADS and floating limbs connected by loose fabric midriffs, which may conceal a bellows voice-box operated by a pull string.

MOULD, METAL Expensive, durable iron moulds, finely cut and chased.

MOULD, WOOD Hinged moulds that are less durable but cheaper than metal ones; used for mould-blown, hollow glass.

MOULD-BLOWING A technique for forming GLASS similar to FREE-BLOWING, but involving the shape of a GATHER by blowing it into a hinged wooden or metal mould. The technique was used by Roman glassmakers in the 1stC AD. It is useful for producing wares of a uniform size or diameter, such as DECANTERS, and for objects that are too complex to be formed by CORE-FORMING or free-blowing. Two main methods are used: blowing a gather into a part-mould, then removing it and free-blowing it further to expand the shape or impressed pattern; or blowing a gather into a mould to shape an entire object.

MOULDED EARS Ears cast as an intrinsic part of the head mould of a DOLL.

MOULDED GLASS A type of 19thC glassware produced in large quantities and in the same pattern by forcing GLASS into a mould. *See also* PRESSED GLASS.

MOULDED HAIR Hair that forms an intrinsic part of the head of a DOLL.

MOULDING Originally, any ornament cast in a mould; now the term refers to any shaped projection, carved in wood or stone or cast in plaster.

MOULINS FAIENCE centre in central France; noted for its ROCOCO designs.

MOUNT Pieces of BRASS, BRONZE, gilt-bronze, or ORMOLU found on late-17thC French, and 18thC English, French, and American FURNITURE, and originally intended to protect susceptible areas. Also refers to other metal parts found on furniture such as ESCUTCHEONS, HANDLES, hinges, and LOCKS. In addition, SILVER or SILVER-GILT mounts have been used on GLASS as handles and lids, especially in the 18th and 19thC. Silver mounts were secured using plaster of Paris, so they are difficult to replace if damaged or worn. The hallmarks on silver are a valuable method of dating glass. Check that the mount fits tightly around the neck – a good sign that it is original.

MOUNT VERNON Blown and moulded GLASS made during the 19thC at the Mount Vernon Works, New York, USA.

MOUNT WASHINGTON GLASS CO. American glassworks established in Boston, Massachusetts, USA, in 1837. It made utilitarian GLASS until it closed in 1870. William Libbey, the owner of the glassworks, opened a new factory in 1870 in New Bedford, Massachusetts, and made mould-blown and pressed ART GLASS until 1894. The "Royal Flemish" pattern was made solely by Mount Washington from c.1890, as well as the "Burmese" pattern. The original trademark is found on a paper label. Forgeries are acid-etched.

MOURNING JEWELLERY Black JEWELLERY worn in the 19thC during a period of mourning. It was usually made of JET, often with a lock of hair from the deceased; GLASS, ENAMEL, and onyx were also used. Morbid associations limit its appeal, but early, hand-carved pieces, and brooches with glass-covered lockets in the reverse are collectable. *See also* MEMENTO MORI JEWELLERY.

MOURON, ADOLPHE (1901–68) Better known as CASSANDRE, a Russian-born, French-based artist known for poster designs such as *Normandie* (1934). His *Dubo, Dubon, Dubonnet* (1934) poster was the first designed to be viewed from passing cars. His work had a great influence on 20thC advertising.

MOUSTIERS Based in southern France, one of Europe's chief production centres of FAIENCE from the 17thC. It is noted for BLUE-AND-WHITE decoration based on the engravings of Jean BÉRAIN, and for grotesques.

MOVIE MEMORABILIA *See* FILM MEMORABILIA.

MUCHA, ALPHONSE MARIA (1861–1931) Czech-born artist and illustrator who worked in Paris, France, and the USA; best known for his ART NOUVEAU posters such as those publicizing Sarah Bernhardt. His graphic art is predominantly floral and richly intricate. He was also a designer of JEWELLERY, textiles, FURNITURE, and applied art.

Silver MUFFIN DISH by Willim Hutton & Sons, London, 1896.

MUDGE, THOMAS Important 18thC clockmaker based in London, England, and credited with the invention of the LEVER ESCAPEMENT.

MUDJUR Turkish PRAYER RUGS, characteristically with bright green, blue, and yellow designs on a deep-red ground.

MUFFIN DISH Made in SILVER PLATE from the late-Victorian period (late 19thC) until the 1930s. Examples can be bought at reasonable prices.

MUG A lidless drinking vessel with a handle attached to the side. Made from the mid-17thC, early SILVER mugs mirrored the shapes of POTTERY – with bulbous bases and slender necks. Most common in the early 18thC were BALUSTER-shaped mugs with cast handles, and only engraved coats of arms or initials for decoration. In the late 18thC, mugs and their handles were made from cylinders of sheet metal. From the 1830s until *c*.1900, small, often lavishly decorated silver mugs were given as christening presents, sometimes in a cased set with a knife, fork, and spoon. Mugs featuring mottos such as "Pause, ponder, sift!" are more valuable than those that are simply initialled. A mug of baluster shape and a spreading foot is a common form. Most collectable are christening mugs engraved with scenes from nursery rhymes. Until the end of the 18thC, marks were made in a group under the base; later pieces are marked in a line by the handle. Check handles and rims for signs of weakening or splitting, and examine sides for signs of erased armorials or inscriptions. This makes the silver thin and prone to damage.

MULE CHEST A 17thC CHEST with one or two drawers in the lower part.

MÜLLER FRÈRES Founded by Henri Müller in 1895, a leading French manufacturer of CAMEO GLASS. The firm is known for its ART DECO lampshades, and VASES decorated with landscapes.

MÜLLER & STRASSBERGER German makers of 19thC PAPIER-MÂCHÉ DOLLS.

MUNTZ'S METAL Early-19thC copper-and-zinc alloy used for decorative objects because of its resemblance to GOLD.

MURANO Alternative name for VENETIAN GLASS.

MUROMACHI Or Ahikaga era, period of Japanese history AD 1338–1573.

MURRAY, KEITH (1892–1981) A New Zealand-born artist, hired by WEDGWOOD to create modern CERAMICS designs. Bold, geometric shapes in muted shades and simple patterns are typical of his style. Modern shapes with monochromatic glazes (matt, semi-matt, or CELADON), and engine-turned decoration are sought after. Murray designed glass for STEVENS & WILLIAMS.

MURRAY, WILLIAM STAITE (1881–1962) English art potter influenced by Chinese STONEWARE. He made finely thrown pieces with sparse decoration.

MURRHINE GLASS Delicate but strong Roman GLASS containing murra. It was revived as a trade name for a similar ART GLASS in the late 19thC.

MUSICAL BOX A mechanical device with a set of pins on a cylinder, used to create music by striking tuned teeth on a comb-like metal plate, first made in the 19thC. Musical boxes must be in working order to achieve good prices. Movements can be repaired, but damage to the comb or cylinders cannot. After 1875, most musical boxes were mass-produced and of inferior quality. Earlier pieces with a wooden, inlaid flap or glass top are most in demand. Rare types with special effects or features that improve the sound, are prized, particularly "Overture", "Mandoline", and "Orchestra" boxes.

MUSICAL CLOCK A type of CLOCK with a cylinder and pins, which drive a series of hammers that strike bells and play one or more tunes.

MUSICIAN'S CHAIR Distinct type of CHAIR of elegant appearance with a low back and sides and usually on CABRIOLE LEGS.

MUSKET Infantry soldiers' FIREARM from the 16th to the 19thC. The length of the barrel was progressively reduced, and the firing mechanism developed from the match, to the wheel, and then to the flintlock.

MUSTARD POT Until the mid-18thC, unpierced ("blind") casters used to hold the dry condiment, which was prepared on the plate. From the 1760s, pots for paste mustard came into fashion, made in a range of sizes and designs. The tankard form is the basic shape of the earliest mid-18thC mustard-pots. A blue-glass liner was used to prevent the silver from being corroded by the acidic vinegar in the mustard. Mustard spoons have drop-shaped bowls. A slightly curved stem and elongated bowl makes it easier to serve the mustard. Beware of pots converted from small mugs by adding a cover.

MYOTT, SON & CO. Factory that made an ART DECO range of adventurous, original shapes, hand-painted in contrasting colours in Staffordshire, England. JUGS, VASES, and table CENTREPIECES are popular. The more inventive the shape – such as fan- or pyramid-shaped vases – the more desirable the piece.

MYRIOPTICON A mid-19thC, American, mechanical PEEP-SHOW, in which pictures printed on a reel are wound from spool to spool.

MYSTERY CLOCK Novelty CLOCK in which the movement, hidden in a base, slightly rotates a figure from left to right. The motion makes the pendulum swing, but the figure holding it seems unconnected to the mechanism.

N

NABESHIMA Japanese PORCELAIN of rich, enamel colours and UNDERGLAZE-BLUE designs, made only for the aristocracy.

NAIL-HEAD DECORATION Carved decoration resembling square heads of nails and found from the Middle Ages to the 17thC.

NAILS Early nails, known as clout or rose-head nails, had narrow heads and were handmade, so each was slightly different in size. The heads had five distinct surfaces, where the molten tops of the nails were hit five times to make the flower-shaped heads. By the mid-18thC, nails were stamped from metal sheets; they became uniform in size and have regular machine-made heads. Old nails can be difficult to identify – viewed from the top, a rusted modern upholstery tack with a reshaped head is the same as an old clout nail.

NAILSEA A factory founded in the late 18thC near Bristol, England, it specialized in CROWN (window) GLASS and BOTTLE GLASS. It became better known for domestic pieces, such as JUGS and DECANTERS, flecked or striped in white or coloured glass. Nailsea flasks and decanters feature looped, white-trailed or combed decoration, although pink and blue are also known. These were not intended to be used for serving wine and spirits, but were for ornament only. "Nailsea" is now the general term for small decorative items made in this style from glass left over at the end of day and produced outside working hours. These were made at glassworks in the Midlands and other provincial centres, and include items such as walking sticks, bells, rolling pins, and witch balls (large, silvered-glass spheres). Bells are among the most popular items of Nailsea glass – the majority of these have coloured bodies, most commonly red ones, joined with plaster of Paris to clear-glass handles. Decoration includes KNOPS on the handles and writhen moulding or ribbing on the bodies. Among the most common types of useful ware made from left-over, green crown glass are dumps, or doorstops. Some commemorative pieces can be found, such as those celebrating the jubilee of Queen Victoria. Doorstops were subjected to heavy wear and tear and are therefore often damaged, with internal "bruises".

NAIN From central Iran, a CARPET with naturalistic, all-over flower decoration.

NANKIN(G) Chinese wares exported through the port of Nanking in the late 18th and 19thC, especially those with the "WILLOW" PATTERN. "Nankin yellow" are those with a yellow glaze, often in association with BLUE-AND-WHITE wares.

NANTGARW PORCELAIN William BILLINGSLEY, England's foremost flower painter on PORCELAIN, opened the Nantgarw works near Cardiff, Wales, in 1813, although shortly afterward he moved to SWANSEA. A few years later, he returned to Nantgarw, which mainly produced PLATES, cups, saucers, and small ornaments. Beautifully painted floral, subjects were made at both Nantgarw and Swansea, and the marks are often the only way to tell the two apart. Thomas Pardoe took over the decoration after Billingsley left in 1819 to work at Coalport; Nantgarw closed in 1822. Welsh porcelain is scarcer than that from other factories, so it commands a premium. Nantgarw wares were marked with an impressed "NANTGARW CW" (for china works).

NAPKIN HOLDER (Napkin ring) A SILVER clip for attaching the napkin to a shirt, or a ring for tidying away a rolled napkin. ART DECO, ceramic, napkin holders were made in novelty shapes by ROYAL DOULTON and other firms.

Art Deco, ceramic-dog NAPKIN RING.

NAPLES PORCELAIN factory founded in Naples, Italy, under royal patronage in the late 18thC. Noted for Classical figures in glassy, SOFT-PASTE PORCELAIN.

NARA Period of Japanese history AD 710–794.

NASHIJI Japanese LACQUERWORK design incorporating strewn GOLD particles.

NATIONAL WATCH CO. Makers of mass-produced but fine-quality WATCHES from 1864 to the 1960s, based in Elgin, Illinois, USA.

NAUTILUS Large seashell, with a MOTHER-OF-PEARL interior, mounted on a silver stand and ornamented with nautical figures; used as a drinking vessel.

NECK RING Ring around the neck of GLASS DECANTERS that helps in dating.

NEEDLE GUN First gun in which the cartridge was fired by the impact of a needle; an early -19thC, German invention. *See also* FIREARMS.

NEF Highly ornate, SILVER salt container, usually of French or German origin.

NEO-CLASSICAL STYLE (Neo-classicism) Style of architecture, FURNITURE, and ornamentation, using CLASSICAL motifs but in an entirely new way. Interest in the new discoveries made at Herculaneum and Pompeii in Italy – which uncovered ancient Roman artefacts – combined with an adverse reaction to ROCOCO exuberance, led to this new style, which dominated the mid- to late 18thC. Neo-classical objects are decorated with Classical motifs such as GADROONING, BEADING, REEDING, stylized foliage, masks, SWAGS, and columns. Carving is in low relief and usually symmetrical. The furniture is light and elegant in appearance. Straight, tapering legs are typical of chairs made during this time, as are geometrical forms and the use of Greek and

Ivory NETSUKE mask of Hannya, by Koichi, form the Meiji period, 1868–1912.

Roman ornament. Neo-classicism was pioneered in England in the work of the furniture designer Robert ADAM; it is also reflected in the designs of George HEPPLEWHITE and Thomas SHERATON. *See also* PALLADIAN.

NEO-GREEK Classical-revival FURNITURE in the USA, made *c.*1815 – 40.

NE PLUS ULTRA An American DOLL body, patented in 1833, with joints at the knees and body. The doll has a SHOULDER-HEAD in BISQUE, COMPOSITION or leather arms, and jointed elbows. The body forms part of the thigh.

NETSUKE Japanese carved toggles, used from the 16thC to secure SAGEMONO ("hanging things") to the OBI (waist belt) from a cord. They were usually made of IVORY, LACQUER, SILVER, or wood. Signed *netsuke* by acknowledged masters of the art, and those depicting rare or novel subjects are sought after. The best pieces are hand-carved. Ivory is not necessarily more valuable than wood, but inlaid *netsuke* often command a premium. Copies and fakes are numerous. Some are genuine, period ornaments (*okimono*), converted to *netsuke* by boring a cord hole. In genuine *netsuke*, the hole is almost invisible; in fakes the holes are obtrusive. The grain in genuine ivory is only visible at certain angles, whereas simulated ivory grain is always visible and regular. Signatures on fakes are often moulded, not carved.

NETTLE FIBRE Material resembling linen used by STEIFF when materials were scarce during World War I.

NEVE, HENRY Huguenot clockmaker, active in London, England, 1700–20.

NEVERS French centre of FAIENCE production since the 16thC. Also, POTTERY decorated with pastoral scenes produced all over France in the 18thC.

NEW AMSTERDAM GLASS from one of two 17thC producers working in the Dutch colony that became New York, in North America.

NEW BREMEN GLASS tableware from the 18thC works in Maryland, USA.

NEW CANTON SOFT-PASTE PORCELAIN made at Stratford-le-Bow, London, England, in the mid-18thC. *See also* BOW FACTORY.

NEWCASTLE GLASS Type of light, BALUSTER wineglass made at glassworks in Newcastle-upon-Tyne, England, in the 18thC. They were often decorated by skilled Dutch engravers, because the GLASS has a bright and lustrous material that displayed engraved motifs to best advantage.

NEW CHELSEA Reproductions of CHELSEA and other 18th and 19thC PORCELAIN made at an early 20thC factory in Longton, Staffordshire, England.

NEW CHELSEA nursey teapot, inscribed "This Little Brown House Is Set On A Hill, You Only See Jack But Inside You'll Find Jill", *c.*1936.

NEWCOMB POTTERY American ART NOUVEAU pottery founded in 1895 in New Orleans by Mary G. Sheerer. Newcomb VASES are decorated with designs based on the flora and fauna of the surrounding bayou country. The decoration is created by drawing into the wet clay and painting with oxides after the first firing. Wares were then given a transparent, high-gloss glaze in a palette of blue, green, yellow, and black. Designs were rarely repeated.

NEW ENGLAND GLASS CO. American manufacturer of lead GLASS, based in Massachusetts. Its British-born designer, Joseph Locke, developed "AMBERINA" glass. The firm was the earliest producer of PAPERWEIGHTS in the USA, making them from 1850. Its fruit weights are among its best designs, but the firm is also known for flower and MILLEFIORI weights. They sometimes used a white LATTICINIO ground for weights with fruits or flowers. A bright-green colour, and clearly delineated veins on the leaves are typical of the firm's work.

NEWHALL After LONGTON HALL, the second pottery in Staffordshire, England, to make PORCELAIN successfully. The usual date given for the founding of the factory is 1782, when it was known as Hollins, Warburton & Co. Newhall used the Cookworthy method of making a hybrid, HARD-PASTE PORCELAIN. The porcelain is a greyish colour when held to a light and is seldom crazed. Duvivier, who had worked at DERBY and WORCESTER, also painted at Newhall, from 1782 to 1790; some of his work at Newhall may have been wrongly attributed to another factory. Around 1812, a new BONE-CHINA body was introduced, and at this time the factory became known as Newhall. After 1820, the BONE-CHINA wares seemed to lose some quality, and the factory closed in 1835.

NEW JERSEY GLASS made in southern New Jersey, USA, from the late 18thC.

NEWRY Irish manufacturer of FLINT GLASS in the late 18th and early 19thC.

NEW STONE CHINA A type of STONEWARE containing potash FELDSPAR and developed in the early 19thC by SPODE.

NICKEL Any of various white alloys of copper, zinc, and nickel, used in ELECTROPLATING as a base for coating with SILVER.

NICKEL SILVER Used as an alternative to SILVER for cutlery and coinage, a white-coloured alloy of 25 per cent nickel and 75 per cent copper.

NIDERVILLER Mid-18thC, FAIENCE factory in Alsace-Lorraine, France; noted for figures that rivalled the finest PORCELAIN, and for delicate, floral decoration.

NIELLO Black metal alloy or ENAMEL used for filling in engraved designs on SILVER. A black compound consisting of silver, lead, copper, and sulphur is first heated, then reduced to a powder. A design is engraved into the silver,

NIDERVILLER **figure of an apple vendor,** c.1775.

filled with the black compound, and heated until the powder granules fuse together. The object is polished after firing, leaving the carved decoration filled with niello, and the surface smooth. Because niello is a metallic alloy, it is stronger than enamel and less prone to damage. Most examples of niello are from France, Russia, and the former Austro-Hungarian Empire, and date from the 18th to the early 20thC. Some of the finest niello SNUFFBOXES decorated with townscapes, architectural scenes, or floral designs were made in Russia.

NIGHT TABLE *See* BEDSIDE CABINET.

NIGHT WATCHMAN TOBY JUG in the form of a watchman holding a lantern.

NIGOSHIDE ("Milky white") Extremely fine, white ceramic body used to make Japanese KAKIEMON porcelain.

NIM Literally "half", used to denote the size of a CARPET. *See also* ZAR.

NINSEI (1596–1666) Japanese potter credited with making the country's first PORCELAIN in 1616.

NODDING FIGURE Popular from the 19thC, a PORCELAIN figure with the head mounted on a pivot or spring, so that it nods when touched.

NON-FLAM CELLULOID Nonflammable celluloid acetate, discovered in 1926 and used widely in the 1930s and '40s for electrical equipment.

NORITAKE From *c.*1900, a prolific and successful Japanese manufacturer of PORCELAIN aimed at the European market. Early pieces reflect the influence of ART NOUVEAU and ART DECO. Noritake is marked with a fleur-de-lis motif.

NORTHERN CELADON Early Chinese, grey-green, glazed wares with a brown fabric or body, as distinct from the red fabric of SOUTHERN CELADON.

NOTTINGHAM STONEWARE SALT-GLAZED MUGS and vessels with pierced and engraved decoration, made by several potters in Nottingham, England, from the late 17th to the early 19thC.

NOVELTY DOLL Wooden DOLL made in the 18thC to satirize or honour celebrities and professions, such as hermaphrodite dolls, probably a satire on George III (1760–1820) and Queen Charlotte. Members of holy orders were venerated and admired, so dolls were made in honour of them.

NOVELTY WARE Cheerful, inexpensive EARTHENWARE made in Britain in the gloom of the 1920s and '30s. Designers produced whimsical designs to brighten up everyday tableware such as jugs, CRUET SETS, and jam pots.

12thC, NORTHERN CELADON, conical dish with incised decoration.

NULLING Decorative carving in the form of irregular fluting; usually found on early oak furniture.

NUREMBERG EGG Early German watch worn as a neck pendant; possibly so-named because Uhrchen – "little clock" – sounds like Eichen, or "little egg", or perhaps simply because they were oval in shape.

NUREMBERG POTTERY A type of 18thC FAIENCE, noted for blue-on-white scenes, based on engravings, with crosshatched shading.

NUREMBERG SCALE Scale used for modelling German toy soldiers: 30mm (1⅛in) high for foot soldiers; 40mm (1⅝in) for cavalry.

NURSERY WARE Many nursery articles have survived in good condition, often because they were given as christening presents. Novelty items such as rattles were made in large numbers in silver, silver gilt, and gold from the mid-18thC. Most rattles feature a coral handle or teether, but sometimes the teether was made of ivory. Look out for loose or damaged bells or coral, or replacements. Child-sized knives, forks, spoons, MUGS, and BOWLS were presented in boxed sets. The bowls were often engraved with scenes from nursery rhymes, Mother Goose stories, or other childhood themes. Christening bowl-and-spoon sets by well-known makers such as TIFFANY & CO. or the GORHAM MANUFACTURING CO. are desirable. Cutlery sets of a knife, fork, and spoon often incorporated the birthday or name of the child. Makers such as the firm of Georg JENSEN produced children's utensil sets in a variety of styles from the 1950s. Mugs have also been given as christening presents, sometimes in sets with other nursery ware; they were produced in large quantities from 1850 to 1900. Other items to commemorate a christening include APOSTLE SPOONS. Many forms can be found in ceramic, too, including bowls, plates, and mugs. Wares from the 1930s featuring Walt Disney cartoon characters are popular, as are designs commissioned by major firms, such as Mabel Lucie ATTWELL's range commissioned by SHELLEY in the 1920s, and E.H. Shephard's "Christopher Robin" series, made from c.1927 for Ashstead's. Clarice CLIFF and Susie COOPER worked on nursery ranges, as did the potters Charlotte RHEAD and Barbara vernon.

Rare Susie Cooper NURSERY WARE Paris-shape jug, c.1930.

NYMPHENBURG FACTORY Established in the mid-18thC, a German manufacturer of fine PORCELAIN figures. The firm is known for its sophisticated handling of porcelain, and its figures have subtle ROCOCO-style poses, with upwardly spiralling movements. Elongated bodies and delicate faces with exaggerated expressions are typical of their figures, which were made of a creamy coloured, lightweight, slip-cast body. Key modellers include Franz Anton Bustelli, J.P. Melchior, and D.J. Auliczek, who is famous for his hunting scenes. The figures were marked with an impressed or incised shield mark, often placed at the front of the base.

Derbyshire OAK **centre table from the second half of the 17thC.**

OAK A rich chocolate-brown or paler, golden-brown, coarse-grained wood, oak (*Quercus*) is strong, durable, and resists damp and woodworm.

OAK FURNITURE The principal material for making all FURNITURE up to *c.*1670 and used into the 19thC for COUNTRY FURNITURE. Early oak has character, and although originally a golden honey colour, it ages to a warm chestnut to black colour, with a rich PATINA after years of polish and handling. Stripping and refurbishing destroys colour and sheen, and devalues a piece. Wear and damage consistent with use is inevitable, but avoid pieces so damaged as to require repair, which reduces value. Avoid pieces that have been "embellished" at a later date. VICTORIAN-STYLE carving will be in relief with sharp edges. Original carving protrudes and will be worn smooth. Later VENEERS and INLAY are thin, machine-cut, often distinguished by insensitive treatment of grain or anachronistic patterns. Many early oak TABLES are small and therefore popular, because they fit modern room sizes. Avoid tables reduced in size, as these tend to lack patination to the cut edges. Oak tables can be dated by their legs and stretchers. The earliest are simple and square; lathe turning was mastered *c.*1640, and this allowed more decorative legs with twists, bobbins, and BALUSTERS to be introduced. Turning from the 18thC is more restrained and architectural in style. Later oak furniture often has heavy, bulbous mouldings or overly elaborate imitations of earlier styles, especially BARLEY-SUGAR TWISTS. Period CHESTS in solid, well-worn oak, with good decoration, are highly desirable. The best oak DRESSERS were made in the 17th and 18thC for the parlour. The fashion for stripping painted furniture has ruined some fine pieces. Early painted pieces are more valuable in original condition.

"OAR" PATTERN SPOON A spoon with an oar-shaped handle and FINIAL.

OBI In Japanese costume, the waist sash from which SAGEMONO ("hanging things") are hung, in lieu of pockets.

OBI-HASAMI NETSUKE with a hook, which is designed to catch on the lower edge of the OBI (waist sash).

OBJET DE VERTU An object, usually small, of beauty or rarity; such items are made with precious materials and display the finest skills of craftsmanship.

OBRIST, HERMANN (1863–1927) Leading artist of JUGENDSTIL, the German ART NOUVEAU movement.

OCCASIONAL TABLE Small, portable TABLE, known in France as a GUÉRIDON. The opulent French style of the 1720s and '30s was fashionable again from 1830 to 1930, when vast numbers of small tables in the LOUIS XV STYLE were made in England and France. Various woods were used and often combined to produce MARQUETRY decoration. Before buying a table, make sure that the top and platform STRETCHERS are of matching form. The marquetry should be in good condition, with no pieces missing; look also for quality metal mounts.

OCHEL German manufacturer of flat-cast toy soldiers, since 1925.

OCTANT Invented in 1731, an instrument in the form of one-eighth of a circle, used for measuring angular distances. Octants often have frames made of MAHOGANY, EBONY, or BOXWOOD. *See also* SCIENTIFIC INSTRUMENTS.

OEBEN, JEAN-FRANÇOIS (*c.*1720–63) Leading French cabinet-maker. After his death, the business was continued by his widow, until she married Jean RIESENER in 1767, after which time the firm took his name.

OEIL DE PERDRIX French for "eye of the partridge", a pattern consisting of a small blue circle surrounded by darker dots, randomly scattered as a background decoration on PORCELAIN.

"O" GAUGE Introduced *c.*1900, one of the gauges used for model railways, signifying 32mm (1¼in) between the tracks.

OGEE Double-curved shape, which is convex at the top and becomes concave at the bottom. Often found on the feet of Georgian FURNITURE.

OGEE CLOCK From New England, USA, a type of 19thC MANTEL CLOCK with OGEE mouldings framing the case.

OHR, GEORGE Prolific American craftsman, "the Mad Potter from Biloxi" made more than 10,000 pots and crammed them into barrels in the family attic. Ohr produced STUDIO POTTERY in innovative forms that anticipated many of the developments of contemporary ceramics. Unctuous glazes, richly mottled in metallic colours, bizarre forms, and thin walls are distinctive of his work. Pieces are impressed "GEO E OHR/BILOXI, MISS."

OIGNON WATCH ("Onion" watch) A French WATCH, common in the late 17th and 18thC, and so-named because of its shape.

OIL LAMP A lamp with a reservoir for holding oil. Few all-glass OIL LAMPS exist because they were hard to make; the majority had glass reservoirs, but metal or ceramic supporting columns. Oil lamps are collected in their own right, but sometimes they are converted to electric use.

OJIME Sliding bead threaded by a cord between a NETSUKE (toggle) and an INRO (medicine box). When the *ojime* is pushed down, it keeps the *inro* closed, while slid up, it allows the *inro* to be opened.

OLBRICH, JOSEPH MARIA (1867–1908) Pupil of Otto Wagner at the WEINER WERKSTÄTTE, and one of a group of Austria-based, young, progressive artists who produced fanciful but disciplined ART NOUVEAU designs.

"OLD ENGLISH" PATTERN A simple pattern on FLATWARE, where the handle remains undecorated, and the terminal features a central inward point, or "pip". Made from *c.*1760, it is a derivative of the "HANOVERIAN" PATTERN.

OLDFIELD WARE A type of SALT-GLAZED STONEWARE made during the 19thC in Derbyshire, England.

OLD SHEFFIELD PLATE SILVER vessels made in Sheffield, England, in the 19thC. By the 1820s, Sheffield silversmiths were posing a threat to London makers by mass-producing wares more cheaply. Sheffield-made silver, which used the same dies and stampings as the plating industry, was produced on a large scale, without sacrificing quality to mechanization. This Sheffield plate is now often referred to as "old Sheffield plate" to avoid confusion with ELECTROPLATE on copper – patented *c.*1840 and sometimes termed "Sheffield" or Sheffield plate by 20thC manufacturers. Notable makers of old Sheffield plate include the firms of J. Wright & G. Fairbairn and Messrs Creswick.

OLEOGRAPHS Prints made from the mid-19thC to resemble oil paintings. They were often made onto embossed paper, then varnished, and framed.

OLIVE WOOD Hard, dark-greenish wood with black streaks. Used as a VENEER.

OMNIUM Victorian name for a WHATNOT.

ON POINT In quilting, the mounting of a square block or patch at an angle so that it appears as a diamond. *See also* QUILT.

"OO" GAUGE (Double O, or Dublo) A gauge used for model railways. This type, introduced in the 1930s, is half the width of an "O" GAUGE, with 16.5mm (⅟₁₆in) between the tracks.

OPALESCENT GLASS Type of GLASS in which phosphate, such as powdered, calcined, animal bones, is added to the batch. While the glass initially appears milky blue, it will have a fiery red tint when held up to the light.

OPAL GLASS ("Beinglas") A translucent, white glass made in the 17th and 18thC in Venice, Italy, and late 17th to 19thC in Germany and Bohemia.

OPALINE GLASS A GLASS made by adding gold oxide to the batch to create a richly translucent BODY, often coloured with other metallic oxides; it has a fiery, orange-red tint when held up to the light. At first glance, opaline glass may look as though it is made from PORCELAIN. It was first made in France in the 19thC, where production was prolific. It was also made in many colours other than white, notably a turquoise blue. Bohemian and English glassmakers produced opaline glass from the mid-19thC, but their wares lack the rich opalescence of French pieces. Quality can vary – the best examples are made from LEAD CRYSTAL and are heavy.

Hunt Roskell scent bottle made from OPALINE GLASS, with a gold top, 1860.

OPAQUE-TWIST STEM A stem on DRINKING GLASSES with an opaque twist produced by inserting rods of white or coloured glass into a GATHER of clear glass, then pulling and twisting the stem to draw out the rods into fine threads. The main difference between an opaque- and AIR-TWIST STEM is that the former is cut from a long rod, with the bowl and foot made separately and applied, while the latter is made individually, so that each one is unique. The cut end of an opaque twist, where it was sliced from a longer rod, will be visible. Glasses with opaque-white-twist stems are known as "COTTON" TWISTS, because the fine white rods have the appearance of cotton. Opaque-twist stems are usually white, because different colours of glass have varying cooling rates, making coloured rods more prone to breaking. Blue and yellow twists are rarer than red and green. Most opaque-twist stems are "double series", with one spiral within another; single-series opaque twists are rare. As with air twists, KNOPS on opaque-twist stems are unusual, because compressing the glass to create the bulbous ring risked breaking the twist pattern inside the stem. A plain, bell-shaped bowl is common on glasses with opaque-twist stems – few were engraved. The neatness and evenness of the twist are a sign of high-quality craftsmanship. Continental European copies often have uneven and poorly formed twists, because soda glass cools more rapidly than English lead glass. Few opaque twists were made after 1777, when an Excise Act raised a tax on coloured glass. *See also* COMPOSITE STEM GLASS, and MIXED-TWIST STEM.

OPEN-CLOSED-MOUTH DOLL A DOLL with a mouth that appears to be open but with no opening between the lips.

OPEN FRETWORK Fretwork that is not carved into or applied to a solid surface, but is left open so that it can be seen through.

Victorian, walnut whatnot or cantebury with OPEN FRETWORK on the sides and the gallery.

OPEN HEAD The open section on the crown of the head of a DOLL. It is covered with a PATE (cork on French dolls, cardboard on German) and is the section to which the wig is attached. BISQUE dolls often have open heads.

OPEN-MOUTH DOLL A DOLL on which the mouth is modelled in such a way that it appears to be open, with a space between the lips.

19thC, Paris, porcelain, oil-lamp base with ORMOLU mounts.

OPENWORK A type of PIERCED DECORATION.

ORANGE PEEL In quilting, a PATCHWORK design using curved patches in the shape of orange segments. *See also* QUILT.

ORGAN CLOCK A CLOCK in which the hours are sounded by bellows operating on organ pipes instead of bells.

ORIENTAL CARPET A CARPET made in the Near East, rather than in China.

ORLÉANS PORCELAIN Wares produced from the mid-18th to early 19thC at Orléans, in the Loire Valley, France.

ORMOLU Gilded BRONZE or BRASS; the term, literally "gilt bronze", is sometimes loosely used to describe any yellow-coloured metal. Originally used for FURNITURE handles and mounts, from the 18thC it was also used for INKSTANDS, CANDLESTICKS, CLOCK cases, and other smaller objects.

ORREFORS Glassware manufacturer established in Orrefors, Sweden, in 1898. The factory made affordable TABLEWARE and a range of engraved GLASS that was shown at the Stockholm Exhibition of 1930 and toured Britain in 1931. Orrefors' success led to may imitations – early copies are more desirable than those still being made in Eastern Europe.

ORRERY CLOCK A CLOCK named after the Fourth earl of Orrery. It shows the positions of the earth, moon, and sun, and sometimes also the planets.

ORVIETO MAIOLICA Some of Italy's earliest TIN-GLAZED EARTHENWARE, with production dating back to the 14thC. PLATES, JARS, and jugs of that period survive, decorated with GOTHIC-style ornamentation. deruta, faenza, FLORENCE, and NAPLES were other main Italian centres of production. *See also* MAIOLICA.

OSIER (Ozier) Basket-weave decoration found on the rims of PORCELAIN PLATES, introduced at MEISSEN in the 1730s.

OTT & BREWER PARIAN manufacturers of Trenton, New Jersey, USA. They produced a range of busts of famous people including George Washington, Abraham Lincoln, Ulysses Grant, Benjamin Franklin, and Cleopatra, all by the sculptor Isaac Broome. *See also* AMERICAN CERAMICS.

OTTWEILER PORCELAIN Established during the mid-18thC, this German PORCELAIN manufacturer produced figures and FLATWARE.

OUDE LOOSDRECHT Dutch, late -18thC PORCELAIN, decorated with rural landscapes and peasant scenes.

OVERCOIL In a CLOCK mechanism, a second spring attached to the BALANCE SPRING to ensure that it retains its regular shape. Invented in the late 18thC.

OVERGLAZE A decoration technique in which a second glaze is laid over a first and refired. The second glaze is made from a mixture of metallic oxides and molten glass, and fired at a lower temperature in a muffle kiln, causing the glass to fuse with the glaze. Overglaze enamels may be less hard-wearing than UNDERGLAZE colours, but were available in a wider range of colours. Also known as ENAMELLING, overglaze enamel, and PETIT-FEU ENAMELS.

OVERGLAZE PRINTING Developed in the mid-1750s, the earliest form of TRANSFER PRINTING, in which the design is applied over the glaze and refired at a lower temperature.

OVERLAY GLASS A technique in GLASS decoration that involves fusing a coloured layer to a clear BODY. The term is now interchangeable with CASING. To form the decoration, an outer vessel is partially blown and placed in a mould, and a second GATHER (either clear or in a contrasting colour) is placed inside and blown into it, so that the layers fuse and expand together. The process is complex, because different colours of glass cool at different rates, making the object susceptible to cracking when annealed. The process was popular in Bohemia in the BIEDERMEIER period, and during the 19thC in England; it was also used in France by Emile GALLÉ. The best examples are sometimes cut or engraved to reveal the contrasting colour underneath; opaque layers on PAPERWEIGHTS were often cut with facets or "printies" to show the design within. Casing and overlay can be distinguished from FLASHING or staining by the thicker layers: the greatest number of layers is four, otherwise the object becomes opaque. *See also* CAMEO GLASS.

OVOLO The moulding of convex, quarter-circle sections. Sometimes found around the edges of drawers to form a small overlap onto the carcass.

OWL JUG An owl-shaped, slipware jug in which the head is detachable and forms a cup. The marbled effect found on many of these jugs was created by dipping the piece into brown and cream SLIPS, and combing the two to mix them slightly. Owl jugs have been faked, therefore, to determine an original, look for breaks and cracks in the glaze and wear on studs around the eyes. The handle should be irregularly shaped and heavy – on a fake it would be more even and finer. The base should be thickly potted and uneven – similarly, on a fake it would be thinner and regular in finish.

OXBOW Reverse SERPENTINE curve, which is exaggerated inwards.

OYSTER VENEER Decorative, veneered pattern produced by the VENEER being cut across the branch, then laid to create a geometric ringed effect.

P

PADDINGTON A TEDDY BEAR named after the railway station in London, England, where he arrived as a stowaway from darkest Peru, according to his creator Michael Bond. In fact, he came from Selfridges, where Bond was searching for a last-minute Christmas gift for his wife and thought the bear looked lonely. The story he devised was published in 1958, and illustrator Peggy Fortnum established the bear's shaggy appearance in a bush hat, duffle coat, and, later, Wellington boots. He is produced in the USA by Eden, and in Britain by Shirley Clarkson of Gabrielle Designs, who began by making a couple for her children one Christmas.

George III (1760–1820) silver PAIR-CASED WATCH by John Wilter, the outer case repoussé-decorated.

PAD FOOT Rounded foot resembling the padded foot of an animal. Very similar to a CLUB FOOT, but a little more exaggerated and larger.

PADOUK Hard and heavy, reddish wood with darker FIGURING, best known for its use in making military CHESTS.

PAGODAS Popular in the 19thC, CHINOISERIE figures of elderly men, some with nodding heads.

PAINTED BISQUE DOLL DOLL with a BISQUE head covered with a layer of paint but not fired, and hence susceptible to flaking.

PAIR-CASED WATCH A watch with a double case, standard from 1650 to *c*.1800. The movement itself was encased, and this fitted, for protection, into another outer case, like a jewellery box. The outer case was often ornate.

PAIRPOINT MANUFACTURING CO. A leading American GLASSmaker at the turn of the 19thC, Pairpoint was best known for its "Puffy" lamps, with mould-blown, glass shades in high relief, and hand-painted on the inside with flowers, such as roses and pansies. They also made a glass DECANTER with an inventive, circular shape, with the body similar to the shape of a doughnut.

PAKTONG CANDLESTICKS, fireside furniture, and ornaments made of an alloy of copper, zinc, and nickel in China for export to Europe in the 18thC.

PALAS Alternative name for a KELIM or flat-woven RUG.

PALLADIAN Items influenced by the designs or architecture of Antonio Palladio (1518–80). He was influential in reviving CLASSICAL Roman motifs.

PALLET Set either side of a CLOCK linkage, the arms that alternately engage and release the ESCAPEMENT wheel to regulate its movement.

PALMETTE Stylized, palm-leaf motif, used on Oriental CARPETS and FURNITURE.

PANACHE The plume on a helmet; also the plumes of feathers with which many 17thC TESTER beds were embellished. *See also* BED.

PAN COVER In FIREARMS, the lid over the pan that holds the priming powder – designed to protect the powder from rain and accidental firing. In early firearms, the cover had to be lifted manually. In the FLINTLOCK mechanism, it moves aside automatically as the serpent descends.

PANEL An area that is raised from or sunk into the surface of its framework.

PANEL CUT Decorations cut into GLASS using the face, rather than the edge, of a grinding wheel.

PANTIN ART GLASS made at Pantin, in France, in the second half of the 19thC.

PAP DISH Cup or BOWL with a spout for feeding infants or invalids.

PAPER KNIFE SILVER utensil designed for opening letters or turning the pages of large books to avoid soiling the pages. Many large paper knives were made in the shape of swords or scimitars. Smaller knives were probably used as bookmarks. Novelty paper knives are desirable, especially lavishly decorated examples with intricate handles.

St Louis, panelled, MilleFiori, closepack PAPERWEIGHT, c.1850.

PAPERWEIGHT Popular in the 19thC, a GLASS hemisphere encapsulating decorative coloured glass, or objects such as seashells. Paperweights made in the 1840s by the French glassmaking factories of BACCARAT, ST LOUIS, and CLICHY are regarded as some of the finest ever made. They can be grouped into two main categories: MILLEFIORI weights and "subject" weights. Millefiori weights have bases made of clusters of multi-coloured glass CANES encased in clear glass. Subject weights, reflecting the 19thC vogue for naturalistic ornament, incorporate naturalistic flowers, fruit, vegetables, animals, insects, and birds, created by manipulating glass RODS over an open flame or lamp. Some of the most expensive weights are those overlaid with white and coloured glass and cut with facets, showing the design inside. These were made by all three aforementioned French firms. Different colours, shapes, and arrangements of canes are associated with particular firms, such as a rose used by Clichy. You can often identify the maker of a paperweight by the type of rods it contains and the way in which they are arranged; paperweights are sometimes signed and dated in the canes, or they may be marked with initials. While the highest-quality weights were made by the three major

French factories, a number of firms elsewhere in Europe and the USA also produced weights from the 1850s to 1900. In England the WHITEFRIARS GLASSWORKS in London and George BACCHUS & SON of Birmingham created millefiori paperweights. For the Scottish factories, Caithness and MONCRIEFF'S GLASS WORKS, Paul YSART (b.1904) produced designs featuring flowers, fish, insects, and butterflies. Paperweight production flourished in the USA from the early 1850s, especially after craftsmen from the leading French factories emigrated there. The leading exponents were the NEW ENGLAND GLASS CO., the BOSTON & SANDWICH GLASS CO., the MOUNT WASHINGTON GLASS CO. (all in Massachusetts), and GILLINDER & SONS of Philadelphia. American and British weights are less expensive than the best French pieces. All French weights are highly collectable, and value is determined by rarity of colour or design. Size can be a determining factor in the value of a paperweight. Most weights measure 5–10cm (2½–4in) in diameter: weights over 10cm (4in) in diameter are known as "magnums", those less than 5cm (2½in), as "miniatures". Beware: reproductions of antique paperweights abound, but can be identified by their lighter weight.

PAPERWEIGHT CLOCK A 19thC CLOCK with a glass dome and brass base.

PAPERWEIGHT EYES Realistic, blown-glass "eyes" with white threads running through the irises, giving the impression of depth. Also known as spiral glass eyes, they are found on French BÉBÉS, especially those by JUMEAU.

PAPIER-MÂCHÉ Used from the early 18thC, paper pulp combined with glue was moulded to form small objects such as BOXES, wine COASTERS, and TRAYS, then painted with elaborate decoration of flowers, birds, or rural scenes, or JAPANNED. The material was sometimes applied over a metal frame to make large items of FURNITURE such as TABLES and CHAIRS. Sheets of wet paper were also pasted together and pressed in moulds to make a great deal of papier-mâché furniture in England in the Birmingham area, between 1820 and 1870. Once dried, the furniture was coated with layers of (usually) black LACQUER and decorated with gilt, painted decoration, and thin slivers of MOTHER-OF-PEARL. The firm JENNENS & BETTRIDGE is particularly associated with papier-mâché furniture; its stamp on a piece will add value. Spiers of Oxford, Henry CLAY, and B. Walton & Co. are other manufacturers popular among collectors; look for objects decorated by Edwin Haseler (flowers) and Frederick Newman (peacocks).

Victorian, Jennens & Bettridge PAPIER MACHÉ tray.

PAPIER-MÂCHÉ DOLL A DOLL with a PAPIER-MÂCHÉ head, introduced in Germany for commercial manufacture in 1800. However, papier-mâché dolls had been made in a lesser way in France, England, and elsewhere in Europe. The German dollmaker Friedrich Müller reputedly learned how to make papier-mâché from a French soldier. He then had the substance pressed into shape by moulds instead of making the dolls individually, so that production was almost mechanical and costs were reduced – thus the Sonneberg doll industry was founded. When dry, the heads were painted and varnished. The deep-yolked SHOULDER-HEADS of pre-1870, German, papier-mâché dolls were glued to bodies of KID or calico. They were unjointed, with narrow waists and wide hips. Joining points may be covered with a paper band, usually pink. Some dolls had wooden or kid lower limbs. Their hair was usually moulded, and their features were naively modelled, resembling WOODEN DOLLS of the same period, with moulded and painted black hair, painted eyes, and single-line eyebrows. Flesh tones vary between pinkish and yellowish. Hands are spoon-shaped, with only a separate thumb. Papier-mâché dolls are rarely marked. Sometimes known as milliners' models, dolls from the BIEDERMEIER period (1815–48) in Germany were the precursors to French FASHION DOLLS and are the most sought-after, 19thC, papier-mâché dolls. Elaborate hairstyles, high-waisted dresses, long necks, and thin faces are attributes from the 1820s and '30s. After this date, waists are lower and necks may be shorter. The hairstyles are also less complex, and the faces are chubbier and more childlike than on earlier examples. Some German heads were exported to France. French bodies were mostly made from pink kid, with one-piece limbs and a V-shaped, central seam on the lower torso. Some have hip and knee gussets and separately stitched fingers. Papier-mâché is difficult to restore, so condition is vital. Heads often crack, and this reduces value. Arms are usually straight, so if they are made of COMPOSITION and wire to allow them to bend, they are of a later date.

PARAGON Firm founded c.1903 in Staffordshire, England, and by the 1930s a leading maker of china tableware with printed and enamelled decoration. The firm's reputation was enhanced by royal patronage – much of its TEA WARES are stamped "Replica of service produced for Her Majesty Queen Mary". Its NURSERY WARE was used by the British princesses Elizabeth and Margaret.

PARAISON Bubble of molten GLASS that has been partially inflated on the end of a PONTIL ROD or blowpipe. *See also* FREE-BLOWING.

PARASOL Umbrella-like device for providing shade when outdoors. Silk parasols with IVORY handles, fitted with richly decorated SILVER mounts were produced in large numbers in the 19thC for the hot climates of colonial settlements in India and the Far East. Local silversmiths were employed to fashion the silver mounts for walking canes, swagger sticks, riding crops, and parasols, which are rarely hallmarked. A parasol in good condition can be affordable.

PARCEL GILDING SILVER that has been gilded to make it resemble GOLD, as well as to protect it from tarnishing. The technique is used for highlighting decoration. The dangerous method of mercury gilding was replaced by the safer electrogilding in the mid-19thC. Silver DRINKING VESSELS were often gilded on the inside to preserve the metal from corrosion caused by the acid present in wine.

Bone china, lion-handled cup by PARAGON to commemorate the 80th birthday of the British Queen Mother, 1980.

Copeland PARIAN figure after an original by Joseph Durham, entitled "Go to Sleep", stamped with "Art Union of London", 1862.

PARCEL GILT A wood object that is partially gilded with GOLD.

PARIAN A fine white BISCUIT PORCELAIN, named after Roman marble quarries at Paros. It was a popular 19thC material used to make small, inexpensive CLASSICAL statuary in imitation of marble sculpture. COPELAND and MINTON both claim to have invented Parian in the 1840s, and, by the mid-19thC, many other factories were also producing it. Other leading factories that used the material include WEDGWOOD and Robinson & Leadbeater, a firm specializing in Parian. Copeland called the substance "statuary porcelain" in the early days, while Wedgwood termed its version "Carrara ware" after another famous Italian marble quarry. Parian contains a high proportion of glass crystals, and its vitreous nature means that dirt does not adhere to it. Parian figures depicting famous royal, political, and literary figures were popular; copies of famous works from antiquity were also made. Value depends on a piece's maker, its decorative appeal, and its size. Parian figures are usually marked by the maker on the base or back of the model. Some pieces may also be titled and have a date code. Parian figures are often stamped with names such as "The Crystal Palace Union" or "Art Union of London". To raise funds for the arts, "art unions" ran lotteries where art lovers could buy tickets to win an original work such as a Parian figure. Copeland was one of the firms who made figures for art unions.

PARIAN DOLL A DOLL with a head made from unglazed, untinted, HARD-PASTE PORCELAIN. PARIAN dolls were made from 1870 to the end of the 19thC, using the same porcelain paste that was employed for china dolls, but with the paste left unglazed for a matt finish. The dolls have a white, marble-like skin tone. Most of these dolls were made in Germany. Bisque lower limbs were attached to stuffed bodies, which had narrow waists and wide hips. Parian dolls tend to have a sugary appearance due to the paste used, and this is usually emphasized by fancy garments with lace and frills. Blonde hair is most common, and on the best dolls hair is in elaborate styles, sometimes adorned with moulded ornaments or applied flowers. Parian dolls were often moulded with pieces of JEWELLERY or clothing, which were painted and fired with facial details. Many examples have pierced ears. Late -19thC dolls may have moulded bonnets, and the faces became more rounded and childlike, with short necks and simple hairstyles set low on the forehead. Due to their fragility, parian dolls are rare. Some restoration or unrestored damage is acceptable, and even heads without bodies are collectable.

PARIS Products of a number of CERAMICS factories in the French capital, but principally the late -18thC PORCELAIN in the SÈVRES style.

PARISIENNE DOLL Term first used by JUMEAU to describe its FASHION DOLL, but basically any French, BISQUE-head doll with a stuffed KID body. Made by various manufacturers from the 1860s to the '80s. *See also* DOLL.

PARKESINE Early form of plastic invented by Alexander Parkes and produced between 1862 and 1868. It was used for making toys, combs, and buttons.

PARQUETRY Popular in the 17th and early 19thC, MARQUETRY decoration, in which the whole surface of the wood is made up of separate, geometric-shaped pieces of wood (like a parquet floor). Due to its elaborate nature, parquetry is found on smaller furniture, such as REGENCY tables and tea caddies.

PARTRIDGE WOOD Brown-and-red wood with streaks suggesting plumage. It was imported from Central and South America and used as a VENEER.

PASSGLAS A German, 16thC GLASS BEAKER marked into sections, each showing the measure to drink as it was passed round during a toast.

PASTILLE BURNER Ceramic object for burning pastilles of compressed herbs as air fresheners. Burners in the shape of cottages or castles (with smoke going through the chimney or tower) were popular in the early 19thC.

PATCH BOX A small BOX made to hold tiny, cut-out paper shapes that were originally worn by women to mask unsightly smallpox scars. In the 18thC, it became fashionable among ladies of fashion – and male beaux – to apply the patches as imitation beauty spots. Such dainty boxes are now used to hold pills, mints, and powder. *See also* BEAUTY SPOT.

PATCH FIGURES Term for early English PORCELAIN figures, with unglazed patches on the base, where they were supported during firing.

PATCH STAND Dating from *c*.1710 to *c*.1760, a small TAZZA on a BALUSTER STEM with an upturned rim. Probably used to hold BEAUTY SPOTS in the 18thC.

PATCHWORK QUILT A QUILT comprising scraps of cloth sewn together to form a patterned surface. In the USA, there are numerous regional types with characterful names. These quilts were popular in New England from the late 17thC, but most of the surviving examples date from the 19thC.

PATE The covering of a doll's head aperture to which the wig was attached. The pate gives a rounded rather than a flat or indented effect. French DOLLS used cork pates, harvested from Portuguese "cork oak" trees. German dolls had cardboard pates, which were moulded and cut to fit snugly into the aperture and glued with light fish glue. The German firm of KESTNER & CO. was known for making "plaster" pates, which were difficult to remove.

PÂTE-DE-CRISTAL (French for "crystal paste") Translucent glassware made from finely powdered GLASS made into a paste and shaped using the "lost-wax" method.

18thC, enamel, combination scent bottle and PATCH BOX, possibly of French origin.

PÂTE-DE-VERRE (French for "glass paste") An ancient Egyptian technique reinvented by ART NOUVEAU glassmakers, whereby GLASS was ground up into a paste, moulded into the desired shape, then fired like POTTERY, producing a translucent, soft-edged glass.

PATERA Small, flat, circular ornament, often in the form of an open flower or rosette. Used as a ceiling or FURNITURE ornament.

PATERSON REVOLVER Progenitor of the Colt pistol, made at Paterson, New Jersey, USA, in the first half of the 19thC. *See also* FIREARMS.

PÂTE-SUR-PÂTE A refined, cameo-like, applied decoration, created by building up layers of translucent white PORCELAIN SLIP on a contrasting BODY, and carving back to create a low-relief design. The technique was used by the SÈVRES factory in the 19thC, and it was introduced to the MINTON, and the English market, by Marc-Louis Solon, a former employee of Sèvres.

PATINA (Patination) The surface colour and sheen of FURNITURE and SILVER that is built up from years of use and careful polishing – an effect that is hard to fake or reproduce. A rich, mellow colour is one of the most important features of any item of furniture. The glow that wood develops over the years is from an accumulation of wax polish and dirt. Most furniture is not the same colour all over – grooves and carving will look darker, while surfaces exposed to sunlight may be lighter. Deep patina is less favoured by the European market, where furniture is often stripped and repolished to give an almost "new" look. However, repolished English furniture is often devalued in the English market. On silver, years of use and an accumulation of scratches, knocks, and bruises cause a soft glow to develop. This patina is important to value. Repolishing old silver on a buffing wheel can destroy the patina of a piece and is always considered undesirable. *See also* FURNITURE CARE.

PATINATED The desirable, dull-green colour of ancient BRONZE, caused by oxidization of the metal, as distinct from the undesirable, bright-green verdigris, which occurs when bronze is attacked by an acid solution.

PATTERN-MOULDED GLASS A type of GLASS in which the molten material is pressed into a mould to impress the pattern, before the vessel is then blown into its finished form.

PATTERN NUMBER Introduced on PORCELAIN *c.*1790 and used until it was superseded by the design REGISTRATION MARKS of 1842. These numbers are useful for dating porcelain patterns and, occasionally, for identifying the precise place of production – although few patterns were unique to one factory.

PAW FOOT Foot that somewhat resembles a paw, usually with claws.

PEACH BLOOM Pale red to brown glaze with a silvery bloom like a peach's skin. Developed in China and used in the West in the late 19th and early 20thC.

PEACHBLOW Late -19thC, peach-coloured ART GLASS, first made by the NEW ENGLAND GLASS CO., USA.

PEACH OPAL A clear opalescent GLASS to which golden iridescence is added.

PEACOCK & SONS Founded in 1853, a British maker of TEDDY BEARS, taken over by CHAD VALLEY in 1930, although it retained the Peacock name. Their bears are noted for their angular heads, chunky arms, and arched, square snouts with heavy black stitching, and have red-and-white Peacock labels on the right foot.

PEAR DROP Descriptive of a pear-shaped DROP HANDLE.

PEARLWARE A variation of CREAMWARE with a slightly blue tinge. Developed by WEDGWOOD in 1779, and also popular with other POTTERY manufacturers in the 19thC, it was used to produce a variety of decorative figures and novelty wares, and was left white or decorated with coloured enamels. Late -18th or early -19thC models of sheep are favourites, as are figurative groups. Pearlware figures in high-fired colours are often called PRATTWARE.

PÊCHÉ MORTEL Meaning "mortal sin", the name of a French SOFA made of a STOOL and EASY CHAIR placed together.

PECK, MRS LUCY English maker of poured-wax DOLLS, active 1891 – 1921.

PEDESTAL DESK Introduced in the 1670s, a WRITING TABLE with two pedestals of drawers below the writing and working area. GEORGIAN and REGENCY pedestal desks, with leather-lined tops and well-figured VENEERS, are popular. Some were designed to be free standing, and have drawers on one side and cabinets on the other; the back was plainly veneered or, if it was to stand against a wall, left unfinished. Others are known as partners' desks and can be used by two people at the same time. Partners' desks have drawers on both sides of the frieze, and their pedestals have drawers on one side and cupboards on the other. The cupboards sometimes have dummy drawer fronts. Small desks are sometimes called KNEEHOLE DESKS. The Victorians (1837–1901) improved the simple, Georgian pedestal design by adding a gallery and banks of drawers on top, and an upholstered footrest in the space between the pedestals. Kidney and serpentine forms are popular shapes on small, drawing-room pieces. Other quality features to look for include metal mounts or carved decoration, and good-quality locks.

PEDESTAL STEM Early to mid-18thC wineglass STEM that is fluted and thicker at the top than at the base.

Staffordshire, PEARLWARE figure group – musicians with a flock of sheep, c.1810.

19thC PEDLAR peg doll, holding a pedlar tray containing miniature dolls, needles, threads, and glass-bead jewellery.

PEDESTAL TABLE Also known as a PILLAR TABLE, and made continuously from the 18thC to the present day, a practical table with legs attached to one or more central pedestals. Pedestal DINING TABLES were featured in the late 18thC pattern books of George HEPPLEWHITE and Thomas SHERATON, but they had become less fashionable by the 1820s, by which time multi-legged styles were favoured. At the beginning of the Edwardian period (1901–10), when smaller tables were more desirable, dealers often rounded the corners of sections from large pedestal tables to make them into two or more BREAKFAST TABLES. Original 18th- or early 19thC tables, especially those with three or more pedestals, are now rare. Pedestal dining tables are copied today, often to a high standard. Reproductions are smaller, with thinner tops and legs, and do not have the depth of PATINA that you would see in a period example. Value depends on age and the number of pedestals. Before you buy one, fit any extra leaves in the table to check that they haven't warped. Signs of age include a solid MAHOGANY top (usually without CROSSBANDING or INLAY), "reeded" edges to tops, and brass casters – plain or cast as lion's paws.

PEDIGREE SOFT TOYS English, London-based, firm responsible for the popular doll "Sindy". It also made "Pedigree", a 1950s', all-plastic, "walking" doll with "FLIRTY" EYES, which move from side-to-side if the head is shaken. A feature of this doll is that children can shampoo its hair without causing any damage. The firm was taken over by Dunbee Combex Marx, then Tamwade.

PEDIMENT Decorative feature on top of CASE FURNITURE or LONGCASE CLOCKS.

PEDIMENT BAROMETER Mid-18th to early 19thC stick barometers, so-called because the top housing is carved in the shape of a pediment. Elaborate examples incorporate thermometers and hygrometers.

PEDLAR DOLL An early form of GRÖDNERTAL DOLL (some date back to the 1830s), pedlar dolls carried trays or baskets of wares in imitation of pedlars.

PEEP-SHOW Box with a small front aperture and a series of painted-glass or printed-card scenes designed to create a three-dimensional effect. Originally an architectural aid, but produced as a toy from the early 19thC.

PEG Used to hold MORTISE-AND-TENON joints in FURNITURE until the late 17thC. Early pegs were handmade and slightly protrude from the surface, because wood shrinks across the grain over time. Later, machine-made pegs are symmetrical, and are either flush with the surface or slightly recessed.

PEG DOLL (Peg wooden) An early WOODEN DOLL with simple peg joints.

PEG TANKARD Late -17thC form of TANKARD with internal peg markers, used for communal drinking. Peculiar to northern England and Scotland.

PEMBROKE TABLE A small rectangular, serpentine, circular, or oval TABLE, with curved corners, drop flaps supported on small, hinged members known as "flys", and drawers. It was introduced in the mid-18thC, and named after the Countess of Pembroke, who supposedly ordered the first one. "Pembroke" table was used interchangeably with BREAKFAST TABLE; both were used for light meals – breakfast and tea – or as WORK TABLES. SHERATON-style Pembroke tables were copied in the late 19th and early 20thC. Later reproductions are covered in thin, machine-cut VENEERS.

PEN, DIP From the 1840s, the most widely used writing instrument until ink-flow systems became standard in fountain pens from the late 19thC. Many SILVER dip pens were made, including some examples that were part of desk sets or that had stands or trays. Decorated versions were produced as symbols of wealth, and incorporated FILIGREE, REPOUSSÉ, NIELLO, and engraving. Examples bearing makers' MARKS are particularly sought after by collectors.

PEN, FOUNTAIN A pen containing a cartridge or other reservoir in the pen's barrel, which supplies the nib with ink for writing. Fountain pens have been made since the 17thC, in an array of imaginative styles. They became widely available from the late 19thC, and most examples date from this period. The quality and originality of the decoration, the maker, and the quality and size of the nib determine the value of these pens. Condition is important, because fountain pens can be expensive to restore; check for signs of excessive wear. Avoid pens with replacement parts, which have often been forced or glued to the body. In particular, look out for specially designed, large, and oversized pens. Quality pens (before 1945) by these makers are especially desirable: Parker (before 1930), Waterman, Montblanc, Dunhill-Namiki, Wahl-Eversharp, Sheaffer, and Mabie Todd (Swan).

PENCIL, SILVER A thin rod of lead fitted into a SILVER case, these pencils were made by silversmiths who bought the internal mechanisms and produced fitted pencil cases, as well as by large specialist manufacturers. Many elaborate novelty pencils were made by leading jewellers, and these can be valuable. Notable makers include Hicks of New York, Butler, Fairchild, and Sampson Mordan & Co. By the mid-19thC, retractable examples that could be attached to CHÂTELAINES were fashionable.

PENDULUM A brass or steel rod with, at the bottom (usually lead cased in brass), a metal disk, or BOB, used to control the speed of a CLOCK by swinging in a regular arc. On a VERGE ESCAPEMENT the bob is on a threaded rod; on an ANCHOR ESCAPEMENT, the bob slides on the rod and can be locked in place by tightening a nut. Adjusting the bob on the rod alters the clock's timekeeping.

PENDULUM CLOCK Any CLOCK regulated by the swinging of a PENDULUM. They have been made and widely distributed since the mid 17thC.

Rare Sheaffer engraved, gold-plated lever-fill FOUNTAIN PEN, 1920s.

PENKNIFE Originally, a knife used for cutting a point on a quill pen. Made from *c.*1750, sometimes in novelty shapes or with ornate handles.

PENNER A portable writing set, consisting of a tubular casing for holding a short quill with an INKWELL (often stuffed with wool to absorb the ink and reduce leakage) at one end and a POUNCE holder at the other. Fittings stored inside the casing include: tubular sections incorporating a PENKNIFE; folding rules with scales; dividers; and nib sections for holding quill nibs. Less-valuable penners were made *c.*1800 in Birmingham, England, by makers such as Joseph Taylor and Samuel Pemberton. Fine examples are collectable.

PENNINGTON BROTHERS English, Liverpool-based potters, active from *c.*1769 to 1799 and noted for jugs and BOWLS painted with ships.

PENNSYLVANIA BABY Late -18thC, North American DOLL of carved and painted pine. *See also* WOODEN DOLL.

PENNSYLVANIA DUTCH STYLE A provincial art style developed from German and Northern European immigrants who settled in Pennsylvania, North America. From the Colonial period, simply constructed FURNITURE is brightly painted, or sometimes carved and painted with a pastel-coloured "milk" paint. From the 19thC, POTTERY was made of REDWARE, often decorated with SGRAFFITO; TINWARE items such as COFFEE-POTS are also typical. The most common motifs found on Pennsylvania Dutch items are simple but stylized tulips and birds, or a pinwheel. Red, yellow, and blue colours are favoured.

PENNY FARTHING One of the first forms of the bicycle to be produced in quantity, from *c.*1870, so-called because of the relative sizes of the large front wheel (penny) and small back one (farthing).

Glass PENNY LICK, *c.*1910–20.

PENNY LICK A robust small GLASS with a thick-walled, moulded bowl, short, sturdy stem, and wide, flat foot. "Penny licks" were made from the 19thC to the early 20thC for ice-cream vendors to sell an old British penny's worth of ice cream. A slightly larger version was called a "tuppenny lick".

PENNYWEIGHT Smallest measure in the TROY WEIGHT system of weighing SILVER, GOLD, and PRECIOUS STONES. It is usually abbreviated to "dwt".

PENNY WOODEN A crudely carved, WOODEN DOLL sold at fairs and market stalls, especially toward end of the 19thC. "Penny" reflects the cost.

PENWORK Decoration techinque whereby a piece is JAPANNED black, painted with designs in white japan, then more clearly defined by detailed line work.

PEPPER BOX (1) American term for a PEPPER CASTER.

PEPPERBOX (2) Repeating FIREARM with a revolving barrel with five or six chambers; an early -19thC progenitor of the revolver.

PEPPER CASTER A caster for serving pepper. Most early -18thC examples were cylindrical with high-domed covers. The covers then became lower, with simpler piercings, and single scroll handles were added. Long-necked examples with slightly baluster-shaped bodies were popular *c*.1735. By 1730, casters no longer had handles, and the pear shape was the most typical. The FINIALS and handles are prone to wear and may have been replaced. Watch out for MARRIAGES of a body and a cover; a difference in the colour of the PATINA of the two parts is a good indication that they have been married. The covers of pepper casters should be original and fit snugly.

PERCUSSION LOCK Early 19thC FIREARM that is fired by the impact of a sharp-nosed hammer on the cartridge cap. It superseded the FLINTLOCK.

PERFUME BOTTLE *See* SCENT BOTTLE.

PERIOD When used as an adjective such as a "period table", it means that the item was made at the time that the design would suggest and is not, for example, a later copy.

PERIWIG CHAIR A late -17thC CHAIR with a tall, caned back and a carved, arched CRESTING RAIL, often with a similarly carved STRETCHER at the front legs.

PERPETUAL CLOCK CALENDAR CLOCK with a dial marked with a one-year (and sometimes a four-year) calendar, as opposed to one marked with the numerals 1 to 31. It therefore never needs adjusting.

PERSIAN KNOT *See* SENNEH KNOT.

PETIT-FEU ENAMELS (French for "little fire"). Low-temperature colours used in FAIENCE decoration, allowing the use of a wider range of colours and tones than high-temperature colours. *See also* FRENCH FAIENCE.

PETIT PORCELAIN Made in the 19thC, revivals of ROCOCO figure groups and ornate CLOCK cases from the factory of Jacob Petit of Fontainebleau, France.

PETUNTSE China stone. A granite used to make HARD-PASTE PORCELAIN and hard, white, porcelain glazes.

PEWABIC POTTERY Art pottery established by Mary Chase Perry (1868–1961) in Detroit, Michigan, USA, in 1903. It produced thrown vases decorated with IRIDESCENT, crystalline, or matt glazes, as well as architectural ceramics and tiles, until the 1950s.

A Jacob PETIT Paris porcelain flask and stopper modelled as a seated monkey wearing 18thC women's attire, 19thC.

A 1960s Rosenthal soap dish showing Peeping Tom and Lady in the Bath, by Raymond PEYNET.

PEW GROUP English, 18thC group of two or three EARTHENWARE figures seated on a church pew. Reproduced in the 19th and 20thC.

PEWTER Also known as "poor man's silver", an alloy made of tin and lead in varying proportions. The most commonly found objects are 18thC PLATES, but pewter was also used to make FLATWARE and TANKARDS. Until *c*.1826, the Pewterers' Co. laid down stringent standards for the industry: the size and weight of pewter objects was controlled, MARKS were used to designate the fineness of the alloy, and a maker was required to stamp his productions with his own mark. After 1826, capacity marks were required by law on tavern pieces. In the USA, pewter was imported from Europe until the 18thC. Some early US pewter bears an "X" mark to indicate quality. From *c*.1750 to 1850 American-made pewter became more available, and the quality was usually good. In Britain and Germany, high-quality ART NOUVEAU pewter was popular. Decorated with Celtic motifs, the "TUDRIC" range of LIBERTY & CO. included TEA and COFFEE SERVICES as well as CLOCKS, tableware, BOWLS, and VASES. The chief German exponent was Engelbert KAYSER (1840–1911). Owners' marks and coats of arms on old pewter can enhance its value. Pewter more than 50 years old develops a dull, glowing PATINA. Most modern copies are noticeably lighter in weight than old British and American pieces. Look for signs of wear consistent with age: the undersides of objects should be covered with a fine patina of scratches, and the edges of plates and hollow wares should be smooth.

PEYNET, RAYMOND (1908–99) French illustrator of stylized people, using linework and pastel colours. After the firm of ROSENTHAL approached Peynet in 1952, his illustrations featured on much pottery over the subsequent decade. His work is also found on items by the Danish company Nymolle.

PHENAKISTOSCOPE A 19thC form of MAGIC LANTERN in which the pictures are mounted around the rim of a disc and spun to simulate movement.

PHILADELPHIA CHIPPENDALE FURNITURE made in the USA in the style of Thomas CHIPPENDALE, notably work by Thomas AFFLECK and William SAVERY.

PHOENIX GLASS Made in Pittsburgh, USA, in the late 19thC by the Phoenix Glassworks, a specialist in MILK GLASS (known locally as "mother-of-pearl").

PHOENIXVILLE Pennsylvanian maker of MAJOLICA in the mid- to late -19thC.

PHONOGRAPH Predecessor of the record player, patented by Edison in 1877; plays a recorded drum cylinder rather than a disc. It developed over the next three decades, and successive innovations can be dated by the patent number. All early models are of interest to collectors, especially ones with finely decorated cabinets and shapely horns. Prices fall substantially for post-1920 models. *See also* GRAMOPHONE.

PHOTOGRAPH A printed image of a person, object, or scene, taken with a CAMERA. Old negatives and photographs are collectable. Prior to 1870, the main interest is in their technical merit; afterward the subject, photographer, and aesthetic merits are paramount. Be cautious of an attribution to a famous photographer that cannot be proved. Many fakes are now known. Pictures of famous subjects are collectable, but the price should reflect the quantity of prints in circulation and the age of the print.

PHOTOGRAVURE A 19thC process for printing a photograph in which a negative is applied to a metal plate, which is etched or engraved.

PHRENOLOGICAL SKULL Ivory or wood object in the form of a human skull, mapped out with lines showing how variations in skull shape, from one person to another, are supposed to determine character and fortune.

PHYFE, DUNCAN (1768–1854) Scottish-born master cabinet-maker who worked in New York, producing designs with roots in English REGENCY (SHERATON) and french EMPIRE STYLES. His FURNITURE is both elegant and distinctive, and often incorporates the LYRE motif. He retired in 1847.

PIANO BABY Made by GEBRÜDER HEUBACH, an all-BISQUE figurine of a baby, intended for display on a piano. Piano babies and larger, mantelpiece babies should bear the Heubach mark. Other firms made similar DOLLS, but these are unmarked and much less valuable. *See also* BÉBÉ.

PIANO-TOP A DAVENPORT desk that has a curved, rising top, shaped like that of a piano.

PICHET Used from the 16th to 18thC, a small, French, pear-shaped TANKARD with a foot-ring.

PICTURE CLOCK A CLOCK with a case painted with a scene that places the dial in an appropriate setting, such as in a church tower in a rural landscape.

PICTURE FRAME A frame used to display a photograph. In the 1880s, the CAMERAS made for the amateur photographer, and the development of roll film made photography accessible to a wider audience. Frames were created in standard sizes to meet the demand for a place to display these images. Picture frames come in a variety of styles, with doubles being especially popular. The frames contain little silver, and frequent polishing over time leaves many in a damaged condition; such examples should be avoided. All picture frames, unlike mirror frames, have detachable backs held on with swivel clips. The mount, velvet backing, and strut should be in good condition, and modern reproductions, where the pattern is weakly stamped out of thin metal, should be avoided. If picture frames still have their

Victorian burr walnut PIANO TOP by Davenport, c.1860.

Glass diamond-cut PIGGIN with fan-cut handles, Irish, c.1815.

original glass, check the latter at the corners to ensure it is not chipped. Better-quality frames feature BEVELLED glass. With American frames, be suspicious if you encounter English marks, because they are usually fake.

PIECRUST Carved and scalloped decorative edge, commonly seen on dish-top TRIPOD TABLES and on SILVER. It resembles the rim of a crusty pie.

PIERCED DECORATION SILVER decoration created by making tiny cuts through the material to create a decorative design, or for a more practical purpose, such as to make holes in the top of a sugar caster. The tedious and time-consuming process, which was carried out by hand until the late 18thC, initially involved using a chisel to punch out the patterns. From the 1770s, this was done with a fretsaw. Hand piercing was eventually replaced by mechanical piercing. In the 18thC, pierced decoration was favoured for decorative tableware, including ÉPERGNES, MUSTARD POTS, SALT CELLARS with glass liners, DISH RINGS, and CAKE BASKETS. Hand-pierced decoration tends to be slightly rough, while machine piercing is more precise and consistent. The thin-gauge silver used from the late 18thC is vulnerable to damage if pierced.

PIER GLASS Made from the mid-17thC, a MIRROR partnered by a PIER TABLE.

PIEROTTI FAMILY London-based makers of poured-wax DOLLS, active in England in the 19th and early 20thC.

PIER TABLE A table designed to fit in a pier – the wall space between two windows; made from the 18thC, usually in pairs. They are similar to CONSOLE TABLES, but have back supports. Expensive woods were used, such as ROSEWOOD, MAHOGANY, and GILTWOOD. Examples with a decorative appearance and in semi-circular or serpentine shapes are desirable. REGENCY-STYLE versions often have MIRRORS below to reflect light, and original glass is a bonus on these. Look for ones with original or traditional gilding.

PIETRE DURE Italian term, meaning "hard stones". Slivers of hard and semi-precious stones used to decorate FURNITURE and JEWELLERY, notably from Florence.

PIGEONHOLE Open compartment found in the internal fittings of a BUREAU.

PIGGIN A small, cylindrical, GLASS, CERAMIC, or SILVER vessel. Glass types, used for ladling milk, were popular, especially in Ireland, c.1800. Silver ones, a variation on the cream pail, were used to hold clotted cream; they were popular from the 1740s to the 1760s, particularly in Scotland, and are rare.

"PIGS IN CORN" American glassware pattern found on a pair of pressed-glass GOBLETS, with the design on one mirroring that on the other. Coloured DRINKING GLASSES are scarce.

PILE Fine fibrous surface, or nap, of a CARPET. It is created by looping yarn through the WARP, so that the loops form a dense mat.

PILGRIM FURNITURE Early American FURNITURE. A pilgrim chair refers to an open ARMCHAIR made with turned elements and a rush seat.

PILKINGTON'S TILE & POTTERY CO. British company known for its ART NOUVEAU ceramics, notably those with IRIDESCENT and colourful glazes.

PILLAR CLOCK A CLOCK in which the hour hand moves up and down a vertical scale.

PILLAR-CUTTING A type of decorative cut found on GLASS wares, such as DECANTERS, featuring broad flutes cut in relief with rounded edges.

PILLAR TABLE *See* PEDESTAL TABLE.

PILL BOX *See* PATCH BOX.

PIN-BACK BADGE Circular, transfer-printed badge with a pin for attaching it to clothing. The earliest and most collectable examples date to *c*.1918.

PINCHBECK Early -18thC, copper-and-zinc alloy invented by Christopher Pinchbeck for use as a GOLD substitute, especially for watch cases and JEWELLERY.

PINCHED GLASS Decorative motifs on GLASS made by pinching the BODY with hand tools while it is still soft.

PINCUSHION FIGURE A DOLL'S head, designed to be sewn into a pincushion, and sometimes the arms and trunk as well. Usually only the head was sold, and the purchaser then made up the pincushion.

PINE A soft, pale, honey-coloured, straight-grained wood, pine (*Pinus*) was used in England as a secondary timber and for drawer linings. Pine is easy to carve and was used as a base for gilt MIRRORS. In provincial areas in the early 18thC, it was sometimes used for the sides of WALNUT pieces and stained to match. It was also used as a base for painted and JAPANNED furniture and, more commonly from *c*.1800, as a carcass wood, especially for the backs of CASE FURNITURE. Many inexpensive items of bedroom and kitchen furniture were made from pine, then painted. The most common type of pine is the European redwood, or "Scots" pine. In North America, hard, yellow, and white pines were used as secondary woods. *See also* PINE KITCHEN FURNITURE.

PINEAPPLE WARE Yellow-and-green, glazed POTTERY in the shape of the fruit, made in the 18thC.

Free-standing PINE plate rack, c.1880.

PINE KITCHEN FURNITURE From the late 18thC onward, PINE was used for inexpensive FURNITURE that was painted. The techniques for decorating pine were often inventive, and included scumble (softening the painted finish by applying an opaque top coat of a different shade), faux marbling, and graining to simulate expensive woods. In recent years, there has been increased demand for old pine with its original painted finish. Much early pine kitchen furniture was built into a room. As the fashion for stripped pine grew in the 1960s, many pieces were removed and converted into free-standing pieces. It is rare to find a piece of pine furniture in its original condition; most has been adapted, stripped, or converted to suit modern tastes. However, these pieces can be just as valuable. Watch out for pine furniture that is made from old floorboards; it is still worth buying, but do not pay the price of a genuine antique. High-back, pine ARMCHAIRS are common, especially those constructed with shaped, flat-slatted backs and turned legs and stretchers. LADDER BACKS are another popular style of pine kitchen CHAIR. A single chair is of little value, but its value might double if it were part of a set of six or more. Look for late Victorian (1860–1901) and Edwardian (1901–10) extending tables with winding mechanisms. Make sure that the leaves are original by comparing the colour and grain of the wood. Before buying a plank-top table, try sitting at it first. A table with a deep frieze can be uncomfortable if it has been reduced in height, particularly if you are tall. About 76cm (30in) will be high enough to suit most people. Look out for small, pine kitchen items such as washboards, meat safes, plate racks, clothes airers, and spoon racks. Beware: plate racks and airers are in short supply, and reproductions have been made. Check the joints of stripped pine furniture carefully for strength and firmness; any glued joints may be seriously weakened. *See also* DINING CHAIR and DINING TABLE.

PIN HINGE Simple hinge of two linked loops, found on early CHESTS.

PINXTON Founded by William BILLINGSLEY in the English village of Pinxton, Derbyshire, a PORCELAIN factory in which SOFT-PASTE PORCELAIN was made between 1796 and 1801. From 1804, the factory was under the management of John Cutts. In the early stages the porcelain, GLAZE, and designs were similar to those found on wares produced by DERBY. The BODY has good translucency, and the palette has a yellow-brown look; these wares are sought after. A fine, creamy-white glaze with the occasional suggestion of blue was used, and the enamels tend to have subdued or pastel tones. The factory is well known for its flower painting (some no doubt by Billingsley). It closed in 1813.

PIONEER SWORD Issued to pioneers from the late 18thC, a SWORD with a saw-edge. It was used as a tool as well as a weapon.

PIPE-BACKED BLADE Early -19thC blade with a solid, cylindrical rib running down the back edge for two-thirds of its length.

PIPKIN *See* BRANDY SAUCEPAN.

PITCHER Large jug of BALUSTER form, with tall, narrow neck and lug handles.

PITKIN GLASS Small oval bottle or flask with moulded ribbing made in America (Connecticut) from *c*.1800.

PITTSBURGH High-quality, American, pressed GLASS made in the late 17thC at various glassworks in Pittsburgh.

PLANCK, ERNST German mass-producer of toy locomotives from *c*.1890.

PLANISH In SILVER, the stage before polishing to finish the surface of plate. A flat-headed hammer removes the marks that are made in raising.

PLANISPHERE SCIENTIFIC INSTRUMENT for calculating distances in relation to points such as stars or planets.

PLASTERWARE Figure groups or sculpture cast in plaster of Paris from the early 18thC.

PLASTIC DOLL A DOLL made from hard plastic after World War II. By the mid-1950s, they had been replaced by VINYL. The AMERICAN ALEXANDER DOLL CO. was one of the best-known makers of early plastic dolls. PEDIGREE SOFT TOYS made "Pedigree", a 1950s, all-plastic, walking doll. Plastic dolls had moulded hair or wigs, while vinyl dolls have rooted hair. The wigs were usually attached to a cardboard or cork PATE. A doll must be in excellent condition in order to be valuable, preferably with the hair still as originally set. *See also* VINYL DOLL.

PLASTIC SOLDIER Toy soldier made of various plastics by injection moulding, introduced *c*.1947.

1950s Pedigree hard PLASTIC DOLL.

PLASTIQUE An object made from an early form of plastic, such as PARKESINE or BAKELITE.

PLATE (1) Originally applied to GOLD and SILVER domestic wares, this term now refers to objects made of base metal and covered with silver, either by fusion, such as SHEFFIELD PLATE, or by ELECTROPLATING.

PLATE (2) A shallow object for holding food, forming part of a DINNER SERVICE. With the exception of border decoration, SILVER plate design changed little in the 18th and 19thC. Plates were rarely made in different sizes or shapes, so border decoration is the key to determining the date. Early plates have broad, flat borders, are decorated with engraved crests or coats of arms,

and are usually marked underneath. New borders were often added, and rims reshaped according to contemporary fashions, which commonly resulted in lost or damaged MARKS. Elaborate borders were popular during the REGENCY period, when fine, silver dinner services were commissioned by aristocratic families from such leading silversmiths as Philip RUNDELL, Paul STORR, and Benjamin Smith. By the 1840s, PORCELAIN services were popular, and most silver plates were made as additions to or replacements for earlier services. Soup plates are distinguished from dinner plates by deeper central wells, and in general are less valuable than dinner plates. The most desirable sets are those with 12 plates. Often, the number and weight of each item in a set was inscribed on its base. This may show how many items were in the set and, by a change in weight, if a piece has been altered.

PLATE PEWTER An early form of PEWTER, made of TIN and COPPER rather than tin and lead, and used for making FLATWARE in the 16th and 17thC.

PLATFORM BASE Flat base found below the column of a TABLE.

PLAYING CARDS Made since the 14thC, if not earlier, and originally hand-painted, playing cards were printed from copper plates from the 17thC, often with satirical or propagandist themes. Their development is linked with that of the printing press. The "joker" first appeared in American packs in the 1860s, and in Britain by the 1880s, which is when most cards had rounded corners. In the 20thC, playing cards were widely used for marketing, and these are collectable by those interested in advertising memorabilia.

PLINTH Base around the bottom of an item of FURNITURE not raised on feet.

PLIQUE-À-JOUR Rarely found on English SILVER, a form of ENAMELLING that was popular for small objects, such as spoons and ladles, in Scandinavia, France, and Russia. The enamel is held in an unbacked metal framework, which creates the effect of a stained-glass window. This technique was favoured for items decorated in the delicate and sinuous, ART NOUVEAU style.

PLUG BAYONET Dating to the 17thC, the earliest form of BAYONET, designed to plug into a musket barrel after it had been fired. *See also* FIREARMS.

PLUM PUDDING A type of FIGURING, with dark oval spots in the wood, in some types of VENEER. It is found particularly in MAHOGANY.

PLUSH Fabric with a long, loosely woven, cut PILE, used as fur on TEDDY BEARS.

Northern European PLUG BAYONET, c.1680–90.

PLYMOUTH The first factory to make HARD-PASTE PORCELAIN in England, it was founded in *c.*1768 by Cookworthy, who had discovered KAOLIN on the estate of Lord Camelford. In 1768, he took out a patent for the use of this material with PETUNTSE. The wares had a blackish UNDERGLAZE BLUE. The most recognized products are the bell-shaped TANKARDS painted with dishevelled birds. The shell salt, also known at WORCESTER, DERBY, and BOW, is the most commonly found piece. Cookworthy moved the factory to Bristol in 1770.

POCKET SUNDIAL Portable SUNDIAL made by Michael BUTTERFIELD; the most desirable ones have SILVER, octagonal, base plates, and a bird-shaped gnomon.

POERTZEL, PROFESSOR OTTO (b.1876) Prominent German sculptor specializing in ART DECO figures of actors, dancers, and mythological deities. He worked with Johan Philipp Ferdinand PREISS, whose figures share many stylistic similarities.

POISON BOTTLES Vessels made of blue GLASS to a distinctive design to prevent confusion with other BOTTLES. They are often decorated.

POKER WORK Decoration on 17th- to-19thC, wooden objects, achieved by placing the point of a hot poker on the wood to burn the surface.

POLE In CARPETS, a linear motif linking a series of medallions.

POLE ARM Long-handled weapon, such as a spear and lance.

POLE GLASS A tall -16th to -17thC, German BEAKER with a trailed spiral design, like a barber's pole.

POLE SCREEN A FIRESCREEN with a tripod or platform base. Its screen can be moved up and down and locked at different heights. Pole screens are no longer in demand and are often made into TILT-TOP TABLES.

POLICHEH Oriental RUG measuring a standard size of 2.1m x 1.2m (7ft x 4ft).

POLLARDING Artificial production of knotty FIGURING in timber by removing the crown and top branches of a young tree and then trimming the new shoots that grow thereafter. A large, club-shaped mass is produced, which can be sliced through to provide a highly figured VENEER.

POLONAISE Fine, 17thC, Persian, silk CARPET with a free floral design. So-named because many were commissioned by Polish aristocrats.

POLYCHROME Many coloured; often used to describe the range of colours on low-temperature, TIN-GLAZED EARTHENWARE such as MAIOLICA and FAIENCE.

POLYURETHANE FIBRE Synthetic fabric developed in Germany during World War II. Used as fur in TEDDY-BEAR production.

One of a pair of late -18thC, mahogany POLE SCREENS with needlework panels, c.1795.

POMANDER Derived from *pomme d'ambre* (French for "apple of amber"), for the strong-smelling secretion of the sperm whale used in the production of perfume, a pomander is a small, spherical, SILVER box, often with a pierced lid, originally made as a neck or wrist ornament and filled with sweet-smelling herbs. In their simplest form, pomanders, which were believed to protect the wearer against the plague, were merely oranges stuffed with cloves and held in the hands, or silver cases containing balls of solid spices and worn as pendants from chains or CHÂTELAINES. However, even from an early date, elaborate, novelty-shaped examples were also made. Some contained up to 16 compartments, each for a different scented oil or spice.

POMMEL (1) A bolt that passes through the front of a DRAWER to secure a HANDLE in place.

POMMEL (2) Terminal piece of a SWORD or DAGGER hilt, often spherical.

POMONA Late -19thC frosted, pale-orange, ART GLASS. Made by the NEW ENGLAND GLASS CO., USA, it was mould blown and etched with floral designs.

POMPADOUR A style associated with Madame de Pompadour, mistress of Louis XV. It incorporated designs based on flowers and idealized rural scenes, typically in pastel colours, especially pink and blue.

POMPEIAN Objects decorated with motifs based on frescoes rediscovered when the city of Pompeii, Italy, was excavated in the 18thC.

PONIARD Small, easily concealed DAGGER, with a narrow blade.

PONTI, GIO (1891–1979) Italian designer and architect who combined elements from Italy's CLASSICAL heritage with modern industrialization to create CERAMICS, FURNITURE, GLASS, lighting, and textiles.

PONTIL MARK A rough bump under the stem of a GLASS object, where it was cut from the PONTIL ROD.

PONTIL ROD Rod that is attached to the base of a GLASS vessel to hold it steady while it is finished (after it is blown).

POOLE POTTERY British firm established by Jesse Carter in 1873. Among the earliest pieces are terracotta JARDINIÈRES, some designed by Archibald KNOX for retail through LIBERTY & CO., and LUSTREWARE. Other designers who worked for Carter include James Radley Young, who designed wares in an ethnic style, and Roger Fry, whose work was retailed through the Omega Workshops. In 1921, the company took on new partners Harold and Phoebe Stabler and John Adams to form the firm of CARTER, STABLER & ADAMS. Under the influence of the new partners a range of sculptural pieces was introduced. Figures include "The Bull" and "Picardy Peasants", as well as "Piping Faun", designed by Phoebe Stabler. Other important designers at Poole are Truda Sharp (later Truda Carter), who made bold, geometric and floral designs, and Olive Bourne, who produced plates decorated with stylized, female faces. Among the most sought-after pieces of Poole POTTERY are the large, handmade, ornamental wares produced in the 1920s and '30s. Architectural ceramics are also among Poole's large output. During the 1960s and '70s, the company continued to produce highly innovative studio wares. A wide range of marks was used – they usually include the name of the company and the decorator's initials or pattern code.

POP EPHEMERA *See* ROCK AND POP EPHEMERA.

POPE, JOSEPH American clockmaker, active in Boston from 1790 to 1810.

POPLAR Hard, close-grained wood that is whitish-yellow in colour. Used for INLAY and MARQUETRY work.

PORCELAIN Ceramic bodies made of porcelain are divided into two categories: hard paste, a mixture of china clay and PETUNTSE; and soft paste, a mixture of crushed glass or quartz and white clay. HARD-PASTE PORCELAIN has a smooth texture resembling icing sugar. It was first discovered by ancient Chinese potters, and was subsequently made by MEISSEN in Germany and in other European factories in the 18thC. SOFT-PASTE PORCELAIN is slightly more granular, and chips may have a rougher appearance compared to hard paste. It was developed in Italy from the 16thC, in an attempt to replicate true, Oriental porcelain. The colour of the soft-paste body varies between pure white and grey, depending on the minerals used. Colour can help with identification, because certain factories are associated with bodies of a particular shade. Porcelain is a fine material, which gives a musical note if gently tapped, and may be semi translucent if held to the light. The glaze on hard-paste porcelain has a glassy, thin appearance. The glaze on soft-paste porcelain is thicker, softening detailed modelling, and pooling in the curves and crevices of a piece. GLAZES on porcelain vary according to the factory concerned, and often have a distinctive appearance ranging from matt to glassy, opaque to translucent. Glazes can also give porcelain a characteristic tinge of colour; some glazes appear to be pure white, while others can seem bluish, yellowish, greyish, or greenish in appearance. Many pieces bear manufacturer's marks of some type. These can provide useful information about both origin and date, but they are no guarantee of authenticity. Value is usually a matter of size, age, rarity, decorative appeal, and condition. European, 18thC porcelain is expensive, but you can often buy damaged pieces for a fraction of the cost of those in perfect condition. See also PORCELAIN, CHINESE; PORCELAIN, BRITISH; and PORCELAIN, EUROPEAN.

19thC, Meissen, PORCELAIN figural salt.

19thC, Rockingham, PORCELAIN, floral-encrusted scent bottle and stopper.

PORCELAIN, BRITISH Early English porcelain made before the late 19thC may seem unsophisticated, but to many collectors this simplicity is appealing. One of the first English porcelain factories, CHELSEA, was founded in *c*.1745, nearly 50 years after porcelain had first been made in Germany and France. British porcelain factories also opened at BOW and BRISTOL in the 1740s. Other important factories founded in the 18thC include DERBY and WORCESTER. With few exceptions, all these early factories produced soft-paste porcelain, and most made luxury items as well as domestic wares. Most minor, 18thC, English porcelain factories produced useful items such as tea and coffee wares and DINNER SERVICES. BLUE AND WHITE was the most popular form of decoration, but some factories also used a POLYCHROME palette based on the FAMILLE ROSE of Chinese porcelain. Of the minor factories, Limehouse was the first to be established in 1745 (until 1748), followed by VAUXHALL in 1751 (until 1764), LOWESTOFT 1757 (until 1799), and CAUGHLEY (*c*.1775–99). Several factories were established in Liverpool; among the most important were Richard CHAFFERS (active 1754/5–65), Samuel GILBODY (active 1754–61), Phillip CHRISTIAN (active 1765–78), and Seth PENNINGTON (active 1778–99). Caughley, the most prolific of the minor English factories, is less sought after. Porcelain-making was an expensive and precarious business, and, by the end of the 18thC, most of the early factories had closed or amalgamated with their rivals. Among the most successful and long-lived centres were Worcester and Derby, where factories continued to make porcelain throughout the 19th and 20thC. Industrial development in the 19thC led to the introduction and perfection of new porcelain-making techniques. The development of BONE CHINA meant that less-expensive porcelain became widely available. DINNER, dessert, and TEA SERVICES were made in large quantities, many of them with decoration added by TRANSFER PRINTING, which was also developed in this period. Some of the most affordable collectables are items such as statuettes and ornaments with printed decoration produced by the GOSS factory during the second half of the 19thC. At the other end of the spectrum, ROCKINGHAM, SPODE, and MINTON made a variety of ornamental wares using lavish gilding, elaborate, high-relief, floral decoration, and new techniques such as PÂTE-SUR-PÂTE. The most valuable pieces are from the 18thC, or larger, elaborately decorated 19thC pieces. Smaller 18thC pieces in less-than-perfect condition are available for low sums. Expect to pay more for hand-painted decoration. Any elaborately decorated piece will command a premium. Do not confuse hand-painting, which increases value, with hand-enamelled print, which is less desirable. If an item is hand-enamelled, you will probably be able to see the transfer print underneath the enamel. *See also* MARKS, CERAMIC.

PORCELAIN, CHINESE Porcelain evolved from the high-fired white wares made in China in the TANG dynasty (*c*.618–906) – the earliest pieces were greyish or creamy and slightly gritty in appearance. By the SONG dynasty (960–1279), forms were increasingly sophisticated, their shapes and decoration often inspired by flowers, such as the lotus, chrysanthemum, and peony. In the northern region of Dingyao, potters began producing carved and moulded porcelain BOWLS and dishes with an ivory or buff-coloured appearance. UNDERGLAZE-BLUE decoration on porcelain first appeared *c*.1330, and most early wares were decorated in bands or registers of pattern, each of which could be completed by a different hand. The overall effect is crowded and complex when compared to the balanced and spacious designs of early Ming. By the 15thC, the first POLYCHROME wares were being made, but some of these later wares are not as skilfully painted as the DOUCAI porcelain of the Chenghua period (1465–87). When Dutch traders began importing Chinese porcelain to Europe in the 17thC (the late MING period), no European maker had yet been able to produce such fine-quality wares, and there was a huge demand for Chinese porcelain – as well as a scramble to find out how it was produced. Most Chinese porcelain was blue and white until *c*.1700. Later wares can be identified by complicated designs, more evenly applied blue, and a thinner glaze. In the 18thC, varied colour schemes such as FAMILLE ROSE and FAMILLE VERTE were introduced. The decoration on Chinese ceramics has symbolic significance: dragons represent authority, strength, wisdom, and the Emperor; pairs of ducks symbolize marital bliss; the traditional twin fish design denotes marital fidelity and harmony; the peony shows love, beauty, happiness, and honour; the pine, prunus, and bamboo together denote spiritual harmony; and cranes show longevity and were traditionally a form of transport for Immortals. The many objects made for the European market, often using Western shapes but decorated with traditional Chinese designs, are known as CHINESE EXPORT WARES. Ming ware is rare and expensive, and Imperial Ming porcelain is among the most valuable of early Chinese ceramics. In southern Qinghai, huge quantities of bluish and greenish bowls survive, and these are modestly priced. Marks were first used regularly during the Ming dynasty in the reign of Xuande *c*.1426, and usually comprise four or six characters. Do not rely on dynasty reign MARKS for dating Chinese porcelain – by *c*.1500 as many as 80 per cent were retrospective, and used simply to show respect for earlier wares. Imitation "Tang" pieces were produced in the early 20thC, after the genuine items became widely available following excavations in China. Imitation pieces made in the Far East from *c*.1920 are sometimes identifiable by heavy potting and poor-quality calligraphy. Emil Samson, son of Edmé SAMSON, made good-quality copies of later Chinese and Japanese porcelain, usually marked with a square-shaped "S". *See also* CHINESE DYNASTIES.

Late Ming CHINESE PORCELAIN *wucai* dish for the Japanese market, 1621–27.

PORCELAIN, EUROPEAN A millennium after porcelain was discovered in the Far East, the tantalizing secret of how to make it was still undiscovered by European potters. By the late 16thC, as Portuguese traders began to export Oriental porcelain to Europe, demand outstripped supply, prompting European potters to try to discover the elusive formula. Although various factories in France and England managed to make SOFT-PASTE PORCELAIN in the 17thC, it was not until 1708 that a German alchemist, Johann Friedrich

Finely painted, Sèvres, PORCELAIN trembleuse cup and saucer, 1782.

BÖTTGER, found a formula for HARD-PASTE PORCELAIN. In 1710, the MEISSEN factory opened near Dresden; it dominated porcelain production for the next 50 years or so, but as the secret leaked out, factories such as VIENNA, FÜRSTENBERG, and NYMPHENBURG began hard-paste production too. Meissen's pre-eminence was challenged by SÈVRES, which began making wares with spectacularly coloured GROUNDS, and raised gilding of unrivalled quality. Many of the most famous European factories continued to produce porcelain throughout the 19thC and beyond, although from the mid-19thC, few new ideas and styles evolved, and the majority of production remained heavily retrospective until after World War I, when some factories began making innovative designs. For collectors, European porcelain offers a vast range of prices and objects, from modestly priced cups and saucers to elaborate figurative groups. Value is largely a matter of maker or factory, style, quality of workmanship, and condition. Identification is usually a case of recognizing the characteristic features of each factory's wares, such as the shapes, colours, and type of paste and GLAZE they used. Decoration can also give away the maker's identity. It is the combination of these factors, together with the MARK (if there is one), that can tell you whether a piece is genuine or not. However, dating some types of European porcelain can be confusing, because, during the 19thC, factories such as Sèvres often repeated earlier shapes and decorative styles. It is also a mistake to attach too much importance to marks, because many were copied – more than 90 per cent of the Vincennes/early Sèvres linked "L"s appear on later copies. One way of detecting fakes is by looking at the paste from which the piece is made – most copies are on hard-paste porcelain, but the original mark was used only for soft-paste porcelain. Figures were made by many factories, and the differences between the figures are often so small that they are overlooked. Details such as the modelling, the shape of a base, the colours, and the glaze can tell you when a piece was made, and by whom.

PORCELAIN, FRENCH The first known French firm to make porcelain successfully was at St Cloud, near Paris, in the 1690s. Among the other factories to follow suit in the 18thC, the most important were CHANTILLY and MENNECY. French factories made tablewares, figures and small decorative objects such as SNUFFBOXES, ÉTUIS, and nécessaires. Decorative styles and proportions were influenced by Chinese and Japanese ceramics, but some slightly later pieces also reflect fashions introduced by MEISSEN. Until 1769, all porcelain produced in France was SOFT PASTE, and, compared with German porcelain of the same date, it looks softer and creamier, and is not gilded. Pieces are often unmarked and can be difficult to attribute, because factories often changed the pastes they used. In general, 18thC French porcelain is less widely available than that made by leading German factories, but the naive quality of the French product (except SÈVRES) makes it less expensive than more sophisticated pieces made in Germany. From the late 18th to the mid-19thC, Paris blossomed as a centre of porcelain manufacture, and dozens of factories and enamelling shops began producing DINNER SERVICES, TEA WARES, and ornamental pieces for the newly affluent population. The fashion for Egyptian subjects, a hallmark of French EMPIRE STYLE in the early 19thC, was fuelled by Napoleon's campaigns in North Africa. Scale and ostentation were typical of many of the decorative items produced, and pictorial plates featuring Louis XVI and Marie Antoinette were popular after c.1850. As the 19thC progressed, many manufacturers moved near LIMOGES, where labour was cheaper, and raw materials were readily available. Sèvres continued to be France's best-known porcelain factory, but other leading names include: Jacob PETIT, Dagoty & Honoré, Darte Frères, Discry, Talmour, Pouyat, Nast, Clignancourt, all based in Paris; and Denuelle, Michel & Valin, Alluaud, Ardant, Gibus & Cie, Jouhanneaud & Dubois, HAVILAND, Ruaud, all based in Limoges. The majority of French factories relied heavily on earlier designs from Sèvres and elsewhere for inspiration. All these factories produced only HARD-PASTE PORCELAIN (although some also made pottery), and marked their wares erratically. Many unmarked pieces, and pieces with spurious Sèvres marks survive; these are often catalogued either as "Paris" or as "Sèvres style". NANTGARW, in Wales, produced imitations of French-style porcelain in the early 19thC, and these are collectable. English manufacturers including COALPORT and MINTON made imitations too, mainly of larger Sèvres pieces.

PORCELAIN, ITALIAN Italy was the first European country to try to produce porcelain. In 1575, Duke Francesco de Medici opened a short-lived factory in Florence, but the first successful porcelain factory, VEZZI, was not established until 1720, when a former MEISSEN employee, Christoph Hunger, stole the formula and took it to Venice. Other leading factories at DOCCIA and COZZI soon followed suit, and the most famous Italian porcelain of all was produced from 1743 at CAPODIMONTE, Naples. Some Italian porcelain is characterized by its greyish, granular appearance, and is easily confused with pieces from minor German factories. Italian factories made a range of figures. A CLASSICAL subject is less desirable than a group in contemporary dress, and pieces should always be in good condition. The forms used by Italian porcelain-makers are often idiosyncratic, and distinct from those from elsewhere in Europe. Tentative, fussy gilding is characteristic of much Italian porcelain. One feature of late 18th- and 19thC decoration is the use of relief-moulded decoration. Prices tend to be high and the most readily available pieces tend to be from Doccia, mostly in the quasi-Oriental or NEO-CLASSICAL STYLE. The most common MARK is the red or gold anchor of Cozzi – this is much bigger than the similar CHELSEA mark. After 1757, Doccia marked with a star; a red, blue, or gold "F" was used between 1792 and 1815.

Doccia ITALIAN PORCELAIN **teapot and cover, c.1770.**

PORCELLANEOUS Having some of the characteristics of true PORCELAIN; sometimes used of ceramic developed before the discovery of porcelain ingredients, including soft porcelains using frit or soapstone.

PORRINGER From the French term *potager*, for "soup bowl", a vessel made between c.1650 and c.1750 from SILVER or PEWTER, originally for holding porridge or broth. The earliest British examples date from the mid-17thC, and, until c.1800, most were plain. Porringers were often given as presents to women following the birth of a child. Like CAUDLE CUPS, porringers are two-handled bowls, sometimes with covers, but they have straight sides and are larger and deeper. Used for a variety of drinks or thick soups, porringers were still made well into the 18thC. In the USA, a shallow bowl with a pierced handle is known as a porringer, although this is called a bleeding bowl in Britain. The light body and thin handles of the porringer are fragile and susceptible to damage, which would be detrimental to the value.

PORRORN Originally made in Spain in the 17thC, a drinking vessel of GLASS with a long spout used for pouring liquid down the throat.

PORTER'S CHAIR *See* HALL PORTER'S CHAIR.

PORTLAND VASE JASPER WARE vase made by WEDGWOOD and modelled on a celebrated, Roman, cameo-glass vase in the British Museum, London.

PORTMEIRION Originally known as Grays Pottery, a British ceramics firm taken over in 1960 by Susan Williams-Ellis. She designed striking coffee and tableware items, and gold LUSTRE features heavily on her early work. Black-and-white engravings of VICTORIAN-STYLE imagery were in vogue in the mid-1960s, and Susan created an innovative decoration with her "Totem" design, which, combined with her "Cylinder" range of shapes, made the factory famous. Storage jars with GREEK-KEY decoration were a successful line, and the black-and-white images were updated in the late 1960s and placed on psychedelic mugs and fancies for the younger generation. Portmeirion's most famous pattern is "Botanic Garden", used from 1972.

PORTRAIT DOLL A DOLL representing a particular person.

PORTUGUESE SWELL Bulging, bulb-like part of a support or leg found on some 17thC FURNITURE. Sometimes referred to as bulb or melon bulb.

POSSET JUG A British mid-17th to mid-18thC jug, often in DELFTWARE, used for an alcoholic gruel or porridge, which was drunk from the spout. Often has a bulbous body with two handles and a curving spout.

POST BED A BED with two or four posts supporting a TESTER.

POSTCARD First used in Austria in 1869, a card with a picture on one side, used to send a message via the post. Some collectors look for cards that illustrate developments in postal history, others specialize by subject. Cards made in the 19thC are more valuable than those from the 20thC, and used cards are preferred because the postmark is a guarantee of date and authenticity. Continental European souvenir cards of the 1880s and '90s, and "patriotics" of the Franco-Prussian war are sought by collectors of early cards. Cards that illustrate changes in postal regulations, such as imprinted stamps, and those that restrict messages to the front are also desirable. Cards published for national events (exhibitions, jubilees, coronations) with a commemorative postmark sell for a premium. Postcards from 1900 to 1940 are numerous, and value depends on subject, artist, and condition, although gimmick cards, cards of unusual materials, and album sets perform best. Patriotic, propagandist, and satirical cards form an important collecting category. Cards dating from World War I are more valuable if posted from the Front and bearing Field Post or censor's marks. Irish Home Rule and Easter Rising cards, and Nazi, Communist, and Fascist cards of the 1930s find a ready market. Cards signed by artists achieve high prices. Key names are: MUCHA, Kirchner, WAIN, Thackeray, Browne, May, Hassall, Hardy, Payne, and McGill. Social historical subjects, transport, and ethnographical subjects, and cards illustrating coins, flags, and heraldry are more collectable than architecture, scenery, and portraits. Unusual postmarks enhance the value of a card, particularly commemorative marks, early machine franking, and postmarks from remote places.

POSTER A printed medium used to advertise products, transportation, and events. Those made before World War II are particularly collectable. The growth of the ART NOUVEAU movement coincided with the development of several versatile, lithographic, printing techniques. Prominent artists such as Jules CHERET, Alphonse MUCHA, and Adolphe Mouran (Cassandre) exploited the new mediium with unrivalled originality. The designer, aesthetic appeal, and condition of a poster influence value. Transport posters form a rich field, because shipping and railway companies, motor manufacturers, and petrol companies all commissioned work of high artistic merit to promote their names. The value of a poster is increased if it has become famous through reproductions. Posters advertising products that have become household names, and whose slogans have become part of the language are valued. War recruitment posters include the famous James Montgomery FLAGG'S. finger-pointing Uncle Sam, which George Orwell used to sinister effect in his book *1984*. Some collectors specialize in derivatives of this theme. Many original Art Nouveau posters were printed on cheap paper and have suffered from foxing, creasing, tearing, fading, or staining. Avoid those that are damaged or glued onto a backboard. ART DECO posters have simple but striking designs, and focus on a single, dominant image, with strong emphasis on lettering such as those by Cassandre. Art Nouveau and Art Deco posters have been much reproduced in recent years; reproductions are identifiable by thicker, usually glossy, modern paper and colour printing made up from tiny dots that you can see with a magnifying glass – lithographs have flat areas of colour. Contact the International Vintage Posters Dealers Association for a list of fakes.

POSTER **for London Transport by John Minton, 1951.**

POSY HOLDER Device designed to hold nosegays or single flowers and attached to the bodice of a dress. Posy holders were fashionable in the mid-19thC. A SILVER funnel containing a moistened sponge holds the posy stem, which was secured by a small pin or spike. Some posy holders are designed to be worn as brooches, while others have finger rings attached to small chains, which could be used when they were carried in the hand. If a ball FINIAL is pulled, the handle turns into a three-legged stand to make a posy vase.

POTASH GLASS A strong GLASS made from potash, lime, and silica, first made in Bohemia in Northern Europe and associated with northern and central Europe. Glassmaking was introduced into these areas during Roman Imperial rule, and at first, soda glass made with the ashes of marine plants imported from the Mediterranean was produced. By the 10thC, northern and central European glassmakers began to use potassium-rich ashes (potash) of beechwood, oak, and ferns or bracken found in local forests as a flux. This type of glass, characterized by a yellowish-green or brownish colour, due to impurities in the raw materials, was known in German-speaking countries as WALDGLAS (forest glass) and in France as VERRE DE FOUGÈRE (fern glass). A thick, hard glass, potash glass has a longer working life than SODA GLASS but is unsuitable for cutting, and is usually decorated with applied PRUNTS or TRAILING. By the late 17thC, following experiments to produce glass imitating natural rock crystals, Bohemian glassmakers had perfected a fine-quality, clear potash glass by adding lime, in the form of chalk or limestone, to the batch. This potash-lime glass was more robust than earlier types, with greater brilliance, and could be blown sufficiently to be cut and wheel-engraved.

POTATO-FLOWER Usually painted in cobalt blue and yellow, a fashionable motif on European POTTERY from the early 18thC.

POTEMKIN Late -18thC Russian GLASS factory established to supply the tsar. It briefly produced commercial wares in the 19thC.

POTICHE High-shouldered VASE of Oriental shape, often with a cover.

POT LID A pictorial, colour-printed lid found on small ceramic pots made to contain paste or ointment. More than 300 designs were produced between 1840 and 1900. The best lids are the early flat tops (1845–60) and convex tops (1860–75). Later lids have weaker colours and heavy texture. Post- 1900 re-issues can be detected by the lack of crazing. Lids made by the firm of Felix PRATT, especially those signed by the engraver Jesse Austin, are particularly collectable. Avoid lids with poor colour and bad registration– where layers of colour do not precisely overlie each other.

POT METAL Used both of a copper-lead alloy and cast iron. Each of these was used for making large pots for suspending over an open fire.

POTSDAM Glass from the works founded in the late 17thC near Berlin, Germany; famous for engraved RUBY GLASS and MILK GLASS.

POTTERY EARTHENWARE and STONEWARE, but not BONE CHINA or PORCELAIN, and handmade rather than cast. The earliest vessels were made from an earthenware body, where clay is fired at a low temperature of under 2,200°F (1,200°C). Depending on the minerals in the clay, earthenware pottery is white, buff, brown, red, grey, or black in colour; it is coarser in texture than porcelain, and the body is opaque if held to the light. Unglazed earthenware is porous, and has to be glazed in order to hold liquids. There are three main types: LEAD GLAZE, TIN GLAZE, and SALT GLAZE. The types commonly seen today include Islamic pottery, Italian and Spanish MAIOLICA, French and German FAIENCE, DELFTWARE, SLIPWARE, WHIELDON ware, items from the STAFFORDSHIRE POTTERIES, CREAMWARE, PRATTWARE, PEARLWARE, and MAJOLICA.

POTTERY, BRITISH Most British pottery dates from *c*.1650 onward; earlier pieces are scarce. In the 17th and early 18thC, lead-glazed EARTHENWARE dominated production, and today their naive charm and colourful decorative appeal make them sought after. As the 18thC progressed, new materials and glazes evolved, and certain makers such as WHIELDON and WEDGWOOD were associated with certain types of ware. English pottery is categorized by the type of body (earthenware, STONEWARE, CREAMWARE, BASALTES, AGATEWARE, REDWARE); its GLAZE or decoration (SALT GLAZE, LEAD GLAZE, LUSTRE); or by the name of the potter with whom it is associated (e.g. PRATTWARE). Common types of pottery made before *c*.1770 are SLIPWARE, DELFTWARE, salt-glaze stoneware, Whieldon, agateware, and creamware. The production of all CERAMICS depends on the ready availability of the raw materials, and for this reason the Staffordshire region, where there were rich deposits of clay and available fuel, dominated pottery production from the late 18thC onward. Among the potters who flourished in the region, known as the Staffordshire Potteries, were Whieldon, SPODE, and Wedgwood. Potteries became mechanized during the 19th and 20thC; output increased, and these pieces are available for modest sums today. Firms such as Pratt & Co. perfected colour TRANSFER-PRINTING from *c*.1840 and POT LIDS, BOXES, PLATES, and other wares were decorated with images of the British royal family, the Crimean War, and the Great Exhibition of 1851. Royal events, such as Queen Victoria's wedding, the coronation, and jubilees, inspired a huge number of decorated wares. Many of these are now avidly sought after. Other popular collectables from this period include Staffordshire figures, BLUE-AND-WHITE, transfer-printed WARES, WEMYSS WARE, and IRONSTONE. In the late 19thC, the reaction against industrialization inspired a revival of hand-crafted pottery, and studio potteries such as the MARTIN BROTHERS and William de MORGAN flourished. In the 20thC, modern designs became an important element in industrial pottery. Today designs by Clarice CLIFF, Eric RAVILIOUS, and Keith MURRAY are sought after. Copies of early stoneware, slipware, and agateware were produced in the 1920s.

Prattware farmer's jug, c.1790 (BRITISH POTTERY).

POTTERY, CHINESE There are few extant examples of pottery made before the HAN dynasty (206 BC–AD 220), but Han funerary pottery wares have survived. These were made to accompany the deceased into the afterlife. They are stylized and primitively modelled, and include figures, animals, models of buildings, and vessels. Models of contemporary buildings include watchtowers, storehouses, barns, well-heads, gatehouses, and granaries. During the T'ANG dynasty (AD 618–907), figures became refined and naturalistically modelled; some objects were unglazed, others were decorated with pigment or straw-coloured glaze, or POLYCHROME glaze known as SANCAI (three-coloured glaze). Unglazed or straw-glazed figures are less expensive than those with three-coloured glaze. Horses and camels are among the most sought-after objects. They were made in different sections: the neck, legs, and rump of a horse, for example, were probably all separately moulded and joined together. Figures should be crisply modelled and powerful. Unusual poses can add to value – a horse with a foot raised or rearing is more valuable that one in a plain standing pose. Fakes of horses have been made since the 1920s. The best fakes can be hard for novice collectors to identify. Examine the glaze carefully for signs of authenticity. Points to note are translucent glaze that shows imperfections in the body beneath; crackling in the glaze; unevenness (the glaze usually pulls to the base); and an element of iridescence caused by being buried in the soil.

POTTERY, EUROPEAN The Arab invasion of Spain in the 8thC marked an important turning point in European pottery. The Moors introduced LUSTRE DECORATION and other sophisticated GLAZES. These new techniques enabled potters to make objects of unrivalled sophistication, and pieces of pottery achieved the status of decorative works of art rather than being utilitarian objects. During the centuries that followed, potters in Italy, France, Germany, and The Netherlands evolved their own decorative styles and potting techniques. The earliest European pottery that collectors are likely to see is TIN-GLAZED EARTHENWARE, one of the largest pottery "families". Other early wares include STONEWARE, discovered in the Rhineland by potters who also developed SALT GLAZES. As more refined bodies such as CREAMWARE were developed in the 18thC, and new glazing techniques evolved, so too did new styles of decoration. The patterns with which pottery is adorned reflect the prevailing fashion for BAROQUE, ROCOCO, and CLASSICAL ornament. For collectors, European pottery offers a diverse and fascinating collecting area at a similarly varied range of prices. *See also* DELFTWARE, FAIENCE, and MAIOLICA.

POTTERY, GERMAN STONEWARE was made in the Sieburg and Cologne areas of the Rhineland from the late Middle Ages, and evolved independently from that made in China. Regional specialities became more pronounced, and, by the 17thC, WESTERWALD, Cologne, Frechen, RAEREN, and KREUSSEN were all important centres of stoneware production. Features typical of

Westerwald pottery include moulded and applied, and incised motifs; a blue- wash ground; and detailing in manganese. German potters also made faience, a TIN-GLAZED EARTHERNWARE, and the industry was well established by the mid-to -late 17thC in Frankfurt, Hanau, and, later, in Berlin. Spirally moulded forms derived from SILVER shapes, were produced in Frankfurt, HANAU, ANSBACH, and NUREMBERG; a scattered floral decoration is typical of Frankfurt FAIENCE. German faience is easily confused with Dutch DELFTWARE. Early wares were confined to bulbous JUGS such as the BIRNKRUG and ENGHALSKRUG, and the deep dish known as a Buckelplatte, while in the 18thC, the cylindrical Walzenkrug TANKARD was produced in large quantities. The last has a hinged, PEWTER lid and foot rim and is available for modest sums. One of several minor producers of German faience in the late 18thC, the Wiesbaden factory specialized in scattered floral decoration painted in green, a form of decoration known as *en camaïeu vert*. (Pieces are sometimes marked "WD" on the base.) Earlier stoneware styles were revived in the 19thC, and copies are discernible by their flat rather than concave bases. Copies of 18thC MEISSEN were made throughout the 19thC by the SAMSON factory and others; wares were also imitated by minor factories in the 18thC. *See also* BELLARMINE.

GERMAN POTTERY (stoneware) Westerwald tankard, from the second half of the 17thC.

POTTERY, ITALIAN The technique of making MAIOLICA developed in Italy in the 15thC in the important centres of Deruta and GUBBIO. The earliest pieces were adorned with primitive designs and a limited palette, but decoration became increasingly sophisticated – often based on engravings of ornamental subjects or narrative scenes – and an increasingly wide range of colours was used. LUSTRE DECORATION was probably introduced to Italy from Spain in the late 15thC, and Deruta emerged as an important pottery centre. By the 16thC, Castel Durante, URBINO, and SIENA emerged as leading areas of production, and a fully developed style evolved, known as "beautiful style". Shapes became increasingly ambitious, and many pieces were based on Mannerist SILVER forms. Highly decorative, narrative scenes were depicted on ISTORIATO dishes. In the 17th and 18thC, high-quality pottery was produced in VENICE and CASTELLI, and the influence of Chinese porcelain and an interest in CLASSICISM are reflected in much of the decoration. Ulysse CANTAGALLI was one of the most prolific makers of late -19thC reproductions. Early Italian pottery is only sporadically marked. Later wares are more frequently marked, often with the words "Faenza" and "Made in Italy". MARKS often refer to the individual potter and the town of production.

POTTERY, IZNIK Among the most famous examples of Islamic ceramics are wares made by Turkish potters around Iznik. These colourful pieces were made from the 15thC onward, and their distinctive patterns include flowers that grew wild in the surrounding area, such as tulips and carnations. Many Iznik designs were loosely derived from Chinese PORCELAIN. Turkish potters produced a range of wares including tiles for buildings, and objects such as

19thC Satsuma koro and pierced cover (JAPANESE POTTERY).

CANDLESTICKS and LAMPS, and tablewares, including bowls, PLATES, and cups.

POTTERY PIG Earthenware MONEY BOX made in the mid-17th and 18thC.

POTTERY (AND PORCELAIN), JAPANESE STONEWARE has been produced in Japan from Neolithic times, but the Japanese did not make PORCELAIN until the early 17thC. Many Japanese ceramics reflect ideas from China, mingled with Japanese colour schemes and patterns. Stonewares show the influence of BLACKWARE and CELADON in regional styles. According to legend, the first Japanese porcelain was made in 1616, in the town of ARITA. Early porcelain wares were made in white or blue, and these have three distinctive features: granular, porcelain material; dark or soft UNDERGLAZE BLUE; and three or possibly more spur marks on the underside of the piece. By 1650, the Japanese had established a market in export wares with Dutch traders. Designs on late -17th and early -18thC porcelain are often stiffly painted, because the decorators worked from crudely copied wooden patterns given to them by the Dutch. VASES were popular export items, and have a distinctive shape with straight, conical sides on a ridged foot, and a deep cover with flanges that protrude at a sharp angle. Covers may have FINIALS in the shape of a tall flame, an animal, or a figure. KAKIEMON and IMARI, two types of Japanese, coloured - enamel decoration, were developed in the second half of the 17thC. The Chinese began to produce less expensive porcelain than the Japanese, and, by 1757, the Dutch had ceased trading with Japan. The Japanese export market enjoyed a revival in the late 19thC, when trading links with the Western world were re-established. Most 19thC ceramics repeat earlier styles, often with complex shapes. As production increased, underglaze blue was often applied by stencil, and decoration appears stiff by comparison with earlier wares. SATSUMA stoneware enjoyed a heyday in the late 19th and early 20thC. From *c.*1900, NORITAKE became another prolific maker of porcelain aimed at the European market. With a few exceptions, the only marks on Japanese porcelain are borrowed from the Chinese reign marks of the MING dynasty.

POTTERY, PORTUGUESE Repeating patterns were used on Portuguese pieces after the 15thC, and knot patterns and geometric designs were popular. Loose, flowing brushwork is a feature of much 17thC Portuguese pottery, which was often based on Chinese MING designs; however, they were sometimes westernized with European additions.

POTTERY, SPANISH Spain is noted for its fine lustreware that was made from the 14thC onward in the centre of Málaga and Manises. Production of Spanish LUSTRE continued until the 18thC and beyond, but the finest and most valuable pieces are those of the 14th and 15thC. Early wares are dominated by Islamic motifs; later on, European designs prevail. Repeating patterns were used on Spanish pieces after the 15thC, and intricate knot patterns and geometric designs were popular. Other leading Spanish pottery centres where POLYCHROME wares were produced include Talavera de la Reina, Puente del Arzobispo, and, later, Alcora. During the 19thC, primitively decorated EARTHENWARE replaced the sophisticated pottery of earlier times. Reproductions of early designs were made in Spain from the last quarter of the 19thC onward. Decoration that has a crowded, mechanical appearance points to a date in the late 19thC. Early examples of Spanish pottery are rare, and fetch extremely high prices; prices for small bowls and dishes from the 17thC are inexpensive. It is rare to find early Spanish pottery that has been marked by its factory; however, some later pieces may have factory marks.

POUNCE BOX (Pounce pot) An 18thC, SILVER box or bottle with a pierced top for sprinkling pounce, a talcum powder used to soak up excess ink before the invention of blotting paper. A pounce pot was a glass vessel used for storing pounce and often made as part of a set with INKWELLS.

POUNCET Worn as a wrist ornament or pendant, a POMANDER in the shape of a box, rather than spherical, with pierced sides and top.

POUNCEWORK Decorative pattern on SILVER consisting of numerous, small, closely spaced dots.

POUPARD Popular 19thC DOLL without legs – often mounted on a stick.

POURED-WAX DOLL A DOLL with a head moulded from wax, with the head and limbs being only hollow shells. They are formed by pouring molten wax into a mould, allowing an outer crust to harden, draining off the excess, and repeating the process, until the required thickness is achieved. The head and shoulders are modelled in one piece, and the dolls have stiff muslin or fabric bodies, and wax arms and legs. Closed mouths and inserted eyes and hair (added along the hairline with a needle) are typical. Two Italian families dominated the manufacture of wax dolls. Henry PIEROTTI supposedly invented the first "Royal Model Babies". The dolls often had turned heads and calico, machine-stitched bodies. Augusta Montanari, Pierotti's biggest rival, gave her dolls petulant expressions, hand-stitched linen bodies, and elaborate costumes. Dolls are described as Pierotti-type and Montanari-type, because few are marked. English maker John Edwards established his factory in 1868. He reputedly produced up to 20,000 wax dolls a week in 1871, ranging from the inexpensive to commissions for Queen Victoria. An "E" has been found on the shoe of an Edwards' doll, but many still remain unmarked and unidentified. Look out for dolls by famous makers, as well as those with softly modelled features, glass eyes, and well-defined fingers and toes. It may be hard to check for repairs on a wax doll, because the clothes may be sewn on, and there is no fastening. Pale wax colour may show light damage. The worst damage is malformation of extremities due to heat (direct sun or central heating). Cracks are easy to restore, but malformation is not, and reduces the value.

Scottish, horn POWDER FLASK, c.1780.

POUTY DOLL Generic term for character DOLLS with a pouting expression. KÄMMER & REINHARDT's model 117 is a famous example.

POWDER BLUE Specks of blue used as an UNDERGLAZE on PORCELAIN, and formed by blowing powdered pigment onto the greased surface of the vessel.

POWDER BOX A small BOX for holding powder, often forming part of a DRESSING-TABLE SET. The lid on the box usually featured a MIRROR on the inside and fitted tightly, so that the powder would not dry out. From c.1915 until the 1930s, it was fashionable to decorate powder boxes with ENAMEL.

POWDER FLASK Device for measuring out a quantity of priming powder and made to be hung from a belt or bandolier. Sporting flasks are often made of antler and carved with hunting scenes. Flasks can be found dating back to the 16thC, but the most popular ones are the early 19thC copper and brass pieces. Sought-after manufacturers include Dixon, Sykes, Hawksley, and Bosch. American, colonial horn flasks carrying vignettes or scrimshaw command high prices in original condition. Other desirable American flasks are those made for use with the New England FLINTLOCK pistol and the early COLTS. Designs included "Clasped Hands" and "Stand of Arms". Reproductions of these are sold, some of which are aged and faked to appear original. Look inside the flask: traces of new solder, combined with the bright metal of the "new" thread, indicate a fake. Flasks made of leather attached to a tin frame were intended for shot – not powder – and these are also collectable. *See also* FIREARM.

POWELL, JAMES & SONS A British, London-based, GLASS firm that operated under this name from 1834 until 1962. It was originally known as WHITEFRAIRS glassworks and reverted back to the original name in 1962. During the ownership of James Powell (1774–1840), the glassworks designed ecclesiastical and domestic, stained-glass wares, influenced by the ARTS AND CRAFTS MOVEMENT. The firm is associated with the "pumpkin seed" DECANTER, with an austere, almost geomteric form. The decoration is restrained or absent, so that the transparency of the material is emphasized, and simple, moulded feet are common to add visual balance and increase the amount of light reflected through the glass. The BODY is light in weight and thinly blown – later copies are much heavier in feel.

POWELL, HARRY (active 1873–1919) Grandson of James Powell, he joined JAMES POWELL & SONS, and was responsible for most of the firm's designs until his retirement in 1919. He had a passion for historical glass and a fascination with the natural world, both of which are often represented in his work.

POWOLNY, MICHAEL (1874–1954) One of the founders of the SECESSION and WIENER WERKSTÄTTE, an Austrian artist who made CERAMICS and sculptures. He is known for his white FAIENCE figures painted in black.

PRATTWARE A distinctive, lead-glazed EARTHENWARE mainly decorated with relief moulding and high-fired colours, developed by the Pratt family in Staffordshire, England. Wares of this type were also made in vast quantities by other factories in Staffordshire, Yorkshire, and Scotland, between *c*.1775 and 1835. The name Prattware is now used to describe PEARLWARE: earthenware decorated in a distinctive palette of blue, green, yellow, orange, brown, and purple. Themes for the hand-decorated earthenwares included rustic subjects, such as milkmaids, CLASSICAL figures, political and royal subjects, and animals. The figures include Admiral Nelson, the Duke of York, and Napoleon Bonaparte. Wares include hollow domestic objects, and novelty and decorative items such as MONEY BOXES, and are rarely marked. Figural groups were intended as mantel ornaments, and were made by pressing clay into a mould and adding extra details by hand. Prattware is also the term used to describe a stippled, colour printing developed by Felix Pratt in the mid-19thC. The technique was often used to decorate POT LIDS. Commemorative Prattware is popular with today's collectors. Value relies on the decoration and the rarity of the form. Fake commemorative Prattware jugs are recognizable by their softer or weaker colours and regular CRACKLE GLAZING.

PRAYER RUG Islamic RUG intended for kneeling on during prayers, with a design based on the MIHRAB or pointed prayer niche. *See also* PERSIAN RUG.

PRECIOUS STONES *See* GEMS.

PREISS, JOHANN PHILIPP FERDINAND (known as Fritz; 1882–1943) A leading ART DECO sculptor who made ivory and bronze figures of dancers, children, and athletes. Figures embossed with a "PK" monogram were made by the company he founded with Kassler in Berlin in 1906.

PRESIDENT'S WREATH In quilting, early Colonial APPLIQUÉ block pattern; also published as "Rose of Sharon" and "Wreath of Roses". *See also* QUILT.

PRESS CHEST *See* LINEN PRESS.

PRESS CUPBOARD Made from the mid-17C, an enclosed CUPBOARD with a slightly recessed top that evolved from a COURT CUPBOARD. They were among the most prestigious forms of furniture used for storage and display. Press cupboards were always made of solid wood; the wood was usually OAK, but ELM was occasionally used for boards. Elements of architectural decoration, such as broad pilasters and inverted BREAKFRONT corners, increase the value. A LUNETTE-carved frieze was popular in the Charles II period, and STRAPWORK and GUILLOCHÉ were used too. Butterfly hinges, either plain or with curled tails, were used in the 17C. Look for genuine signs of age on pre-1700 pieces – imitations were made in the late-Victorian period (1860–1901), from early wood or wainscoting. On later pieces, the carving is often more complex.

Ivory figure on a base, by JOHANN PREISS, c.1920.

Edwardian, PRESSED GLASS inkwell with hinged, star-cut cover and brass collar (1901–10).

PRESSED GLASS Items of GLASS made using a mechanized, PRESS-MOULDING technique. The development of pressed glass enabled high-volume production of inexpensive glassware such as PLATES, cups, MUGS, and DRINKING GLASSES. While fashioning glassware by blowing molten glass into a shaped mould was known from Roman times, and DECANTER stoppers and RUMMER bases had been produced by using small hand-operated presses in the 18thC, it was not until the 1820s that mechanized production of glassware was introduced in the USA. The technique of pressing glass involved pouring a measured quantity of hot glass into a metal, hinged mould, then lowering a plunger to force the glass into all parts of the mould; as the glass cooled it retained the shape of the mould on one side and that of the plunger on the other; from *c.*1870, the advent of FIRE-POLISHING – which involved placing the object in a furnace – enabled the ridges left by the mould to be removed. The invention of the steam-powered press in the early 1860s increased the rate at which mould-pressed items could be made, and further reduced costs. Pieces of glass with extremely complicated patterns can be produced by press moulding, either with a machine or by hand, although the definition is not as good as on original cut glass. At first, the technique was used to produce copies of heavily cut glass, but distinctive, pressed-glass styles emerged. Early press-moulded wares are associated with New England glassmakers in America, but production later spread to the Midwest factories, and to Europe.

PRESSED GLASS, AMERICAN It is not certain who first invented it, but PRESSED GLASS was used for small tableware by the late 1820s at the NEW ENGLAND GLASS CO. and the BOSTON & SANDWICH GLASS CO. The MOUNT WASHINGTON GLASS CO. is also known for pressed glass. The technique came into widespread use from the 1830s, and, after the introduction of the steam-driven, mechanized press in the 1860s, it was employed for most glass tableware and domestic ware made in the USA. Pressed glass was made in a huge range of named patterns and colours, owing to the rivalry that developed between manufacturers. One of the most sought-after types was "lacy" glass. Spoon racks and holders, distinctly American designs, were made in pressed glass in many styles throughout the 19thC. The "Jumbo" pattern spoon rack, made in Carlton, Ohio, commemorates P.T. Barnum's famous elephant Jumbo. It is a good example of the type of pressed glass produced by the new factories that emerged in the Midwest.

PRESSED GLASS, EUROPEAN GLASS produced by the PRESS-MOULDING technique was introduced into Britain and Continental Europe from the USA in the late 1830s. English firms were among the most prolific pressed-glass manufacturers – in the early 19thC, most were based in the Midlands. Production expanded throughout the 1850s. From this period, the leading producers were in the North, for example Molineaux, Webb & Co. of Manchester, Henry GREENER & Co. of Sunderland, and SOWERBY ELLISON GLASSWORKS and George Davidson & Co., both of Gateshead. As well as

TABLEWARE, English firms also manufactured ornamental figures, and items commemorating important national events, such as Queen Victoria's golden and diamond jubilees. Many items were made in the style of more expensive cut glass. Animals were among the most popular subjects for pressed-glass figures. PLATES, perhaps because of their simple form, were among the most commonly produced, and can still be found at reasonable prices today. Many pressed-glass makers tried to create VASES decorated with a marbled effect. These small pieces were often souvenirs brought home from a day trip away, and are still available today. As moulds were expensive to cut, such pieces were made over long periods, in many styles and colours.

PRESSED-WAX DOLL Made until 1840, a DOLL with a solid-, carved- or moulded-wax head. They usually had small heads, with glass-bead eyes, stylized features, solid wax arms and legs, real hair wigs, and unseparated fingers and toes. *See also* POURED-WAX DOLLS.

PRESS MOULDING Method of producing ceramic objects by forcing clay into a mould. Also a method of creating GLASS vessels by pressing molten glass into a patterned mould to make PRESSED GLASS.

PRIE-DIEU From the French for "pray to God", a CHAIR with a low seat and a tall back. They were made during the 19thC, and were designed for prayer.

PRINCE-OF-WALES FEATHERS A motif, comprising three feathers tied loosely at the base with a ribbon, used by George HEPPLEWHITE on CHAIR backs.

PRINCE'S METAL Reputedly invented in the late 17thC by Prince Rupert, a copper-tin alloy made to resemble GOLD.

PRINCESS FEATHER In quilting, an appliqué block probably derived from the PRINCE-OF-WALES FEATHERS. *See also* QUILT.

PRINT DECORATION As distinct from hand decoration; introduced in the mid-1750s, and used for the mass production of inexpensive tablewares.

PRINTED DOLL Features of a DOLL printed on fabric for home assembly.

PRINTIES Hollows cut into GLASS for decoration, especially on PAPERWEIGHTS.

PRISM CUTTING Zig-zag, or chevron ornament found on the necks of DECANTERS made in the late 18th and early 19thC.

PRISONER-OF-WAR WORK Objects made for sale or barter by soldiers and seamen held in prison camps, especially during the Napoleonic Wars (1792–1815). Subjects include ships, toys made of bone or wood, and boxes.

A Czechoslovakian opalescent PRESSED GLASS vase depicting poppies, marked "BAROLAC", c.1928.

PROJECTION CLOCK Night CLOCK with a lamp behind the pierced dial to cast a shadow of the time on the wall. First used in the early 18thC.

PROTECTOR REVOLVER Patented 1888, a small FIREARM designed to be hidden in the palm and fired by clenching the fist.

PROTO PORCELAIN Chinese HAN dynasty STONEWARE, so-called because it resembles and is the predecessor of true PORCELAIN.

PROVINCIAL FURNITURE made in the provinces that look country-made, and are generally of a lesser quality than those made in a city.

PROVINCIAL SILVER English SILVER assayed at any office other than London.

PRUNT A form of GLASS decoration, in which blobs of molten glass, usually found on the stems of German DRINKING VESSELS such as ROEMER, are either left plain or impressed to form textured "raspberry" prunts, which gave the drinker a secure grip. Early medieval CLAW BEAKERS feature drawn-out prunts, one end of which is fused to another part of the vessel. Occasionally the prunts take the form of LION MASKS, representing the LION OF ST MARK, and, on later Roemer, the prunts were drawn out into points or loops.

PUGIN, AUGUSTUS WELBY (1812–52) English architect of French descent, whose writings on the GOTHIC style inspired the English neo-Gothic movement. He designed stained glass, metalwork, FURNITURE, and other woodwork, all noted for its lavish ornamentation. His style was copied by other contemporary craftsmen, whose work is often styled "Puginesque".

PUIFORCAT, JEAN (1897–1945) A renowned French ART DECO SILVER designer, who made solid silver TEA SERVICES and BOWLS in a rectangular or cylindrical form in the 1920s. In the 1930s, the forms became sleeker, and the silver was combined with IVORY, amber, jade, and exotic woods.

PUMPKIN HEAD A WAX-OVER head on a DOLL with moulded hair. Dolls of this type were popular in England and Germany in the mid-19thC.

PUNCHBOWL Large, SILVER bowl with two ring handles and a ring foot for mixing and serving punch, often with a matching LADLE or ladles. It was first produced in Britain in the late 17thC, after punch was introduced from India. Punch was often mixed by the host at the table after dinner. Punchbowls have fixed, straight rims, and are deeper than MONTEITHS. Over time, the bowls became larger and the feet higher. Early punch-bowls from the late 17thC were decorated with embossed work; those made from the 18thC were not as elaborate. Today, punchbowls are often found gilded inside, but this was a later fashion with the purpose of protecting the interior from corrosion. Many later punchbowls were made as prizes or presentation pieces, some with matching ladles. Most 18thC examples are marked underneath in the points of a compass. The earliest and many later examples are marked in straight lines below the rim. Be suspicious of punchbowls without decoration – bowls usually have at least an engraved coat of arms or armorial.

PUNCH LADLE Long-handled LADLE used to serve punch from a punch bowl. Those from the George III era (1760–1820) may have stems fashioned from twisted whalebone, and bowls raised from silver coins, with beaded rims to add extra strength. Ladles produced from coins were made in large numbers from the 1760s. Fully marked, better-quality, early -18thC examples, decorated with embossed scenes or bright-cut engraving are desirable.

PUNCH POT An 18thC china pot, shaped like a large TEAPOT, with a rounded base intended to sit over a heated stand and used for punch.

PURDY, JAMES Leading British gunsmith, active in the mid-19thC.

PURITAN Simple and unadorned, 17thC, American FURNITURE.

PURITAN SPOON A mid-17thC SILVER spoon with an unadorned stem, squared off end without a FINIAL, and a simple, ovoid bowl.

PURITAN WATCH Plain, early -17thC, English watch of oval shape.

PURPLEHEART *See* PURPLEWOOD.

PURPLE LUSTRE Wares made in the 19thC in Staffordshire, England, with a pink-to-purple lustre made by applying a mix of tin and gold over the glaze.

PURPLEWOOD Also known as PURPLEHEART, a pen-grained wood from Central and South America. Used for MARQUETRY and INLAY, it is brown in its natural state but turns purple when exposed to the air.

PUTTI A cherub, or nude boy or infant, used as decoration and portrayed in art and statuary from the 15thC, often alongside female deities.

PUZZLE JUG DELFTWARE form made from the 17thC with several spouts and a syphon system, none of which will pour unless the others are blocked.

PYREX® Wares made from a heat-resistant glass, first patented by the Corning Glassworks, New York, USA, in 1915. A range of heat-resistant, oven-to-table wares was made in different forms, colours, and patterns. Early pieces in shapes and patterns typical of a particular decade, such as the brightly coloured vegetables of the 1950s, are most collectable.

An 18thC pearlware pratt-style PUNCH POT inscribed "WW".

Blue and white printed PUZZLE JUG with sprays of flowers, c.1840.

QIAN LONG (Ch'ien Lung) Chinese QING dynasty emperor, 1736–95.

QING Alternative spelling of Ching, the ruling dynasty in China 1644–1916.

QUADRANT A quarter circle, marked with degrees of a circle and with a weighted line or pointer. Used for navigation. *See also* SCIENTIFIC INSTRUMENTS.

QUADRANT DRAWER Quarter-round drawer, which is pivoted and swings out, in the frieze of a TABLE or DESK.

QUAICHE (Quaigh) SILVER DRINKING VESSEL resembling a shallow PORRINGER, with two flat handles, in a form that originated in Scotland. Small quaiches were for individual use, while larger ones were passed round on ceremonial occasions. The earliest examples were made of wood, and featured vertical staves, silver rims, and silver-mounted handles. Many quaiches were given as christening presents. Examples made in the late 17th or early 18thC are rare, and command high prices.

QUARE, DANIEL (1648–1724) An English, London-based clockmaker, credited with inventing the repeating watch. He also made barometers.

QUARTER CLOCK A CLOCK that strikes on the quarter, half hour, and hour.

QUARTER-VENEERED Four pieces of identical VENEER, which are laid opposite each other to create a decorative mirrored effect.

QUARTETTO TABLES (Nesting tables) Four graduating, matching tables that can be stored inside one another. They were first made between *c.*1780 and 1820 in England, and revived in the last years of the 19thC. Practical for modern-day interiors, they have remained popular in the 20th and 21stC. MAHOGANY was most common; SATINWOOD was rare. PAPIER-MÂCHÉ was also used in the 19thC. GEORGIAN tables had solid, generous proportions; later versions tend to have thinner legs and lighter trestles. Tables with attractive, painted decoration in the French or NEO-CLASSICAL STYLE are desirable. Look for sets in reasonable condition, as they are vulnerable to damage.

Mahogany, Georgian-style set of QUARTETTO TABLES, *c.*1890.

QUARTZ GLASS In the USA, opaque GLASS with marbling that resembles quartz. STEUBEN GLASSWORKS used the term as a trademark for a type of "CLUTHRA" GLASS with a matt finish, such as a pink glass known as "Rose quartz".

QUATREFOIL Four-cusped figure that resembles a four-lobed leaf or flower.

QUEEN ANNE BARREL FIREARM originally made in the early 18thC in the reign of Queen Anne, with a barrel that unscrewed for loading.

QUEEN ANN DOLL American term for English, carved-and-jointed, wooden dolls made in the 18thC during the reign of Queen Anne (1702–14).

QUEEN ANNE STYLE (Queen Anne) Uncluttered elegance and restraint are associated with the reign of Queen Anne (1702–14). The style was popular in England from *c*.1688 until *c*.1720 (and, with increased ornament, until *c*.1730). WALNUT was the prevailing wood of the period, and CABRIOLE LEGS made their first appearance. Chairs with cabriole legs, as well as vase-shaped SPLATS, curved backs, and rounded STILES, are the elements that epitomize the Queen-Anne style. Many metal wares were made in BRITANNIA STANDARD SILVER, mostly by casting, and inspired by Huguenot silversmiths. Silver forms were plain with clean lines. Decoration was minimal, at most perhaps a coat of arms or an ARMORIAL, with little applied ornament, but FACETING was popular to reflect the light. The style was revived in the late 19th and early 20thC.

"QUEEN'S" PATTERN Used from *c*.1820, a FLATWARE pattern similar to the "KING'S" PATTERN, although more elaborate, with a convex-shell motif.

QUEENSWARE English CREAMWARE by Josiah WEDGWOOD, who christened his products in deference to Queen Charlotte, wife of King George III. Wedgwood's "Queensware", generally used for tea and coffee services, was popular from *c*.1765. Its fame spread to Continental Europe, where it was copied. Wares were decorated with moulded designs, TRANSFER PRINTING, or hand-painted decoration. The name was also borrowed by SOWERBY.

QUEZAL GLASS Early -20thC maker of IRIDESCENT GLASS in New York, USA.

QUILLING TRAILED-glass ornament made by pulling the GLASS while still soft.

QUILT A textile consisting of two layers of fabric (which in a PATCHWORK QUILT is pieced together from patches of material) with wadding in between. Some have APPLIQUÉ and decorative stitches. The majority of quilts available date from the 19th and early 20thC, and are popular with collectors in Europe and the USA, where many of the finest were made. Some American examples are considered FOLK ART. Newspaper or scrap-paper templates were often used to stiffen the fabric patches in old quilts. You might find accompanying laundry lists, letters, or news stories, and these can indicate the date of the quilt.

QUIMPER FAIENCE TIN-GLAZED EARTHENWARE made at a factory established in the late 17thC in Brittany, France. Closely modelled on ROUEN wares.

QUEEN ANNE, walnut side chair, *c*.1710.

R

Early, cartoon-like RAGGEDY DOLL with cardboard heart, attributed to the Volland company, c.1918.

RABBET (Rebate) Groove used to hold a removable shelf.

RABERY & DELPHIEU French, doll-making firm that was granted a patent for DOLLS in 1856, and introduced "talkers" in 1890. It purchased heads and arms from GAULTIER, and made assorted versions with swivel or stationary heads, and pink or white KID, COMPOSITION, or wood bodies. Look for an impressed "R.3.D" on their BÉBÉS, a type that appears regularly on the market.

RACK The structure of shelves at the top of some DRESSERS.

RACK STRIKE From c.1676, a CLOCK refinement where the movement of the hour hand regulates the strike mechanism. Also called a rack-and-snail strike.

RADEN Japanese wares in LAQUER decorated with INLAY of MOTHER-OF-PEARL, SHELL, GOLD, or SILVER.

RADIGUET French firm mass-producing toy locomotives from c.1890.

RAEREN WARE Late -16thC, brown, SALT-GLAZED STONEWARE JUGS and DRINKING VESSELS from the Rhineland.

RAG DOLL Cloth DOLL stuffed with rags. *See also* FABRIC DOLL.

RAGGEDY DOLL A FABRIC DOLL designed by John Gruelle, who wrote a story based on a doll of that type found in his attic. His family made "Raggedy Ann" dolls with a wooden heart and six lower lashes on hand-painted faces. In 1918, Volland & Co. began to produce the dolls. "Raggedy Andy" was created in 1920. Second versions appeared in the 1920s, with printed faces and four eyelashes. The Georgene Novelty Co. also made Raggedy dolls.

RAIL In FURNITURE, the horizontal piece of a joined frame or panelling.

RAILWAY EPHEMERA Objects connected with the railway industry. Items bearing insignia – lamps, crockery, clocks, office equipment, carriage equipment, and posters – are the most valuable. Tickets, timetables, and route maps or posters of defunct companies are prized. Railway locomotive nameplates fetch the best prices of all railway relics, headed by those from famous engines, followed by those with florid lettering or unusual insignia. Railway relics in Britain fall into one of three periods: pre-1921, when more than a hundred companies operated services; 1921–47, when companies were amalgamated into four regional groups; and post-1947, when railways were nationalized to form British Railways. The value of relics from the earliest period depends on the size and longevity of the company. Relics of small, short-lived companies are rarer and more valuable than those of the larger firms. Relics of the second and third periods are still plentiful. Interest focuses on the lines that remained outside the major groups' control, especially narrow-gauge lines, or relics of lines that closed after the Beeching Report of 1963. Items connected with the Great Western Railway are desirable.

RAISED WORK Also known as STUMPWORK, embroidery that includes areas of decoration raised up with padding to create a three-dimensional effect. Among the earliest and most valuable English needlework textiles are raised work pictures made in the 17thC. They often contain inconsistencies of scale – figures may be dwarfed by gigantic insects, huge flowers loom over tiny houses, etc. – but this is part of their charm. *See also* TEXTILES, CARE OF.

RAISING Also known as PLANISHING, a labour-intensive, shaping technique used for producing SILVER dishes and other hollow wares. The silver is raised from a flat disc that has been hammered or cast from a silver ingot, then cut to size and formed into the desired shape with a series of hammer blows. The silversmith works in a series of rings from the centre of the base toward the rim, forcing the metal outward and upward over an iron block or anvil. The silver at the rim is hammered to make it thicker and stronger. The invention of the rolling mill in the mid-18thC revolutionized the raising process, and facilitated the commercial production of sheet silver, because it enabled the sheet silver to be made in a standard gauge. When the silver is hammered it becomes harder and tougher, but the metal must be ANNEALED (heated and cooled) at regular intervals to strengthen it and prevent it from becoming brittle. Hammer marks, which can be seen on the interior of hand-raised pieces, are removed from the surface with a special broad-headed hammer to create a smooth finish.

RAKU Japanese tea-ceremony BOWLS in STONEWARE, with a black or earth-brown matt finish.

RAMSDEN, OMAR (1873–1939) Leading early -20thC, British metalsmith and exponent of ARTS AND CRAFTS and ART DECO movements. SILVER marked and inscribed "Omar Ramsden me fecit" ("Omar Ramsden made me") is valuable.

RAM'S HEAD Decoration resembling the head of a ram, which was used in mask form by Robert ADAM.

RANDOLF, BENJAMIN (*c*.1745–*c*.1805) American furniture-maker based in Philadelphia; known for his flamboyant ROCOCO-STYLE pieces in MAHOGANY.

Great Western Railway circular plaque with central painted shield, from the early 20thC (RAILWAY EPHEMERA).

343

RAPIER SWORD with a pointed blade for piercing rather than cutting.

RATAFIA Dating from the 18thC, a tall, narrow DRINKING GLASS, in which the slender, conical bowl forms one continuous line with the stem.

RATING NUT Nut and screw at the base of the BOB, or weight, of a CLOCK pendulum, allowing minor adjustments to the rate of swing.

RATSKANNE STONEWARE jug made in the Rhineland, Germany, in the 16thC.

RAT TAIL Tapering support, often decorated, that joins the bowl of a spoon to its handle.

RAVENSCROFT GLASS marked with a raven's head seal in honour of the inventor of LEAD CRYSTAL, George Ravenscroft (1618–81), and made from the late 17thC by the London Glass Sellers' Co., Henley-on-Thames, England.

RAVENSTEIN PORCELAIN From the German factory in Thuringia, made in the late 18thC in imitation of MEISSEN.

RAVILIOUS, ERIC A British illustrator who worked for WEDGWOOD in the 1930s. He designed alphabet NURSERY WARE, a zodiac set, a boat-race cup and bowl, and a commemorative TANKARD for the coronation of Edward VIII, which was then adapted for the coronations of George VI and Elizabeth II. Ravilious was killed while working as a war artist in 1942, before many of the wares printed with his designs had been produced.

RAZOR Steel blade for removing facial hair. The earliest surviving examples date to the late 18thC, and many have ornate handles and decorated blades. Boxed "seven-day" sets are notable.

REBATE American term for RABBET.

READING CHAIR CHAIR fitted with candle holders and a bookrest; also known as a LIBRARY CHAIR.

RÉCAMIER A type of French DAY BED in the Grecian style, with upwardly curved ends.

RECESSED CARVING Mainly used in the 17thC, carving in which the background is removed, leaving the pattern exposed.

RED FIGURE Ancient Greek method of decorating POTTERY, whereby the whole vessel is painted black, and figures are incised through the black SLIP to reveal the red-brown body of the clay beneath. Revived in the 19thC.

A Wedgwood earthenware mug designed by ERIC RAVILIOUS to commemorate the coronation of King George VI and Queen Elizabeth, 1937.

RED STONEWARE Chinese TEA WARES imported from the 17thC and copied at MEISSEN and FULHAM before the development of true PORCELAIN.

RED WALNUT Another name for BLACK WALNUT.

REDWARE Red EARTHENWARE was made by the earliest American settlers at Jamestown, Virginia, and Plymouth, Massachusetts. In the South, as the plantation owners prospered, slave-made POTTERY was relegated to the kitchen, while imported wares were used by the masters. In New England and the Middle States, there was demand for storage and kitchen wares made by local potters. Before the end of the 17thC, potters decorated their wares with simple, slip-trailed designs. Inspired by the folk pottery of the Rhine Valley and Switzerland, SGRAFFITO and slip-decorated redware became popular on pie plates – those decorated with figures are rare and valuable; floral decorated ones are more common. Redware was also made in Staffordshire, England.

REED, HENRY GOODING (1810–1901) American, Massachusetts-based silversmith and exponent of ELECTROPLATE. Founded Reed & Barton in 1840.

REEDING Fine, parallel, convex fluting used as a decorative motif on CHAIR and TABLE legs and SILVER items.

RE-ENTRANT CORNER A corner that has been cut away with a decorative indentation, usually seen on the corners of table tops made c.1720 to 1740.

REFECTORY TABLE Long, joined TABLES popular from c.1550 to 1700. Some have huge, single-plank tops, but most have two or three pieces of wood cleated together. These tables are usually made from OAK, but some are made from ELM or a combination of the two. Many refectory tables have been altered or repaired, but attractive, good-sized examples are still desirable. Copies, often made from oak floorboards, were produced at the turn of the 19thC. An original table top should have a rich PATINATION. Look for filled holes at even spaces – this could mean that the planks were originally nailed to joists as part of a floor. Also, check the difference in colour between the underside of the top and the inside of the skirt. Heavy, bulbous legs are preferable. Hard, square edges on the feet suggest that they are replacements, as do legs that are thin. Originally, the STRETCHER would have been several inches off the ground, so that people could avoid the cold stone floor by resting their feet on it. If the stretcher is close to ground level, the feet have been worn away, suggesting that the components are original. Attractively shaped brackets between the legs and APRON are a sign of quality. The joints should be pegged with dowels that slightly protrude, due to the drying out and shrinkage of the wood; these are sometimes replaced with screws. The carving typically covers only one side because the tables were kept pushed against walls. Carved dates may be original, but spurious dates are often carved onto friezes.

REDWARE jar from Connecticut, 1810–20.

One of a set of six, late-REGENCY, mahogany dining chairs, c.1825.

RÉGENCE STYLE Style found on objects made in France in the early 18thC. Precedes the ROCOCO.

REGENCY STYLE (Regency) Strictly, items from the period when the Prince of Wales was Regent (1811–20), although more generally used to cover the new style that evolved from *c.*1790 and remained fashionable until 1830 and the succession of William IV. Compared with the objects of the preceding NEO-CLASSICAL period, styles became heavier and more sober, inspired by CLASSICAL prototypes. Decorative motifs were drawn from Ancient Egypt, Greece, and Rome. MAHOGANY was the favourite wood, but ROSEWOOD, ZEBRAWOOD, and MAPLE veneers were also used. Key furniture designers were Thomas SHERATON, Thomas HOPE, Henry Holland, and George SMITH.

REGIMENTAL BADGE British military badge worn on helmets, belts, buckles, or shoulder belts, and an important aid to dating military uniforms.

REGIMENTAL BUTTON From 1767, buttons made of PEWTER embossed with the regimental number were found on military tunics; after the mid-19thC, they were made of BRASS.

REGISTRATION MARK A diamond mark with the letter R in the centre found on English PORCELAIN from 1842 to 1883 to register patterns. Letters and numbers in the corners of the diamond refer to the date of the design – some designs continued in production for years, so the date is not necessarily a reliable guide for dating. Although registration began in 1839 following the Copyright of Design Act, the insignia was not used until 1842. After 1883 "Rd No" (the registered number) followed by the number itself was used. *See also* MARKS, CERAMIC.

REGULATOR Accurate CLOCK sometimes used to check other timepieces.

REICHSADLERHUMPEN Late -16th and 17thC, German, lidded GLASS BEAKER ("Imperial Eagle Beaker"), enamelled with the double-headed eagle of the Habsburgs, and intended to show allegiance to the Holy Roman Emperor.

REIGN MARK, CHINESE MARKS found on PORCELAIN that record the dynasty and the emperor's name. They should be regarded with caution, because the Chinese often added early MING marks to pieces made in the later QING period – not to deceive, but as a mark of veneration for their ancestors. Square seal marks are sometimes used instead of character marks. The characters read from the top right down. In a mark of six components, the characters are: 1. character for "Great"; 2. dynasty; 3. emperor's first name; 4. emperor's second name; and 5. and 6. period made. *See also* CHINESE DYNASTIES.

REINICKE FIGURE A mid-18thC, MEISSEN figure modelled by Peter Reinicke.

RELIEF A design raised above the surrounding surface. *See also* BAS RELIEF.

RELIGIEUSE French for religious. A type of late -17thC CLOCK with a simple wooden case, although sometimes adorned with delicate INLAY.

REMINGTON Mid-19thC American, New York-based gunsmiths famous for Civil War revolvers, but also makers of rifles and pepperbox pistols.

REMONTOIRE Clockwork device, usually in the form of a small ancillary spring, designed to convert the power from the MAINSPRING into a constant force. It is continually rewound to maximum tension by the mainspring and acts as the power source rather than the mainspring itself.

RENAISSANCE Revival of CLASSICAL ideas and styles, in rejection of the GOTHIC. It began in Florence, Italy, *c*.1400 and spread slowly across Europe. In England, the Renaissance style did not influence art until the early 17thC.

RENDSBORG Blue-painted wares from a pottery founded in the mid-18thC in Denmark.

RENNES French, 18th and 19thC centre of FAIENCE production, influenced by the ROUEN style.

RENT TABLE TABLE that usually takes the same form as a DRUM TABLE, but was traditionally used for keeping account of rents paid and owed. Some rent tables have initials on the drawers to help with this purpose.

REPEATER CLOCK or watch with a lever or button to repeat the strike of the preceding hour. It was invented in 1676 to tell the time in the dark.

REPOUSSÉ French for "pushed out". Method of embossing SILVER or other metal by hammering into a mould from the reverse side. *See also* EMBOSSING.

Newlyn School, copper, REPOUSSÉ tea caddy, *c*.1890.

REPRODUCTION A piece that is a copy of an early design; many are now antique themselves. The term "reproduction" is often used in a derogatory sense to suggest something that is inferior to an original, but much fine reproduction FURNITURE has been produced since World War I. The best pieces copy not only design but also the original proportions and construction. Some reproductions are artificially patinated and distressed to give a semblance of age, but, critically, there is no attempt to pass the piece off as a genuine antique. The negative status that is awarded to reproductions is a recent phenomenon. In the 19thC, it was acceptable for a collector to have antique pieces copied, if originals were not available. Reproduction furniture made between the two world wars was scaled down to fit smaller modern living spaces. *See also* FAKE; FURNITURE, ALTERNATION OF, and MARRIAGE.

RESERVE An unworked and unpainted area in the decoration on an object.

RESIST LUSTRE On CERAMICS, a lustrous pattern, often in silver, applied by painting a pattern in wax or grease and dipping it in a pigment, which coats the untreated areas. *See also* LUSTRE.

RESTORATION (1) Repairing of a piece, including the discreet replacement of any irreparably damaged or missing parts.

RESTORATION (2) Term used to describe English FURNITURE made in the reigns of Charles II (1660–85) and James II (1685–89).

RETICELLO Rim or edge on a GLASS vessel ornamented with twisted strands of coloured glass. *See also* GLASS, COLOURED.

RETICULATED An interwoven or pierced net or weblike pattern found on GLASS, CERAMICS, and SILVER.

REVEILLE-MATIN Early alarm CLOCK, made in quantity in the mid-19thC.

REVERE, PAUL (1734–1818) American patriot and silversmith whose work reflects the American Colonial and Federal styles. Incorporating bright-cut decoration, his post-war SILVER is more refined than his earlier pieces.

REVERSED AREAS Parts of a ceramic body painted with grease or wax so that they repel GLAZE or LUSTRE when dipped.

REVIVAL STYLES Historical styles that were revived in the Victorian period (1837–1901), including GOTHIC, ROCOCO, and NEO-CLASSICAL. Eclecticism – where motifs from different periods were combined – was also in vogue.

RHEAD, CHARLOTTE (1885–1947) Daughter of Frederick Alfred RHEAD, a designer of hand-painted wares for Burgess & Leigh and the Crown Ducal range of A.G. Richardson & Co. She produced a range of shapes and patterns for CHARGERS, wall plaques, and VASES, and used tube-lined decoration.

RHEAD, FREDERICK ALRED (1856–1929) British POTTERY designer who worked for WEDGWOOD and several other firms. He was a member of a well-known family of potters, whose members worked in Britain and the USA.

RHEINSBERG German FAIENCE factory, founded in the late 18thC.

RHINELAND STONEWARE Jugs, jars, and TANKARDS of blueish-grey and brown, SALT-GLAZED STONEWARE, often with applied or relief-moulded decoration. Made from the 16thC in Germany, and widely reproduced.

RICE GRAIN Decoration used on Chinese household wares from the 16thC. The PORCELAIN body is pierced at random intervals, and the glaze fills over the perforations in firing but leaves dimples the size of a rice grain; the glaze is semi-translucent when held up to the light.

RICKETTS Name of early -19thC glassmakers, from Bristol, England. Their BOTTLES are often stamped, usually on the neck, with the wine-merchant's seal.

RIDGWAY POTTERY factory in Hanley, Staffordshire, England, in which a vast range of wares were produced from the 19thC.

RIEDEL, GOTTLIEB FRIEDRICH (1724–84) German PORCELAIN painter known for his landscapes and birds. He worked for top factories including MEISSEN (1743–56), FRANKENTHAL (1756–79), and LUDWIGSBURG (1759–79).

RIE, LUCIE Austrian studio potter who came to London in 1938. Rie experimented with GLAZE techniques, which she often used to give texture to her pots. She used an impressed seal of "LR". *See also* STUDIO CERAMICS.

RIESENBURGH, BERNARD VAN (d.1767) French cabinet-maker, who produced some of the most highly prized work of the LOUIS XV STYLE. His ROCOCO designs involve exquisite MARQUETRY and BOULLE decoration.

RIDGWAY **ice pail and cover, c.1825.**

RIESENER, JEAN (1734–1806) French cabinet-maker who enjoyed royal patronage as master *ébéniste* to Louis XVI of France. His FURNITURE is rich and ornate, but has clear lines and a solid look. He was trained by Jean-François OEBEN, whose business he continued after the latter died.

RISING SUN *See* SUNBURST.

RITTENHOUSE, DAVID American (Philadelphian) maker of CLOCKS and SCIENTIFIC INSTRUMENTS of outstanding quality, active between 1750 and 1790.

ROBERTSON'S BROOCH *See* GOLLIWOG.

ROBINIA Another name for ACACIA.

ROBINEAU, ADELAIDE ALSOP (1865–1920) American, New York-based, studio potter influenced by the ARTS AND CRAFTS MOVEMENT. Her small, ovoid, PORCELAIN vessels were decorated with pale, crystalline GLAZES.

ROBINSON & LEADBEATER Based in Stoke-on-Trent, England, a maker of PARIAN ware, figures, and busts, from 1864 to 1924.

ROCAILLE Shell-and-rock motifs found in ROCOCO work.

Signed Bob Dylan poster, early–mid 1960s (ROCK AND POP EPHEMERA).

ROCK AND POP EPHEMERA Items associated with the popular music industry of the 20th and 21stC. Almost any object connected with a well-known star can be collectable. The most sought-after pieces are those closely linked with the stars themselves, especially musical instruments that were played at memorable concerts. Posters relating to important concerts are among the more affordable memorabilia. Items from the 1950s and '60s tend to be scarce compared with those of the following decades, so concert programmes and magazines are keenly collected, especially those that relate to the big names whose popularity endures today, such as The Beatles, Elvis Presley, Buddy Holly, Bill Haley, and Bob Dylan. The 1970s marked the heyday of rock-star rebels, and items associated with Led Zeppelin, David Bowie, Bruce Springsteen, Iggy Pop, The Ramones, and The Sex Pistols are collectable. The advent of the pop video was responsible for the emphasis on extravagant costumes in the 1980s and '90s. Costumes from the top five stars of this period – Michael Jackson, Madonna, Prince, Elton John, and Queen (in particular, anything connected with Freddie Mercury) – are desirable.

ROCK CRYSTAL LEAD GLASS engraved to simulate the natural facets of rock crystal. The technique, used only on the most expensive GLASS items in the 19thC, involved engraving with the item an angle, then polishing the facets so that the finished product imitated carved, natural rock crystal. The process was first employed by the English firm of STEVENS & WILLIAMS in 1878, and used by BACCARAT in France and Thomas G. Hawkes & Co. in the USA.

ROCKING CHAIR A CHAIR mounted on a pair of bent rockers or some other mechanism that allows it to rock. Large numbers of rockers were made in the 19thC in the USA, where the design was invented. Makers include George Hinzinger, and designs were often made in the EASTLAKE taste, a practical and simplified, Gothic Reform style. *See also* BOSTON ROCKER and SALEM ROCKER.

ROCKINGHAM A British PORCELAIN factory founded in Yorkshire in 1826 by the BRAMELD family; the company took its name from its financial backer, the Earl Fitzwilliam, Marquis of Rockingham. Highly elaborate, moulded-and-flower-encrusted decoration is typical of its wares, as are lavish gilding and accomplished, painted decoration. In 1830, the firm began making a service for King William IV – a move that ultimately led to its financial ruin and closure in 1842. Despite the limited output, pieces made by the factory, including their animal figures, are popular with collectors. Most Rockingham was marked with a griffin taken from Earl Fitzwilliam's arms, first printed in red, then purple after *c.*1830, when "Manufacturer to the King" was added.

ROCKINGHAM WARE The American term for EARTHENWARE decorated in Rockingham glaze, a lustrous coating with a rich brown colour, created with manganese. Wares were made in the USA, notably by BENNINGTON, Britain, Canada, and Australia. Forms include TOBY JUGS, PITCHERS, and animal figures.

ROCOCO REVIVAL Huge revival in the 1830s of everything in the ROCOCO STYLE. Unlike on a genuine Rococo piece of the 1750s, the carving on a revival piece is not as light or attenuated, and the detail is crowded and fussy.

ROCOCO STYLE (Rococo) Developed in France in the early 18thC, "rococo" comes from the French *rocaille*, a fancy STONEWORK and shellwork for fountains and grottoes. Rococo objects are typified by a lighter, more fanciful, decorative style than those of the BAROQUE, which preceded it. Ornament is often assymetrical, and motifs include shells, ribbons, and flowers. The Rococo style spread across Europe from *c.*1740 to 1760. The designs in the *The Gentleman and Cabinet-Maker's Director* (1754) of Thomas CHIPPENDALE reflect the English vogue that emerged for the French, Chinese, and GOTHIC tastes. There was a departure from CLASSICAL order and a move toward fantasy and asymmetry.

ROD Metal shaft of a CLOCK pendulum. Made of BRASS and steel to equalize and cancel out variations in the length caused by temperature changes.

ROD BEAR An early type of STEIFF TEDDY BEAR with metal-rod jointing.

ROEMER A German vessel for drinking white wine, it usually has a spherical bowl, a wide, hollow STEM decorated with PRUNTS, a flared foot, and perhaps a domed cover. *Roemer* have been made for at least 500 years.

ROENTGEN, DAVID (1743–1807) German cabinet-maker who enjoyed royal patronage in Germany and France, and made items with elaborate VENEER.

ROHLFS, CHARLES (1853–1936) New York-based furniture-maker who combined the ARTS AND CRAFTS style with ART NOUVEAU to create OAK FURNITURE carved with sinuous motifs. Some pieces were made for Buckingham Palace.

ROHMER DOLL A French DOLL made by Marie Antoinette Léontine Rohmer's company, from 1857 to 1880. The firm made a variety of heads on differing body types, so identification is difficult. A high-quality doll with glass eyes and a SWIVEL HEAD is more valuable than one with a rigid neck and painted eyes.

RÖHRKEN German PEWTER TANKARDS of slender cylindrical form, tapering out slightly toward the rim and, with hinged lids. Made in the 17th and 18thC.

ROIRO In Japanese INRO work, a polished and reflective, black background.

ROLLED EDGE Edges of SHEFFIELD PLATE or fused-plate articles rolled to conceal the copper centre, which would otherwise be visible.

ROLLING PIN Decorated, GLASS rolling pins were sold as seaside souvenirs from the late 18thC. They were given as love tokens, and many feature girls' names and declarations of love. Some have corks at one end, and it is thought the rolling pins may have been filled with salt. When empty they could be filled with cold water and used to work pastry. NAILSEA rollings pins of coloured glass and commemorative pins are especially collectable.

ROLL-TOP DESK A type of WRITING FURNITURE with a cylindrical top that rolls up to reveal a flat writing surface. Roll tops were derived from DESKS used by kings to stand beside when they received guests. Prices for roll tops are lower than those for BUREAUX, because there is a tendency for the cylinders in roll tops to jam. The earlier styles were often reproduced in the late 19th and 20thC. An Edwardian (1901–10) roll-top desk made from satinwood will have a much deeper colour than you would find on an original 18thC piece. Small proportions are also typical of a later period. A desk made in the 18thC will be far larger and grander than a later reproduction. Many plain, OAK roll-top desks were produced in the early 20thC, probably as functional pieces of office furniture. An example with two pedestals will be worth more than one with a single pedestal.

ROLY-POLY BEAR A TEDDY BEAR fixed to a curved, wooden base and made between 1909and 1914 to entertain babies by rolling to and fro when knocked.

ROMAN STRIKING CLOCK A late -17thC CLOCK with two bells, one of which was used to strike the Roman numeral I, the other the numerals V and X. The maximum number of strikes heard was four.

ROMAYNE WORK A decorative carving showing a head in profile within a roundel, and with further embellishment such as scrollwork.

ROND BOSSE The earliest solid, three-dimensional toy soldiers, made in France from *c*.1870, with round bases.

ROOKWOOD POTTERY American, Ohio-based factory established in 1880 by Maria Longworth Nichols to produce high-quality ART POTTERY. Their wares were influenced by Japanese design after the arrival of the Japanese artist, Kataro Shirayamadani, in 1887. Edward Diers was another prominent Rookwood artist. By 1890, the factory was offering "standard" wares, slip-cast and decorated in dark brown, red, orange, and yellow under a yellow-tinted, high-gloss glaze. "Iris" and "Sea Green" glazes were used from 1894, and matt glazes by 1902. Vellum, a matt glaze transparent enough to be used over coloured-slip decorations, was introduced in 1904. Rookwood is impressed with the "RP" mark. A flame over the mark was introduced in 1886, and another flame added each year until 1900, when a Roman numeral was added to indicate the year. Many pieces are also signed by their artists.

ROOTED-HAIR DOLL A DOLL with tufts of real or synthetic hair.

ROPE BACK A CHAIR made during the REGENCY period (1811–20) with a moulding of twisted rope appearance in the back. *See also* CABLE MOULDING.

RÖRSTRAND A Stockholm FAIENCE firm founded in the 18thC, it pioneered TRANSFER PRINTING and specialized in ceramic vessels made to imitate SILVER. It was one of the main Swedish factories to use modern designs in the 20thC. The designer Marianne Westman created their design "Pickwick" in 1956.

ROSE & CO. Pottery founded in the 1790s by John Rose at Coalbrookdale, England, and known from the 1820s as COALPORT. Produced PORCELAIN to rival the best of SÈVRES and MINTON in the mid-19thC.

ROSE BOWL SILVER or GLASS vessel, varying in size from a finger BOWL to a PUNCHBOWL, and used from the late 19thC for flower arrangements, or for filling with water and scattering the surface with petals.

ROSEBUD A black, British DOLL made by the Northamptonshire maker T. Eric Smith, who registered it under the trademark "Rosebud". His factory, Nene Plastics, merged with American Mattel Inc. in 1967.

ROSE-CUT Jewel with a flat base and faceted upper surface; one with 24 facets is known as a "Dutch Rose"; one with 36 is "Rose Recoupée".

ROSE-ENGINETURNED POTTERY decorated with flowing patterns of incised wavy lines or basketwork designs, achieved by turning the body on a rose-engine, or lathe.

ROSEHEAD NAIL Handmade NAIL used to secure iron fittings.

ROSE IN A RING In quilting, a design of roses arranged in a wreath; one of many APPLIQUÉ block patterns using flowers. *See also* QUILT.

ROSENTHAL German (Bavarian) PORCELAIN factory founded in 1879, and noted for its ART NOUVEAU and ART DECO wares, especially its figures.

ROSETTE Circular floral ornament.

ROSEVILLE POTTERY CO. American, Ohio-based factory (1890–1954), noted for its "Rozane" vases with richly coloured glazes, produced 1900–1920.

ROSEWOOD A figured, dark red-brown wood with blackish streaks from the East Indies and Brazil, rosewood (*Dalbergia nigra*) was popular in Britain during the REGENCY and VICTORIAN (1837–1901) periods for high-quality FURNITURE. It was also used in the CHIPPENDALE period as a VENEER on French-style furniture, and was popular with French ART DECO *ébenistes*.

RÖRSTRAND **pottery vase by Gunnar Nylund, Sweden.**

ROSSO ANTICO Burnished RED STONEWARE vessels made by WEDGWOOD in imitation of ancient Greek black-and-red-figure wares.

ROUBILAC FIGURES English PORCELAIN figures based on sculptures by the French sculptor Louis François Roubilac (1705–63).

ROUEN Founded in Normandy in the mid-16thC, and at its peak in the early 18thC, an important centre of French FAIENCE, renowned for its lacy, painted designs. A blue and red palette, and formally painted style of decoration are typical of POTTERY produced at the Rouen factories during the late BAROQUE period. SILVER shapes provided the inspiration for many domestic pieces made from the early 18thC, and, throughout the 18thC, potters moved away from the use of hot, high-fired colours to PETIT-FEU, a more refined, delicate palette.

ROUNDABOUT Another name for a CORNER CHAIR.

ROUNDEL A circular motif, which may include additional decoration.

ROUSSEAU, CLÉMENT (1872–1950) French, ART DECO furniture designer, who used simple forms and rich materials such as IVORY, sharkskin, EBONY, and other exotic woods.

ROUT STOOL Another name for a CORRIDOR STOOL.

ROVINE Italian for "ruins". Ruined buildings in a romantic landscape were popular as decoration on late -18thC PORCELAIN.

ROYAL ARMS A factory MARK found on POTTERY after 1800.

ROYAL BARUM WARE *See* DEVON POTTERIES.

ROYAL CAULDON British, Staffordshire-based firm (active 1774–1960s) that made high-quality BONE-CHINA wares and was granted a royal warrant in 1924. It produced NURSERY WARE in EARTHENWARE in the 1920s and '30s.

ROYAL COPENHAGEN PORCELAIN factory established in Copenhagen, Denmark, in 1760, with the help of German craftsmen from MEISSEN and FÜRSTENBERG. The factory made SOFT-PASTE PORCELAIN in its early years (these pieces are rare), and began making HARD-PASTE PORCELAIN after 1783. Royal Copenhagen is renowned for the massive "Flora Danica" service produced for the Russian Empress Catherine the Great between *c.*1780 and1805, in which each piece was adorned with a different botanical study; the pattern is still used today. Pre-1900 services are more valuable. Early painted decoration looks lively and robust; the porcelain on modern versions is finer and more

1950s, ROYAL COPENHAGEN, Marselis vase in a celadon-dappled tear-moulded glaze.

glassy in appearance. Royal Copenhagen also made a range of tablewares in styles derived from MEISSEN and other European centres. Their figures have enjoyed huge popularity with collectors, and are among the most popular pieces. Groups in historical dress form a favourite theme, as do figures in regional dress. Groups of elegant couples made in the 20thC are well modelled and painted in detail, in subtle shades. Among the firm's other successes are ART NOUVEAU-style pieces in pale-grey, and animals.

ROYAL CROWN DERBY Factory founded in the late 19thC under royal patronage, and noted for its fine BONE CHINA. It was first known as the Derby Crown Porcelain Co. Ltd, then later became Royal Crown Derby; it absorbed all its surviving predecessors in the town, including the Derby King Street factory. The two factories were rivals, and made similar pieces based on designs by SÈVRES with coloured grounds and raised gilding. Derby PORCELAIN is famed for its high-quality decoration – the finest pieces made after 1895 were signed by the artist. Derby's most famous decorator is Désiré Leroy, a French decorator who had worked at Sèvres. William Dean was a specialist in yachts and ships, and Cuthbert Gresley and Albert Gregory are well-known flower painters. IMARI wares were another Derby speciality, and reached a peak of perfection from the 1890s to 1915. The "Old Witches" pattern, the "Cigar" pattern, and the "King's" pattern are popular. Miniature pieces are among the most valuable of all Imari wares, and rare shapes include milk churns, flat irons, and casseroles. A range of popular figures, many of which were originally made in the 18thC, were produced by the King Street factory. After World War I, production deteriorated, and later pieces from the two factories are less sought after today. Derby pieces are usually clearly marked, usually in red, with a printed crown and cipher and a year code; these marks are rarely faked. The King Street factory used the original Derby painted mark with the initials "SH" on each side.

ROYAL DOULTON Name given to DOULTON products after 1900, notably hand-painted VASES and figures, and SALT-GLAZED EARTHENWARE art pottery.

ROYAL DUX PORCELAIN firm founded in Dux (now Duchov), Bohemia, in 1860. Known for its in ART NOUVEAU VASES and ART DECO figures and FACE MASKS.

"ROYAL FLEMISH" PATTERN Made by the MOUNT WASHINGTON GLASS CO. of Massachusetts, USA, from *c*.1890, a pattern with elaborate, Oriental, bird, and flower motifs, and abstract designs. It is sometimes marked "RF".

ROYAL WINTON The trade name of Grimwades Ltd, based at the Winton Pottery (established 1885) in Stoke-on-Trent, England. The firm made a diverse range of TABLEWARE and decorative designs in moulded EARTHENWARE, including lamp-bases, CANDLESTICKS, jug-and-basin sets, DRESSING TABLE SETS, JARDINIÈRES with stands, novelties, and cottage ware. During the 1930s, Royal

ROYAL DUX, mid-1930s, porcelain figure.

ROYAL WORCESTER **flatback jug, c.1909.**

Winton became known for its CHINTZWARE. The factory's breakfast sets and stacking TEA SERVICES are popular. Among the most sought-after patterns are "Evesham", "Hazel", "Julia", "Royalty", "Sweet Pea", and "Welbeck".

ROYAL WORCESTER Wares, ranging from humble domestic goods to the finest pieces, exquisitely decorated by leading painters, from the Worcester Royal Porcelain Co. Ltd, founded in England in 1862. Worcester excelled in designs of Eastern inspiration: as Japanese art infiltrated the Western world the factory began producing patterns inspired by Japanese CERAMICS and Indian ivories, Persian ceramics, and Oriental metalwork. Worcester is also famed for unusual finishes such as "blush ivory", which provided a background for formal, floral decoration. Most blush-ivory vases were decorated by hand, applying colour to a black, printed, etched outline of the design. The best designs are by Edward Raby, who sometimes signed his work with his initials in the printed design. On some pieces, the blush ivory ground was painted entirely by hand, and this adds to the value. This finish was copied in Germany and Austria in the late 19th and early 20thC. Among the most sought-after pieces of Royal Worcester are signed pieces by leading names such as Charley Baldwyn, Harry Davis, and the Stinton family. Harry and his father John Stinton specialized in painting Highland cattle in mountains. James, John's brother, painted game birds. In the 19thC, James Hadley modelled blush-ivory figures, which are popular with collectors today. Freda Doughty, a popular Worcester modeller in the 1930s, produced a series of children at play. Royal Worcester also produced animal models by Doris Lindner. Value depends on the rarity of the figure. Standard Royal Worcester marks are date-coded with a series of letters and dots. From 1862, "Worcester Royal Porcelain Works" within a circle surmounted by a crown enclosing a cipher and crescent, with the date code beneath was used. After 1891, the words "Royal Worcester England" were used. From 1938, the words "Bone China" appear in addition to the standard mark.

ROYCROFT *See* HUBBARD, ELBERT GREEN.

ROZENBURG Early -20thC pottery from The Hague, in The Netherlands. Noted for VASES in the ART NOUVEAU style and Indonesian-influenced vessels.

RUBINGLAS *See* RUBY GLASS.

RUBY GLASS (Or "Kunckel red" or Rubinglas.) Glass containing copper oxide to give it a rich, brilliant-red colour. It was invented in the late 17thC by Johann Kunckel at POTSDAM. It was also made at Nuremberg, and in southern Germany and England.

RUDD'S TABLE Distinct variation of the DRESSING TABLE with three deep, fitted drawers, the central one containing a writing slope. The end drawers each have a swivelling MIRROR, and can themselves be swung out to give the mirrors maximum versatility.

RUG A small-scale (up to 2.6m/8ft 6in long) CARPET, which could hang on a wall. Most are categorized by their place of origin or the tribe who made them; distinctive colours, patterns, motifs, and weaves are characteristic of each type. The size, richness of the colours, fineness of the knots, intricacy of design, and condition are important when valuing a rug. Collectable rugs should be made by hand, with the design visible on the back as well as on the front. Loops in the PILE rather than knots indicate a machine-made rug. The foundation material of a rug (the WARP and WEFT) is usually wool, cotton, or silk. The best-quality wool is fine, soft, and shiny. Inferior-quality wool is coarse and lacks lustre. The best colours are those made from natural vegetable and insect dyes. Blues and reds predominate in most old rugs. Warm red colours are often derived from the plant madder. Blue comes from indigo. Sometimes crimson comes from insect dyes such as COCHINEAL. This indicates a date after c.1850, when cochineal was first imported to the East. Chemical (ANILINE) dyes were introduced c.1890; they tend to be harsher in tone, and are not colourfast. CHROME DYES were first used in the early 20thC. They can be difficult to distinguish from natural dyes because they are colourfast, but they lack the subtlety of natural dyes, and come in a wider colour range. To check a rug's age look at the pile with a magnifying glass. If the fading is soft and gradual, it signifies an old piece; if you can see three distinct bands of colour the rug may be artificially aged. Lick a handkerchief and rub it on the carpet – dyes that come off copiously may be chemical – an indication that the carpet is not old. *See also* AUBUSSON, KAZAK, KELIM, LADIK, SHIRVAN, and SOUMAC.

RUGS, CAUCASIAN AND TURKISH Oriental rugs noted for geometric designs. Caucasian rugs were made in the region between the Black and Caspian Seas by villagers using small looms. Each region has its own distinctive characteristics. Among the most famous Caucasian rugs are KAZAKS, SHIRVANS, and SOUMACS. Turkish rugs were made by nomadic tribal weavers, or in urban or Imperial factories. The colours have a significance: red indicates happiness; black, rebellion and devastation; brown, plentitude and fruitfulness; white, cleanliness, serenity, and purity; green, rejuvenation; and gold, prosperity. Look for vibrant colours – preferably coloured with vegetable dyes; finely textured weaving; good condition, unless early; and complete rugs – cut down ones are less desirable. *See also* KNOT, and LADIK.

RUGS, CHINESE Highly distinctive rugs, peppered with real and imaginary beasts and symbols of power, wealth, and good luck. Most Chinese rugs date from the 19thC or later, and were made for the Western market. Post-World War II Chinese carpets that drew on French designs and look less "Chinese" are not as valuable as traditionally patterned ones.

RUGS, EUROPEAN Rugs made in Europe, where the art of carpet-weaving was introduced by Moorish invaders in the 8thC. Among the most popular and abundant Western rugs are AUBUSSON rugs.

RUGS, INDIAN Rugs made in regions of India. PILE carpets, first made in the 16thC for the Mongol rulers, often reflect the influence of Persian rugs. In the 19thC, large numbers of woven and piled carpets were made in Indian jails, such as Agra, Amritsar, and Hyderabad. India is also famed for its flat-woven DHURRIES. Carpets made for the European market were often large; rectangular ones are more desirable than square ones. Pile AGRAS are among the most valuable, while dhurries are the least expensive. White or yellow grounds are more valuable than red or blue, which are more common.

RUGS, PERSIAN A rug made in Persia (present-day Iran). The finest, richly coloured and exotic Persian rugs are made from silk, and are among the most expensive of all Oriental carpets. Most Persian carpets date from the 19th and 20thC, and can be either tribal village pieces woven both for trade and for use, or town-made factory-woven pieces, made for the Western market. Garden motifs recur in many Persian rugs, and are inspired by the Islamic notion of the Garden of Paradise. PRAYER RUGS show the garden through a MIHRAB or arch. The town of Heriz in northwest Iran was a prolific centre of carpet production. *See also* KELIM and KNOT.

RUHLMANN, JACQUES-ÉMILE (1879–1933) Maker of FURNITURE, highly renowned in Paris, France, in the 1920s. His designs are of simple form, and executed in exotic and expensive woods, often with INLAYS of IVORY.

RULE HINGE Another name for an ELBOW HINGE.

RULE JOINT Edging found on PEMBROKE and other DROP-LEAF TABLES. Enables the leaf to fold without leaving a gap.

RUMMER A large-bowled, short-stemmed GOBLET for drinking rum and water in England in the 18th and 19thC. While the shape of the rummer remained constant through the period, decoration, which was concentrated on the bowl, was varied. The most expensive examples have heavy cutting in geometric patterns, a type of decoration linked with Irish glassmakers. A combination of different types of cutting – diamond around the top of the bowl, with facets at the bottom and around the KNOP, for example – is characteristic of GLASS made in Ireland during the REGENCY period. On elaborate examples the foot is also cut. Rummers made in the 19thC are larger and have sturdier feet than 18thC versions. Most are plain glass – coloured ones are rare. In the early 19thC, a much simpler style of cutting emerged; this involved cutting flat, vertical slices from the glass, usually around the bottom of the bowl on DRINKING GLASSES, and was known as

Small, 19thC RUMMER engraved on a lemon-squeezer base.

"broad-flute" or facet-cutting. Cutting glass is labour intensive, so makers used MOULD-BLOWING to produce inexpensive rummers in imitation of hand-cut pieces. A petal-moulded rummer is so-called because a flower shape is visible when you look into the bottom of the bowl.

RUNDELL, BRIDGE & RUNDELL English, London-based firm founded by the silversmith Philip Rundell (1743–1827). He took John Bridge into partnership, then his nephew Edmund Rundell, and the firm gained its name in 1805. Rundell was known for quality craftsmanship in the CLASSICAL style, and made items for the royal family. Paul STORR worked for them 1807–19.

RUNNER (1) Another term for the rocker of a ROCKING CHAIR.

RUNNER (2) Strip of wood on which a drawer slides in and out in FURNITURE.

RUNNING FOOTMAN Another name for a DINNER WAGON.

RUPERT BEAR TEDDY BEAR created in 1920 by the cartoonist Mary Tourtel in the *Daily Express*. He has "human" hands and feet and wears a red jumper and yellow checked trousers with a matching scarf. He lives in the village of Nutwood, and has magical adventures. A soft-toy example was made in the UK by Bedy Toys and is embossed with the copyright "Beaverbrook Newspapers".

RUSH SEAT (Or flag seat.) Seat made out of rushes woven together.

RUSKIN POTTERY Firm founded by William Howston Taylor (1876–1935) in West Smethwick, England, active 1901–35, and named after the ARTS AND CRAFTS exponent John Ruskin (1819–1900). The shapes of the wares were inspired by Chinese forms, using a clay BODY developed by Taylor. He also widely experimented with GLAZES, and is known for high-fired, vibrant colours.

RUSSELL, SIR GORDON (1892–1980) British furniture-maker influenced by the ARTS AND CRAFTS MOVEMENT. He began using machine tools in the mid-1920s to lower his production expenses. *See also* FURNITURE.

RYA Shaggy, hand-woven, Finnish CARPETS patterned with human and animal figures and religious symbols.

RYE POTTERY Small, English family-run producer of POTTERY founded in Rye in 1947 by Walter and John Cole. A distinctive style was formed with the use of TIN GLAZES and MAIOLICA decoration. Hand-thrown and SLIP-CAST pieces are decorated with stars, dots, stripes, and SGRAFITTO.

RYUSA NETSUKE formed by joining two hollowed-out sections, each with a perforated or cut-out design.

S

SAARINEN, EERO (1910–61) A Finnish-born architect and FURNITURE designer, who emigrated to the USA in 1923. His most popular pieces include a 1956 sculptural "Tulip" chair and matching table made by KNOLL ASSOCIATES.

SABIJI Japanese LACQUERWARE made to imitate the appearance of metal.

SABOT On FURNITURE, a metal foot to which castors are fixed.

SABRE A curving SWORD used mainly by cavalrymen. It was used from the 7thC, and introduced to Europe in the 15thC.

SABRE LEG Also known as a TRAFALGAR LEG, an elegant, outward-curving, tapered leg, associated with REGENCY furniture, but first made in the late 18thC.

SADDLE SEAT (1) A seat that is cut away in a downward direction from the centre. Often found on WINDSOR and other COUNTRY CHAIRS.

SADDLE SEAT (2) A seat shaped like a bicycle saddle, as on a READING CHAIR.

SADLER & GREEN Liverpool pottery that pioneered the technique of TRANSFER PRINTING on EARTHENWARE and PORCELAIN in the early 19thC.

SAFAVID Between the 16th and 18thC, a Persian dynasty under whose rule the production of CERAMICS and CARPETS underwent a renaissance.

SAFF (Saph, Saaph, Sarph) Turkish, silk PRAYER RUGS characterized by MIHRABS.

SAFFRON TEAPOT Small, 18thC TEAPOT in SILVER. Used for saffron tea.

SAGEMONO Japanese for "hanging things"; items suspended from the OBI (waist) and secured by the NETSUKE (toggle).

SAKU Japanese term meaning "made by".

SALEM ROCKER Produced in Salem, Massachusetts, an American version of the WINDSOR CHAIR.

SALEM SECRETARY Made in Salem, Massachusetts, USA, a type of SHERATON-style SECRÉTAIRE BOOKCASE.

SALEM SNOWFLAKE Carved decoration in the form of a six-pointed snowflake. Found on some FURNITURE from Salem, Massachusetts, USA.

SALON CHAIR A general term for a French or French-style ARMCHAIR.

SALON SUITE A seating arrangement comprising a SETTEE, an open ARMCHAIR (called a "grandfather"), and a LOW CHAIR (called a "grandmother"), made from *c*.1840 onward; some suites also had matching side chairs. Good early suites are not easy to find complete, but they often cost less than a good-quality modern equivalent. The frames might be made from WALNUT, ROSEWOOD, or MAHOGANY. A pierced back can look elegant, but it is not comfortable. Buttoning was popular in the 19thC and often covers the entire back and seats of settees. *See also* BUTTON BACK.

SALTCELLAR Also known as a "salt", a GLASS, SILVER, or PORCELAIN dish or cellar designed for holding salt. From the late 17thC, the most popular type of silver saltcellar was the TRENCHER SALT. By the 1730s, this style had been superseded by the circular "cauldron" saltcellar on three feet. At 18th and 19thC tables, each diner had a small saltcellar. Salts are among the most varied and attractive small items of silver. Condition is vital with silver examples – the corrosive nature of salt, particularly when damp, means that many salts are corroded or stained with black spots, which reduces the value. Avoid salts with retouched decoration, and plain 18thC examples with later embossing. *See also* CONDIMENT ACCESSORIES.

Fine, mahogany, Hepplewhite-period SALON CHAIR with silk upholstery, 18thC.

SALT GLAZE Used on STONEWARE, a hard, translucent GLAZE achieved by throwing common salt into the kiln during firing at a high temperature. The sodium in the salt fuses with silicates in the clay to form a glassy surface. Some salt glaze has a distinctive pitted surface – often described as looking like the skin of an orange. *See also* SALT-GLAZED STONEWARE.

SALT-GLAZED STONEWARE A lightweight, white STONEWARE in which Devon clay and powdered flint are used to make the EARTHENWARE body, which is fired in the kiln to a high temperature (2,500°F/ 1,400°C); as items were fired, salt was thrown in the kiln to form a SALT GLAZE. The technique was developed in Germany and spread in the late 17thC to England, where it was patented by John Dwight of Fulham, London. In the 18thC salt-glazed wares were made in quantity in Staffordshire and Nottinghamshire. Tea and tablewares were the most common products, but decorative items were also made, including PEW GROUPS, loving cups, cats and other animals, JUGS formed as owls, and quirkily shaped teapots. Most salt-glazed stoneware was finished with moulded decoration, then covered in a cream-coloured GLAZE. After *c*.1745, there was wider use of FAMILLE ROSE-type ENAMEL colours to imitate Chinese PORCELAIN, notably in Staffordshire from the mid-18thC. Pieces decorated with coloured enamels are less common and collectable.

Incised or scratched SGRAFFITO decoration was used on stoneware from the third-quarter of the 18thC. Simple foliate subjects and inscriptions typically painted in blue are characteristic. Later pieces were sometimes decorated with TRANSFER PRINTING. Early sculptural pieces tend to attract high prices, but moulded PLATES and other small objects are available at reasonable prices. *See also* NOTTINGHAM STONEWARE and STAFFORDSHIRE POTTERIES.

SALVER A flat PLATE (often with feet), made for placing underneath other dishes, usually of SILVER or SILVER PLATE. From the mid-17thC, salvers were used to serve food and drink, or as stands for PORRINGERS and CAUDLE CUPS, as well as for presentation pieces. Small salvers are known as WAITERS, while a salver on a stemmed foot is sometimes called a TAZZA. Most salvers are circular or oval shaped, and the finest ones are gilded and decorated with chased-and-engraved ornament. Large, decorative salvers often graced SIDEBOARDS as displays of wealth and status. Massive, heavily decorated examples, featuring FLAT-CHASED decoration depicting wildlife, flora and fauna, or architectural scenes, were made in large numbers between the 1820s and '40s by top silversmiths. In the mid-19thC, flat-chased decoration was sometimes applied to vessels of an earlier date; decoration that is contemporary with its manufacture will enhance the salver's value. Many silver salvers survive from *c.*1700. A glass salver is a type of low *tazza* with a spreading foot; such items were made in many sizes, ranging in diameter from 15–45cm (6–18in), and were probably used for serving wine in the 18thC. *See also* TRAY.

SAMADET Based in southwest France, a FAIENCE factory active in the mid-18th to 19thC, and noted for green painted wares and CHINOISIERE grotesques.

SAMARKAND From Sinking, Chinese CARPETS formerly distributed through Samarkand, now in Central Asia. They are made of loosely knotted wool PILE on cotton WARP and notable for subtle colours (especially creams and yellows) and fine floral designs, including the flowering pomegranate tree.

SAMHAMMER, PHILIP German wax-doll maker, active in the late 19th and early 20thC. *See also* DOLL and WAX DOLL.

SAMOVAR A Russian term for any metal URN used to store hot water for tea or coffee. Not all examples are designed to keep water hot, but later ones on platforms tend to have burners. *See also* TEA URN.

SAMPLER Needlework pictures using different stitches and designs to teach children the craft. They often bear the maker's name and date of production. Look out for examples with subjects such as houses, figures, alphabets, animals, birds, insects, and flowers. Place names may increase local interest. Samplers are rare from before the mid-17thC, but common in the 19thC, when nearly every schoolgirl made one. Samplers in wool are more desirable than those in silk, but check that they are in fair condition. Examples made after 1850 are less desirable. *See also* EMBROIDERY and TEXTILES, CARE OF.

SAMSON, EDMÉ ET CIE One of the most prolific imitators of early CERAMICS, a French firm established in 1845 by Edmé Samson, who made copies of Oriental, German, French, and English ceramics in Paris. Much of the output was marked with an entwined or squared "S", crossed batons, or the "WORCESTER" seal mark. As values have risen in the 20thC, these imitations have become collectable in their own right. The company's fakes of MEISSEN and Chinese PORCELAIN are excellent.

SANCAI Used on Chinese POTTERY, a GLAZE of three colours.

SAND BABY Produced by Käthe KRUSE, a DOLL with a heavy head, loosely attached to a body filled with sand.

SANDBLASTING Technique of decorating GLASS by blasting sand through a stencil to etch a superficial pattern.

SAND-CAST FIGURES ALUMINIUM, as distinct from lead, toy soldiers that were sand-casted (moulded in damp sand). Commonly made since the 1950s.

Large, Chinese, SANCAI-glazed camel from the Tang dynasty, AD 618–907.

SANDERSON SILVER Rare, 17thC American SILVER produced by Robert Sanderson in Boston, Massachusetts.

SANDWICH GLASS From the BOSTON & SANDWICH GLASS CO., an American GLASS firm founded in 1825 in Cape Cod, Massachusetts.

SANG DE BOEUF French for "bull's blood", a rich, deep-red GLAZE made using copper oxide. It was first developed in China in the early 18thC and not successfully imitated in the West until the late 19thC.

SARAB North-western Iranian, CARPET-making centre, noted for runners.

SARCOPHAGUS Descriptive of an item shaped like a stone coffin of the same name. A common shape for a CELLARET or TEA CADDY.

SARREGUEMINES In the Lorraine region, a French CERAMICS factory specializing from 1800 in reproductions of old MAIOLICA.

SARUK From southwest Teheran, top-quality CARPETS in traditional Persian floral designs and, more recently, Western-influenced designs for export.

SASHA DOLL A dark-skinned VINYL DOLL designed by the Swiss maker Sasha Morgenthaler (1893–1975), who wanted to create internationally identifiable

Edwardian, Perophone, SATINWOOD bow-fronted cabinet gramophone.

dolls, not just examples with pretty features. Trendon Toys began producing them in Britain in 1965, and they were also made in Germany and the USA.

SATIN GLASS Late-19thC ART GLASS heated with hydrofluoric acid fumes to give a lustrous, satin-like finish.

SATINWOOD A light, close-grained, yellow-coloured, West-Indian wood, satinwood (*Chloroxylon swietenia/Xanthoxylun flavium*) was popular in England during the SHERATON period (1790–1800), at the time of the REGENCY Revival of the 1880s, and around the Edwardian era (1900–14). It was usually used in a VENEER, sometimes with painted decoration.

SATSUMA From the port of Satsuma, early Japanese STONEWARE, influenced by Korean designs. These decorative pieces with crackled creamy GLAZES, heavy gilding, and subdued colours were popular in the late 19th and early 20thC, and are now widely available. They often featured elaborate figurative subjects such as women and children gathering blossom; *geisha* and holy men were also popular. Prices depend on the size and visual appeal of the decoration. Good Satsuma often carries the potter's name.

SAUCEBOAT A narrow, boat-shaped, SILVER vessel with a wide spout, foot, and handle, sometimes with a matching spoon, introduced in the reign of George I (1714–27) for serving gravy or sauces for fish and meat dishes. Most were made in pairs, or sets of four or six for larger services. Early, double-lipped sauceboats, introduced to England from France *c.*1717, have spouts at each end and handles on either side of the centre. Later sauceboats had shallow, boat-shaped bodies, and were plain, with only GADROONED rims and engraved crests or coats of arms for decoration. Helmet-shaped sauceboats with deep bowls and accentuated spouts were popular in the 1760s. After a hiatus in the REGENCY period, sauceboats were popular with the Victorians (1837–1901), but in 18thC-Revival styles. HALLMARKS are usually underneath in a straight line; sauceboats made in the 1770s sometimes have marks under the lip. Check that the legs are not bent or pushed through the body, and examine the handles, as these can be vulnerable. Look also at rims, which often split. Pairs are worth at least three times the value of singles. *See also* ARGYLL and SAUCE TUREEN.

SAUCE TUREEN Made for serving sauces, a covered vessel that became fashionable in the 1770s because it was better at keeping its contents hot than a SAUCEBOAT. Sauce tureens are similar in design to soup tureens, only smaller. Some have matching LADLES and stands, which protected the table from the heat. Cast decoration, such as FINIALS, feet, ram's-mask handles, FESTOONS, and PATERAE, add to the value of NEO-CLASSICAL tureens. The boat shape was popular from the late 18thC. Pairs or multiples command a premium. Check that covers match and fit, and bear the same marks as the base. *See also* ARGYLL.

SAVERY, WILLIAM (1721–87) American cabinet-maker who worked in Philadelphia. He produced furniture in the style of Thomas CHIPPENDALE.

SAVONA WARE MAIOLICA from the Italian town near Genoa. Made in the 17th and 18thC, it is distinguishable by its blue CHINOISERIE designs.

SAVONNERIE French CARPETS and TAPESTRIES by a firm founded in 1627. Originally hand-knotted in Oriental style, their designs were later of cut PILE.

SAWBUCK TABLE A type of TABLE with a plain or X-shaped frame, from New England, USA.

SCAGLIOLA Imitation marble made from a mixture of marble chips and plaster, and used for tabletops from the 18thC.

SCALLOPED Often used on the rims of vessels, decoration of depressions resembling the shape of a scallop shell. Also, any shell-shaped ornament.

SCARAB Antique gemstones cut in the shape of scarab beetles, typically with INTAGLIO designs cut into the flat underside. Often used as SEALS.

SCEAUX FAIENCE Ceramics made near Paris, France, in the late 18thC, and distinguished by their ROCOCO, flower-and-bird decoration as seen on SÈVRES.

SCENT BOTTLE A small portable flask, known since ancient Egyptian times, when small glass vessels made by CORE-FORMING were used for storing perfume. The earliest modern, European glass bottles were made in the 18thC; many were embellished with gilding, GOLD and SILVER mounts, enamelling, cutting, and CAMEO decoration, reflecting the value of the scent. Before the mid-19thC, scent was sold in commercial glass phials and decanted by the owner into bottles. Some bottles were designed for travelling – these often came in pairs (one for perfume, one for smelling salts), and were kept locked in a box. Only the tops of the stoppers were decorated, because these were the only parts visible when the box was opened. Portable, double-ended scent bottles were popular in the late 19thC. They were often made of coloured glass with silver or SILVER-GILT mounts, and are the most affordable bottles available. Coloured glass helped to protect the scent from harmful ultra-violet light. Many high-quality 19thC bottles have glass stoppers inside the silver caps to keep the bottle airtight. Scent bottles and INKWELLS were often in identical styles, and it can be hard to distinguish between them. However, the glass stoppers on scent bottles are usually decorated, while those on inkwells are plain. Novelty silver scent bottles were made in quantity from *c*.1890 until 1900, especially in Germany and the Netherlands. These bottles should bear English import marks of *c*.1900; 18thC marks are spurious. In the early 20thC, makers such as René LALIQUE designed bottles (now collectable) for the major perfume houses.

Turquoise, opaline glass, gilded, and enamelled SCENT BOTTLE, *c*.1890.

Bruno SCHMIDT character doll with pale bisque head, closed mouth, and bent-limb composition body, c.1910.

SCHAPER, JOHANN (1621–70) German-born Schaper ornamented GLASS with black enamel, specializing in landscapes, usually on BEAKERS.

SCHERZGEFAS (Or "puzzle goblet".) A DRINKING GLASS popular in 17thC Germany, and designed to make drinking difficult by partially obscuring the opening of the bowl with a detachable figure. These joke glasses came in a variety of frivolous shapes, including shoes, boots, and various animals.

SCHILLING, BARBARA AND FERDINAND MAX German, late-19th and early-20thC makers of DOLLS. Specialists in PAPIER-MÂCHÉ and WAX DOLLS.

SCHLESWIG FAIENCE Fine wares from a late-18thC, Danish factory noted for ROCOCO-STYLE figures and manganese-purple decoration.

SCHMELZGLAS Predominantly white, marbled glass intended to imitate precious minerals such as opal and onyx. *See also* OPAL GLASS.

SCHMIDT, BRUNO Active 1900–25, a German maker of CHARACTER DOLLS.

SCHMIDT, FRANZ Based at Georgenthal, near Waltershaüsen, 1890–1930, a German makers of DOLLS. He was the first to make a BÉBÉ with "sleeping" eyes, and also introduced "tongues" that trembled in 1914.

SCHMITT & FILS Originally French toymakers, but also producers of BISQUE and bisque-headed BÉBÉS (1863–91). In 1877 the firm was granted a patent for decorating SHOULDER-HEADS in PORCELAIN by a method that made it possible to have bisque heads in any shade. A layer of wax was later added to improve the appearance of the DOLL and make the piece more durable. Schmitt dolls typically have bodies with eight ball-joints, are extra long, and have slender feet and flat-bottomed torsos. Straight, rather than jointed, wrists signify an early date. The bodies have well-formed upper arms, and the heels are usually more pronounced than on other dolls. From 1885 Schmitt developed eye movement in dolls. There are many different "looks" to these dolls, starting with early round faces and changing expressions. The firm became famous for an "indestructible" "Bébé Schmitt", which was sold in France from 1879 onward. The paler, long-faced examples are more desirable. Schmitt often used JUMEAU bodies, but purist collectors buy heads on Schmitt bodies only. The last are usually stamped with black shields and two hammers under the bottom; the mark should also appear on the heads. Do not confuse Schmitt with later Franz SCHMIDT German dolls, which carry a similar trademark.

SCHNEEBALLE From the German "snowball", a vase decorated with May blossoms. They were first made by MEISSEN in the 18thC, but several 19thC factories, including a number of factories in the Dresden area, continued the tradition by covering the entire surface of objects with tiny florets.

SCHNELLE Made in the Rheinland, Germany, from the 16thC, a tall, upwardly tapering TANKARD in STONEWARE. Relief decoration and PEWTER lids are common.

SCHOENAU & HOFFMEISTER German maker of DOLLS. Active from 1901.

SCHOENHUT CO. American, Philadelphia-based dollmaker, active in the early 20thC. Specialized in DOLLS with spring-jointed limbs.

SCHOFIELD, JOHN An eminent, 18thC, British silversmith who produced CANDLESTICKS, CANDELABRA, and CRUETS in the NEO-CLASSICAL STYLE.

SCHREZHEIM FAIENCE Mid-18thC, TIN-GLAZED EARTHENWARE of a German (Bavarian) factory, notably its large figures modelled by J.M. Mutschele.

SCHUCO German manufacturer, established in 1912 by Heinrich Muller and his partner Schreyer, and noted for toy cars, boats, aircraft, and a range of novelty toys including Disney characters, as well as mechanical TEDDY BEARS and miniatures. Production ceased when Muller and Schreyer were drafted to fight in World War I. Schreyer left after the war, but Muller restarted production with a new partner. High-quality vehicles were produced in large numbers between the two world wars – look for examples with clockwork mechanisms, streamlined designs, and good-quality, rubber tyres. Pieces should be made from both lithographed and painted TINPLATE and marked "Made in Germany". Schuco also made DIECAST vehicles from the 1960s to 1976. Small facial features and feet are characteristic of early Schuco bears. The 1920s' black-and-white miniature is rarer than the golden 1930s' miniature. Unusual colours such as pink, purple, and green command high prices, provided that the bears are in excellent condition. Schuco miniatures were constructed with metal bodies. The earliest and smallest were only 6cm (2⅓in) tall, but over the years they grew larger and sturdier. By the 1950s, the firm was selling throughout North America, including Canada, and at this time their bears were beige with short PLUSH coats, stitched snouts, glass eyes, swivel-jointed bodies, growlers, and short plush pads. The arms were no longer straight, and the feet were noticeably bigger than those used on earlier bears. The firm went bankrupt in 1970.

Pre-war, clockwork SCHUCO musical clown.

SCHWANHARDT Strictly, GLASS engraved by Georg Schwanhardt and his sons in Nuremberg, Germany, in the 17thC, but generally used to describe any fine glass engraving of similar style and quality.

SCHWARZHAFNER Black IRONSTONE produced in the 15th and 16thC in southern Germany and Austria.

SCHWARZLOT Painting or enamelwork on GLASS or PORCELAIN in black, similar in appearance to an engraving. The technique was used mostly by

19thC, William Salmon of London, lacquered brass microscope (SCIENTIFIC INSTRUMENTS).

German HAUSMÄLER from the mid-17th until the mid-18thC, mostly on porcelain. Schwarzlot was introduced on glass at Nuremberg and used by Bohemian glassmakers in the early 18thC. Designs consisted mainly of battle scenes, mythological subjects, landscapes, and hunting scenes. Gilding and an iron-red enamel ("EISEROT") were also used, and fine details were etched with needles. Reproduction Schwarzlot glassware was popular in the 19thC.

SCIENTIFIC INSTRUMENTS Tools made for measuring or viewing. Most early instruments were made for amateur scientists, who regarded them as objects of beauty, or for professionals, such as surveyors, navigators, and architects, for whom these were everyday tools of the trade. Rare examples of 18thC, handcrafted objects are always in demand. Many instruments are ornately decorated and incorporate materials such as BRASS, SILVER, IVORY, and EBONY. Machine-made precision tools were first made in the 19thC. The same design was often repeated over long periods, but some instruments were marked by their makers, and this usually helps with identification and dating, as well as adding to the value. Fakes and reproductions of early instruments exist. Never attempt to polish an old scientific instrument without checking with an expert first, because this may damage the patina and reduce the value dramatically. *See also* MICROSCOPE, OCTANT, SEXTANT, SUNDIAL, and TELESCOPE.

SCISSOR TOYS From Saxony in Germany, traditional wooden, figure toys mounted on a criss-cross concertina to simulate movement.

SCONCE Strictly, a wall-mounted plate or bracket to which lights or candle-holders could be attached. In the 18thC, they were made of SILVER or other metal. Nowadays, the term is also used to refer to the CANDLESTICKS.

SCOOP PATTERN With a band of carved decoration in the form of round-ended gouges, which have been scooped from the wood.

SCRATCH BLUE Incised decoration overpainted in blue. Typical of 18thC SALT-GLAZED STONEWARE.

SCRATCH CARVING On 16th and 17thC joined FURNITURE, a simple form of decoration, whereby a design is formed by an outline scratched into the wood.

SCRATCHWEIGHT Note made of the weight of a SILVER article at ASSAY, and often hand-engraved on the base or reverse. Any change from the original weight indicates that the piece has been altered or overly polished. With sets, such as PLATES, the number of the individual piece was often also inscribed on the base, and this may help when building up a complete set.

SCREEN A series of tall, hinged frames used to form a private section within a room. There are usually three or four folds, but there may be more. Oriental

LACQUER, PAPIER-MÂCHÉ, leather, and wood with textile panels are among the range of materials used for screens. Oriental-style screens were popular until World War I. A screen with castors and hinges that allow the sections to fold either way are desirable. The value of a screen lies in its decorative appeal rather than its age; original embroidery raises value.

SCREW Used in FURNITURE to hold a join together. Early screws were handmade from iron, and have uneven threads. The earlier the screw, the cruder it will be. The groove in old screw heads tends to be off-centre and the top irregular. Unlike on modern screws, the threads on old ones run the entire length of the shank. Old screws were not as tapered as modern ones, and can be difficult to extract if they have rusted in. *See also* FURNITURE.

SCRIBING LINE Inscribed mark made by a cabinet-maker when preparing to cut joints. They are often seen on the dovetail joints of drawer linings.

SCRIMSHAW Dating from the late 17thC, objects of whale and walrus tusk, whalebone, or teeth, engraved by sailors using knives and needles.

SCROLL Curved decoration, particularly used for handles. Often found shaped as an ornate "C", in which case it may be called a C-SCROLL.

SCRUTOIRE American term for an ÉSCRITOIRE.

SCULPTURE, ART NOUVEAU AND ART DECO Inexpensive scaled-down figures epitomizing the ART NOUVEAU and ART DECO styles. In the early 20thC, as new technology enabled sculptors to create smaller-scale models of monumental pieces, sculpture (hitherto an expensive artistic medium) became popular. One recurring subject is the female form – Art Nouveau sculpture shows women in dreamy poses, or draped around functional objects such as lamps. Form, function, and decoration are intermingled into fluid shapes that were favoured by French sculptors, while English pieces are less stylized. Sculpture from the Art Deco era reflects the Jazz Age, and typically depicts elegant ladies dancing, playing golf, and smoking. The bases of Art Deco sculptures are often integral to the composition and can provide clues as to the identity of the maker – those by Demêtre CHIPARUS, for example, tend to be impressive, with an architectural quality. The most valuable Art Deco sculptures are those made from CHRYSELEPHANTINE. Many less-valuable figures from that period were made from SPELTER combined with IVORENE.

SCUTCHEON Shield-shaped ornament or fitment. *See also* ESCUTCHEON.

SEAL Object used to impress the writer's personal crest or monogram into sealing wax on an envelope. Until the practice of sending letters in envelopes became widespread with the introduction of the "penny" post in the 19thC,

George I wine SEAL BOTTLE, with seal marked "Welman 1723".

letters were sealed using wax and branded with seals. Hardstones were used for this purpose since CLASSICAL times. Striated glass seals were made in the 19thC. Fob seals, which were suspended from chains attached to waistcoats, were among the various seals made for men. Other types of seal include ring seals with the seal in the signet of the ring, FINIAL seals attached to the ends of pencils or pens, and seals that were worn suspended from CHÂTELAINES or watch chains. *See also* SEALING-STICK HOLDER.

SEAL BOTTLE A wine bottle with an applied-glass medallion or SEAL. In the 18thC, wine bottles were filled directly by the merchant from barrels, so owners identified their bottles by impressing seals with coats of arms or initials, and sometimes a date, onto a blob of molten glass applied to the body of the bottle. Seals were also used by taverns and colleges.

SEALING-STICK HOLDER Made for holding and protecting blocks of wax. Some examples had built-in tapers and SEALS. Because sticks of wax used to seal documents were brittle, they were often kept in protective tubes with slider mechanisms for pushing out the wax.

SEAL SPOON A mid-16th to late 17thC spoon, with a finial shaped like a wax seal – sometimes even engraved like one.

SEAT RAIL A frame that supports a CHAIR seat and holds the legs together.

SEAWEED MARQUETRY Distinctive MARQUETRY in the form of flowing-and-curling, thin, leafy patterns, which often cover most of the visible parts of the piece. Associated with the William and Mary period of the late 17thC.

SECESSIONIST The Austrian ART NOUVEAU Movement, dominated by Josef HOFFMANN and influenced by Charles Rennie MACKINTOSH and the GLASGOW SCHOOL. Objects of this style, are also described as Secessionist.

SECRÉTAIRE A writing cabinet with a flat front and a deep drawer. The front of the drawer conceals compartments, and is hinged to pull down and form a smooth writing surface. The disadvantage of the design is that the desk is unstable when the flap is lowered. Secrétaire drawers were often added to other FURNITURE. *See also* WRITING FURNITURE.

SECRÉTAIRE À ABATTANT A French WRITING TABLE with a fall front.

SECRÉTAIRE BOOKCASE First popular in the late 18thC, a BOOKCASE above a SECRÉTAIRE. Some have cupboard doors, which conceal shelves below; others have drawers. The bookcase should be slightly smaller than the base, but made of matching wood. Beware of bases and tops that are flush sided – they could be a MARRIAGE or a cut-down library bookcase.

SECRETARY American term for a SECRÉTAIRE or BUREAU.

SEDAN CLOCK A CARRIAGE CLOCK resembling a large watch and designed to be suspended from its bow-shaped handle.

SEDDON, GEORGE (1727–1801) English cabinet-maker of the 18thC. His large-scale, London business produced fine-quality FURNITURE.

SEDJADEH Alternative name for the "standard" size of Oriental CARPET, measuring about 1.5m x 2.5m (5ft x 8ft).

SEHNA CARPETS Fine, dense, floral, short-PILE RUGS from the town of Kurdistan, on the Iran/Iraq border. These carpets gave their name to the Sehna (SENNEH) knot, but, paradoxically, were often made using the GHIORDES KNOT.

SELVEDGE Designed to prevent fraying, a strip of flat material made by weaving the WARP threads, at the short edges of a CARPET.

SEMI-FLATS Toy soldiers produced in quantity from the 1930s, and intermediate between FLATS and SOLIDS. Usually made of lead cast in a mould, they are regarded as being of mediocre quality because they lack fine detail.

SEMINOLE In quilting, an American PATCHWORK method developed by the Seminole Indians of Florida. Narrow strips of fabric are joined, then cut in segments, and rejoined to form many patterns. *See also* QUILT.

SEMI-PRECIOUS STONES *See* GEMS.

SENNEH KNOT (SEHNA, Sinneh; also known as the PERSIAN KNOT.) One of two knotting techniques used in RUG-making and typical of Persian rugs. The WEFT is looped under and over one WARP thread and under the adjacent one.

SEREBAND In Iran, near Teheran, a town producing RUGS with all-over BOTEH designs. Also used to describe any similarly styled rug.

SERPENTINE An undulating, shallow, double S-shape. A form often used on the fronts of quality FURNITURE.

SERRE-PAPIER Another name for a CARTONNIER.

SERVING DISH Generally made en suite with PLATES, and often part of a larger DINNER SERVICE, a dish used for presenting the main course to the table. They were made in a variety of designs and sizes for different purposes. Elongated oval platters were made to hold fish; meat dishes were produced in all sizes from 22.5cm (8½in). From the mid-18thC, serving dishes were sometimes fitted with pierced inserts, known as a MAZARINES. Other serving wares include two-handled TRAYS, used for serving drinks and often made with matching tea or coffee services. Two-handled trays were produced in two pieces (the flat central section and the border) and are flimsy. Avoid examples that are not made of solid SILVER, and those in poor condition. Stacking may have caused denting, and an absence of scratches or knife marks may be the result of overpolishing, which will have left the silver thin. *See also* ENTRÉE DISH, FISH PLATTER, and VEGETABLE DISH.

SERVING SPOON Medium to large spoon (33–38cm/13–15in long), first used in the mid-17thC, and common from the 1700s. *See also* FLATWARE.

SERVING TABLE Long, rectangular TABLE placed against a dining-room wall and used for serving and preparing food. Some had raised edges on three sides. Although not as practical as SIDEBOARDS, they can be among the most attractive of tables. Some have elaborately carved legs and friezes embellished with garlands and masks. The earliest examples date from *c*.1750.

SETTEE A long seat with an upholstered back and sides, for two or more people. They generally have a square-ended appearance, and may have a space between the seat and the back and sides. The word "settee" was derived from "SETTLE", and its usage often overlaps with "SOFA". Nowadays, the term usually refers to a seat that is both smaller and more formal than a sofa. Perhaps in order to protect expensive upholstery from the fashionable, powdered wigs of the 18thC, the backs of settees became lower at that time. In France, the undulating backs of sofas were sometimes designed to fit into the moulding of similarly curved wall panelling. Painted furniture was fashionable in the late 18thC. Look for examples with ornate features, such as elaborate camel backs and double-serpentine seat-rails, which add to the value.

SETTING SUN *See* SUNBURST.

SETTLE A long wooden seat with a back and arms, and possibly a BOX SEAT, this was the earliest form of seating for two or more people. The tall backs of settles are similar to those of CHAIRS of the same date.

Carved oak SETTLE, 1900.

SÈVRES France's most famous PORCELAIN factory, first established at Vincennes in 1738, when it began to produce SOFT-PASTE PORCELAIN. In 1756, the factory moved to Sèvres, near the home of its patron Madame de Pompadour, mistress of Louis XV; soon after, it fell under the king's ownership. After 1769, Sèvres began making HARD-PASTE PORCELAIN; after *c*.1803 it stopped making soft paste. Sèvres porcelain is famed for its lavish gilding and colourful GROUNDS and panels decorated with flowers, figure subjects, or landscapes. Sèvres introduced the pink ground known as "Rose Pompadour" *c*.1757, but it was probably discontinued after Madame de

Pompadour's death in 1764. Green was introduced in 1756. Other Sèvres colours include: *bleu lapis* (lapis blue), 1749; *bleu céleste* (sky blue), 1752; *jaune jonquille* (pastel yellow), 1753; *violette* (violet), 1757; *rose* (pink), 1758; and *bleu royal* (royal blue), 1763. Knowledge of these colours can help with dating and spotting fakes, because some pastiches combine late colours with early date marks. Sèvres GILDING is soft and richly applied, and the factory developed a wide range of distinctive techniques, such as the ŒIL-DE-PERDRIX (partridge eye) gilding, and *caillouté* (pebble) decoration. On some pieces, gilding was raised and tooled to create detailed bouquets of flowers and foliage. All Sèvres forms are named – for example, a double-handled VASE made *c*.1755 is called a *vase Duplessis à fleurs*, after the sculptor employed by the factory to create interesting shapes. Pear-shaped JUGS with tripod feet, and ovoid teapots with ear-shaped handles are typical of 18thC Sèvres forms. The factory also produced figures in BISCUIT modelled by E.M. Falconet, often after the designs of the 18thC painter François Boucher. Like other European factories in the early 19thC, Sèvres began making more formally decorated pieces, using semi-mechanical methods of gilding. The factory's reputation has attracted numerous imitators. MARKS and styles were copied throughout Europe, and confusion also arises because at the time of the French Revolution (1789–99) the factory was taken over by the state, and many blank pieces were sold in the white (undecorated) to independent decorators in France and England. Some of them marked these wares as though they were genuine Sèvres. Coloured grounds are prone to faking; probably about 90 per cent of all *bleu-céleste* pieces are imitations. The interlaced Sèvres "L"s were centred with a date letter from 1753. This is one of the most commonly faked of all porcelain marks. Look for strong definition on genuine pieces – a weak, attenuated mark is usually suspect.

One of a pair of 19thC, SÈVRES porcelain vases.

SEWING ACCESSORIES Tools used in sewing, such as thimbles, bobbins, pincushions, tape measures, ribbon threaders (used as aids to weaving ribbons through garments), scissors, hemming gauges (guides for measuring the hems of trousers or skirts), and ÉTUIS are now sought after. Many sewing accessories were made at least partly of SILVER, often in imaginative designs and with detailed decoration. Numerous British examples were made in SHEFFIELD PLATE, because the blades were usually made of steel; the handles were often of "loaded" (weighted) hollow silver. Different sewing accessories were sometimes combined in one design such as a needlecase, bobbin holder, and thimble set. American silversmiths excelled in the production of novelties, such as silver-plated tape measures in the shape of turtoises. Pincushions, used for keeping pins, needles, and decorative hatpins or hairpins safe, often feature loaded, sheet-silver bases and velvet-covered padded tops. They were made in huge numbers in the Edwardian period (1901–10), often in animal and bird forms. Other collectable sewing tools include bodkins, bodkin cases, crochet hooks, needlecases, nécessaires, shuttles, stilettos (used for piercing cloth), and tatting sets.

SEXTANT Navigational instrument invented in 1757, so-called because its frame is one-sixth of a circle. It measures angular distances using reflective mirrors. Sextants were usually framed in BRASS and were more accurate (and are now often more expensive) than OCTANTS. *See also* SCIENTIFIC INSTRUMENTS.

SEYMOUR, JOHN (*c*.1738–1818) American, Massachusetts-based cabinet-maker. Inspired by George HEPPLEWHITE and Thomas SHERATON and their NEO-CLASSICAL STYLE, he made elaborate FURNITURE using exotic woods, and incorporating complex banding and inlay.

S.F.B.J. *See* SOCIÉTÉ FRANÇAISE DE FABRICATION DE BÉBÉS ET JOUETS.

S.G.D.G. On French DOLLS, an unregistered trademark meaning "without government guarantee (*Sans Garantie du Gouvernement*).

SGRAFITTO From the Italian word meaning "little scratch", the technique of scratching into the BODY of a piece of POTTERY before firing to create an incised design, sometimes revealing a contrasting colour through a top layer of SLIP. *Sgraffito* has been used on EARTHENWARE and STONEWARE, and remains popular with studio potters such as Lucie RIE. "Scratch blue" was a type of incised decoration, where *sgraffito* designs were rubbed with cobalt oxide or other coloured pigments before the piece was fired. The technique was used on early English stoneware, and by the DOULTON factory in the late 19thC. Scratched or incised decoration is also used on GLASS.

SHAGREEN Untanned leather, originally the skin of the shagri, a Turkish wild ass, but now used to refer to any granulated leather, including the skin of shark or ray fish. It can be found on SWORD grips and decorative BOXES.

SHAKER FURNITURE Simply designed FURNITURE made by members of the Shaker community, a self-sufficient religious group that flourished in the USA in the 19thC. The Shakers followed strict codes of behaviour and believed that the furniture they built should be as simple as possible to bring them closer to God. It was also designed to be practical – for example, some CHESTS have large, flat tops and were used as work counters. North American woods such as PINE, MAPLE, butternut, and CHERRY were typical. Today, Shaker simplicity fits well with modern interiors and is highly sought after. It is still produced.

SHAKUDO Gold bronze alloy used by Japanese makers of INRO.

SHAMSIR (Shamshir) Eastern SWORD with a curved blade, short quillons, and a POMMEL set at right angles to the grip.

SHANG YIN In Chinese history, the period *c*.1532–1027 BC.

Georgian, SHAGREEN and silver-mounted draughtsman's instruments case, c.1810–20.

SHARPS, CHRISTIAN Leading American gunmaker, active in the mid-19thC.

SHAW, JOSHUA Leading American gunmaker, active in the early 19thC.

SHEARER, THOMAS An English, 18thC cabinet-maker and author of *The Cabinet-maker's London Book of Prices* (1788). His designs are similar to those of Thomas SHERATON, and, to this day, his two contemporaries George HEPPLEWHITE and Sheraton are given much of the credit really due to him.

SHEEP'S-HEAD CLOCK Late-17thC type of CLOCK with an outsized dial, which hides the case from view.

SHEET METAL A process introduced commercially in the late 18thC to produce BEAKERS, TANKARDS, and other cylindrical objects. An oblong sheet of SILVER or SHEFFIELD PLATE is cut to the required size, then wrapped to form a cylinder. The seam where the two sides meet is soldered together, and a disc of silver is soldered to the base. Features such as feet, handles, and borders are cast and applied. Items made of sheet metal are lighter than cast wares.

SHEFFIELD PLATE Introduced *c.*1740 by Thomas Bolsover as a less-expensive alternative to SILVER, wares made from a fusion of copper between two sheets of sterling silver. Sheffield plate could be rolled or hammered into sheets and made into objects. Decoration is usually FLAT-CHASED rather than engraved, as the latter meant cutting through to the copper. In the late 18thC, a method was developed for decorating Sheffield plate with an engraved crest: a hole was cut into the object, and a heavily plated or solid-silver shield soldered into place. During the early 19thC, a patch of pure silver foil was burnished onto Sheffield plate to provide a base for crests. The introduction of the ELECTROPLATE technique in the 1840s caused the rapid decline of the Sheffield plate industry. You can usually identify Sheffield plate by its pinkish tinge caused by areas of silver wearing thin and revealing the copper body. Most Sheffield plate is unmarked, but some late 18thC pieces had HALLMARKS similar to those on silver. A piece with "Sheffield plate" stamped on it is probably electroplate, and not genuine silver Sheffield plate, which is also referred to as OLD SHEFFIELD PLATE. Try not to over-polish Sheffield items, because this may wear away the thin surface of silver.

SHELL Decorative motif used in the 18thC, and revived in the Edwardian era (1901–10). Also known as SCALLOPED, after the type of shell usually shown.

SHELLAC (1) Made from the shell of the lac beetle, a substance produced in France and used in the process of French polishing.

SHELLAC (2) Invented 1868, an early form of plastic, used principally for gramophone records, but also (more rarely) for moulded ornaments.

SHELLEY POTTERY LTD First known as Wileman & Co., then as FOLEY, Shelley is best known for its ART DECO-style tablewares made in the 1920s, along with NURSERY WARE and figures based on illustrations by Mabel Lucie ATTWELL. The most valuable pieces are Art Deco tablewares painted with bold designs in distinctive colour combinations. Less striking (and less desirable) pieces with floral decoration were made in the 1930s and '40s. Wares are categorized by their design and by their shape, for example "Eve", "Vogue", and "Regent". Shelley also made commemorative pieces, the value of which depends on the rarity of the design. Most pieces are marked with a signature in a CARTOUCHE and serial number. Marks that include "Fine Bone China" are post-1945. A serial number beginning with "2" shows that the piece was a second.

SHENANDOAH VALLEY Simple EARTHENWARE and slip-decorated REDWARE produced by several valley towns in Virginia, North America, from 1800. Examples by the Bell family are the best known.

SHEN-LUNG Chinese dragon motif found on CARPETS and PORCELAIN.

SHEPHERD'S-CROOK ARM Fashionable in the 18thC, a curving chair or settee arm shaped like a shepherd's crook.

SHEPHERD'S SUNDIAL Portable SUNDIAL with a complex scale. Designed for year-round use, it takes into account the sun's seasonal movement.

SHERATON REVIVAL FURNITURE produced in the style of Thomas SHERATON, notably during the Edwardian period (1901–10).

SHERATON, THOMAS (1751–1806) English FURNITURE designer renowned for his practical books on furniture design, widely used by cabinet-makers, linking the NEO-CLASSICAL and REGENCY STYLES. He used INLAY work extensively, with MARQUETRY taking the place of much of the carving employed by previous makers. Sheraton produced a variety of lightly framed pieces, his favoured wood being SATINWOOD. He is said to have invented the kidney-shaped table, and is known for his SIDEBOARDS (often with convex corners).

SHERRAT, OBADIAH Active *c.*1815–1830s, a British, Staffordshire-based potter, who made brightly coloured groups with themes such as bull baiting and fairgrounds. Many of his large pieces required table bases for support.

SHIBAYAMA Decorative INLAY named after the Japanese artist, Shibayama Dosho. It usually comprises IVORY, MOTHER-OF-PEARL, coral, GOLD, or SILVER, inlaid into a lacquered ground.

SHIBUICHI Silver-bronze alloy used by Japanese makers of INRO.

Superb Japanese ivory and SHIBAYAMA case, c.1890.

SHIELD BACK Designed in the 18thC, a type of CHAIR with a back shaped like a shield. It is mainly associated with George HEPPLEWHITE.

SHIPPING FURNITURE Term usually applied to lesser-quality FURNITURE intended for export.

SHIPS IN BOTTLES Made by sailors from *c*.1870 to 1920, but mass-produced from 1900.

SHIRAZ Centre of distribution in central Iran for RUGS decorated with simple geometric designs.

SHIRVAN A Caucasian RUG, typically with fine knots, short PILE, and small geometric patterns, in which dark blues and strong reds predominate. Modern Shirvans can be identified by their long pile and cotton WARP and WEFT. *See also* RUGS, CAUCASIAN AND TURKISH.

SHISHI Japanese name for DOG OF FO.

SHOE BRACE (Or shoe piece.) At the bottom of a chair back, a piece into which the central splat is fitted.

SHOE-BUTTON EYES *See* BOOT-BUTTON EYES.

SHOO-FLY American rocking horse patented in 1859, and consisting of two horse-shaped, cut-out boards on rockers and joined by a seat.

SHOULDER-HEAD Type of head found on many early DOLLS, with the shoulders, neck, and head moulded in one piece. The SHOULDER-PLATE reaches the top of the arms. The head might be glued into a KID body, or sewn, using specially made holes, onto a cloth body. This type of head was introduced with the earliest PAPIER-MÂCHÉ DOLLS. Adding a shoulder-head was more versatile and often cheaper than making the head as part of a whole doll.

SHOULDER-PLATE The area of a doll's SHOULDER-HEAD below the neck.

SHOW WOOD Visible wood on an upholstered piece of FURNITURE.

SHUNZHI (Shun Chih) Chinese QING dynasty emperor, 1644–61.

S.I.C. (Société Industrielle de Celluloid) A French organization, the initials of which are found on some CELLULOID dolls.

SICILIAN POTTERY Italian wares made in several centres in Sicily, most notably in Palermo. It commands a premium.

East Caucasian SHIRVAN rug, c.1880.

SIDEBOARD A piece of dining-room FURNITURE with CUPBOARDS and DRAWERS for holding PLATES, CUTLERY, wine, table linen, and other DINING ACCESSORIES; it was popularized by Robert ADAM from *c*.1770. As imported MAHOGANY became available, sideboards became increasingly elegant and sophisticated in the 18thC. Most English sideboards have brass galleries that originally would have been hung with silk curtains to protect the wallpaper from the juices that splashed as the meat was carved. Dining was a lengthy process in wealthy homes during the 18thC, and sideboards usually had cellaret drawers on one side for storing wine and cupboards on the other side for storing chamber pots. On later versions, the central arches were lowered and often turned into drawers without handles. The shape of a sideboard, as well as the FIGURE of the wood, can affect the value of a piece: SERPENTINE and bow-fronted versions are more expensive than examples with straight fronts. A wide range of sideboards was made during the 19thC, including heavy pedestal versions in the reign of William IV, and the eclectic range of styles such as GOTHIC reform, ART NOUVEAU, and SHERATON REVIVAL that were produced in the 19thC. Many 19thC sideboards are more than 2m (7ft) long, and can be overpowering if placed in modern dining rooms. If you can find one to fit, it will probably cost about half as much as one made in the 18thC. Although some sideboards reflect the styles of the previous century, a high back, bevelled, oval mirror, and elaborate inlays are in the style of the late Victorian and Edwardian eras (1860–1901 and 1901–10 respectively). Turned legs, features of later sideboards, were often replaced with the earlier, square, tapering style of leg to make 19thC sideboards look older (and more valuable). The legs should form part of the carcass and not be joined onto it. During the 19thC, the Victorians sometimes "improved" a piece by adding an INLAY. Although a purist might think that this alteration reduces the value, it appeals to some decorators, and will not affect the price unduly. Deep drawers converted into cupboards are common, and do not seriously affect value.

SIDE CABINET A type of FURNITURE for displaying objects, first made in the 18thC. They were plain and unfashionable until the early 19thC. In Britain, the late Victorians and Edwardians (1860–1901 and 1901–10 respectively) were fond of side cabinets for displaying decorative objects, and they made a vast range, with many examples lavishly decorated with MARQUETRY, porcelain plaques, and metal mounts. At the end of the 19thC, many were made with upper sections of shelves, mirrors, and porcelain niches. Check the condition of a piece before buying, as damage to decoration can be costly to repair.

SIDE RAIL (Also known as an UPRIGHT.) One of the two outer, vertical members that form the back of a CHAIR.

SIDE TABLE The forerunners of the SERVING TABLE, side tables were made from the 16thC to stand against walls. Their backs are plain, and there is often a drawer in the front frieze. The rectangular tops were made from planks. The wood varies according to date, but OAK was often used. Look for attractively shaped legs (double-BALUSTER legs are a bonus), a shaped STRETCHER (if there is one), good PATINATION (this adds to value, whatever the wood), and original or appropriate handles. *See also* LOWBOY SIDE TABLE.

SIENA In Tuscany, Italy, a centre of production known for Renaissance MAIOLICA, often with Moorish-influenced designs and using burnt "sienna" – the orange-brown colour named after the town.

SIGILLATA Relief-decorated POTTERY cast in a mould, in imitation of ancient Roman Samian or red-gloss wares.

SIGNPOST BAROMETER Alternative name for an ANGLE BAROMETER.

SILEH An S-shaped motif found on Caucasian RUGS.

SILENT-STRIKING CLOCK A CLOCK with a device to shut off the strike at certain times: during the night for example.

SILESIAN STEM On DRINKING GLASSES, a distinctive hexagonal or octagonal MOULD-BLOWN STEM, flaring up to a pronounced shoulder, with a hollow centre. Originating in Silesia, it was popular for a short period (*c*.1710–30), although this style continued to be used on TAZZAS, CANDLESTICKS, and other wares throughout the 18thC. The number of sides on the PEDESTAL STEM is a useful method of dating Silesian-stem glasses: the earliest have four sides, while later ones have six or eight. English versions were made from LEAD CRYSTAL, but versions in SODA GLASS were produced in Continental Europe – these are lightweight, and have a dull colour and lack of ring when tapped.

SILICA Fine sand, the basic material for GLASS. It requires FLUXES (such as soda) to reduce the melting temperature to a practical level.

SILICON WARE Colourful vitreous, or enamel-like STONEWARE made by DOULTON in England in the 1880s and '90s and imitated by other potteries.

Doulton Lambeth SILICON WARE amphora vase by Edith Lupton, 1885.

SILVER A malleable, greyish-white metal used to mint coinage and make practical items for the household, as well as for precious objects reflecting wealth and status. Silver has been used throughout history, and encompasses all the major decorative arts styles. Pure silver is unworkably soft, and has to be mixed with other, more resilient base metals before it can be made into objects. A silver standard was introduced in Britain in 1300, and all silver objects made after this date had to be tested and marked to show that they contained more than 92.5 per cent pure silver. Much Continental European and American silver was also marked in some way, but in many countries the system was less rigorously applied than in Britain. In the 16thC, the conquest of the Americas

Edwardian, Barker Brothers, SILVER pedestal bowl, 1903.

by the Spanish, and the discovery of vast silver deposits there led to a surge in production. Over years of use, silver develops a soft glow, or patina, caused by accumulated scratching and knocks and bruises. This patina is important to value. With the exceptions of early 18thC English and 18thC American silver, which was generally unembellished, various forms of decoration were usually applied to the surface of the metal according to contemporary taste. New decoration was often added to an old piece of plain silver to accommodate changing trends, and engraved ARMORIALS and initials were frequently removed and replaced with new ones. The practice of altering silver reached its peak in the Victorian period (1837–1901), when many 17th and 18thC plain silver vessels were chased with lavish ornament of flowers and foliage. It has also been common practice across the centuries to alter or convert silver items from having redundant functions into useful ones. Many TANKARDS, for example, were converted into TEAPOTS when tea became more popular than beer in the 18thC. These alterations are illegal, and any alteration to an original piece of silver, whether in function or decoration, will reduce the value. Signs of alteration include crude joins, suggested by roughly soldered patches (typical on hollow wares) and thin, vulnerable patches of metal, where an original inscription may have been polished off to make way for new engraving. Pushing gently on a suspicious patch will reveal if any original engraving has been removed. All detachable components of a piece should be at least partly marked. Check all parts such as handles, feet, and finials carefully. Sometimes silver objects are cast from originals, with the old HALLMARK deleted and new marks applied, but this practice of copying is acceptable. However, reproducing an item with only its original hallmarks demonstrates an intent to deceive, and is illegal. Pieces intended to deceive are often easy to detect. The craftsmanship and quality of detail of a master cannot be reproduced by mass-production methods, and the lack of quality is often self-evident in a piece of faked silver. Forged marks can be identified by soft outlines and a lack of definition. A common method of faking silver involves removing the marks from an older or a more valuable item, or one in poor condition by a celebrated maker, and soldering them into a less-valuable piece. Most objects have characteristic configurations of hallmarks. For example, MUSTARD-POTS usually bear a cluster of marks on the base, while SALVERS are nearly always marked in a straight line. Marks that have been added are often positioned incorrectly, distorted, or missing. Any repair will reduce the value of silver, unless the piece is rare or by a top silversmith. Inspect areas that are vulnerable to damage: feet may be pushed up through the base; the metal of the body might be pulled away by the handle; hinges can be broken and are often difficult to repair; and PIERCED DECORATION is fragile and prone to damage. *See also* BRITANNIA STANDARD; ELECTROPLATE; HALLMARK; SILVER, CARE OF; and STERLING SILVER.

SILVER, CARE OF SILVER develops black spots and becomes tarnished when in contact with sulphur, which is found in the air, especially in polluted cities, or in fumes from burning oil and gas. Sulphur is also found in foods such as eggs, peas, and Brussels sprouts. Ammonia will also discolour silver. If you acquire heavily tarnished silver follow expert advice, because tarnish is hard to remove. If an object is not heavily tarnished, clean it with a proprietary cleaner or wadding polish. Never use an abrasive cleaner. After the first cleaning keep the silver in good condition by regular washing with warm, soapy water (use a mild detergent), rinsing, and drying with a soft cotton or chamois cloth. SILVER-GILT and plated wares can be treated in the same way, but take care when washing and drying silver-gilt objects with delicate decoration such as FILIGREE and ENAMEL. Silver should be rubbed over occasionally to prevent the build-up of tarnish, but too frequent rubbing or polishing will destroy the patina and wear away the marks and BRIGHT-CUT, ENGRAVED, or FLAT-CHASED details. Similarly, overzealous polishing of plated wares will wear away the thin layer of SILVER PLATE, allowing the base to show through. Take care when cleaning and polishing plated wares with protruding features such as scroll feet, which are vulnerable. Silver dips may be effective for larger items such as TUREENS, and for cleaning objects with complex shapes or decoration. However, use them sparingly: always use a non-metallic bath, and do not leave the objects in the dip for too long – the chemicals may turn the silver dull. Carefully clean pierced silver, especially pieces made of thin-gauge metal from the late 18thC, with a fine soft brush and soapy water to avoid splitting the piercing. This method is also good for removing abrasive cleaning powders from older pieces. Use a weak solution of washing soda and water to clean stained TEAPOTS and coffee-pots. Many CANDLESTICKS from the last 150 years are "loaded" with tar, plaster of Paris, or resin for stability. Do not immerse them in hot water, or leave them exposed to direct sunlight, because the tar or resin will expand under heat, pushing off the base. Knife handles are also sometimes loaded – do not clean them in hot water or put them in the dishwasher, as the loading in the handle will expand. On knives, forks, and other FLATWARE take care with IVORY or MOTHER-OF-PEARL handles that have steel tangs (shafts) running down the centre, joining the handle to the blade. Do not put them in water because the steel will rust, and the tang will swell and split the handles.

SILVERED GLASS A double-walled, GLASS vessel lined with SILVER to produce a mirror-like glass, patented in 1849 by Edward Varnish and Frederick Hale Thomson. Much silvered glass is plain, but some pieces are in coloured glass, sometimes embellished with cutting or engraving.

SILVER GILT Solid SILVER covered with a thin layer of GOLD.

SILVER LUSTRE On CERAMICS, a silvery, iridescent LUSTRE achieved by painting the vessel with a platinum-based pigment.

SILVER TABLE A small rectangular TABLE, often with a fretwork gallery and used for displaying objects and serving tea in the 18thC. French-style tables with metal galleries were popular. MAHOGANY was used in the 18thC, and various woods after that. Look for pierced galleries and wide CASTERS on 18thC tables, and good-quality metal mounts on 19thC versions.

SILVERWOOD A name used for harewood in the 18thC. *See also* SYCAMORE.

SIMON & HALBIG One of Germany's earliest, most prolific manufacturers of BISQUE dolls' heads, supplying other German and French firms. They produced SHOULDER-HEADS until 1880, then SOCKET-HEADS, with fine heads for CHARACTER DOLLS after 1900. "Sleeping" eyes and real-hair eyelashes were introduced on some DOLLS from 1895 onward. Almost all heads have a mould number, which is important for collectors. Simon & Halbig were prolific makers of brown dolls, and specialized in Oriental girl dolls.

SINCENCY Early-18th to mid-19thC FAIENCE factory near Paris, France. Wares are noted for their muted colours and CHINOISERIE scenes.

SINDY The best-selling teenage fashion DOLL made in Britain, "Sindy" was created by Dennis Arkinstall of PEDIGREE SOFT TOYS in London in 1962. She was originally modelled on an adolescent girl; in 1971, a more sophisticated version was introduced, with a long, flick-up hair-style instead of the original short version to which a hair piece could be added. By 1966, Sindy had a little sister called Patch and a boyfriend named Paul. Both had fashionable, specially designed outfits – Paul's often matched Sindy's. Patch was discontinued in the early 1970s, and other minor friends also came and went. Until 1966, Sindy had plain eyes with straight limbs. Bendable limbs were introduced later, and in 1968 more realistic eyelashes were added. In 1971, the first "walking" Sindy was made, with moving head, shoulders, elbows, waist, hips, and knees. Pedigree made a new collection of clothes for her every six months. They were made in Hong Kong and embroidered labels were sewn into each garment. A huge range of Sindy accessories was produced in the early 1970s, including a kitchen, bedroom, fillable bath, and piano. For "out-of-doors" she had a horse called Peanuts and a scooter. Many of these items are collectable. Only 250 black Sindys were made, and a model in her original box is very desirable. Look for the identification mark under the hair on the back of the head on all Sindy dolls.

SINGERIE Motif based on monkeys, often dressed in clothes. Popular during the fashion for CHINOISERIE in the 18thC.

SINGLE-TRAIN MOVEMENT A movement in which all the functions of a CLOCK are performed by one mechanism.

SIPHON BAROMETER Generic term for barometers with a vertical column of mercury and a vertical scale, as distinct from the WHEEL BAROMETER, which has a dial and indicator hand.

SIVAS From Turkey, Persian-influenced CARPETS noted for delicate colours.

SIX-CHARACTER MARK *See* REIGN MARK, CHINESE.

SIX DYNASTIES Period in Chinese history AD 265–589.

SIX-HOUR DIAL A CLOCK dial with six divisions instead of 12, often with the hours 1–6 in Roman numerals and 7–12 superimposed in Arabic numerals.

SKÅNSKA Noted for its simple forms, GLASS from the Swedish works founded in the late 17thC.

SKEAN-DHU Short, Scottish DAGGER carried in the stocking top in the 19thC.

SKEAPING, JOHN (1901–80) CERAMICS modeller who specialized in animal figures in matt GLAZES. He made designs in 1927 for WEDGWOOD for a group of animals, including deer, a polar bear, kangaroo, bison, and monkeys, in various glazes, and was paid £10 for each model. Animals are typically marked both with the designer's name and that of Wedgwood.

SKELETON CLOCK A CLOCK designed to display as much of the working mechanism as possible by cutting the plates to the minimum requirement for supporting the movement. The origins of skeleton clocks lie in Continental Europe, but the most complex and elaborate pieces are English. Many of these clocks had protective glass domes.

SKELETON ESCUTCHEON Simplest form of lock ESCUTCHEON, which merely outlines the shape of the keyhole.

SKEWER, MEAT The earliest SILVER meat skewers date from the mid-18thC, when it was fashionable for the hostess to carve meat at the table. Most skewers have rings at one end to withdraw the skewer or hang it on a hook, but some have decorative terminals. They were sometimes made in graduated sets and decorated to match FLATWARE patterns. Meat skewers were rarely used by the 1850s, and today are often seen used as paper knives.

SKEWER, POULTRY A smaller version of the meat SKEWER – some examples measuring only 7.5cm (3in) in length – made for poultry. Produced mainly in Continental Europe, early (pre-1770) poultry skewers are rare and collectable, especially those featuring cast, heraldic terminals.

SKIPPY Manufactured by EFFanBEE Toy Co., a 1930s' DOLL with a jointed COMPOSITION body and moulded-and-painted hair. It was based on a comic-strip figure created by Percy L. Crosby, and played in a film by Jackie Cooper – hence "Skippy" was often referred to as a "Jackie Cooper" doll.

Victorian, brass, SKELETON CLOCK without its glass dome.

SKIVER Thin leather used as a writing surface on WRITING TABLES and DESKS.

SLAT BACK A type of COUNTRY CHAIR with a back formed of curved vertical strips or slats of wood.

SLEEPING EYES (Or sleep eyes.) On a DOLL, eyes that can open when upright and close when horizontal. They were used on some WAX-OVER-COMPOSITION and PAPIER-MÂCHÉ DOLLS. At first, the eyes were operated by wire levers, but by the end of the 19thC they were controlled by weights.

SLEEVE VASE Oriental VASE of narrow, tubular form.

SLEIGH BED American bed made in the EMPIRE STYLE and resembling a sleigh.

SLICE Made from the 18thC, a SILVER knife with a broad, trowel-shaped blade, sometimes pierced or engraved.

SLIDE *See* BRUSHING SLIDE and CANDLE SLIDE.

SLIP Clay mixed with water. Often used to decorate POTTERY.

SLIP CAST POTTERY made by pouring SLIP into a plaster mould, which absorbs the water and leaves behind the moulded clay. The technique is used for producing varied forms.

SLIPPER CHAIR A 19thC, upholstered, drawing-room CHAIR, with a back that is more reclined than usual and continuous through the seat in a curving line.

SLIP TRAILING Application of slip onto a ceramic form as a way of decorating the surface.

SLIPWARE Red or buff EARTHENWARE body decorated with SLIP. Pieces were usually dipped into white slip, with extra details later applied by TRAILING, dotting, and COMBING other slips of varying russet and chocolate colours onto the surface of the body. Zig-zag, feathered, and marble designs predominate. Decorated pieces were then coated in thick lead GLAZES that turned white clay yellow when fired. The overall effect has a primitive charm that collectors in Britain and the USA find appealing. Wares were produced in Staffordshire, Wrotham in Kent, Bideford, Barnstaple, Wales, Wiltshire, and Sussex from the 17th to mid-18thC. Early slipware can fetch high prices. Makers of this kind of ware did not generally mark their pieces; most names or initials refer to the owner rather than the maker. Look for dishes and MUGS, and named or dated wares, especially those of best-known maker Thomas TOFT, who occasionally signed his wares on the front. Other names to look for include: George Talor, William Talor, John Wright, John

Simpson, and Samuel Malkin. Beware of skilful fakes. Slipware continued to be made in Britain throughout the 19thC by firms such as DOULTON and MOORCROFT. The tradition was revived by studio potters such as Bernard LEACH in the 20thC. *See also* OWL JUG and STAFFORDSHIRE POTTERIES.

SLIT HEAD A wax-over-papier-mâché DOLL made in England in the early-19thC. A slit ran across the PATE into which hair was inserted, to fall either side and simulate a parting. *See also* PAPIER-MÂCHÉ.

SMALLSWORD Any short SWORD, under 75cm (29½in) in length, designed for hand-to-hand fighting, duelling, thrusting, or fencing.

SMITH & WESSON Major American gunmakers, founded in the mid 19thC.

SMITH, GEORGE Active from 1790 to 1826, an English cabinet-maker and FURNITURE designer who helped revive the Egyptian and NEO-CLASSICAL STYLES.

SMOKER'S BOW Variation of the WINDSOR CHAIR but with a low back, and arms formed from a continuous hoop, above spindles.

SMOKER'S COMPANION A contraption used to perform a range of tasks for a smoker. The hollow body of the vessel can store cigars, cigarettes, and cheroots, or serve as an ashtray. The "guillotine" is for snipping off the ends of cigars. Two small containers, one on each side, with hinged lids and finials are for holding vestas or small tapers. The TAPERSTICK is for igniting tobacco and lighting the room. High-quality examples are sought after by wealthy, cigar-smoking collectors, and achieve high prices.

SMOKEY A TEDDY BEAR named after an Assistant Chief of the New York City Fire Department, "Smokey Joe" Martin. "Smokey" was dressed in blue jeans, a special hat, silver badge, and belt buckle, and carried a blue plastic shovel; he first appeared on posters for an American, forest-fire prevention campaign in 1944. One of the first licenced Smokey bears was made with a vinyl head, hands, and feet and a brown PLUSH body by IDEAL in 1953. By 1954, only the head was vinyl.

A silver-mounted tusk double cigar cutter by Sampson Morton & Co., London, 1910 (SMOKING ACCESSORIES).

SMOKING ACCESSORIES Items associated with tobacco, which first appeared in 16thC France, when snuff – pulverized tobacco taken by both men and women and sniffed up the nose – was considered beneficial to the health; the custom was introduced to Britain a century later. Small boxes for storing snuff were made in the early 18thC. However, by the mid-19thC, cigar and cheroot smoking became fashionable, and few SNUFFBOXES were produced after this date. The Spanish introduced cigars to Europe shortly after the discovery of America in 1492, but the first European cigar factory only opened in Hamburg in 1788. In Britain, the taste for cigar smoking was well established by the end of the 18thC. The custom of retiring for a smoke after a meal became fashionable among gentlemen from the mid-19thC, reaching its peak of popularity between 1880 and 1910. Cigars and cheroots were expensive luxuries to be savoured, and, as a result, considerable ceremony was attached to their enjoyment. Items produced to enhance the pleasure of the smoking ritual include CIGAR CUTTERS, LIGHTERS, which were usually non-portable and designed to stand on a table, and combination SMOKERS' COMPANIONS, used to perform a range of tasks by the smoker. Novelty designs were favoured, and these remain popular with collectors today. From the end of the 19thC, cigarettes became fashionable, and their popularity was accompanied by the production of CIGARETTE CASES. During the 19th and 20thC, British, Birmingham-based makers produced a variety of accessories, from cigar boxes to VESTA CASES for matches.

SNAKEWOOD Hard, deep, reddish-brown wood with dark spots. Imported from South America and used as a veneer.

SNAPE A thin metal strip used for fixing pear-drop handles and early bail handles to the drawer front. The snape was bent back on the inside of the drawer front and secured.

SNUFFBOX A small PORCELAIN or SILVER box for storing snuff, made from the early 18thC to the mid-19thC. Snuffboxes have interior lips tucked under the lids, which help to keep the snuff dry and prevent spillage; early examples have integral rasps and spoons. Many examples were made of inexpensive SHEET SILVER. They were embellished using a variety of decorative techniques, from simple, engine-turned examples to lavish embossed or enamelled ones, adorned with scenes of battles or hunting. Many snuffboxes have engraved initials, presentation inscriptions, or coats of arms. Some of the finest NIELLO snuffboxes were made in Russia, and these are often decorated with townscapes, architectural scenes, or floral designs. Large, table snuffboxes were used after dinner, when a host would offer his guests snuff from a communal box. They were often commissioned from such makers as A.J. STRACHAN and Nathaniel MILLS and made as presentation gifts. PORCELAIN boxes often had metal mounts. The decoration on the box has a bearing on its price: hunting scenes are sought after, and a recognizable view such as Windsor Castle, St Paul's Cathedral, or scenes of Edinburgh are collectable. The less-expensive pieces tend to be those made in the 19thC; earlier objects are scarcer, and can be highly priced. Check that the hinge is not damaged. Make sure the marks on the base are the same as those on the lid – if they don't match, the box may have been altered.

Rare Royal Worcester "Town Girl" SNUFFER, 1881.

SNUFFER A metal device used to extinguish candle flames. Scissor-shaped snuffers were made in large quantities in the 19thC. They were essential for trimming and collecting the wicks of tallow candles, which burnt more quickly than wax candles, and needed to be frequently trimmed. Many had steel blades and a box-like device at the end to hold pieces of wick, but this was no longer necessary with the invention of the self-consuming wick *c.*1800. Snuffers were produced by specialist makers, together with small oblong trays or stands that were sometimes made en suite with CANDLESTICKS. Early 18thC snuffer stands mirror the style of contemporary candlesticks, with faceted, BALUSTER stems and bases, and engraved ARMORIALS as the only decoration. The scissor-like snuffers were contained upright inside the body. Some snuffer stands feature hooks at the front of the body to support candle extinguishers. Watch out for splitting around joins at the handle or the base of the stem, and for solder repairs, as any such damage will reduce the value. In the mid-18thC snuffers had "waisted" or oblong-shaped stands, like trays. Later trays, in oval or boat shapes, were made from flat SHEET SILVER, often with applied, pierced borders. These are more lightly made than early examples. A tray and matching pair of scissor-action snuffers are rarely found together, and fetch a premium.

SNUFF GRATER Rasp used for grating compacted, dried tobacco leaf to make snuff powder. Sometimes incorporated within a snuffbox.

SNUFF HORN Used for storing tobacco or snuff, an 18thC vessel made of a sheep's horn, or sometimes a hoof. Many examples have silver MOUNTS.

SNUFF MULL The name "mull" is dialect for "mill"; snuff mulls featured devices for mashing snuff. They were made of ram's horn, usually date from 1790 to 1840, and are often unmarked.

SOAP BOX An 18thC SILVER sphere with a cover and a foot, often with pierced or fretted ornament.

SOCIÉTÉ FRANÇAISE DE FABRICATION DE BÉBÉS ET JOUETS Usually known as "S.F.B.J.", an association of major French dollmakers who feared the intrusion of German makers, and teamed up anonymously to form a consortium against the competition from 1899 to 1950. Its main period of activity was before 1930. Based at the JUMEAU factory, they made boy and girl CHARACTER DOLLS, coloured dolls, and BÉBÉS, mostly producing BISQUE-HEADED bébés on jointed wood and COMPOSITION bodies. The dolls were numbered according to the mould used. The most frequent moulds are No.s 60 and 301. A doll from mould No. 301 usually has a jointed wood-and-composition body. These dolls are likely to be of slimmer proportions than earlier dolls with high-cut legs, and are distinguishable from their German counterparts by the lack of separate ball joints at the elbow and knee. By 1911, the S.F.B.J. was making character dolls to compete with the realistic German ones, and these are much better made than the association's bébés. Despite the intense rivalry, doll parts were sometimes imported from

Germany. Most notable were the SIMON & HALBIG heads used 1900–14. Many dolls were sold in French colonies and in South America and Australia, but the Americans tended to buy German dolls. Their dolls were sent to Paris to be dressed in the latest styles, and the result was stylish dressing, with less attention paid to the actual doll. "S.F.B.J." was stamped on the back of the head of most of these dolls from 1905, along with the mould number. Circular stickers may also be found on the body.

SOCKET BAYONET A late-17thC, French invention – used until the 19thC – enabling a musket to be fired while the bayonet was in place. See also FIREARM.

SOCKET-HEAD A swivel head on a DOLL with a rounded base at the neck, enabling the head to fit into the top of the body. This is the most common head type on the majority of French and German dolls and babies.

SODA GLASS The earliest type of GLASS, in its simplest form it comprises only silica and soda (the soda was derived from the ashes of burnt seaweed), but this mixture is not durable, and dissolves in water to form a syrupy liquid known as water glass, now used for commercial fireproofing, and as a sealant. The addition of lime in small quantities, usually 10 per cent lime to 15 per cent soda and 75 per cent silica, stabilizes the batch and makes the material workable. Soda glass has a short working life – it hardens quickly when cooling – so the amount of soda is often increased to combat this. It is generally bubbly in appearance, with a slightly greenish colour, and is thin and fragile when blown, and difficult to engrave or cut. Also known by the Italian term CRISTALLO, soda glass was made in Venice from the 13thC, because the molten glass had a malleable quality that allowed glassmakers to create elaborate shapes. Soda glass is still the most common type of glass used today to make cheap, disposable items such as bottles and light bulbs.

Regency SOFA TABLE with a single frieze drawer.

SOFA Long seat that was developed from the French DAY BED. The word "sofa" is of Middle Eastern derivation (denoting the "dais" on which the Grand Vizier sat) and did not appear in England until the 18thC. Nowadays, "sofa" usually refers to a seat that is both larger and more comfortable than a SETTEE. An important development changed the appearance of many sofas made after 1830 – earlier sofas were stuffed with layers of horsehair and wadding; spring upholstered sofas, introduced from c.1830, had seats and backs filled with coiled metal springs that were supported on hessian webbing and covered in layers of horsehair and wadding, making them far more comfortable. In order to make room for the new springs, sofas became deeper and wider, and buttoning was often used to make them look more sumptuous. *See also* BUTTON BACK, CHAISE LONGUE and SALON SUITE.

SOFA TABLE An elongated, rectangular TABLE with drop flaps and drawers. First made c.1790, it was a longer, narrower version of the PEMBROKE TABLE.

The best sofa tables have two end-supports connected by a stretcher. Tables with central pedestal bases are less valuable. Such tables were designed to stand near sofas, to be used by ladies for writing, drawing, and reading. The first ones were made of MAHOGANY, and various exotic woods were also used for VENEERS. MARQUETRY decoration in the NEO-CLASSICAL STYLE is found on fine pieces. The position of the stretcher on a sofa table can give an indication of the table's date. A high stretcher points to an early date of *c.*1790; a decade later, stretchers were lower or had been replaced by central pedestals.

SOFT-PASTE PORCELAIN Developed by English potters in the mid-18thC as a by-product of the search for true PORCELAIN, soft-paste porcelain used ground frit, soapstone (or steatite), and bone-ash instead of the PETUNTSE of true porcelain. As the name suggests, soft-paste porcelain is more vulnerable to scratching than HARD-PASTE PORCELAIN. Soft paste can often be identified because the GLAZE sits on the surface, feeling warmer and softer to the touch, and looking less glittering in appearance than hard paste. Chips in soft paste look floury, like fine pastry, while chips in hard paste look glassy. Soft-paste porcelain was first produced in Italy in the 16thC. Later factories using it include ST CLOUD, CHANTILLY, VINCENNES, and SÈVRES in France, CAPODIMONTE in Italy, and CHELSEA in Britain.

SOFT TOYS A child's plaything made of cloth, usually in the shape of an animal. Soft toys took off only after Margarete STEIFF created felt pincushions as gifts in 1880. Before long, Steiff had created a menagerie, with designs ranging from pigs and donkeys to monkeys and camels. These toys sold so well that other makers quickly began to imitate them. Children took to the animals, which, like TEDDY BEARS, were cuddlier than traditional toys, even when they incorporated clockwork movements or could be pulled along on wheels. In Germany, numerous small companies made animals in cloth, felt, leather, and PLUSH; however, in the USA, the teddy-bear craze was so great that there was little room for competition until the 1930s. DEAN'S, FARNELL, CHAD VALLEY, and MERRYTHOUGHT were among the first makers in Britain. Look out for animals from children's literature, especially characters by Beatrix Potter. When the maker cannot be identified, look for quality in the material, design, and stitching. Some animals by other makers were as good as those by Steiff, but are less expensive today. The soft toys made by Steiff before World War I are the most desirable. After teddy bears, the most sought after of the early animals are jointed rabbits and elephants. Look out for cats with green eyes, rabbits and hares with yellow eyes, dogs such as dachshunds, poodles, or sheepdogs, and characters from film and television if they are in soft material and jointed, and also have their label and name showing. American toymakers made up for lost time in the production of soft toys. North American animals to look out for are known characters inspired by the film industry. In England, toys by the old established firms such as Dean's are the most desirable. The most valuable, later soft toys are

Two 1930s TOY SOLDIERS from Britain's Austro-Hungarian Infantry of the Line set.

African safari-type animals, such as lions and zebras, and polar bears. The value of later animals depends on several factors. Good condition is essential, and 1950s' toys are preferable to those of the 1960s or later. The average size is 23cm (9in) tall or long, and larger creatures are more costly. Rarity and attractiveness can make others more desirable. Look out for toys by named makers (most animals of any value have labels), known animal characters, and particularly cuddly and cute toys. Such is the demand for early Steiff designs that in the 1980s the company began to make limited-edition replicas of animals; many dealers sell reproductions as well as originals. Such toys can complement the originals, but take care not to confuse them. Watch out for genuine buttons (the Steiff trademark) added to incorrect animals. Damaged fur reduces value.

SOLDER Molten substance, often lead, applied to repair cracks and holes.

SOLDIER, TOY First made in the mid-18thC, a miniature replica of a soldier. The first models were two dimensional and made of TIN in Germany. Early DIECAST lead soldiers are more popular among collectors; these were flat or semi-flat. Solid, three-dimension soldiers were first made *c*.1890. The HOLLOW-CAST technique, patented by William BRITAIN Ltd, led to a wider range of more realistic figures from 1900. Toy soldiers cast in ALUMINIUM, as distinct from lead, are common from the 1950s. High-quality, solid and hollow-cast lead soldiers were produced by firms such as LUCOTTE, HEYDE, and William Britain, and these are among the most collectable items available today. Examples with oval bases and paper labels in their original boxes fetch the best prices.

SOLID-DOMED HEAD On a DOLL, a head that is solid, without an opening for a separate PATE. The few BISQUE-headed dolls with solid domed heads are called "Belton" heads. They can be SOCKET-HEADS, a later form of SWIVEL-HEAD, or SHOULDER-PLATE heads. Wigs are stuck on with glue, and sometimes the head has holes, with the wig attached using string.

SOLIDS Three-dimensional toy SOLDIERS, introduced *c*.1890 as distinct from FLATS, SEMI-FLATS or "cut-out" figures. They are now the most collected form.

SOLID WAX *See* PRESSED WAX.

SOLITAIRE A tea set for one person. *See also* TÊTE-À-TÊTE.

SOUMAC A richly coloured and decorated KELIM, and one of the easiest of the Caucasian RUGS to identify because they are flat-woven rather than knotted. Unlike other kelims, they are patterned on one side only, with the weft left uncut for warmth. Trappings such as bags, saddle covers and tent hangings are always popular with collectors, and can be surprisingly expensive. *See also* RUGS, CAUCASIAN AND TURKISH and KNOT.

SOUTH BOSTON GLASS Early-19thC, American GLASS by an unrecorded Massachusetts factory, and showing the influence of BOSTON & SANDWICH.

SOUTHERN CELADON From the southern province of Chekiang, early Chinese wares with a distinctive deep red fabric and grey-green GLAZE.

SOUTH JERSEY GLASS Simple, free-blown glassware (often coloured) made by many firms in South Jersey, USA, in the late 18th and early 19thC.

SOUTHWARK South London POTTERY centre, active in the 17thC and noted for the earliest English DELFTWARE. *See also* DELFTWARE, ENGLISH.

SOVEREIGN HOLDER A small SILVER case employed to keep pocket money handy when it was attached to a chain or CHÂTELAINE.

SOWERBY ELLISON GLASSWORKS (1881–) Previously Sowerby & Neville (1855 72) and Sowerby & Co. (1872–81), a British GLASS firm established in Gateshead, England. It produced inexpensive pressed, slag, and spangled glass, and their "Opal" vases are among the most collectable PRESSED GLASS today. Wares were marked from 1876 onward. A signature was moulded, usually under the base, although sometimes in the interior.

SOY FRAME A smaller version of the CRUET stand, made from the 1760s to hold four to eight small bottles of sauces and condiments. Most soy frames had wooden bases with pierced sides, similar to wine COASTERS. By the late 18thC, larger soy frames were made, to hold up to ten bottles. Miniature versions of wine labels, engraved with the names of sauces, were hung around the bottles, and these – especially those with unusual names such as Anchovie or Chile – are sought after by collectors today. Soy frames were often poorly constructed of thin SHEET METAL, so few survive in good condition.

SPADE FOOT Tapering foot with a square section. Usually found on TABLES, CHAIRS, and SIDEBOARDS of the late 18thC.

SPADE HANDS Crude hands found on early German wooden DOLLS.

SPA GLASS Made in Germany, a heavy BEAKER or footed tumbler engraved with views of a spa town. Spa glasses were purchased as souvenirs by visitors seeking to "take the waters" at popular resorts, and they were customized and made to order. Trade was so prolific that glass engravers set up workshops in most resort towns.

SPANDREL Usually associated with the four corners on a CLOCK dial, the area between the corner and the central arch. This part of the clock is often filled with either BRASS or painted decoration.

SPANGLED GLASS coated in a mineral such as mica to glittering effect.

SPANISH FOOT A chair or table foot with elegant, outward-curving vertical lines, slightly reminiscent of a hand resting on its knuckles.

SPARTA Turkish CARPETS intended for European export. They were made and marketed in Smyrna, but are of better quality and finer colour than Smyrna carpets.

SPARVER BED Another name for a TENT BED.

SPATTERWARE Inexpensive British POTTERY produced by Staffordshire potters from 1820 to 1860 for export to the USA. It featured random mottled patterns and came in a wide range of colours. It is now rare.

SPECIMEN CHEST Designed for housing a collection of items, a small CHEST with many small drawers and sometimes also with enclosing doors.

SPECULAR Meaning "mirrorlike", a CARPET design in which the two halves, either the top and bottom or left and right, are symmetrical.

SPELTER An inexpensive patinated BRONZE made from a zinc-alloy base and used for making sculptures. To identify spelter, scratch the metal underneath – a silvery tone indicates spelter and means that the piece is less valuable than one made of bronze. *See also* SCULPTURE, ART NOUVEAU AND ART DECO.

SPICE BOX A late-16thC, SILVER casket with numerous internal divisions for storing precious spices, and a lid often in the form of a shell.

SPICE-BOX SPOON Spoons designed for dipping into SPICE BOXES. They usually have broad bowls and short curved "swan" handles.

SPILL VASE Made to contain spills for lighting candles, a porcelain VASE, often with a flat back for hanging on a wall.

SPLAT The central, flat piece of wood in a CHAIR back.

SPLINT SEAT A seat made of interlaced strips of wood, usually OAK or HICKORY, and found mainly in 18thC, American COUNTRY FURNITURE.

SPLIT BALUSTER Turned BALUSTER that has been split in half vertically to provide two flat surfaces.

SPLIT-BALUSTER GATELEG A TABLE leg in which the gate is part of the end leg. The leg splits in half down its length when the gate opens.

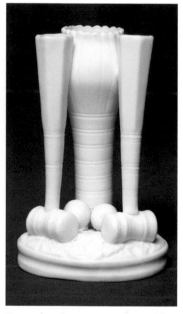

Unusual parian ware SPILL VASE with croquet theme, *c.*1870.

SPODE In England, a large Staffordshire factory founded in 1776 by Josiah Spode (1733–97). From the end of the 18thC through the 19thC, it produced a vast range of domestic EARTHENWARES and PARIAN, as well as grander, BONE-CHINA services (it was one of the first factories to use bone china), and ornamental pieces reflecting the prevailing taste for CLASSICAL and ROCOCO STYLES. The company was bought out by COPELAND & GARRETT in 1833, and is still in production today. Decorators at Spode did not usually sign their work, and their names are not generally known, but their high-quality decoration attracts high prices. Spode's most distinctive products include the IMARI patterns popular c.1815–25, pieces with coloured grounds, and wares embellished by decorators such as C.F. Hürten. Lavish gilding is also a feature of many of the best pieces. Patterns are identified by numbers – 1166, a floral design on a deep-blue, gilded "scaly" ground, is one of the most popular. Products by this factory may be less distinctive than those by some others, but they range from highly ornamental items to humbler wares decorated by BAT-PRINTING. On pieces made before 1830, the Spode name is usually hand-painted on PORCELAIN and impressed on pottery. After 1833, the names "Copeland & Garrett" usually appear, with "Late Spode" in the middle. "Copeland" is used alone after 1847.

Spode porcelain "Botanical' dessert plate, c.1830.

SPONGED WARE Akin to SPATTERWARE, inexpensive china produced for export from Britain to the USA in the 19thC, and decorated by dabbing at random a sponge soaked in SLIP over the surface of the vessel.

SPOOL FURNITURE Introduced in the USA in the 1850s, a form of decoration based on BOBBIN TURNING, which had been popular in the 17thC. It was used on many types of FURNITURE, including CHAIRS, BEDS, and TABLES.

SPOON BACK The back of a CHAIR that has a central SPLAT shaped somewhat like the handle of a spoon.

SPOON HANDS Wooden DOLLS manufactured with simple hands, with only the thumb articulated.

SPOONMAKER Term used to describe a maker of FLATWARE.

SPOON RACK A small hanging rack dating from the 17thC and earlier. Spoon racks are typically made from OAK or country woods and, although usually fairly simple in their design, they can be very decorative.

SPOON TRAY Early-18thC, small, silver TRAY, used to hold teaspoons before the saucer came into general use.

SPORTING MEMORABILIA Encompasses a wide range of items connected with sporting events, from equipment and clothing used in a match or game (such as bats, balls, bails, stumps, clubs, gloves, and boots) to autographs,

Silver golfing trophy on an ebonized base with winners' shields, 1914 (SPORTING MEMORABILIA).

presentation awards (including medals, trophies, belts, plates, and caps), decorative items (from commemorative ceramic wares to items of jewellery), and even literature. Five of the most popular sports among collectors are football, cricket, tennis, golf, and, particularly in the USA, baseball.

SPOUT CUP With a spout and two handles, a covered cup used for feeding invalids from the early 18th. *See also* CAUDLE CUP.

SPRIGGING Relief decoration – usually of a foliage motif – made from separate pieces of PORCELAIN, clay, or moulded SLIP, and applied to the BODY of a piece; the stems were modelled by hand. MEISSEN and many other leading factories applied "flowers" to ornamental objects.

SPRIGMONT, NICHOLAS (1716–70) A Flemish HUGUENOT who was a leading exponent of the ROCOCO STYLE in SILVER and PORCELAIN. His decoration was inspired by sea-related items such as shells, dolphins, and crabs. He founded the CHELSEA factory *c*.1745.

SPRING AND AUTUMN ANNALS In Chinese history, the period 770–480 BC.

SPRING DRIVEN Clockwork movements powered by the tension in the MAINSPRING, rather than by weights or a PENDULUM.

SPRINGFIELD TYPE DOLLS with moveable limbs. Similar to ELLIS DOLLS, but made by other companies in the region of Springfield, Vermont, USA.

SPRING-LOADED BAYONET Early-20thC BAYONET, with a release button to allow its swift removal from the gun barrel, and a hooked quillon, enabling the piece to be used as a hand weapon. *See also* FIREARM.

SPRUCE Wood of the fir family. Soft and white in colour.

SPUR MARK In the GLAZE on the base of a POTTERY vessel, an indentation caused by small stilts used to support the object during firing.

SQUAB Detachable or loose cushion for a bench or seat.

SQUAB STOOL Joined 16th and 17thC STOOL, with a seat with a slightly raised rim designed to hold a loose cushion.

SQUEEZER Late-19thC, small FIREARM designed to be concealed in the hand and fired by clenching the fist.

STAFFORDSHIRE BANK Early ceramic MONEY BOX or "piggy bank", of many forms. Made by STAFFORDSHIRE POTTERIES in the mid-18th to late 19thC.

STAFFORDSHIRE FIGURES A range of colourful CREAMWARE and PEARLWARE pottery figures produced in the small potteries in the North Staffordshire region of England in the early 19thC. Some were made in Scotland and Wales, but the majority came from the STAFFORDSHIRE POTTERIES, and hence all examples of this type are known as "Staffordshire figures". The earliest represented idyllic themes – shepherds and shepherdesses, musicians, and courting couples – and were brightly enamelled and crisply detailed, with modelling in the round, although they were mainly viewed from only one side. From *c*.1840, potters began making simpler, flat-backed figures. Most later figures were less well modelled, and the backs were not detailed. There was a strong use of red and ochres between *c*.1850 and 1860. Despite their primitive qualities, Staffordshire figures have great decorative appeal and enjoy huge popularity with present-day collectors. Prices are affected by the quality of the modelling and enamelling, as well as the subject matter – collectors' favourites include sporting and theatrical subjects, and rare and exotic animals such as elephants and lions. Figures of royal, political, and military subjects are also desirable. Dogs are particularly popular, especially spaniels, poodles, and greyhounds. Most examples are unmarked, so the style of each piece should be carefully examined. Less-valuable Staffordshire figures were reproduced in the 20thC, often from the same moulds as genuine 19thC pieces. These copies can be identified in several ways. A genuine piece will have crisp modelling, detailed painting, colourful decoration, finger or tool marks inside (from PRESS MOULDING), thick, heavy walls, erratic, widely spaced crackling in the GLAZE, soft gilding, and kiln grit and glaze on the foot. A copy or fake will have soft definition, little detail or colour, a smooth inside (from slip casting, or pouring SLIP into a mould), thin fragile walls, regular, exaggerated crackling in the glaze, bright gilding, and glaze wiped from the foot.

STAFFORDSHIRE-**pottery, pearlware figure of Britannia, c.1840.**

STAFFORDSHIRE POTTERIES The centre of the English pottery industry since the 18thC. An enormous number and variety of inexpensive ceramic household and decorative objects were produced by factories in the Staffordshire area, which came to be known as the Staffordshire Potteries in the 19thC. At that time, these pieces were very inexpensive, costings just a few shillings or less, and they are still abundantly available. Although popular with collectors, they have remained relatively affordable. *See also* STAFFORDSHIRE FIGURES.

STAINING A decoration technique that involves brushing the surface of GLASS with pigments of various colours to create a pictorial or decorative design. In the Middle Ages, silver chloride – producing a yellow stain – was painted into glass panes to create stained-glass windows. The technique was used on decorative glass from the early 19thC. The Bohemian glassmaker Friedrich EGERMANN had his own method of staining glass; this involved painting an object with a coloured stain, then firing it at a low temperature

Victorian Tunbridge-ware STAMP BOX, inlaid with a stamp on rosewood ground.

to produce the effect of FLASHING. His technique was used to mass-produce glassware in the 19thC.

STAKED LEG On FURNITURE, a simple way of fitting a leg to a seatboard. The top of the leg is pushed through a hole in the seat and secured by a wedge.

STALKER AND PARKER Firm that greatly popularized the art of JAPANNING in the late 17th and early 18thC.

ST AMAND-LES-EAUX An 18thC FAIENCE factory in northern France. It is noted for lacy patterning on a pale-grey GLAZE.

STAMP BOX Boxes produced from 1845 for storing and dispensing postage stamps. Often made in silver but also in TUNBRIDGE WARE.

STAMPED Design impressed into the BODY of a ceramic while it is still soft.

STAMP HOLDER Container used to store stamps. They were made in a huge variety of shapes and sizes, often with a postal theme, for example envelope-shaped pockets. Some were made in novelty forms such as tiny CHESTS OF DRAWERS. Such small dainty items can be valuable.

STANDARD (1) Required amount of pure SILVER in an alloy.

STANDARD (2) A dome-topped, iron-bound, travelling CHEST with handles.

STANDARD (3) A DINING CHAIR without arms.

STANDARD TIME COMPANY Founded in 1876, a firm specializing in highly accurate electric CLOCKS, mostly made for business firms.

STANDING CUP Usually a purely ornamental, highly elaborate, SILVER or GOLD vessel, used as a display piece.

STANDING SALT Large, ornate vessel for storing salt. Used in the 17thC, when salt was a precious commodity and a symbol of wealth.

STANDISH Before the 18thC, the common term for an INKSTAND in SILVER.

STANGENGLAS Produced in Germany in the 16th and 17thC, a tall, cyclindrical glass BEAKER decorated with PRUNTS.

STANHOPE A small souvenir made in novelty shapes from metal, wood, bone, or plastic in the mid-19th to 20thC. It incorporates a miniature lens, which was used to view a tourist scene on a transparency inside the piece.

STAR-CUTTING A method of glass cutting whereby multiple cuts meet at a central point in order to create a star pattern.

STAR OF BETHLEHEM In quilting, a block PATCHWORK pattern in which each of eight points of a star is pieced from diamonds. *See also* QUILT.

STATUARY PORCELAIN Alternative name for mid-19thC PARIAN ware, so-called because of its resemblance to marble.

STAUDENMAYER A leading English, London-based gunmaker, active in the early 19thC.

ST CLEMENT Late-18thC FAIENCE factory in Lorraine, France.

ST CLOUD French manufacturer based near Paris and famous for SOFT-PASTE PORCELAIN in the first half of the 18thC. The factory made a range of small decorative items, including SNUFFBOXES. Some wares were decorated in KAKIEMON style; some were made in BLANC-DE-CHINE. St Cloud paste is greyish-white and often peppered with black flecks. There are variations of the St Cloud mark, which includes the initials "St C" and "T" with a cross, found in blue and red or impressed. *See also* PORCELAIN, FRENCH.

STEEPLE CLOCK Early-GOTHIC CLOCK case with pinnacles resembling a church tower. Also refers to 19thC clock cases of similar form.

STEIFF mohair BEAR with boot button eyes, c.1908.

STEIFF BEARS The name Steiff is virtually synonymous with collectable TEDDY BEARS. Margarete Steiff opened a clothes shop in 1877 in Giengen, Wurtenburg, south Germany. She created tiny, elephant-shaped pincushions as presents, and went on to make fabric dolls and different animal toys, including, in 1884, the first bear standing on all fours, which she sold at local fairs. She set up business with her nephew Richard, who devised the first jointed bear. In 1903, Steiff sold 12,000 teddy bears and had toy outlets in Berlin, Hamburg, Leipzig, London, Paris, Amsterdam, and Florence. The following year Margarete registered the elephant trademark, which was attached to all Steiff products; from 1904, a blank button was used, replaced by a button with the company name in 1905–6. The company has continued since her death in 1909. With their pointed snouts, long arms and feet, humped backs, close-set eyes, and round, widely spaced ears, early Steiff bears look much more like real bears than most teddies of today, and are the most valuable of all collectable bears. Later bears can be recognized by the less-prominent humps on their backs. Long, curved limbs and large, oval felt paws, with narrow wrists and ankles are also characteristic of early Steiff bears, but the arms lost their deep curve and the feet became smaller on later bears. Steiff made bears using red, apricot, and white MOHAIR, and even a few, sought-after, black bears. Steiff bears sometimes have seams

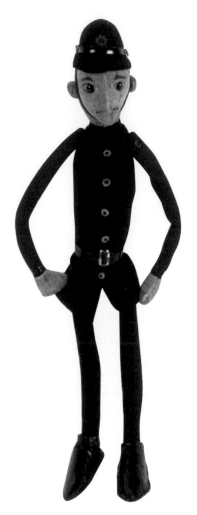

Rare STEIFF DOLL with accurate felt policeman's uniform and velvet face and hands, c.1901.

running down the front of the face marking where one bolt of cloth ran out and the next was started; these bears are especially valuable. The first Steiff bears were filled with EXCELSIOR. The shavings' thickness increased over the years, giving the bears a firmer feel. KAPOK was used later, sometimes together with excelsior around the voice boxes of early bears. Voice boxes with papered bellows were introduced in 1905. In 1908, these were replaced with automatic ones, and, in 1912, voice boxes were inserted. Brown stitched noses are characteristic of white, blond, or silver PLUSH bears; black noses of brown or gold bears. Stitches are generally vertical on larger bears, but may be horizontal on smaller ones. From 1927 to 1930, Steiff made bears known as "Petsys"; these had wired ears that could be moved into different positions and they are sought after. Steiff made some miniature bears that peaked out of the pocket on clothing worn by a larger bear. These tiny bears can be worth as much as their larger counterparts. The firm also made many novelty bears, including somersaulting bears, muzzled bears, and ROLY-POLY BEARS. Their cinnamon-coloured bears are prone to ageing because of the dye used. Many Steiff bears have new pads because the felt used was fragile. These do not reduce the value of a bear if correctly replaced, but missing ears or fur are irreplaceable. Steiff bears in excellent condition are sought after, as are pre-World War I bears with black BOOT-BUTTON EYES (later examples have glass eyes). Metal-rod bears, identifiable only by x-ray, are the most sought after. Sealing-wax noses are unique to early, rod-jointed bears. Look for bears with a naturalistic style as in pre-1940 bears. Steiff made several thousand miniature bears, but, in the 1970s, the firm produced several hundred life-sized, highly realistic bears. The size affects the value of the bear up to a point, but life-sized bears are difficult to house, and thus the price does not rise accordingly after 76cm (30in) high. The most distinctive feature of later Steiff bears is the button and paper label. Look for the distinctive button in a Steiff bear's ear. The high prices that Steiff bears can now command have resulted in an increasing number of fakes, and some have fake buttons in the ear. Others, and these are more misleading, have genuine buttons taken from less-expensive STEIFF DOLLS or worn-out bears.

STEIFF DOLLS Manufacturer of fabric dolls and STEIFF BEARS, founded by Margarete Steiff. There are several features typical on Steiff fabric dolls. The seaming runs vertically down the centre of the face, facial details are painted, button eyes are standard, the ears are not integral but applied, and large feet enable the doll to stand. Bodies were made all or partially from felt stuffed with wood-shavings until 1908. From 1909, PLUSH and velvet were sometimes used instead of felt. Heads and hands were usually covered in felt even if the bodies were not. Steiff had a great penchant for comic figures, for example the rare dolls made as musicians and known as "Dachau Peasants". Their black-button eyes and large feet are typical of Steiff CHARACTER DOLLS, but their integral ears and horizontal facial seams are unusual, as is the presence of Steiff buttons in both ears and on their costume. Steiff was one of many makers to produce GOLLIWOGS. At first, the firm marked dolls with paper labels, then in 1904 metal ear buttons (either blank or embossed with an elephant) were introduced. From 1905, the button was printed with "Steiff", and in 1908 a cloth label was added underneath bearing a product number. Blue-plated or blank tin buttons were sometimes used during World War II. If the identifying buttons have been removed, the residual holes should still be visible.

STEINER A French, Paris-based firm established in 1855 by Jules Nicholas Steiner (active 1855–91), who created a walking, talking DOLL known as an "AUTOPERIPATETIKOS CRYING DOLL". A wind-up mechanism was patented in 1890, which makes a doll walk while its hand is held. The MOTSCHMANN-TYPE doll, with a SHOULDER-HEAD in BISQUE and "floating" limbs attached to a loose, fabric midriff incorporating a voice-box, was also made by Steiner. The best period for Steiner dolls is the 1880s, when J. Bourgoin was involved in the production. "Wire-eyed" dolls, made in 1880, have wire levers at the side of the head that opens and closes the eyes. The company was taken over in 1890 by Lafosse, and quality gradually declined. The dolls may not be marked, but look out for narrow, almond-shaped eyes and delicate eyebrows. Early BÉBÉS have stubby hands and jointed PAPIER-MÂCHÉ bodies, which are coloured purple beneath the flesh paint. The mouth is positioned close to the nose. Later Steiners have slender fingers and well-defined big toes. Steiner dolls have open mouths with two rows of teeth, and, also, fixed glass eyes. The faces of Steiner bébés were painted by different artists, so details vary. Management changed often, so there are many different Steiner marks. Some mechanical dolls are marked only on the mechanism; some heads are marked "J. Steiner" or "Ste"; in 1889, however, a trademark was registered showing a baby holding a flag, and this was used as a body stamp. The finest dolls may be stamped by both Steiner and Bourgoin. A blue ink stamp on the left hip of a Steiner doll indicates a Bébé Le Parisien Médaille D'Or Paris. This means it was made in 1889, when Steiner won the medal in Paris. If the body is fully jointed except for the wrists, the head is marked "Steiner Bté S.G.D.G. Bté" meaning that it is patented, but without government guarantee of the patent. The GESLAND label was used from the end of the 19thC for bébés with German heads on Steiner bodies. The dolls were assembled by the doll-repair and spare-parts firm, the Gesland Co., which operated from 1860 to 1915, and had interests in making French regional-costume dolls.

STEINER, HERMANN Active 1921–5, a German maker of CHARACTER DOLLS.

STEINGUT German CREAMWARE produced from the late 18thC.

STEM Shank joining the bowl to the foot of a wineglass. It is made in many forms, which can help date or place the manufacture.

Jules STEINER doll with bisque head, glass paperweight eyes, and closed mouth, c.1890.

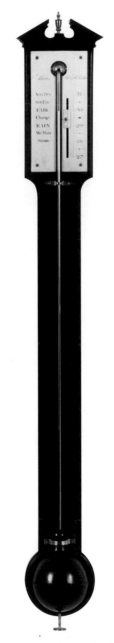

Mahogany STICK BAROMETER by Adams, Fleet Street, London, c.1780.

STEP-CUT Foot of a GLASS bowl or wineglass cut in a rising series of concentric circles of diminishing radius.

STEREOSCOPE Binoculars used for viewing two slightly different versions of the same picture to achieve a three-dimensional effect.

STERLING SILVER Silver that is at least 92.5 per cent pure – the minimum standard for English silver since 1300. From that time, sterling silver was stamped with a leopard's head; by 1478 the leopard had a crown, and from 1544 the sterling mark changed to a lion passant, shown walking to the left (after this date the leopard's head was used as London's town mark). *See also* BRITANNIA STANDARD, HALLMARK, and SILVER.

STEUBEN GLASSWORKS An American firm established in 1903 in Corning, New York, by English-born Frederick CARDER and known as Steuben Glass, Inc. from 1933. Carder developed an innovative range of ART GLASS to compete with firms such as TIFFANY, including "AURENE" (1904–30) and "CLUTHRA", typified by large bubbles. After 1934, the Steuben specialized in elegant tableware and ornamental wares. Its mark from 1903 to 1932 was an acid-stamped fleur-de-lis with "Steuben" on a scroll. The mark after 1932 was STEUBEN in script writing.

STEVENS & WILLIAMS England GLASS firm established in 1847 near Stourbridge, and renamed Royal Brierley in 1919. It was responsible for developing new types of 19thC ART GLASS, including ALEXANDRITE. It produced fine cut glass and engraved glass, sometimes with the help of designers such as Keith MURRAY, who was involved with the firm in the 1930s.

STEVENS CO. American makers of mechanical MONEY BANKS in the 19thC.

STICK BAROMETER A barometer with a vertical scale and register plate.

STICKLEY, GUSTAV (1857–1942) American furniture maker who espoused the ideals of William MORRIS and developed, from 1898, a famous range in the Craftsman style. *See also* AMERICAN ARTS AND CRAFTS.

STICK SCREEN *See* POLESCREEN.

STIEGEL GLASS Pre-revolutionary, American glass manufactured in the Pennsylvania glassworks of Henry William Stiegel.

STIFF-JOINTED DOLL A type of DOLL with limbs hinged so that they only move backward and forward in one direction. *See also* BALL JOINT.

STILE Outermost vertical part of a panelled construction.

STIPPLE ENGRAVING In GLASS, a decoration technique that is similar to DIAMOND-POINT ENGRAVING but much more skilled and time-consuming. It involves tapping a diamond-pointed needle against the surface of the glass with a light hammer to produce patterns of tiny dots – light areas are dense with dots, while darker areas have fewer. This type of engraving can be identified by the delicate designs and indented matt surface, and it was particularly suitable for thin-walled vessels. It is associated with 17thC glass from the Netherlands, where it was introduced in the early 1620s, and is also found on English glasses.

STIRRUP CUP First made in the 1770s, a drinking vessel used for making toasts at hunts. Most are in the shape of fox masks, although some are modelled as rabbit, stag, and horse heads. They are sought after, especially if in pairs or large sets, or traceable to a specific hunt. Marks are usually in a line around the neck.

ST IVES Pottery founded in Cornwall, England, in 1920 by Bernard LEACH and Shoji HAMADA, and renowned for its handmade pieces.

ST LOUIS GLASSWORKS Founded in the late 18thC in Lorraine, France, a large glassworks that became a pioneer of PRESSED GLASS, and is famous for coloured-glass vessels. It is known for fine-quality cut glass, CAMEO GLASS, engraved glass, and PAPERWEIGHTS, and produced many fine, hand-carved, cameo-glass pieces. In the mid-19thC, the firm became known for its fine LATTICINIO wares. Many of these consist of a clear-glass body worked with an intricate lattice of pink or blue and white canes. Bouquets of flowers, buds, and leaves are characteristic of St Louis paperweights, which may be marked with initials. Large single-flower heads are also common, sometimes laid on a *latticinio* ground. Brightly coloured fruit weights are among the most notable paperweights made by the firm. The most common fruit are grapes, pears, cherries, and apples, often with leaves. St Louis overlay weights often have six facets with one on top (BACCARAT and CLICHY examples have five).

German, fox-mask STIRRUP CUP with gilt interior, by Naresheimer of Hannau, c.1895.

STOCKELSDORFF FAIENCE Wares from a late-18thC factory in Schleswig-Holstein, Germany. Especially notable are large VASES, stove tiles, and TRAYS.

ST OMER Late-18thC FAIENCE factory near Calais, northern France. Noted for its lively, ROCOCO-STYLE decoration.

STONE CHINA Stoneware containing china stone (PETUNTSE). It was developed in the 19thC by SPODE and resembles PORCELAIN but is heavier.

STONEWARE A fine water-resistant BODY created by firing clays at a high temperature, stoneware was first used by ancient Chinese potters of the Shang dynasty (1700–1027 BC). It is made from a type of clay that can withstand firing to temperatures of 2,500°F (1,370°C). At these high temperatures components of the clay melt, forming a water-resistant body that is extremely robust. Western stoneware was independently developed in Germany in the Middle Ages. There are two distinct types of stoneware: the first is a fine, white-bodied variety such as Sieburg and, later, STAFFORDSHIRE (from England); the second, a grey-bodied ware sometimes covered in a brown salt glaze – which looks pitted like an orange skin – was produced in Cologne, WESTERWALD, and FULHAM in London. Some stoneware is slightly translucent and can sometimes resemble PORCELAIN. Stoneware was also produced in the USA by such potters as Remmey and Crolius in New York, and Norton in Bennington, Vermont. Among the wide range of stoneware objects made are CROCKS, JUGS, jars, chamber pots, colanders, butter tubs, and PITCHERS, often decorated with incised or painted, cobalt-blue designs. Various new types of stoneware were developed in the 19thC, including brown-glazed ROCKINGHAM WARE and flint enamel, a process developed by C.W. Fenton in Bennington. Decoration on American stoneware determines value; jugs and crocks with cobalt, floral decoration are less valuable than those with figures, birds, and animals. Incised designs bring a premium.

STONEWARE, CHINESE Stoneware began to be produced in China in the Shang dynasty (1700–1027 BC), and, by the Han dynasty (206 BC–AD 220), it had become refined enough to be considered more than just a utilitarian material. A range of small objects for the educated élite, such as water-droppers (used in calligraphy), OIL LAMPS, and VASES, began to be made, often in the form of animals such as frogs and rams. These pieces were often decorated using a roulette wheel with incised or carved repeating patterns. CELADON, the most famous type of Chinese stoneware, was produced in two main centres. Among the other important types of stoneware made in China was CIZHOU WARE, which was produced mainly in the northern provinces of Henan, Hebei, and Shaanxi. JUN WARE is another highly sought-after type of Chinese stoneware. Although larger examples of Chinese stoneware are keenly collected, and often attract high prices, small, less rare items such as tea bowls are readily available for modest sums.

STOOL The simplest type of seat FURNITURE, with legs and a seat but no back. A status symbol, a seat, and something to put your feet on – the humble stool has played many roles since it first appeared in ancient times. At medieval courts the stool showed rank, and only honoured guests could use them. Among the most elegant and expensive stools are those inspired by antiquity. Robert ADAM designed a stool modelled on a Roman cistern (a water tank), and the "X-form" stool, used by ancient Egyptians, Romans, and Greeks, became enormously popular in the REGENCY period. American stools often reflect European designs. The joint stool, for example, which was usually made of OAK, was produced from the 17thC onward in both continents; it was also reproduced in large numbers in the 1930s. There are several signs of age to look for in a stool. These include: a mellow sheen with variations in tone where the stool has been exposed to wear; genuine wear on the STRETCHERS; irregular-shaped pegs that protrude (but beware – copies have machine-cut pegs that sometimes protrude to give an impression of shrinkage); and a dry appearance underneath. X-form stools were popular in the late 18C, and piano stools were first seen in the late 18C. Look out for late-19thC, Moorish stools. A good 18thC or REGENCY stool will be expensive, but you can often find 19th and 20thC examples at more affordable prices. Pouffes – cylindrical or rectangular cushion-like stools – are among the least expensive stools available.

STOOL TABLE A joined STOOL that is fitted with falling leaves that can be raised for use as a TABLE.

STORE KONGENSGADE FAIENCE Leading Danish factory, producing blue-painted wares from the mid-18thC, and noted for large TRAYS and bowls made in the shape of a bishop's mitre.

English oak STOOL TABLE, c.1650–80.

STORR, PAUL (1771–1844) English silversmith who is closely associated with the London firm of RUNDELL, BRIDGE & RUNDELL, for whom he produced fine silver. He is probably the most acclaimed REGENCY silversmith. One of his later marks is "P.S" within an outline of two conjoined circles.

STOTER, MARIA LONGWORTH NICHOLS Founder, in 1880, of the ROOKWOOD POTTERY in Cincinnati, Ohio, USA. The wares were strongly influenced by Japanese designs.

STOURBRIDGE Based in Worcesteshire, England, a glassmaking centre noted for imitations of Venetian GLASS and 19thC ART GLASS. The first factories were founded in the early 17thC by HUGUENOTS, who concentrated on producing flat glass. Coloured and decorative glass was made from the mid-18thC. As well as numerous small workshops, several important large firms, including STEVENS & WILLIAMS and Thomas WEBB & Sons, produced glass in Stourbridge in the 19thC.

STOVE TILE TIN-GLAZED EARTHENWARE tiles with scenes painted in blue. They were made principally in the Netherlands and Germany from the 16th to the 18thC for decorating the walls of a stove recess.

ST PETERSBURG PORCELAIN *See* IMPERIAL PORCELAIN FACTORY.

STRACHAN, A.J. (d.c.1845) A British silversmith, Alexander James Strachan was especially noted for his production of small objects such as SNUFFBOXES, including large, specially commissioned examples. Wares should bear his mark, the initials "AJS".

STRAINER A pierced vessel used to strain lemon or orange juice for the preparation of spiced wine and punches. Most early strainers are perforated with a simple dot pattern and have only one handle, with a hook or ring on the opposite side that would be clipped onto the rim of the PUNCHBOWL; later, mid-18thC, examples have two handles. Few strainers were made after 1800, because by then drinking punch was no longer in vogue. Strainers should be fully marked on the bowl, but sometimes HALLMARKS have been lost in the PIERCED DECORATION. The handles are susceptible to damage.

STRAINING SPOON A spoon with a bowl pierced with fine holes, often forming a pattern, and a long handle. Used for straining tea and other liquids from the early 18thC.

STRALSUND FAIENCE In the once-Swedish (now-German) town, a factory producing large vases and trays in the latter half of the 13thC.

STRAPWORK An interlacing decorative motif, resembling the appearance of carved fretwork or leather straps. It was originally used from the mid-16th to the mid-17thC, but was revived again in the later 18thC.

STRASBOURG A long-time important centre of ceramic production in the Alsace region. Noted for fine, naturalistic flower painting on 18thC FAIENCE, animal-form dishes and for imaginative CHINOISERIE designs.

STRASS A fine GLASS paste, named after the 18thC jeweller Georges-Frédéric Strass (1701–73).

STRAWBERRY DISH Made from the late 17thC and often gilded, a shallow circular dish with a fluted edge. However, the name is misleading, because these dishes were used not only for strawberries but also for all types of dessert. This type of dish was a speciality of HUGUENOT silversmiths who fled to Britain and the Netherlands. Made in various sizes, strawberry dishes are often undecorated or simply engraved with coats of arms or crests.

STRAW WORK A type of FURNITURE decoration, with small strips of coloured straws arranged to form geometric patterns or pictures.

STRETCHER A horizontal component found on some CHAIRS joining and strengthening the legs. A stretcher going into a square block on the leg usually denotes Continental European manufacture – English chairs of early date or of provincial origin usually have legs joining stretchers of matching form. Many chairs have stretchers joining all four legs together, but, by the time of QUEEN ANNE, quality London cabinet-makers were able to make seat-rails with sufficient strength to manage without the additional support of stretchers, thus giving a less cluttered and more flowing line to the legs.

Set of four George I silvergilt STRAWBERRY DISHES with scalloped rims and a central engraved coat of arms, 1715.

STRIKE Of CLOCKS, sounding the hours or quarters on only one bell, as opposed to a multiple chime.

STRIKE RING On a CLOCK, a dial or ring that turns the striking mechanism either on or off.

STRINGING A narrow line of inlaid wood or brass around a piece of FURNITURE. The Victorians and Edwardians (1837–1901 and 1901–10 respectively) often added it to earlier furniture to make it more ornate. *See also* INLAY and VENEER.

STRING PIECING A quilting technique of joining lots of scraps of fabric until they form a piece large enough to cut out patches of the required size and shape for a block. *See also* QUILT.

STRIPPED FURNITURE that has been reduced to bare wood, having had the old surface removed.

STRIPPY QUILT A QUILT in which the top is made from strips in alternating colours running lengthwise. Patterns are often worked within the strips.

STRUT TABLE CLOCK A 19thC TABLE CLOCK with a back strut for stability.

STUART The period 1603–89, including the Commonwealth Interregnum.

STUDIO CERAMICS Individually hand-crafted pottery made since World War II. Pieces produced by certain leading potters have enjoyed a rapid increase in popularity and price in recent decades, but value depends on quality rather than upon the name of the potter concerned, and only a handful command high prices. Bernard LEACH is regarded by many as the founder of the revival in British studio ceramics. Lucie RIE – along with Hans COPER, with whom she worked closely from 1946 – is renowned for strong innovative forms and unusual glazes. James Tower is one of a new generation of studio potters, whose work is increasingly collectable. Other potters whose work is also achieving notable success include Elizabeth Fritsch, Sue Mundy, Alison Britton, Gabriele Koch, and Abdo Nagi.

STUDIO GLASS One-off pieces, usually designed and produced by independent artist-craftsmen.

STUMP BEDSTEAD A BED of simple construction, comprising a wooden framework on four short legs and no headboard. If it has a headboard, it is known as a "STUMP-END BEDSTEAD".

STUMP DOLL DOLL carved from a piece of wood, with fixed head and limbs.

STUMP-END BEDSTEAD *See* STUMP BEDSTEAD.

STUMP LEG Plain, slightly curved rear leg found on some QUEEN ANNE-STYLE and CHIPPENDALE CHAIRS.

STUMPWORK *See* RAISED WORK.

ST VÉRAIN STONEWARE Dark-blue glazed vessels – especially tiles – decorated with RENAISSANCE relief motifs. Made from the 16thC until the 18thC in the Nièvre region of France.

STYLE RAYONNANT Decorative pattern common on late 17th and 18thC French CERAMICS, consisting of a pattern of lines radiating from the central point of a circle, terminating in ornate designs derived from LACEWORK, wrought ironwork, or BAROQUE flower SWAGS.

STYLIZED Pattern based on an object – often a flower – reduced to a geometric pattern.

STYLOGRAPH Patented in 1879, the earliest form of the fountain PEN, with an integral ink reservoir.

SUBSIDIARY DIAL On a CLOCK or watch face, a smaller dial that shows, for example, the seconds or phases of the moon.

SUCKET FORK/SPOON Used from the late 17thC, an implement with a spoon bowl at one end and a two-pronged fork at the other.

SUE Early Japanese CERAMICS, with a grey-green mottled GLAZE.

SUF Persian for "embossed". The technique of cutting the PILE of a CARPET to create a design in shallow relief.

SUFFOLK CHAIR *See* BALL BACK.

SUGAR BASKET A vessel for holding sugar. The boat-shaped basket with a short stem and a swing handle was introduced in the 1770s. Sugar baskets, which are fashioned from plain SHEET SILVER, are often decorated with pierced FESTOONS and stylized leaves and flowers, and are fitted with glass liners; they remained popular throughout the 19thC, although at this period containers for sugar were usually produced as parts of TEA SERVICES. They were often used for holding sweetmeats as well as sugar. Sugar baskets paved the way for the development of the open SUGAR BOWL in the 19thC. One quirky variation on the basket style, for which the Victorians were renowned, was a double-ended, ELECTROPLATED sugar scuttle by the renowned designer Christopher DRESSER.

George III swing-handled SUGAR BASKET with pierced sides, 1790.

SUGAR BOWL A vessel for storing sugar. Sugar was stored in a box until the late 17thC, when the fashion for drinking tea led to the introduction of the sugar bowl – until that time the consumption of sugar was largely associated with sweet drinks such as punch. Sugar bowls were often made as part of a cased tea-caddy set. The earliest sugar bowls were hemispherical, resembling PORCELAIN tea bowls, and were usually simply decorated with only engraved coats of arms. Most had loose, reversible covers; these were surmounted by rings, which could be used for holding teaspoons; however, few bowls with covers survive today. A distinctive variation on the hemispherical sugar bowl form includes an inverted lip and is found in Scotland and Ireland, but rarely in England. Most Irish examples are chased and stand on three feet, while in Scotland these sugar bowls usually feature a circular foot and are rarely decorated. Sugar vases on pedestal bases became popular in the NEO-CLASSICAL period. Decoration was minimal, confined to simple fluting or EMBOSSING and a decorative bud FINIAL on the fitted cover. The upturned handles served as hooks or holders for SUGAR-SIFTER SPOONS. Sugar vases typically came in suites of three, and cased sets of three are rare and desirable. Urn-shaped sugar bowls topped with finials instead of rings became popular in the mid-18thC, but, by the 1770s, this type of sugar holder had been replaced by the SUGAR BASKET. In the 19thC, sugar bowls were made in a range of styles and colours, often in vividly coloured late-Victorian fancy glass, with ornate rims and handles. One variation on the open sugar bowl, made from a coconut shell and lavishly decorated with silver mounts, illustrates the Victorian taste for the exotic. Sugar bowls were also produced as parts of TEA SERVICES. A variety of devices have been employed for serving sugar, including sugar casters, SUGAR NIPS, and SUGAR TONGS. Beware: sometimes original inscriptions are polished off to make way for new engraving, causing the silver to become thin and prone to creases and dents.

SUGAR NIPS Produced from the early 18thC, a utensil with a scissor-like action, used to lift a lump of sugar from a SUGAR BOWL. Early sugar nips have straight arms, are delicate, and are rare and valuable, especially if they bear a maker's mark. VICTORIAN-STYLE sugar nips were made in many elaborate forms. Nips made in the USA are particularly sought after.

SUGAR-SIFTER SPOON An ingenious device used to sprinkle powdered sugar over sour fruit. Sugar-sifter spoons are often found in fitted cases alongside spoons for serving fruit. Beware of converted sauce ladles, which have been pierced with a scrolling pattern at a later date. These are easy to spot, because the bowl of a sugar-sifter spoon is generally flatter and shallower than that of a sauce ladle.

SUGAR TONGS A utensil employed to lift a lump of sugar from a sugar bowl. The earliest were shaped like fire-tongs; later, they were of scissor form, with claw or spoon ends. Early tongs were made from the late 17thC.

Silver SUGAR NIPS by John & Henry Lias, London, 1865.

Magnificent-quality Baccarat SULPHIDE plaque of Louis XVI, c.1820.

Sugar tongs, which are widely available, are easily damaged, and if repaired are worth little, making them among the most affordable SILVER available to collectors. Scottish and Irish provincial tongs are more expensive and highly sought after. Cast-arm tongs, in which the arms have been cast separately and soldered onto a U-shaped spring section, are sought after in good condition, but they tend to have flaws or damage. *See also* SUGAR NIPS.

SUI DYNASTY Period in Chinese history AD 589–617.

SULPHIDES White ceramic medallions enclosed in clear GLASS. The first tentative experiments in producing sulphides were made in Bohemia in the mid-18thC, but, in 1818, a method was patented in France by Pierre-Honoré Boudon de St-Amans (1774–1858). In England, Apsley Pellatt (1791–1863), owner of the Falcon Glassworks in London, patented the sulphide technique, which he called "crystallo-ceramie", in 1819, the year after St-Aman's patent in France. Although sulphides were also made in the USA, the leading producers were Bohemia, France, and England. As well as being made as decorative plaques, sulphides were also incorporated into a wide variety of useful glassware, such as DECANTERS, JUGS, GOBLETS, and TUMBLERS. While the medallions known as TASSIES generally depicted personalities, the subject matter of sulphides was much broader, also including coats of arms, landscapes, and, especially on French examples, religious scenes such as images of the Madonna and child. The medallion often seems silvery rather than opaque white in appearance, owing to the thin layer of trapped air formed during manufacture.

SUMACK A rich, mauve-blue colour in CARPETS, named after the plant from which the dye is obtained.

SUNBURST (Or rising sun.) A decorative motif of a sun surrounded by rays, found on 17thC BAROQUE furniture. A linear, stylized version was a popular motif of the late ART DECO period. It was especially used on mass-produced items as late as the 1950s.

SUNDERLAND Cheap EARTHENWARE made from the late 18thC in County Durham, England. Also, CREAMWARE decorated with purple-pink mottles.

SUNDIAL Object for measuring time, using shadows cast by pointers placed around a graduated dial. It was mostly used before watches and CLOCKS became widely accessible and reliable. The two main types of dial are: the pedestal, most commonly used in the garden, and the pocket, designed to be used at any latitude. *See also* POCKET SUNDIAL and SCIENTIFIC INSTRUMENTS.

SUNG DYNASTY (or "Song") Ruling Chinese dynasty from AD 960 to 1279, split into the Northern and the Southern Sung Dynasties, the latter from 1127.

SUNRAY CLOCK A clock with a dial in the form of a stylized sun, often with gilded, radiating rays in relief. Popular under LOUIS XIV.

SUNSHINE AND SHADOW QUILT pattern composed entirely of rows of squares arranged diagonally in alternating colours. Particularly popular with Amish quiltmakers, and also known as "Trip Around the World".

SUPPER CANTERBURY Another name for a CUTLERY STAND.

SUPPER TABLE Introduced in the 18thC, and set on a tripod base, a circular TABLE, the top of which displays around its edge a circle of eight dished areas, each about the size of a plate.

SUPPORTER In heraldry, the figures either side of a shield, such as a lion, unicorn, or griffin.

SURGICAL INSTRUMENT Ivory- or wood-handled implement used for surgery until 1872, when the surgeon Joseph Lister (1827–1912) discovered the value of sterilization. Thereafter metal instruments that could be boiled became standard.

SUTHERLAND TABLE DROP-LEAF TABLE with end columns joined by a central STRETCHER and a distinctive narrow centre section when not in use. It was introduced during the 19thC and is named after Harriet, Duchess of Sutherland, Queen Victoria's Mistress of the Robes.

SWADLINCOTE In Derbyshire, England, a factory noted in the 19thC for TOBY JUGS.

SWAG A suspended FESTOON of foliage, flowers, fruit, or drapery.

SWAGGED Of SILVER, applied strips of ornament made in a mould, not necessarily of swag or garland shape.

SWAN NECK Another name for a BROKEN PEDIMENT.

SWAN-NECK HANDLE A handle with sinuous curves at either end. Popular in the mid-18thC.

SWANSEA PORCELAIN Much prized, SOFT-PASTE PORCELAIN of the early 19thC, noted for William BILLINGSLEY'S flower painting. Swansea POTTERY and PORCELAIN factories were active from 1765 under the banner of the CAMBRIAN WORKS, but Swansea's reputation was earned from the fine, soft-paste porcelain made from 1814 in the factory started by Dillwyn, Billingsley, and Walker. (In 1816, Billingsley left to start up again at NANTGARW.) The

Small, Victorian, walnut SUTHERLAND TABLE.

A European hunting SWORD with scabbard, *c*.1820–50.

Glamorgan Pottery was active at Swansea from 1813 to 1839. Swansea produced a superb translucent body with an excellent GLAZE, and in many ways it is one of the best porcelain bodies produced in Britain. The body may be one of three types, and this can affect value. Early pieces were made from "glassy" paste; the most sought-after pieces are made from "duck-egg" paste, with a slight greyish tinge; later pieces were made from a "trident" paste and are considered somewhat less desirable. Swansea was famed for tea and dessert services, cabinet pieces, and decorative objects such as TAPERSTICKS and INKWELLS. Many pieces were sold in the white and decorated in London. Pieces painted in Wales are more sought after than those decorated elsewhere – the most famous decorators include Thomas Baxter and William Pollard as well as Billingsley himself. A close study of marked pieces will give an idea of Billingsley's work, but unless actually signed by him pieces should be considered "possibly by Billingsley". The decoration was inspired by French taste of the late REGENCY period, with delicately painted ROCOCO-STYLE flowers on a white ground being typical. On pieces moulded with floral cartouches, the moulding can be detected on the other side of the rim, unlike the heavier COALPORT wares, which later utilized the same moulds. Many Swansea pieces were marked in red with a painted, stencilled, or impressed "SWANSEA". The Swansea mark is often faked, particularly on French porcelain in the late 19th and early 20thC. Fake Swansea marks are also known to have been added to English porcelain to make it more valuable.

SWATOW WARE From the MING DYNASTY, Chinese PORCELAIN made for export from the 16thC, and decorated with bright enamel colours.

SWEET GUM Reddish brown, close-grain American wood, sometimes used as a substitute for MAHOGANY, which it can easily be stained to resemble.

SWINTON English factory near Leeds. Noted for its late-18thC CREAMWARE.

SWIVEL HEAD On a DOLL, a type of head in which the head and SHOULDER-PLATE are separate. A ball shape at the bottom of the head fits into a cup on the shoulder-plate (which may be lined with KID), enabling the head to swivel. The family firm MAISON HURET at Montmartre, Paris (1850–1920), renowned for its jointed dolls, patented the socket swivel head in 1858.

SWORD AND OTHER EDGED WEAPONS A long-bladed weapon, designed for both cutting and thrusting, and with quillons (crosspieces that provide some protection for the knuckles) and a hilt, is known as a sword. Other sharp-edged weapons include SABRES, DIRKS, and BAYONETS. Long-bladed, medieval swords often had POMMELS of shaped metal at the top of the hilt, to balance the blade. The shape of the pommel may give a clue as to dating. Few genuinely old swords have their original scabbards. Made of thin wood, leather, or velvet, scabbards deteriorated quickly. Swords made in the 17thC are sought after, particularly those of the English Civil War period. MARRIAGES and reproductions are not unknown, so look for pitting and other signs of genuine wear, and check that the hilt matches the blade correctly. The 18th and 19thC are the most fruitful and rewarding periods for the sword or dagger collector. There are a number of clearly defined areas in which to specialize, with genuine pieces being readily available at reasonable prices, depending on condition. American swords go back to before the War of Independence in the 18thC. Hilts are similar to European designs, while pommels and quillons often carry an eagle's head motif. Japanese swords are also collectable. Those of fine workmanship, that are genuinely old, and examples with signatures, justifiably command high prices. However, such swords were mass-produced during World War II, and since then reproductions have become widely available. Make certain that you know what you are buying, and that the price is right. Middle Eastern and Indian swords can be found in a great variety of types and designs. Many are of quite recent date, being produced well into the 20thC. Always wipe a blade with an oily cloth after it has been handled. This prevents rust marks caused by sweaty fingers. When cleaning, do not use a metal brush – one with a soft bristle gives the best results. Hot water with a small amount of detergent should remove deeply ingrained dirt or grease. Dry thoroughly to prevent rust. A non-abrasive, silicon-based paste will remove tarnish. Leather scabbards should be treated regularly with a good leather polish. The decoration on a sword usually reflects the status of its original owner, and always adds to value. Fake engraving is sometimes added to swords to increase their value – be suspicious of harsh, bright edges, and expect there to be signs of ageing such as dirt and grease between the lines. When fake engraving is added to a piece that already has some decoration it will often be of a different depth from the original and have a different background colour.

SYCAMORE Close-grained white wood with a slight fleck. It was used mainly as a VENEER, but was also stained green and called HAREWOOD.

SYLLABUB DISH Used from the early 18thC, a SILVER cup, like a CAUDLE CUP, with handles for mixing cream, egg, and wine syllabub.

SYLVAC Founded in Stoke-on-Trent by William Shaw and William Copestake in 1894, this firm first used the name "SylvaC" in the mid-1930s. It responded to the ART DECO demand for ornaments and wall decoration with a range of moulded and matt-glazed EARTHENWARE. Common pieces include VASES, POSY HOLDERS, WALL POCKETS, ashtrays, eggcups, and small animal figures in muted colours, including beige, blue, green, and brown.

1930s SYLVAC jug with moulded floral decoration, No. 1114.

SYMPIESOMETER In barometers, a device that uses gas instead of mercury to measure air pressure.

T

TABACHI The poorest quality wool, taken from dead animals. It produces coarse CARPETS. *See also* RUGS.

TABA-TABRIZ Recently made Tabriz RUGS, as distinct from old ones.

TABERNACLE CLOCK A 16thC German CLOCK, often in the shape of a tower, with elaborate open fretwork, and, sometimes, four dials.

TABLE A piece of FURNITURE consisting of a flat, horizontal surface and legs. The many types of table include DINING TABLES and myriad small tables dating from the 18thC or later. Before this, SIDE TABLES were mainly general purpose and often rectangular in shape. Tables in the 17thC were made from planks. As fashionable society became increasingly sophisticated, FURNITURE became more varied and elegant, and numerous small tables were designed for specific purposes, such as tea-drinking, card-playing, or sewing. Many types of small table were used for serving tea or coffee, which were then seen as expensive commodities that deserved to be presented on extravagant stages. CONSOLE and PIER TABLES were decorative objects, designed for the large rooms of grand Georgian houses; they were expensive when made, and have remained so. The most successful 18thC designs for small tables were often repeated in the late 19thC. The decoration on better-quality tables can add greatly to their value – the most desirable features are: carved decoration on legs and feet; tops decorated with elaborate INLAY made from differently coloured woods or specimen stones; painted decoration (popular in the late 18thC and early 20thC Edwardian period); gilt-metal MOUNTS; and LACQUER, or JAPANNING. You can distinguish Georgian painted SATINWOOD tables from their early 20thC counterparts by the pale, mellow colour of the wood and the less-colourful painted decoration. Later tables are less valuable. Small tables fit easily into most modern homes and have hence remained sought after. Pairs are always desirable. *See also* CARD TABLE, DRUM TABLE, PEMBROKE TABLE, QUARTETTO TABLE, SOFA TABLE, TRIPOD TABLE, and WORK TABLE.

TABLE À OUVRAGE Another name for ÉTAGÈRE.

Chinese, black-laquered and gilt TABLE CABINET with six drawers, c.7cm (2¾in) high, c.1900.

TABLE CABINET A type of small CABINET, made from EBONY and inlaid with engraved bone panels, and designed to sit on top of a TABLE. Larger versions were also made, and these were sometimes placed on stands. Small pieces are rare and desirable today. The majority of examples were made in Antwerp during the 17thC.

TABLE-CHAIR (Or chair-table.) A 17thC ARMCHAIR that can be converted to a TABLE by means of a pivoted back that drops across the arms of the CHAIR.

TABLE CLOCK An early domestic CLOCK, often in a drum shape and with the dial set vertically. Thought by some to be the predecessor of the WATCH.

TABLE PLATEAU Used to support a CENTREPIECE on a TABLE, a circular TRAY in GLASS with a pedestal foot.

TABLEWARE, AMERICAN GLASS Early American settlers imported European GLASS tableware, but from the late 18thC, enamelled, cut, and engraved, mainly colourless, tableware was produced at the factory of Henry William STIEGEL at Manheim, Pennsylvania, and the New Bremen glassworks of John Frederick Amelung in Frederick County, Maryland. The popularity of mould-blown glass and the 1820s invention of PRESSED GLASS led to the mass production of inexpensive tableware for the domestic market – most was similar to that found in Europe, but some distinctively American forms emerged, such as the banana stand, the SPOON RACK, and CUP PLATES. Complete table services and domestic ware were available in a huge range of named patterns and patented colours. Domestic and tablewares in animal shapes made before World War I are popular today, and have been copied.

TABLEWARE, GLASS Matching GLASS table services were produced from the late 18thC to compete with those in PORCELAIN and CREAMWARE. England and Ireland led the way in producing glass items for the DINING TABLE, perhaps because their LEAD CRYSTAL was more durable than the SODA GLASS and POTASH GLASS from Continental Europe. The greater demand for glassware for tea and DINING TABLES was sparked by the increasing refinement of dining etiquette, which demanded specialized utensils for each aspect of eating and drinking. This was especially the case among the middle classes during the Victorian period (1837–1901). Not only were larger items such as DECANTERS and TAZZE decorated to match, but also the wide range of DRINKING GLASSES and huge array of smaller items, such as WINEGLASS COOLERS, SALT-CELLARS, pickle jars, and finger bowls. While PUNCHBOWLS were generally made of SILVER, glass was used for small drinking vessels and decanter-shaped serving implements known as TODDY LIFTERS. Glass PLATES were rare before the advent of PRESSED GLASS. Most early plates have simple decoration and low, flat rims, and were used for fruit or dessert. Other wares, such as patty pans, that were originally made in glass were superseded by cheaper metalware. There is a large variety of modestly priced small glassware items available today. The most collectable items are those made in the late 18th and early 19thC and often decorated with simple-cut patterns. Pressed-glass tableware made from the mid-19thC onward is more accessible, but less valuable.

TABOURET Low, upholstered French STOOL made in the 17th and 18thC.

Japanese samurai TACHI sword, *c.*1930.

TABRIZ CARPETS, often finely woven, from the old capital of Persia. They were the first to be exported to Europe. *See also* RUGS.

TACHI Long, gently curved, single-edged, Japanese Samurai SWORD.

TAILLE D'ÉPERGNE Linear decoration on wares in SILVER, in which an area is filled with coloured ENAMEL.

TAIT, JESSIE One of the most influential designers at MIDWINTER. Her VASES, CANDLESTICKS, and flask-and-beaker sets, made from 1956, were based on hand-thrown shapes, and decorated with SLIP TRAILING or TUBE-LINING in black, with contemporary textures or motifs, and are among the most popular Midwinter collectables. Many of Tait's designs were inspired by textiles. Her "Red Domino" pattern of hand-applied white spots on a red ground, found on Midwinter's cube-shaped "Stylecraft" range, was a huge success when launched in 1953, and was copied by many factories. Her hand-decorated items are more valuable than those with floral transfers. Tait's name featured on most of the backstamps on Midwinter wares.

TAKA-MAKIE Japanese LACQUERWARE decorated with low-relief designs.

TALAVERA DE LA REINA (Or Talavera MAIOLICA.) In Castille, a leading Spanish POTTERY centre, where polychrome wares were made from the mid-16thC. Tiles formed the bulk of production until the 17thC, when the factories began making household pottery. Crude, feathery decoration in cobalt, manganese, and ochre is characteristic of these wares.

TALBOTYPE An early (mid-19thC) form of photographic print named after Fox Talbot, the inventor of photographic papers and film.

TALE GLASS Poor-quality GLASS, made from the first metal from the melting pot and containing a high proportion of scum and impurities.

TALLBOY American term for a CHEST-ON-CHEST.

TALLCASE CLOCK American term for a LONGCASE CLOCK.

TALWAR (Tulwar) Hindi word for SWORD. Used especially to describe Indian, long-bladed weapons with disc-shaped POMMELS.

TAMBOUR Flexible sliding shutter made of strips of wood stuck side by side onto a canvas backing.

TAMMANY HALL BANK Late -19thC mechanical MONEY BOX in the form of a fat man who swallows coins.

TANG DYNASTY Period in Chinese history, AD 618–906, during which PORCELAIN was first developed.

TANKARD Straight-sided SILVER or PEWTER vessel with a hinged lid, handle, and thumbpiece. Made for drinking ale, mostly between c.1600 and 1780, they became less prevalent as wine and spirits became more popular. The earliest British tankards date from the mid-16thC, when simple examples of EARTHENWARE, STONEWARE, or GLASS were made with silver MOUNTS. Solid-silver tankards, decorated with ENGRAVED or CHASED designs of STRAPWORK and fruit, were favoured by the end of the century. These had a simple, cylindrical form and flat, stepped lids. This shape was also produced in North America in the late 17thC, with a volute thumbpiece, a speciality of New York silversmiths. In Germany, large SILVER-GILT tankards were chased with biblical and mythological scenes, strapwork, masks and flowers, and occasionally even decorated with coins. By the second half of the 17thC, the most popular tankards were drum-shaped with flat, moulded bases, scroll handles, and simple, stepped covers. This form was succeeded in the 1730s by the BALUSTER tankard, with a pronounced domed cover, double-scroll handle, and an applied plain or reeded band around the body. Decoration was usually confined to an engraved ARMORIAL or a monogram. Tankards made in the 19thC (often for presentation) were usually elaborate, although handles were generally only minimally decorated, possibly with motifs or rows of graduated beads. In the 19thC, many plain tankards from earlier periods were embellished to suit the Victorian taste for elaborate decoration. CLASSICAL ornament of PUTTI, fruiting vines, masks, shells, flowers, and grapes was frequently added. While attractive, this later decoration diminishes the value. It was also common in the 19thC to convert tankards into jugs, which were thought to be more practical. However, avoid conversions, because alterations lower the value and are illegal if the additions are not marked. Variations on the tankard form were many in the late 19th and early 20thC, including examples in the "CYMRIC" silver range for the London firm of LIBERTY. Look for HALLMARKS on one side of the body or base and on the lid; earlier tankards have marks in a line on top of the lid; on later ones, they are in a group inside. Tankards may have been heavily used, so check for cracks, especially on vulnerable points around the handles. Check handle sockets, which may have become weak. Examine the thickness of the cover – if it is domed and thin, it may have been reworked from a flat lid. Check also for tankards on which the original decoration has been removed; tell-tale signs include traces of hammering and white marks on the surface of the metal.

TANNER, JOHN American clockmaker, active 1740–60, in Newport.

TANTALUS On DECANTERS, a locking frame named after the mythical Greek king who was forced to stand surrounded by water that receded when he tried to drink it. The tantalus was a late -19thC phenomenon. Rare ART DECO examples were luxury items. *See also* DRINKS TABLE.

TANG DYNASTY **stoneware amphora,** C.AD **618–906.**

TAPERSTICK Made from the late 17thC, a vessel designed for holding a taper, or thin candle, and used to melt sealing wax at a WRITING TABLE, to light a tobacco pipe, or provide illumination. Most were in the form of small CANDLESTICKS, and measured only 10cm (4in) in height. Early SILVER examples are usually cast and mirror the style of contemporary candlesticks. Some tapersticks were made in the form of CHAMBERSTICKS, often also with candle extinguishers. Replacement conical extinguishers or SNUFFERS are common, and detract from the value. Some tapersticks incorporated INKSTANDS. Silver tapersticks are usually marked under the base. Faceted GLASS tapersticks were made between the 17th and 19thC. Tapersticks, which are rarer than candlesticks and sought after, were generally made in pairs but rarely survive as such, particularly those from the early 18thC, so surviving pairs are particularly desirable. In the mid-18thC, tapersticks were replaced by WAXJACKS. Tapersticks are small and fragile and hence were prone to damage, which will considerably diminish their value.

TAPESTRY Hangings used to provide an essential source of warmth in draughty 17th and 18thC interiors. It was only as wallpaper became popular, and houses warmer, that tapestries dwindled in popularity. Look out for door hangings (*portières*) and seat covers, or fragments of large tapestries, such as small snippets of flowery AUBUSSON, or finely woven Beauvais tapestry, because these are often inexpensive. Tapestry cushions are often fragments of a larger piece. *See also* TEXTILES, CARE OF.

TAPE TWIST Broad, white spiral band in the STEM of a wineglass.

TAPPIT HEN Scottish lidded ("tappit") PEWTER measure in many sizes.

TARSIA Type of Italian MARQUETRY, which usually represents a pattern of flowers or ribbons and is mainly used on TABLES and CHAIRS.

TASSIES Opaque, white, GLASS portrait medallions, developed in the mid-1760s by the Scottish stonemason James Tassie (1735–99) to satisfy the fashion in the 18thC for CAMEOS decorated with CLASSICAL-style motifs. The medallions usually represent politicians, royalty, and other prominent contemporary figures, and they were made by modelling a portrait in wax, casting it in plaster, removing the wax, and pouring a molten white glassy paste into the plaster mould. Tassies continued to be made in London after James's death by his nephew William Tassie (1777–1860). Early examples feature portrait medallions mounted on a sheet of glass of contrasting colour to simulate true hardstone cameos. Later pieces were cast complete with a background. *See also* SULPHIDES.

TASTEVIN Usually of French or German origin, a small flat SILVER bowl, 8cm (3in) in diameter, with a simple ring handle. Used for tasting wines.

18thC, Scottish, pewter TAPPIT HEN.

TAVERN CLOCK Alternative name for an ACT OF PARLIAMENT CLOCK.

TAVERN TABLE Small, rectangular, four-legged TABLE usually with one or two drawers. Used in taverns in the 18thC.

TAZZA The Italian word (plural: *tazze*) for "cup", a wide, shallow or flat bowl or dish on a stemmed foot. CERAMIC and metal *tazze* were made in antiquity, and the form was revived by Venetian glassmakers in the 15thC; *tazze* were also made in SILVER from the 16thC. The earliest glass examples were probably inspired by Islamic footed glass bowls, with wide, hollow cylindrical stems, and by similar engraved items made in silver. VENETIAN GLASS *tazze* were luxury items, intended as wedding gifts – some feature enamelled portraits of a bride and groom in the centre – or for important ceremonies. The finest pieces are decorated with enamel and gilding in the centre, sometimes with coats of arms, as well as around the rim. Such items were copied by 18thC English glassmakers in LEAD CRYSTAL, with elaborate stems following the style of DRINKING GLASSES. These may have been used not only for display but also for serving fruit and sweetmeats at the end of a meal, or by servants for presenting a glass of wine. In the 19thC, the term *tazza* (often also called "COMPORT") was used in a much broader sense to describe any type of stemmed glass dish or bowl for serving a variety of delicacies at the dinner- or tea table, or simply for display. While some flat-topped *tazze* in the 18thC style were still produced in the 19thC, they were made mechanically by PRESS-MOULDING rather than by the more expensive and laborious earlier method of hand "spinning". While 18thC *tazze* were generally made in clear glass, later versions were produced in a great variety of colours and decorative finishes, from cutting and engraving to LATTICINIO and ENAMELLING; some of the most expensive items, especially those by French glassmakers, also have elaborate figural handles. Sets of *tazze* of different sizes, usually with matching sets of flat glass PLATES, were often given as wedding gifts in the second half of the 19thC. However, single *tazze* remain popular with glass enthusiasts, because they are useful for serving fruits, chocolates, and cakes. Reasonably priced examples in both clear and coloured pressed glass were a speciality of American manufacturers, who made *tazze* only from the 19thC; some American pieces feature high-quality cutting on the bowl and occasionally also the stem and foot. A SALVER in SILVER on a stemmed foot is sometimes called a *tazza*. The earliest silver *tazze* were made of thin-gauge metal with central trumpet-shaped feet, which were sometimes detachable; however, in the reign of George I (1714–27) these trumpet-shaped feet were replaced by three or four small cast feet, which made them more robust than their late -17thC counterparts. There are several types of silver *tazza* – some were used as drinking cups, some for serving drinks, and others for holding delicacies. Silver *tazze* should be marked on both the flat top sections and on the feet. Look out for the initials of specific designers stamped next to the HALLMARKS, because these add considerable value.

TAZZA, ENGLISH Inspired by Venetian examples, the *tazza* (plural: *tazze*) was among the earliest type of glassware produced in England from the early 18thC. They are thought to have been used as all-purpose serving dishes, or were stacked one on top of the other in decreasing sizes to create CENTREPIECES for DINING TABLES or to display desserts and sweets. They were expensive items affordable only by the rich. Most early and mid-18thC pieces were plain and shallow, sometimes like flat dishes on stemmed feet, in styles similar to those on wineglasses. English *tazze* made in the early 18thC feature two styles of stem: the BALUSTER and the moulded-pedestal SILESIAN STEM. The former was made only until *c.*1730 and is rare, while the Silesian type, produced from *c.*1750, remained popular well into the 20thC. Early pieces are smaller than later ones. The 19thC versions can often be identified by thicker stems, heavy weight, and unevenly balanced shapes. As with early 18thC English DRINKING GLASSES, copies of baluster and Silesian-stemmed *tazze* were made in Continental Europe. Made of SODA GLASS and with hollow stems, they are lighter in weight than English pieces, and lack the distinctive grey tone of LEAD CRYSTAL. *See also* TAZZA, VENETIAN and GLASS.

TAZZA, VENETIAN A TAZZA made in Venice, Italy. The form was closely associated with VENETIAN GLASS, with some of the finest surviving examples made there from the 15th to the 18thC. Unlike later examples, these early pieces nearly always have distinctive low, hollow, spreading feet, and shallow bowls with upturned lips or rims, inspired by contemporary examples in SILVER. As with many early Venetian wares, *tazze* may be decorated with geometric patterns inspired by Islamic glass. Most are made of clear glass with enamelled and gilded decoration, usually the coats of arms of the owner, allegorical scenes, or formal diaper patterns. These *tazze* were made for the wealthy, and, although their precise function is unknown, they were used only on special occasions, such as weddings, probably as a show of wealth. They are prized by collectors today. Copies of early *tazze* were made but can be identified by their heavier weight (they were made of LEAD CRYSTAL rather than the original SODA GLASS) and more uniform shape; coats of arms on such pieces are mostly fictitious.

TEAK A heavy brown wood that is strong and durable. It was used for military CHESTS and ships' FURNITURE, which required a strong wood.

TEA KETTLE A vessel introduced in the 1730s, and intended for boiling water at the table to provide a supply of hot water to replenish small TEAPOTS and COFFEE-POTS. Made in SILVER or other metals, tea kettles were made in two or three parts, notably a kettle, stand, and burner. Early examples are of circular form and plain. Some original, ROCOCO tea kettles have ivory swing handles, although most have metal handles bound in WICKER or covered with a thick leather outer casing to protect the hands from the hot metal. Some made in the Victorian period (1837–1901) feature hinged mechanisms, attaching the kettle to the base, so that the heavy kettle could be tilted forward to fill the teapot more easily. Tea kettles waned in popularity after the 1760s, when they were replaced by TEA URNS, which were more practical and safer; however, many were made in the mid-Victorian period as parts of TEA SERVICES. Spirit burners were often lost, so look out for replacements. If a kettle is still complete with its original stand and burner, all separate parts (including the cover) should bear the same maker's mark. They are usually marked underneath, but the HALLMARKS have often been rendered illegible by carbon deposits and erosion from the flame of the burner.

TEAPOT, SILVER A vessel used for making tea, which became fashionable in the late 17thC. Many early teapots were small, reflecting the high cost of tea. The first ones were not used for brewing tea but for pouring hot water over tea leaves into cups. In the 17thC, SILVER teapot shapes imitated the tapering cylinder and straight spout of contemporary COFFEE-POTS, hexagonal wine pots, or globular PORCELAIN teapots imported from China. Early 18thC teapots were pear-shaped and octagonal. The spouts on pear-shaped pots were often faceted, sometimes with hinged flaps at the end to retain the heat, although this feature was abandoned in the 1720s. Examples in good condition are rare and valuable. Most of these teapots were of heavy-gauge silver, with separately made foot rims, spouts cast in two halves, and minimal surface decoration. The bullet-shaped teapot was a speciality of Scottish silversmiths and fashionable from the 1730s until *c.*1760. The silver handle is also a feature of Scottish teapots – most English teapots had wooden handles. "Bullet" teapots are highly prized, and often faked today. The inverted pear-shaped teapot, on a short stem with a wide foot rim and a low domed cover, was briefly produced in the 1750s, and enjoyed greater popularity in North America than in Britain. A simple vase form with a pedestal base and decorative beading around the body of a teapot are hallmarks of the taste for the NEO-CLASSICISM that became fashionable in the latter part of the 18thC. The severe forms of American teapots in this style – produced mainly in Boston and Philadelphia – were influenced by English prototypes of more than a decade earlier. These had elongated proportions and double-domed covers with decorative FINIALS. Reflecting the influence of the Neo-classical period of the mid-to late -18thC, drum-shaped teapots of plain cylindrical form and oval cylindrical teapots were made from the 1770s. Most oval teapots had flat bases, so many were initially made with matching stands to protect FURNITURE from the heat of the pot; however, by 1800, most were designed with feet that were more practical. Tiny versions of this form, for one or two cups, are known as "bachelor", "spinster", or "afternoon" teapots. By the 1770s, thin-gauge, rolled SHEET SILVER had become widely available, facilitating the mass-production of silver objects. This also sparked the production of matching TEA SERVICES. From *c.*1790, many teapots were made with ivory handles, instead of the earlier wooden ones. In the REGENCY period, low, boat-shaped teapots resembling Classical OIL LAMPS

Silver melon-shape TEAPOT, c.1844

Victorian burr-walnut and walnut-veneered TEAPOY with two lidded compartments.

were popular. Most 19thC teapots, created as parts of larger services, were made in a range of historical revival styles. With the exception of the original ARTS AND CRAFTS and ART DECO styles, most 20thC teapots copy or reinterpret earlier designs. Because many 18thC styles were repeated in the 19th and 20thC, check the HALLMARKS on the base to tell if the piece is a later reproduction. Decoration can help with dating: for example BRIGHT-CUT ENGRAVING was popular in the late 18thC, while some 19thC teapots were elaborately decorated. The maker's mark on a handle may be different from that on the body, because handles are often later replacements, particularly if they are made of silver. Lids should also be marked. Bear in mind that teapots were made to be used, and many have become well worn as a result – before you buy one examine it carefully for damage, which can be expensive to restore. Sheet-silver teapots are not as sturdy as those raised from heavier-gauge, metal and they are prone to splitting along the body seams and around the spout. Check lids carefully before buying – if the hinge is weak it may be impossible to restore. Wooden handles and finials are vulnerable to splitting, rotting, and cracking; however, this will not reduce the value because they can be easily replaced.

TEAPOY Small container used in the drawing room for the storage and mixing of tea, and often resembling a casket on a pedestal stand. Because tea was expensive, teapoys were usually fitted with good-quality locks. Quality features to look for include zinc-lined caddies that fit perfectly, heavy, cut-glass mixing bowls that are still intact, a lock by a premier maker such as Bramah, and a GILLOWS stamp (this can add 30 per cent to the value).

TEAR A drop-shaped air bubble enclosed in a GLASS, usually in the stem of an early 18thC wineglass. The AIR-TWIST STEM evolved from the tear.

TEA SERVICE Serving vessels for making tea. A basic tea service comprises a TEAPOT, MILK JUG, and SUGAR BOWL, all with matching decoration; in addition to this there might be a hot-water jug, slop bowl, COFFEE-POT, and TRAY. Although a handful of tea services are known from the early 1700s, most were made after the mid-18thC, with the advent of new production technology. A set with identical marks on each piece is worth more than a composite service.

TEA TABLE A small TABLE used for serving tea and dating from the 18thC onward. Tea was expensive, thus tea tables were often elaborate. MAHOGANY was usually used for them, and JAPANNING was popular in the 18thC. The most desirable ones have well-figured wood, swivel tops (these were added to some to make serving easier), good decorative detail, and original casters.

TEA URN First introduced in the mid-18thC, tea urns provided a supply of hot water to replenish TEAPOTS and COFFEE POTS. They are larger and less portable than TEA KETTLES, and they have horizontal taps (spigots) near the base for drawing hot water more safely than tilting a kettle. The earliest tea urns were heated with charcoal burners, but, from the 1770s, a heated iron rod (billet) was inserted into a socket or tube inside the urn, around which water circulated. Most urns are vase-shaped on stemmed feet, with restrained decoration of CLASSICAL ornament or engraved coats of arms. Occasionally, the spout of the tap is cast and chased in the form of an animal or a bird. Vase-shaped urns, introduced in the 1770s, were popular in North America in the Revolutionary period. Globular or barrel-shaped urns were made from the first half of the 19thC, and were popular until c.1840; these urns rested horizontally on pedestals. Tea urns sometimes formed integral parts of 19thC TEA SERVICES. The spigot, finial, and handles are often made of IVORY or hardwoods such as apple or pear, and this insulated the user from the hot metal. Many tea urns were produced in SHEFFIELD PLATE because the cost of making such a large item in SILVER was prohibitive. Tea urns can be affordable, but unusual or imaginative examples command high prices. Be sure to check that the internal fittings are intact. Watch out for tea urns that have been converted from two-handled cups by attaching spigots and lids. Some tea urns have been changed into cups by the insertion of a plate of silver or "patch" over the hole left by the spigot. Such patches are often disguised with engraving. In some cases tea urns have been fitted with electrical elements, and these conversions are best left well alone. *See also* SAMOVAR.

TEA WARES Vessels for serving tea. They were first used in Europe in the 17thC, when tea was introduced from China. Tea was expensive, and drinking it became fashionable among the wealthy and aristocratic classes in the 18thC, thus sparking the need for suitable vessels in which to prepare and serve the beverage. TEAPOTS, TEA KETTLES, and TEA URNS were made in SILVER, alongside MILK JUGS, spoons, SUGAR BOWLS, and CADDIES. By the end of the 18thC, tea wares had become a major part of the silversmith's trade. Large quantities of these wares were made at the time, many of which still survive.

TEBO FIGURES French, ROCOCO-style figures produced at BOW and CHELSEA in the mid-18thC, and so-called after the modeller's mark.

TECO POTTERY (Also known as the American Terra Cotta and Ceramic Company, or the Gates Pottery.). An Illinois-based company that registered a trademark in 1895, Teco is known for its architectual CERAMICS, some designed by Frank Lloyd WRIGHT. A silvery, matt green, inspired by matt glazes on French ceramics, is typical of Teco POTTERY. The firm produced 500 shapes in various matt colours, including brown, grey, blue, rose, purple, and yellow. Teco is marked with a long "T" and the "e", "c", and "o" arranged under each other.

TEDDY BEAR A soft toy bear. The earliest bears were STEIFF BEARS, made in Germany in the early 20thC, and those made by Morris Michtom, founder of the American IDEAL NOVELTY & TOY CO. Opinion is divided between which of

All-original 1930s silk plush Merrythought TEDDY BEAR.

the two is the first teddy-bear creator. Bears were produced by increasing numbers of toy companies on both sides of the Atlantic. During World War I, and in the years that followed, British bear manufacturers expanded to fill the void left after German imports were banned. Prominent companies such as CHAD VALLEY, MERRYTHOUGHT, DEAN'S RAG BOOK COMPANY LTD, CHILTERN, and J.K. FARNELL enjoyed considerable success with their high-quality products. Few bears were made during World War II, but, after the war, production resumed, although the appearance of bears subtly changed, as they became less realistic and more like the teddy bears of today. Children's books and cartoons featuring bears also affected the market, prompting reproductions of well-loved characters such as WINNIE-THE-POOH, PADDINGTON, Sooty, and RUPERT BEAR. Prior to 1945, most bears have beige or gold silk MOHAIR plush, made from the wool of the angora goat. Dual-coloured mohair plush, which had dark tips and a pale base, was fashionable in the 1920s. Synthetic fibres became common after World War II and are much shinier and harder to the touch. Makers also began to experiment with more unrealistic colours. Not surprisingly, natural fibres are more desirable. Felt was the most usual material for early bear paws, with the most popular colours for paws being beige, brown, and cream, although black bears might have black paws. Leather paws have been used throughout the 20thC. Cotton, velveteen, and woven cotton were popular between 1930 and 1950. Wrexine, a type of oil cloth, was used from the 1930 to '50s. Synthetic plush paws came in after 1950. Long limbs were standard among early bears, although they shrank at a varying rate. Over the years, the shape of bears became more barrel-like, and this change is most noticeable after World War II. The first German bears had BOOT-BUTTON EYES. Shortly before World War I, GLASS eyes attached by wire shanks became common, but other types are also seen, including moving GOOGLY EYES, enamelled metal eyes, and painted clear-glass eyes. Earlier bears tended to have eyes set closer together than later ones. From 1955 onward, plastic eyes were used because they were safer for children. Later plastic eyes are usually larger. Long, clipped snouts gradually gave way to stubbier, often hairier, versions. Early noses were made from sealing wax or hand-embroidered, with the shape and direction of the stitching varying according to the maker. Rubber noses were introduced after 1950, and many modern bears have plastic noses. Early German bears were stuffed with EXCELSIOR. Other bears were sometimes stuffed with KAPOK, while some teddies were filled with a mixture of the two. Post-war bears often have a synthetic, machine-washable stuffing that is lighter than shavings or kapok. Most bears are disc-jointed at the hips, shoulders, and neck. American bears were often unmarked but have distinctive, wide, barrel-shaped bodies, narrow arms and legs, and small feet. Some have humps – often the case on German bears. The most valuable bears for collectors are early examples, in good condition, made by famous makers. In general, Steiff bears remain the most valuable because of their unique historical appeal and high-quality workmanship. The Steiff invention of a button in the ear was copied as a method of labelling by various firms, including Merrythought and Chad Valley. Because of the Steiff patent, BING

TOYS placed their buttons under the arms. Unfortunately, anxious parents often removed such buttons, as they were potentially dangerous. Fabric labels were often stitched to feet or inserted in seams, but these may have been lost if the paws have been replaced. Paper labels were frequently attached to bears' chests, but these rarely survive. Prices depend on the age, colour, condition, rarity and the maker. The collectability of old bears has led to the artificial "ageing" of traditional, new bears and the adding of spurious labels or buttons to genuinely old bears of unknown makes. Because many genuine old bears are unmarked, novice collectors need to be especially careful. It is difficult to stitch the head or snout of a bear, and this is a key area to observe. An incorrect shape and mis-stitching is a good indication that a bear is not genuine. Pay attention also to the jointing at the shoulders and hips and to over-stuffing with straw, because this creates a rigid effect. *See also* TEDDY BEAR, AMERICAN; TEDDY BEAR, BRITISH; TEDDY BEARS, CARE OF; TEDDY BEAR, GERMAN; and TEDDY-BEAR PARAPHERNALIA.

TEDDY BEAR, AMERICAN The first American TEDDY BEARS were made by Morris Michtom's IDEAL NOVELTY & TOY CO., but its bears were never labelled. Other important makers included the KNICKERBOCKER TOY CO., whose bears have labels reading "Knickerbocker Toy Co. New York" in their front centre seams. The Fast Black Skirt Co. made bears with novelty features such as squeaking, growling, whistling, laughing, tumbling (the most desirable), and musical effects. Columbia Teddy Bears in New York produced "Laughing Roosevelt", a jointed bear with two rows of white glass teeth; squeezing a mechanism in the stomach causes the mouth to open and close. Some bears were made with two faces: one of a teddy-bear face, one of a doll. Another variation was a bear's body with a doll's head, known as a "Teddy Doll" and produced by Hahn and Amberg in New York in 1908. This was followed in 1909 by E.I. Horsman's "Billiken" dolls, with teddy-bear bodies and grotesque elfin features. By 1920, Ideal and other firms were still expanding, as teddies caught on worldwide. Features often associated with American bears are long, narrow bodies, straightish arms, small feet, and short, bristle-type MOHAIR. However, the shapes changed and became more stylized as rival firms vied for attention. Besides bears made by Ideal and Knickerbocker, look out for bears by GUND MANUFACTURING CO. and CHARACTER TOY CO. American firms were bad at labelling their bears, so identification is often a matter of speculation. Ideal grew into an international concern owning companies worldwide, until it was taken over in 1982 by C.B.S. Inc, which then stopped the firm's line of bear production. The new collectables among American bears are ARTIST BEARS. Teddy bears adverstising a product are collectable, as are spin-offs from television programmes, such as Radar's teddy linked with *M.A.S.H.* Be suspicious of teddy bears that show no obvious sign of wear or restoration. There is also a growing number of American fakes.

TEDDY BEAR, BRITISH World War I led to the growth of the TEDDY BEAR industry in Britain. Imports from Germany were banned and companies such

1950s, Chad Valley, gold-plush TEDDY BEAR with glass eyes, jointed body, and velvet pads.

as DEAN'S, FARNELL, and CHILTERN stepped in to fill the gap. Farnell are probably the most desirable early English bears, although Dean's, CHAD VALLEY, MERRYTHOUGHT, and Chiltern are collectable too. Numerous firms were established to meet increasing demand. World War II disrupted the European teddy-bear industry, and teddy-bear factories ceased most production from 1939 to 1945. However, some endeavoured to keep production going through World War II, with bears joining the Burma Campaign and even parachuting into Arnhem. During this period, "Hugmee" bears were popular. They have a sorrowful look, with the head and nose angled downwards, and their ears are small and sit far up on the head. Various features such as the STEIFF identity button were imitated, but British bears are stubbier in shape. They are often also softer than German bears, because British makers preferred KAPOK stuffing to EXCELSIOR. After the war ended, makers began to use synthetic fibres. Bears with synthetic coats are generally less valuable. While the larger teddy-bear manufacturers were involved in take-over battles in the 1960s and '70s and cheap bears flooded in from the Far East, smaller British producers were also beginning to proliferate. With so much variety available, collectors should look for limited editions as future investments.

TEDDY BEAR, GERMAN With the success of STEIFF BEARS, many German firms were quick to jump on the TEDDY-BEAR bandwagon in the early 1900s. Their bears were frequently unmarked, and this can make them difficult to identify. Among the most notable makers were HERMANN (whose bears were similar to Steiff bears), SCHUCO, and BING, some of whose mechanical novelties, such as somersaulting bears, are highly prized. Examples are rare, since production was disrupted by World War I, when other countries banned imports from Germany. By the end of the war, increasing numbers of doll and toy manufacturers brought out their own teddy bears, because this popular new toy was easy to produce, as long as the aspiring manufacturer had a talented seamstress, a pattern, and a sewing machine. Hermann, Schuco, and Bing remained Steiff's biggest rivals in Germany. Steiff, noted for their attention to detail and the durability of their bears, were emulated by other German manufacturers, but continued to lead the market. However, bears' body shapes began to change, and features became less exaggerated. The hump almost disappeared, the nose became shorter, the arms lost their deep curve, and the feet grew smaller. After World War II, manufacturers began to use synthetic fibres, and these are generally less valuable.

TEDDY-BEAR PARAPHERNALIA The craze for TEDDY BEARS has led to a wide variety of related items being produced – bear accessories or artifacts represent bears at both work and play. POSTCARDS with bears were popular at the beginning of the 20thC, and bear annuals proliferated with the growing number of famous bear characters such as RUPERT BEAR. Games, especially jigsaws, were popular. The overall condition must be good, and check also that the game or jigsaw is all there, because any missing pieces can reduce the value to virtually nothing. Many leading pottery factories such as WEDGWOOD, who made children's services, made wares decorated with teddy bears. Sadly, many pieces were broken, and whole services are rare. Watch out for chips and cracks. The most valuable examples are PLATES and bowls with a centre bear and maker's marks on the reverse. Teddy bears sometimes had a dual purpose. SCHUCO is known for making bears that held lipsticks or perfume holders; these were often small bears. Look for a belly with a mirror on one side, powder on the other. Greetings card manufacturers were also fond of teddy bears. The affection indicated by a teddy bear further led to the adoption of bear-related items as love tokens. Also look for bears on biscuit tins and other ephemera that are in the best condition.

TEDDY BEARS, CARE OF Dirty bears should be cleaned by a specialist – if they are left untreated, the dirt can cause the fabric to rot. Holes in a bear can be mended without detracting from the bear's value. When patching, always try to use similar, preferably old, fabric, and leave as much of the original fabric as possible. Paw pads made from felt often suffer some damage, but it is always much better to patch them than to replace them completely. The extent to which the value of a bear is affected by pad replacement varies considerably, so even if you think there is no alternative, it is best to check first. Put new additions to your collection in a plastic bag with mothballs over night to kill any insect infestation.

TEDDY CLOWN With a hat and ruff, the "Teddy Clown" has distinctively large glass eyes set close together and is soft to cuddle because it is stuffed with KAPOK instead of EXCELSIOR. It was patented by STEIFF in North America in 1926. It was made in pink, gold, or brown-tipped MOHAIR plush, and sold in 11 different sizes, from 23cm (9in) to 114cm (45in) tall. These clowns were so popular that 30,000 were manufactured in 1928.

TEHRAN Now the capital of Iran, noted for fine and now-rare CARPETS decorated with animals set against intricate floral and foliage designs.

TEKKE Nomadic tribe of the Azerbaijan/Iranian border region noted for their deep-red CARPETS decorated with GUL motifs.

TEKNO Founded in Denmark in the 1930s, a maker of TINPLATE toys. One of its most collectable DIECAST cars is the Mercedes-Benz 230SL, which has a fingertip steering action. Commerical vehicles in unusual liveries are desirable.

TELESCOPE Series of wood, parchment, or brass tubes containing lenses designed to magnify distant objects. John Dollond, a leading 18thC London maker, perfected the use of achromatic lenses, which eliminated the problem of colour fringing (caused by the distortion of light) in telescopes. Handmade, 18thC examples of MAHOGANY and BRASS have the greatest appeal

Austrian TERRACOTTA plaque of a lady singing, stamped "Ernest Wahliss, Turn Wien", c.1900.

to collectors. Large floor models on CABRIOLE LEGS are priced higher than hand-held or table top versions. Decoration and famous names (Dollond, Bradley, Molyneaux, Scarlet, and Hearn) add value. Instruments made by John Dollond or his sons, Peter and John Jnr, are signed "J." or "P. Dollond London". In the early 19thC, unscrupulous dealers attempted to cash in on the Dollond reputation by selling telescopes falsely inscribed Dolland. These are still collectable but less valuable. Machine-produced 19th and 20thC telescopes are inexpensive, unless they have regimental insignia or an owner's name. Avoid any telescope with damaged lenses or dented cases. *See also* SCIENTIFIC INSTRUMENTS.

TELL-TALE CLOCK Used in banks and other establishments in the early 19thC, a CLOCK to check that a night watchman was doing his rounds. The most common type has a series of pins, which can only be depressed at a precise time, around the dial.

TENT BED (Also known as a SPARVER BED.) An 18th and 19thC BED with a domed canopy. Resembles a tent when covered with drapes.

TERM Pillar or pedestal terminating in a sculpture of a human head and torso.

TERRACOTTA Italian for "baked earth". A red-coloured EARTHENWARE, often unglazed, used for tiling, garden statuary, and pots.

TERRY CLOCK A CLOCK made by Terry, active between 1792 and 1852, in Plymouth, Connecticut, USA. Also, a MANTEL CLOCK with architectural side pillars and pediment, and a painted glass panel below the dial.

TESTER The wooden canopy over a bedstead. It may cover only half the BED and is supported by two or four posts, hence full tester or HALF-TESTER BEDS.

TÊTE-À-TÊTE (1) (Also known as a CABARET.) French term for a small tea set, comprising enough pieces to serve tea for two, and fashionable in the mid-18thC. (A SOLITAIRE is a tea set for one.)

TÊTE À TÊTE (2) In FURNITURE, another name for a "love seat", which was usually made of two seats facing each other and joined at the sides.

TEXTILES, CARE OF Textiles are vulnerable to fading, discolouration, and spotting, and should be hung away from strong sunlight and damp. Framed textiles can be protected by being mounted behind light-resistant glass. If storing pieces in a drawer, roll, rather than fold them to prevent damage from pressure and creasing. Also make sure that they are well protected from moths, by using plenty of mothballs. Unless they are fragile, most textiles can be washed with warm soapy water.

THEODOLITE First made in 1730, a surveying instrument for measuring and mapping heights above sea level. Pre-1840 versions by top SCIENTIFIC INSTRUMENT makers, such as the Troughton brothers and William Simms, command a premium over more utilitarian, but more accurate, later models.

THERESIENTHAL GLASS Wares from the Theresienthaler Kristallglassfabrik, a glasshouse founded in 1836 in Bavaria, Germany, by Prague natives Frans and Wilhelm Steigerwald. The factory was directed by the Poschinger family from 1861. It achieved fame for its engraved, cased, and flashed glass, and for DRINKING GLASSES that mirrored earlier German and Venetian fashions. In the earlier 20thC, it produced decorative, iridescent glass in the TIFFANY style, as well as tablewares based on the ideas of designer Hans Christiansen.

THIMBLE A small cap, made of SILVER, hand-painted PORCELAIN, IVORY, or other materials, for protecting the fingertips while sewing. It is rare to find one made before the 18thC. As a general rule, the price of thimbles reflects the intrinsic value of the material and the fineness of the decoration. GOLD thimbles are rare, and even plain examples are costly. Silver thimbles tend to be next in value, followed by those in base metals. Hand-painted enamel and porcelain examples have high value because of their rarity, whereas prices for other materials, such as ivory, TORTOISESHELL, MOTHER-OF-PEARL, and GLASS, are dependent upon the fineness and quality of the thimble. Flowers and scenery were the most common form of decoration on silver; less-valuable thimbles often have the name of a town inscribed round the base, or feature a crude picture; intricate, skilfully modelled scenes attract higher prices. Thimbles celebrating important royal or national events are highly prized. Trademarks and advertising slogans can increase the value of base-metal thimbles, but most sought after are patented types: the Dorcas ventilated thimble, the non-slip, and those with needle-threaders or cutters attached. Thimble cases are collected in their own right but are worth more with the original thimble inside. Look especially for pre-1850 silver, gold, enamel, hardwood, and leather examples, and for cases with needle compartments and novel shapes. Beware of modern silver thimbles, which resemble 18th and 19thC originals but lack patina.

Charles Horner silver THIMBLE, Chester, 1907.

THIRTY-HOUR MOVEMENT A CLOCK that needs rewinding after 30 hours.

THISTLE BOWL Made of GLASS, a BOWL resembling the shape of a thistle flower, with a tapering upper section and rounded base.

THISTLE MUG A small vessel made in Scotland in the late 17th and early 18thC. Such mugs are of flaring form, with central applied bands and the lower body decorated with applied flutes imitating thistles.

THOMAS CLOCK Similar in form to a TERRY CLOCK but made by Terry's former apprentice, Seth Thomas (active 1810–30), in Connecticut, USA.

THONET, MICHAEL (1796–1871) An innovative, 19thC, German designer who developed a technique for mass-producing "bentwood" FURNITURE, by steaming and bending wood. By 1900, he had factories throughout Europe and the USA, and had made over six million CHAIRS . His four sons helped to run the business, hence its name: Thonet Brothers. Look for the original Thonet brand mark or label under the seat rim or that of the lesser-known maker, Kohn. Chairs should be in good condition – they are quite easy to find and, therefore, not worth buying if damaged.

THREADING In GLASS, decoration consisting of fine threads of metal, used around the neck or rim of a vessel.

THREE-FACED DOLL First produced in the late 19thC, a DOLL with a revolving head and three distinct faces.

THREE KINGDOMS Period in Chinese history, AD 221–265.

THREE-PIECE GLASS Vessel made of three parts welded together, for example the bowl, STEM, and foot of a wineglass.

THREE-TRAIN MOVEMENT A movement with three separate sets of mechanisms: one for turning the hands, one for striking the hours, and another either for an alarm or the quarter hours.

THROUGH DOVETAIL A DOVETAIL JOINT that has the end grain showing on both sides of the angle.

THROWN CHAIR The old name for a TURNER'S CHAIR.

THUMB MOULD Rounded projecting edge to a tabletop.

THUMBPIECE Concave depression on the flange or handle of a hinged vessel lid. Helps in lifting the vessel or is pressed to raise the lid.

THUYA Reddish brown wood imported from Africa and used as a VENEER.

TIANQI (Tien Chi) Chinese MING DYNASTY emperor, 1621–27.

TIED QUILT A QUILT in which the three layers are joined and secured by a series of knots tied at intervals.

TIEFSCHNITT On GLASS, a type of INTAGLIO design that has been cut in, as distinct from HOCHSCHNITT, or high-relief decoration.

T'IEN LUNG Dragon of the skies. A motif on Chinese CARPETS and PORCELAIN.

TIE PIN Ornamental pin, used from the early 19thC (when cravats succeeded stocks as gentlemen's neckwear) to attach the tie to a shirt.

TIFFANY & CO. Founded in 1837 by Charles Louis Tiffany (1812–1902), a leading American, New York-based manufacturer of GLASS, JEWELLERY, POTTERY, and SILVER. Louis Comfort Tiffany (1848–1933), America's most influential ART NOUVEAU designer, took over the firm after his father's death. He founded the Tiffany Glass Company in 1885, intending it originally to produce stained glass. The firm also traded under the names Tiffany Glass and Decorating Co. (1892–1902) and Tiffany Studios (1902–1933). Tiffany was especially known for its range of "FAVRILE" glass. "Favrile" glass lamps have bronze or gilt-bronze bases, and shades made of a lattice of bronze, set with small pieces of glass. They are marked on applied bronze pads. Fake "Tiffany" lamps are identifiable because they do not usually have the marked pad on the shade. Tiffany began making pottery in the Art Nouveau style, in organic forms, in 1904, but this was less successful than the firm's glass and was discontinued after 1917. Light yellow-and-green tones were favoured on early pieces. Most Tiffany pottery is marked with the "LCT" cipher, and "L. C. Tiffany", "Favrile Pottery", or "Bronze Pottery" are sometimes etched on the base. Tiffany also made silver objects decorated with other metals in the Art Nouveau style. Tiffany marks on silver changed over the years. From 1873 until 1965 they included the letter or the surname of the company president. *See also* MIXED METALS.

TIFFANY & CO. **sterling silver cup and saucer, c.1873–91.**

TIGERWARE German, salt-glazed, EARTHENWARE jugs from the Rheinland with a glaze-pattern resembling a tiger's stripes. The term is sometimes also used to describe trailed white-SLIP decoration on a coloured BODY, creating a similar appearance.

TILL (1) Original name for what is now called a DRAWER.

TILL (2) Old name for the small lidded compartment found in some CHESTS. Now commonly known as a CANDLE BOX.

TILT-TOP TABLE Any table with a hinged top that can be tilted over in one piece for ease of storage when not in use.

TI-LUNG Earth dragon motif on Chinese RUGS and CERAMICS.

TIN Silvery-white metal, normally used in alloys, such as PEWTER, or as a coating (TINPLATE) for other metals. The firm of HUNTLEY AND PALMER pioneered the use of tins as packaging; the earliest ones, dating from the 1840s, were handmade with intricately decorated paper labels glued onto the surface. Such tins are now rare and valuable, and rust-free examples are desirable. Next in terms of value and rarity are the machine-made, transfer-printed tins of 1860 to 1880; the few that survive in good condition are very collectable. With the invention of cheaper, offset lithography for colour printing on tins, production expanded in the 1880s and '90s, and only the more ornamental and attractive designs of this period are of any value. The first shaped tins were made *c.*1888 and are valuable if they can be dated unequivocably to this first stage of shape experimentation. Most are embossed to simulate picture frames, or gently curved. Between 1900 and 1920, imaginative shapes of every description were made in quality. Tins that resemble wood, wicker, or leather, and unlikely shapes such as "book" tins, now sell well if they are in good condition. Christmas and commemorative tins are popular but are too numerous to be valuable; however, food tins printed with messages of encouragement and sent to World War I troops are collectable. The latest tins of interest are those with moving parts made between 1920 and 1939. Those in the forms of windmills, aeroplanes, vehicles, prams, coconut shies, and shooting galleries must be in perfect condition to be valuable.

London Delft TIN-GLAZED EARTHENWARE plate, 1680.

TINDERLIGHTER A 17th and 18thC pistol-shaped tinder box with a FLINTLOCK mechanism.

TINE A prong of a fork. Early forks have two tines; later ones, three.

TIN GLAZE A GLAZE containing tin oxide, which gives an opaque-white appearance, similar to PORCELAIN.

TIN-GLAZED EARTHERNWARE POTTERY with an EARTHENWARE body, which has been covered with a lead glaze to make it watertight. Tin glaze was applied to the fired BODY, which was then decorated with enamels, and finally coated with a clear lead glaze before the piece was returned to the kiln for refiring. The tin glaze was so opaque that it allowed potters to simulate the effect of white PORCELAIN. Tin-glazed pottery is given different names according to its country of origin. In Italy and Spain it is called MAIOLICA, in France and Germany it is known as FAIENCE, and in the Netherlands and England, it is termed DELFTWARE. The richly coloured designs and motifs found on Continental European pottery of the 17th and 18thC provided inspiration for 19thC and later makers, whose wares are known as MAJOLICA. Most of these later copies are highly decorative and collectable in their own right. Some genuine pieces of maiolica, faience, and Delftware have fake inscriptions to make them seem more valuable. Be suspicious if the calligraphy seems to lack fluidity and if there are any grey specks in unglazed areas – a sign the piece has been refired.

TING-TANG Name for the quarter chime on 19thC BLACK FOREST CLOCKS.

TING YAO Dating from the SUNG DYNASTY, Chinese PORCELAIN with a thick, white glaze and incised, floral patterns.

TINNED Interior of a base-metal or plated vessel, treated with a flux of TIN to give a silvery appearance and to prevent liquids being tainted by contact with the metal itself.

TINPLATE Metal objects, usually FLATWARE in iron or steel, covered in molten TIN to give them a silvery coating.

TINPLATE TOYS Toys made of TINPLATE in the late 19th and early 20thC, including horse-drawn carriages, boats, submarines, cars, and even airships, which reflect contemporary developments in transport. German toy companies led the field in the manufacture, and toys made by well-known firms such as BING, MÄRKLIN, and LEHMANN are famed for their accurate representations and quality. Toy trains were first made in the 1830s, and have remained popular since. With the onset of the "space race" and the advent of science-fiction films such as *The Forbidden Planet*, tinplate robots and space toys became popular. Rare, early robot toys can be extremely expensive.

TINWARE Cheap household items made of beaten-and-soldered TIN that is similar in appearance to PEWTER but less durable.

TIPP & CO. (Also known as Tippco.) German, Nuremberg-based company founded in 1912, and known for its toy motorcycles, cars, trucks, and aeroplanes. After World War II, it produced TINPLATE toy cars based on American prototypes. Tipp & Co. were also licensed to make Disney merchandise such as "Mickey Mouse" and "Minnie Mouse" on a motorcycle, one of the rarest Disney toys today. *See also* DISNEYANA.

TOASTING FORK Long-handled fork designed for toasting bread or muffins at the fireside, and relatively common after *c.*1720. Telescopic versions were made from *c.*1800.

TOASTMASTER'S GLASS With a thick-walled bowl, a GLASS that appears to hold more liquid than is actually the case.

TOAST RACK Item for serving toast at the DINING TABLE. The earliest toast racks date from the mid-18thC, and were fashioned from SILVER wire. In the REGENCY period, heavier, elaborately decorated examples were favoured, and, in the Victorian era (1837–1901), novelty forms (often in pairs) were popular. Toast racks were made in great quantities in OLD SHEFFIELD PLATE and ELECTROPLATE. Expanding, concertina-style examples are desirable.

TOBEY FURNITURE CO. An American firm, established by Charles and Frank Tobey in Chicago and active from 1875 to 1954. It manufactured architectural-style furniture influenced by the local architects Frank Lloyd WRIGHT and Louis Sullivan.

Welsh wrought-iron TOASTING FORK, *c.*1780.

TOBY JUG One of the amusing novelty objects produced after *c*.1750 in the STAFFORDSHIRE POTTERIES region of England, using coloured lead GLAZES. Toby jugs resemble comical men wearing tricorn hats, and were based on Harry Elwes, a character nicknamed Toby Philpot because of his capacity for drink. They were first made by Ralph Wood of Burslem in the mid-18thC. Many forms of Toby jug were made, and each is known by a special name; one of the most commonly seen "traditional" types depicts a man sitting and drinking beer, with a glass held to his mouth and a jug balanced on his knee. Other forms include the "Thin Man", the "Sharp Face", "Admiral Lord Howe", the "Coachman", and the "Fiddler". Toby jugs originally had covers in the hats; most are now missing, but an original cover can considerably increase the value of the piece. During the late 18th and early 19thC, brightly coloured PRATTWARE Toby jugs were made. Numerous, poor-quality copies were also produced in France and elsewhere.

TODDY LADLE Made primarily in Scotland and Ireland, toddy ladles have long, slim stems and small, shallow bowls, and were used to serve hot toddy from a PUNCHBOWL. Complete sets of six (the standard number) and provincial ladles are highly desirable.

TODDY LIFTER A hollow GLASS vessel used for transferring punch from the bowl to the DRINKING GLASS, the toddy lifter was popular between *c*.1810 and 1830 in England and Ireland. Shaped like a miniature DECANTER, with the capacity of a single wine glass, it has holes in both the top and bottom and is used like a pipette – the bulbous base is dipped into the punch to collect the liquid; a vacuum is created by placing the thumb over the top hole, ensuring that no liquid leaks out. The punch is released into the glass by uncovering the hole. Some pieces have collars as grips for the fingers when the thumb is placed over the top hole. The body is usually decorated with simple cutting or optical moulding. The body should have a grey tone characteristic of English and Irish LEAD CRYSTAL. Check carefully for cracks or chips around the top and bottom holes, as these areas are particularly prone to damage.

TOFT, THOMAS (d.1689) One of the best-known makers of SLIPWARE.

TOFT WARE Dishes made in Staffordshire, England, in the 17thC by Ralph and Thomas TOFT. They are decorated with SLIP TRAILING, often portraying a mermaid, pelican, or the head of King Charles II.

TOGI-DASHI In Japanese LACQUERWORK, pictures resembling watercolour painting covered with a thin layer of translucent lacquer.

TOILET MIRROR A MIRROR used by both ladies and gentlemen, and originally designed for travelling. The earliest examples from the late 17thC and the QUEEN ANNE period were fitted in boxes, along with such accessories

Victorian, mahogany, swing TOILET MIRROR.

as bottles, combs, brushes, and toilet boxes. The easel-back support allowed the mirror to stand upright, thus making it easier to consult when washing, shaving, or powdering. Several reputed French silversmiths such as Cardheillac, Jean-Baptiste Claude Odiot, and, later, Jean PUIFORCAT made high-quality toilet mirrors, which are usually highly priced.

TOILETRY *See* DRESSING-TABLE ACCESSORIES, DRESSING-TABLE SET, and GENTLEMEN'S TOILETRY.

TOKUGAWA Better known as the Edo era, the period in Japanese history, 1615–1867, when Tokyo became the capital of the country.

TOLEWARE From the French *tôle peinte* ("painted sheet iron", or "painted metal"), a French, 18thC technique of varnishing sheet-iron vessels so that the surface could be painted upon – and by derivation, painted metal panels applied to furniture. Toleware (sometimes "Tolerware") was used for hollow wares, such as TRAYS, and lampshades.

TOMPION & BANGER Company co-founded by Thomas TOMPION in the early 18thC. Noted for fine WATCHES.

TOMPION, THOMAS (1639–1715) Active 1671–1710, a famous English maker of CLOCKS and WATCHES. Known as the "father of English clockmaking".

Early-19thC TOLEWARE wine cooler with hinged top.

TONGUE-SCRAPER Made in a variety of designs in SILVER and OLD SHEFFIELD PLATE and used to scrape residue from the tongue. In one design, the flexible U-shape is held by the twisted ends and drawn across the tongue to eliminate the pink stain caused by drinking red wine; in another, the scraper is in the form of a small rake. Early SILVER examples are very rare. Tongue-scrapers are sometimes found in toothbrush box sets. They are often unmarked.

TONGZHI (T'ung Chih) Chinese QING dynasty emperor, 1862–74.

TONKA TOYS American firm first established in an old schoolhouse in Minnesota in 1947. It was originally called the Mound Metalcraft Co., but the name Tonka Toys was inspired by nearby Lake Minnetonka. The firm is known for its range of durable, pressed-steel toys, including its famous dump truck, introduced in 1964. DIECAST vehicles were made to a 1:64 scale in the 1960s and '70s. Tonka was purchased by Hasbro in 1991.

TONKOTSU Small, carved, Japanese tobacco pouch made for suspending from the waist sash (OBI).

TOOL An instrument used for making or fixing an object. Tool-collecting is still in its infancy, and interest focuses on the famous makers, because their work is easiest to date. Given that many craftsmen made their own tools, there are many examples that have potential value by anonymous or unknown makers. Price differentials emerge between the good and the mediocre, and the rare and the common, with premiums for complete sets of tools in boxes fitted with individual compartments. Prices for pre-1830 tools are higher than those for later examples, although rarity and quality are also important. Thus 18thC planes are preferred to 19thC models, except for metal planes by Spiers, Norris, and Preston, because these are admired for their sophisticated construction. Smoothing planes are less valuable than tools made for a specific task, such as mitre, dovetail, and moulding planes. Wooden braces, particularly of ROSEWOOD or BOXWOOD, are generally preferred to metal ones. An exception is the Marples brass-framed "Ebony Ultimatum", which is most valuable in mint condition. Lathes attract the highest prices of all tools, especially if they are well equipped. Those made by Holtzapftel or Evans are highly prized.

TOOLING Working of a pattern onto a leather SKIVER.

TOOSTIE TOYS American firm that created the first DIECAST toys in 1906, and went on to produce a fine range of diecasts in the 1930s. Their most famous models are of Graham and La Salle cars, but Tootsie also made diecast versions of cars by Ford, Lincoln, De Soto, and Auburn. These models were both attractive and affordable, and, from the mid-1920s, included details such as recessed lines around the engine compartments and doors. After World War II, quality declined, and the products became cruder in appearance. By the 1970s, their toys had become simple in design and were made of plastic.

TOOTHBRUSH BOX SET A portable SILVER box with a double-hinged cover and two compartments, designed to accommodate coarse and finely milled toothpowders as well as a toothbrush. Some sets also include a TONGUE-SCRAPER. A hallmarked toothbrush set in its original tooled leather box is rare and desirable.

TOP RAIL The highest horizontal bar on the back of a CHAIR.

TOPSY A black DOLL named Topsy, after a character from the *Little Black Sambo* books. "Topsies" were made in COMPOSITION by several firms, including ROSEBUD English from the 1930s to the 1950s. The better examples have defined fingers and extrovert hairstyles. Avoid dolls that have lost their hair. Examples with original clothes are more valuable than those without.

TOPSY-TURVY DOLL A DOLL with two heads and two trunks, joined at the waist. A reversible skirt covers one or the other as required.

TORCHÈRE *See* CANDLESTAND.

American composition TOPSY doll, c.1940.

TORELLI MAIOLICA An Italian, Florence-based firm that reproduced RENAISSANCE wares in the 19thC.

TORPEDO BOTTLE A BOTTLE with a pointed base and intended to be laid on its side. It was used by drinks manufacturer Jacob Schweppe from the late 1790s. The liquid, in contact with the cork, helped to keep the bottle airtight.

TORQUAY TERRACOTTA COMPANY *See* DEVON POTTERIES.

TORRICELLIAN TUBE Simple early form of barometer, named after its inventor, Evangelista Torricelli (1608–47).

TORTOISESHELL Mottled brown GLAZE on late 18th and early 19thC CERAMICS (especially WHIELDON ware), resembling real tortoiseshell.

TOUCH HOLE On a FIREARM's firing mechanism, a hole through which the combustion from the priming powder to the main charge is carried.

TOUCH MARK Maker's mark stamped on much, but not all, early English PEWTER. Its use was strictly controlled by the Pewterers' Company of London. Early examples consist of initials; later ones are more elaborate and pictorial, sometimes including the maker's address.

TOUCH PIN On the dial of a CLOCK, protrusions that enable the time to be felt in the dark.

TOULOUSE FAIENCE Now extremely rare, early -18thC pieces of TIN-GLAZED EARTHENWARE from the southern French town of the same name.

TOURNAI FACTORY The largest producer of PORCELAIN, notably figures, in The Netherlands. Their figures were usually unglazed and often depicted pastoral themes, as in their "Four Seasons" group. Although wares from this factory are readily available in Denmark, few examples are found elsewhere.

TOU T'SAI Anothere spelling of "DOUCAI".

TOY, WOODEN A toy carved from wood. They are often less sophisticated than those made from other substances, and hence have an appealing naivety. Wooden toys were produced in quantity by German makers in the 18th and 19thC, and some collectable examples were made in the USA by the Schoenhut Co. Noah's ark was a popular subject for German carvers; value depends on size, quality, and the number of animals included. Many 20thC wooden toys are affordable. Although chips and dents are inevitable and acceptable, a toy in mint condition or with its original packaging is sought after. Repainting reduces the value.

Staffordshire TORTOISESHELL-glazed teapot and cover, with bird finial, and raised on mask and claw feet, c.1750.

TOY SOLDIER *See* SOLDIER, TOY.

TRACERY Carved GOTHIC decoration that resembles the stone openwork typically found above Gothic windows.

TRADE LABEL Label placed on an item by the maker or the retailer.

TRADE TOKEN Coins produced by shopkeepers, innkeepers, and factory owners from the mid-17thC, and used instead of the legal coinage for the exchange of goods.

TRAFALGAR CHAIR With SABRE LEGS and a ROPE BACK, a DINING CHAIR made during the REGENCY period.

TRAFALGAR LEG Another name for a SABRE LEG.

TRAILED DECORATION On CERAMICS, SLIPWARE decoration resembling piped icing sugar.

TRAILING A glass-decoration technique in which thin rods of molten GLASS are applied around the vessel to create a spiralling pattern. It is found on pieces of ancient Roman glass and ART DECO-style glass. Coloured trials can be "combed". Pincering is a method of squeezing or nipping trails or other types of decoration to create a frilled edge.

TRAIN (1) In a CLOCK movement, a set of cog wheels and pinions often used for a specific function such as moving the hands or regulating the strike.

TRAIN (2) At first, a crude representation of a real train, an important form of transport that developed from the mid-19thC. Trains provided toymakers with a fertile source of inspiration and are among the most sought-after of collectable toys. The earliest toy trains, made in the 1830s, were designed to be pulled along the floor or powered by steam, but by the 1850s and '60s clockwork versions were being made. Electric trains were produced in substantial numbers in the late 19thC. By 1920, toy trains were accurate-scale models of the real thing. Collectors look for early MÄRKLIN, BING, and HORNBY models.

TRANSFER-PRINTING A method first used in the mid-18thC to make the decoration of CERAMICS less costly. Transfer-printing decoration involved taking an impression from an engraved copper plate onto transfer paper (the bat) and applying it to the ceramic body using an ink consisting of glaze mixed with oil. The paper, which is laid over the body of the vessel, burns off in firing, leaving an outline. Transfer-printing may be OVERGLAZE or UNDERGLAZE, and was used on both PORCELAIN and POTTERY. Early examples were printed in monochrome, sometimes with hand enamelling. Colour-printed designs were developed in the 1840s by F. & R. Pratt. Patterns had to be specially amended for differently shaped wares, and interesting variations are sometimes seen. Transfer-printing was also used on GLASS.

TRANSITIONAL STYLE Chinese PORCELAIN made between *c.*1620 and 1680, during the transition between the MING DYNASTY (1368–1644) and the QING Dynasty (1644–1916). The finely decorated objects, which were mostly in blue and white, usually depicted landscapes and everyday scenes with naturalistic elements, such as flowers and foliage, animals, and figures, instead of the imperial scenes found on earlier pieces. The "transitional" style was one of the most important influences on European pottery in the latter 17thC.

TRAPUNTO Quilting method in which small pieces of BATTING are inserted from the back of the QUILT to give a raised contour to parts of the pattern.

TRAY Made from the end of the 18thC, and initially conceived for clearing away as well as for the presentation of delicates. Trays have handles, while SALVERS do not. Borders used to decorate trays (and other types of SILVER) can help to date them, although many designs were repeated in the 19thC; these include borders decorated with GADROONING (1690–1700), scrolled borders (1730–40s), thread borders (1790s), and shell-and-scroll borders (*c.*1850–*c.*1895). Trays often had their owners' ARMORIALS engraved in the centre – if the crest belongs to a well-known family it can increase the item's value. Armorials that are contemporary with the piece are preferable to later ones. Many were erased on change of ownership, so check that the metal in the centre is not thinner than the rest (indicating removal of original metal). There should be a full set of HALLMARKS on the body – usually in a straight line – but applied borders may be separately marked.

TREEN Any small wooden object associated with everyday domestic, trade, professional, or rural life. Most articles of treen have been turned on lathes and are not normally the work of a cabinet-maker or joiner. The term is not applied to articles larger than a spinning-wheel. Carving, POKER WORK, INLAY, and painting are all common forms of decoration. There are a large number of possible subject areas in which to specialize. The earliest examples available date from the late 17thC, although these are difficult to distinguish from later reproductions. Treen drinking vessels made in the 18thC and other utensils are often attractive pieces, with fine turning and in a variety of quality woods such as MAPLE, WALNUT, MAHOGANY, and LIGNUM VITAE. Such 18thC pieces are sought after, but the collector has to be on guard against late-Victorian (1860–1901) reproductions, which tend to be of poorer-quality mahogany, and are cruder and less elegant in execution. Fine carving, especially if combined with skilful turning and attractive graining, adds greatly to value. Mottoes and quotations, carved or in poker work, are also desirable, but beware of later additions to genuine but plain items.

Scottish mixed-boxwood TREEN box with lid, *c.*1880.

Rare Chelsea cup and saucer
TREMBLEUSE, Raised-Anchor period, in
blanc de chine, 1749–52.

TREFID SPOON French-style spoon that was introduced to Britain in the mid-17thC. It has an egg-shaped bowl and broad, flat stem ending in a TREFOIL (sometimes notched), and tapering rib, or "rat's tails", at the junction of the bowl and stem for extra strength. These spoons were often stamped or engraved with decorative scrolls, foliage, or beading.

TREFOIL Three-lobed, GOTHIC decorative motif, like a stylized clover leaf.

TREMBLEUSE Saucer with a deep well, designed to steady a cup in place.

TRENCHER CASE Made in the 17thC, a small, decorative display shelf for the storage and presentation of GLASS, TREEN, PEWTER, and other objects.

TRENCHER SALT Dating from the late 17thC, the most popular type of SALTCELLAR, usually made in pairs or sets. The trencher salt had a circular, octagonal, or triangular form, with a central well.

TRESPOLO Elegant, three-legged, Italian TABLE designed to stand against a wall and carry a CANDLESTICK or small *objet d'art*.

TRESTLE (Also known as a DORMANT.) Horizontal beam with diverging legs, used as a support for some early tabletops.

TRIAD The owner's initials, sometimes on PEWTER, often with just three letters.

TRI-ANG Founded in 1919 by William, Arthur, and Walter Lines, sons of the founders of LINES BROTHERS. In 1935 the firm began to make its "Minic" series of small TINPLATE vehicles to compete with the popular and successful DIECAST cars on the market. When World War II broke out, toymaking was suspended. Production continued afterward until 1963. Collectable pre-war Minic cars should be pocket-sized, depict a contemporary British vehicle, be made of painted tinplate, have a clockwork mechanism and its original key, and have white tyres. Post-war Minics are more plainly coloured, designed to a scale to fit them into the popular "O" GAUGE railway layouts of the day, have well-illustrated boxes, and be fitted with black tyres. They may also have clockwork mechanisms, but later vehicles have "push-and-go" flywheel friction drives. Tri-ang entered the diecast market with a range called "Spot-On". They were modelled to a 1:42 scale and came with fully fitted interiors and windows, as well as "Flexomatic suspension". Electric headlamps were added from 1961–2. Examples complete with their box are sought after. The range of cars comprised contemporary vehicles such as the Austin A60, Vauxhall Cresta, and Morris 1000, and haulage vehicles were made between 1960 and 1963. The London "Routemaster" bus of 1963 was their most popular vehicle. In 1964, Lines Brothers took over MECCANO, which included their competitor DINKY, so Spot-On toys were discontinued in 1967.

TRICOTEUSE Small, French, galleried, sewing table.

TRIDARN (Or cwpwrdd tridarn.) The Welsh variety of the PRESS CUPBOARD, with three tiers.

TRIFLE PEWTER PEWTER made of 79 per cent tin, 15 per cent antimony, and 6 per cent lead. It was the best-quality pewter until the development of higher grade "hard metal" c.1700.

TRIO A tea set consisting of a matching cup, saucer, and plate.

TRIPLE-TOP TABLE Another name for a HARLEQUIN TABLE.

TRIPOD TABLE A small TABLE with a top that can be tilted, supported by a central pillar on a three-legged base; it was first made c.1700. Tripod tables were used for tea or dessert in the 18thC. Most tripod tables have tops that can tip up into a vertical position when not in use. The least expensive versions are those with plain circular tops. Those with decorative details such as a piecrust top with a shaped edge; a fluted and leaf-carved baluster (most tables have only simple turned decoration); and hairy paw feet (simple pad feet are more common) are more desirable. The classic, 18thC tripod table has a top that is made from a single piece of solid MAHOGANY, but some American WALNUT tables have two-piece tops. Country tripod tables were made from OAK, FRUITWOOD, and ELM; some were decorated with veneers. Tripod tables were sometimes made from papier-mâché. *See also* BIRDCAGE SUPPORT.

Chinese black laquered TRIPOD TABLE, c.1880.

TROIKA A pottery founded in St Ives, Cornwall, England, in 1963. It initially produced small, decorative items, but graduated to larger sculptural pieces as it expanded. By 1964, the factory was producing wares for the top London stores LIBERTY, and HEAL & SON. In the early days, the factory produced both textured ware and less-distinctive, white, glaze-finished pieces. The rugged Cornish coastline inspired the shapes and decoration, and circle patterns and clean abstracts remain popular. The firm closed in 1983.

TROLLEY *See* DRINKS TROLLEY.

TROMPE L'OEIL Any flat, decorative motif intended to deceive the eye into seeing the third dimension of depth.

TROY WEIGHT System of weights used for quantifying GOLD, SILVER, and precious stones.

TRUCKLE BED (Also known as a TRUNDLE BED.) Early bedstead that can be moved by means of wooden wheels under the uprights.

TRUMPETER CLOCK A CLOCK similar to a CUCKOO CLOCK but with a model of a military bugler that sounds the hours.

TRUNDLE BED *See* TRUCKLE BED.

TRUNK *See* COFFER.

TSUBA Guard of a Japanese SWORD, often with an ornamented plate.

TSUGE Japanese for "BOXWOOD", one of the most common materials used for carving NETSUKE.

TSUIKOKU Carved Japanese LACQUERWARE in black, the natural colour, as opposed to TSUISHU, which is coloured red.

TSUISHU Japanese carved LACQUERWARE in red. *See also* TSUIKOKU.

TUBE-LINING Decoration on ceramic vessels in which thin trails of SLIP are used to outline areas of coloured glaze. Technique used by Charlotte RHEAD.

TUCKER PORCELAIN Wares made by Philadelphia-based William Ellis Tucker (active 1826–38), the second firm in North America to make PORCELAIN. Similar to pieces by SÈVRES, Tucker is noted for its fine painting and gilding. The vase-shaped pitcher is a form unique to this firm, with prices dependent on the painted decoration – Philadelphia views are sought after. Much Tucker is hard to distinguish from the French and Italian prototypes on which it was based. Most is unmarked, although some pieces are marked "Tucker and Hulme" or "Tucker and Hemphill". Early examples can be identified by their greenish cast when held up to the light. Later pieces seem orange or straw-coloured.

TUDOR A period in England from 1485 to 1603. FURNITURE made during that time may also be referred to as "Tudor", although furniture made during the reign of Elizabeth I (1558–1603) is more likely to be called "Elizabethan".

TUDRIC High-quality range of Celtic-inspired, ART NOUVEAU pewter, designed for mass production by Archibald KNOX and sold by LIBERTY.

TULIP ORNAMENT A type of ornament, in the shape of a tulip flower, in vogue from *c.*1650 to *c.*1700.

TULIP TANKARD In PEWTER an 18thC TANKARD resembling a tulip flower.

TULIP WARE Pennsylvanian Dutch, 18th and 19thC POTTERY, decorated with SGRAFFITO to create stylized tulips in yellow or green.

TULIPWOOD A pale olive-green to brown, straight-grained wood imported from Brazil, tulipwood (*Dalbergia*) was used for VENEERS and borders decorated with crossbanding. It often appears on quality French FURNITURE, usually with KINGWOOD. In England, it was often used as crossbanding for ROSEWOOD.

TUMBLER (1) A flat-bottomed, stemless GLASS, with parallel or tapering sides. Made since ancient Roman times, the tumbler is the most widely produced, practical form of drinking vessel. In the 18th and 19thC, English GLASS firms made a variety of decorative examples, with ornamentation ranging from fairly crude DIAMOND-POINT ENGRAVING on the least expensive versions to enamelled hunting and sporting scenes, flowers, fruiting vines, landscapes, and coats of arms on those made for the wealthiest clients. The subject matter on most tumblers consists of humorous scenes, commemorative themes, and hunting. Tumblers are among the most affordable items of glass available today. *See also* BEILBY GLASS.

TUMBLER (2) Inside a firing mechanism, a notched wheel that controls the sear and hammer, causing the latter to rest at half or fullcock or to fall and strike the steel or cap. See also FIREARM.

TUMBLER CUP Round-bottomed drinking vessel.

TUNBRIDGE WARE Items decorated with intricate pictures made from long strands of differently coloured woods glued together and sliced transversally into thin sheets. Tunbridge decoration was mostly made in the Tunbridge Wells area of Kent, England. Value depends on the fineness of the decoration.

TUREEN A large BOWL with a foot and, often, two side handles. Used for serving soup from the early 18thC. *See also* SAUCE TUREEN.

TUREEN, SOUP A TUREEN used for serving soup From the early 18thC, soup was served as part of the first course, alongside boiled meats, fish, and vegetables. Soup was served to guests at the table with great ceremony, and hence the soup tureen became a vehicle for the display of wealth; it was often the most opulent and highly prized piece in the DINNER SERVICE. The earliest, mid-18thC soup tureens were commonly oval-shaped with decorative, cast side handles and domed covers, with FINIALS, perhaps cast as artichokes, crayfish, or simple KNOPS. They usually stood on four cast feet, and were often fitted with detachable drop-in liners of thin sheet SILVER, or, later, SHEFFIELD PLATE, which were easy to clean. Most early tureens are of heavy-gauge silver and feature engraved coats of arms. From the 1730s, some extravagant soup tureens were crafted by such master silversmiths as Paul de LAMERIE, Juste-Aurèle Meissonnier, and Thomas Germain, and these are among the most celebrated items of influential ROCOCO silver. By the mid-18thC, tureens were made with matching stands and ladles, and sometimes

TUNBRIDGE WARE **counter box, 1830.**

Victorian, marquetry and parquetry-banded whatnot with spiral-TURNED column supports and TURNED feet.

also with liners. In the mid-to-late 18thC simple, boat-shaped NEO-CLASSICAL-STYLE soup tureens came into vogue; most were oval (vase form), on single pedestal feet, with domed covers, high loop handles, and urn-shaped finials. Soup tureens produced in the 1790s were made from a minimum amount of sheet silver, so they are lighter and more susceptible to damage than examples made in the early 18thC. By the early 19thC, sumptuous designs were popular. Tureen covers and stands have often been lost and then replaced in the more fashionable style of the moment, so original examples are rare. In general, soup tureens are valuable – those made before the mid-18thC or by a major maker are especially rare and valuable.

TURKEY RED Dye obtained from the root of madder plants and used in carpet-making. They are dark red but with an orange tint, as distinct from the brownish-red of Turkoman CARPETS. *See also* RUGS.

TURKEYWORK European-made imitations of Turkish CARPETS. They were often made by stitching wool to a canvas background and used for FURNITURE covering and upholstery from the 16thC. *See also* RUGS.

TURKISH CARPET Traditionally of deeper pile than Persian CARPETS and decorated with geometric or stylized motifs rather than floral. *See also* RUGS.

TURKISH KNOT Alternative name for the GHIORDES KNOT. Typical of – but not exclusive to – Turkish-made CARPETS as distinct from Persian. *See also* RUGS.

TURKISH RUG *See* RUGS, CAUCASIAN AND TURKISH.

TURKOMAN CARPET Woven by the nomadic tribes of the region that stretches from the Caspian Sea to Sinkiang in southern China. The CARPETS are predominantly decorated with GUL motifs. *See also* RUGS.

TURNABOUT DOLL RAG DOLL with two faces, one on the front, one on the back, either of which could be covered by a reversible bonnet.

TURNED FURNITURE Pieces made by turning on a lathe.

TURNER BLACKWARE Late -18th and 19thC black PORCELAIN made by John Turner of Staffordshire, England, in imitation of WEDGWOOD'S BASALTES.

TURNER'S CHAIR A CHAIR made entirely from turned parts.

TURNIP FOOT On American FURNITURE, a foot similar to a BUN FOOT but narrower, and with a ringed moulding around the top.

TURN-OFF PISTOL A pistol with a barrel that unscrews for loading.

TURNOVER RIM A rim on a GLASS bowl in a classic style associated with Irish Regency cut glass. The rims are sometimes uneven because of the difficulty of manipulating hot glass into this form.

TURNOVER DOLL *See* TOPSY-TURVY DOLL.

TURN-UP BED CHAIR or SOFA that can be converted into a BED.

TURRET CLOCK Strictly, the type of CLOCK installed since the Middle Ages in towers and driven by a weight suspended from a rope wound round a drum. Also, smaller clocks with a similar drive, and usually hung on a wall.

TURTLE BACK A 16thC, decorative ornament resembling a turtle's shell.

TWIST *See* AIR-TWIST STEM, MIXED-TWIST STEM, and OPAQUE-TWIST STEM.

TWIST-OVER Revolver with a twist action to align each of the chambers in succession with the firing mechanism and barrel.

TWO-FACED DOLL A DOLL with a waking face on one side and a sleeping face on the other. It was patented in 1868, as a development of the laughing and crying dolls made by BRU JEUNE. The SWIVEL HEAD is rotated to reveal the alternative face. JUMEAU also made a version with a crying and laughing face. The face is typically switched by means of a knob on top of the head.

TWO-TRAIN MOVEMENT A CLOCK movement that has two separate mechanisms, one for turning the clock hands, the other for the strike.

TYG A type of CUP with three handles.

TYPEWRITER A machine with a keyboard designed to print letters onto a sheet of paper. Patents were taken out on typewriters as early as 1828 in the USA, but REMINGTON made the first commercially successful machine in 1873; demand soared, and hundreds of manufacturers filed patents after 1890. Collectors look for pioneering machines that represent a stage in the development of typewriters, and rare, pre-1900 models. Post-1914 machines hold little interest for collectors. Patent numbers are a useful guide to date; most machines were made within three years of a patent being filed. Early manufacturers of note include Fitch, Yost, New Century, Williams, Empire Fay-Sho, Oliver, Crandall, and Blick. Condition is paramount in assessing value, and a perfect machine, with contemporary ribbon, undamaged transfer motifs, gilding, enamelling, and paintwork, sells for much more than a damaged or restored item. Accessories such as the instruction manual and carrying case, add further value. Avoid machines with defective nickelling to the metal parts, because this is expensive to repair or restore.

Doulton Lambeth TYG by Frank Butler, 1878.

UNDERGLAZE BLUE POTTERY and PORCELAIN decorating technique in which a design is painted onto a BODY made of BISCUIT with cobalt oxide before a piece is glazed. First used on 13thC Persian pottery, the method was later adopted by the Chinese to decorate porcelain. Underglaze-blue decoration was used from the late 18thC by factories in England such as CAUGHLEY, LIVERPOOL, and WORCESTER, who decorated wares with underglaze-blue TRANSFER PRINTING.

UNDERGLAZE DECORATION Decoration applied to a ceramic BODY prior to glazing and final firing.

UNDERGLAZE PRINTING Technique in which a colour or design is applied to the BISCUIT-fired BODY before glazing.

Jug designed by Karl H.L. Muller for UNION PORCELAIN WORKS, 1875.

UNDERWEISSBACH White-glazed PORCELAIN figures based on sculptures by Ernest Barlach, and made at the Schwarzburger Werkstätten, Germany, in the early 20thC.

UNION GLASS CO. American, Massachusetts-based glassworks, founded in 1851. The factory made clear cut and PRESSED GLASS until 1934. *See also* GLASS.

UNION PORCELAIN WORKS Founded in 1861, an American, New York-based factory that produced utilitarian PORCELAIN such as door knobs and PLATES, but is better known for its "Century" vases made to commemorate the Centennial in 1876, as well as for oyster plates and whimsical items modelled by Karl L.H. Miller (1820–87).

UPRIGHT (Also known as a SIDE RAIL.) A vertical pillar on a CHAIR back.

URBINO MAIOLICA Major Italian centre of production of MAOILICA. Noted for ISTORIATO and Raphaelesque painting in bright colours in the 16thC.

URN *See* TEA URN.

URN STAND A support for a JARDINIÈRE or small *objet d'art*.

URUSHI Japanese for "raw lacquer", a sap from varieties of the ash tree.

USHAK From Turkish Anatolia, long-pile, loosely woven CARPETS, usually with a central medallion on a plain ground.

V

VALENCIA From the 14thC, an important centre of MAIOLICA production in Spain, where Moorish potters introduced TIN-GLAZED EARTHENWARE techniques, and from where itinerant potters took these new methods to all parts of Europe.

VAN BRIGGLE, ARTUS A decorator at the American ROOKWOOD POTTERY, van Briggle set up his own pottery in Colorado Springs in 1901. Influenced by ART NOUVEAU, his designs combine figural, floral, and plant forms. His "Lorelei" vase, reflecting the influence of the French sculptor Auguste Rodin, was produced at Rookwood by van Briggle in 1898. The van Briggle pottery still produces Lorelei vases today.

VAN DER ROHE, LUDWIG MIES *See* MIES VAN DER ROHE, Ludwig.

VAN DE VELDE, HENRY (1863–1957) A Belgian architect who also designed FURNITURE, influenced by both the ARTS AND CRAFTS and MODERNIST MOVEMENTS. Van de Velde's sculptural furniture had fluid, curving lines, and although he used studded upholstery, he used little applied decoration.

VAN ERP, DIRK (1860–1933) A Dutch metalworker who emigrated to California, USA, where, from 1908, he worked in the Dutch medieval style, inspired by the ARTS AND CRAFTS MOVEMENT. His VASES, writing equipment, and table lamps, made of hammered copper with exposed riveting, are sought after today.

VASE Any tall vessel with a primarily ornamental use. They were made in every variety of style, shape, and ornament. Most available GLASS pieces date from the 19th and early 20thC, the most productive period of technical and artistic innovation in glassmaking. Vases specifically for holding flowers were introduced in the late 19thC, with the vogue for exotic flowers sparked by the new interest in Japanese art at that time. Such examples were often tall and narrow. Many earlier vases were made in pairs, to sit on either side of a mantelpiece, and often had covers – typical of these ornate pieces are those made in France, in coloured or OPALINE GLASS with ORMOLU mounts, often of CLASSICAL motifs. Elaborate centrepieces known as ÉPERGNES were also made from the 19thC to hold impressive floral displays. Vases were the perfect vehicle for manufacturers to show off their skills in producing the unusual surface treatments and colours, elaborate shapes, and ornate, applied decoration typical of so-called ART GLASS – ornamental blown and pressed wares – made from the 1870s in Europe and the USA. American

One of a pair of late-19thC Bohemian opaque glass VASES.

firms are associated with experiments in iridescence, and some of the "FAVRILE" vases created by TIFFANY are among the most highly priced available today. At the same time, simpler practical pieces such as CELERY VASES (part of matching sets of tableware) were made.

VASE, AMERICAN From the late 19thC, many American glassmakers turned their attention from domestic tableware to the development of luxury ART GLASS in a range of dazzling colours created by unusual techniques. Some of the best examples of American art glass are ornamental VASES from this period. The leading exponent was Louis C. TIFFANY, known for his lamps with shades made of leaded panels of iridescent "FAVRILE" glass; he also made a range of ART NOUVEAU vases in iridescent and CAMEO GLASS. The popularity of Tiffany's wares led to the manufacture of a variety of iridescent wares and other, similarly creative, art glass by firms including QUEZAL in Brooklyn, New York, and the STEUBEN GLASSWORKS in Corning, New York.

"VASE" CARPET Persian RUG with a vase of flowers as the central motif.

VASE, CONTINENTAL In Continental Europe, the most innovative VASES in GLASS were produced in France and Bohemia during the 19thC. Such vases are often in a style different from that of contemporary English pieces, and were often inspired by ornamental wares in luxury materials such as PORCELAIN and HARDSTONES. However, as in England, the vase proved the best medium for exploring new developments in glass technology, particularly colouring. Bohemian glassmakers were the leaders in developing new colours, with Friedrich Egermann patenting his marbled LITHYALIN GLASS in 1829, and, in the 1830s, Josef Riedel developing yellow- and green-toned glass by adding small amounts of uranium to the batch. Bohemian makers were also the pioneers in the development of CASING, OVERLAY GLASS, FLASHING, and STAINING techniques for colouring glass in the 19thC. In France, many fine-quality vases were produced in OPALINE GLASS. More restrained forms began to appear in Continental glassware toward the end of the 19thC, through the influence of reforming designers. Vases enamelled with a Japanese-inspired pattern, such as chrysanthemums, are sought after today.

VASE, ENGLISH The heyday of the English VASE was from *c*.1850 to *c*.1900, a period in which a large number of firms experimented with coloured, enamelled, and silvered GLASS. The highest-quality and most sophisticated pieces were produced by the leading Midlands manufacturers of luxury tableware, including W.H., B. and J. Richardson, George BACCHUS & SONS, STEVENS & WILLIAMS, and Thomas WEBB & Sons. Initially, designs were somewhat restrained, typically with CLASSICAL inspiration, but, from the 1870s, ornate trailed and pincered forms and, frequently, vibrant colours were fashionable.

VASELINE GLASS (Also known as yellow opaline.) A type of GLASS developed in the late 19thC and so-called because of the slightly greasy look of its surface. Characteristic shades include blue, yellow, and green.

VAUNCANSON, JACQUES Early -18thC maker of mechanical toys.

VAUXHALL FACTORY One of the minor English PORCELAIN factories, active between 1751 and 1764. It made bottle VASES in bulbous shapes with long thin necks; these proved popular in London. The vases usually sagged slightly in firing – a defect characteristic of this firm. Because Vauxhall is a recently discovered factory, it has a keen following, and wares demand a premium. Spurious Chinese MARKS are occasionally found on Vauxhall porcelain.

VAUXHALL GLASS Products of the Duke of Buckingham's glassworks at Vauxhall. Founded in the third-quarter of the 17thC, the factory chiefly producing plate GLASS and silvered glass for mirrors.

VEGETABLE DISH A variation on the ENTRÉE DISH, usually of shallow, circular form with a high, domed cover. Some have glass liners, while some have dividers, so that the dishes could hold several types of food.

VELOCIPEDE Meaning "fast feet", the earliest form of bicycle, invented *c*.1760. It was originally powered by the feet pushing along the ground, but later versions had pedals attached to a large front wheel.

Webb VASELINE/cranberry-glass footed vase, 1900.

VENEER Thin sheet of decorative wood applied to a solid body (a carcass), which is made from a different (less-expensive) wood. This secondary wood, as it is known, is most commonly PINE or OAK. Veneering is an economical way of using expensive woods, and it allows the maker to create decorative effects from the figuring of the wood. The earliest veneers were of WALNUT, followed by the superbly patterned MAHOGANY in the late 18th and early 19thC. Walnut returned to favour in the Victorian period (1837–1901). Many other woods were also used as veneers, notably SATINWOOD, ROSEWOOD, and MAPLE. The technique of veneering was imported to England by Dutch craftsmen in the late 17thC. Early veneers were cut in a saw pit and vary in thickness between 2mm and 4mm (⅟₁₆in and ⅛in). All modern veneers are less than 2mm (⅟₁₆in) thick if cut with a circular saw, and paper thin if machine planed. From the mid-18thC onward, band saws allowed more even and even thinner veneers to be made. Veneers may be cut from the tree in various ways: if they are cut lengthways, the grain will be longitudinal; if cut across the roots, a burr effect is achieved. Another variation occurs if they are cut across the top, where the tree was pollarded. Once the thin layers of veneer are cut, they are laid in a variety of ways to create a decorative effect such as QUARTER-VENEERING and an OYSTER VENEER. The quality of veneering has an important bearing on price. Plain veneer panels

Venice and Murano Glass Co.

Large, ruby VENETIAN GLASS goblet and dish, c.1900.

on an otherwise decorated piece could indicate replacement of the original veneer. Look at hinges on the doors – if there is little dirt or grime around them, the veneer has probably been steamed off to repair the carcass wood beneath, and replaced. *See also* BANDING, CROSSBANDING, and PARQUETRY.

VENICE AND MURANO GLASS CO. A glassworks established (using British capital) by Antonio Salviati, who brought together skilled craftsmen on the Venetian glassmaking island of MURANO, Italy. From 1866 to 1909, the factory produced mainly tableware, including VASES, BOTTLES, GOBLETS, and TAZZAS with elaborate STEMS, freely based on VENETIAN GLASS styles from the 16th and 17thC, but usually more richly coloured. These purely ornamental, pastiche copies of early Venetian glass were popular, influencing glassmaking in Europe and the USA. The quality of Salviati glass varies, from superbly crafted vessels to crudely coloured examples. On some pieces, Salviati used an unusual lacy decoration, achieved by using lace covered with enamel. When the enamel was fired, the material burned away, leaving the delicate lacy pattern on the surface.

VENETIAN GLASS SODA GLASS and coloured glass, blown and pinched into intricately ornamented vessels. Made on the island of MURANO, near Venice, Italy, and copied from the 15thC. *See also* DRINKING GLASS, VENETIAN; LION OF ST MARK; and TAZZA, VENETIAN.

VENETIAN MIRROR A MIRROR first produced on the island of MURANO, near Venice, Italy, in the late 19thC. They are still made today.

VENETIAN PORCELAIN Now rare, an early SOFT-PASTE PORCELAIN produced in Venice, Italy, in the early 18thC.

VENINI (est. 1921) One of the major Italian glassworks, celebrated for its bold use of colour and original forms and decorative techniques, as seen in the "Tessuto" VASE – named after its fabric-like decoration – designed by Carlo Scarpa. One of the firm's quirky, early -1960s designs is a decorative fish PAPERWEIGHT, which shows off the company's mastery of form and colour.

VENTURI, ROBERT (b.1925) American architect who has also designed post-modern FURNITURE, manufactured by KNOLL ASSOCIATES.

VERGE ESCAPEMENT Found on CLOCKS made as early as the 14thC, and still in use in 1900, it consists of a bar (the verge) with two, flag-shaped pallets that rock in and out of the teeth of the crown or escape wheel to regulate the movement.

VERNIER Sliding scale, used in conjunction with the fixed scale on a barometer for taking accurate pressure readings.

VERNIS MARTIN Lacquers and varnishes used in France on CLOCKS and FURNITURE in the 18thC. It is named after the Martin brothers, who were permitted to copy Japanese LACQUER, and is found in many colours, especially green.

VERRE DE FOUGÈRE French term meaning "fern glass". *See* FOREST GLASS.

VERRE DE NEVERS Toys and figures made from differently coloured rods of GLASS. It was first made *c.*1600 at Nevers in France, but was widely copied.

VERRE DE SOIE French for "satin glass". A type of GLASS with a satin finish.

VERRE DOUBLE Early form of CAMEO GLASS, developed by Emile GALLÉ and first shown in 1899. Coloured glass is sandwiched between two layers of plain glass, and areas are carved or etched to reveal the colour underneath.

VERRIÈRE The French term for a MONTEITH.

VESTA CASE Small SILVER case made to hold vestas – friction matches invented *c.*1840. These small cases were adapted from SNUFF BOXES with the addition of serrated strikers. As smoking became fashionable from the late 19thC, small rectangular boxes with rounded corners and closely fitting hinged lids (vital to prevent matches from combusting) were produced specifically for vestas. They were made in a variety of shapes, with ENGRAVED, CHASED, or ENAMELLED decoration. Many vesta cases made in the late-Victorian and Edwardian periods (1860–1901 and 1901–10 respectively) were enamelled with nudes in erotic poses. These risqué designs adorn some of the most highly treasured vestas. Some of the most common novelty vesta cases are in the form of birds and animals. The finest vesta cases are enamelled, although others are chased or engraved. Fine, pictorial vesta cases were a speciality of makers such as Sampson MORDAN & Co. and Henry William Dee. Novelty vesta cases were made in the USA in great numbers between 1890 and 1910. The interiors were often gilded to prevent the phosphorous match heads from reacting with the silver. Cases may be designed with a loop for suspension from a SILVER chain. From *c.*1890, Birmingham was the major centre of production of vesta cases in Britain, although the highest-quality workmanship is usually found on London-made cases. Some vesta cases have double compartments for matches, or were combined with other objects such as a PENKNIFE, CIGAR CUTTER, or STAMP HOLDER. From the late 19thC, novelty examples were produced in great numbers. With the introduction of the more durable petrol lighter, the production of vesta cases stopped after World War I.

Edwardian champagne-bottle VESTA CASE.

VETRO A FILI Italian "thread glass"; a type of FILIGRANA. Other types include *vetri a reticello* ("glass with a small network"), *vetri a retortoli* ("glass with a twist") and *vetri di trino* ("lace glass"). *See also* GLASS.

VEUVE PERRIN One of the most prominent French FAIENCE factories was that of the Veuve (widow) Perrin, in the Marseilles region. The firm made highly prized and colourful faience in the latter half of the 18thC. Many wares from this factory are marked "VP", but the mark is also seen on copies, so always check the quality of the painting – painters from the factory were sent to the French drawing academies.

VICAR AND MOSES Figure group, depicting a parson preaching while his clerk sleeps, made in quantity in Staffordshire, England, in the late 18th and early 19thC. *See also* STAFFORDSHIRE FIGURES and STAFFORDSHIRE POTTERIES.

VICTORIAN STYLE A wide variety of styles were popularly revived in the reign of Queen Victoria (1837–1901) – usually divided into early Victorian (1837–1860) and late Victorian (1860–1901). Much of the FURNITURE produced at this time exhibits a hybrid of Neo-GOTHIC, ROCOCO, and NEO-CLASSICAL STYLES. However, the Victorians kept a style popular even when they had discovered a new one, whereas in the 18thC one style superseded another. The decoration of Victorian furniture is often elaborate with a profusion of carving; INLAY and metal MOUNTS, often made by industrial machines, were popular. The later Victorian style encompassed the AESTHETIC MOVEMENT (epitomized by the "Japanese" designs of E.W. Godwin), the ARTS AND CRAFTS MOVEMENT, and ART NOUVEAU – all of which helped to drive out overly fussy Victorian ornamentation.

VIENNA FACTORY The second European factory to produce HARD-PASTE PORCELAIN, the Vienna factory was founded by Claudius Innocentius DU PACQUIER, who managed to extract the secret of porcelain making from disgruntled MEISSEN employees. Porcelain from the du Pacquier period (1719–44) is rarer than Meissen, and few pieces have survived. It is similar in composition to early Meissen, and often has a greenish tone. Wares are usually decorated with CHINOISERIE and formal, Baroque, STRAPWORK borders. Dominant colours are puce, iron red, and monochromes, and, compared with that on Meissen, the manner of painting is naive. Figures are rare and idiosyncratic. In 1744, the company was taken over by the state, and production increased. Vienna continued making similar wares to Meissen until the 1780s. In 1784, a new director was appointed, and wares were made in the NEO-CLASSICAL STYLE, with elaborate painted scenes and heavy gilding of similar appearance to wares from centres such as BERLIN and ST PETERSBURG. Topographical scenes, which were often named on the base, were among the specialities of Viennese decorators. Although tableware formed the bulk of the factory's output, it also made accessories. The Vienna Factory closed in 1864, but many imitations of its more elaborate wares were made by other European firms in the late 19thC. Highly desirable are pieces from later periods decorated by Joseph Nigg, a renowned flower painter. Prices for other late pieces are dependent on their decorative appeal. Vienna was marked with a shield, which was much copied on later pieces "in the style of" Vienna. From the 1780s, the factory also used three impressed numerals denoting the last three numbers of the year of manufacture: for example, the mark 817 indicated a piece made in 1817.

VIENNA REGULATOR An early -19thC, Austrian PENDULUM CLOCK with a glass-fronted case, which reveals the fast-swinging pendulum.

VILE, WILLIAM (d.1727) Prominent English cabinet-maker and upholsterer to George III. Worked in partnership with John COBB.

VINAIGRETTE Inspired by POMANDERS, and made from the late 18th until the late 19thC, a tiny hinged box (smaller than a SNUFFBOX) designed to hold sponges soaked in perfume, aromatic salts, or vinegar and concealed under a pierced, hinged SILVER grille. They were carried in pockets and sniffed to combat fainting fits or unpleasant smells created by primitive sewage and water systems. Early vinaigrettes were small, making them convenient to have about the person, and they had simple grilles and engraved tops; by the 1830s, they were larger, with more elaborate decoration and fancier grilles – vinaigrettes are often collected for their grille decoration, so these later 19thC ones can be very popular. British examples often bear the Birmingham anchor HALLMARK, because, from the late 18thC, silversmiths in this area produced small silver items in the thousands. Among the most sought-after vinaigrettes are those known as CASTLE-TOPS. The Victorian fancy for novelties found expression in an unlimited variety of vinaigrettes made in the mid-19thC, including examples in the shapes of shells, fish, watches, crowns, flowers, and purses. Book-shaped vinaigrettes often celebrated popular authors, including Sir Walter Scott or Lord Byron. Other vinaigrettes were made to commemorate historical events such as Admiral Nelson's victory at Trafalgar in 1805 or the Great Exhibition of 1851. Those in fanciful designs – hunt or battle scenes, military trophies, animals, birds, musical instruments, or filigree work – are the most valuable. Engine-turned scrollwork and floral motifs were popular, as was the fashion of engraving vinaigrettes with the owner's initials or a crest. The interiors of vinaigrettes were gilded to protect the silver from corrosion caused by the perfume oil. Makers who are celebrated for their vinaigrettes include: Sampson MORDAN & Co. of London, Nathaniel MILLS (particularly famed for castle-top vinaigrettes), Thomas Shaw, and Joseph Taylor of Birmingham. Pre-19thC pieces are scarcer and can be highly priced. Check that the hinge isn't damaged, and make sure the MARKS on the base are the same as those on the lid – if they don't match, the box may have been altered. Sometimes snuffboxes are turned into vinaigrettes by adding grilles – just as vinaigrettes are sometimes turned into PILL BOXES by removing their grilles.

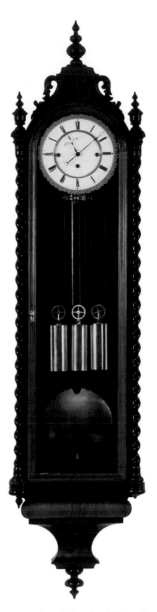

Rosewood and ebonised "Grande Sonnerie" Biedermeier VIENNA REGULATOR, c.1850

VINCENNES French national manufacturer of wares made of SOFT-PASTE PORCELAIN from 1738 until 1756, when it moved to SÈVRES. The factory's early production was generally of indifferent quality and inferior to the contemporary productions of ST CLOUD and MENNECY. Toward the end of the 1740s, probably influenced by MEISSEN, coloured GROUNDS were introduced at Vincennes. In the 1750s, lightly tooled GILDING was used to heighten reserve panels. The coloured grounds were: "bleu" (blue) from the late 1740s; "bleu celeste" (sky blue) from 1752; "jaune jonquille" (daffodil yellow) from 1753; and "Rose pompadour" ("Pompadour pink") from 1757.

VINEGAR STICK A small box, made in SILVER or other metals, and pierced and mounted on a stick. They were designed to hold vinegar-soaked sponges and were used as air fresheners.

VINELAND FLINT GLASS WORKS An American, New Jersey-based GLASS producer owned by the French-born Victor Durand. ART GLASS was made by Vineland from 1924 after the arrival of Martin Bach Jr (1865–1924), who had worked at QUEZAL. Vineland wares are signed with the name "Durand" or "Durand" superimposed over a large "V".

VINE TRAIL Repeated band of carved decoration in the form of leaves, flowers, and grapes.

VINOVO PORCELAIN Wares in PORCELAIN made at a factory active briefly in the late 18thC near Milan, Italy.

VINYL A non-flammable, flexible yet tough plastic that was used for DOLLS from the 1940s. It had virtually replaced hard plastic by the 1950s.

VINYL DOLL Made from the mid-1950s, a DOLL with a hollow VINYL head, which was much softer than the hard ones on plastic dolls produced before then. It is possible to determine if a doll is vinyl or plastic by its hair: a vinyl doll has synthetic rooted hair inserted in clumps, while the hair on a plastic one is moulded or in the form of a wig. Vinyl dolls have jointed limbs and painted or inserted eyes, and they had registered trademarks on the heads or bodies. The ALEXANDER DOLL CO. was a well-known maker. Popular, more recent, vinyl examples include BARBIE, SINDY, "Action Man", "Bionic Woman", and SASHA DOLLS. Excellent condition is crucial to value (vinyl fades in the sun), and the best dolls are those that have not been taken out of their boxes. If boxes are lost or the dolls damaged, the value will plummet. Watch out for inferior copies made in the Far East (usually stamped "Made in Taiwan" or "Made in Japan").

VIOLETEER A pot to hold petals and herbs.

VIRGINIA WALNUT Another name for BLACK WALNUT.

VISSCHER GLASS Made in the early 17thC and now rare, Dutch GLASS engraved by the Visscher sisters.

VITRINE French term for a display CUPBOARD that is often of BOMBÉ or SERPENTINE outline and decorated with MARQUETRY and ORMOLU.

VITRINE TABLE Another name for a BIJOUTERIE TABLE.

VITRO PORCELAIN Alternative name for MILK GLASS. Also a late -19thC form of English ART GLASS made from slag and having a streaked, marbled appearance, somewhat like a ceramic material.

VITRUVIAN SCROLL Used in CLASSICAL ornament during the 18thC, a decorative motif that uses wavelike patterns of repeating VOLUTES.

V-JOINT The technique of joining the terminal of a SILVER spoon to the STEM. It involves cutting the two ends to form opposing V shapes.

VOICE BOX The internal device that enables a DOLL to "cry" or "sing".

VOISINLIEU French ART POTTERY, made from the mid-19thC, near Beauvais.

VOLKSTEDT German centre of PORCELAIN production in the late 18th and 19thC. Noted for MEISSEN-style tableware.

VOLMAR, CHARLES (1841–1914) American studio potter who trained in France. His work is technically sophisticated and artistically skilful.

VOLUTE A spiral scroll or coil, supposedly inspired by the shape of a ram's horns, as on an Ionic capital. A common CLASSICAL motif.

VONÊCHE GLASSWORKS An innovative, Belgium GLASS firm, founded in 1778 by a Frenchman. The firm employed many Irish glassworkers, and made elaborate lead-crystal wares, including VASES, GOBLETS, dishes, and clockcases, in the English style from 1802 to 1830. Many of the most ornate designs were created by the talented glassworker Alexandre CHARPENTIER, who worked at Vonêche before establishing the firm of Escalier de Cristal in Paris.

VOYSEY, CHARLES FRANCIS ANNESLEY (1857–1941) Influential English architect who also designed FURNITURE and textiles in the ARTS AND CRAFTS tradition. His furniture was plain, functional, and simply decorated. He was also a pioneer in the Modern Movement in industrial design.

VULLIAMY Important Swiss family of clockmakers. They worked in London from *c.*1750 to 1854, making fine timepieces under royal patronage.

Victorian, walnut VITRINE with boxwood-inlaid frieze and ormolu-mounted inlaid pilasters.

Large, late-19thC, continental WAGER CUP.

WAALS, PETER VAN DE Dutch cabinet-maker who worked with Ernest GIMSON and the BARNSLEYS, designing FURNITURE in the ARTS AND CRAFTS style from 1901 to 1937.

WADDING Layer of filling placed between the top and backing of a QUILT. Known as "batting" in the USA.

WADE Famous for its range of endearing PORCELAIN and cellulose nursery figures and animals, the Wade factory was founded in 1922 in Burslem, Staffordshire, England, by George Wade. The firm also established a factory in Ireland, where it made porcelain for the tourist industry and export market. Price depends on the rarity and popularity of the subject. The most sought after are early -1930s Disney figures. A vast range of animals were produced by Wade in the 1950s. Apart from animal figures, the firm manufactured many other small decorative objects, including novelty egg cups, VASES, MONEY BOXES, jugs, and TRAYS. Most of these are less valuable than the figures. Pieces by Faust Lang, a leading Wade modeller, are keenly sought after and command a premium. Condition affects value, so look out for flaking paint, small chips, and imperfections. Figures are not always marked and do not have serial numbers. *See also* DISNEYANA.

WAGER CUP Found in Britain and The Netherlands, a cup used for drinking games or making toasts. Usually in the form of a woman holding up a cup that tilts on an axle, or a windmill, where the drinker blew down a tube in the cup to make the sails spin, then drained the cup before the sails stopped or lost the bet.

WAGER TANKARD A late -17thC, Scandinavian TANKARD in SILVER, with pegs on the inside to set wagers for drinking games. The vessel had three ball feet and was embossed and chased with flowers, foliage, and scrolls.

WAG-ON-THE-WALL Popular name for a PENDULUM CLOCK without a case, so that the pendulum is visible.

WAIN, LOUIS WILLIAM (1860–1939) A British illustrator renowned for his cat drawings. His work was popular among his contemporaries and often appeared on POSTCARDS.

WAISTED Describes the shape of a wineglass bowl that tapers into a well-defined waist and flares outward to form a rounded base.

WAITER A small SALVER, measuring 15cm (6in) in diameter and used for presenting calling cards or messages. Due to their small size, waiters were often made in pairs. They have feet, commonly of hoof, scroll, or pad form, which are delicate and prone to damage. The centre of a waiter should be checked to ensure that it has not been over-polished or that a crest has not been removed, because this leaves the SILVER thin. The London silversmith Robert Abercromby specialized in making them in Britain in the 18thC. Square salvers were popular in the 1730s. By the turn of the 19thC, waiters were put to a variety of practical uses such as stands for CRUET sets. Salvers made in North America before the War of Independence (1775–83) are round; most salvers made after the Revolution are oval.

WAKE TABLE Long, thin TABLE, which may or may not have drop leaves, on which a coffin rested prior to the funeral. The table was then used by the mourners to eat and drink at after the funeral.

WALDENBURG From the Rhineland, a jug in STONEWARE characterized by a chevron pattern around the rim and base.

WALDGLAS Literally "FOREST GLASS", a natural, green-coloured GLASS, made in the Black Forest region of Germany from the Middle Ages, using a potash (potassium carbonate) flux that is derived from the ashes of burned wood or ferns. The sand used contained iron, which produced the green colour. Thick and robust, Waldglas was mould-blown in large, simple forms, and decorated with designs ranging from the Biblical and mythological to scenes of daily life. In France, it is known as VERRE DE FOUGÈRE *See also* POTASH GLASS.

WALKER COLT Colt revolver of the mid-19thC with a barrel over 37.5cm (14¾in) in length, as designed by Captain Samuel Walker.

WALKER, IZANNAH F. Based in Rhode Island, an American dollmaker who patented the first mass-produced RAG DOLLS in 1873. His DOLLS have closed mouths, oil-painted, brown eyes and hair, applied ears, and cloth bodies. The hair is usually painted in curls around the ears, but dolls have been found with painted, ringleted hair. Hands stitched with separate thumbs are characteristic of Izannah Walker dolls, as is the use of patterned cotton to cover the body. Original clothes add to value.

WALL CLOCK A CLOCK hung on the wall to accommodate the length of the driving weight and chain mechanism.

WALLENDORF In Thuringia, Germany, a late -18thC PORCELAIN factory producing Meissen imitations. It was re-founded in the late 19thC.

WALL PERIOD Period 1751–74 when Dr John Wall managed WORCESTER.

WALL POCKET Ornament with a flat back and half-cone shape, intended for hanging from the wall to hold flowers, spills, or letters.

WALNUT A nutty or honey-brown, highly figured wood, walnut (*Juglans regia/J. nigra*) has been used in England and France since the RENAISSANCE. The range and variety of cuts and grains can be confusing, and polished walnut can look black. The wood was good for carving, although susceptible to WOODWORM, and it was noted for its excellent finish. Walnut was used in a solid form on English and some French FURNITURE between *c*.1660 and *c*.1690 and as a VENEER from *c*.1690 until *c*.1735, when it was supplanted by MAHOGANY. It was equally prized in Continental Europe. Fine Italian, French, and German furniture in the 16th and 17thC commonly made use of walnut. It returned to favour in the Victorian period, from 1850 to 1880. Walnut was also popular in the USA in the 19thC. *See also* BLACK WALNUT.

WALNUT FURNITURE Walnut imported from France and Spain became the principal material for FURNITURE from *c*.1670 until *c*.1730, when France prohibited further exports. The period coincides with the Restoration of Charles II in England; the plain, Puritan styles of the previous 20 years were superseded, as the exiled aristocracy returned to England with a taste for flamboyance. Walnut lent itself to the new taste because of its rich colour and FIGURING, and its suitability for VENEER work. Early walnut furniture has twist-turned legs and STRETCHERS, and detailed MOULDING. English walnut furniture, which makes subtle use of the figuring and grain for embellishment, is more desirable than that from Continental Europe, where pieces were often over-decorated. English furniture is generally also stronger. Joints were mortised, and tenon pegged and dowelled, while Continental European furniture was often simply pegged, with stretchers on the legs for stability. All walnut pieces are desirable if in prime condition. Small CHESTS and BUREAUX, SECRÉTAIRES, BUREAU BOOKCASES, and CHESTS-ON-STANDS are especially valuable. Do not confuse early walnut with BLACK WALNUT – some later -17th and early -18thC pieces were made in the latter, but it was mostly used from 1830.

1930s enamelled and gilded vase by JOHN WALSH WALSH.

WALSH, JOHN WALSH (1850–1951) British GLASS maker known for high-quality wares. The firm made VASES and flower holders, lampshades, and tableware in the late 19thC, and was especially innovative in producing and decorating glass in the 20thC. W. Clyne Farquharson, who joined John Walsh Walsh in 1924, created a range of outstanding designs for the firm from the mid-1930s to 1951. One of his most popular designs was the "Leaf" pattern, launched in 1936, and used on large bowls, vases, DECANTERS, JUGS, and TUMBLERS. His pieces are signed "Clyne Farquharson" on the base.

WALTHAM WATCH CO. Founded in 1850 in Boston, Massachusetts, the first American company to mass-produce watches. A CLOCK, noted for its simple elegance and fine quality, is known by the firm's name.

WALTON, JOHN Based in Burslem, England, in the early 19thC, a modeller of Staffordshire BOCAGE figures. *See also* STAFFORDSHIRE FIGURES.

WANDERING-HOUR CLOCK OR WATCH A CLOCK or WATCH in which the hour numeral, engraved on a revolving disc and revealed through an aperture, moves around the perimeter of the dial and points to the minute divisions marked around the fixed edge of the dial.

WANLI (Wan Li) Chinese MING DYNASTY emperor, 1573–1620.

WARBURTON Principally CREAMWARE made by WEDGWOOD and decorated by members of the Warburton family in the 18thC.

WARDROBE Made from the mid-19thC onward, a CUPBOARD fitted with shelves, pegs or hooks, or drawers, for storing clothes. Rails and hangers were first added in the 1870s, but were not common until after 1900. By the late 19thC, wardrobes were made as parts of bedroom suites, not individually. The late -20th and early -21stC passion for fitted FURNITURE has caused a fall in the demand for wardrobes. However, old wardrobes, especially those from Continental Europe, are often handsome. The internal fittings in a wardrobe are often altered or removed, but, as long as this has been done in a sympathetic manner, it should not affect the value. *See also* ARMOIRE and CLOTHES PRESS.

WARMING PAN Predecessor of the hot-water bottle, a metal pan on the end of a long handle that was filled with glowing coals and used to warm the bed. Produced from the mid 17th until the mid 19C.

WARP Long threads of yarn used to make a CARPET or textile. The warp is the first thread to be stretched across the loom, and the WEFT is woven into it. The warp is not visible on the surface, but it forms the fringes.

WARRING STATES Period in Chinese history 484–221 BC.

WARSAW FAIENCE wares produced in the 18thC in Warsaw, Poland, and decorated in IMARI and CHINOISERIE style. Some pieces with Kufic inscriptions were made for the court of the Ottoman Sultan.

WARWICK CRUET CRUET stand with a cinquefoil frame featuring a central scroll handle. It is designed after a 1715 example by Anthony Nelme, once in the collection of Warwick Castle, England. This was a popular, mid-18thC design, and many such cruets were produced by Samuel Wood, a specialist cruet and CASTER maker.

WASHED CARPET Used to denote a modern CARPET treated in a chemical wash to reduce the brilliance of the colours and achieve an aged appearance.

Georgian mahogany WASHSTAND.

WASHSTAND (Washing stand; also known as a basin stand.) A stand designed to hold a basin and jug for washing in the bedroom, and usually with drawers for toiletries. Washstands vary from simple tripod stands with round tops to hold the basins, and triangular shelves with drawers (sometimes wrongly called "wig stands"), to small cabinets with basins let into the top, sometimes with enclosing flaps. Look for one with a bowl and jug, because replacements could cost as much as the washstand itself. In the Victorian era (1837–1901), some large, marble-topped washstands were made as part of bedroom suites.

WASSAIL A bowl, often made of wood and used for drinking hot, spiced ale.

WATCH A small portable timepiece, often in SILVER, GOLD, or gilt metal, and either plain or decorated with techniques including ENGRAVING and ENAMELLING. The earliest watches were designed to fit into the pocket, often attached to chains, and were made from the second half of the 16thC; two hands are typical of watches made after the late 17thC. Wristwatches were introduced in the early 20thC. Calendars, moonphases, and repeating features can add value.

WATCHCOCK (Or watchbridge.) The metal plate that protects the balance wheel of a WATCH, it is often ornate and engraved with the maker's name.

WATCH KEY Used for winding a WATCH, and collectable in its own right.

WATCHMAN'S CHAIR Another name for a HALL-PORTER'S CHAIR.

WATCH STAND An item designed to hold a pocket WATCH, converting it into a miniature CLOCK for standing on a table.

WATCOMBE TERRACOTTA COMPANY *See* DEVON POTTERIES.

WATERBURY WATCH CO. An American, New York-based, watch-making firm – one of the first to produce inexpensive WATCHES in the 1880s and '90s.

WATERFORD Centre in Ireland that has made CUT GLASS, LEAD CRYSTAL, especially DECANTERS, since the late 18thC. Also a glassworks in New Jersey.

WATER LEAF Decorative, carved motif representing a narrow leaf with a central stem and horizontal undulations.

WATERMELON MOUTH A thin-lipped, smiling mouth on GOOGLY DOLLS.

WATERS POTTERY Brightly decorated EARTHENWARE produced in the early 19thC in England at the Lambeth factory of Richard Waters.

WAX CASTING *See* LOST-WAX CASTING.

WAX DOLL A type of DOLL that evolved from the funeral effigies and religious figures produced throughout Europe in the Middle Ages. Wax can be made to resemble the colour of human skin, when tinted and mixed with substances such as animal fat and turpentine. However, wax was expensive, and only wealthy parents could afford to purchase dolls of this kind for their children. Wax dolls were made by two different methods. Dolls with solid, carved-wax heads, known as PRESSED-WAX DOLLS, were made until 1840. The heads and limbs on POURED-WAX DOLLS were made in moulds and hollow. Between 1830 and 1890, WAX-OVER-COMPOSITION DOLLS were made from a moulded core of COMPOSITION or PAPIER-MÂCHÉ dipped in or painted with a layer of wax.

WAX JACK A device designed to hold a coiled wax taper, so that the end of the taper pointed upward, and the flame could be used to melt sealing wax. Waxjacks replaced TAPERSTICKS from the mid-18thC.

Fine, George III, silver WAX JACK, 1777 8.

WAX-OVER-COMPOSITION DOLL (Also wax-over-papier-mâché doll.) A DOLL with a hollow, moulded head, or SHOULDER-HEAD of ready-painted COMPOSITION or PAPIER-MÂCHÉ, which was dipped into a layer of molten wax. These dolls were developed as cheap alternatives to POURED-WAX DOLLS, and are still inexpensive. They were mass-produced in Britain, France, and Germany in the 19thC. The three types are known as SLIT HEADS, PUMPKIN HEADS, and wax-overs. Slit-head dolls, also known as "Crazy Alices", were made in England from 1830 onward. They have a slit in the crown, into which hair was inserted in a block – a fast and inexpensive process. Their faces were crudely modelled, but the wax gave a soft appearance. Most have glass eyes without pupils and fabric bodies with KID forearms. Made in England and Germany *c.*1860, pumpkin-heads – so-called because of their large heads – gradually replaced slit-heads. They usually have moulded hair, but dolls that have real hair and moulded bonnets, known as BONNET HEADS, are especially desirable. Dolls made of wax-over-composition, but of neither slit head nor pumpkin-head type, were made in the 1870s in Germany and France. They often appear similar to BONE-CHINA and PARIAN dolls of the same period. Dolls made in the late -19thC appear more realistic. Dark hair was rarer than blonde. French dolls have blue, PAPERWEIGHT EYES made of glass, similar to those on fashionable but more expensive BISQUE dolls, while German examples have flatter, spun-glass eyes. A deep-pink flesh colour is a distinctive feature of later dolls. Make sure that the doll is in good condition. Slit-head dolls should have a reasonable abundance of hair. With pumpkin-head dolls, the more elaborate the hairstyle and moulded bonnet, the better. Damage to the heads of later dolls reduces their value. Wax-over dolls of all types are susceptible to crazing. The cracks are a result of the expansion and contraction – which occurs during changes in temperature – of the different materials from which they are made. However, colourful and elaborate original costumes increase their value considerably.

WEARDALE CHAIN Quilting pattern of interlinking oval shapes imitating the effect of a metal chain. Named after the region in northeast England, where the pattern evolved. *See also* QUILT.

WEBB GLASS Stained GLASS or tableware designed by Philip Webb, friend and partner of William MORRIS, in England in the latter half of the 19thC. Also used to refer to glass made by Thomas WEBB & Sons.

WEBB, THOMAS & SONS English GLASS firm established near Stourbridge in the West Midlands. It is renowned for its ART GLASS, including CAMEO GLASS, ALEXANDRITE GLASS, and IRIDESCENT GLASS. It was first established as John Shepherd & Thos. Webb at White House Glass Works (1833–40). After various mergers it has also been known as Thos. Webb's glassworks "The Flats" (1840–55), Thos. Webb, Dennis Glass Works (1835–59), and Thos. Webb & Sons, Dennis Glass Works (1859 onward).

WEB FOOT Another name for DUCK FOOT.

WEBLEY, PHILIP AND JOHN English (Birmingham), 19thC gunmaker.

WEBSTER Noted family of English, London-based, makers of CLOCKS. Robert was active 1680–99; William, 1730–50.

WEBSTER, WILLIAM English gunmaker, active in the early to mid-19thC.

WEDGE Either a triangular thumbpiece on the hinged lid of a TANKARD in PEWTER or SILVER, or a silver stand designed for resting a dish at an angle.

WEDGWOOD Pottery founded by Josiah Wedgwood (1730–95) at Stoke-on-Trent, noted for its numerous innovations and high-quality wares that achieved renown throughout the rest of England, Europe, and the USA. The factories at Burslem and Etruria were the first to introduce industrial production techniques to POTTERY. Wedgwood's name is synonymous with many types of body: AGATEWARE, black basalt, CANEWARE, CREAMWARE, JASPER WARE, and ROSSO ANTICO. Wedgwood was the first potter to commission leading artists to create designs for his products. John Flaxman was responsible for many of the "jasper ware" designs of the 18th and 19thC. A. Walker painted naturalistic scenes, which were popular in the late 19thC. The tradition continued unabated throughout the 20thC. Designers include John SKEAPING, Richard Guyatt, Keith MURRAY, Eric RAVILIOUS, and Daisy MAKEIG-JONES. The range of Wedgwood available is so vast that many collectors tend to concentrate on particular objects, on specific types of body, or on certain designers. Value depends on the size and elaborateness of the decoration as well as on the reputation of the designer concerned. Early marked pieces tend to attract the highest prices. Although early pieces were

18thC, WEDGWOOD, blue jasper-ware plaque with the bust of "Rev. Willett".

unmarked, the majority of wares made after 1768 were marked "Wedgwood & Bentley", "Wedgwood", or with initials. From 1860, a system of date coding was used. Works by designers are usually marked with printed signatures or the words "designed by…" plus the name and the Wedgwood mark. Letter date marks were also used; after 1929, the last two years of the date appear in full. In the 19thC, a rival factory called Wedgewood (note the additional "e") also marked its products with its name. Wares by Wedgewood are of inferior quality and far less valuable. Wedgwood's success spawned numerous imitations, the most successful of which was Turner of Lane End; ADAMS and SPODE also made many Wedgwood imitations. Wedgwood wares were also imitated on the Continent by factories such as SÈVRES, but few fakes are marked.

WEDGWOOD-ARBEIT German for "Wedgwood-work", used to refer to blue porcelain with applied, white, relief decoration made in imitation of the JASPER WARE range made by WEDGWOOD from the late 18thC.

WEESP Dutch PORCELAIN factory, founded in the 18thC.

WEFT Crosswise threads that are interwoven between the long threads, or WARP, in the making of CARPETS or textiles. The weft is predominantly responsible for the design. *See also* KNOT.

WEI DYNASTY Period in Chinese history AD 386–557.

WEISWEILER, ADAM (b.1750) German cabinet-maker trained by David ROENTGEN. Weisweiler was in business in Paris before 1777, where he was employed by royalty and the aristocracy.

WELL Hollow or interior of a bowl or dish.

WELLINGS, NORAH Initially a designer for the firm of CHAD VALLEY, Wellings established her own soft-toy factory in Shropshire, England, in 1926. She patented a form of doll's head made of fabric or felt, backed with buckram (stiffened cloth) and incorporating some "plastic" wood. The dolls she created were chiefly CHARACTER DOLLS, and they were often more successful than those of some larger manufacturers. Output continued until 1960. Costumes are always colourful, and the heads are well modelled, especially on the large DOLLS. Some faces were made in pressed brown velvet; others in slightly rough felt, in which case the body may be cloth. Eyes were sometimes painted and sometimes glass and glancing sideways. The eyebrows are lightly painted in a single line, and the ears are applied. Dolls' heads were given waterproof coatings, so that the faces could be washed. North-American Indian, brown-velvet dolls are typical of the wide range of character dolls Wellings produced. Others include "Britannia", with a plumed fabric helmet and coat of mail, "Little Bo Peep", "South-Sea

1930s, NORAH WELLINGS Mountie cloth doll.

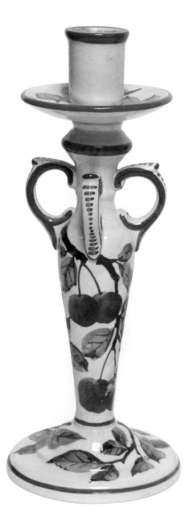

One of a pair of WEMYSS WARE Kantor candlesticks, c.1900.

Islanders", "Canadian Mounties", "Sailors", and "Cowboys". The "Jolly Toddlers" were made from 1933. Many of Wellings' dolls were sold as mascots on American ocean liners. The "Noreen" range of foreign dolls was introducted in 1937. The top-priced dolls are those modelled on the Royal Family or other famous people. So many of Wellings' dolls are readily available and inexpensive that condition and original clothing are important. All her dolls have cloth labels reading "Made in England by Norah Wellings" either on wrists or under the feet. Look for sculpted faces, zig-zag stitching on the head, attention to detail (this denotes better dolls), and dolls with colourful, original clothing.

WELLINGTON CHEST A tall, narrow CHEST OF DRAWERS, usually with six or seven drawers. They became popular in England and France, where they were known as *semaniers* in the early 1800s. Instead of each drawer having its own lock, English Wellington chests have single locking mechanisms, and the hinged flap on the right locks over the drawer fronts to stop them opening. The most valuable Wellington chests are those with SECRÉTAIRE drawers, often contained in the second and third drawer fronts.

WELSH DRESSER Made in Wales, a high DRESSER, with a boarded rack. As skirting boards (baseboards) became popular, dressers were pulled away from the wall, and open backs were filled in with boards.

WELSH WARE Late -18th and 19thC rustic FLATWARE, decorated with trailed-and-combed SLIP.

WEMYSS WARE Charmingly naive, hand-painted, lead-glazed EARTHENWARE figures first produced in Fife, Scotland, in the 1880s. Ornamental "pigs", often covered with "cabbage roses", are among the best loved of Wemyss wares, but there is a wide range of MUGS, VASES, jugs, and jam pots. The simple wares were decorated in a distinctive, colourful style using underglaze ENAMELLING. Flowers are a recurring theme, and other hand-painted motifs include, fruit, birds, and farmyard animals. Many Wemyss designs were by Karel Nekola, a Bohemian artist. Cockerels and hens were one of Nekola's most popular designs. The pieces were sold through Thomas Goode in London. In 1930, the Scottish factory closed, and the moulds were sold to the Bovey Tracey Pottery in Devon, where the same designs continued to be produced until the 1950s and beyond. Prices for Wemyss vary according to the age and rarity of the particular piece. Look for good-quality painting; tableware with red borders (these are early); figurative subjects, especially "cockerels", "cats", "bees", and pigs; and large pieces. Early Wemyss ware bears an impressed MARK and the words "Wemyss Ware R H & S" in a semicircle. The single word "Wemyss" was used as a mark in the 19th and 20thC. The words "Thos Goode" usually indicate an early production. After 1930, "Made in England" can appear with the Wemyss mark.

WESLEY FIGURES Popular late -18th and early 19thC STAFFORDSHIRE FIGURES of the founder of Methodism, based on the bust sculpted by Enoch WOOD.

WESTERN HAN Period in Chinese history from 206 BC–AD 24.

WESTERN ZHOU (Chou) In Chinese history, the period from 1027 to 770 BC.

WESTERWALD Blue-glazed jugs from the Rhineland in Germany. They are manufactured in STONEWARE with impressed and incised decoration.

WESTLEY RICHARDS, WILLIAM English gunmaker, active in the 19thC.

WESTMORELAND GLASS COMPANY Pennsylvanian-based factory that specialized in reproductions of early American glassware in the late 19thC.

WET-PLATE CAMERA Earliest form of CAMERA, made between 1840 and 1880, often from brass-bound MAHOGANY and with bellows.

WHATNOT Tall stand with four or five display shelves and sometimes a drawer in the base; some were made to stand in a corner. The whatnot first became popular in the late 18thC, when it was used for the display of ornaments. In the Victorian period (1837–1901) it was known as an OMNIUM. *See also* DUMB WAITER and ÉTAGÈRE.

WHEAT EARS Carved, decorative ornament suggesting ears of wheat, mainly associated with George HEPPLEWHITE.

WHEATON, CALEB Clockmaker, active 1785-1822, in Rhode Island, USA.

WHEEL BAROMETER A barometer with a circular register plate. A weight floating on the mercury surface is attached to a pulley-and-wheel mechanism, and the vertical motion turns the pointer round the arc of the circular dial.

WHEEL ENGRAVING First used in the 1stC AD, a method of decorating GLASS using abrasive discs. The object to be engraved is held under the wheel, and the surface incised by rotating copper (now composition) discs and an abrasive paste (usually oil combined with emery). The discs are of progressive fineness to add detail to the pattern. The finest exponents were central European craftsmen, who used a fine-quality POTASH GLASS, in the 16th to 18thC. Wheel engraving is classified in two ways: HOCHSCHNITT, where the design is cut in relief, so that it protrudes slightly above the surface, and TIEFSCHNITT, in which the pattern is cut into the surface. Most engraved surfaces are left matt to enhance the light and shadow, but in rock-crystal engraving, developed in the 19thC, deeply engraved areas are polished to imitate carved rock crystal. Wheel engraving was the most common form of British engraving from the 18thC.

18thC, WESTERWALD **stoneware pitcher.**

WHEELING GLASS A type of GLASS manufactured by one of several early 19thC factories in Wheeling, West Virginia, USA.

WHEEL LOCK Early -16thC firing mechanism superseded by the FLINTLOCK but used into the 18thC for hunting weapons. Pulling the trigger caused a steel wheel to spin against a piece of mineral pyrites; the friction made sparks, which ignited the priming powder.

WHIELDON, THOMAS (1719–95) A famous British, Staffordshire potter who used distinctive mottled GLAZES. The effect was created by using coloured lead glazes that mingled during firing. Whieldon was probably the first potter to develop the coloured, lead-glaze technique in the mid-18thC, but many other potters in the region also made similar objects; because wares of this type are not marked, they are usually called "WHIELDON TYPE". Colours were limited to olive-green, brown, grey, and blue. A large proportion of Whieldon ware consists of domestic items such as PLATES and tea ware, or decorative objects such as figurative groups and animals; large hollow wares such as COFFEE-POTS are rarer and command the highest prices. Look for well-modelled animals, such as dogs, TOBY JUGS, candlestick figures, COW CREAMERS, and cottages with figures. Naturalistic moulds of cauliflowers, cabbages, lettuces, melons and pineapples were used by all the STAFFORDSHIRE POTTERIES from the mid-18thC for teapots, coffee-pots, TUREENS, and other objects. In the 19thC, the Victorians made copies of many of these shapes, but these objects tend to be more heavily potted and larger, and less desirable than earlier ones. Several characteristic features can help identify Whieldon ware: irregular glaze, blurred colours that typically run together, a limited palette, a thinly potted body, and a slightly iridescent surface covered with crazing. They are never marked. *See also* STAFFORDSHIRE FIGURES.

WHIELDON TYPE *See* WHIELDON, Thomas.

WHIMSIES Small GLASS objects such as hats, shoes, and animals originally made in the craftsman's spare time, but then mass-produced in the 19th and 20thC as commercial trinkets.

WHISTLE TANKARD A TANKARD in SILVER with a hole in the handle – this permitted air to escape from the hollow formed during manufacture, but traditionally drinkers blew on it to "whistle" for a refill.

WHITEFRIARS In London, a long-established English glassworks, making imitations of VENETIAN GLASS as early as the 17thC. It was noted in the 19thC for the fine ART GLASS designed by Philip Webb, and for the innovative, coloured and textured glass designed by Geoffrey Baxter (b.1922) in the 1960s. It was sold to James Powell in 1834, and was known as James Powell & Sons until 1962; from then until 1980, it was known again as Whitefriars Glassworks.

Streaky green, WHITEFRIARS bubble vase by Geoffrey Baxter, no. 9788, c.1971.

WHITE METAL Hard alloy of copper and zinc used as a base in ELECTROPLATE.

WHITNEY FIREARMS made by Eli Whitney in Connecticut, USA, from the end of the 18thC. They were among the first to be made with standard, interchangeable parts.

WHITNEY GLASS Wares, principally bottles and flasks, from an American factory founded in the late 18thC in Glassboro, New Jersey.

WHOLECLOTH QUILT A QUILT top made from a single piece of fabric. The quilting may be stitched in decorative patterns or in a simple, utilitarian style.

WHORL Decorative circular ornament, the distinctive characteristic being that the enclosed carving radiates from a central point in a curve.

WICKER FURNITURE Weaving of boiled-and-dried willow shoots, called withies, to make items such as cradles, CHAIRS, and baskets. Wicker is a light material, making it ideal for conservatory and garden furniture that is often moved. Wicker furniture (or "wickerwork") was popular between 1920 and 1940. *See also* LLOYD LOOM FURNITURE.

WIENER WERKSTÄTTE The "Vienna Workshops", founded in 1901 by Josef HOFFMANN and Ludwig MOSER, and a leading producer, until 1932, of GLASS, FURNITURE, CERAMICS, and other wares in the ART NOUVEAU (SECESSIONIST) style.

WIINBLAD, BJORN Danish potter who began producing wares in the mid-20thC. His distinctive style was inspired by folk tales of elves and sprites. His early work for the Danish Nymolle factory also features bold portraits or tells a story. His output for the German factory ROSENTHAL includes illustrated series and dated PLATES, delicate PORCELAIN fancies, and relief patterns. He also designed shapes for ranges of tea ware with simple banded decoration.

WILKINSON, A.J. LTD At Newport, Staffordshire, a British POTTERY firm that employed Clarice CLIFF and other leading artists of the 1930s.

WILKINSON, NORMAN (1878–1971) British artist known for his travel POSTERS, produced for the British railway companies in the 1920s and '30s.

WILLARD CLOCKS Made by an American, Massachusetts-based family of clockmakers. Simon Willard, active in the late 18th to mid-19thC, is credited with inventing the BANJO CLOCK; his nephew, Aaron, the LYRE CLOCK.

WILLIAMITE GLASS A rare English GLASS from the 1740s that features engraving commemorating the victory of William III over James II at the Battle of the Boyne in 1690. Motifs on these glasses include busts of William III

Simon WILLARD, mahogany, and parcel-gilt banjo clock, 1800–25.

and Mary II, as well as William III on horseback, with the date of the battle and/or the inscription "To the Glorious Memory". Many copies were made *c*.1900, so careful examination is necessary to ensure the glass is genuine.

WILLIAMSON, JOSEPH English clockmaker active in the late 17th and early 18thC, and credited with inventing the EQUATION CLOCK.

"WILLOW" PATTERN A scene, based on an actual garden in Shanghai and a story about two lovers, painted in blue on Chinese export PORCELAIN and copied, with slight variations, by numerous English potters from the late 18thC.

WILTSHAW & ROBINSON English, Stoke-on-Trent-based pottery, founded in 1897 and renowned for its ART NOUVEAU/CARLTON WARE.

WINCANTON An 18thC English manufacturer of DELFTWARE, produced at Wincanton. Wares were similar to the products of nearby Bristol.

WINCHESTER, OLIVER F. American gunsmith, active in the mid 19thC.

WINCHESTER RIFLE Semi-automatic rifle invented by B. Henry Taylor and manufactured in Connecticut after the American Civil War.

WINDMILLS, JOSEPH Active in London in the late 17th and early 18thC, a noted English maker of CLOCKS and WATCHES.

WINDSOR CHAIR A COUNTRY CHAIR, usually with a SADDLE SEAT, HOOP BACK, and simple turned legs. Country woods, such as ELM, OAK, ASH, and YEW were used to make Windsor chairs, which usually date from after *c*.1700. Yew Windsors are the most sought-after. The higher and more elaborate the back, the more expensive the chair will be. Heavy-turned legs can date a chair to *c*.1825–50; an earlier chair would have CABRIOLE legs. The turning on the back legs should match that on the front – if it does not, some of the legs may be replacements. A crinoline (curved) STRETCHER, most commonly seen on 18thC chairs, adds value. Check the SPLAT, TOP RAIL, and arms for cracks – especially important on chairs made of yew, which is more brittle than ash.

WINE CELLAR *See* CELLARET.

WINE COOLER A container, normally placed beneath or to the side of the SIDEBOARD, and used for the short-term storage of wine in the dining-room. Originally a French refinement, wine coolers were produced by immigrant HUGUENOT silversmiths in the early 18thC. By the 1800s, the terms "CELLARET" and "wine cooler" were interchangeable. Most wine coolers are based on the form of an antique CALYX crater or bucket shape. CLASSICAL ornamentation features on the massive REGENCY coolers in SILVER-GILT by makers such as

Victorian, octagonal, walnut WINE COOLER with acorn finial.

RUNDELL, BRIDGE & RUNDELL and Paul STORR. From c.1730, all wine coolers were made with removable, drop-in liners around which ice could be packed to chill the bottles. Early examples were made with separate collars, but by the early-Victorian period (1837–1860) the collars and liners were integrated into one. Wine coolers in the form of wooden buckets or pails were made in large quantities in OLD SHEFFIELD PLATE, particularly in the 1790s. Many have swing handles and are decorated with engraved, vertical lines simulating the staves on a wooden pail or with reeded hoops and engraved ARMORIALS. Most Victorian coolers combine GOTHIC or Egyptian styles with naturalistic decoration. Sheffield makers used far less silver to produce wine coolers than other British silversmiths, because the handles and borders of acanthus leaves and flowers on their wares were added by DIE-STAMPING from a thin foil of silver, then lead filled, and soldered, rather than cast or embossed. With regular use, some Sheffield-made examples with elaborate decoration are prone to damage, so check for dents in the body, broken and repaired handles, or cracked ornamentation. Check that collars and liners have not been replaced and, with silver examples, that they bear the same HALLMARKS as those found on the body of the cooler. Many wine coolers were made in pairs, and in general a single is much less desirable than a pair.

WINE FUNNEL Produced in great numbers from the late 18thC until c.1830, a cone-shaped vessel with a spout for decanting wine. Made in two parts – a funnel and a pierced bowl to strain the sediment – they are minimally decorated. Early examples tend only to have beaded or reeded rims, while some later ones feature chased ornamentation around the bowls. A typical funnel from the George III period (1760–1820) would have a straight OGEE bowl or a plain tulip- or dome-shaped one. The curved spout allows the wine to trickle down the side of the DECANTER, although as the necks of decanters became narrower, these spouts were sometimes trimmed. Provincial wine funnels, magnum funnels, and funnels made in the USA, Scotland, Ireland, or by known makers are most desirable. The bowl, spout, and collar (if appropriate) of a wine funnel should all be marked. Look for alterations – a funnel with a trimmed spout is worth less than one in original condition.

WINEGLASS COOLER (Or rinser.) A GLASS bowl for washing or cooling DRINKING GLASSES between courses – there was one for each diner. Wineglass coolers can be identified by the pouring lip on either side of the bowl, preventing the stem of the glass from rolling around the rim. One lip was sufficient, but most have two, because that was quicker to make with a hot iron rod. Early wineglass coolers have deeper bowls than their 19thC counterparts, because drinking glasses in this period had long STEMS and small bowls. Simple narrow fluting around the base of the bowl is characteristic of GEORGIAN pieces, but less common from the mid-19thC, when it was more popular to have different styles of drinking glass.

Silver wine coaster with floral, applied rim and pierced body, Birmingham, 1838 (WINE-RELATED WARES).

WINE-RELATED WARES From the mid-18thC wine became increasingly popular in Britain, and SILVER vessels and gadgets associated with wine drinking were made in vast quantities. The service of wine was an elaborate procedure demanding its own silver items in many forms, from massive WINE COOLERS to wine JUGS and EWERS for serving wine and spirits, COASTERS for holding glass DECANTERS, WINE FUNNELS for decanting the wine, BOTTLE LABELS and collars for labelling, and CORKSCREWS for opening bottles. A variety of wines was served to complement the different dishes of each course, thus increasing the need for a range of designs from which to serve each beverage. Other vessels used for serving wine include MONTEITHS and PUNCHBOWLS. Decoration of Bacchanalian motifs (vine leaves and bunches of grapes, for example) is characteristic on these wares.

WINE TASTER Shallow circular vessel employed by vintners for judging the taste, clarity, and colour of wine since the 15thC. SILVER was considered to be the most suitable material for wine tasters, although they were frequently gilded on the inside to protect the silver from corrosion by the wine. The earliest surviving English silver example dates from 1603. The majority of wine tasters have raised domed centres that enable the colour of the wine to be seen more easily; most designs with flat centres were intended for decoration. English wine tasters usually have two wire handles, and body decoration of chased fluting or a pattern of circular bosses on one side. William Maddox produced such items in great numbers in England, and his fully marked examples are desirable. French examples had shaped handles with flanges at the top from the mid-18thC and ring handles in the form of serpents in the late 18th and 19thC – they were usually undecorated, but engraved mottos, message, initials, names, or pastoral scenes on shaped handles increase value. Rare, marked, provincial examples are highly collectable, as are those made prior to the French Revolution in 1789. Wine tasters are prone to damage – the wire handles are susceptible to breaking, and the decoration on English types may have been polished away. Those in poor condition are not desirable.

WINGED GLASS Made in 16th and 17thC Venice, Italy, a goblet with a stem decorated with designs of applied threading in coloured GLASS. The design was copied in the Low Countries (now Belgium and the Netherlands).

WINGED STEM Wing- or ear-shaped ornamental mouldings of fine GLASS, attached to the stems of wineglasses and bowls. Typical of VENETIAN GLASS.

WINKLE, KATHIE (b.1932) British CERAMICS designer who joined James BROADHURST & Sons Ltd. in 1950 and produced "Pedro", her first design for the factory, in 1958. Many of her designs are simple borders, but she also created all-over patterns. Winkle was given credit as designer on the back of her designs from 1964. The firm also used her name on some patterns that she had not designed.

WINNIE-THE-POOH BEAR Created by the writer A.A. Milne in 1926, a character inspired by the FARNELL bear purchased for his son Christopher Robin. The illustrator Ernest Shepard based "Pooh" on his own son's STEIFF BEAR. "Winnie" was a North American black bear in London Zoo, while "Pooh" was Christopher Robin's favourite swan. Disney Pooh bears are made in the USA by Sears, Roebuck and Co. The most sought-after makers are CHAD VALLEY and MERRYTHOUGHT, but even those by unknown makers are collectable.

WIREWORK Any metal object, such as a fruit basket or toast rack, made of strands of wire.

WIRKKALA, TAPIO (1915–85) A Finnish designer at the forefront of GLASS design in the early post-war years. In 1946, he joined the Ittala glassworks, for which he designed a range that included elegant domestic pieces as well as sculptural ART GLASS. He preferred organic shapes and textured surfaces, and his love of the Finnish landscape inspired the textured, frosted, ice-like finishes seen on much of his clear colourless glass.

WISTAR GLASS Early American GLASS made by Caspar Wistar, who founded a glassworks in Salem, Massachusetts, in 1739.

WITHDRAWING TABLE A TABLE with two additional leaves (usually hidden within the carcass), which can be pulled or drawn out to increase its length. Also known as a DRAW-LEAF TABLE.

W.M.F. Popularly used abbreviation for the Austrian Württembergishe Metallwarenfabrik, one of the principal producers of SILVER and SILVER-PLATED objects in the ART NOUVEAU style in the early 20thC.

WOLFE & CO. Liverpool PORCELAIN factory, active c.1795–1800. Noted for its attractively painted polychrome wares, which are now sought after.

WOOD (1) From one of many species of trees, a material used to construct furniture and other items. Developing a knowledge of which type of wood was used and when is the basis of learning how to date a piece. It is easier to learn to identify polished rather than unpolished woods, because most woods look different when polished. *See also* ASH, BEECH, BIRCH, BOXWOOD, CALAMANDER, CEDAR, CHERRY, COROMANDEL, EBONY, ELM, KINGWOOD, MAHOGANY, OAK, PINE, ROSEWOOD, SATINWOOD, TULIPWOOD, WALNUT, and YEW.

WOOD (2) Family of Staffordshire potters: Ralph Wood I (1715–72) and his nephew Enoch Wood (1759–1840) were noted for fine PORCELAIN figures and TOBY JUGS. Aaron Wood (1717–85), brother of Ralph I, worked as a modeller for WHIELDON and other companies. Ralph Wood II (1748–95), the son of Ralph I, continued to make figures, but with enamel colours.

WOOD, JOHN Philadelphia clockmaker, active in America 1770-93.

WOOD & SONS English CERAMICS firm, active 1865–2005 in Stoke-on-Trent, and known for its post- World War II production of decorative and functional ranges. It is best known for its single-colour services, and the "Berol", "Jasmine", and "Iris" ranges are some of the best utilitarian designs. The decorative "Piazza" ware, the height of fashion in its day, was painted by hand on matt white GLAZES with bright colours on a broad range of organic sculptural shapes.

WOODEN CLOCK A CLOCK with a wooden movement, which is usually driven by a pendulum.

WOODEN DOLL Early DOLLS, first made either from turned or carved wood in the wood-carving areas of Germany and Austria. In England, wooden dolls were made from the 17thC until the early 1900s, and were normally dressed as adults. The bodies of wooden dolls are shaped like skittles, because this was straightforward to make on a lathe. The arms and legs were carved and turned in the same way and attached separately. Pegged disc joints at the shoulder, elbow, hip, and knee were often used in the 17th, 18th and 19thC to enable the doll to move. The dolls' upper arms were wired and padded and ended in wooden wrists with rather large hands, carefully carved with long fingers. The best early wooden dolls had hair attached to cloth caps, which were nailed to the heads. English wooden dolls made before 1740 had round, rouged faces with long wide necks, while mouths were slightly enigmatic. The heads and torsos were usually in one piece, the waists were tapered, and the upper arms possibly cloth. The eyes of a 17thC wooden doll sometimes have unusual white spots to accentuate the pupils, and both eyes and eyebrows were painted. Some of the eyes of 17thC dolls have single lines above to denote the upper lids; others have lines below as well. The eyebrows are usually single lines with dashes above and below the line creating a herringbone effect. Fixed black eyes made of glass and without pupils were more common in the 18thC. They tend to be duller and can render the doll less valuable, because eyes are one of the most important facial features and contribute greatly to the appeal. Beauty spots are typical on late-17thC dolls. The clothes of 17thC wooden dolls reflected contemporary fashions. The *fontange*, an elaborate ribboned-and-wired headdress, can be found on dolls with SWIVEL HEADS. These had heads attached by metal rods or wires to rings in the bottom, which allowed the heads to be moved. The most important wooden dolls date from the 18thC. Well carved and elaborately dressed, they were the playthings of children of wealthy families. English dolls were noted for their finesse, and were completed by one maker. In Europe, where the guilds' traditions were stronger, several different craftsmen and seamstresses were involved in carving, painting, and dressing a single doll. Subtle changes appear between early- and late-18thC dolls, and this can affect their value.

From 1740, wooden dolls had slimmer necks, sloping shoulders, and skittle-shaped torsos with high busts and no waists, although after 1780, the necks thickened again and the features became cruder. Developments in fashion through the 18thC are important in helping to date a doll, although the original clothes may have worn out, and outfits may have been replaced over the years. The quality of dollmaking deteriorated toward the end of the 18thC, due to imports from German makers and the introduction of PAPIER-MÂCHÉ and WAX DOLLS. The size and attractiveness of the doll and a known history add to the worth of a particular doll. Those that have survived with original clothes and wigs, as well as original limbs and paint, are the most valuable, and the larger the doll, the better. English, wooden, novelty dolls in unusual outfits, or those that were erotic or satirical – sometimes made to poke fun at the monarchy – are also increasing in value. Wooden dolls are rare, so be careful not to be persuaded that you have spotted one just because you want to. Seek all the proof you can of the doll's provenance. Restoration will reduce value. Beware also of wooden dolls that have been "aged" to fake an early doll.

WOODWORM A wood-boring beetle, *Anobium punctatum*, that normally attacks softwood such as BEECH and PINE. Woodworm attacks are difficult to treat – although fumigation will help, the grubs are capable of remaining dormant after treatment, and when they wake up they will attack untreated wood. Never underestimate the gravity of woodworm – you might only see half a dozen holes, but underneath there may be a maze of tunnels weakening the structure of the wood. To identify active woodworm, examine the holes in spring, when the grubs are active; dust around the holes or on the floor is a sign of this. The beech seat rails of 18thC CHAIRS are particularly vulnerable. Woodworm rarely attacks hardwoods such as MAHOGANY, but it can attack a softwood carcass with a mahogany VENEER, in which case flight holes (caused when the beetle hatches and leaves the wood) may appear.

WORCESTER Founded in 1751, Worcester is one of the most successful PORCELAIN manufacturers of the 18thC. A British-based firm, it is famous for the vast amount of tea and coffee wares it produced. The porcelain made by Worcester contained soapstone, which made it stable and able to withstand boiling water. As a result, huge quantities of hollow ware have survived, and the range available is so daunting that collectors often concentrate their efforts on a particular area, such as early wares, designs decorated with TRANSFER PRINTING, teapots, or coffee cups. Worcester is classified according to the factory's owners: Dr Wall or First period (1751–74); Davis period (1774–83); Flight period (1783–92); FLIGHT & BARR period (1792–1804); Barr, Flight, & Barr period (1804–13); Flight, Barr, & Barr period (1813–40); Chamberlain & Co. (1840–52); Kerr & Binns period (1852–62); and Worcester Royal Porcelain Co. Ltd (from 1862). Early wares were inspired by Chinese decoration, and the body had a bluish tone. Floral

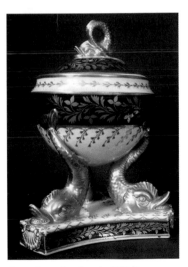

One of a pair of early-19thC, Chamberlain WORCESTER sauce tureens.

patterns inspired by Oriental designs were the most popular form of hand-painted design in the 18thC, and continued well into the 1770s. Coloured grounds were popular from the 1760s to '80s, although they had a tendency to blotchiness – a problem often overcome by using a blue ground printed with an overlapping, fish-scale pattern. Yellow, green, and claret grounds were also used. Worcester started using UNDERGLAZE TRANSFER PRINTING from c.1757. Printed wares are less expensive than hand-painted pieces of a similar date, but are still collected. Among the most readily available and collectable printed designs are the "Three Flowers", "Fence", and "Fisherman and Cormorant" patterns. Lavish gilding and detailed, painted decoration are hallmarks of Worcester porcelain of the early 19thC. CHAMBERLAIN PORCELAIN was a rival factory, producing wares in similar styles. The factory amalgamated with Flight, Barr & Barr to become Chamberlain & Co. in 1840, and pieces were marked "Chamberlains Worcester". The usual Worcester MARK is an open crescent, either painted or printed. The factory also marked with a square, Chinese fret with crosshatching, and used pseudo-Chinese or alchemical marks. Worcester's 18thC wares were copied in Paris in the 19thC. *See also* ROYAL WORCESTER.

WORK TABLE Designed for ladies to store sewing materials, a small table with drawers and a pull-out bag. Dating from the late 18thC onward, the work table varies considerably in form. The majority have silk bags underneath that pull out; some have hinged lids that open to reveal interiors fitted for sewing materials; others have hinged flap tops and pull-out slides. The 18thC cabinet-maker Thomas SHERATON even designed one with a retractable fire-screen. Because they are small, work tables were often veneered in the most expensive woods of the day. Look out for beautifully figured woods, such as burr WALNUT, or exotic timbers such as COROMANDEL, SATINWOOD, or KINGWOOD. Replacement legs and handles reduce value, but replacement bags are acceptable, provided that they are made from suitable materials. A late -19thC work table may have a scene painted on the top – children playing is a typically nostalgic, Victorian subject.

Regency, rosewood-banded and boxwood-inlaid WORK TABLE.

WRIGGLEWORK Wavy engraved designs on SILVER or PEWTER.

WRIGHT AND MANSFIELD Cabinet-makers of fine, reproduction, English FURNITURE in the 19thC in the style of Robert ADAM and Thomas SHERATON.

WRIGHT, FRANK LLOYD (1869–1959) Influential and accomplished American architect who also designed FURNITURE in the MODERNIST style.

WRIGHT, RUSSEL (1904–76) American designer who created organic, yet practical forms. As a CERAMICS designer he had a huge influence on the industry. His "Casual China", which has a soft, sculptural quality, was popular in the 1950s. He used speckles in the GLAZE colours and a mix-and-match palette that are both typicle of the period. He is also known for his "American Modern" dinnerware, which was produced by the Steubenville Pottery from 1939. Wright designed FURNITURE such as the "Pony Skin chair", which was more comfortable than other more-angular furniture made at the time. The Imperial Glass firm made his blown glass range in 1949.

WRITING CHAIR Another name for a CORNER CHAIR.

WRITING FURNITURE A type of FURNITURE that provides a flat surface for writing on. The writing slope, a portable and slant-lidded box that was hinged at the top, was the precursor of the BUREAU. During the 17thC, as householders became more settled, writing slopes on stands or chests of drawers began to be made. Writing furniture evolved during the 17thC. By the reign of QUEEN ANNE (1702–14), walnut-veneered bureaux were popular. Throughout the 18thC, writing furniture became increasingly varied and sophisticated. Bureaux were combined with shelves for books to make BUREAU BOOKCASES, and PEDESTAL DESKS were produced. A new form of writing furniture that appeared in the 18thC was the CARLTON HOUSE DESK. Other REGENCY innovations in writing furniture include the BONHEUR DU JOUR, an elegant ladies' desk, and the DAVENPORT. Among the more varied types of writing furniture are SECRÉTAIRES, which usually have concealed stationery compartments. Bureaux are generally more sought after than *secrétaires*. WRITING TABLES were also popular in England. All writing furniture is sought after today, and prices can be high for quality pieces. *See also* DESK; DESK ACCESSORIES, AND DESK SET.

WRITING TABLE Any TABLE designed for writing at, usually with an inset leather top. Inspired by the French BUREAU PLAT, it was popular in England from c.1740. Similar to LIBRARY TABLES, they have drawers fitted for stationery. In the 18thC, the leather tops were often covered in baize.

WROCKWARDINE WOOD FACTORY In Shropshire, England, a factory that made GLASS wares with splattered, white-glass decoration in the 18thC. Their pieces are rare and collectable.

WRYTHENING Decoration of diagonally twisted ribbing used on early VENETIAN GLASS and 18thC ALE GLASS. Revived by WHITEFRIARS in the late 19thC.

WUCAI PALETTE (Wu ts'ai palette) From the Chinese for five colours, although more than five colours were often included in the palette. Red or black were often used for outlines, blue was applied as an UNDERGLAZE, and the other colours were applied as ENAMELLED OVERGLAZES.

WÜRTTEMBERG METALWORK FACTORY *See* W.M.F.

WYCH ELM A variety of ELM.

Painted satinwood Sheraton-revival ladies' WRITING TABLE, c.1905.

X

X-FRAME The X-shaped construction of some CHAIRS and STOOLS.

XIANFENG (Hsien Feng) Chinese QING dynasty emperor, 1851–61.

XUANDE (Hsuan Te) Chinese MING DYNASTY emperor, 1426–35.

XUANTONG (Hsuan T'ung) Chinese QING dynasty emperor, 1909–11.

XYLONITE Made from 1868, a rare, early form of plastic, simulating wood.

Y

19thC, gilt, X-FRAME stool.

YALLAMEH Iranian RUGS decorated with colourful geometric shapes.

YAMI-MAKIE Japanese LACQUERWARE in which black designs are made on a subtly contrasting, black ground.

YAO Chinese for "kiln", used to refer to the wares of a specific region. Jian yao, for example, is POTTERY from the Jian region of Fukien province.

YATAGHAN Turkish SWORD with a short hilt and no guard.

YAYOI Early Japanese bronze and CERAMICS, dating from *c.*300 BC to AD 1stC.

YEAR CLOCK A CLOCK that runs for a year without rewinding.

YELLOW METAL Early -19thC, copper-and-zinc alloy made to imitate GOLD.

YEN YEN Perhaps derived from the Chinese "yen" (meaning "beautiful"), a European term for a BALUSTER VASE with a broad, flaring neck.

YES/NO BEAR A mechanical TEDDY BEAR that nods or shakes its head when its tail is moved. These popular bears came in various sizes.

YEW A hard, reddish-toned, indigenous hardwood, yew (*Taxus*), sometimes used in the 17thC (until 1730) as a VENEER. Quality, provincial FURNITURE was often made from solid yew, and it was always used for the arms of high-quality WINDSOR CHAIRS. It is sometimes used today for reproduction pieces.

YEZD Modern, handmade CARPETS from the Kirman region of central Iran.

YI HSING Chinese tea-ceremony vessels in unglazed STONEWARE.

YING QING Chinese SUNG and YUAN dynasty PORCELAIN that has been decorated with carved or moulded floral patterns and covered with a pale, blue-green, translucent GLAZE.

YIN-YANG Chinese motif found on CARPETS, bronzes, and CERAMICS. Consists of a circle divided into two comma-shaped portions in contrasting colours, symbolizing the unity of opposites.

YOMUD From the Iranian border region, CARPETS with diamond patterns on deep red or blue grounds.

YONGLE (Yung Lo) Chinese MING DYNASTY emperor, 1403–24.

YONGZHENG (Yung Cheng) Chinese QING dynasty emperor, 1723–35.

YORKSHIRE CHAIR (Also known as a DERBYSHIRE CHAIR.) Type of mid-17thC CHAIR with a tall back and ornately carved arched rails.

YORKSHIRE CLOCK A bulky, grandiose LONGCASE CLOCK of the late 18th and early 19thC, not necessarily from Yorkshire.

YORKSHIRE CLOTH Cloth often used as an alternative to MOHAIR plush by J.K. FARNELL in making TEDDY BEARS. Also used by other manufacturers.

YORKSHIRE POTTERY Made by many factories in Yorkshire in the 18th and 19thC, lead-glazed EARTHENWARE decorated with cream SLIP.

YSART, PAUL (1887–1956) A Spanish-born GLASS designer, known for his PAPERWEIGHTS. Ysart moved to Scotland in 1915 with his family, including his father Salvador, who also worked in the glass industry. He worked for the Scottish factories Caithness and MONCRIEFF'S GLASSWORKS, where he produced designs featuring flowers, fish, insects, and butterflies. His paperweights often feature mottled grounds and butterfly and dragonfly motifs. His designs are usually signed "PY" in one of the canes.

YU A Chinese vessel for storing food. Usually in bronze.

Oak YORKSHIRE CHAIR, 1620–30.

YUAN DYNASTY Period in Chinese history AD 1280–1368, during which the art of UNDERGLAZE painting was developed.

YUE WARE (or "Yueh") Chinese STONEWARE with a green GLAZE and delicate, low-relief decoration, produced from the HAN DYNASTY to the 10thC. Made in the Yueh district of Chekiang province.

YURUK Loosely woven, brightly coloured, geometric-design CARPETS made by southeast Turkish nomads.

ZAANCLOCK A 17thC, Dutch WALL CLOCK with a case extending above and below the dial. The case accommodates a PENDULUM pivoted above the movement rather than below it.

ZANESVILLE Early -19thC coloured GLASS made in Zanesville, Ohio, USA.

ZANZIBAR CHEST Elaborately decorated CHEST, usually made in India and shipped via Zanzibar.

ZAR Unit of measure for CARPETS: one zar is 1m (1yd) in length.

ZARANIM One and a half ZARS (1.5m/5ft). The width of many Oriental RUGS.

ZEBRAWOOD Brown wood from South America. It has distinctive black stripes and was used as a VENEER.

ZECHLIN An 18thC glassmaking centre in Silesia, central Europe. Specialized in GLASS ornamented with applied portrait medallions, often gilded.

ZERBST FAIENCE Short-lived, 18thC FAIENCE factory near Leipzig, Germany.

ZHENGDE (CHENG TE) Chinese MING DYNASTY emperor, 1506–21.

ZIEGLER Persian CARPETS imported by the British, Manchester-based firm of that name in the latter half of the 19thC.

ZINNSOLDATEN Toy soldiers of lead or tin alloy made in the Nuremberg area of Germany from the 16thC, and widely exported in the 18th and 19thC. Also known as "flats" because they are two-dimensional, with a narrow base. *See also* TOY SOLDIER.

ZOETROPE Revolving cylinder into which a circular strip of pictures is placed. When spun, the figures in the picture seem to move.

ZURICH PORCELAIN FACTORY PORCELAIN factory established in 1763 at Scoren near Zurich, Switzerland, by the painter Salomon Gessner; production ceased in the late 19thC. The factory began by making SOFT-PASTE PORCELAIN, but, by 1765, this was replaced by HARD-PASTE PORCELAIN. Wares include TEA and COFFEE SERVICES; tea bowls and saucers are among the most affordable pieces of their 18thC porcelain. Gilt dentil (indented) rims are characteristic. Zurich's painted decoration generally followed fashions established elsewhere in Europe, although the style in which flowers and landscapes were painted was often sparse and stiff. The hard paste used by the factory is greyish and sugary in texture, and it has a glassy, greyish GLAZE. Colours before 1780 are soft; after this date, a strong russet and yellow were introduced. The factory also made a wide range of figures throughout the 18thC, and these are recognizable by their static poses and simple bases with little decoration. The modelling is so loose that the hard paste almost looks like soft paste, and a lack of detail in the face and rudimentary hands and clothing are typical. Soft autumnal or pastel shades are often found. Among the range of figures produced by the factory are: street vendors, fisherfolk, musicians, craftsmen, fashionable ladies and gentlemen, Classical figures, hunters, and shepherds and shepherdesses. The factory also produced a range of miniature figures, which are more affordable than larger ones. Although Swiss porcelain is less available than that made by major German and French factories, it is not too scarce and remains popular with Swiss and other European collectors. Values are similar to those for smaller German factories, with the highest prices being paid for early rarities. Pieces are usually marked with an incised or UNDERGLAZE-BLUE "Z". Dots and incised letters and numbers are also sometimes found.

ZWISCHENGOLDGLAS Meaning "gold between glass" in German, a double-walled DRINKING GLASS made by fitting one vessel inside another and fusing them together. The outer surface of the interior vessel is decorated with gold-leaf ornamentation (sometimes with silver leaf, in which case it is known as "Zwischensilberglas"). Zwischengoldglas was used on German and Bohemian BEAKERS and TANKARDS in the mid-18thC. Heraldic designs, hunting scenes, and religious subjects were popular. The leaf was sometimes engraved with a pictorial or decorative design, or combined with enamel colours. Zwischengoldglas plaques were also inserted into plain goblets and beakers. Examples of this type of GLASS are relatively rare, because the application of a sleeve could easily rub off the delicate gold leaf underneath.

German cardboard ZOETROPE, c.1900.

BUYING & SELLING

No matter what you collect – whether it's 18thC tea caddies, 19thC carriage clocks, pressed glass, Art Deco teapots, or Googlie dolls – there are many ways in which you can acquire items for your collection. If you want to dispose of items in your collection, you can also sell them in the same way. There are pros and cons to each method – it's up to you to decide which one best suits you.

AUCTION

One of the most exciting ways in which to buy antiques and collectable is at an auction, with potential buyers bidding for items. You'll find almost every type of collectable, from objects worth millions to boxes of inexpensive bric-a-brac. Auctions are not limited to the big city salerooms such as Sotheby's, Christie's, Phillips, and Bonhams – there are local auctioneers throughout the country. Going to auctions regularly is an excellent way to learn about the area you are interested in before beginning to collect. If you attend saleroom previews often and read the auction catalogues carefully, you will soon acquire a sound knowledge and a feel for prices.

VIEWING THE SALE

A "sale preview" occurs about two or three days before an auction. All the objects to be sold will be put on display, so that buyers can examine them. If you are hoping to buy at the sale, it is important to attend one of these preview days because on the day of the sale it may be impossible to view properly. Always examine thoroughly any object on which you intend to make a bid. Pay particular attention to the condition of the piece and take into account the potential cost of restoration, which may be considerable, before deciding on your bidding limit.

CATALOGUES, ESTIMATES, AND RESERVES

When attending an auction, make sure you acquire a catalogue. This publication is used to identify items to be sold at auction. Whether it's a typed sheet or a glossy illustrated publication, it will list and give "lot" numbers of the objects in the order in which they will be sold. Next to each catalogue entry there may be a suggested price range, which is known as the "estimate". The suggested price range, for example £250–380, is a rough guide to the value of an object; they are never a guarantee of the price for which something will be sold. At auction, any item on sale, no matter how rare or valuable, is ultimately only worth what two or more people are willing to bid for it. The price the item is sold for may be lower or higher than the estimated price. There may also be a reserve: the minimum price for which the auctioneer may sell your property at auction. It can be an important safeguard if the sale turns out to be poorly attended.

If there are no estimates printed in the catalogue they may be pinned up in the saleroom; if not, ask the auctioneer. When at larger auction houses, pay careful attention to the exact wording of each catalogue entry. Read the explanations at the beginning of the catalogue, which tell you the significance of words such as "attributed to", "style of" and "after". This catalogue terminology is like a code that tells you the valuer's opinion of the date and authenticity of a piece, and will have an important bearing on its value. Ask to speak to the expert in charge of the sale if you would like more information about a particular piece.

BIDDING

The process of offering a price for an item for sale at auction is known as bidding. The auctioneer will start the bidding at a figure that is usually slightly below the lower estimate. As the people present signal to him by waving or nodding he will call out their bids in regular sums, called increments. Depending on the value of the piece, the bidding could rise in £5s, £10s, £20s, £100s, £1,000s, or more, the increments increasing as the price rises. The auctioneer will indicate that the bidding is finished by banging a small hammer, called a gavel, on the rostrum, and recording the sale and the name or number of the successful bidder. You may need to register before bidding. Some salerooms will issue you with a number to hold up should your bid be successful; in others you simply call out your name and fill in a form at the time. If you can't get to the sale you can often leave a bid with the commissions clerk, who will bid on your behalf.

HAMMER PRICE AND COMMISSION

The actual price achieved by an antique at auction as opposed to an estimate is known as the hammer price. The auctioneer's commission and tax on the commission will usually be added to the hammer price. The auctioneer's fee, usually about 10-15 per cent is added onto the hammer price.

INTERNET AUCTION

With the explosion in computer use, auctions are now appearing on the Internet. Antiques are included in on-line auctions held by some major auction houses, as well as in more general websites. It is advised that you use the former, because the descriptions of the lots and conditions of sale should be similar to those you encounter when bidding in person at a major auction house. The disadvantage of on-line auctions is that you cannot handle the object (although you can usually view an image). However, you can bid for several lots at once, the bidding process is confidential, and you can often quickly find whether there are any items that you are interested in by enetering keywords into the website's search facility. Bear in mind that on-line auctions can last for several days or weeks, usually at the descretion of the lot's seller, and are not linked to real-time auctions held in the auction house itself.

To bid you will normally need to register your name, contact information, and usually a credit card number – in return you will be asked to select a user name and password that enables you to bid. Use the search facility, if available, to find the lots you are interested in – each lot should have a photograph, a catalogue description, and the e-mail address of the seller in case you need to find out more information. If you wish to bid, click on the appropriate button and enter your bid; remember that many on-line auctions of the major auction houses are centred in the USA, so prices may be given in dollars. You

will be identified to other bidders only by a paddle number (as in normal auctions), and a list of the bids should be given, with the paddle numbers of the other bidders so that you can see how many people are bidding against you. The bidding is carried out using normal increments. If you are unsuccessful you should receive an e-mail saying that you have been outbid, while, if you are successful, you will be notified that your credit card has been debited with the hammer price, commission, taxes, and if necessary, shipping costs.

ANTIQUE DEALERS

A professional who sells antiques, often in a permanent establishment but also at fairs, is known as an antiques dealer. There are many advantages to buying from a dealer rather than at auction. There is no pressure to make up your mind in an instant as to how much you are willing to pay, which you may have to do in the heated atmosphere of an auction. You will also know exactly how much you will pay for the piece – there is no need to worry about adding the auction house premium onto the price quoted. Unlike auction houses, where furniture may be quite dilapidated, most quality dealers offer furniture in a good state of repair and will have the piece restored, if necessary, before offering it for sale. This means that there are no extra restoration costs to take into account. If you get on well with your dealer, you might build up a long-lasting relationship that will be beneficial to both of you. Most dealers are great enthusiasts about their stock, and will probably be happy to share their knowledge of the subject as you build your collection. They might look out for special pieces that they do not have in stock for you, or offer to buy back pieces they have sold to you, so that you can upgrade your collection.

BUYING FROM A DEALER

If you see something that you want to buy, ask for as much information about the piece as possible. A good dealer will spend time talking to you, explaining the pros and cons of the pieces in which you are interested. The dealer should be able to tell you how old an item is, what it is made of, and from where it came (auction, private property, or deceased estate). There may also be some interesting history or provenance to the piece. You should also ask what, if any, restoration has been carried out on the piece. When it comes to agreeing the price there are no hard and fast rules, but in many antiques shops the first figure you are quoted is not the "best" price and if you discuss the sum you will often find that you can reduce it a little.

When you pay for the piece, make sure that you are given a detailed receipt by the dealer, which should include: the dealer's name and address; the date; the price; a clear and accurate description of the item, including the approximate date that it was made. Beware of descriptions that use the word "style" and give no date of manufacture. A description that reads "Queen Anne-style" without a date could mean that the piece was in fact made during the 20thC in the earlier style; whereas if it reads "Queen Anne c.1702", it means that the piece was actually made during Queen Anne's reign.

SELLING THROUGH A DEALER

Many people assume that they will get the best price by selling through an auction house, but this is not always the case, and it is always worth comparing the price a specialist dealer can offer you with the saleroom's valuation from an auction house before you decide how to sell. Before approaching a dealer, make sure that he specializes in the sort of piece you have to offer. If the piece is large and difficult to transport, it is a good idea to telephone the dealer beforehand to ask whether he might be interested in what you have to offer or to show him a photograph first. If he is interested, he will probably be happy to come to see the piece. Selling to a dealer has many advantages. The price you agree is the amount that you will receive – there are no hidden costs, such as the auction house premium, photographic charges, insurance and taxes, which would be taken from the hammer price if you sold at auction. If you agree to sell a table to a dealer for, say, £500, you should receive a cheque for that amount almost immediately. If, on the other hand, your item fetches £500 in a saleroom, you will receive a cheque for £400.71 (based on a rate of 15 per cent commission, 1½ per cent insurance, £2 handling, and taxes). If the piece appears in black and white in the sale catalogue, this could cost an additional fee. You will also have to wait for a few weeks while your item is catalogued and entered in the appropriate sale. In many cases, you will not receive your cheque until several weeks after the sale. Bear in mind, too, that in the unlucky event of the piece not reaching its reserve at auction, this may make it more difficult to sell to the local trade.

In certain circumstances a dealer might agree to take a piece "on consignment". Be sure to obtain a signed contract from the dealer and to agree who is responsible for insurance. The contract should clearly state an agreed rate of commission.

TRADE ASSOCIATIONS

There are organizations that oversee retail dealers. In Britain the two major trade associations are the LAPADA and BADA; the equivalent American bodies are the AADLA and NAADA. Those dealers who wish to become members of these bodies have to undergo a rigorous selection procedure. This assesses both their stock and knowledge. Once members, they are bound to keep to a strict code of practice. Member dealers must tell a buyer as much about the piece as they can; and this includes pointing out any restoration the piece may have had. If, after buying something from a member dealer, you discover it is not genuine, the organization will themselves organize a panel of independent experts to investigate your claim and make sure, if it is upheld, that you get a refund. Remember that even the best-intentioned dealers can make the odd genuine mistake.

JUNK SHOPS

There is a world of difference between an up-market dealer's showroom and a junk shop. Most junk shop owners find their stock from house clearances that will have been scoured by dealers first. However, they are a great source of less-expensive pieces of furniture (in particular 20thC furniture). With a little care and attention, any such pieces can become just as attractive as more expensive antiques. If you buy from a junk shop do not expect the same level of expertise that you would find at an established antiques dealer's outlet. Ask questions, but also make sure that you examine the piece as carefully as possible and make up your own mind as to its age, origins, and authenticity.

KNOCKER

In Britain a "dealer" who calls at your door uninvited, or who leaves an advertisement telling you that he will pay cash for valuables and will return in a day or two is called a "knocker". Many knockers are of dubious integrity, particularly when convincing the elderly and vulnerable into selling their property for less than its true value. There is also the added risk of allowing into your home an unknown person, who may be using the visit as an opportunity to plan to return later without an invitation.

FAIRS & MARKETS

Each year various major and minor antiques fairs take place throughout Britain, continental Europe, and the USA. Attending some of the larger antiques fairs is an interesting way for an amatuer to learn about the area in which he or she wants to collect. There will be dealers specializing in a variety of styles, all under one roof. Such a range gives you a chance to compare stock as well as prices. You will be able to decide what you like best, and who offers the best value. The larger fairs usually charge an entry fee, for which you may also be given a list of the exhibitors, perhaps in a glossy catalogue. This list is a useful reference because it will include the stand numbers of exhibitors at the fair, as well as their business addresses and telephone numbers. Dealers use fairs as an important way of making contacts with potential new customers, as well as making sales.

Vetting is a procedure established at larger fairs to offer the safeguard that all the exhibitors have been carefully selected for their reputations and the quality of their stock. Each piece is examined by a panel of independent experts (auction-house valuers, museum curators, and specialist dealers) to make sure that it is authentic and has not been over-restored. At some fairs, anything exhibited must have been made before a specified date. This is known as a date-line.

OTHER FAIRS

As well as the large fairs, numerous smaller antiques fairs take place. The goods may not have been vetted, and the exhibitors may not have the same degree of expertise, but the goods offered will usually be less expensive. Fairs such as these can be great places to find "bargains", but you need to determine for yourself the age and authenticity of any piece you buy. Whether going to a large or small antiques fair, get there early to find the best bargains, try to get to know the dealers personally, and always make sure that you get a proper receipt.

ANTIQUE MARKETS

Established areas with a concentration of antiques dealers with stands or shops, markets may take place one or two days a week, or even every day. Some well-known antiques markets such as Portobello Road in London, the Flea Market (*Marché aux Puces*) in Paris, or the Annex Antique Fair & Flea Market in New York City are the haunts of collectors. Some reputable dealers have stands and shops in markets, but there are also less scrupulous dealers. Keep in mind the adage, *caveat emptor* (buyer beware) before you part with large amounts of money over a market stall where the dealer is not a member of a recognized trade association. Try to obtain a clearly written receipt for your purchase – one that includes the name and address of the dealer, with a description of the object and its approximate age. In this way, should you find out that the object you have bought is not authentic, you will be covered by the laws of consumer protection.

CAR-BOOT SALES

In Britain, goods are sold from the boot (or trunk) of a car in a site hired for the occasion such as a farmer's field, school playground, or large car park (car lot). Each year there are several well-publicized "discoveries" that are bought at car boot sales and, after being identified as valuable works of art, they are resold for thousands of pounds. Stories such as these contribute greatly to the popularity of car boot sales. They are advertised in local newspapers, the classified columns of various magazines, or on notices pinned to trees or lampposts in the area. Some boot sales are regular events held throughout the year, usually at weekends, while others occur just once. You can sell anything at boot sales, and from the buyer's point of view they can be inexpensive sources for a collection. Obviously, the pieces that you find at car-boot sales tend to be smaller – a local boot sale might be a good place to hunt for a Lloyd Loom wicker chair or laundry basket, but do not expect to find a Chippendale side chair or an oak dresser very often.

As always, the old adage "the early bird catches the worm" is true. The first to arrive are often the dealers, who may arrive well before dawn. Try to arrive at the sale as early as possible and always carry a torch (or flashlight). The light can be poor if it is early in the morning or late in the afternoon, and you need to be able to inspect items closely before you part with any cash. If you find something that catches your eye, the prices at a boot sale are usually flexible, so it really is worth bargaining (gently, but firmly) with the person selling. Bring coins and low value notes. If you are in any doubt, ask a few questions about the provenance of the piece. You should try to obtain a written receipt with the name and address of the person from whom you are buying. It is also a good idea to note the license-plate number of the seller's car.

SELLING AT A BOOT SALE

If you intend selling at a boot sale, you will usually be charged an entrance fee according to the size of your vehicle. Arrive early to get a good position and to give yourself time to set up properly. It is worth packing the car the night before to make sure that everything you want to take fits. Also, decide what price you want for your property before you go to the sale and, if possible, mark each item with its price; this will save you having to make quick decisions that you might regret with hindsight.

TAG SALE

The American equivalent method for selling household items is known as a tag sale. It is usually run by an indivudual household from a garage (also called a garage sale) or in the front garden (yard sale).

ADVERTISING

A source for buying or selling items in the classified columns in a wide variety of publications, including national newspapers, local papers, and the specialist collector's magazines. If you see an advertisement that looks promising, try to find out as much about the piece as possible before you make the journey to see it. Ask for the price and a full description, including size, material, age, condition, and whether it has been repaired.

If you are selling through an advertisement, have a good idea of the value of the piece before you advertise it. Show a photo or the object itself to a few reputable dealers or auction houses to get an idea of its market value. Look at descriptions of similar objects in auction catalogues for an idea of how to describe the piece, word the advertisement clearly, and always include the object's dimensions, its age (if you know it), and a note of any decoration that could make it more attractive to buyers. Include a telephone number, but do not, in the interests of security, include your name or address. Be prepared to name the price you are looking for (you should negotiate if necessary) and to give the prospective buyer a full description of the piece and its condition. If you find a buyer, never part with your property before you have been paid in full with cash or the cheque has cleared.

CONDITION

The amount of wear and tear, or lack of it, on an item determines its "condition" and value. Dealers use there own terms when referring to the condition of a piece. An object in near perfect condition – as new – may be called "pristine". A piece that has been stored away for years and has escaped use or restoration is called a "sleeper". A fine piece by a leading maker, especially one that has been shown at exhibitions or featured in text books is referred to as "important". A "collector's piece" originally denoted a fine piece of interest to connoisseurs, but it is now often used to describe pieces that appeal only to a minority taste. An "old friend" is an antique that has been resold at auction many times.

"As found", often abbreviated to AF, refers to an item with some flaw or damage, usually unspecified. "As bought" is used for an item of uncertain date or provenance, meaning that the seller takes no responsibility for the accuracy of the description. A dealer may refer to a piece as "right" for something that is genuine and authentic, as opposed to "wrong", which means it is faked, altered, or restored. A piece that has been made into a smaller, more saleable item is known as "cut down". A piece is "made up" if it has been constructed from old materials but is not genuine. See also MARRIAGE.

A toy collector may use "Sunday fresh" for a toy only played with on Sunday under supervision. "Enjoyed" is a toy-collectors' term for an object that has been played with and has suffered an acceptable level of damage, as opposed to "playworn" or badly damaged, which is only worth collecting if rare.

FOR THE RECORDS

Keep a detailed record of every collectable object as you acquire it in an inventory book. Write down where the piece came from, the date you bought or acquired it, the price you paid for it, the value for insurance purposes if your collection is insured, a full description of the piece – including its size, material, and any decorative features – a report of its condition, including cracks, chips, alterations, or restoration (update this if you have the piece restored); and anything else you know about the object's history, or "provenance". The provenance of an object can help in a piece's correct identification and valuation. Even minor details can help a valuer. Keep the receipts of any items you have purchased in the same place. It's a good way to show proof of ownership in the event of an insurance claim.

INSURANCE AND VALUATION
A way of recuperating the monetary value of a valuable item if it has been stolen or damaged through fire, flood, or certain other causes is to insure it. Most insurance companies call for a professional valuation for any object worth more than a certain sum, usually based on a percentage of your overall policy. Many will accept valuations by an independent valuer, an auction house valuer, or an individual dealer.

A valuation is a statement from a professional valuer that includes a full description of an antique item, together with its dimensions and a value for insurance purposes. The value placed upon the object depends on where you would go to replace your property – for example, an auction house or well-known specialist dealer. The price an insurance valuer puts on your property will probably be at least 20 per cent higher than what you could expect to get should you decide to sell. You can opt for "market valuations" – in other words auction prices – instead. But if the valuation is too low you may not be able to replace lost items satisfactorily. The price that you have to pay for a valuation can vary considerably, so shop around for the best deal. The cost is calculated in one of three ways: as a percentage of the total value of the property involved (usually between ½ and 1½ per cent); on a daily rate plus additional travelling expenses; by a flat fee. Before the valuer begins an assessment, make clear at what level you want your property valued.

SECURITY
A burglar who sees an open window or door is more likely to break into your home than the professional antiques snatcher. The best way to deter this type of theft is to not leave obviously valuable objects on display, and to make your home uninviting. Window locks, good-quality locks on all your doors, effective burglar alarms, and bright security lights are all readily available for a moderate cost. If you need advice on how to make your home more secure, talk to a local police officer.

You can assist the recovery of stolen property by marking your valuables with a security pen. However, many collectors prefer not to do so, because the pen is indelible and could deter potential buyers. Good photographs are an effective way of helping the police to recover stolen items. Photograph small or ornate objects against a plain background. A ruler beside a small object will act as a scale reference. Photograph the object from as many angles as possible. Include close-up shots of distinctive decoration and of defects, which can help to identify your item from similar ones. Keep one set of photographs with your inventory and another with your solicitor or bank. There are also various firms and publications, such as *Trace* and the *Antiques Trade Gazette*, that can help to track down stolen antiques, using photographs. In addition the Art Loss Register, a database of stolen property, can help to trace stolen pieces sold through auction rooms and dealers both in Britain and abroad.

PERIODS & STYLES

Dates	British monarch	British period	French period
1558–1603	Elizabeth I	Elizabethan	Renaissance
1603–1625	James I	Jacobean	
1625–1649	Charles I	Carolean	Louis XIII (1610–43)
1649–1660	Commonwealth	Cromwellian	Louis XIV (1643–1715)
1660–1685	Charles II	Restoration	
1685–1688	James II	Restoration	
1688–1694	William & Mary	William & Mary	
1694–1702	William III	William III	
1702–1714	Anne	Queen Anne	
1714–1727	George I	Early Georgian	Regence (1715–23)
1727–1760	George II	Early Georgian	Louis XV (1723–74)
1760–1811	George III	Georgian	Louis XVI (1774–93) Directoire (1793–99) Empire (1799–1815)
1812–1820	George III	Regency	Restauration (1815–30)
1820–1830	George IV	Regency	Charles X (1820–1830)
1830–1837	William IV	William IV	Louis Philippe (1830–48) 2nd Empire (1852–70)
1837–1901	Victoria	Victorian	3rd Republic (1871–1940)
1901–1910	Edward VII	Edwardian	
1910–1936	George V (Edward VIII 1936)	George V	
1936–1952	George VI	George VI	Vichy (1940–44) Provisional Government of the Republic (1944–47) 4th Republic (1947–58)
1952–present	Elizabeth II	Elizabeth II	5th Republic (1958–present)

German period	U.S. period	Style
Renaissance (to c.1650)	Seventeenth Century / Pilgrim (1640–90)	Gothic Baroque (c.1620–1700)
Renaissance/Baroque (c.1650–1700)	William & Mary (1700–30)	Rococo (c.1695–1760)
Baroque (c.1700–30)	Queen Anne (1725–55)	
Rococo (c.1730–60)	Chippendale (1755–90)	
Neo-classicism (c.1750–1800)	Federal (1790–1815)	Neo-classical (c.1755–1805)
Empire (c.1800–15)	Classical/Empire (1815–40)	Empire (c.1799–1815)
Biedermeier (c.1815–48 and 1880–1920)	Restauration / Pillar & Scroll (1830–65)	Regency (c.1812–30)
	Gothic / Elizabethan Revival (1830–65) Rococo Revival (1840–70)	Eclectic (c.1830–80)
Revival (c.1830–80)	Renaissance / Neo-Grec / Egyptian Revival (1855–85)	Arts & Crafts (c.1880–1900)
Jugendstil (c.1880–1920)	Innovative / Patented / Exotic / Victorian (1850–1900)	Art Nouveau (c.1890–1920)
	Design Reform / Arts & Crafts / Architect (1875–1920)	
Bauhaus / International (c.1920–45)	International / Art Deco ("Roaring Twenties" & New Deal of 1929–41)	Art Deco (1918–40)
Postwar / Modern (post c.1945)		

FURNITURE LEG & FEET STYLES

The variety of legs and feet found on tables, chairs, and other furniture can help to date a piece. However, many styles were revived and reproduced in later periods; the style of a leg, therefore, is no guarantee of age and you should also take into account the appearance of the wood when dating.

Feet on caned furniture are frequently replaced, as damp floors often caused them to rot. Replacement feet will not necessarily reduce the value of a piece dramatically if their style is consistent with the date of that piece. Replacement legs, however, especially if they have all been replaced, should be viewed with more scepticism.

Having casters that are original to a piece is always desirable, especially if they are attached to decoratively carved feet.

Here is a small selection of the types of legs and feet you may come across on furniture.

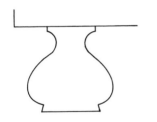

Flattened bun foot, late 17thC

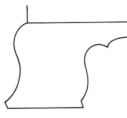

Double ogee bracket foot, mid-18thC

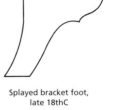

Splayed bracket foot, late 18thC

Ogee bracket foot, c.1725

Leather wheel caster, c.1750

Late Regency gilt metal caster

Victorian porcelain caster

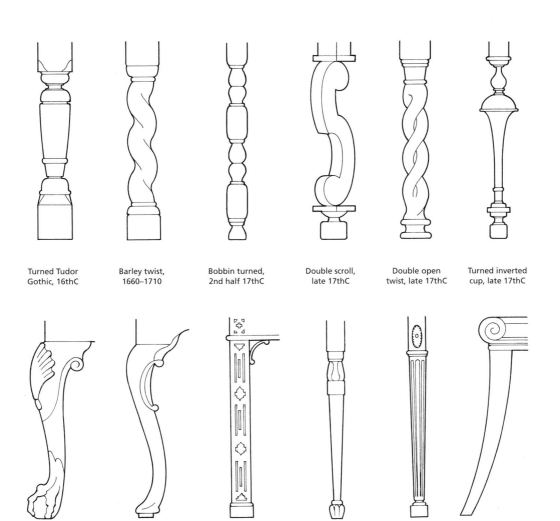

Turned Tudor
Gothic, 16thC

Barley twist,
1660–1710

Bobbin turned,
2nd half 17thC

Double scroll,
late 17thC

Double open
twist, late 17thC

Turned inverted
cup, late 17thC

Claw and ball foot,
1730–1750

Cabriole leg with
carving on inside of
knee, 18thC

Fretted, mid-
18thC

Turned,
late 18thC

Adam fluted,
late 18thC

Sabre leg,
early 19thC

GLASS FORMS & STYLES

Hot molten glass can be manipulated into a vast array of shapes and patterns using the main methods of free-blowing, mould-blowing, and press-moulding. Designs, even of practical glass tableware such as drinking glasses and decanters, have changed considerably over the centuries. A good knowledge of styles and decoration can certainly help the budding collector in dating and authenticating glass.

Glass from the 18thC and 19thC is more commonly found today than that of earlier centuries. 18thC-styles of lead-glass drinking glasses and decanters are generally much simpler and plainer than later ones. Early 18thC English drinking glasses had small bowls – mainly because the wine and spirits drunk at the time had a much higher alcohol content than those of today. The decoration, such as air and opaque twists and faceting, focused on the stem, which often had a knop or decorative bulbous form made by compressing the hot glass rod of the stem during manufacture. Decanters of the same period are either plain or with restrained engraving, and with matching stoppers. Heavy cutting, another speciality of Irish and English glassmakers, is characteristic of the early 19thC and is found in a wide variety of patterns, according to the type of cutting wheel: flat, curved, or V-shaped. Some of the most common patterns are shown above on the right.

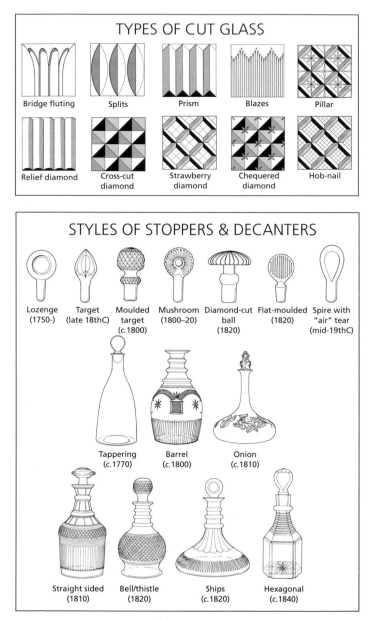

TYPES OF CUT GLASS

Bridge fluting — Splits — Prism — Blazes — Pillar

Relief diamond — Cross-cut diamond — Strawberry diamond — Chequered diamond — Hob-nail

STYLES OF STOPPERS & DECANTERS

Lozenge (1750-) — Target (late 18thC) — Moulded target (c.1800) — Mushroom (1800–20) — Diamond-cut ball (1820) — Flat-moulded (1820) — Spire with "air" tear (mid-19thC)

Tappering (c.1770) — Barrel (c.1800) — Onion (c.1810)

Straight sided (1810) — Bell/thistle (1820) — Ships (c.1820) — Hexagonal (c.1840)

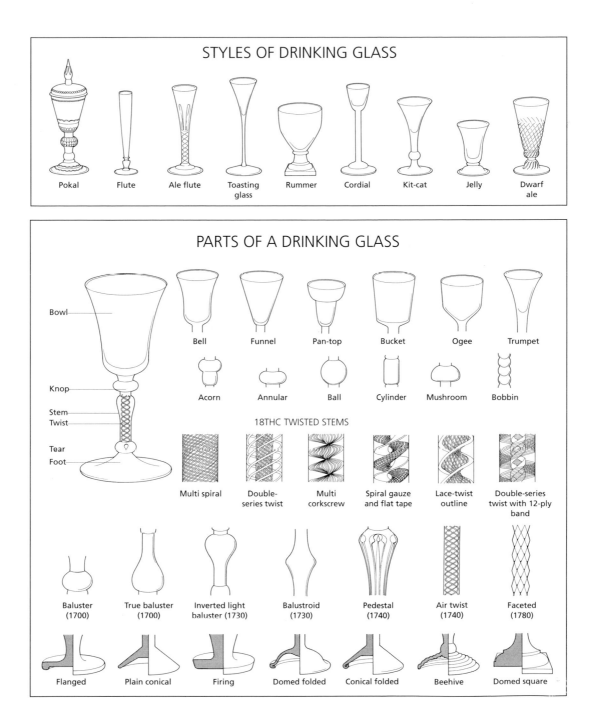

STYLES OF DRINKING GLASS

Pokal • Flute • Ale flute • Toasting glass • Rummer • Cordial • Kit-cat • Jelly • Dwarf ale

PARTS OF A DRINKING GLASS

Bowl

Knop

Stem
Twist

Tear
Foot

Bell • Funnel • Pan-top • Bucket • Ogee • Trumpet

Acorn • Annular • Ball • Cylinder • Mushroom • Bobbin

18THC TWISTED STEMS

Multi spiral • Double-series twist • Multi corkscrew • Spiral gauze and flat tape • Lace-twist outline • Double-series twist with 12-ply band

Baluster (1700) • True baluster (1700) • Inverted light baluster (1730) • Balustroid (1730) • Pedestal (1740) • Air twist (1740) • Faceted (1780)

Flanged • Plain conical • Firing • Domed folded • Conical folded • Beehive • Domed square

CERAMIC MARKS

One of the most useful marks on later ceramics is the Design Registration Mark. Registration began in 1839 following the Copyright of Design Act but the insignia shown on the right was used from 1842. The table on the right shows which piece of information each area of the insignia represented and which letters were used to denote the years and months of registration (which were not used in sequence). The positioning in the insignia changed after 1867 and from 1884 consecutive numbers were used to represent the year instead, nearly always prefixed by "Rd" or "Rd No." A guide to the year from the number is given in the table below.

REGISTRATION MARKS 1842–83

1842–67		1868–83
a – class		a – class
b – year		b – day
c – month	Rd	c – bundle
d – day		d – year
e – bundle		e – month

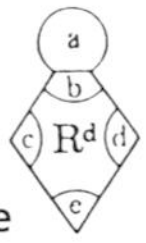

1842–67

A = 1845	N = 1864
B = 1858	O = 1862
C = 1844	P = 1851
D = 1852	Q = 1866
E = 1855	R = 1861
F = 1847	S = 1849
G = 1863	T = 1867
H = 1843	U = 1848
I = 1846	V = 1850
J = 1854	W = 1865
K = 1857	X = 1842
L = 1856	Y = 1853
M = 1859	Z = 1860

1868–83

A =1871	L = 1882
C = 1870	P = 1877
D = 1878	S = 1875
E = 1881	U = 1874
F = 1873	V = 1876
H = 1869	W = 1878
I = 1872	(1–6 March)
J = 1880	X = 1868
K =1883	Y = 1879

Month letters for both periods are as follows:

A = December
B = October
C or O = January
D = September
E = May
G = February
H = April
I = July
K = November
(and December1860)
M = June
R = August
(and 1–19 September 1857)
W = March

TABLE OF REGISTRATION NUMBERS 1884–2003

1 = 1884	658988 = 1917	860854 = 1950	978426 = 1977
19754 = 1885	662872 = 1918	863970 = 1951	982815 = 1978
40480 = 1886	666128 = 1919	866280 = 1952	987910 = 1979
64520 = 1887	673750 = 1920	869300 = 1953	993012 = 1980
90483 = 1888	680147 = 1921	872531 = 1954	998302 = 1981
116648 = 1889	687144 = 1922	876067 = 1955	1004456 = 1982
141273 = 1890	694999 = 1923	879282 = 1956	1010583 = 1983
163767 = 1891	702671 = 1924	882949 = 1957	1017131 = 1984
185713 = 1892	710165 = 1925	887079 = 1958	1024174 = 1985
205240 = 1893	718057 = 1926	891665 = 1959	1031358 = 1986
224720 = 1894	726330 = 1927	895000 = 1960	1039055 = 1987
246975 = 1895	734370 = 1928	899914 = 1961	1047799 = 1988
268392 = 1896	742725 = 1929	904638 = 1962	1056078 = 1989
291241 = 1897	751160 = 1930	909364 = 1963	2003720 = 1990
311658 = 1898	760583 = 1931	914536 = 1964	2012047 = 1991
331707 = 1899	769670 = 1932	919607 = 1965	2019933 = 1992
351202 = 1900	779292 = 1933	924510 = 1966	2028115 = 1993
368154 = 1901	789019 = 1934	929335 = 1967	2036116 = 1994
385180 = 1902	799097 = 1935	934515 = 1968	2044227 = 1995
403200 = 1903	808794 = 1936	939875 = 1969	2053121 = 1996
424400 = 1904	817293 = 1937	944932 = 1970	2062149 = 1997
447800 = 1905	825231 = 1938	950046 = 1971	2071520 = 1998
471860 = 1906	832610 = 1939	955342 = 1972	2080158 = 1999
493900 = 1907	837520 = 1940	960708 = 1973	2089210 = 2000
518640 = 1908	838590 = 1941	965185 = 1974	2098500 = 2001
535170 = 1909	839230 = 1942	969249 = 1975	3000500 = 2002
552000 = 1910	839980 = 1943	973838 = 1976	3009770 = 2003
574817 = 1911	841040 = 1944		
594195 = 1912	842670 = 1945	After a European Directive	
612431 = 1913	845550 = 1946	was implemented in the UK in	
630190 = 1914	849730 = 1947	December 2001, the numbering	
644395 = 1915	853260 = 1948	started again at 3000000.	
653521 = 1916	856999 = 1949		

MOTIFS & DEVICES

There are many motifs used in ceramic marks. Such marks might be used to help distinguish a company from others, and they can be very useful in dating a piece as variations often occur throughout a company's manufacturing period. Here are some examples.

Scroll marks

Coalport Porcelain
This "ampersand" mark appeared painted in gilt c.1861–75.

Sèvres
Crossed "L"s, for Louis XV and XVI, were used from 1749, with date letters inside them from 1753.

Anchors

Geminiano Cozzi
This factory ran from 1765 to 1812. An anchor mark in red, or more rarely gold, was used.

Squares

Worcester
This mark varies in style. It was hand-painted in underglaze blue c.1755–75 and on reproductions.

Triangles

Hubaudière
Hubaudière took over this faience factory in 1782 (d.1794). Also used in the 19thC.

Globes

Minton
The standard printed Globe mark, without "S" or the crown, was used c.1863–72, and this version from c.1873, with "England" added from 1891.

Crowns

Royal Worcester
This mark was used from 1891, when "Royal Worcester England" was added.

Derby Porcelain
This mark was used 1861–1935. The intials "S" and "H" stand for "Stevenson & Hancock".

Animals

Ulysee Cantagalli
Cantagalli made malolica reproductions 1878–1901. The cockerel mark appears in various forms, and can be very abstract.

Belleek Pottery
This standard mark was used 1863–91, and one with the addition of "Co. Fermanagh" and "Ireland' is still used.

Swords

Meissen
First used in 1724, the crossed swords mark went through various changes. The first mark shown here (left) generally appeared between 1763 and 1774. From 1774 until 1814 the star below the handles denoted the Marcolini period. From 1818 until 1924 the swords were long with slightly curved blades.

Crescents

This painted mark was used on tin-glazed wares by this German company (est. 1661) 17th–18thC.

SILVER MARKS & FORMS

Because gold and silver were of such commercial importance it became necessary by the end of the 13thC to establish and maintain reliable standards which everyone dealing in the metals must follow. The first mark in England guaranteeing such a standard was stamped on silver in 1300, by the Goldsmiths' Company, of Goldsmiths' Hall in London. From then on such marks were known as "Hall" or "Town" marks. In Britain all silver wares, with a few minor exceptions, carry such marks, which provide precise information on place of origin, quality, and date. On the Continent and in North America marking has never been systematized in this way and is therefore not always a reliable method of identification and dating. Town and manufacturer's marks can, however, provide useful clues.

> **Beware**
> • Early silver marks are far from uniform, because the punches were handmade. Often there is considerable variation even for the same year.
> • Silver hallmarks should never be taken as a sole guarantee of authenticity. They are easily – and frequently – faked.

British silver marks

There are four main types of mark, in addition to less common ones:

1) *The specific "Hall" or "Town" mark*, which was different for each assay office. Variations to the basic mark occur over the years.

2) *A "standard" or quality mark* to indicate 92.5% silver (Sterling), frequently placed first, before the hallmark. From 1300 this was a leopard's head (which also became recognized as the London mark and by 1478 had a crown); in 1544 it was a lion walking to the left (*passant*); and from 1820 it was an uncrowned lion's head (as shown below).

When, between 1697 and 1719, the silver standard was raised, the existing town or hall mark was replaced by "Britannia", and the

Lion passant replaced by a lion's head in profile (as shown below).

When the lower standard was restored in 1719, the original marks were revived. However, the "Britannia" marks were, and are, still permitted and used on silver that reaches the higher standard.

In Scotland the Edinburgh standard mark is a thistle (used since 1759) and the Glasgow mark is a *Lion Rampant*, which has had a thistle since 1914 – both are shown below.

The Irish Republic has no standard mark, the Dublin town mark (a crowned harp) doubling for it on Irish silver.

3) *An annual date letter.* Each assay

office allocates its own specific letter for each year. This letter and the shield enclosing it are distinctive in form, enabling the piece to be dated precisely. An alphabetical sequence is normally followed (although "J" is often omitted). The example below is the letter "D", used by the London office in 1719.

4) *Maker's mark or initial* (such as "P.S." for Paul Storr, as below).

5) *Other silver marks include:* the "Sovereign's Head" mark, indicating duty paid (1884–1890); the letter "F" (for "foreign") indicating imported silver from 1843; and marks to commemorate King George V's Silver Jubilee (on articles assayed between 1933 and 1936) and Queen Elizabeth II's coronation.

The shapes, styles, and production methods used in silver have evolved over time, resulting in a fascinating variety and useful indicators of date. Spoons, for example, were generally made from two separate pieces of silver (bowl and handle) up to the end of the 18thC. Also, in the United States, since early silversmiths produced pieces to order, each item possessed its own characteristics – but style trends can still be identified. The examples below give a taster of the progression of key shapes.

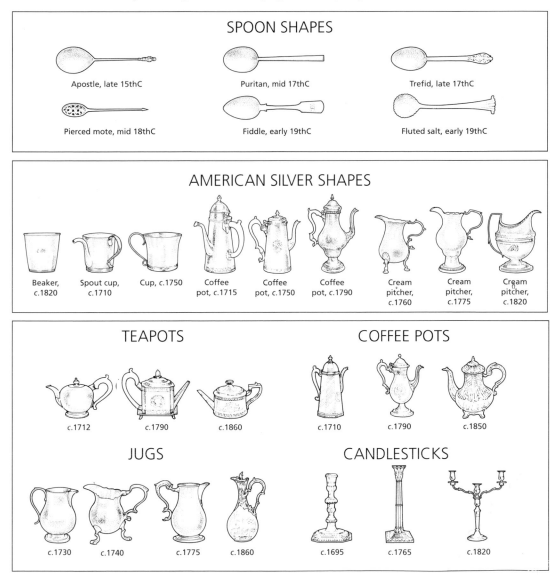

SPOON SHAPES

Apostle, late 15thC

Puritan, mid 17thC

Trefid, late 17thC

Pierced mote, mid 18thC

Fiddle, early 19thC

Fluted salt, early 19thC

AMERICAN SILVER SHAPES

Beaker, c.1820

Spout cup, c.1710

Cup, c.1750

Coffee pot, c.1715

Coffee pot, c.1750

Coffee pot, c.1790

Cream pitcher, c.1760

Cream pitcher, c.1775

Cream pitcher, c.1820

TEAPOTS

c.1712

c.1790

c.1860

COFFEE POTS

c.1710

c.1790

c.1850

JUGS

c.1730

c.1740

c.1775

c.1860

CANDLESTICKS

c.1695

c.1765

c.1820

DOLLS BODIES & HEADS

The variation in dolls' bodies is enormous, especially with bisque. The heads are the same material, but the bodies may not be, nor the construction or the quality. A knowledge of different body types is invaluable in identifying and in spotting "wrong" replaced limbs. Here are some of the bodies most commonly found.

Early wooden
English wooden pre-1740 dolls were round-faced with long wide necks, a head and torso usually in one piece, a tapered waist, forked hands, and possibly cloth upper arms .

Papier mâché
The shoulder heads of German pre-1870 papier-mâché dolls were moulded with deep yokes. They had unjointed kid/calico bodies, with a narrow waist and wide hips, and possibly wooden lower limbs.

Fashion shapes
Fashion dolls often had a gussetted kid body (tenon-jointed) with wide shoulders and hips to suit the dresses of the period. Forearms were sometimes bisque.

Ball joints
Some bisque head dolls have eight-ball-jointed or floating-ball-jointed bodies. In this case the limbs slide over an unattached floating ball joint.

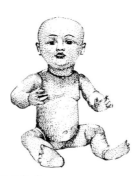

Bent limb
Five-piece bent-limb composition bodies were used on various babies and characters 1910–39. Some examples were extremely well modelled.

Jointed todler
German jointed toddlers had wood or composition bodies with pronounced side-hip joints and fat tummies, as used on character dolls produced after 1910.

Dolls are classified according to head type. The style and quality of the head can assist in dating and identifying a doll, while knowledge of the right combinations of heads and bodies is vital in authentication. The following examples are among the most common or distinctive head.

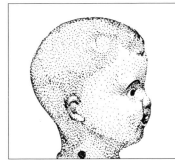

Flange neck
The flange neck is often used on soft-bodied dolls such as Dream Babies. The neck is open and the base curves outwards with two holes positioned so that the head can be sewn onto the body.

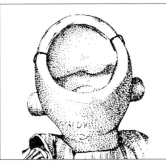

Open head
Bisque dolls very often have an open head. The open section is the crown. This is covered with a separate pate, cork on French dolls, cardboard on German, and is the section to which the wig is attached.

Swivel head
On a swivel-headed doll the head and shoulderplate are separate. The head fits into a cup on the shoulderplate, which may be lined with kid, enabling the head to swivel.

Shoulder head
Many early dolls have shoulder heads (where the shoulders, neck, and head are moulded in one piece). The shoulderplate reaches the top of the arms. The head might be glued into a kid body or sewn, using specially made holes, onto a cloth body.

Socket head
The most common head type on the majority of French and German dolls and babies is the socket head. The base of the neck is rounded so that the head fits into a cup shape at the top of the body.

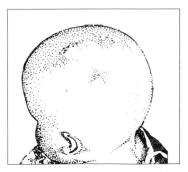

Solid domed
The few bisque-headed dolls which have solid-domed heads are generally called Belton heads. They can be either socket heads, a later form of swivel head, or shoulderplate heads. Wigs are stuck with glue. Sometimes the head has holes, with the wig held by string.

ACKNOWLEDGMENTS

The Publisher would like to thank the following people and organizations for allowing their pieces to be illustrated in this book:

ACAC Afonwen Craft & Antique Centre; AH Andrew Hartley; AJP A J Photographics; AMC Amelie Caswell; APC Antique Photographic Company; APO Apollo Antiques; AUC Aurea Carter; BaN Barbara Ann Newman; Bbe Bourton Bears; Bbo Bazaar Boxes; BD Banana Dance; BEV Beverley; BEX Daniel Bexfield; BHa Judy & Brian Harden; BKJL Brenda Kimber & John Lewis; BOW David Bowden; BRU Brunel Antiques; BrW Brian Watson; BtoB Bac to Basic Antiques; BURA Burford Antiques Centre; BWDA Brightwells Decorative Arts; BWL Brightwells Fine Art; CAL Cedar Antiques Ltd; CAu Cotswold Auction Company Ltd; CBB Colin Baddiel; CDC Capes Dunn & Co; CH Chris Halton; CHAC Church Hill Antiques Centre; ChC Christopher Clarke (Antiques); CHI Chinasearch; CHTR Charterhouse; CO Cooper Owen; COBB The Cobbs Auctioneers LLC; CoHA Corner House Antiques and Ffoxe Antiques; CoS Corrinne Soffe; CRU Mary Cruz; CSA Christopher Sykes Antiques; CSK Christie's South Kensington; CSM C.S. Moreton Antiques; CSt Chuck Steffes; DA Dee, Atkinson & Harrison; DAD Decorative Arts @ Doune; DEB Debden Antiques; Del Ann Delores; DJH David J Hansord & Son; DLP The Dunlop Collection; DM David Merryweather; Dma David March; DML David Moulson; Do Liz Farrow trading as Dodo; DOL Dollectable; DRA Derek Roberts Antiques; DSA David Scriven Antiques; Ech Echoes; EG Emma Gillingham; F&C Finan & Co; FAC Faganarms; Fai Fair Finds Antiques; FHF Fellows & Sons; FRD Fragile Design; G&G Guest & Gray; G(B) Gorringes Auction Galleries; G(L) Gorringes Auction Galleries; GAK Keys; GaL Gazelles Ltd; GAU Becca Gauldie; GAZE Thomas Wm Gaze & Son; GEO Georgian Antiques; GGD Great Grooms Antiques Centre; GIL Gilding's Auctioneers; GLAS Glasstastique; GLD Glade Antiques; GLEN Glenda-Antiques Dolls; GN Gillian Neale; GRe Greystoke Antiques; GRI Grimes House Antiques; GTM Gloucester Toy Mart; H&G Hope & Glory; HAD Henry Adams; HAL John & Simon Haley; HAYS Hays & Associates Inc; HeA Heanor Antique Centre; HEM Hemswell Antiques Centre; HIS Erna Hiscock & John Shepherd; HL Honiton Lace Shop; HO Houghton Antiques; HOB Hobday Toys; HOW John Howard; HUM Humbleyard Fine Art; HUN The Country Seat; HWK H W Keil Ltd; IB Ian Booth; ICO Iconastas; JAA Jackson's International; JAS Jasmin Cameron; JE Julian Eade; JFME James Ferguson; JHa Jeanette Hayhurst Fine Glass; JHo Jonathan Horne; JM Jeremy Martin; JPr Antique Textiles & Lighting; JSG James Strang; JTS June & Tony Stone, Fine Antique; JUN Junktion; JUP Jupiter Antiques; KEY Key Antiques of Chippping Norton; KW Karel Weijand; L&E Locke & England; LaF La Femme; Lbe Linda Bee; LBr Lynda Brine; LGr Langton Green Antiques; LLD Lewis & Lewis Deco; LP Lynda Pine; MAA Mario's Antiques; MALT The Old Malthouse; MARK 20th Century Marks; MB Mostly Boxes; McP R & G McPherson; MDL Michael D Long; MI Mitofsky; Mit Mitchells Auction Company; MiW Mike Weedon; MMc Marsh-McNamara; Mpe Michael Pearson; MSh Manfred Schotten; NAW Newark Antiques Warehouse Ltd; NB Nigel Benson; NoC No1 Castlegate Antiques; NORTH Northiam Antiques & Interiors; NS Nicholas Shaw; ORI The Originals; P&T Pine & Things; PA Peter Anderson; PAY Payne & Son; PICA Piccadilly Antiques; POLL Pollyanna; POW Sylvia Powell; PP Premier Photography; PR Peter Rixon; PrB Pretty Bizarre; PWA Paul Weatherell Antiques; RAN Ranby Hall – Antiques; RAY Derek & Tina Rayment; RD Roger Dixon; RdV Roger de Ville; REN Paul & Keren Rennie; ROS Rosebery's Fine Art Ltd; RPh Phelps Antiques; RS Robin Saker; RUSK Ruskin; SAACScottish Antique and Arts; SAF Michael Saffell Antiques; SAS Special Auction Services; SAT The Swan at Tetsworth; SCO Peter Scott; SEA Mark Seabrook Antiques; SERE Serendipity; SGA Stair Galleries; SHa Shapiro; SiA Simply Antiques; SJH S.J.Hales; SK(B) Skinner, Inc; SLh À La Façon De Venise; SLI Sanda Lipton; SOO Soo San; Spe Sue Pearson; SPUR Spurrier-Smith Antiques; ST Steve Tanner; SV Sutton Valence Antiques; SWO Sworders; TAC Tenterden Antiques Centre; TCG 20th Century Glass; TDG The Design Gallery 1850-1950; THE Theriault's; TL Telephone Lines; TLA The Lanes Armoury; TMA Tring Market Auctions; TOP The Top Banana Antiques Mall; TYE Typically English Antiques; UD Upstairs Downstairs; VEC Vectis; VHA Vanbrugh House Antiques; VK Vivienne King; VSA Vennett-Smith Auctioneers; WAA Woburn Abbey Antiques Centre; WADS Wadsworth's; WW Woolley & Wallis; YC Yesterday Child

Acknowledgments in source order, with page numbers (except jacket, which is in picture order):

Front cover, top left: OPG/GN/ST; *Front cover, top centre:* OPG/PP/CSK; *Front cover, bottom left:* OPG/AJP; *Front cover, bottom centre:* OPG/NB/ST; *Back cover, left:* VEC; *Back cover, right:* OPG/MPe/SPe

ACAC/RS 263; AH 237; AMC/RS 290t; APC 477; APO/RS 266; AUC/RS 90, 335t; BaN/RS 145, 366; BaN/EG 387; BBe/RS 127, 397, 422; Bbo/RS 258; BD/RS 293; BEV/RS 225; BEX 429; BHa/RS 273; BKJL/RS 132t; BOW/RS 94, 330; BRU/RS 228; BrW/RS 129, 150, 408; BtoB/RS 290b, 392; BURA/RS 170; BWDA/RS 148; BWL 68, 466; CAL/RS 280; CAu 343; CBB/RS 137; CDC 425; CHAC/RS 8, 27, 238; ChC 70; CHI/RS 326; CHTR 308, 322, 383, 468; CO 181, 350; COBB 17; CoHA/RS 134, 152b; CoS/RS 297t; CRU/RS 341; CSM/RS 439; DA 149; DAD/RS 171, 204; DEB/RS 432; DEL/RS 314; DJH/RS 301; DMa/RS 220; DML 59; Do/RS 91; DOL/RS 255; DRA 57, 76, 198, 400, 451; DSA/RS 239; Ech/RS 105; F&C/RS 214; FAC 60, 318; Fai/RS 458; FHF 167, 398; FRD/RS 126; G&G/RS 96, 323; G(B) 14, 75, 122, 300, 364; G(L) 3, 6, 10, 22, 24, 32, 36, 48, 52, 77, 79, 86, 93, 102, 123, 136, 140, 153, 158, 169, 172, 187, 201, 234, 253, 261, 265, 279t, 282b, 291, 295, 297b, 302, 306, 309, 324, 336t, 368, 370, 379, 380, 390, 396, 409, 424, 433, 438, 442, 443, 450, 467; GAK 28, 270; GaL/RS 114; GAU/RS 112, 313, 340; GGD/RS 337, 361, 386; GIL 107, 332; GLAS/RS 154, 336b; GLD/RS 44, 80, 363; GLEN/RS 34, 461; GRe/RS146, 212; GRI 101, 356; GTM/RS 256, 275; H&G/RS 303, 344; HAD 63; HAL/RS 367; HAYS 342; HeA/RS 289; HEM/RS 49; HIS/JM 430; HL/RS 250; HO/RS 310; HOB/DM 226; HOW/RS 395; HUM/RS 449; HUN/RS 464; HWK/RS 184; ICO 174; JAA 12; JAS/RS 128, 155; JE/RS 30; JFME/RS 411; JHa/RS 205, 235, 246; JHo/RS 193, 331, 463; JPr/RS 39; JSG/RS 241; JTS 180; JUN/RS 264; JUP/RS 259; KEY/RS 54, 74, 218, 294, 403, 416, 475; KW/RS 377; L&E 453; LaF/RS 58, 427; Lbe/RS 207; LBr/RS 355; LGr 19, 73, 304, 346, 375; LLD/RS 355; MAA/RS 236, 281; MALT/RS 472; MARK/RS 194, 248, 353; MB/RS 441; McP/RS 177; MDL/RS 410; MI/RS 125; MI 335b; Mit 231; MiW/RS 55, 69, 284, 447; MMc/RS 151; MSh/RS 394; NAW/RS 157, 243; NoC/RS 216, 474; NORTH/RS 372; NS 459; OPG/CH 268; OPG/CS/ST 116; OPG/LP/ST 120; OPG/PA/CSt 85; OPG/PR/RD 115; OPG/S/IB 108; ORI/RS 164, 168; P&T/RS 316; PAY/RS 240; PICA/RS 142; POLL/RS 317; POW/RS 5, 132b; PrB/DM 312; PWA/RS 473; RAN/RS 138; RAY/RS 166; RdV/RS 307; REN/RS 327; ROS 321, 374, 471; RPh/RS 66t; RUSK/RS 462; SAAC/RS 276; SAF 7, 33; SAS 283; SAT/RS 84, 286, 385, 407; SCO/RS 339b; SEA/RS 329, 334, 431; SERE/RS 111; SGA 179, 465; SHa/RS 373; SiA/RS 376; SJH 311, 460; SK(B) 81; SLh 175; SLI 31; SOO/RS 415; SPUR/RS 436; SV/RS 257; SWO 9, 21, 43, 47, 50, 56, 64, 71, 72, 78, 103, 104, 152t, 160, 182, 197, 203, 215, 249, 254, 262, 267, 278, 282t, 292, 298, 339t, 349, 354, 388, 393, 412, 419, 420, 426, 446; TAC/EG 208; TAC/RS 61, 213, 227; TCG/RS 456; TDG/RS 279b, 347; THE 144, 178, 260; TL 40; TLA/RS 414; TMA 161, 233, 305; TOP/RS 469; TYE/RS 106, 211; UD/RS 11, 434; VHA/RS 141; VK/RS 365; VSA 99; WAA/RS 121, 244; WADS/RS 133; WW 15, 18, 26, 46, 66b, 82, 97, 113, 119, 131, 143, 147, 156, 159, 173, 191, 192, 229, 232, 242, 325, 358, 401, 404, 406, 435, 448, 454; YC/RS 38, 219, 222, 399